ENVIRONMENTAL QUALITY
AND WATER DEVELOPMENT

ENVIRONMENTAL QUALITY AND WATER DEVELOPMENT

Edited by

Charles R. Goldman

James McEvoy III

Peter J. Richerson

University of California, Davis

W. H. Freeman and Company
San Francisco

Library of Congress Cataloging in Publication Data

Goldman, Charles Remington, 1930-
Environmental quality and water development.

1. Water resources development—United States.
2. Human ecology—United States. I. McEvoy,
James, 1940- joint author. II. Richerson,
Peter J., joint author. III. Title.
TC423.G64   333.9'1'00973   72-83739
ISBN 0-7167-0256-8

Printed in the United States of America

International Standard Book Number: 0-7167-0256-8

1 2 3 4 5 6 7 8 9

CONTENTS

PREFACE

The National Water Commission was established in 1967 for a period of five years by an Act of Congress, as a response to growing concern on the part of the American people for the rapidly diminishing natural resources and steady deterioration of the quality of our environment. The Commission undertook a variety of individual studies on water development including environmental quality, the legal aspects of water development, and aesthetics, a subject that is particularly difficult to quantify. Our study attempts to evaluate the causes of conflict between environmental quality and the development of the nation's water resources and to suggest some possible solutions. We have described the attitudes and values of Americans toward their environment: attitudes and values that have caused us to define environmental quality in different terms during different periods in the past. The report upon which this volume is based attempts to identify basic principles that are necessary for more realistic environmental planning and decision-making, and our recommendations to the Commission are included in the first chapter.

We acknowledge the extremely valuable assistance that was provided us by the staff of the National Water Commission, particularly Mr. Theodore Shad, Mr. Victor Koelzer and Dr. Tom Scott. We are grateful to the Commissioners who gave permission to publish this study, and we are particularly indebted to our own staff of Ecological Research Associates—Miss Barbara Johnston and Mrs. Mary Major—who assisted in the research and production of the original report.

Charles R. Goldman,
Division of Environmental Studies
University of California, Davis

October 25, 1972

CHAPTER 1

ENVIRONMENTAL IMPACT
AND WATER DEVELOPMENT

Charles R. Goldman

INTRODUCTION

In June 1970 I undertook a study for the National Water Commission on the problem of balancing environmental considerations and water development. I was assisted in this study by my colleagues, Dr. Peter Richerson,

a limnologist, and Dr. James McEvoy, a sociologist. We were to pay particular attention to the environmental movement and how environmental interests might be incorporated in water development planning to achieve a better balance between water development and environmental quality. This volume—a result of that study—contains reports from individuals who, by virtue of their research and experience, provide excel-

From a paper presented on June 8, 1972, at Session 33 of the American Water Works Association's 92nd Annual Conference in Chicago.

lent counsel on dealing with the host of conflicts which frequently accompany major water developments.

PUBLIC ATTITUDES AND VALUES

There was a time when extreme alteration of the landscape was accepted without protest, and development of any kind, regardless of its environmental impact, was almost universally condoned in the name of progress. This "frontier" attitude has been gradually modified during the first half of this century, and in the past decade we have seen the rapid evolution of widespread public concern over the progressive deterioration of the environment. The purpose of the study was to compile an evaluation of the basic causes of conflict and present recommendations for their reduction. It was hoped that a functional scale of values could be established against which development could be measured and from which functional trade-offs could be drawn. By studying the history of attitudes and values that people hold toward environmental quality, as well as the history of the conservation movement, it became evident that such a scale would not be valid over time and space. Attitudes and values change so rapidly that water projects planned in response to a current public attitude may well be outdated and a source of conflict before the project is completed.

One example of the rapid change in attitudes is that of the advertisement for a small American city some 40 years ago. The picture of a busy and prosperous community with large billows of smoke curling upward from its factory smoke stacks would today have a decidedly negative connotation as it would serve to signal air pollution and a poor environment to most people. Despite the rapidly changing attitudes, very little scientific work has been done on the measurement of human values such as aesthetics. Still, it is generally recognized that there is now rather widespread disenchantment with machines,

technology, and the quantitative (as opposed to the qualitative) view of what constitutes progress.

William Everson, a poet we consulted, describes a growing feeling, particularly among the young, that we must somehow return to the spirit of life with nature. Inherent in this movement is the idea of renewal of life, requiring abstinence from too much manipulation as well as petition for environmental wisdom, not merely a proficiency in programming the physical world.

The Small Watershed Improvement Act, a product of the 1950s, illustrates how values and attitudes have changed in twenty years. This legislation's single purpose was flood control—providing funds for stream channelizations which were called "improvements." These "improvements" are now being challenged for degrading fish habitat, causing accelerated bank erosion, flooding, lowering the water table, and increasing variation in stream flow, and in contrast, flood plain management and zoning now appear to be sounder flood control policy. Despite this change in public values, Congress has again appropriated funds under this act for still further channelization.

The history of attitudes toward the environment in general and rivers in particular dramatizes the rise of enthusiasm for wilderness throughout the last century. We are currently witnessing an increase in wilderness appreciation with preservationist views being accepted.

Roderick Nash, a historian, has described the evolution of American attitudes toward wild rivers. From considering them as a commodity—the source of transport, power, irrigation—we have moved to treating them as a "symbol of the spirit." This change evolved as conflicts between preservationists and water developers in 1913 began over whether or not there would be a dam built at Hetch-Hetchy. Interestingly enough, this is the conflict that split the conservation movement into two factions: the preservationists, led by John Muir, wished to preserve natural beauty, and the conservationists, exemplified by Gifford Pinchot and Theodore Roosevelt, wished to use a resource, but to use it wisely.

The battle over Hetch-Hetchy was bitterly contested and although it was lost by the preservationists, they were able to raise the consciousness of the American public during the twenties, thirties, and forties when new organizations such as the Wilderness Society and the National Parks Association were founded. These groups, then, helped stop the Echo Park Dam in 1950. With these struggles Americans began to realize that most of their frontier had already vanished and that any remaining wilderness is precious. The next major confrontation occurred when developers sought to construct dams at Marble Canyon and Bridge Canyon on the Colorado River in 1963—which turned into a victory for the preservationists that gave a real measure of the movement's increasing strength. These victories proved very costly, however, as the preservationists were to lose the beautiful and valuable Glen Canyon in the compromise.

In the course of the years between 1910 and 1960 the "burden of proof" shifted from the preservationists to developers as far as public attitudes are concerned. The present level of public concern appears to be linked to increasing awareness of pollution and resurgence of preservationist thinking among much of the public at large.

There are few undeveloped rivers of significant length left in the continental United States, and water development planners should know that construction is often proceeding on the basis of the plans and attitudes of a previous generation. These plans urgently require review in the light of current needs and attitudes.

In the past decade there has been enormous recreational expansion into the wilderness areas so that now the National Park Service and the US Forest Service are having to take regulatory steps to prevent serious damage from crowding in the areas that remain undisturbed. The increase in the number of recreational river travelers down the

Colorado River through the rapids of the Grand Canyon illustrates this point (Figure 1).

ANALYSIS OF HUMAN ATTITUDES AND VALUES

Human attitudes and values are conditioned by man's response to his environment, and this is complicated by the different ways in which different individuals respond to the same stimulus. A wilderness traveler may become very disturbed by the overhead flight of an airplane or the passing of a snowmobile as it disturbs the serenity which he has worked so hard to find. In contrast, it is reported that some people cannot sleep without the humming noise of an air conditioner in the bedroom (Swan, this volume). Such is the different acquired response to the stimulus of noise.

The concept of stress in man has received considerable attention by psychologists, and causes of stress can be both physiological and psychological. Physiological "stressors" may be further subdivided into those which can readily be perceived, such as loud noises, congested traffic, and visual blight, and those which cannot be readily perceived, such as mercury, asbestos, or radiation. Some chemicals that produce physiological stress or death at high levels can in small quantities reduce an organism's ability to withstand physical stressors of another sort. For example, it was found that herring gulls from Lake Michigan with high concentrations of persistent pesticides in their bodies are less able to withstand stress induced by adverse weather conditions than are gulls without traces of pesticides (Swan, this volume).

INCORPORATING PUBLIC VALUES AND ATTITUDES

To incorporate contemporary attitudes toward environmental quality into water development projects, it is necessary to coordinate

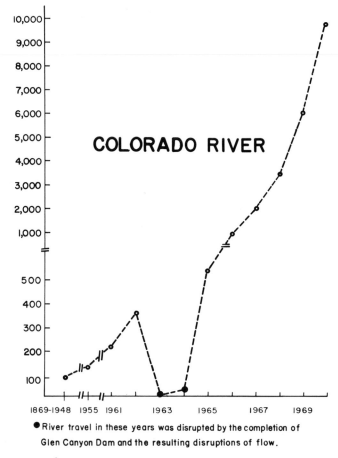

FIGURE 1
Recreational river travelers on the Colorado River.

environmental and developmental interests to relate to all stages of water development, particularly planning. To be effective however, this must be done early in the planning stages.

How can the values of the public be incorporated into the planning and decision-making process of water developments? Survey research is an important tool for assessing attitudes and values and has great potential for use by the decision-maker. Unfortunately, there are not yet many national polls available on attitudes of Americans toward their environment. The 1970 Gallup Poll found that citizens considered environ-mental pollution to be the second most important problem of this decade. We hope that water resource planners will make greater use of survey research tools in analyzing the potential effects of their decisions on public values.

The kind of planning that is done, as well as the manner in which the results are submitted for final decision, is very influential in the formation of public opinion. Gilbert White noted that in the 1950s there was much emphasis placed on water-based recreation resulting in only mild tensions in the readjustment of the planning activities needed to provide for this new emphasis.

In the 1960s and early 1970s values changed rapidly, and old methods conflicted with new ideas. This made for great technical difficulty in the formulation of plans and resulted in a buildup of tensions. Conventional procedures in the decision-making process have proved particularly inadequate so that radically different devices may be required to respond to a more dynamic ordering of priority in all types of resource planning. There is particular need for a more effective means of consulting that sector of the public that is concerned with environmental quality.

Furthermore, White feels that there has long been a myth that resource management is an optimizing process. Actually, there is considerable evidence that in resource management decisions an economically efficient choice is neither sought nor achieved. Benefit-cost calculations are used to help justify the choice made rather than to determine which choice is best. The evidence presented suggests that there is an almost total lack of advance planning in an attempt to predict what will actually happen when a project is in operation. Although needs are presented and supposedly economically feasible plans are outlined, there is rarely a comprehensive analysis of the full range of consequences resulting from the development. Thus, a pressing need exists to work the various interest groups into the decision-making process early if we are to reduce conflicts which are now or will soon be the rule rather than the exception wherever water developments are proposed.

The question of how to incorporate public values and attitudes into the decision-making process is vital to the success of planning. It is encouraging that a number of governmental agencies that have been involved in water planning are attempting to respond to this need. This volume includes a case study of such an example by Margaret Petersen who worked for the Corps of Engineers on the Morrison Creek Project near Sacramento, California. An approach of a different sort in the Susquehanna Basin is described by Gilbert White in another paper on a Corps of Engineers project, which employed a variety of workshop techniques. By examining the decision-making network of interest groups, twelve different elements are identified by White. Conservation groups are conspicuous by their absence, and it is usually after the decisions have been made that they enter into the adversary proceedings that are likely to decide, if not resolve, the controversy. Thus, public involvement in the early planning stages is essential to reduce the conflict between the growing conservation movement and the national needs for the storage and transport of water.

Public involvement in the whole decision-making process, the first part of which is planning, is important. In this country most decisions for water resources are made at federal or regional levels because of the large-scale impact of these developments and the great resources needed to deal with them. Charles Ross, a former member of the Federal Power Commission, recognizes that there are two major problems associated with the decision-making process in this country. First, he believes that most of the frustration, cynicism, and disillusionment so prevalent today with many of our institutions stems from a lack of real public involvement in the decision-making process and second, he believes that inadequate staffing of resource agencies making the decisions makes it difficult to improve matters. He points out that the man in the street has a sense of helplessness regarding his ability to have any impact on the decision-making process. This general erosion of confidence now threatens our form of government, and it is of the greatest importance that confidence be restored at all levels. A basic change must occur in the philosophy of the decision-makers; that is involving the public rather than excluding them, and the elimination of the attitude that public involvement will only be asking for unnecessary trouble and delay.

SEPARATE PLANNING AGENCY

Toward this end our study has recommended that the planning of water projects be completely separate from the construction and regulatory agencies, and that physical, biological, and social scientists be part of the planning team, together with the traditional engineering and economic components. This planning agency should probably be established at the federal level because of the size and scale of most water projects.

The political climate of the past, which encouraged the sole use of the frequently biased benefit-cost analysis, is changing with the recent emphasis on environmental problems. Economic evaluation seems destined to play a lesser role as an instrument of consensus building and a greater role as one method of technical evaluation in forming a multi-objective framework. The Water Resource Council's multi-objective policy statement records the necessity of incorporating environmental considerations into water resource plans. With the requirement for agencies to file 102 statements under the NEPA, this may become a reality. Although it is possible to embrace this philosophy it should be remembered that no miraculous balancing scheme will correctly deliver any agency from the necessity of making hard decisions. Further, chief administrators should be willing to sign decisions so that there is a higher degree of identification and responsibility associated with them.

PLANNING METHODS

Methodologies are currently being developed which will allow planning for a quality environment. What now remains to be accomplished is effective procedures for incorporating environmental quality into benefit-cost analyses, and it must be recognized that strictly monetary terms are insufficient for evaluating environmental quality. There remains a good deal that is still possible within the framework of benefit-cost analysis, such as the dollar value of anadromous sport and commercial fish losses versus the dollar value of reservoir fish and flood control when a stream is dammed.

We generally agree that proper planning can prevent many difficulties in water development, and, further, that it can serve as a major compromising force in considering alternatives. Ian McHard (1969) has taken an ecological view in his approach to planning. We studied one of his plans in detail, and as an example it gives a good idea of this sort of innovative approach. The project was the Skippack Watershed near Evansburg, Montgomery County, Pennsylvania, where in 1960 the Corps of Engineers proposed to establish a large reservoir. McHarg and his associates were retained by the county to make an ecological study of the Skippack Watershed. They considered impact of the dam development and inventoried local resources and their potential for withstanding future land-use demand. A rather complete inventory was made of natural and cultural processes covering climate, geography, physiography, ground water hydrology, pedology (soils), plant ecology, limnology, and cultural history. The social values associated with these categories were assessed. They included agricultural resources, developable resources (construction limitations), ground water supply limitations in areas requiring protection, historical resources, scenic resources (in closed places, visual bowls, long views), as well as surface water resources. In the final stages of the study all prospective land uses related to a watershed resource and possible future alternatives were analyzed. Matrices were constructed which rated all of these resources by classification for physical, cultural, and social values. Finally, a synthesis overlay map was prepared showing land use alternatives and recommended allowable land use. In their ecological study, development also was simulated through four uncontrolled growth models which assumed *status quo* planning. In the final evaluation of the Evansburg project, water yields in both quantity and quality were examined, and it was concluded that the large reservoir would be highly eutrophic (excessively fertile) unless existing and projected water quality was improved.

The study was supported by a detailed list of the consequences of building the project, which included considerations of changes in the stream ecosystem, loss of cultural heritage, disruption of major highways in the vicinity, and the inevitable acceleration of urbanization around the project so that the large reservoir plan was therefore abandoned.

The Evansburg study was unique in providing an ecological approach to planning wherein alternative courses were presented and an analysis of natural processes considered. Planning for the high dam had considered projected demand for water, engineering feasibility, and economic feasibility, but lacked adequate coverage of water quality and historical and aesthetic values.

The kind of information collected by this sort of total land use planning provides a data base essential for evaluating any planning proposed thereafter and may well deliver the least cost and most benefit for a desired objective.

Other new techniques are simulation models such as those being developed at Harvard (Steinitz, 1970) and the use of impact analysis during the planning stage of a project. The impact statement is now required by law under the NEPA, and if used during the planning stage and not during the authorization stage, it can be a useful tool in planning.

Perhaps basic to all good planning is resource inventory and land-use zoning. Wisconsin has been a leader in this field with its Shoreland Protection Law that was enacted in 1966 to protect the resource value of shoreland in a joint state and county regulatory effort. It is an example of the states establishing minimum standards for local land use and retaining the authority to adopt regulations if the local government fails to act. Wisconsin's Shoreland Protection Law is an approach to the protection of resource values by state and local governments by the establishment and enforcement of zoning regulations.

We look forward to a day when land-use zoning based on land capability will be the rule rather than the exception. This is evidenced by the conclusions of the President's Water Pollution Control Advisory Board and the President's Air Quality Advisory Board. They recommended that financial assistance be given to state and local governments that develop "comprehensive land-use plans" and take action against those "unwilling to carry out effective land use programming."

Unfortunately, in the past very few water resource planners have viewed their role as one to maximize social benefits. As a result most water development plans have not really implemented public goals through good management. Management and planning agencies often begin with a development project and sometimes even a range of alternative plans. From this beginning there is a tendency to construct a plan merely to justify its implementation. Again, the public at large is presented with a self-fulfilling prophecy (Lukens and Langlois this volume).

A good example of this sort of planning is the ambitious California Water Plan, that is predicated upon supplying water to Southern California. It now appears that the best public interests in this case may be served by attempting, through planning, to spread the population away from arid regions into areas with ample water supply. As more information has become available reassessment of the plan is taking place and more is likely to occur before the project is set in concrete (Seckler 1971).

The following recommendations were generated by this study and were submitted to the National Water Commission for their consideration. They incorporate the author's hope for a change in future water development planning through more public participation, through better assessment of the natural and social environment by a separate governmental planning agency, and finally, through a realistic evaluation of the effectiveness of past planning. And when some of these goals are realized, we hope to make better decisions in the future.

RECOMMENDATIONS

I. *Public participation in planning must be greatly increased in order that human and environmental values may be given more nearly appropriate weight in balancing the engineering and purely economic aspects of water development.*

In considering water developments, there arise questions of public values necessitating public judgments and participation in the formulation of development alternatives. There are encouraging signs that governmental agencies are moving toward fuller public participation, and this trend should be encouraged and intensified along the lines of subsequent recommendations. Real public involvement is the best antidote to the prevalent attitude of frustration, cynicism, and disillusionment concerning governmental institutions. Such involvement increases public confidence in decision-making and will do much to reduce the divisive political conflict common in the development field. (Allee and Chapman; Beeton; Fox; Hedgpeth [Bodega Head]; McCloskey; Ross; Swan; White.)[1]

1. To eliminate one of the key weaknesses in present water resource planning, public participation should be sought at the outset so that viable alternatives may be generated. In the past there has been an unfortunate tendency for development agencies to present the public with single, take-it-or-leave-it plans, for communication with the public to be in the nature of salesmanship rather than

two-way exchange, for hearings to be scheduled in various ways to prevent the full participation of groups representing an interest in environmental values, and to use overall practices which result in development along narrowly conceived lines.

In the future, we must make possible real choices among real alternatives (including that of no development). To this end, proposed developments should be well publicized and comment should be invited from groups and individuals representing consumers, conservationists and preservationists, and the public at large. (Edmondson; McCloskey; Swan; White.)

2. In addition to direct participation of the public, which is essentially a political aspect of the planning process, perhaps even more can be accomplished through what can be thought of as indirect participation—the use of various techniques to measure and incorporate attitudes and value judgments. To this end there is pressing need for increased research in the field of environmental attitudes and opinions. Existing survey data are adequate only for tracing the gross outline of the changes in attitudes toward the environment, and many important details remain to be understood. Research support is necessary to continue present studies and encourage new ones in the quantitative and overlay methods dealing with aesthetics and other social aspects of the natural environment. (McEvoy; Swan; White.)

II. *Evaluation of proposed water development projects must go far beyond traditional methods to include analyses of aspects of the social and natural environment that can be assessed with new innovative techniques.*

Water development is too important to be undertaken without knowledge of all its potential effects. Present planning methods depend largely upon economic and engineering evaluations which are far too narrow in

---

[1] All references cited in these Recommendations are to papers in this volume.

conception and method. Progress to date on incorporating measures of environmental effects is woefully inadequate, and several of the subsequent recommendations suggest specific techniques now available for better incorporation of environmental quality into project evaluation.

1. The water development planning process must utilize integrative and innovative techniques. These techniques include resource inventory and map overlay planning techniques, impact studies for evaluation, and systems analysis (where data is available) for gross resource planning. Political techniques include land-use zoning. (Henwood and Coop; McHarg and Clarke; Yanggen.)

2. To provide a data base for planning, environmental impact analysis, and land-use regulations, the federal government should encourage the states to make natural resource inventories.

All analytical methods for balancing water development and environmental quality require geological, biological, climatological, cultural, and demographic data. Such inventories would provide much of the required information for any assessment, and although considerable initial expense is required, subsequent savings in the costs of planning and impact assessment should more than justify the outlay. (Henwood and Coop; McHarg and Clarke; Yanggen.)

3. Every attempt should be made to incorporate dollar equivalents of environmental costs and benefits into economic evaluations of proposed water developments, although no pretense should be made that such evaluations are descriptive of all such effects.

Benefit-cost analysis is a powerful evaluation tool if properly used, but its conceptual limitations prevent its serving as the sole method of impact evaluation. (Allee and Chapman; Henwood and Coop; McCloskey; McHarg and Clarke.)

4. New guidelines requiring environmental impact evaluation procedures of sufficient detail to portray accurately all the important positive and negative effects of proposed development alternatives should be developed to replace the present inadequate guidelines. The National Environmental Policy Act now requires impact statements, and the Water Resources Council Task Force Report has proposed full evaluation of environmental quality as part of the planning process. However, present impact reports suffer from inadequate funding, too few staff members with training in the biological and social sciences, and a prejudice in favor of development. The reports prepared thus far are well below the excellence possible with existing measurement and evaluation techniques. (Henwood and Coop; Ross.)

5. In all programs calling for federal approval of plans, the government should require the states and cities to undertake comprehensive land-use planning and zoning based upon environmental as well as social and economic criteria. Such an approach has proved of great value in regulating the everyday uses of water, waterfronts, flood plains, and watersheds of insufficient magnitude to require full-scale impact analysis and planning, and thus preventing environmental deterioration through uncontrolled housing and commercial and industrial construction. The previously recommended natural resources inventory would furnish much of the data for such regulation. Waterfronts in urban areas, usually highly developed or at least susceptible to intense development, are often most in need of environmental quality enhancement. A special federal effort is needed to encourage wise use of these resources. Public access to waterfront areas needs to be increased, and impact statements should incorporate evaluations of public access changes to result from development. Much of the activity on waterfronts is influenced by federal agencies and policies, including military installations and many aspects of navigation. Also, federal grant programs to cities can be enlarged and coordinated to encourage greater attention to considerations of environmental quality.

(Luken and Langlois; McCloskey; Scott; Yanggen.)

6. The federal government can assist states which are attempting to set up regional goals and controls but are frustrated by local interest groups. Examples can be seen in the experience of the Tahoe Regional Planning Agency, Bay Area Development Commission, International Joint Commission for the Great Lakes, and the Morrison Creek Plan. It can deny federal funds for highway construction, sewage disposal, and other projects to counties within these regional organizations which are not complying with state or national goals. Legislation is presently being introduced to attach a rider to the Water Quality Control Act which would strengthen the states' position on subdivision sewage disposal because most environmental problems are regional in character and any effective action should be on a regional scale. (Beeton; Edmondson; Hedgpeth [Estuaries]; Scott; Yanggen.)

7. Demographic projections as a basis for predictions of water requirements should be used with extreme caution because they are very likely to become self-fulfilling prophecies. Thus, the use of present demographic projections may be considered bad planning. When it is successful it is likely to foster excessive population concentrations. A better approach to the problem would be to apply demographic planning to disperse the population into areas of good water supply. (Hollis and McEvoy; McCloskey.)

8. Further research on measurement, planning, and evaluation techniques should be encouraged. Although understanding of such fundamental processes as eutrophication in aquatic ecosystems is far from complete, there is much information that can be applied now in assessing the quality of the aquatic environment. Further improvements in measurement techniques is certainly warrented; these should include development of more useful systems analysis, measures of aesthetic and recreational values, and demo-graphic projections. Good measurement techniques are essential to good planning and evaluation of water development. (Richerson and McEvoy; Swan.)

9. Regulatory agencies must be supplied with an adequate, expert staff, or the means to hire outside experts to discharge their statutory functions of protecting the public interest, including environmental quality. Without such assistance, it is simply not possible for regulatory commissions and agencies to properly discharge their responsibilities in reviewing project plans or supervising operations. (Fox; Henwood and Coop; Ross.)

10. All planning efforts should be aimed at developing valid alternative plans—including nondevelopment—which incorporate innovative methods as well as the traditional ones to achieve project ends. Because of narrow legal mandates, established interest group relationships, and bureaucratic tradition in federal planning and construction agencies, valid alternatives are rarely developed during the planning process. This problem is as much political and psychological as structural and is the key to other recommendations. (Allee and Chapman; Luken and Langlois; McCloskey; McHarg and Clarke; Richerson and McEvoy.)

11. Independent consultants, technical committees, and lay advisory boards must be included in all water development planning. This mechanism is useful for incorporating the knowledge and independent judgment of imaginative and sometimes controversial persons into the planning process. (Fox; Ross.)

12. Effective monitoring programs need to be developed for areas such as coastal estuaries and river systems near population and industrial centers where monitoring procedures sufficient to evaluate present impacts and provide the historical data base for predicting effects of future development do not yet exist. Enforcement of present standards and planning of future projects are handicapped by the lack of such programs, and existing ones are very likely to have a

major portion devoted to data gathering and lack the rapid evaluation systems so essential for an immediate and effective response to environmental change. (Beeton; Richerson and McEvoy; Teclaff and Teclaff.)

13. Public Law 566 should be amended to require protection of streams or sections of streams. Extensive re-examination of projects approved and being planned under Public Law 566 is called for and should be done in the light of present knowledge and new attitudes and values. Evaluation of projects which have been completed under this law should incorporate an ecological point of view and should be undertaken before further destruction results. Wetlands can no longer be looked upon as wastelands. (Jahn.)

III. *A separate governmental agency should be created to be responsible for the planning of water development in order to eliminate the pro-development prejudice of construction and regulatory agencies. This agency should have broad representation.*

It is difficult to expect an agency to display sufficient objectivity to evaluate nonengineering alternatives to today's development needs if that agency exists because of appropriations for the construction of engineering works and has accumulated skills and traditions in engineering. With a few exceptions, these agencies are not likely to respond quickly to the changing attitudes and values of the American people evoked by the deteriorating environment. A new agency is needed, one free of inherited prejudices and therefore able to develop the best possible plans for the change in attitudes toward the natural and social environment. References: Fox: McCloskey (this volume).

IV. *To benefit from past experience and to improve present and future planning, a large-scale, multi-project program should be undertaken to determine the effectiveness of the planning of completed projects with regard to economic returns as well as their environmental impact.*

Detailed and accurate information regarding the economic, social, and ecological history of a broad sample of completed projects should be collected. These data should be organized in the light of present goals, with an assessment being made of the successes and failures of past planning to try to minimize environmental damage in future water development. These studies should be conducted by the Environmental Protection Agency which in turn should employ independent consultants as investigators and reviewers. As in all phases of planning and evaluation, public review and participation in these studies must be encouraged in every possible way.

The history of water use, population growth, and the present ecology of the Los Angeles Basin is an example of the kind of study we have in mind. Some planning entered into these developments, and it is not too late to try to find out what went so drastically wrong. (Hollis and McEvoy; White.)

References

McHarg, Ian. 1969. Design with nature. The Natural History Press. New York.

Seckler, David, ed. 1971. California Water, a study in resource management. University of California Press, Berkeley.

Steinitz, Carl, ed. 1970. Selected Projects. Laboratory for Computer Graphics and Spacial Analysis. Graduate School of Design, Harvard University, Cambridge, Massachusetts.

CHAPTER 2

The function of a poet in a study otherwise made by scientists, technicians, sociologists, and resource managers is to explore the spiritual, mythical, and emotional aspects of man's relation to his environment. The meaning of water for man is not exhausted by a list of its physical, chemical, and engineering properties. It is also of vital psychological importance.

Water is the source of our existence. An ancient mythical identification between water and woman—their shared nature of fertility, regeneration, strength, and submissiveness—carries a message even for modern, scientific man. Only by acting in accordance with the natural inclinations of water can we ultimately "solve" the problem of the conflict between preservation and development. The key is a change in attitude from the self-centered to the recognition of water's value and importance to us both spiritually and psychologically.

Our present national malaise, of which concern for our mistreated environment is a part, testifies to our past disregard of this primordial truth. Many of our youth understand our alienation and seek to re-establish connaturality with the earth. In this search to live with nature, rather than to exploit it, the poet finds hope of escape from our present dilemma. The same intuition of unity between man and nature underlies the tenets of both our scientific society and mysticism.

THE HOPE WE HAVE

William Everson

My letter of invitation to this study mentions the various participating scientific disciplines, but asks me as a poet to touch on the spiritual, mythical, and emotional content of man's relation to environment.

And indeed the poets of today are very much in the forefront of the battle for environment. Their faces are frequently seen upon the picket lines, protesting this or that threat to wildlife, this or that ecological abuse.

The theme runs like an undercurrent through almost all the poetry now being written, typifying the poet's acuity of response to the changes in our social and cultural atmosphere, an atmosphere within which he tingles like a nerve, the wince of a sensitive antenna.

Thus you can find poems clanging like fire alarms, verse flung bitterly against such a pronouncement as one recently reported from the anti-ecological counter-resistance, namely that "the future of this mighty nation cannot be jeopardized merely to preserve a couple of dozen whooping cranes!"

Such complacencies send the poet leaping

to his pen, his sensitivity acutely engaged in the battle of words and ideas that precedes the battle of legislation by which a people orients its path into the future.

In this discourse I shall not, however, take such a tack. I shall rather ponder the meaning of our subject for the total life of man: his imagination, his dreams and his vision of the future.

For without some sort of meditation on the nature of water, we cannot fully devote our energies to the manner in which it should be deployed. To assume in advance that water is simply H_2O is more than an error in definition. If we persist in it we will be certain to exhaust what we set out to conserve.

In the San Joaquin Valley where I grew up, water means life in the most unequivocal sense. Given an average rainfall of only ten inches a year, the area qualifies on the climate maps as a desert. But the great snow pack in the Sierra Nevada enables man to transform this desert into a garden of subtropical richness.

As a young man I planted a vineyard and took water directly from the vast network of irrigation canals that lace the plains. And in the winter, when the vines are dormant and water has shrunk back to its ancient courses, I worked as a bander on a pipe-laying crew. In this capacity I installed cement irrigation pipe all over Fresno County.

So, too, in the hottest part of the summer, while the grapes are ripening and are best let alone, I worked as a syrupmaker in a great peach cannery, mixing sugar with water, gauging the sacrometer to the precise degree required, and sending the resultant fluid down by gravity flow to the bustling lines of cans.

As I labored with water in the valley, the symbolic nature of everything that I did kept haunting my imagination and my dreams. Water ran through my psyche like a living freshet, and soaked into the roots of my awareness.

And when I came to write poems it emerged there; water became the weather and climate of my poet's thought. For in the valley rain is so rare that its coming is always something breathtaking, something touched with awe.

I learned more about the meaning of water from its lack than from its excess. Now the whole world is learning.

One winter day when one of the rare storms blew in, and work on the pipeline had to be abruptly terminated, I wrote a poem quite spontaneously in an effort to express what I was experiencing. It is in free-form, and is called "The Rain On That Morning." That was over thirty years ago, but to this day it summons up within me the mystery that it celebrates.

We on that morning, working, faced south and east where the sun was in winter in rising.
And looking up from the earth perceived the sky moving,
The sky that slid from behind without wind, and sank to the sun,
And drew on it darkly: an eye that was closing.
The rain on that morning came like a woman with love,
And touched us gently, and the earth gently, and closed down delicately in the morning,
So that all around were the subtle and intricate touchings.
The earth took them, the vines and the winter weeds,
But we fled them, and gaining the roof looked back a time
Where the rain without wind came slowly, and love in her touches.

Here is a young man, a dropout from college, responding simply to the actuality of rainfall, suggesting that water is more than we think it is in our categories of usefulness.

Thoreau indicated as much when he laconically observed, "The only use of a river is not to float on it." But the poem goes beyond that. It is not so much an observation as a witness; it testifies to the fact that water is profoundly feminine. At the heart of the poem is an ancient truth, newly sprung from the contemporary imagination—the archaic, almost menstrual identification between water and woman.

From pre-Socratic days onward, water has been categorized as one of the four cardinal points of material existence and, by a close parallel, also of spiritual life. But such a categorization is only a very late formula evolved from ages upon ages of mythological and spiritual reflection.

The Greek formula of the four elements was derived from the most empirical evidence that primitive man could gather regarding the context of his existence. By dividing the elements into a quadernity, men were able to understand them in an objective way.

Water stands opposite Fire in the scheme. To early man, water was everything that fire was not.

Of the elements, traditionally speaking, two are active (fire and air) and two are passive (earth and water). Hence the masculine, creative character of the first pair, and hence the feminine, receptive, and submissive nature of the second.

It is not surprising, then, that a young poet, working in a sun-drenched region where the light at mid-summer is pure fire, and the temperature often soars to 110 degrees, should compare the coming of rain to the approach of a woman. For in the evolution of consciousness a poet is even more primal than a farmer or laborer, and it is the essence of his role to put first things first.

So we have arrived at the threshold of an answer to the question: what is water? It is an element, yes, but more than that it is a metaphorical entity, a symbolic truth: Water is Woman.

Let us determine what the ancient wisdom has had to say about water. *A Dictionary of Symbols* gives a compact rundown:

> In Egyptian hieroglyphics the symbol for water is a wavy line with small sharp crests representing the water's surface. The same sign, when tripled, symbolizes a volume of water, that is, the primeval ocean and prime matter.

The Chinese consider water as the specific abode of the dragon, because all life comes from the waters.

In the Vedas water is referred to as *matritamah* (the most maternal) because, in the beginning, everything was like a sea without light.

In India, this element is generally regarded as the preserver of life, circulating throughout the whole of nature, in the form of rain, sap, milk, and blood. Limitless and immortal, the waters are the beginning and the end of all things on earth.

Although water is, in appearance, formless, ancient cultures made a distinction between "upper waters" and "lower waters." The former correspond to the potential, or what is still possible; the latter to what is actual, or already created.

In a general sense, the concept of "water" stands, of course, for all liquid matter. Moreover, the primeval waters, the image of prime matter, also contained all solid bodies before they acquired form and rigidity.

For this reason, the alchemists gave the name of "water" to quicksilver in its first stage of transmutation and, by analogy, also to the fluid body of man.

This "fluid body" is interpreted by modern psychology as a symbol of the unconscious, that is, of the nonformal, dynamic, motivating, female side of the personality. The projection of the mother-image into the waters endows them with various numinous properties characteristic of the mother.

A secondary meaning of this symbolism is found in the identification of water with intuitive wisdom. In the cosmogony of the Mesopotamian peoples, the abyss of water was regarded as a symbol of the unfathomable, impersonal wisdom.

In prehistoric times, the word for abyss seems to have been used exclusively to denote that which was unfathomable and mysterious.

The waters, in short, symbolize the universal congress of potentialities, the *fons et origo*, which precedes all form and all creation.

Immersion in water signifies a return to the preformal state, with a sense of death and annihilation on the one hand, but of rebirth and regeneration on the other, since immersion intensifies the life force.

The symbolism of baptism, which is closely linked to that of water, has been expounded by St. John Chrysostom: "it represents death and interment, life and resurrection . . . When we plunge our head beneath water as in a sepulchre, the old man becomes completely immersed and buried. When we leave the water, the new man suddenly appears."

On the cosmic level, the equivalent of immersion is the flood, which causes all forms to dissolve and return to a fluid state, thus liberating the elements which will later be recombined in new cosmic patterns.

The qualities of transparency and depth, often associated with water, go far to explaining the veneration of the ancients for this element which, like earth, was a female principle.

The Babylonians called it "the home of wisdom." Oannes, the mythical being who brings culture to mankind, is portrayed as half man and half fish.

Moreover, in dreams, birth is usually expressed through water-imagery. The expressions "risen from the waves" and "saved from the waters" symbolize fertility, and are metaphorical images of childbirth.

On the other hand, water is of all the elements the most transitional, between fire and air (the ethereal elements) and earth (the solid element).

By analogy, water stands as a mediator between life and death, with a two-way positive and negative flow of creation and destruction.

The Charon and Ophelia myths symbolize the last voyage. Death was the first mariner.

"Transparent depth," apart from other meanings, stands in particular for the communicating link between the surface and the abyss. It can therefore be said that water conjoins these two images.

Whether we take water as a symbol of the collective or the personal unconscious, or else as an element of mediation and dissolution, it is obvious that this symbolism is an expression of the vital potentiality of the psyche, of the struggles of the psychic depths to find a way of formulating a clear message comprehensible to the consciousness.

On the other hand, secondary symbolisms are derived from associated objects such as water-containers, and also from the ways in which water is used: ablutions, baths, holy water, etc.

There is also a very important spatial symbolism connected with the "level" of the waters, denoting a correlation between actual physical level and absolute moral level.

It is for this reason that the Buddha, in his Assaparum sermon, was able to regard the mountain lake—whose transparent waters reveal, at the bottom, sand, shells, snails, and fishes—as the path of redemption.

This last obviously corresponds to a fundamental aspect of the "upper water." Clouds are another aspect of the "upper waters."

In *Le Transformationi* of Ludovico Dolce, we find a mystic figure looking into the unruffled surface of a pond, in contrast with the accursed hunter, always in restless pursuit of his prey, implying the symbolic contrast between contemplative activity—the *sattva* state of Yoga—and blind outward activity—the *rajas* state.

Finally, the upper and lower waters communicate reciprocally through the process of rain (involution) and evaporation (evolution).

Here, fire intervenes to modify water; the sun (spirit) causes sea water to evaporate (i.e., it sublimates life). Water is condensed in clouds and returns to earth in the form of life-giving rain, which is invested with twofold virtues: it is water, and it comes from heaven.

Lao-Tse paid considerable attention to this cyclic process of meteorology, which is at one and the same time physical and spiritual, observing that:

"Water never rests, neither by day nor by night. When flowing above, it causes rain and dew. When flowing below, it forms streams and rivers.

"Water is outstanding in doing good. If a dam is raised against it, it stops. If a way is made for it, it flows along that path. Hence it is said that it does not struggle. And yet it has no equal in destroying that which is strong and hard."

When water stands revealed in its destructive aspects, in the course of cataclysmic events, its symbolism does not change, but is merely subordinated to the dominant symbolism of the storm.

Similarly, in those contexts when the flowing nature of water is emphasized, as in the contention of Heraclitus that "You cannot step twice in the same river; for fresh waters are ever flowing in upon you."

To quote Evola, in *La tradizione ermetica*: "Without divine water, nothing exists, according to Zosimus. On the other hand, among the symbols of the female principle are included those which figure as origins of the waters (mother, life) such as: Mother Earth, Mother of the Waters, Stone, Cave, House of the Mother, Night, House of Depth, House of Force, House of Wisdom, Forest, etc."

One should not be misled by the word "divine." Water symbolizes terrestrial and natural life, never metaphysical life.

Thus for *A Dictionary of Symbols*. I have quoted at such length only to insure that we do not underrate the profound ambiguity of the subject with which we are dealing.

Clearly, then, water is not a merely quantitive entity. Its subjective presence is more meaningful and significant than its objective constitution, being ineradicable not only from our minds, but also from our spirit: the participation of our whole being in the fact of our existence.

Whatever we do to water, we do to ourselves.

Water, then, according to ancient tradition, and according to the spontaneous insight of contemporary poetry, is female. Water is Woman. What inferences can be drawn, and how can we apply them?

The first step appears to be simple: we should stop referring to water as "it," and begin talking about "her." For language is the key to attitude, and in any basic revaluation, attitude is really the point at issue. Attitude is all.

But, conversely, language *directs* attitude, deepens and confirms it. One cannot employ gender in speech without inculcating what is denoted into the substance of one's associations.

For instance, a few years ago the authorities decided to effect flood control along the primary California river-system by stripping the streams and throwing up more levees—an approach that its opponents scornfully indicted as "straight-line engineering."

Whether or not this means was adequate is still disputed. Even its bare effectiveness is contested, and the equation between effectiveness and adequacy is by no means absolute. Be that as it may, the result was ugliness, and the ugly can never be adequate.

If the people who made that decision had been thinking in terms of "she," they would have reflected at greater length before embarking on so irreversible a course. This thought leads us to a further consideration: in the world of woman, consultation is primary. Without it nothing proceeds. To put it bluntly, if one wants a woman to participate, he cannot command her. A man must ask.

Remember Lao-Tse's words above: Water, he said, does not struggle. Yet she has no equal in destroying what is strong and hard. The sexual symbolism, even if unintentional, cannot be concealed. No man can reject the inference save at his peril.

Had those mentioned above approached the confluence of the Sacramento and the San Joaquin, and had they addressed themselves to the feminine presence those rivers constitute, they would have remembered that her ancient watercourse is really the signature of her existence and her intention. It is the hieroglyph of a living purpose and a manifest destiny.

Had they asked how they could help fulfill that destiny, some other solution might possibly have emerged. Something closer to their own fates, and to the river's fate, might have given the answer to periodic flooding.

And if, from this approach, no solution is forthcoming, what then? To the religious mind, very few problems have tangible solutions or yield final conclusions.

Although every problem *appears* to have a solution, most problems are best left alone. When a woman embarks on one of her periodic rampages, it is better to let the fury blow. The broken crockery is nothing, compared with the hell of alienation that results from having her clapped into a straitjacket.

There is an old Forty-niner's song entitled, "On the Banks of the Sacramento." We have much to learn—if not from the song, then directly from the river—on the banks of the Sacramento.

The inference is clear. We cannot chart water's future course without ascertaining her own determination in the matter. In order to solve our problem, we must ask of a given water what she intends to do.

I learned this primal fact on the irrigation ditch many years ago. It did not matter so much what *I* wanted the water to do. I prospered only when I ascertained what *she* wished to do. When I adapted my vineyard to her will, my vineyard flourished.

Scientifically, we can do this same thing by analyzing water, understanding its composition, and proceeding accordingly. This, of course, we have done, and with considerable success, although no scientific inquiry is ever complete.

Or, philosophically, we could speak of ascertaining the constitutive law of the existence of this phenomenon, and proceeding in terms of that law. Here our practice has been more problematical, because philosophic approaches are apt to make us feel impatient.

But in terms of our culture and our collective life, our environment and our spiritual heritage, we must go to the heart of femininity and placate this being with consideration.

Any man who has loved woman knows this. We have behaved like an arrogant bachelor who has structured his career on managerial prowess, hiring and firing women at will, only to discover himself one day falling in love.

Suddenly he realizes, with a shock, that he needs, that he really *desires* a woman. It no longer suffices him to determine what *he* wants; the central relevance now is to learn what *she* wants.

In our impending dryness, the threat of universal drought, we are beginning to wake up. We are at last concerned about water, absorbed in the drama of her existence as it relates to our own. Out of sheer need we are, in a manner of speaking, falling in love.

Although this sounds fanciful, absurd, it is the truth. Water is now something sacred, something to be honored and served. Because water, once so abundant, is becoming rare. And rareness invokes reverence.

So the problem narrows down. How are we to approach this spiritual substance? How can we engage her as a mythological and religious presence?

For we have lost the knowledge that archaic people possess, the knowledge of propitiation and appeasement. In our zeal and our pride we have assumed the power to enforce. And in doing so we have lost the most valuable power we possessed: the power to love.

Not quite. More than one American Indian has retained the ancient secrets, the immemorial mysteries. He knows how to speak to the presence; how to propitiate the maternal spirit in water.

I have said that as a poet I am honored to be asked to participate in this symposium. But if a poet is asked today, who can doubt that a shaman will be asked tomorrow? Poet and shaman are of the same vibration. They speak the same language, even if they do not use the same words.

We are now at a crisis point chiefly because we have thought only of ourselves. We have appropriated and directed and compelled and possessed, and in the end we are left with what? A weary woman.

The polluted rivers crawl to the sea. Our lakes are stinking. The streams ache through the eternal hills. The springs gasp in the parched fissures.

A weary woman. A sullen slave. A listless lover.

And we are weary. A pall infects us, and we are afraid of our shadow. We overreact. The sullenness of the slave whom we have subjugated oppresses our spirit. Our wives are defiant. Our youth is in rebellion. We have jeopardized our manhood.

I wrote another poem, much later in my life than the one I gave earlier. That one spoke of her coming. This one speaks of her going.

I had held her in my arms as a bride, but then I arrogated her presence to myself, and lost her. She left me, the prideful man, to my sterile devices. She left me to myself.

It is thus that our waters withdraw from us.

Wader,
Watcher by water,
Walker alone by the wave-worn shore,
In water woven.

She moves now where the wave glistens,
Her mouth mocking with laughter,
In the slosh unheard
When the sea slurs after;
In the sleepy suckle
That laps at her heel where the ripple hastens.

And the laughing look laid over her arm,
A tease and a wooing,
Through the flying maze when the wave falls
   forward,
From its faultless arch, from its tallest yearn,
To its total ruin.

Lurker,
She leaves with laughter,
She fades where the combers falter,
Is gone where the dream is gone,
Or the sleeper's murmur;

Is gone as the wave withdrawing
Sobs on the shore, and the stones are shaken
As the ruined wave
Sucks and sobs in the rustling stones,
When the tide is taken.

We see in such evocative testaments more than the swan-song of the individual poet.

At root it is the white man's lament, when he feels the whole feminine presence of things withdraw from him, imperceptibly receding before his inexorable conquest of space and time.

But there is a Rain Song of the Sia tribe, one of the pueblo peoples, that was sung in time of drought, in the shrivel of things, the touch of death in the tinder-like grass, the dearth of the dew. It can serve as the paradigm of our lost opportunities.

Though we must make our own Rain Song to meet our own needs, this Sia song will show us how our hearts can be changed, our *attitude* changed.

All who live in this broad land can understand the song, for it is thoroughly American. Our earth was the Indian's earth before we usurped it. Because he never sought to own it, he unquestionably belonged to it. What he knew, we can recover.

White floating clouds.

O clouds like the plains,
Come, water the ground.

Embrace the earth, Sun,
That she may be fruitful.

Moon,
Lion of the north,
Bear of the west,
Badger of the south,
Wolf of the east,
Eagle of the heavens,

Shrew of the earth,
Elder war hero.
Warriors of the six mountains of the world,
Intercede with the Cloud People for us,
That they may water the earth.

Medicine bowl,
Cloud bowl,
Water vase,
Give us your hearts,
That the earth may be watered.

I make the ancient trail of meal,
That my song may pass straight over it—

The ancient trail.

White shell bead woman,
Who lives where the sun goes down.

Mother whirlwind,
Mother Susistumako,
Mother Ya-Ya,
Creator of good thoughts.

Yellow woman of the north,
Blue woman of the west,
Red woman of the south,
White woman of the east,
Amber woman of the heights,
Black woman of the depths—

Intercede,
I ask you,
With the Cloud People!

Today, even as I speak, the more sensitive youth are moving out into the land. Drawn by an ineluctable need, *our* need, they are seeking the places of solitude.

Like poets, quivering in the oppressive climate of our spiritual crisis, the sense of impending catastrophe to our whole environment, they are slipping away.

They are seeking out the fresh lakes and the ponds where Loon Woman cackles crazily in the night. They are finding the rivers that are pure, the streams that are fresh and fierce.

They do not go, as our generation went, for sport. They go not as hunters and fishermen but for reflection and meditation. They go for renewal.

One of them recently described to me in glowing terms the little communes tucked away in the folds of the hills. He asked how I, knowing what I know, could remain apart from them.

I shook my head. I had tried that, too, in my youth, and known disillusionment.

He smiled and said, "We are going to make it. And when the crud really begins to fall, we'll have a place for you."

I shook my head again. When things really got tough, that's when the communes break up. They exist only by a kind of largesse; they endure by virtue of the age of affluence against which they are in revolt.

Only a degree of affluence sustains for long the preoccupation with intangibles. When the crud really begins to drop, the preoccupation with tangibles becomes oppressive, and the communes cannot sustain that kind of pressure.

But my young friends, the youth of America, do not believe this. Conceivably, they won't have to learn it as we learned it in the Depression.

Anyway, the success or failure of the communes is incidental. They are where they are, not as an aberration from the life of conventional communities, but as symptoms of something deeper. The trek from suburbia indicates a primary lack.

Our children are living out the response to our own unconscious alarms. They echo a cry that sounds louder and louder from under the certitude of our affluence and our technology.

They represent the roots of our distress, our deep and repressed desires. The sound of their moccasined feet on the earth as they leave us is the throb of our beleaguered hearts.

They are finding what we intuitively crave but lacked the historic opportunity to discover for ourselves. And yet through them, our sons and daughters, we are discovering it.

And because they are the bridge between us and the future, they are solving our dilemma. They are learning how to shift between the cities and the streams, how to take for granted an urban sophistication even as they discover the ancient techniques of wisdom and knowledge. They are finding out how to propitiate the earth even as they experience her.

They are coming just in time. Thank God they are already here.

For it stands evident that a new world is struggling to be born, and this is the throb of its birth. It is the pulse of renewal through crisis.

Of the fact of crisis there can be no doubt. Our very project confirms it. We would not be concerned with environmental quality, if quality were not in danger.

It is a crisis for which neither our old social solutions (our established riparian legalism) nor our accomplished hydraulic technology will suffice. Although each of them is old, neither is old enough.

Neither is archaic enough, primitive enough. For neither is fundamental or tribal. Because they lacked, from their very beginnings, certain essential ingredients, they could not meet the challenge of their future. Now their future has become our present.

To meet that challenge we must go back—in terms of water—to sources which represent inception points, the emergence of nascent being in its pure spontaneity.

Only the most naive, simplistic assumptions can help us now, for they are the only fresh and unspoiled responses left to us. Everything else has been compromised by dexterity and fluency, technology, proficiency. We have prostrated ourself to Moloch, the beast who devours our children, our future. His other name is Know-How.

Youth must solve the world-wide environmental dilemma. Not that our own generation has capitulated to doddering impotence; but that youth is ever evolving new solutions. Youth is predestined to take the lead.

These young people are attempting to achieve not just a *contiguous* relationship to environment, to woods and fields and streams. Contiguous relationship is a heresy; it has got us where we are today. We have stocked streams with trout; we have controlled breeding programs for the correct ratio between game and fodder. None of these measures has proved sufficient.

Contiguity is a human determinant. Too much human emphasis only results in a human excess: polluted streams, contaminated forests. All our conservation programs collapse because we are using the tactics of mere proximity, not real relationship to the earth.

Everywhere we see monolithic self-edification, the grinning Moloch of self.

In the face of this failure, the youth of today is seeking to achieve a relationship not of contiguity but of something far deeper, what the ancient philosophers called *connaturality* —a relationship based on mutuality of essences.

The denial of this essential relationship is our great contemporary lack, and it is driving our youth to drugs. Our stratified distinctions have placed an intolerable stress on man's spirit.

The young people are right—not in their recourse to drugs, certainly, but in their quest for unity of being.

We must join our children in this quest. We must re-evaluate everything that violates unity of being; reappriase all the immediate gains in terms of ultimate costs.

This is a unity which the Indian, throughout his immemorial centuries in this land, understood and revered. And yet, even to him, it remained mysterious, being neither static nor passive, but vital and dangerous.

Yes, dangerous. Because at its source is not the certitude of rationality, but the incertitude of faith, or of reason through faith.

Many centuries ago Saint Anselm said: "I believe in order that I may know." Today we know all and believe nothing. By virtue of this paradox, our knowledge amounts to ignorance. Why? Because knowledge without belief excludes the ultimate element— namely, wisdom.

Wisdom is not approximation. It demands that we participate, that we recognize mutual essences in the ineluctable relationship of connaturality. Wisdom lies not in the triumph of managerial finesse, but in humility, spiritual empathy—which is another way of saying Love.

And not just the luxurious empathy of something enjoyed, which has come to stand for love, but the painful empathy of something shared: passion, anguish, exaltation, delight.

For five hundred years, ever since the invention of printing gave man the power of duplication to correlate and then implement his inventive formulas, Nature has suffered for us. The time has come when we must suffer for her. This is not a matter of choice. It will be exacted of us or we shall perish.

And youth knows this. Youth is seeking to renew our life through the gifts of the spirit as well as the gifts of the mind. It employs invocation as well as invention; it requires abstinence and petition, not mere proficiency and programming.

Does this seem terribly unrealistic? I don't think it is. One can begin anywhere, anytime. During the War at our camp on the Oregon coast near Yachats, we had a visit from Morris Graves, whose Northwest paintings are almost painfully beautiful in their accessibility to spiritual perspectives. This artist arrived unannounced, quietly locating at the mouth of Big Creek. Before we knew he was there, he was established.

Eager to be of use we workers rushed down with axes and saws to help him hack a trail up the slope through dense stands of shore pine and brush. With consummate delicacy he checked us. "Please," he said. "Before we begin we had best consult the spirit of this place."

In our profound ignorance we sat down and waited, questioning him with our eyes. He himself was questioning the hill. "Let us regard the underlying purpose," he began. "Let us discover why things are as they are."

"Observe the inclination of the slope, and above it the drift of the foliage. Do you sense the slight depression there where the leaves have drifted? It is the clue to the vector, the stress-line in the rock below. It is the flaw that enables us to enter into the presences here, and understand their disposition."

Then, with supreme deliberation, the tact that comes only from an achieved authority, he reached in his arm and extracted a dead branch. "The trail begins here," he said simply.

Very nice, I can hear it retorted. But can one live with such immediacy in the congestion of a city? There everything is already established, and creative "moments" like this are not possible. Under such oppressive conditions, how does one induce contemplation from natural forms, extract spiritual essences from life movements?

Actually, a great deal is possible. When you step out onto the street of a city, look not at the highrises but at the light that shafts between them, the long oblique slant of significance speaking either of morning or evening, or telling of that straight, enveloping descent of solar energy we know for high noon. Massive as they are, the office buildings have only a participating role. They have no more meaning than the light allows.

Or watch the wind whip the surface of pools left in the street by rain, the water wrinkling its skin for every change in direction as the air veers, quivering with responsive tactility. In this scruffed mirror thrown up from one's feet, the scene momentarily transmutes to another octave of reality, takes on a new being.

And most especially wait for the dark, the vast enveloping involvement of night. The blessedness of its erasures enfolds convolution within convolution, the solidarities of our thought, quenching with unspeakable aptness the psychological stresses that daytime imposes on the soul.

In every city there is day and night, water and wind. No more than this, than these, seen as presences rather than as facts, is needed to change the face of the earth from drab to dazzling.

Let every privation be the key to a new penetration of vision. Then the whole of reality will respond, correcting the imbalance that our inordinate will has caused. What we have destroyed with utility suddenly leaps to life.

It is the secret of the American Indian's relation to the land. He was blessed with being; for him the whole earth stood up and smiled. And if aboriginal Indian life seems too primitive for us, remember that the Japanese evolved an advanced culture out of just such affinities.

But speaking for myself, I cherish the native American approach—the thrust of the Indian, back and down, probing the archetype of all wildness in the aperture of the divine—the numen, the sacred instinct in animal, earth, and plant, as sources of mystery and wonder.

And I do not find this approach unrecoverable. In appropriating a life-style, we adopt not its customs, but its attitudes. For that is all custom is essentially: the clue to attitude.

But still, practices are meaningful. When I find a wild animal beside the road, struck down by traffic, I often carry it home and skin it out. After the skin is cured, I nail it to my wall so that the numen, the mystery it contains, may radiate into my life.

Nor do I feel that this is inimical to my Christianity. In the incarnation of Christ I perceive the term of all Nature divinized in participation with God. Nothing less shines to me from the skin of the weasel, the pelt of the badger, the feather of the grebe.

So in his great *Canticle of Brother Sun* Saint Francis of Assisi began his invocation. His chant was his witness to actuality as he perceived it.

> *Be praised, O Lord, in what you have created,*
> *Above all else in Brother Sun,*
> *For he lights up the day.*
>
> *He is beautiful and radiates splendor.*
> *Of you, Most High, he gives signification.*
>
> *Be praised, O Lord, in Sister Moon and the Stars.*
> *You shaped them in the heavens,*
> *Clear and beautiful and precious.*
>
> *Be praised, O Lord, in Brother Wind,*
> *And in the air and clouds,*
> *And fair and other weathers.*
> *Through them you give your creatures sustenance.*

> *Be praised, O Lord, in Brother Fire,*
> *With whom you light up the night,*
> *He is beautiful and strong,*
> *Robust and jocund.*
>
> *Be praised, O Lord, in our sister, Mother Earth,*
> *She governs and sustains us,*
> *Brings forth varied fruits,*
> *Gaudy flowers and grass.*
>
> *Be praised, O Lord, in all who for love of you grant forgiveness,*
> *Bearing infirmity and tribulation.*
> *Blessed are they who endure with a peaceful heart.*
> *By you, Most High, they will be crowned.*
>
> *Be praised, O Lord, in our Sister: Bodily Death,*
> *Whom no living thing can escape.*
> *Alas for those who die in spiritual blindness!*
>
> *Blessed are they who find themselves in your most holy will!*
> *To them the second death shall bring no harm.*
>
> *Praise and extoll my Lord and give him thanks.*
> *Serve him in profound humility. Amen.*

Such is the religious spirit, primitive, exalted, revivifying, true. Like the Rain Song of the Sia tribe, this canticle addresses all things as living and new, fresh-sprung from the great Hand of Being, without blemish or taint.

Let us praise our youth. They are seeking to see again, to throw off the blindness of our insensible pragmatism which, having brought us many rich and manifold things, now threatens to destroy us.

Let us rejoice with our sons and our daughters that they are experiencing the instinctive reawakening of religious faith, so tentative and vulnerable, so quickening and true.

Like the first pussywillows around the landlocked valley ponds, when Spring, not yet in the air, hovers beyond the horizon, our children emerge. They serve as talisman of the full awakening yet to come.

Sister Water, bride of the chinook, prophetess of spring and mistress of renewal, let us learn from your gifts even as we utilize your attributes. Give us all you have to offer of the ancient, underlying rhythms: when to rise, when to flow, when to bend, when to rest.

Suffer us to change with your changes, to move, respond to the quick of your indirections. Deliver us back to the source from which we have sprung, the source which you are, which we have lost, and are groping to recover.

In your presence we encounter the ancient paradox, the mythlike subjectivity of all analysis: Man, at the heart of his probing, meets only himself.

So it is with you. At the end of our study, everything we are stands measured. You, like a mirror of judgment, confront us. The quality of our water puts us face to face with the quality of our life. *Whatever we do to water we do to ourselves!*

In defining the type of relationship necessary to correct our rigidifying objectivity, I pointed to the ancient principle of connaturality, the clue of mutual identity which enables even radically distinct essences to participate in the well-being of one another.

If we call water the source from which we have sprung, we refer, of course, to the widely accepted evolutionary theory that all life emerged from the sea.

This hypothesis continues and extends its direct conceptual forerunner, the ancient tradition of esoteric wisdom we found in *A Dictionary of Symbols*, namely, that water is the universal potential from which emerged the multiplicity of specified forms.

I will conclude by bringing these tangential themes to focus in Robinson Jeffers' famous poem, "Continent's End." In a sense this poem is their unconscious synthesis. Jeffers invokes the sea as a presence, the mode that can correct our attitude toward water in the crisis of our dwindling resources.

This poem employs the principle of connaturality as the efficacious bond between even organic and inorganic substances. But it has the advantage, here, of being based more on the evolutionist's view than on the mystic's. For it is necessary, in closing this paper, to get back to the point from which we began.

Jeffers was capable of profound mysticism. But when he came to reflect on the situation of modern man as having reached the term of the historic westward migration, he was impelled to speak in scientific and evolutionary concepts. His poem is religious, but the religious intuition seems to arise spontaneously within the context of a scrupulously reserved point of view.

Today we think much more in scientific terms than in religious ones, and are wont to consider science and mysticism as incompatible. Jeffers' poem demonstrates that the same intuition of unity underlies both disciplines.

Jeffers is standing on the rock shore at Carmel, looking west. This extremity of position makes him feel a little like the last man, the summation point of human consciousness, the crystallizing awareness that completes the long evolutionary process.

The immensity of it all gives him a kind of detachment, an essential reserve and loneliness. Freed from self-preoccupation, he sees things, as the philosopher says, "under the aspect of eternity."

The poet's gaze to the horizon takes his mind over the rim, touching, beyond it, the enormously distant Orient, the origin of civilization that instituted the long trek westward to his outpost on the California shoreline. But the vast water at his feet takes his mind down and under to the origin of life itself—and even deeper to the fundamental floods of energy that shape the cosmos.

But it is principally the water that is the focusing symbol. And all we have been discussing seems taken up and resolved in a point of view that is consonant with the mind of modern man, alienated as our minds are from the intuition of the Sia aborigine chanting his Rain Song, or the medieval mystic's cry of joy and celebration that we heard in the *Canticle of Brother Sun*.

Jeffers knows that the modern spirit is lonely in the midst of a staggering cosmic vastness, but in his poem that alienation is somehow annealed of its corrosive acidity. Man's loneliness takes on a strange religious dimension, consonant with the same scientific objectivity that has so caged man's spirit.

As men of the modern world, may we gain solace from such meditation, even as it shows us how we, too, may place ourselves in line with the ancient movements of earth and sea, the growth of plants, the episodic periods of transient civilizations.

And yet if Jeffers' poem is indeed the terminus of a certain direction in human thought, it does shape for us a place where we may stand, gazing both ways down the steep watersheds of the past and the future, making this continent's end our vantage point in the long summation of consciousness.

Sadder and wiser, we are a people who despoiled a land, raping what we cherish— a people who, taking Nature for very God, yet have spat in His face with filth and pollution. How can sadness and wisdom console us now? How can they absolve us?

They certainly do not make for our happiest thoughts. We blithely subjugated the earth with optimism and ingenuity, because a selfish happiness has been our curse. But they are the best hope we have—sadness for the past, wisdom for the future—the only hope the poet can hold out to us:

> At the equinox when the earth was veiled in a late rain, wreathed with wet poppies, waiting spring,
> The ocean swelled for a far storm and beat its boundary, the ground-swell shook the beds of granite.

> I gazing at the boundaries of granite and spray, the established sea-marks, felt behind me
> Mountain and plain, the immense breadth of the continent, before me the mass and doubled stretch of water.

> I said: You yoke the Aleutian seal-rocks with the lava and coral sowings that flower the south,
> Over your flood the life that sought the sunrise faces ours that has followed the evening star.

> The long migrations meet across you and it is nothing to you, you have forgotten us, mother.
> You were much younger when we crawled out of the womb and lay in the sun's eye on the tideline.

> It was long and long ago; we have grown proud since then and you have grown bitter; life retains
> Your mobile soft unquiet strength; and envies hardness, the insolent quietness of stone.

> The tides are in our veins, we still mirror the stars, life is your child, but there is in me
> Older and harder than life and more impartial, the eye that watched before there was an ocean.

> That watched you fill your beds out of the condensation of thin vapor and watched you change them,
> That saw you soft and violent wear your boundaries down, eat rock shift places with the continents.

> Mother, though my song's measure is like your surf-beat's ancient rhythm I never learned it of you.
> Before there was any water there were tides of fire, both our tones flow from the older fountain.

References

Astrov, Margot (editor). 1962. *American Indian Prose and Poetry.* ("Rain Song," p. 243) New York: Capricorn Books.

Cirlot, J. E. (editor). 1962. *A Dictionary of Symbols.* ("Water, p. 345–347) New York: Philosophical Library, Inc.

Everson, William. 1968. *The Residual Years.* ("The Rain on That Morning," p. 22; "Wader" from "In the Fictive Wish," p. 185) New York: New Directions, Inc.

Jeffers, Robinson. 1937. *The Selected Poetry of Robinson Jeffers.* ("Continent's End," p. 87) New York: Random House, Inc.

Reinhold, H. A. (editor). 1944. *The Soul Afire.* ("Canticle of Brother Sun," p. 37) New York: Pantheon Books, Inc.

CHAPTER 3

The course of water development and its relation to environmental quality from earliest antiquity to the present is reviewed, particularly the history of water development in the United States.

The present legal-political structure of water use has its antecedents in both the European context of abundant water for all, and the appropriative-rights scheme developed in the western United States. Although our society is far more complex than that of ancient Mesopotamia and Egypt, similarity to these early fluvial civilizations is apparent in the highly centralized planning and development of our water resources. Many examples of modern development are cited in which environmental quality has been disregarded. The results of this disregard have had ever more widespread effects on our land. With an eye to what happened to early water-dependent civilizations when their supply system broke down, we point to the growing cost of providing new sources of water and say:

> *There is a point in water resources development when water can no longer be matched to the economy, but the economy must be matched to the water available. In the light of past experience, one thing above all should be asked of modern, scientific water management—that major projects be undertaken only when all their potential effects on the totality of the environment have been assessed by all available means.*

A HISTORY OF WATER DEVELOPMENT AND ENVIRONMENTAL QUALITY

Ludwik A. Teclaff and Eileen Teclaff

In nature there are neither rewards nor punishments—there are consequences.
R. G. Ingersoll "Some Reasons Why."

Man's yesterday may ne'er be like his morrow; Nought may endure but Mutability.
Shelley *Mutability.*

Water development is an activity so old that it goes far back into the mists of legend. If irrigation agriculture was practiced in Jericho in 7000 B.C., then water development has existed for almost nine millennia. Its history is far from being a story of continuous progress. It reached a high level of sophistication in antiquity in certain regions where climatic and hydrologic conditions combined required an all-out effort to make irrigation agriculture possible. The remarkable feats of engineering that were required were achieved solely with the energy output of work animals and human workers, through administrative organization and discipline imposed on the population with efficient ruthlessness. But because of this low level of energy output, the impact on the environment was not one of dramatic transformation. There is a tendency to think of the fluvial civilizations in the context of a swift bursting into bloom, followed by a catastrophic decline, and a long period of quiescence. It was the other way about. The benefits were slow in coming, but cumulative and durable, and so were the defects. In Mesopotamia, salt and sand had reclaimed a great part of formerly irrigated fields and gardens long before the Mongols delivered the *coup de grace* in the thirteenth century. In Egypt, by contrast, the techniques of water development adopted early in antiquity persisted until very recently with little change and little apparent detriment.

Outside the regions of the fluvial civilizations, water use techniques did not reach a comparable level until the eighteenth or even the nineteenth century, and water-rich Europe was especially slow in moving ahead. From an historical perspective it can be shown that the physical limitations of individual river basins imposed quite powerful constraints on water use. Very little could be done, for example, to increase the amount of water available for irrigation, power, or municipal supply until modern technology permitted large-scale diversion from basins amply endowed with water. Similarly, until the advent of concrete dams for storage and of long-distance transmission of electricity, power from water could be used only on-site and was subject to seasonal fluctuations.

In linear progression, the next stage in water development did not begin until the Industrial Revolution, as demand for water for industry, population, and later, irrigation agriculture, increased—a trend which is now turning even water-abundant parts of Europe and the eastern United States into shortage areas, comparable in this respect to the ancient fluvial civilizations. However, for a discussion of the environmental aspects of water development, the long ages of slow progress in water-rich areas have a great deal of importance and must be included, because extensive water use in those areas did have an impact on the environment, although only in a sporadic way, and also because potential for the next leap forward was accumulating.

The new stage in water development that began with the Industrial Revolution in Europe and the United States is not confined, as past stages were, to selected regions, but is spreading rather uniformly over the whole world. In this growth lies its greater promise for man and also its greater danger for the environment, because the sheer scale of the activities is so much larger than anything attempted in the past, even in the fluvial civilizations. To escape disaster the developers must read aright the message of the fluvial civilizations and of medieval Europe.

With the aid of modern data-gathering, and through the science of ecology, the impact of various types of water development and use can be gauged far more effectively than in the past. It is known, for instance, that the reduced streamflow resulting from diversion from rivers and lakes causes changes in the ecology of the water body itself and of its riparian lands right down to the estuary (see Hagan and Roberts, and Hedgpeth, this volume). Channelization, or the straightening and regulating of streams, increases flow and thus the rate of erosion; it can contribute to siltation downstream and also to the severity of floods. Large reservoirs effect changes in local climate which are sometimes felt a considerable distance away, especially in the direction of the prevailing wind. The drowning of valleys behind dams and the raising of lake levels (and with them the ground water table as well) destroy existing wildlife habitat and vegetation, not to mention cropland and sometimes whole villages and towns. The damage is not always offset by an increased water supply, the new aquatic habitat, or the aesthetic values provided by the new artificial bodies of water. Ground water extraction in excess of the replenishment rate of the resource may cause changes in vegetation (for example, trees dying due to the progressive desiccation of the upper layers of soil) and this, in turn, may produce changes in wildlife habitat, in land use, and in the character of the landscape itself. Likewise, draining and reclamation lower the water table, cause shrinkage of the soil, alter or destroy existing ecosystems, and can add to the severity of flooding.

It is possible to distinguish between types of water development and use which have an irreversible impact (reclamation of swamps, creation of reservoirs, total exhaustion of a deep underground aquifer) and those which have not (some kinds of pollution). Certain developments and uses have an immediate impact and others a slowly cumulative one. Some harmful impact may result from neglect, some from intentional choice between economic benefit and environmental quality, and some from factors which only modern techniques of data processing and model-making can evaluate. The key to the ensuing study of water development and environmental quality in history, therefore, lies in awareness of the nature of water and water systems, of their interdependencies, and of their interrelationships with other elements in the physical environment. The historical analysis that follows attempts to show the consequences of that awareness or lack of it.

THE FLUVIAL CIVILIZATIONS: PROGRESS AT THE DAWN OF HISTORY

Legends referring to "supermen" who tamed floods and brought water to thirsty lands attest to the antiquity of water development in the basins of the Nile, the Tigris-Euphrates, the Indus, the Yellow, the Yangtze, and other rivers of the Old World, as well as in parts of Mexico, coastal Peru, the American Southwest and various other localities in the New World. The legends give a picture of order achieved out of chaos through grand projects, heroic labors, and the strong leadership of a king or god. More likely, the first works were undertaken by small communities or local chiefs, rather than by individual rulers of large areas. Such development goes back, it is believed, to 7000 B.C. at Jericho, and was probably practiced long before 4000 B.C. in Mesopotamia and 3400 B.C. in Egypt, where we hear of major river-taming projects. It came somewhat later in China, in the Chou age (1100–221 B.C.), but again legend would indicate a much earlier origin.

The initial ventures were undoubtedly small in scale, designed to cope with localized problems, but the very intensive development which came to characterize the fluvial civilizations arose out of great and widespread need. The environmental spur in North Africa, the Middle East, and central Asia, for example, was aridity, and in some other areas, such as China, it was a variability in rainfall so pronounced that one writer terms the natural process of water supply in China as "not only unreliable, but positively disastrous." Another environmental spur was the size of the rivers to be controlled, and the fact that most of them required flood control measures and drainage of riverine lands.

Thus, both climate and the rivers imposed water management as an imperative for the survival of settled communities. The economic base of these civilizations was irrigation agriculture, dependent upon development of surface and ground waters, associated with and sometimes conflicting with the use of water in industry, navigation, and municipal supply. The political and social structure was close-knit, highly centralized, managerial and bureaucratic, influencing and influenced by the high level of water development. Water became synonymous with political power, and power with water control. The ruler of a land that was naturally better endowed with water was like Baudelaire's king of a rainy country, "rich but impotent." Indeed, an entire study of a non-western system of total power through the ages and its modern legacy in bureaucratic totalitarianism —Wittfogel's *Oriental Despotism* (1963)— has been based on research into the "hydraulic economy." Mastery of water use for agriculture permitted many people to occupy areas where before only a few had lived, but the price paid was overcrowding and loss of freedom. The intricate waterworks needed cheap, mass labor, along with conditions conducive to the production of such labor. The state grew more and more powerful and prosperous—for a time—but the majority of individuals probably lived under conditions not much better (if not worse) than did their ancestors before the advent of the water works.

The fluvial civilizations developed hydraulic engineering to a degree that was not equalled or surpassed until modern times, and their means of data gathering and awareness of the nature and interdependencies of water systems were quite sophisticated. The intricate works for the reclamation of the left bank of the Nile were constructed more than three millennia before our era, at the time of Egypt's unification under Menes. The great diversion canal to carry excess flood waters from the Nile mainstream to the Faiyum depression and to provide storage in time of low flow dates from about a thousand years later. In Mesopotamia the Nahrwan Canal paralleling the Tigris for 250 miles, the 370-mile-long Pallacopas Canal that discharged the surplus floodwaters of the Euphrates into the Chaldean marshes, and the Shatt-el-Hai Canal joining the two rivers, which was built by Entemena to celebrate his conquest over a rival city state, are equally impressive feats of engineering skill undertaken at a very early period. In Armenia, the qanat system of irrigation by underground tunnels was probably well developed by this time, for Sargon of Akkad borrowed it and introduced it into the lower Tigris-Euphrates basin. The Persians later built the complex systems of upland dams and water works described by Herodotus, which distributed waters to subject lowland peoples according to need, shutting off the supply to one group before releasing it to another.

Labor-saving machinery for raising and distributing water seems to have come very much later, perhaps because labor was cheap, plentiful, and expendable. Archimedes invented one such device, based on his study of the screw. A more sophisticated version with a longer lift used buckets attached to an endless chain on a rotating drum. Drawings of such machines have been found on Egyptian papyri of the second century B.C. and this system is believed to have been used to raise water for the Hanging Gardens of Babylon. The period between the third century B.C. and our era was a fruitful one for new techniques. Knowledge of the equilibrium and pressure of water was applied by the Romans, with great precision of surveying and leveling, to municipal water supplies, and resulted in the remarkable Roman aqueducts, such as the one built in 312 B.C. that ran for 10 miles underground. Another important development was the rotary grain mill driven by water power, which began to be used around 100 B.C., and of which Antipater of Salonica wrote in awe, "Mill girls touch the quern no more; for Demeter hath bidden the Nymphs perform your work."

The credit for building waterworks was, as a rule, appropriated by the kings and princes, but a few names of hydraulic engineers have been preserved through the ages, attesting to the high esteem in which they were held. Such engineers were Chen Kou, whose reputation was so great that he was brought from his native state to build the canal between the King and Lo rivers in the state of Ch'in, and Li Ping, designer of the irrigation system developed in the Red River basin of Szechuan around 250 B.C., who had his precept for effective river control—"Dig the channel deep: keep the spillway low"— engraved in stone that it might endure for all time (Jones, 1954).

In the fluvial civilizations the distribution of surface waters was in the hands of public officials and was closely supervised. A Chinese classic, the *Li Ki* of the Chou period, outlines the duties of local officials in seeing to the repair of dikes and dams, in inspecting land, in ensuring that canals and ditches were free from silt, and in opening channels. There were heavy penalties laid upon everyone for neglecting the upkeep of works; Section 55 of Hammurabi's Code prescribed compensation in an amount equivalent to the value of the crop lost by the injured party. Even more severe penalties were imposed in China, where an official might lose his life if the flood overtopped the dikes. In certain areas and at certain periods, waters were appropriated for private use in excess of requirements, and there was often a seesaw struggle between the private interests and the administration. Thus, the Chinese *Book of the Tang* (618–905 A.D.) describes how in one province a number of water-driven wheels for power were abolished and how nearly 100 privately owned reservoirs were ordered destroyed because they held back the flow of irrigation water to lower lying land.

Ground water had a separate, though also closely controlled, regime. If its occurrence and nature were not always precisely understood, the body of law that grew up around it in ancient times gave evidence of its importance. One of the oldest systems of irrigation, of land use, and of administration evolved about the use of ground water. This system was the so-called Well-Land system of China which flowered in the Chou period and probably before. The unit was a portion of land, divided into nine parts; the central one, containing the well, was the public field, and the surrounding eight were each cultivated by a family and irrigated from the well. The notable feature of this scheme was that it ensured a supply of water for all, and prevented wells from being too closely spaced and depleting the underground resource. A similar concept is expressed in the Indian *Code of Manu*

(believed to date from between 200 B.C. and 200 A.D.), which prescribed that wells and fountains be built where land boundaries coincided, thus obviating individual monopoly of a particular source of supply, and also in Moslem customary law, which to this day prescribes a reserved or prohibited area (the *hareem*) around each well.

Elaborate laws were developed quite early to regulate the use of ground water. Ancient Talmudic law provides a precise system of priorities governing the relations, in every circumstance, between those who lived close to a well or spring and strangers. It refers to a spring owned by the people of a city (Hirsch, 1959):

> their lives and the lives of others—their lives take precedence over those of others; their beasts and the beasts of others—their beasts take precedence over the beasts of others; their laundering and the laundering of others —their laundering takes precedence over the laundering of others; the lives of others and their laundering—the lives of others take precedence over their laundering.

The benefits of a truly well-conceived, well-administered water development system were not utilitarian alone. There was an early association between water development and aesthetic values. The pleasures derived in arid lands from the sight of pools and fountains and water running in channels, from the coolness and shade of trees, from the scent of flowers and the presence of wildlife, must have been sharpened intensely by the contrast between the watered oasis and the sterile wilderness beyond its bounds. The pleasure garden, watered either naturally or artificially, is a motif central to all the fluvial civilizations. Plans for water gardens have been dated back at least to 1500 B.C. in Egypt. Around 700 B.C., in the Tigris-Euphrates basin, Sennacherib formed an artificial swamp in one of his royal parks— perhaps the earliest known instance of wetlands conservation. And there were the famous Hanging Gardens of Babylon, a "pleasaunce" of trees and flowers, built on the topmost of a series of arches 75 feet high, and kept in a state of perfection by water raised from the Euphrates. That water development enhanced the quality of life in every way is aptly described in *Isaiah* 58, 9–14:

> thou shalt be like a watered garden, and like a fountain of water whose waters shall not fail. And the places that have been desolate for ages shall be built in thee: thou shalt raise up the foundations of generation and generation: and thou shalt be called the repairer of the fences, turning the paths into rest.

The different natures of the great rivers made it necessary to devise different systems for their development. In the Egyptian sector of the Nile valley, which received no rainfall and no increment in flow from tributary streams, the problem was to provide a more even distribution of the life-giving autumn Nile flood—*aut Nilus, aut nihil*. Menes reputedly reclaimed the left bank in 3400 B.C., leaving the right bank as a kind of safety valve to be swept by floods. A longitudinal dike was cut parallel to the mainstream and a network of cross dikes and canals conducted water into basins. Under the Pharaohs of the twelfth dynasty, the right bank was reclaimed and the Nile confined to its main channel. Then the channel was cut to the Faiyum depression, which became a storage reservoir. The system of basin irrigation developed was to last until well into the nineteenth century A.D., constantly renewing the fertility of the soil. Not until perennial irrigation was introduced did Egypt begin to experience serious problems, or attempt to solve them by building ever-larger dams and waterworks.

In the Tigris-Euphrates basin the problems were more complex. This was a land of some rainfall (which the Egyptians, who had no experience of it at home, called a "Nile in heaven") and of spring flood fed by snowmelt. There were two rivers to be controlled instead of one, a broad instead of a narrow floodplain, very erratic floods, and river beds so built up by sedimentation that the rivers ran high above the plain. Here perennial irrigation had to be used, for the crops were already standing in the fields when the floods came. Massive barrages and banks were built to regulate the flow, and canals were cut at carefully calculated levels. The two rivers were treated differently—the Euphrates was controlled by escape channels into the desert and the Tigris was protected by parallel canals.

Perennial irrigation, as in Mesopotamia, posed problems. The building of dams and canals without adequate drainage, the salinization of soils, the flooding, erosion, and siltation of irrigation works from forest destruction on the watersheds eventually brought about a total breakdown of the once-great water development system. The Mongols have been charged with destroying Mesopotamia's irrigation agriculture, but the damage was done before they came. By the twelfth century deterioration was so far advanced that one chronicler, Otto of Fresing, wrote: "But what now is Babylon? —a shrine of sirens, a house of lizards and ostriches, a den of serpents" (Helfrich, 1970). The harmful effects were due not so much to siltation or soil deterioration per se, but to human failure to sustain a social system permitting maintenance of the works. Nicholson (1970) has distinguished between the development in Egypt and China and that of Mesopotamia:

> Of their areas of operation the Nile and the Yellow River continue to perform similar roles for populations not even now sufficiently richer or denser to contrast unduly with results achieved in very early times. Only, perhaps, in Mesopotamia are there indications that erosion and other misuse of the land may have contributed towards rendering beneficial use of certain community sites impossible. Not so much directly as by encouraging excess growth and concentration of population over wide surrounding areas, which became deforested, overgrazed or overcropped and eroded, did the new cities and states become an instrument for severely degrading their natural environment" (p. 38).

The Egyptians, it must be admitted, had an easier time of it. Their flood season and their growing season came in orderly sequence. They scarcely needed to plough, but could sow directly into the film of fertilizing mud left by the flood. Field canals were not required, for the land was left fallow after the winter cropping until the next flood, and return water drained naturally into the river or downward to replenish ground water in the sand and gravel beds underlying the alluvial layer. They were wise enough to leave well enough alone, for, as Hamdan (p. 125) points out:

> There can be . . . no doubt that either through its silt deposit or fallow period, the basin system is biologically sound, making for soil conservation and regeneration. It has survived through millennia because it maintained the "ecological balance" of the soil and provided a "workable connexion" with the natural environment. Since it needed few main canals and no field ditches or drains, it was likewise in tune with the principle of space economy, so imperious in such a limited "finite universe" as the land of Egypt.

Close observance of their physical environment was so rooted in the Chinese character that one of the most ancient Chinese books of wisdom and philosophy, the *I Ching*, bases its entire scheme for the regulation of human conduct upon the observance of patterns of change in nature (Legge, 1969). Indeed, its very symbolism is supposed to have derived from the legendary "River Map" given forth by the Yellow River, and the attributes of the various kinds of water—rainfall, springs, mountain torrents, streams, rivers, lakes, marshes, and water artificially contained in ponds, tanks, and wells—provide analogies for nearly half the book. The *I Ching* reveals an awareness of the hydrologic cycle and of the nature of monsoon rains ("When the airs of spring begin to blow, from the collections of water on the earth the moistening vapors rise up and descend again"), as well as of the action of ground water. A rising ground water table was a symbol of good

fortune, but there could be too much of a good thing, for a forest submerged in water indicated excess and destruction, on which the commentator said (Legge, 1969, p. 303):

> The waters of a marsh moisten and nourish the trees. When here it is said that they destroy and extinguish the trees, their action is very extraordinary.

The microclimatic effect of a body of water, such as a marsh, upon surrounding terrain was duly noted (Legge, 1969, p. 318).

> The waters of a marsh are continually rising up in vapor to bedew the hill above it, and thus increase its verdure; what is taken from the marsh gives increase to the hill.

The book also contains a clear warning that encroachment upon the floodplain by building was dangerous, whereas on the river terrace it might be acceptable. There were equally clear precepts concerning the upkeep of wells and the need for tiling a well to prevent seepage. In fact, the advice is so timeless that the statement, "A city may be moved, but not a well" (Legge, 1969, p. 164-165) seems to sum up the entire history of water development versus environmental quality.

But the good advice was by no means steadfastly implemented. Periods of efficient water administration were followed by periods of disruption and political instability. During China's feudal times, water control became a weapon in interstate struggles, as described by a later historian (Chi, 1936, p. 64):

> Those feudal states which quarreled for water-benefits, constructed dikes to enclose the fertile valleys and river channels for their own benefit. Those who were anxious to avoid the dangers of flood also constructed dikes to force water into their neighbour's country, regarding the latter as a reservoir for surplus water . . . more and more dikes were built day by day and they encroached so much upon the natural channel of the river that the dikes were burst and floods became frequent.

The uncoordinated building of dikes and embankments reveals the lack of effective central direction of flood control measures, which increased the danger of floods. A commentator of the last decade B.C., Chia Jang, gives a vivid account of how rings of dikes were built inside each major embankment of the Yellow River. The land between the dikes was drained and the government gave it to people who had lived there for ten years. Permanent settlements were established in the floodplain and another embankment went up to turn the river in a different direction. Thus, he says (Chi, 1936, p. 91):

in a distance of over a hundred *li* [about 33 miles] the river was turned twice westward and three times eastward.

Other evils developed later, notably the drainage and appropriation of the so-called Wei-land, or lake and river bottomland, during the Sung dynasty in the twelfth century A.D. This action brought the twin and alternating curses of drought and flood to the lands of the common people. The dangers could have been avoided by effective government control but since it was largely government officials themselves who were responsible for the drainage and who owned the choicest land, little was done about it. Wei Chin, a more public-spirited official of the times, wrote angrily (Chi, 1936, pp. 136–137):

Thus the people were deprived more and more of the benefit of reservoirs and lakes. What used to be rivers, lakes, and marshes has all become land in the last thirty years . . .

The rise of Wei-land and the construction of dikes and embankments have blocked the outlet of the waters. During slight drought, the owners of Wei-land take possession of the upstream sections of the rivers and monopolize the advantages of irrigation, and the people's land is deprived of the use of water. When the water of the rivers and lakes overflows, the surplus water is sent downstream and the people's land is used as a watershed.

Even in Egypt, where the beneficent basin system of irrigation left perhaps slightly more margin for error, any neglect of the waterworks added to the perils of a too high or too low flood, bringing famine in its wake. When control from the center declined, land went out of cultivation, especially on the desert margins where salt and sand were ever waiting to move in. Apathy and neglect are believed to have been the reasons why Egypt lost forever some 1.5 million acres of land—the Beraris of the delta—in the period of late Roman and early Arab rule. The canal network broke down, hindering drainage to the sea, and all that once-fertile land, on which the excess water evaporated into a saline crust, became an alkali desert (Hamdan, 1961).

EUROPE FROM THE MIDDLE AGES TO THE INDUSTRIAL REVOLUTION: SLOW MOTION

The water development techniques of the fluvial civilizations persisted in the regions of their origin until well into our own era, and had some influence on Europe through the Romans, who borrowed and adapted them from the Middle East, and through the Moors, who introduced a highly sophisticated irrigation agriculture into Spain. On the whole, however, humid western Europe went its own way in water management and did not make much use of the examples bequeathed by the Romans, except in water law.

The economic base in this period was rainfall agriculture (apart from scattered areas of intensive irrigation, such as the Po Plain and parts of Spain), with a gradually increasing amount of industry, dependent to a considerable extent upon water power and scattered mining and metal working. Flour milling was the most widespread industrial use initially. Domesday records of the eleventh century show more than 5,000 grist mills in southern and eastern England, of the sort that Kipling described in *Puck's Song*:

See you our little mill that clacks
So busy by the brook?

> She has ground her corn and paid her tax
> Ever since Domesday book.

This type of mill was also early adapted to the fulling of cloth, and the technique spread from southern to northern Europe. It is recorded that at the beginning of the twelfth century the Italian city of Prato had a large number of cloth-working mills, and that to accommodate their needs the Bisenzio River was diverted into a network of small canals. By the end of that century the fulling industry was well established in England, especially in upland areas with rapid streams and clear water.

There was scattered water development, too, for placer mining and iron manufacturing. Tin streaming, for example, reached such a level of activity in southwestern England by the mid-fourteenth century that the tinners developed their own law and their own courts to settle disputes. Iron manufacture was carried on all over medieval Europe and required increasing amounts of water, especially after the switch from the bloomery hearth to the blast furnace, for which a larger water wheel was needed. The blast furnace was another industrial technique which, like cloth fulling, spread gradually northward and northwestward. It made an appearance in the Rhineland in the fifteenth century, in southeastern England around 1500, in the English midlands by the mid-sixteenth century, and to the Welsh marshes by the beginning of the seventeenth century.

Navigational improvements on the whole came later. It is true that the Romans had introduced some artificial canals, which were refurbished (the Foss Dyke in England, a relic of the Roman occupation, was deepened and made navigable in 1121), and that Charlemagne had had plans for a system of waterways connecting the Main, Rhine, and Danube. But very little could be done to make more use of the rivers until locks were built to overcome differences of level. Whether the Dutch or the Italians are credited with this invention—Leonardo da Vinci

is known to have completed six locks uniting the canals of Milan in 1487—it was not until the seventeenth century in France that modern-type canals made their appearance— the Briare canal (1605–1642), and the Canal du Midi (completed in 1681) with its 119 locks.

The localized need for drainage and reclamation, as in the Netherlands and in the English fenland, did give rise to some quite large-scale projects at this period of European history. Schemes for the draining of the fenland, for instance, were prepared during the later years of the sixteenth century, and when James I came to the throne in 1603 he showed a lively interest in the matter, declaring that he himself would undertake the work in return for 120,000 acres of marsh. He called in the Dutch engineer, Vermuyden, to draw up plans, but died before anything could be done. His successor, Charles I, also showed an interest in fen-draining, which was somewhat abruptly terminated by the Civil War. However, in 1649 an act was passed "for the draining the Great Level of the Fens" and the work was put in charge of the Earl of Bedford and a group of associates. Great things were expected of the project and the drained fen was to be made (Darby, 1936, p. 450)

> fit to bear coleseed and rapeseed in great abundance, which is of singular use to make soap and oils within this nation, to the advancement of the trade of clothing and spinning of wool, and much of it will be improved into good pasture for feeding and breeding of cattle, and of tillage to be sown with corn and grain, and for hemp and flax in great quantity, for making all sorts of linen cloth and cordage for shipping within this nation; which will increase manufactures, commerce, and trading at home and abroad, will relieve the poor by setting them on work, and will in many other ways redound to the great advantage and strengthening of the nation.

On the whole, however, technological achievements in water development in

Europe at this time were few and rather small scale, not because the engineering skill was lacking, but rather because the political and social systems were discouraging to major effort. It was a loose-knit, decentralized, fragmented society, unable to command the enormous labor resources that had made feasible the complex storage and distribution works of the fluvial civilizations, and not really needing them anyway. The legal system, too, was in tune with this attitude toward water. In most of Europe, by the Middle Ages, the major streams had lost the public character that they possessed under the Romans, and were parcelled up between the land magnates and the cities, thus precluding any cooperative effort at water development. The influence of Roman law, which held that the use of major streams, although public and open to all, should be regulated by the state, and the strengthening of the central government brought the navigable streams back into the public domain soon after the close of the Middle Ages. Thus, Venice, influenced in part by scarcity of water, made all its waters public in the sixteenth century and required authorization for their use. Almost a century later, in the Edict of 1669, France reasserted control of all navigable streams by the crown.

On the other hand, the riparian elements in Roman law which emphasized the maintenance of the natural flow and quality of water reinforced local customs which tended to preserve the use of at least the smaller streams as they had always been used in the past, as exemplified in the maxim, *Aqua currit et debet currere ut currere solebat.* Thus, favorable conditions were created for the development in the nineteenth century of a full-fledged riparian rights doctrine. This early European riparianism reflected perhaps the only way in which a society with neither the technical ability nor the overwhelming need to manipulate water could adapt itself to the interdependence of flowing waters.

The rather protective influence of riparianism did not mean, however, that there was not a cumulative environmental impact of innumerable small uses. This impact is indicated by the nature and frequency of conflicts and by the measures taken to resolve them. One development, dating from the thirteenth century and perhaps even earlier, was the introduction of weirs on rivers that were used by water mills for power—the "bonnie milldams o'Binnorie" of the ancient ballad. These did not altogether impound the flow as in the later canal lock, but were supposed to maintain a sufficient depth of water for boats. That they evidently did not do this is shown by edicts forbidding any construction that obstructed navigation, as for example, the document of John of Bohemia of 1337 concerning the Oder River, Magna Carta (c. XXIII), an English act of 1472 "for the taking Away of Wears and Fishbgarthes," and a French edict of 1515 "Concerning Revocation of Unauthorized Tolls Established on the Loire within the Past 100 Years, and the Verification of Titles of Said Tolls, Fisheries, Mills, Etc." Some effort was also made in keeping the channels clear to protect the spawning runs of anadromous fish. These had been jeopardized not only by the navigation weirs and stationary fish traps, but also by the older type of floating mill operating actually in the stream. Thus, as early as the seventh century, the Lex Visigothorum, an amalgam of Spanish, Roman, and Germanic law, provided that:

> No one shall for his own private benefit, and against the interests of the community, obstruct any stream of importance; that is to say, one in which salmon and other sea-fish enter, or into which nets may be cast, or vessels may come for the purpose of commerce (Dobkins, 1959, p. 73).

As the centuries advanced there was concern also over pollution and siltation. For example, so intense was the activity of the tin streamers in southwestern England in the thirteenth and fourteenth centuries that there were many complaints of destruction of arable land and diversion of streams. The tinners (early counterparts of the hydraulic miners in nineteenth century California, who ravaged the valleys of the Mother Lode country—see below) were believed to be responsible for the silting up of harbors at river mouths as well.

Changes in water flow were often caused in the Middle Ages by the damming up of outlets to marshes to form fish ponds. Great numbers of such ponds were created for monasteries and landed proprietors. They frequently became polluted and, in southern Europe especially, a source of epidemics. Changes in flow caused by weirs, mill ponds, and flood protection works appear also as the cause of numerous actions in the English case law. Frequently the building of a new mill diminished the water supply for an older one. This was the complaint, for example, in *Russell v. Handfords* (1583),[33] *La Countee de Rutland v. Bowler* (1622),[16] and *Sands v. Trefuses* (1639).[34] Or the mill-dam backed up water behind it to the detriment of someone else's land, as in *Prince v. Moulton* (1697).[31] Or, as in *Duncombe v. Randall* (1628),[68] suit was brought "for diversion and stopping of a river."

As for ground water, it was almost universally the property of the owner of the land to do with as he liked, even if in digging a well or opening a spring he reduced the flow of a neighbor's well or spring. Such use was recognized by the Spanish *Siete Partidas* of the thirteenth century. The interrelationships of ground and surface waters were not well or widely understood, although some individual observers had a remarkably clear conception of how ground water behaved. The French philosopher Bernard Palissy (1510–1589), for example, was well aware of the processes of infiltration, and wrote (Marsh, 1965, p. 379):

> thou mayest plainly see the reason why there be more springs and rivulets proceeding from the mountains than from the rest of the earth; which is for no other cause but that the rocks and mountains do retain the water of the rains like vessels of brass. And the said waters falling upon the said mountains descend continually through the earth, and through crevices, and stop not till they find some place that is bottomed with stone or close and thick rocks; and they rest upon such bottom until they find some channel or other manner of issue, and then they flow out in springs or brooks or rivers, according to the greatness of the reservoirs and of the outlets thereof.

The fen drainage, as described by Darby (1936) was one of the most conspicuous examples of environmental mismanagement, though in fairness to its proponents, they could hardly have foreseen that their seventeenth century development would contribute to the disastrous effects of mid-twentieth century floods. There were early warnings of trouble, but because of the enormously increased agricultural production in the beginning, these went largely unheeded. The engineer Vermuyden advocated channelization of the main rivers, and this was done over the opposition of a group that wanted the existing waterways merely deepened and cleaned out. The southern fen (or peat fen) which was farthest from the sea was drained first, and the northern part (or silt fen) nearest the sea was tackled later. This sequence resulted in silting up of the river outfalls and poor drainage to the sea. Moreover, the peat fen when drained dried out and shrank, so that quite soon it was lower than the silt fen. Before drainage the peat fen had been some 6 feet higher than the silt fen; within the next three centuries it shrank 16 feet, until it was about 10 feet lower than the silt. Some of these effects were noticeable within a decade or so after work began. It was remarked in the General Drainage Act of 1663 that already drainage in some areas had adversely affected other lands, and the purpose of the act itself was to increase the project area by way of solution. Within just over two decades after initiation of the original work there were disastrous floods. Water had to be pumped out by windmills, and the corporation in charge of the drainage could not undertake a task of this magnitude. It was farmed out to local districts, each responsible only for its own pumping operations. Over the next century-and-a-half these districts proliferated throughout the fenland, uncoordinated and without financial resources to operate effectively when the floods came. Only the advent of the steam engine, which could pump the water off the land faster, saved the fens from that "total ruin" which the Secretary to the British Board of Agriculture had feared in 1805. But nothing could be done about the shrinkage, and with the ruler-straight fen rivers running many feet higher than the land, widespread disaster followed every flood until, in 1953, the gale-whipped North Sea burst over the dikes and forced the already swollen rivers back, drowning the land more thoroughly than it had ever been drowned prior to drainage.

The fenland story is almost contemporaneous with that of another drainage project thousands of miles away, which also destroyed, at enormous cost and suffering, a physical environment that otherwise might have retained its quality for centuries. The Spanish attempt to create a capital city in the Valle de Mexico is not in the mainstream of European water development history of this period, but it illustrates a trend which became much more pronounced in Europe's empire-building phase later. That is exporting European methods regardless of their suitability to local circumstances. The Aztecs, who came into the Valle de Mexico early in the fourteenth century and built their capital, Tenochtitlan, on one of its lakes, Lake Texcoco, had advanced techniques of water management. They had aqueducts for municipal water supply and practiced a unique system of irrigation *a la inversa*, through which they brought land to water, rather than water to land, by building artificial floating islets covered with soil (still to be seen in the famous flower-gardens or *chinampas* of Lake Xochimilco) and watered from below by the lake waters.

The incoming Spaniards destroyed the Aztec "Venice" in 1521 and proceeded to create their own city out of the lake waters. Several times poor drainage and floods almost forced them to seek another site, but landowners objected and, under the Dutch engineer Adrian Boot, a drainage and diversion project was begun in 1607 to carry excess waters through a tunnel into another drainage basin. Completed in 1789 at the cost of 70,000 Indian lives and an untold amount of money, the project was a colossal failure. Mexico City remained one of the New World's worst-drained cities and Lake Texcoco, polluted by centuries of sewage, remained a source of pestilence until 1900 when large-scale drainage works were undertaken. This drainage solved the twin problems of inundation and disease, but the city began to sink at the rate of two inches per year as the drained land shrank. Lake Texcoco was reduced to a shallow, desolate body of water, each falling level marked by salt incrustations around its shores. Other lakes in the Valle, such as Lake Chalco, also shrank through filling and diversion, as noted in the 1910 *Encyclopedia Britannica*, "to the great distress of the natives who have gained their living by fishing in its waters since long before the Spanish conquest."

FROM THE INDUSTRIAL REVOLUTION TO THE ERA OF MULTIPURPOSE WATER RESOURCES DEVELOPMENT: THE MACHINE-AGE INFLUENCE

Western Europe and Its Overseas Dependencies

The era of leisurely approaches to water development in Europe ended with the start of the Industrial Revolution, though it lingered in some areas well into the nineteenth century. When that century began only one major European power was fully in the throes of the Industrial Revolution. That country was Great Britain, where the change-over to large-scale manufacturing had been achieved some decades before the advent of the steam engine. The old-fashioned water wheel had proved adaptable to the new industrial processes and toward the end of the eighteenth century hundreds of grain and fulling mills along the Lancashire and Yorkshire rivers had been converted into textile factories by attaching spinning machines to the source of power. The steam engine gained swift popularity, however, partly because it freed manufacturing from the constraints of location in the narrow, upland valleys, and partly because free water could be obtained from some of the canal companies established in the 1790s. Industrial production rose rapidly, as exemplified in pig-iron output, which almost quintupled in the thirty-year period from 1796 to 1825. Other industrial processes kept pace, decade after decade, and with them grew the demand for water, until in Dickens' *Hard Times* we have Coketown, the city with "its canals black, its river purple with dye."

Other western European countries began to catch up. Around mid-century France attained Britain's 1825 pig-iron production. Germany's modern industries did not begin to develop until the 1840s—partly because the steam engine was slower to supercede the water wheel there. However, from that time on expansion was swift. The output of blast furnace products in the Ruhr multiplied eleven times in the 1850–1860 decade alone, and coal production, which was a little over 1.5 million tons in 1850, almost doubled within the next five years and continued rising at an ever faster rate until it reached more than 60 million tons in 1900. Long before that the Ruhr had its Coketowns too, and pollution was so bad that local communities banded together to form pollution control organizations lest, as the mayor of Essen put it, a city "drown in its own effluvia" (Fair, 1961).

There was no great advance of irrigation agriculture in Europe in the nineteenth century, but a considerable amount of land was brought into production through drainage and reclamation—as in the Garonne basin of France, where the swampy bottomlands were drained, thus providing meadow for pasture and permitting the growth of a thriving dairy industry. Navigation on many rivers declined as other uses of water increased and more attention was paid to flood control, though the loss of natural waterways to navigation was more than offset by the canal building which was enthusiastically pursued throughout lowland Europe. Already all the main English river basins had been interconnected, and on the Continent the first half of the nineteenth century saw the interlinking of the Rhone and Rhine (1832), the Main and Danube (1845), and the Rhine and Seine (1853), as well as the extension of a waterway system in Russia.

This was also an era of immense increase in Europe's population—from 188 million in 1800 to 266 million in 1880, and 401 million by 1900, massive emigrations notwithstanding. Heavy demands were placed on urban water supplies and, partly because of this demand, and also the pollution of local supplies, cities began to look farther and farther afield for water. London had begun the process long before; it had been getting water from springs near Ware, in Hertfordshire, since 1613. Between 1805 and 1822 alone it acquired no less than six new water companies. These and others were eventually placed (in 1904) under a central authority, the Metropolitan Water Board, responsible for "Water London," an area of some 600 square miles. At one time, the London County Council had had a scheme to bring water from the Welsh mountains, but it was never carried out, and the honor fell to Birmingham, which in 1892 received power to acquire the watersheds of two tributaries of the River Wye and proceeded to construct dams and reservoirs.

During the nineteenth century empires were built, and European colonists and administrators brought their notions of water resources development to their farthest outposts. In countries of old-established fluvial tradition such as India and Egypt, the British made a number of serious mistakes at first, and had some rather unfortunate experiences with water development by commercial ventures, though they eventually instituted quite advanced systems of government water control. In the almost empty, arid lands of Australia and Canada they attempted to continue farming as they had done at home—just as the emigrants from the eastern United States did in the semi-arid American West, with much the same results. Finding that settlements were threatened by repeated failures, the governments of these underpopulated countries encouraged an unknown technique—irrigation. The Spanish were already well acquainted with irrigation from centuries of development in their own homeland and in New Spain. They simply expanded it further in their Western Hemisphere possessions and borrowed some administrative trappings from the French in certain areas. The French were also acquainted with irrigation but, like the British, found themselves in a completely different environment—at least in their North African desert possessions, where irrigation was an ancient practice and Moslem tradition held. Like the British they too developed new engineering and administrative techniques to meet the situation.

Twenty years before the French Revolution, Joseph Priestly had written in his *Essay Upon the Principles of Government* (1768):

> Nature, including both its materials and its laws, will be more at our command; men will make their situation in the world abundantly more easy and comfortable; they will probably prolong their existence in it, and will daily grow more happy.

The water engineers of the nineteenth century strove to bring that bright promise within reach—building canals, taming rivers, extending distribution systems, storing water for future use. In the latter part of the century they were able to use reinforced concrete, as well as dynamite and earth-moving equipment. Water began to be used for generating electricity in the last quarter of the century, while power was first transmitted in 1882 from Meisbach to Munich (34 miles) and, during the Frankfurt Exhibition, was experimentally transmitted 109 miles. Data-gathering and the knowledge of the nature of surface and groundwater systems improved. During the first half of the nineteenth century in France, many artesian wells were built, stimulating an interest in ground water. Then came Darcy's law, formulated in 1856 by the French hydraulic engineer Henry Darcy, defining the relations governing groundwater flow in alluvial and sedimentary formations.

As the Europeans of the nineteenth century experimented with new techniques in water resources management, both at home and abroad, so they endeavored to bring their water law regimes up-to-date to meet the challenge of the new industrial age. The Code Napoléon of 1804, which embodied changes brought about by the French Revolution, was immensely influential. It was followed in several other European countries (including Spain during the first decades of the nineteenth century), in French possessions in Asia (where it has remained the heritage of all the countries of Indochina), and in North Africa, and in large parts of South America. It was also borrowed from rather eclectically in such codes as the Mejellé Code of the Ottoman Empire, promulgated between 1870 and 1876 (where it was interwoven with Moslem law). Essentially, the Code Napoléon put the navigable (that is, more important) rivers and streams in the public domain, paving the way for eventual administrative control of all flowing waters. Legislation of the 1790s had already entrusted the French administration with power to issue authorizations for certain uses of navigable rivers (including irrigation) and by mid-century, France was already requiring permits for the taking of water by means of machines from non-navigable and non-floatable streams and for all new construction, such as mills, factories, and dams.

English development took quite a different turn. The principle of ancient use which had evolved into the riparian rights doctrine, making no distinction between navigable and non-navigable streams, protected the community of interests of landowners bordering on flowing waters and, possibly because of the relative weakness of the central government (as compared with that of France), left little leeway for any administrative regulation of water development. The British took their common law system of riparian rights with them in their colonizing ventures, but with varied success. Indeed, it is possible to relate sharp increases in the growth and development of irrigation agriculture toward the end of the century in Australia and Canada directly to the abandonment of riparianism and its replacement by centralized government control of water. In India, the transplantation of an alien system of water management and ignorance of indigenous systems of water development and land use led to grave mismanagement of water resources.

The basic unit of administration in India—the village community—had remained undisturbed for centuries throughout a succession of rulers, and so had the basic organization of water distribution through the village governing body, or *panchayat*. However, the Mogul rulers had introduced a new element which was to have a profound influence on water resources and that was the institution of the *zamindar*, or tax collector. Under the British, the role of the zamindar was confused with that of an English landed proprietor and there was created a distinction between a privileged class of landlords and the vast majority of the population. The abuses of this system have had repercussions on water management to the present day, although it has since been abolished. One recent writer on the distribution of canal water said (Thorner, 1962, p. 16):

The influential get the water first and take as much as they please. Only after they are satisfied do they permit the mass of petty cultivators access to it. For the latter at the period of peak demand water is normally scarce.

Thus, water was frequently wasted by one group, while another larger group went without. The remarkable system of canal water supply for irrigation, by diversion from the great rivers in Bengal, was allowed to fall into decay because the British in the early period misunderstood the purpose of the canals and thought that they were for navigation only. And, in areas of water supply from tanks and wells, the works were neglected because only a small fraction of the receipts from land were used for this purpose. Not the least of the evils was the increasing salinization—the deadly "Reh" and "Kullur" —noted by Henry Medlicott in 1862 over large areas in northern and western India through evaporation of salts leached from the soil by irrigation waters (Marsh, 1965, p. 324).

Europeans attempting to adjust to an alien environment could have been excused their mistakes. There was far less justification for the environmental abuse to which they subjected their water resources at home. One type of abuse was the practice of sinking wells to carry off the effluent from chemical plants and factories. A starch factory in Paris was reported to have discharged 20,000 gallons of polluted water a day into such a well in the winter of 1832–1833 (Marsh, 1965, p. 308). The practice was so widespread and caused such concern that it was the subject of a municipal investigation, because of the danger of seepage into wells used for drinking water supply, but as so often happened, the matter ended with the study. The making of gas was one of the major causes for court cases on grounds of pollution. In a notable English case in 1834, *R. v. Medley* (brought on behalf of fisheries interests which had suffered damage),[32] a gas company was indicted for polluting Thames waters, and eventually, in 1875, the Public Health Act prohibited the deposit in waters of washings or other substances produced in the making of gas.

Coal mining was responsible for a good deal of noxious pollution, as well as unsightly landscapes. Abandoned workings frequently collapsed, as in the Emscher Valley of the Ruhr region, leaving pestilence-breeding watery depressions with no drainage, a convenient dump for all sorts of household and industrial rubbish and effluent. The rivers were no better, for they received all the wastes of the cities and industries crowded along their banks in this German "Black Country." Cities took each other to court and in 1897 the city of Essen was, in effect, enjoined from discharging any of its sewage—a desperate measure resorted to by a desperate downstream community (Fair, 1961).

In England the situation was hardly improved, for although the riparian rights system provided for the enjoining of uses which sensibly affected the quality or quantity of water in a stream, this law could be and was circumvented by statute, prescription, custom, and grant. The statutory provisions superseded all common-law rights, thus giving the polluter a legal right to pollute. Evidence of the type of damage which could result appears in some of the cases. Thus, the washing of mine tailings into a stream was the subject of *Wright v. Williams* (1836),[42] in which the Prescription Act of 1832 was invoked to support a right to pollute as an easement by long user, and of *Carlyon v. Lovering* (1857),[4] invoking immemorial custom. In two other cases, involving public water management agencies against private corporations, the latter had a statutory right to pollute—*Lea Conservancy Board v. Hertford Corp.* (1884)[18] and *Somerset Drainage Comrs. v. Bridgwater Corpn.* (1899).[35]

One clue to the kind of damage being done to the environment in the nineteenth century is provided by international water treaties of the period. While it might turn a blind eye to what its own nationals were doing, no European country in that era of

emergent nationalism was going to permit another country to pollute, divert, or otherwise injure the quality and quantity of the waters it received. Therefore, because of political fragmentation and the large number of boundary streams involved, such treaties must be considered a potent factor in maintaining many bodies of water in a more natural state than would have been the case if only one political unit were involved. A 1779 agreement between Austria and the Elector Palatine provided bluntly that:

> neither of the two Contracting Parties shall be able to alter the natural course of the rivers.[46]

Similarly, the Treaty of Aachen of 1816 between Prussia and the Netherlands, concerning frontier waterways, stated:

> No alterations of any kind can be undertaken, either to the course of the river or to the present condition of the banks, nor will any concession be granted nor water diverted without the agreement and consent of the two Governments . . .[47]

Mutual consent of both parties was required for diversion of waters in the Belgium-Luxembourg treaty of 1842 and the Belgium-Netherlands treaty of 1863 regarding the Meuse.[48]

The Convention of 1879 between Switzerland and the Grand Duchy of Baden, relating to the Rhine, placed on each party the obligation to ensure that any works undertaken, such as the erection of waterwheels, would not substantially impair the flow of water or cause damage to the river banks, and to notify the other state in advance if there were such possibility. The Agreement Relating to Navigation on the Danube between Braila and the Iron Gates of 1883 is very specific as to the siting and nature of structures permitted. It states in Article 5 (Berber, 1959, p. 81):

> Immovable mills erected on the river channel, floating mills, fisheries and irrigation wheels must not hinder navigation. They shall be

erected on those parts of the river which do not serve as channels for ships and river craft, and their location shall be chosen in such a manner as not to injure the free flow of water and not to cause harmful alterations in the bed of the river.

Heavy obligation to maintain the rivers in their natural state is also placed on the participating governments in the Additional Act to the Franco-Spanish treaty of 1886,[44] which requires that:

The lower levels shall be bound to receive from the higher levels in the neighboring country the waters which naturally run down from them, together with whatever they carry along, apart from anything contributed by human agency. No dam, or any obstacle liable to injure the higher riparians shall be built, and the latter shall likewise be forbidden to take any action which may increase the servitudes of the lower levels.

The United States—Setting the Stage

Water development in the United States in the nineteenth century, like everything else, was dominated by the "Go West" drive. Its story divides rather neatly into two distinct periods. In the first, the waterborne activities centered in the humid East, and were directed chiefly to overcoming natural barriers lying across the westward expansion. In the second period, the center of gravity shifted beyond the Mississippi and the main effort and emphasis was on making the semi-arid and arid West into a flourishing garden.

The humid East—a region of rainfall agriculture and heavy industry, and hence of a water use pattern not unlike that of western Europe in the same era—was striving throughout the first half of the century to catch up with the Industrial Revolution in Great Britain. It succeeded by about 1850, when American pig-iron production, some 618,000 tons, reached the annual level that Britain had achieved about a quarter of a century earlier. American industry was still dependent

primarily upon water power rather than steam power and would continue to be so until after the Civil War. Not until 1870 would the use of steam overtake that of water. Mills and mill dams proliferated on every stream in the East with a sufficient head of water, the tumbling streams of New England and the rivers of the Atlantic states from New Jersey to Georgia, where they plunged from the older and harder rocks of the Piedmont over the younger and softer strata of the coastal plain.

This zone of falls and rapids played an important part in the water development and history of the entire eastern seaboard. Frequently, it marked the head of navigation for seagoing vessels, the location of manufacturing, and the sites of most of the seaboard's major cities—New York, Philadelphia, Baltimore, Washington, and many more. It was also a hindrance to navigation, and the young nation devoted considerable energy to overcoming this obstacle. Canal building was enthusiastically pursued to facilitate movement into the West which the natural drainage could not afford. The link between Atlantic and Great Lakes drainage was achieved quite early by the Erie (1825) and Oswego (1828) canals. The problem of surmounting the Appalachian divide was more difficult and took longer. It was met successfully by the Pennsylvania Canal system in 1834 (but only with the aid of a railroad over the Allegheny Front) and by the Chesapeake and Ohio Canal (1850), and unsuccessfully by the James River Canal, which never got beyond the mountain barrier. But the burgeoning West of that period could not wait for the canals to catch up with it. The Louisiana Purchase had given the United States complete control of the huge, ramified Mississippi River system, which through its western tributaries gave access to a land area of over one million square miles. The steamboat opened this inland empire up to the head of navigation and by the end of the first half of the century there were about 1,200 steam packets in service on the Red, the Arkansas, the

White, the Ouachita, the Missouri, and other "western waters."

Here the westward-moving tide of emigrants was brought to a vastly different scene. They had known how to cope with the forest; indeed, they had hacked away at it so mightily that once busy colonial seaports lay idle, clogged with the topsoil of denuded uplands. They were learning how to cope with the treeless prairie and had begun an extensive transformation of its wetter portions through drainage. But on or about the 98th meridian the original tall grass vegetation of the prairie merged into the short grass of the Great Plains. It would take another century before the significance of that fact was truly appreciated, a century in which the plains at times seemed to dissolve in "black blizzards" of dust and the very sun was obscured by the awesome disintegration of a land not meant for the plough. Paradoxically, it was near Beatrice, Nebraska—on the eastern margin of the water-deficient West, just short of the 98th meridian and the 20-inch isohyet—that the first homestead claim was filed, on New Year's Day, 1863. The next decade or so happened to be a wet cycle, in the unpredictable sequence of wet and dry periods characteristic of this region, and the homesteaders who had secured their 160 acres of unappropriated government land actually attributed the increased rainfall to their settlement. "Rain follows the plough," they declared, and in the soaring confidence of those prosperous years was born the so-called Garden Myth.

Meanwhile, in the farthest West, developments were taking place which were to have a profound impact on water management and, ultimately, on the environment. The California Gold Rush and other mining activities in the Mountain West had three consequences: (1) they contributed to the growth of irrigation agriculture; (2) they created, in placer mining, a considerable demand for water on their own account; and (3) they led to the institution of an entirely new legal regime for the use of waters. It was true that the Mormons had begun irrigation works from the time of their arrival in the promised land, and that irrigation had long been known and practiced in the Spanish settlements of the Southwest, but the real impetus came from the demand for food from the mining camps and boom towns, and in the steady stream of people passing through. The Mormon colonies in Utah, Idaho, and Wyoming soon turned their attention to supplying these wants, and after the completion of the transcontinental railroad in 1869, which brought increased imigration to the West, some irrigation was begun in nearly all the arid territories. By 1890, 3.7 million acres were under irrigation, practically all in the seventeen western states, and after a decade the figure had more than doubled to almost 7.8 million acres.

Within a century the United States population, swelled by the influx of Europe's surplus, had grown spectacularly, from some 5.25 million in 1800 to 23.25 million by mid-century, then to 76 million by the end of the period. In the water-scarce West the numbers had multiplied many times over in some states. Since 1850 Utah's population had increased 25-fold, New Mexico's had more than trebled, California's had multiplied sixteen times, and that of Texas fourteen times.

The technology existed to satisfy the varied demands of urban water supply, irrigation, mining, river transportation, and manufacturing. As in Europe, it had steadily risen to and beyond the level of water management in the fluvial civilizations. Now, with the aid of concrete, of steam and electric power, of huge dredges and of dynamiting equipment it was possible, as one technical expert said, to construct more in two decades than during an entire dynasty of rulers in antiquity, employing corvée labor and armies of prisoners.

Technology was one element that contributed to a developmental philosophy, in tune with a belief in the inevitability of human progress and the capacity of man to conquer his environment. Another was the frontier legend, a pastoral epic of rugged, simple, honest folk triumphing over nature to carve out a civilization in the wilderness. This philosophy projected Jefferson's dream of a nation of freehold yeomen, was given substance by Lincoln in the Homestead Act of 1862, and formed the motif of Frederick Jackson Turner's frontier thesis in 1892. The "Go West" drive and the lure of apparently limitless empty land required adaptation to an unfamiliar environment at a pace perhaps unequalled anywhere else in the world at any time. It also absolved people and their leaders in government from the responsibility of correcting environmental mistakes and conserving resources in the older, settled, eastern part of the country. And from river basin to river basin across the land its "manifest destiny" sheltered ignorance, haste, waste, and sheer rapacity in water resources development as settlement drove steadily into a region with 60 percent of the country's land area and only 25 percent of its water. Decades after the frontier closed, around 1890, the frontier legend lived on, a potent symbol defying the evidence of man-altered landscapes, the lessons of flood and drought, the warnings of conservationists, and society's vague unease that it would never again hear the call to "Go and look behind the Ranges—Something lost behind the Ranges. Lost and waiting for you. Go!" (Kipling, *The Explorer*, 1898).

UTILITY THE DOMINANT CRITERION: A LEGAL REGIME TO ACCOMMODATE UNLIMITED DEVELOPMENT

During the nineteenth century in America, as in Europe, water law was molded to cope with the growing demand for water under the spur of industrialization. In the eastern United States, the natural flow version of the riparian rights doctrine was steadily transformed into the reasonable use version, which was much more adaptable to industrial needs.

The natural flow doctrine, by requiring that water not be sensibly diminished or depleted except for domestic uses, reflected the interdependence of waters and the unity of the river basin by recognizing the community of interests of the landowners bordering on the flowing waters. Like the immemorial usage doctrine of pre-Industrial Revolution times, it protected this community of interests by trying to reduce the possibility of change and the scope of new uses. The reasonable use doctrine that appeared around the middle of the century abandoned insistence on an undiminished flow of water, and in its unrestricted version permitted any use of water by a riparian owner which appeared reasonable to the courts. In most jurisdictions, however, permitted uses were restricted to those still pertaining to riparian land; this restriction was by no means detrimental to industry, since the industrial uses were riparian. To the contrary, the reasonable use doctrine had a built-in preference for industry because the great social value attached to manufacturing clothed it with reasonableness when competing with other uses. Even where a use was admittedly unreasonable, the courts still resorted to the balancing of equities in determining whether to award an injunction or merely damages, thus again favoring industrial and developmental purposes. This fact is quite well illustrated by pollution cases.

For example, in *Pennsylvania Coal Co. v. Sanderson* (1886),[30] the Pennsylvania Supreme Court found that pollution of a stream by a coal mine to the detriment of a lower riparian was a permissible use. The court stated:

> The plaintiff's grievance is for a mere personal inconvenience, and we are of the opinion that mere private inconvenience arising in this way and under such circumstances, must yield to the necessities of a great public industry, which although in the hands of a private corporation, subserves a great public interest.

The court neatly disposed of natural flow

requirements that a lower riparian is entitled to receive water in an unchanged condition, with the words:

> It will be observed that the defendants have done nothing to change the character of the water, or to diminish its purity, save what results from the natural use and enjoyment of their own property. They have brought nothing onto the land artificially. The water as it is poured into Meadow Brook is the water which the mine naturally discharged. Its impurity arises from natural, not artificial causes.

Long before any relaxation in the *theory* of the riparian rights doctrine became apparent, however, the developmental trend had inspired the so-called mill laws, which circumvented the doctrine itself. These laws permitted riparian owners, upon payment of compensation, to erect dams that were injurious to other owners. They were justified either on the ground that the authorized mills were in the public interest, or that the state had power to regulate the rights of riparian owners in their interest. A number of the mill acts dated back to colonial times, and most of the older ones pertained to grist mills for grinding grain. In the nineteenth century, however, many mill acts were made applicable to manufacturing establishments of all kinds that used water for power (as, for example, the Massachusetts act of 1824), and the blanket of legislative approval was thrown over a collectivity of uses that added up to grave mismanagement of water resources.

The mill acts were the first opening for governmental incursion into the field of water resources. Another one, and much more important, was through control of navigation. The advent of the steamboat had enhanced the importance of water transport, and the states granted monopolies to private interests, leading to interstate and state-federal conflicts of interest and jurisdiction. The Supreme Court quite early settled the matter in favor of the federal government in *Gib-*

bons v. Ogden (1824),[12] when Chief Justice Marshall delivered his famous opinion that:

> The power of Congress . . . comprehends navigation, within limits of every state in the Union; so far as that navigation may be, in any manner, connected with "commerce of foreign nations, or among the several states, or with the Indian tribes."

But though the federal government thus acquired control over all the navigable rivers in the United States, it did not exercise that jurisdiction to the fullest extent. It was reluctant to engage in the improvement of waterways, and Democratic Party spokesmen of the mid-nineteenth century considered that the government lacked power to appropriate funds for such a purpose. Moreover, by that time the railroads were beginning to capture a considerable share of the river traffic and on the Mississippi system in particular the process was accelerated by the Civil War. Hence the primacy of navigation combined with governmental inertia for a time to operate as a factor preventing excessive tinkering with the natural state of the rivers.

If, during the middle part of the nineteenth century, the federal government lacked the foresight to exercise such regulatory power as was available to it in the eastern part of the country, its reluctance was even more pronounced in the West, where almost all lands were federally owned—and most depended upon irrigation water to make them productive. The combination of federal ownership of land and the lack of federal control of water disposition resulted, in the period immediately following the California Gold Rush, in the application of the rules best known to the people using the water, that is, customs prevailing in western mining camps. This custom, in turn, ripened into that distinctly western system of water law—prior appropriation. In the "Go West" drive the water users literally out-ran the law and the courts. The miners were squatters on public lands and the property-oriented riparian doctrine of the common law could not be applied to them. When, in 1862, the Homestead Act opened most of the area to private ownership of land, prior appropriation had already taken too strong a hold to be dislodged. The riparian rights doctrine did eventually follow, and in a number of states, notably California, became a parallel water regime alongside prior appropriation. In others, however, such as Colorado and Nevada, it was completely repudiated.

Suitability to arid conditions has often been given as the main reason for the spread of prior appropriation throughout the West. It is interesting, however, that prior appropriation did not develop in other arid regions of the world, and when it was transplanted experimentally to Australia (New South Wales in the 1930s) it did not last long there because it was unsuitable to the conditions prevailing in that country.

Apart from an accident of history (the adoption of mining customs in a period of legal vacuum), one major contributing factor to the success of the prior appropriation system in the West was its adaptability to the development rather than to the conservation of water resources. By divorcing water use from land ownership, it opened water resources to a larger number of people than did the riparian rights doctrine. By giving preference to the earlier user over the later, it assured water to the most energetic and developmental-minded elements in the population, and it also minimized interference on the part of the administration. In the initial period after the Gold Rush, the right to water depended solely on the user's actually being the first to put that water to work. This nonstatutory method is still recognized in some states (Colorado, Montana, Idaho), where the administration acts only as a registering agency. California prescribed a statutory procedure in 1872 and other states followed suit. In this more modern form of prior appropriation, first in time means being the one who first lodges an application. The administration has a greatly enhanced role, but still it must observe the preference for prior appropriation, and thus is far from being free, as in truly administrative systems, to grant licenses according to public benefit.

By tying right to water to private beneficial use, prior appropriation rejected the conservationist aspects of the riparian rights doctrine. The water was not to flow unchanged and undiminished, but was to be used to the utmost. Incidentally, the concept of private beneficial use also made it difficult for the appropriator to adopt more scientific methods for the conservation of water, and its influence upon the courts was apparent until well into the present century. As late as 1930, the Idaho Supreme Court affirmed a lower court decision that it was not a beneficial use to flood land in the winter so as to form a cap of ice that would help to retain soil moisture into the growing season (*Blaine County Inv. Co. v. Mays*).[3] And in a 1939 Nebraska decision, *Enterprise Irr. Dist. v. Willis*,[11] it was found that prevailing customs and methods of applying water to the land were to be observed and not the latest and most approved scientific method.

The very nature of the appropriative method itself militated frequently against good conservation practice. In the sequence of appropriation, downstream areas were often developed earlier than upstream ones—usually for reasons of more level land or easier access. Thus, junior appropriators were obliged to send water miles downstream to satisfy a senior appropriator's right, even though large amounts might be lost on the way through evaporation and percolation; the junior appropriator was forced to make up the loss by sacrificing his own needs so that the senior appropriator might receive his legal due. As late as 1940 a senior downstream use was adjudged reasonable, even though the loss of water in transmission was as much as 77 percent. Contrast this with the law of some other semi-arid and arid regions—for example, Moslem law in North Africa where priority goes to the lands farthest upstream.

The anti-conservationist element in the private beneficial use concept was in itself enough to create a severe environmental impact. In addition the application of this concept contributed to the overdevelopment of rivers and waste of water through excessively large appropriations. The appropriative right could be lost if not applied to beneficial use within a specified period of time. Thus, there was small opportunity to make investigation of what environmental damage might result from diversion or the building of water works. How could it have been otherwise? When "first in time" was "first in right," it was imperative to cut in ahead of competitors and file the application or post the notice or begin building the dam, or do whatever the law required as the first act toward appropriation (according to the theory of "relation back," priority in time counted from that first act and not from the time when the appropriation was completed).

The appropriative right was also limited to the amount of water that could be beneficially used—which might seem at first sight a potent restriction on waste, but in reality made the user apply for the maximum quantity which he might possibly use, not for what he actually needed. He had no incentive to save water, because water conserved meant water not put to beneficial use and might cost him his right. Only if the waste were really flagrant was enforcement action taken, as a rule, and the magnitude of some wasteful practices is indicated by a Nevada case, *Doherty v. Pratt*, shortly after the turn of the century, in which an appropriator had caused the loss of two-thirds of a stream by following the line of least resistance and running water into a swamp.

Among the beneficial uses (which were spelled out in many state statutes in order of priority) irrigation, the most consumptive use, ranked first, or first after domestic use. Federal law, too, in the Desert Land Act of 1877 gave irrigation priority in the very restricted number of purposes (the others were mining and manufacturing) for which water might be appropriated on the public domain. The objective was not so much to promote irrigation agriculture per se as to encourage settlement, but the effect was generally to inhibit any change of purpose to a more preservationist use at any time in the future, even if this were ultimately to be considered beneficial, for this would mean losing priority.

As for recreational and aesthetic purposes, they had no place at all in the appropriative scheme of things in the nineteenth century, and would not have for many decades to come. Some western states did eventually enact legislation to reserve a minimum amount of the unappropriated ·flow of a river for boating, swimming, fishing, or other public uses. But, as recently as 1961, the California State Water Rights Board ruled that the undisturbed flow of a river could not be appropriated for such purposes. If it were artificially regulated or impounded, then it might be appropriated for recreational use.

The general attitude of the times toward water development vis-à-vis environmental quality is summarized in a Colorado case in which a power company was pitted against a summer resort attempting to preserve and enhance the natural beauty of its surroundings (*Empire Water and Power Co. v. Cascade Town Co.*, 1913).[10] The summer resort had been established for some decades below a waterfall in a canyon described as "rare in beauty," with "an exceptionally luxuriant growth of trees, shrubbery, and flowers." The resort company had protected the birds, wild animals, and the native flora of the canyon, while at the same time creating a small park, a lake, and a fountain for the enjoyment of its clientele. Then came the power company with plans to develop power from an impoundment above the canyon which would destroy the falls and turn the canyon into a "dry gulch," its luxuriant vegetation, its wildlife, and its scenic and aesthetic value gone forever.

The resort company had obtained a decree perpetually enjoining the power company from interfering with the normal flow of the stream in the canyon, but this was reversed by a higher court in a decision that is worth quoting at some length. The court said:

> The laws of Colorado are designed to prevent
> waste of a most valuable but limited natural
> resource, and to confine the use to needs. By
> rejecting the common-law rule they deny the
> right of the landowner to have the stream run
> in its natural way without diminution. He
> cannot hold to all the water for the scant
> vegetation which lines the banks but must
> make the most efficient use by applying it to
> his land . . . we think complainant is not
> entitled to a continuance of the falls solely
> for their scenic beauty. . . . the trial court
> based its decision of this branch of the case
> largely upon the artistic value of the falls,
> and made no inquiry into the effectiveness
> of the use of the water in the way adopted
> as compared with the customary methods of
> irrigation. . . . It may be that if the attention
> of the lawmakers had been directed to such
> natural objects of great beauty they would
> have sought to preserve them, but we think
> the dominant idea was utility, liberally and
> not narrowly regarded, and we are constrained
> to follow it.

How much environmental damage was
caused by water development under prior appropriation may never be known, except perhaps by a painstaking analysis and piecing
together of old maps and surveys, local histories, and the briefs submitted in cases such
as *Empire Water and Power*. However, where
the damage was sufficiently great to threaten
that highest of all uses in the nineteenth
century—navigation—the federal government
stepped in. This is what happened in the
case of hydraulic mining in California. Conditions in the Sierra foothills were highly
favorable to this mining process, with thick
beds of gravel and abundant water. Initially
the miners used rather primitive methods to
separate the gold from the gravel—first the
pan and later the sluice, with gravel dug by
hand and then thrown in. But as early as
1852 or 1853 the hose, with water under
pressure, came into use and by 1870 this had
become the Hydraulic Giant, with jets discharging more than 3,000 feet of water per
minute at a velocity of 150 feet per second.

The tremendous power of these jets loos-
ened the thick gravel deposits right down to
bedrock and flushed them down to lower
ground, often with large trees and stones.
In nine years alone the bed of the lower Bear
River was raised more than 90 feet in some
places, and that of Sleepy Hollow Creek
136 feet, by the debris washed down from
the mining operations. Thousands of acres
of fertile farmland in the valleys were buried
under gravel; in the lower Yuba alone some
16,000 acres of farmland were lost in this way.
It was a matter of survival for the farmers
and for the valley townspeople, living always
under the threat of disastrous floods from
the high-lying rivers, and in the end they
obtained redress. In *Woodruff v. North
Bloomfield Gravel Mining Company*
(1884),[41] popularly known as the Sawyer decision, it was held that sand and gravel arising
from hydraulic mining and discharged into
navigable rivers in such quantities as to destroy their navigability, bury farming lands,
contribute to the injury and destruction of a
city, and compel property owners, at large
expense, to erect and maintain levees for
their protection, constituted a public nuisance of an aggravated character.

Note, however, that the damage had to be
to a navigable stream. It would be years yet
before the concept of navigability would be
so broadly interpreted (in *Oklahoma v. Atkinson*, 1941)[27] as to include non-navigable
parts of a river and non-navigable tributaries.
But the very fact of a threat to navigability
engaged federal interest, and in 1893 Congress passed an act creating the California
Debris Commission, with power to issue
permits for hydraulic mining (granted only
when all gravel was satisfactorily impounded
and no harm done to streams). The Commission was also to adopt plans to improve
the navigability of the Sacramento and San
Joaquin river systems and restore them to the
conditions existing in 1860 (reconciling as
far as possible the interests of mining and
navigation), and to examine the practicabil-
ity of sites for settling reservoirs or for storage
of debris or water. Except for the Mississippi

River Commission (created in 1879 to deal with flood control and navigation), it was the first federal agency in the water resources field with a multi-purpose objective and so became the harbinger of a whole new era in water management.

The concept of navigability also came to the rescue of environmental quality on a state level in those instances when state law declared streams to be public when navigable for other than commercial purposes. For example, in *Lamprey v. Metcalf* (1893),[17] a Minnesota case, the court said:

> if, under present conditions of society, bodies of water are used for public uses other than mere commercial navigation, in its ordinary sense, we fail to see why they ought not to be held to be public waters, or navigable waters, if the old nomenclature is preferred. Certainly, we do not see why boating or sailing for *pleasure* should not be considered navigation, as well as boating for mere pecuniary profit. Many, if not the most, of the meandered lakes of this state are not adapted to, and probably will never be used to any great extent for commercial navigation; but they are used—by the people for sailing, rowing, fishing, fowling, bathing, skating, taking water for domestic, agricultural, and even city purposes, cutting ice, and other public purposes which cannot now be enumerated *or even anticipated.* To hand over all these lakes to private ownership, under any old or narrow test of navigability, would be a great wrong upon the public *for all time,* the extent of which cannot, perhaps, be now even anticipated." (Authors' Emphasis.)

Under the federal test, however, usefulness for commerce remained the criterion of navigability. In Wisconsin, until changed by statute in 1911, the saw log test of navigability was also based on commercial considerations. Under this definition of navigability, if a body of water were not "commonly useful to some purpose of trade or agriculture" (*The Monticello,* 1874)[12] in the character of a navigable stream, then it could be exploited for any private purpose. Thus, innumerable small lakes and expanses of wetland were drained in order that they might serve some utilitarian end.

Further impetus to the loss of wetland was given by the Swamp Acts of the mid-nineteenth century, whereby the federal government granted the states such lands for the express purpose of drainage and reclamation. In turn, most of the lands were sold off by the states, and although the directive to drain and reclaim was often ignored, years later when the states wanted to preserve portions of these marshlands they were forced to buy them back. In the prairie region, where abundance of water was a problem, drainage was enthusiastically carried out and special districts were formed for this purpose. In Wisconsin, for example, large areas of wooded marsh were ceded by the federal government under the Swamp Act of 1850 and sold by the state to lumbering interests. Fire devastated the area after most of the forest was gone in the 1890s, and the ash deposited on some of the higher ground made it so fertile as to produce bumper crops —for a brief while. With this encouragement, it was decided to convert the marsh to agriculture, and twelve drainage districts, encompassing an area of more than 300,000 acres, were organized in the years 1900 to 1905. Unwise drainage was largely responsible for the fact that within a quarter of a century the experiment had failed on at least half of the land, and much of it was later allowed to revert to marsh.

The history of deterioration of one midwestern river can be read in the findings of the court in a 1921 case, *Economy Light Co. v. United States.*[9] At that time, there had been no navigation on the Desplaines River in Illinois in living memory, but there were records of such from the end of the seventeenth century to the end of the first quarter of the nineteenth century. Then a swamp near the watershed was drained (watersheds in this region are often very ill-defined) and the land was logged over. This action changed the runoff pattern and shortened the higher stages of the river. Its navigable capacity was finally changed by diversion into Great Lakes drainage through the building of the Illinois and Michigan Canal (1848), its deepening (1866–1871), and the construction of the Chicago Sanitary and Ship Canal (1892–1894).

Many other cases from the later nineteenth century and early twentieth century, which were brought on grounds of injury to the navigable capacity of rivers, reveal the damage done to the aquatic environment. The total amount of rubbish deposited in the nation's waterways must have been truly staggering. Take, for example, *Clark v. Peckham:*[5]

> A municipal corporation cannot turn its sewage into a navigable water way in such a way as to *fill it up* [emphasis added] to the injury of navigation.

Or *New York v. Baumberger:*[26]

> A city is entitled to an injunction restraining the discharge of mash from a brewery through the sewer into a navigable river the free use of which for purposes of navigation is impeded by diminishing the depths of water so that vessels will be prevented from coming to the city's wharves, thereby depriving it of dockage and wharfage.

Or *McKeesport Gas Co., v. Carnegie Steel Co.:*[19]

> Equity may restrain a riparian owner on a nontidal stream from depositing slag, cinders, or other refuse below low-water mark and from filling in or otherwise making the slope of the bank from lower water to high water line more than 1 foot to 3 feet—that is, 1 foot rise to 3 feet horizontal distance, if such conduct will tend to fill in the stream and interfere with navigation.

There was little, if any, cognizance at this time of harm to the public health or to the environment through pollution. The outlook was thoroughly utilitarian and the aim to reconcile conflicts between one developmental use of waterways and another. Where the situation became so bothersome as to require remedy on a larger scale, state and federal legislation was passed. Thus Louisiana

enacted a law in 1877 prohibiting the deposit of "offensive matter" in the Mississippi River (except in the middle of the river at the lower limits of the city) by any person, firm, or corporation acting under any ordinance of the parish or city or law of the state. In 1886 Congress passed a law prohibiting the deposit of refuse including "ballast, stone, slate, gravel, earth, slack, rubbish, wreck, filth, slaps, edgings, sawdust, slag, or cinders, or other refuse or millwaste of any kind," but confined its application to New York Harbor. Two years later it passed another law prohibiting deposit in the tidal waters of New York Harbor and adjacent waters, of any kind of matter "other than that flowing from streets, sewers, and passing therefrom in a liquid state." Subsequently, in *United States v. The Sadie,*[40] the deposit of refuse, mud, sand, or dredgings in the Hudson River at a point 60 miles above New York was considered to come within the provisions of this act.

More generally, in the 1890 River and Harbor Act, Congress included a provision making it unlawful to deposit in *any* navigable water of the United States certain enumerated kinds of refuse matter tending to impede or obstruct navigation, and the Secretary of the Army was given authority to issue permits for depositing such material in places where navigation would not be obstructed. This action at least brought the indiscriminate cluttering of the rivers under some sort of regulation and drew attention to the environmental problem, even if it did not help matters very much at the time. It was the Refuse Act of 1899, however, which paved the way for a stricter federal control of changes brought about in the beds and banks of rivers by refuse dumping and the deposition of dredge spoil. Its provisions concerned any kind of refuse matter "other than that flowing from streets and sewers and passing therefrom in a liquid state," and not only applied to navigable waters but also to their non-navigable tributaries from which refuse might be washed into the navigable stream, as well as to the banks of streams and rivers. The drafters of this legislation "builded better than they knew." Not for almost another three-quarters of a century would it be strictly enforced, but now this 70-year-old law has become the kingpin of the federal drive against environmental damage to waterways from a wide variety of sources.

The construction of dams across streams revealed, in the conflict between navigation and industry, yet another cause of environmental deterioration in the water resources of a region with an abundance of water. The mill acts passed in the early part of the nineteenth century authorized the erection of dams that were injurious to the interests of other riparian owners on a stream. They were also injurious to a whole range of public interests as well, but the fact that such dams had legislative approval not infrequently made them immune to attack. For example, in *State v. Elk Island Boom Co.*,[37] it was held that an indictment for maintaining a dam in a navigable stream would fail if the obstruction were authorized by law, unless it appeared that the dam caused unreasonable and avoidable delays in the passage of boats. In *Parker v. Cutler Milldam Co.*,[28] the court found that if the grantee acted in accordance with authority conferred on him by the legislature, he was not liable even though he interfered with navigation or with the flow and reflow of the tides. And in *Clark v. Syracuse*,[6] it was held that legislative permission to construct a dam across a navigable stream would give a right which could not be destroyed by the declaration of a municipal corporation that the dam was a public nuisance, endangering the health of a city.

Nobody worried much about the environmental effects per se, except where fisheries were concerned. The mill-dams were blocking all the eastern seaboard rivers, up which shad and other anadromous fish rushed to spawn. Thoreau (1950) drew attention vividly to the problem. "Poor shad, where is thy redress . . . who hears the fishes when they cry?" he asked, viewing the havoc caused by dams

on the Concord. Many years later, the federal government was empowered to take action on this issue, not arising out of obstruction of streams by private interests, but out of federal improvements to navigable waterways (such as locks and canals) carried out under the various rivers and harbors acts. In 1888 Congress empowered the Secretary of the Army, in his discretion to provide "practical and sufficient fishways" whenever such improvements were found to operate as obstructions to the passage of fish.

VOICES OF CONSERVATION AND CONFLICTS BETWEEN PRESERVATIONISTS AND DEVELOPERS

"The Americans *love* their country, not, indeed, *as it is*, but *as it will be*," wrote Francis Grund (1837) in the 1830s. "They live in the future, and *take* their country as they go on." And another traveler of this period echoes his views: "Their eyes are fixed upon another sight . . . [they] march across these wilds, draining swamps, turning the course of rivers, peopling solitudes, and subduing nature" (Tocqueville, 1945). But not all marched forward in this way. Some paused —to wonder, to reflect, and ever and anon to deplore the transformation of nature that was taking place before their very eyes. Earlier on they were chroniclers, cataloging the contents of a storehouse of wilderness treasure—like William Bartram, whose *Travels* record 5,000 miles of exploration in the Southeast immediately prior to the Revolution. Then came, as Nash describes (1969, pp. 67–83), an appreciation of the American wilderness as something unique, and a hint of recognition that some lessons might be learned from Europe and other lands where little wilderness remained— as in Natty Bumpo's comment in Cooper's *The Prairie* (1827) that the Old World was a *"worn* out, and an *abused* . . . world." A little later we have Catlin, the painter, proposing that the government preserve certain lands "in their pristine beauty and wilderness" in a park for future generations to see and enjoy, and the first stirrings of congressional interest in the park idea in the closing off of Hot Springs, Arkansas, to public entry (1832).

By mid-century the alarm signals were out. Asher Durand, of the Hudson River School of painting, was urging American painters to paint America's "untrodden wilds, yet spared from the pollutions of civilization"—to get them on record before they vanished utterly. There was Thoreau, worrying about the New England fisheries, preaching that "in Wildness is the Preservation of the World," and urging the nation to have preserves "not for idle sport, or food, but for inspiration and our own true recreation . . ." There was George Perkins Marsh in 1847, years before the publication of his famous *Man and Nature*, lecturing the Agricultural Society of Rutland County, Vermont, on the pace of landscape transformation (Marsh, 1965):

> Every middle aged man who revisits his birth-place after a few years of absence, looks upon another landscape than that which formed the theatre of his youthful toils and pleasures.

He also observed the adverse effect of forest clearance upon runoff:

> The suddenness and violence of our freshets increases . . . and there is reason to fear that the valleys of many of our streams will soon be converted from smiling meadows into broad wastes of shingle and gravel and pebbles, deserts in summer, and seas in autumn and spring.

Thoreau had had difficulty in finding storage space for the unsold copies of his *Walden*, but when Marsh published *Man and Nature* (1864), it found an immediate response and went through three editions before being finally reprinted just prior to the 1908 White House Conference on Conservation. A conservationist conscience was emerging. Within that final third of the century, Yosemite and Yellowstone were established as national parks and the Adirondack Preserve in New York State was set aside "forever wild." But at the turn of the century a rift appeared among the conservationists themselves—between those who would conserve *and* develop for use and those who would preserve an unaltered nature. And the focus of the dispute was a water resource—the Tuolumne River in the beautiful Hetch Hetchy valley, designated a wilderness preserve in the act creating Yosemite National Park.

It is significant that the object of chief concern among the conservation movement right from the start was forest. Forest and wilderness were synonymous. Many of the early conservation leaders were foresters, and all of them loved trees. Moreover, the transformation of landscapes and the environmental damage caused by indiscriminate destruction of forests were highly visible. The effect of forest destruction upon streamflow and runoff was duly noted (one of the reasons for setting aside the Adirondack Preserve was to maintain a steady flow of water in the Erie and Oswego canals), but there seems to have been less alarm over the damage to environmental quality caused by water development per se, perhaps because water is such a fluid resource and its effects are more subtle. At any rate, although Marsh had advocated (1874) the regulation of irrigation in the arid West on the basis of a natural unit, the river basin, and John Wesley Powell, in his plans for land use of 1878 and 1888–1889, had proposed equitable sharing of water, the running of water rights with the land, and the organization of water management by drainage basins, these were all just proposals for wiser development. Conservationists were deeply concerned that there might not be enough water for future generations, and preached economy in its use. Water was one of the resources referred to in President Theodore Roosevelt's opening speech to the Governor's Conference of 1908 (Conference of Governors, 1909):

> I have asked you to come together now because the enormous consumption of these resources, and the threat of imminent exhaustion of some of them, due to reckless and wasteful use, once more calls for common effort, common action.

There seems to have been less concern with the techniques by which water was developed, unless such development actively threatened a wilderness area.

Hetch Hetchy was thus the first major test of water development versus environmental quality (see also Nash, this volume), and even then it turned mainly upon scenic and aesthetic values, which weakened the case of the preservationists, because the would-be developers argued (with some justification(that if the dam were hidden by greenery the proposed lake would provide just as great, if not greater, scenic and recreational enjoyment than the untouched valley. Compared with the urgent needs of San Francisco after the 1906 earthquake, the pleas of those with aesthetic sensibilities must have seemed picayune to many. The rift in the conservation movement was deep, and for the future assessment of environmental criteria in water development projects, significant. For on the one hand were ranged John Muir, the advocate of wildness for its own sake, and a group of preservationists; on the other, a group which truly loved wilderness but felt that it must be sacrificed wherever and whenever there was an overriding human need. To this latter group belonged Gifford Pinchot, who said of Hetch Hetchy when it came up for final consideration in 1913 (Nash, 1969, p. 161):

> I am fully persuaded that . . . the injury . . . by substituting a lake for the present swampy floor of the valley . . . is altogether unimportant compared with the benefits to be derived from its use as a reservoir.

No one appears to have asked whether Hetch Hetchy was good for the Tuolumne River, or for the San Joaquin river system into which it flowed, or for the great Delta opening into San Francisco Bay. Perhaps it was not then imperative to ask such a question.

It was precisely in this first decade of the twentieth century, however, that conservation moved into the national arena and into the highest circles of government. While this was a great and remarkable achievement, on a governmental level conservation was channeled into directions which conformed to the (progressivist) philosophy of those of its adherents who believed, like Pinchot, in "the greatest good of the greatest number in the long run." Under the Theodore Roosevelt administration, as pointed out by Grant McConnell (1970):

> [Pinchot] was a powerful agency head, with something like an eighth of the surface of the United States under his command and with the formation of a whole doctrine under his pen. What this all meant in practice was that the question about the *kind* of good was answered—all goods were equal. It was simply a matter of adding them up. Ultimately, it meant those which could be measured were to be regarded as the only values that were hard and real. It is not surprising in the American context of the highly materialistic period of the early twentieth century that the dollar proved to be the best unit of measurement.

This attitude was of immense importance for water development in the twentieth century. For now the nation was moving into an era of multipurpose projects, of planning on a river basin scale, of the construction of vast waterworks by government, and of the resolution of many conflicts between water uses and users at a state level. If good were to be added to good (hydroelectric power, flood control, irrigation, drainage, navigation, pollution control, and recreation), then the sole objective of river basin planning would be to squeeze the maximum number and amount of goods out of a river basin, measurable in dollars and cents. And that is precisely what happened. Nonuse of wilderness was an accepted (if precariously established) principle by the end of the nineteenth century: nonuse of water was not.

THE MODERN ERA OF MULTI-PURPOSE WATER RESOURCES DEVELOPMENT

The United States: Water to Share, Not Water to Spare—Demand Outruns Supply

The United States moved into the new century, not yet a giant in economic production, but well on the way to becoming one. Somewhere between 1900 and 1910 the energy output of mineral fuels and water power began to exceed that of work animals and human workers. From that point production really took off, and so did water use. In the first third of the century, total water use rose from 40 to 110 billion gallons daily Half or more of this amount was accounted for by irrigation agriculture, and practically all of the irrigated acreage was in the water-short western states, where it had increased from just over 7.5 million acres to over 14 million acres between 1900 and 1930.

Around the turn of the century, the development of hydroelectric power and its long distance transmission encouraged the idea that water should serve several purposes at one time. Technology had made this feasible, through the invention of reinforced concrete (back in 1868) and the development of earth-moving equipment. Now really effective dams could be built to regulate a river for storage, flood control, power production, and other uses. As soon as the distribution of electricity was possible over increasingly wide areas, it became apparent that power production not only might be combined with other uses of water, but also might pay for their development. The Inland Waterways Commission, appointed in 1907 by President Theodore Roosevelt to make a study of water resources utilization, adopted this view in its preliminary report, and the Bureau of Reclamation combined power with irrigation in several early projects—Pathfinder dam (1909), Buffalo Bill dam (1910), and Roosevelt dam (1911), which also included flood control.

These projects were on a relatively modest scale, but by the 1930s a new era was ushered in with the authorization of Hoover dam, 726 feet high and with a mass of more than 3.25 million cubic yards, to serve for irrigation, power production, and flood control. At this point also the United States embarked for the first time on the comprehensive development of an entire river basin. Concrete planning on a large scale had begun a few years earlier in 1925, when Congress authorized a comprehensive investigation of the nation's rivers with a view to possible coordination of navigation, flood control, irrigation, and power development, and the Corps of Engineers proceeded to implement it, in the so-called 308 reports, with about 200 separate studies of important river basins. Then, following the market collapse of 1929, basin-wide planning became part of a general development of natural resources to stimulate employment and recovery, and the first basin to receive the benefit of comprehensive development was one of those most badly hit by the Depression, the Tennessee Valley.

By now the role of the federal government in water resources development was solidly entrenched. Federal control over navigation had been paramount for over a century, and in an 1899 case, *United States v. Rio Grande Dam and Irrigation Co.,*[39] it was validated on non-navigable upper segments of a stream so as to protect the navigable capacity of downstream segments. Somewhat earlier, the federal government had begun to show increasing activity in the regulation of water uses, other than navigation, of navigable streams, and in *Green Bay and Miss. Canal Co. v. Patten Paper Co.* (1898),[13] the Supreme Court held that:

> At what points in the dam and canal the water for power may be withdrawn, and the quantity

which can be treated as surplus with due regard to navigation, must be determined by the authority which owns and controls that navigation.

The authority was vested in the Corps of Engineers which, at the beginning of the twentieth century, already had some 75 years of experience in navigational improvement. The Corps was given steadily increasing powers and funds through regular appropriations, as well as a broader base of operations. By special provision in the 1916 National Defense Act, the Army Engineers were authorized to construct *and* operate Wilson Dam for power and navigation on the Tennessee River at Muscle Shoals. The Engineers' data-gathering role (begun in 1871 with observations on the Mississippi River) was expanded until they became responsible for the extensive surveys resulting in the 308 reports, but although they were increasingly called upon to act in a planning and advisory capacity in flood protection, until 1936 they did not have overall supervision over flood control.

It was recognized quite early that major works, vital for the settlement and development of the semi-arid West, were beyond the capacities of private persons or associations of individuals. The federal government assumed this function with the passage of the Reclamation Act of 1902. The Act envisaged the building of works from the proceeds of selling public lands, and the whole scheme was put in charge of the Secretary of the Interior. Initially, its main objective was to aid agriculture by constructing storage works and canals which farmers could not afford to build, and the projects were single-purpose, for irrigation only, but soon other purposes, such as power and municipal water supply, were included.

The 1930s marked the high point of a long progression, a convergence of three distinct concepts—multi-purpose projects, river basin planning, and regional development—along with a parallel convergence of various strands of authority in the federal government. For a time it looked as if the future development of water resources in the United States would be by river basins in which all water-using functions would be intermeshed and, moreover, related to a balance of nature. The influence of the conservationists was strong, and as Lilienthal, one of the architects of the TVA, saw it in the rather heady euphoria of those days (1953):

> For the first time in the history of the nation, the resources of a river were not only to be "envisioned in their entirety"; they were to be developed in that unity with which nature herself regards her resources . . .

But the promise was short-lived. Although the TVA flourished and became the prototype for river-basin development all over the world, none of the other ten basins which the President's Committee on Water Flow had recommended at the same time for similar treatment—the St. Lawrence, Mississippi, Missouri, Sacramento-San Joaquin, Delaware, Columbia, Colorado, Ohio, and Great Salt Lake—were provided with such an administrative structure. The Corps of Engineers and Bureau of Reclamation went their several ways, each with its own constituencies, its own plans, its own projects (see Fox, this volume)—Bonneville and Grand Coulee on the Columbia, Parker on the Colorado, Fort Peck on the Missouri. Twice both agencies prepared comprehensive and overlapping plans for the Columbia River and would not be coordinated. Pleading for a unified administration on TVA lines, President Truman said in 1949 (U.S. Congress, House, 1949):

> we have now reached a point where the growing scope and complexity of the Federal activities in the region require much greater integration and full time attention of top level administration if the tremendous potentialities of the region are to be widely and rapidly developed.

Large-scale water development was becoming more and more a form of regional development through transbasin diversion. Interbasin transfers of water, of course, are an old story in American water resources development (see Fox, this volume). The possibility of tapping the water surplus of the Sacramento River at the Sacramento-San Joaquin delta to aid the water-deficient San Joaquin Valley was studied as early as the 1870s as part of a plan for coordinated development of California's Central Valley; later it formed the core of the Central Valley Project and the State Water Plan. Diversions out-of-basin have been made for a variety of reasons—for irrigation in the arid and semi-arid West, as in the Colorado-Big Thompson project (1938), or to solve a pollution problem, as in the Chicago diversion from Great Lakes to Mississippi drainage. On a major scale, however, the search for out-of-basin sources of water is intimately linked with the growth of big urban metropolises, and with the increasing urbanization of the country as a whole, especially along its eastern and western seaboards. The sequence can be traced in New York's progression from the Croton water system (1842) to the Catskills (1915), to the Delaware Basin (1950s), and in Los Angeles' progression from the Los Angeles River (outgrown by 1905) to the Owens Valley (1913), to the Colorado River (via the Colorado River Aqueduct, 1941). Today , more than half of all the water that traverses drainage basin divides in the United States is destined for municipal and industrial use, and one can predicate the expansion of water resources development by nonbasin units upon urban metropolitan growth.

By the 1960s regional development through transbasin diversion of water had come into its own, and the scale of the diversion projects proposed was staggering. Several involved transportation of water across two or more state boundaries and drainage divides, and their size, measured in amount of water transferred per year, ranged from 1.2 to 110 million acre feet per year. They reflected the anticipation that by 1980, of the nation's twenty-two water resource regions, five (the South Pacific, Colorado River, Great Basin, Upper Rio Grande-Pecos, and Upper Missouri) would have run out of water entirely, and three more (Upper Arkansas-Red River, Western Great Lakes, and Western Gulf) were on the way to doing so within two more decades. Paradoxically, at least two of the major basins running out of water were already supplying, or were destined to supply, areas beyond their drainage divides under some of the proposals. Thus, the Colorado, already water-bankrupt, is required to satisfy demands created by existing diversions through the Continental Divide, as well as the terms of the 1922 Compact and the 1944 treaty with Mexico, while the Missouri, according to the proposed Yellowstone-Snake-Green project, would be required to supply water via its tributary, the Yellowstone, to the Colorado basin via the Snake and the Green rivers and, according to another project, would send water to Texas across almost 1,000 miles of the High Plains.

As the need sharpened, the distance involved in the projects lengthened, and the scale and complexity of the proposed engineering works increased. The progression may be traced from the California State Water Project (an interregional transfer from northern to southern California, adopted in 1959), through the abortive Pacific Southwest Plan (a projected transfer from northern California river basins into the lower Colorado River drainage basin), and the various suggested diversions out of the Columbia River basin (Snake-Colorado, Yellowstone-Snake-Green, and Western Water Project) into Colorado drainage (and directly or indirectly into California), to the most grandiose scheme of all—the North American Water and Power Alliance (NAWAPA) which, if ever undertaken, would interlink Alaskan and Canadian river basins with all the major basins of the West and with the Great Lakes.

The proposals multiplied to the point where, if put into operation, the entire western United States would be carved into huge artificial units of water distribution. In its Appendix to the 1963 Report on the Pacific Southwest Water Plan, the Bureau of Reclamation indicated that the concept of the river basin as an isolated unit of development was virtually outmoded and that "as water needs become more critical in the West, river basin boundaries will become even less rigid in water and land resource development." The California State Water Project is also claimed as an entirely new concept, a stage higher than river-basin planning, and one which carries the "multiple-purpose principle to its logical conclusion." The developmental capacity is not lacking. In addition to the technology required for construction of the huge and complex waterworks envisioned, hydraulic engineers have been able since the 1950s to avail themselves of systems analysis, computers, and model-making in planning for large river systems. These vast projects are technically feasible and are encouraged by the nearly absolute control of the federal government over the nation's water resources.

Parallel with the multiplication of large projects, the regime of water law became increasingly based on authorization. Paradoxically, it was in the humid eastern part of the country that more thorough administrative systems were introduced, in which the states would have power to regulate water uses according to public benefit. In 1933 (again at a time of peak conservationist activity, coupled with governmental initiative), Maryland adopted a statute establishing the requirement of permits for use of both surface and ground water, giving the administration a large discretion in determining public interest in accepting or rejecting an application, and confining the role of the courts to eventual review of the legality of administrative decisions. Minnesota introduced a similar system in 1937, with the same criterion of public benefit, and so did Florida in 1957, without any special directives to the administration, except to conserve and utilize waters in the public interest.

As a corollary to the expanding role of the states in administration of water-use rights, states began to appear as parties to compacts

or agreements for the settlement or obviation of conflicts—another instance of the escalation of water development to a governmental level with the increasing demands upon the resource, just as in the fluvial civilizations of old. The interstate compacts reflected a cooperative as opposed to a contentious approach to water development, and date generally from the second decade of the twentieth century. Beginning with the La Plata and Colorado River compacts of 1922 and the South Platte compact of 1923, these compacts were initially used as a means of resolving conflicts in the arid and semi-arid West, but like interstate litigation they have been increasingly employed in the humid East to help cope with problems of pollution (Ohio River Valley Water Sanitation Compact, 1939, and New England Interstate Water Pollution Control Compact, 1939) and municipal water supply and flood control (Delaware River Compact, 1961). They have also been popular instruments for coordinating the water policies of several states within a river basin, without resorting to a basin authority.

Some compacts have had a broad mandate to plan for multipurpose development of the basin. The commission of the Great Lakes Basin Compact of 1955 (unperfected) was empowered to recommend methods for the "orderly, efficient, and balanced development, use, and conservation" of the water resources of the basin, to improve and maintain its fisheries, and to recommend policies relating to water resources, including the substitution and alteration of flood plain and other zoning laws and ordinances. The Columbia River Basin Compact of 1962 empowers its commission to undertake, by itself or in cooperation with governments or other agencies, the review of all plans for the construction of flood control, navigation, power development, irrigation, or other works. By the Wabash Valley Compact of 1959, a commission was entrusted with the promotion of the "balanced development" of the valley, and with recommending "integrated plans and programs for the conservation, development and proper utilization of [its] water, land, and related natural resources." And the Delaware River Basin Compact of 1961 created a commission (composed of the governors of riparian states and representatives of the federal government), which is empowered to develop plans, policies, and projects related to the water resources of the basin, and to allocate the waters to the signatory states.

"Allocation" and "apportionment" of water resources of a river or a river basin are the outstanding characteristics of the interstate compact as a device for regulating water development. In the eastern United States this was not so very different in essence from the reasonable use version of the riparian rights doctrine, wherein each user's rights are adjusted to those of the entire group of users upon a river. In the prior appropriation jurisdictions of the western United States, however, apportionment goes directly counter to the prevailing water use rights regime, as if to rectify at an interstate level the inadequacies of the system. (It is true that some compacts were based on prior appropriation, but these are in the minority.) Significantly, it has been in the West and Southwest that compacts have led, not to resolution of the problems, but to increasingly acrimonious litigation, as in the Colorado River basin (*Arizona v. California*, 1963).[2] The disposition by contract of the waters assigned by the 1922 Colorado River Compact to the lower basin was upheld by the U.S. Supreme Court in *Arizona v. California* (1963) as apportionment of those waters between the lower basin states, but the matter has not ended there, and the search for out-of-basin sources of water indicates both the compact's failure to resolve the conflict and its unfortunate emphasis upon development rather than conservation in a region of marginal water supply. The 1922 Colorado River Compact's aim was to "secure the expeditious agricultural and industrial development of the Colorado River

Basin," and this same wording appears in the 1948 Upper Colorado River Basin Compact. The Belle Fourche Compact of 1943 was to "recognize that the most efficient use of the waters within the basin is required for the full development of the Basin," and the (unperfected) Cheyenne River Compact of 1950 has a similar theme—to "recognize that the most efficient utilization of the waters within the Basin is required for the full development of the Basin." Not until later does the word "conservation" begin to creep into the stated objectives of compacts—in the 1955 Columbia Interstate Compact (unperfected) and in the Delaware River Basin Compact.

SHORT-TERM GAINS— LONG-TERM LOSS: THE ENVIRONMENTAL IMPACT

The harvest of two centuries and more of environmental exploitation was not truly brought home to the nation until the 1960s when the revived conservation movement drew attention to the damage (see Nash and McEvoy, this volume). There had been plenty of evidence of injury to the land—the erosion of the Piedmont soils all down the Atlantic seaboard and the loss of its hardwood forests—the Appalachian valleys ravaged by suicidal agriculture and timber cutting—the Great Plains blowing the "garden myth" down to the Gulf of Mexico— the charred stumps and cutover remnants of once wonderful forests in the northern lakes area and the Northwest. There was less dramatic evidence of the effects of water use and development, except in pollution, of which perhaps the most horrifying example, revealing the dimensions of the problem and magnitude of the tasks lying ahead, is the fate of Lake Erie (see Beeton, this volume). However, with its built-in bias toward monetary benefits and toward present needs as against future requirements, the developmental approach has been responsible for many other kinds of environmental deterioration which might have been avoided or at least postponed if the development had been balanced with conservation values. This is amply illustrated by the way in which the mandate of the regulatory federal agencies has been interpreted.

Consider, for example, the Corps of Engineers. As late as 1969, at a time when the agency's own attitude had begun to change, a federal district court in Florida interpreted the statutes which authorize the engineers to control development of navigable waters as pertaining solely to navigation and anchorage.[43] The engineers were considered powerless to refuse a permit on ecological grounds, even when it was shown that the projected private dredging and filling would substantially damage the ecology of an entire large bay. At about the same time, a federal circuit court sustained the Atomic Energy Commission's contention that its enabling laws preclude it, when licensing nuclear reactors, from considering any other effects than those of radiation on public health and safety. In this case, the state of New Hampshire argued that the Commission should also consider the effects of thermal pollution on the aquatic habitat of the Connecticut River, and the court characteristically said:[25]

> We conclude that the licensing board and' the Commission properly refused to consider the proffered evidence of thermal effects. We do so with regret that the Congress has not yet established procedures requiring timely and comprehensive consideration of non-radiological pollution effects on the planning of installations to be privately owned and operated.

The Federal Power Commission, another regulatory agency of great importance to water resources, also tended to relegate conservation and recreational aspects of water development to an inferior and secondary position. In the case of the High Mountain Sheep project, it granted a license to build a dam on the Snake River to the Pacific Northwest Power Company without adequate consideration of the Secretary of the Interior's contention that the dam was unnecessary at that time and, if built, would endanger anadromous fish in the river and wildlife in the area. The Secretary in a letter to the Commission stated:[38]

> The examiner's report stated that "(a) comprehensive plan provides for prompt and optimum multi-purpose development of water resources," and that relative merits of the proposed projects "turn on a comparison of the costs and benefits of component developments and on which project is best adapted to attain optimum development at the *earliest* time with the smallest sacrifice of natural values."

Commenting on this, the Court added (p. 448):

> But neither the Examiner nor the Commission specifically found that deferral of the project would not be in the public interest or that the immediate development would be more in the public interest than construction at some future time or *no construction at all.*

The impact on the environment of water diversion and dam projects, especially those associated with interbasin transfers, was perhaps less spectacular than the effects of pollution, but not much less devastating. Problems range from loss of recreational potential in some of California's "areas of origin," to changes in estuarine areas, as in the Delta segment of the California State Water Project (see also Hagan and Roberts, and Hedgpeth, this volume), and there have been warnings of potential earthquake damage and widespread climatic changes if the NAWAPA and similar very large-scale transfers are put into operation.

River estuaries are particularly vulnerable to damage from diversion. Their immense organic productivity (often many times that of the richest farm land) and their amenity value are only now beginning to be more widely recognized, so that the damage done by upstream diversion in the past has often gone unnoticed or been attributed to other causes. However, back in 1922 we have an example in *Antioch v. Williams Irr. District*[1] of a city which sought an injunction because diversions for irrigation had so diminished the flow as to cause salt water to penetrate upstream through tidal action. The court gave its opinion that the irrigation district was not polluting, and that an injunction would prevent the irrigation of thousands of acres of land merely to protect "plaintiff's modest water requirements." Forty-odd years later, in the drought year of 1965, salt water invasion was a central factor in the Delaware Basin dispute between the city of Philadelphia, which took half of its water supply directly from the lower river, and New York City, which derived about a third of its supply by diversion from the upper basin.

The reduction in fresh water flow and the resulting upset in the delicate ecological balance of estuarine areas are a matter of widespread concern. Fishermen and conservationists have objected to both the Texas Water Plan and the California State Water Project as adversely affecting marine life in bays and estuaries. The delta diversion segment of the California State Water Project is estimated to eventually reduce fresh water flow through the Sacramento-San Joaquin Delta to one-seventh of its present average (even less in a dry year) and threatens irreparable harm through downstream pollution and upstream invasion of salt water. A U.S. Geological Survey report in 1970 supports the contentions of ecologists that reduction in the Sacramento River's natural flow to the delta by diversion to the San Joaquin would have these effects. In 1968 a California Fish and Game Department preliminary study had discovered a sharp correlation between salinity and fresh water outflow and the mortality of young striped bass in the delta. The Federal Water Pollution Control Administration also evaluated the project and concluded that it would materially downgrade the quality of delta water.

Another essentially estuarine area in mortal danger from diversion is the Florida Everglades, the "river of grass," which depends for its survival not only upon rainfall, but also upon the annual inundation of innumerable shallow ponds by flood waters from the north and northeast. Prior to man-made alterations of the overland flow, this inundation lasted about nine months. Its duration was reduced almost by half (over a much smaller area) by the flood control and drainage systems of the Central and Southern Florida Project, authorized in 1948, which were devised to remove excess waters of the rainy season from the rich agricultural areas around Lake Okeechobee and the urbanized eastern seaboard of the state. This seasonal surplus, which would find its way under natural conditions into Everglades drainage routes, is diverted and allowed to run off to the sea. During the drought years of 1961–1965, the Everglades suffered severely and there was great loss of wildlife. At the height of this crisis, the Corps of Engineers constructed a levee across the park's principal drainage way, the Shark River, blocking the flow so that no water was released for two years. The situation was alleviated (but not rectified) temporarily by the ending of the drought and by an interim water regulation schedule negotiated between the Department of the Interior, the Corps of Engineers, the Central and South Florida Flood Control District, and the state of Florida. A comprehensive water supply plan was drawn up to accommodate, *inter alia*, the needs of the park until the year 2000, and was authorized by the Flood Control Act of 1968. Still the park is in jeopardy, however, because of the fast-growing southern Florida economy. The Department of the Interior has urged priority for the park against uses resulting from future development, but the Corps of Engineers maintains that it has neither the authority nor the obligation to establish priorities among the users of project water.

Diversion and damming are not the only threats to estuaries and coastal marshes. Drainage and reclamation, spurred by a concentration of population growth along the coasts and by the search for favorable container-port and industrial locations, are no less destructive. Until the passage of the National Environmental Policy Act of 1969, the situation was aggravated by the lack of any mandate to responsible federal agencies to protect estuarine areas on environmental grounds. The states—even those which enacted protective legislation, such as Massachusetts and Connecticut—are hampered by court-imposed limitations on the administrative control of uses of privately owned tidelands and underwater lands. Moreover, there is little legal restraint in the states themselves. The public trust doctrine, according to which these lands are held for the use and benefit of the public, does not as yet bind state legislatures from disposing of tidelands for any use that they choose to call public, as long as the lands so disposed of do not underlie vast expanses of water.

Thus, more than one-third of the nation's wetlands have already been permanently destroyed by development. By 1931, the states of Iowa, Missouri, Wisconsin, Illinois, Ohio, and Michigan had lost nearly 90 percent of their original wetlands. In Florida, statutes passed in 1856 and 1921 gave title to tidelands to the upland owners for the express purpose of filling in and improving the foreshore. Loss of tidelands under the impact of growing population and permissive laws has been so fast that Florida's Attorney General proposed a moratorium in 1967 on all filling and dredging in the state's waters. It is noteworthy that this proposal came ten years after an act ending the Florida land giveaway and vesting title to the state's undisposed-of wetlands to the Trustees of the Internal Improvement Fund, who were required to take ecological factors into consideration when selling such wetlands, and after the dredging and filling had been regulated by an elaborate permit system intended to protect the environment. However, the Florida Supreme Court, in line with similar decisions in other states, held that

denial of a permit on ecological grounds might amount to a taking of property and thus be not valid, thereby weakening the permit system.[43]

San Francisco Bay is another area where, due to permissive laws and fragmentation of jurisdiction, almost one-third of its underwater lands were lost. In contrast to the Florida situation, however, this led to the adoption of an effective regional plan in 1969 and the creation of a commission to implement it, pointing toward a possible solution of problems connected with water development. The act permits filling only for water-oriented uses and even then only when public benefit from filling outweighs the loss of water area and no alternative upland location is available.

In addition to private development, wetlands are being lost in an accelerated manner to development for public benefit which is considered to outweigh their ecological value. Wetlands and coastal marshes seem to be chosen ground for new sea- and airport facilities, simply because they are very often the only large expanses of vacant land still available. Thus, for example, New Orleans is developing a container port in the marshes of the Mississippi Delta, and Jamaica Bay in New York has—for the time being—narrowly missed being an extension of Kennedy International Airport.

Channelization of streams (that is, straightening, widening, and deepening by dredging) is another potent means of altering bodies of water, especially of freshwater swamps, and because it has not in the main affected larger rivers, it has gone almost unnoticed until fairly recently. Along the southern Atlantic coastal plain channelization is the major means of flood control, because few reservoirs are constructed, and for this reason it is a part of most flood control projects of the Soil Conservation Service under P.L. 566. Along the banks of many channelized streams, tree cover is removed in wide strips to permit the deposit of dredge spoil. Moreover, eroded soil has not been redeposited locally, as in naturally meandering streams, but is swept far downstream. Figures from a Soil Conservation Service report itself show that by doubling the discharge rate of a small creek through channelization, the silt load it carried was tripled through slumping of the banks. Kentucky, for instance, reported erosion and slumping in 60 percent of P.L. 566 channels inspected.

Worst of all is the effect of channelization on aquatic life and habitat. A study of habitat alteration associated with stream channelization in eastern North Carolina compared the fish populations of twenty-three channeled and thirty-six unchanneled streams and found a 90 percent reduction in weight and number of game fish per acre in the channeled streams. Moreover, the fish and wildlife populations did not recover for forty years after channelization. Fish and game departments of some states, such as Florida, have urged repeal of P.L. 566 for this reason, and from the director of the Georgia Fish and Game Commission comes this observation of channeling (*Congressional Record*, 1969, H. 11426):

> We are very much disturbed to see an agency of the U.S. Department of Agriculture proposing the drainage of a large acreage of wetlands, while at the same time another federal agency in the Interior Department is spending millions of dollars to preserve and develop wetlands for waterfowl.

> It doesn't make sense for one federal agency to be destroying wildlife habitat as fast as it can, while another federal agency tries to preserve it. During the last 20 years, drainage projects like those of the U.S. Soil Conservation Service have destroyed three to four million acres of bottomland hardwoods in the Southeast of significance to waterfowl.

The loss of free-flowing rivers through regulation for flood control, channeling, and other purposes has been perhaps the least-noted of all types of deterioration until its cumulative effects are brought out, as when it was discovered in 1954 that Wisconsin had only 770 miles left of 10,000 miles of formerly free-flowing rivers.[24] Ultimately, some small portion of the remainder was saved by the Wild and Scenic Rivers Act of 1968, which designated the St. Croix and Namekagon as one of eight initial wild river systems to be preserved and undeveloped. Out of that came an agreement between the states of Minnesota and Wisconsin to conserve about 100 river miles on the St. Croix and 98 on the Namekagon, together with adjacent lands to maintain the area's near-wilderness character (*Congressional Record*, 1969, H. 8635).

The very fact that only eight rivers or parts of rivers (out of twelve initially proposed) were eventually designated for immediate inclusion in the Wild and Scenic Rivers systems is an impressive commentary on the extent of development of all kinds. (The only river included in its entirety was the Feather in California; the other "parts" of rivers—except for the St. Croix above—were on the Clearwater Middle Fork and Salmon Middle Fork in Idaho; on the Eleven Point in Missouri; on the Rio Grande in New Mexico; on the Rogue in Oregon; and on the Wolf in Wisconsin.) Moreover, the status of another twenty-eight rivers named for study and given some protection for five years is precarious indeed, as House Interior Committee Chairman Wayne Aspinall indicated when the bill came up for debate (*Congressional Record*, 1968):

> Friends of the movement to preserve scenic rivers wanted us to go a lot further than we have and to include many more rivers in the system than we have . . . Instead . . . We provided for inclusion of other rivers in the system if the State legislature so requests and if the State will manage such river or rivers at its own, or their own expense . . . Now let me dispel one misunderstanding. We have not "locked up" these rivers. If the Corps of Engineers, for instance, wants to put a development in on any of them, all it has to do is to advise the Secretary of the Interior ahead of time and inform the Congress what the effect of its development will be. Then if Congress says OK, OK it is.

Ground water extraction is another form of water development whose impact may go for a long time unnoticed, but eventually leads to deterioration of the environment. Overpumping of ground water showed up in parts of the Southwest and West early in the century. In the Roswell area of New Mexico artesian wells began to be drilled in the 1890s, were developed on a larger scale after the Reclamation Act of 1902, and were put down in great numbers after World War I, when cheap power could be obtained from auto engines. By 1925, according to Beuscher (1967):

> there were mortgage foreclosures by the thousands on good farm land and virtually the whole valley was in receivership.

A similar problem afflicted the Raymond basin of southern California. This 40-square-mile section of the San Gabriel Valley was originally a citrus growing district. Encroaching urbanization resulted in a rapid lowering of the water table and led to what came to be known as the Raymond Basin Reference, when Pasadena filed suit against the city of Alhambra and about thirty other major users in the basin.[29]

The entire High Plains region is another area threatened by ground water "mining." Underlain by thick layers of silt, sand, and gravel, it is capable of holding millions of acre feet of water. At the turn of the century a U.S. Geological Survey report had warned of the consequences of overpumping this huge subterranean reservoir, but the warning went unheeded. With withdrawals at the rate of 7 million acre feet a year as against replacements of only 50,000 to 70,000 acre feet, it is estimated that the supply will last only about thirty more years.

Cities, especially, are feeling the effects of excessive withdrawal. The wells are dropping at a rate of 4 feet a year in Tucson, 6.5 feet in Nacogdoches, Texas, and 8 feet in Phoenix and Houston (Wright, 1966), and the land is subsiding too in some areas. At one point in California's San Joaquin Valley, it was dis-

covered that the subsidence rate of land was one foot for every 23 feet of lowering of the ground water table (Todd, 1959).

The effect of ground water withdrawals has been especially severe in some coastal areas of California. By 1950, for example, Santa Barbara County was reporting many record-low well levels, Los Angeles County had lowered its water table as much as 70 feet in the Long Beach area, and wells more than a mile from the shore had been abandoned due to invasion of salt water. The Oxnard area, a highly productive agricultural part of Ventura, was even more badly affected (Gregor, 1952). Wells had been uncommon in the early days of its settlement. The district was poorly drained and alkali accumulations discouraged irrigation. Large-scale drainage cured that and irrigation (using ground water) expanded all over the Oxnard Plain until by 1949 it had reached to within less than a mile of the ocean. A rapidly growing population, especially after World War II, posed a new threat to the ground water supplies of the Oxnard, most of which derived from the Santa Clara River by percolation. During dry spells there was less stream discharge and more demand on the underground supplies, so in one dry year, 1947, the Oxnard was drawing twice as much ground water as the estimated annual replenishment. After that the situation literally went "downhill." By the early 1950s the hydraulic gradient of the Oxnard lowland had been completely reversed as a result of the lowered water table; almost two-thirds of it had a water table below sea level, and irrigated lands were being destroyed by the intrusion of sea water, which no amount of replenishment during wet cycles may ever entirely eliminate.

CONSERVATION VERSUS DEVELOPMENT

It is only with the benefit of hindsight that the one-sidedness of water development is clearly seen. Very slow to come was a realization of the fragility of the environment, of its finiteness, and of the necessity to take into account in benefit-cost calculations so-called external values and the value of intangibles. Centuries of development had bequeathed the idea that water was a free gift of nature to man. Fear that water and other natural resources might soon become exhausted had spurred the conservation movement to a peak of activity at the beginning of the century and again in the 1930s. A more widespread understanding of the delicate balance of the environment and of the potential destructiveness of even the best-intentioned human activities came last in the 1960s.

Except during the administrations of Theodore and Franklin Delano Roosevelt, the conservation movement in its earlier stages was on the defensive, unable to gain the ear of top government, and somewhat divided within itself as to its aims. It had fought bitterly against the despoliation of the environment by private interests, and for governmental control of resources in the interest of all the people. Having invested the federal government with stewardship for these resources, and having made it a repository of faith in science and technology to solve the much-prophesied problems of waste and resource exhaustion that had so bothered the 1908 Conference, the conservation movement in succeeding years often found itself supporting the federal government's drive to maximize the benefits from resource use rather than campaigning for conservationist goals. As Hays (1958) has pointed out concerning the Water Power Act of 1920:

> Some apparent victories for the principle of public ownership have actually involved defeats for conservation goals. The Water Power Act of 1920, for example, established the principle of federal administration of hydroelectric power on the public lands in the navigable streams. Yet that act also marked the failure of the fight for one of the major conservation ideas of 1908—multiple-purpose river development . . . In brief, it seems clear that in the Water Power Act of 1920 conservationists sacrificed the essence of their ideas for the single advantage of public control.

Nevertheless, each upsurge of the conservationist movement produced some notable results. With the impetus of the Theodore Roosevelt administration, some forty states established conservation commissions, even if many of them did not last. There were some landmark judicial decisions like that of Justice Holmes in *Hudson County Water Co. v. McCarter* (1908),[14] concerning the planned transfer of water from the Passaic River in New Jersey to Staten Island, New York in opposition to a New Jersey law of 1905 prohibiting export of water. Justice Holmes said:

> it is recognized that the State as *quasi*-sovereign and representative of the interests of the public has a standing in court to protect the atmosphere, the water and the forests within its territory, irrespective of the assent or dissent of the private owners of the land most immediately concerned . . . few public interests are more obvious, indisputable and independent of particular theory than the interest of the public of a State to maintain the rivers that are wholly within it substantially undiminished, except by such drafts upon them as the guardian of the public welfare may permit for the purpose of turning them to a more perfect use.

There was also his famous delivery of the Court's opinion in *New Jersey v. New York* (1931) (283 U.S. 336, 342–343), almost a quarter of a century later, on the dispute over Delaware River waters:

> A river is more than an amenity, it is a treasure. It offers a necessity of life that must be rationed among those who have power over it.

Sometimes in those earlier stages the conservationists were helped by development's too-swift progress, resulting in the abandonment of projects so that nature was allowed to restore (if only partially) the *status quo ante*, aided by federal and local government action. Thus, in Wisconsin, a large area within drainage districts was allowed to revert to marsh after the failure of an unwise drainage experiment at the turn of the century. A somewhat similar fate befell a project devised during World War I to drain North Carolina's largest natural lake, the 40,000 acre Lake Mattamuskeet, and pump the water out via canals into Pamlico Sound. By the late 1920s a large area had been drained and was producing bumper crops, but then the pumping plans and canal system broke down, the crop yields declined, and in 1933 the scheme was abandoned. The following year the federal government acquired the area and turned it into the Mattamuskeet National Wildlife Refuge, a water, marsh, and timberland preserve. The pumping plant still stands, with its commemorative plaque—an ironic comment—from the year 1915 (New York Times, Nov. 1, 1970):

> This plant is dedicated to the spirit of co-operation which has here transformed a great lake into dry land and so created a new and fertile principality for the use and possession of man.

The most outstanding characteristics of the present-day conservation movement are its concern for the totality of the environment and its widespread appeal (see McEvoy, this volume), which reaches down from the Congress and states' assemblies to local town meetings. Its power and drive, though perhaps not yet strongly evident in enforcement action, are shown in the amount of environmental legislation passed in the last few years. In the water resources field there was little federal legislation of any kind pertaining to specifically environmental factors until the Federal Water Pollution Control Act of 1948, and its Amendments of 1956. In the 1960s almost every year brought one or more major pieces of legislation, from the Watershed Protection and Flood Prevention Act Amendments (1961); the Water Resources Research Act (1964, and amendments, 1966); the Land and Water Conservation Fund Act

(1964); the Water Resources Planning Act, the Water Quality Act, and the Water Project Recreation Act, all of 1965; the Clean Waters Restoration Act of 1966; the Wild and Scenic Rivers Act (1968); the National Environmental Policy Act of 1969; and the Water Quality Improvement Act of 1970.

The output of environmental laws in force is already dwarfed by the bills that are proposed almost every day in Congress and in the state legislatures. The most notable result of this legislative avalanche has been a rectification of the federal agencies' lack of concern over environmental deterioration. The National Environmental Policy Act of 1969 mandated this concern generally, and the Water Quality Improvement Act of 1970 mandated it specifically for water resources development. As the conservationist movement is ushered into the seventies, the impact of man on the environment is fully realized, but not as yet fully acted upon.

The Impact of Multipurpose Development in Other Parts of the World

The course of water development in the twentieth century in other parts of the world has tended to parallel that in the United States. First are the multipurpose projects, then river-basin planning and development, then the huge transbasin diversion projects—each strand of development overlapping and merging with the others at various times and places. And, as in the United States, the thrust was almost wholly developmental, without regard to environmental effects.

Already in 1890, Sir William Willcocks had planned the Aswan Dam on the Nile for irrigation and navigation, probably inspired by his studies of ancient hydraulic systems in Egypt and Mesopotamia. By this time the ancient system of irrigation by flooding had given way to perennial irrigation, whereby smaller quantities of water were run onto the land at regular intervals of several weeks throughout the year. This procedure required the construction of deep canals to take the water from the Nile and distribute it to distant fields, and also the building of storage facilities for the seasonal floodwaters. So the Aswan Dam was completed in 1902 and heightened again in 1912 to keep pace with the increasing demand for water by the growing population and the spread of irrigation. The project generated great enthusiasm and Winston Churchill summed up the attitude of his contemporaries toward the "proper" or "beneficial" use of a river (Issawi, 1963, p. 26):

> these giant enterprises may in their turn prove but the preliminaries of even mightier schemes, until at last nearly every drop of water which drains into the whole valley of the Nile . . . shall be equally and amicably divided among the river people, and the Nile itself, flowing for three thousand miles through smiling countries, shall perish gloriously and never reach the sea.

By the end of the 1930s multipurpose projects had become well established in various parts of the world. Work was in progress on the Rhône project in France, for power, irrigation, and navigation, with the first big dam begun at Genissiat in 1937. Plans had been drawn up for the Greater Volga scheme in the USSR for power generation, navigation improvement, and irrigation, and these were put into effect in the next two decades. From 1940 on, the multipurpose project began to spread to Asia, Australia, and South America, with schemes for the development of the Damodar, Snowy, São Francisco, and Gal Oya rivers. This type of project did not become widespread in Africa until the 1960s, but several of the latest developments there (Kariba, Volta, and others) far outstrip the earlier ones in the size of the rivers tackled and the huge power potential harnessed.

The idea that a river basin should be treated as a unit of planning was strongly associated with multipurpose projects from the start. Here again, Sir William Willcocks was one of the pioneers in his plans for harnessing the Nile and the Tigris-Euphrates. It was in Europe, however, that we have the first examples of basin-wide agencies administering a multipurpose development of water resources. The *Genossenschaften* of the Ruhr region, established shortly after the turn of the century to cope with pollution, drainage problems, water supply, and also power generation, were for nearly thirty years the sole representatives of this type of unified administration. However, river basin surveys on a national scale were conducted in several European countries in the 1920s, and in the next decade planning began to be put into practice in the Rhône valley of France. The administrative agency here assumed the form of a stock company in which both public organizations and private interests were represented. The company was slow to start (its first dam was not completed until 1948) and its impact on theories of water resources administration has been much less than that of its contemporary, the Tennessee Valley Authority.

The TVA's influence has been especially pronounced in underdeveloped areas of the world, where planners have tended to regard the river basin as a natural all-purpose region and a suitable unit for the achievement of economic and social goals. Thus was formed the Damodar Valley Corporation with "promotion of public health and agriculture, industrial, economic, and general well-being in the Damodar Valley and its area of operation." The act of 1949 creating the Gal Oya Development Board in Ceylon goes further still. Not merely does it set as a goal the economic and social betterment of the area, but specifically entrusts the governing board with general administration of the undeveloped part of the basin. The Colombian decree of 1960, reorganizing the Regional Corporation of the Cauca Valley, entrusted the Corporation with promotion of agriculture, industry, social welfare, and development of mineral resources, and the statute creating the Comissão do Vale do São Francisco in Brazil is similar in scope.

By that time a UN panel of experts had already recognized a distinction between basin development in developed and under-developed areas. It stated (United Nations, 1970):

> in less developed areas . . . because of the very lack of economic development, water projects may have a more dominating in-fluence. When the works are extended to the physical boundaries of a river basin, there will be a tendency for these boundaries to coincide with those of an economic unit.

This kind of development, for raising the level of the economy of a region, a country, or a group of countries, was the rationale behind the (unsuccessful) Helmand River project in Afghanistan for water supply, hydroelectric power, flood control, improve-ment of old river land, and irrigation. It also lies behind the ambitious international Lower Mekong River Basin Project, on which planning and surveying were begun in 1956, with a view to multipurpose development for navigation, irrigation, flood control, power production, and water supply. In both of these the sponsoring agency was the United Nations itself, which had given the concept of basin-wide planning official endorsement through the Secretary General in 1956 (United Nations, 1956): "River basin devel-opment is now recognized as an essential feature of economic development."

Even while the river basin was receiving this widespread acceptance as the basic unit for water resources development, however, the concept was already being challenged in some areas of fairly acute water shortage. In these areas, just as in the semi-arid and arid West of the United States, planners were turning more and more to interbasin transfers on a very big scale. One such project is the lower Rhône-Languedoc plan to improve land use and water supply in that sun-baked area of southern France between the Rhône River and the Pyrenees by divert-ing water from the lower Rhône and certain coastal rivers and transporting it westward for irrigation. Another is the Snowy Moun-tains Project in Australia, to transfer water and power from the abundantly watered Snowy River basin in Victoria across the mountains to the arid interior of New South Wales via tributaries of the Murray and Murrumbidgee rivers.

Most ambitious of all, however, and on a par with such continental water transfer projects as NAWAPA, are the various Soviet proposals to divert water from the great north-flowing rivers of Siberia (the Irtysh, Ob', Yenesey, and others) southward for irrigation of the arid interior of central Asia. The interesting common denominator of all these transbasin diversion projects is that they appear to be essentially single- or at the most double-purpose, to meet an urgently felt present need. In the United States NAWAPA and similar plans there is re-flected a developing conflict between irri-gation and municipal water supply, but with the galloping urbanization of the Pacific slope municipal water supply will eventually be the prime need. In the projects discussed above, the prime need is for irrigation or irrigation and power combined; any other benefits are secondary, and there is none of the balanced consideration of many different purposes and areas that characterizes a true river-basin approach.

Among the proliferating large-scale devel-opment of water resources, the environ-mental impact has been severe in many cases. In industrialized and heavily urbanized western Europe, the outstanding problem (as in the eastern United States) is pollution. Although it has an international commission for pollution protection and although some of its tributary basins were regulated for this purpose more than half a century ago, the fabled Rhine is 20 percent sewage and in-dustrial effluent by the time it reaches its outlet in the North Sea, and carries at least 30,000 tons of salts alone into the Nether-lands daily, which relies on the river for almost two-thirds of its "fresh" water supply. In the two decades from the 1940s to the 1960s, the amount of chloride in Rhine water increased by 20 percent, ammonia by 7,000 percent or more, phosphorus by 300 percent, whereas oxygen fell by one-third. The immediate and devastating impact has been upon aquatic life. Salmon began to decline before the end of the nineteenth century and have now disappeared from the Rhine, and fish kills by the millions are not a rare occurrence (Helfrich, 1970).

In other parts of the world environmental damage has been directly traced to the construction of large dams, flood control works, and complex water distribution systems. The Aswan High Dam is an awful warning. Within months after it began in 1965 to hold back the floodwaters of the Nile, marine biologists were reporting the failure in the eastern Mediterranean of the phytoplankton which form the basis of a food chain on which the fishery industries of the entire Levantine coast depend. Furthermore, the absence of flood-borne sediment below the dam—sediment which used to be carried both eastward and westward from the delta and settled to the floor of the Mediterranean to form a habitat for bottom-dwelling life—not only adversely affects marine ecological systems and impoverishes the delta, but is expected to result in the scouring down of the existing muddy deposits. The freshwater flow to the sea, already reduced by the impoundment, is further minimized by distribution to newly irrigated lands and by percolation to the ground water table.

The Kariba dam on the Zambesi River between Zambia and Rhodesia has also had unlooked-for, detrimental side-effects. Agricultural failure, which followed an initially bountiful harvest on new land, is believed due to changes in the water table and water level that were not foreseen, and to the need to plow during the rainy season. Moreover, the fish catch in the new lake has been only a tenth of that which was forecast, due to weed growth in the waters. Most serious,

this lake, like the one impounded behind the Aswan high dam and like a number of other such reservoirs in tropical regions, may do more harm to the population by the spread of water-borne diseases, such as schistosomiasis, than it will do good by irrigation. The United Nations took note of this fact in the 1970 report of a panel of experts on integrated river basin development (United Nations, 1970):

> Environmental changes due to the construction of dams and man-made lakes, to the creation or expansion of irrigation systems, or to the draining of swamps and marshes can . . . have far-reaching effects on the health of man and animals in regions affected.

There have also been forecasts of a biological catastrophe if the proposed sea-level Panama Canal is cut, linking eastern Pacific and western Atlantic waters. The less diversified fauna of the tropical eastern Pacific would undergo an inescapable, large-scale extinction (just as some of the dominant Red Sea-Indian Ocean species that have invaded the Mediterranean via the Suez Canal appear to be replacing the native fauna), and the shore life forms of Ecuador, Colombia, Panama, Costa Rica, Nicaragua, Honduras, El Salvador, Guatemala, and Mexico would be radically changed (Briggs, 1969).

Some of the UN flood control studies in Asia and the Far East reveal interesting examples of flood control projects which have done more harm than good and projects which, while achieving the required degree of regulation, have yet been protective of the riverine environment. The usual answer to flood problems has been to build higher and higher embankments, increasing the risk of damage at peak levels of the rivers. Some Indian engineers have doubted the wisdom of this course. Majumdar, the Chief Engineer of Bengal, noted in 1942 that the effect of double embankment on the Damodar had been a gradual rise of the riverbed level and a reduction in its flood-carrying capacity. He concluded, like Willcocks before him, that the fertilizing silt should be allowed to spread instead of being trapped. And Inglis, former Director of the Central Irrigation and Hydrodynamic Research Station in Poona, wrote:

> At the time the bunds (embankments) were built, few, if any doubted that they would be highly beneficial, but where bunds are built, spill is prevented, and so silting occurs on the river-side of the bunds but not outside . . . Consequently where river levels and river berm levels rise, the ground levels outside the bunds remain steady, the head against the bunds increases: so that when breaches occur, the resultant flooding and damage are locally much greater . . . (United Nations, 1952, p. 253)

Often the local people realize better than the engineers the nature of the problem. Majumdar states that "there is widespread belief in India that bunds are the cause of the rise of water levels in the river" (UN, 1950) and in some parts of former French Indochina, people asked for the flood-dike system to be destroyed. Here and there, methods other than solid embanking were tried and found successful. In Burma a Forestry Department officer experimented back in 1914 with bamboo stake fences. These were resorted to in the Yenwe Valley after embankments had failed to contain a series of abnormal floods. With the use of as many as five rows of parallel stake fences and with small silting sluices, water which formerly poured over the bunds spread across the land in thin sheets, depositing fertile silt and eventually collecting in lateral drainage channels. In this way the whole floodplain acted as a retarding basin and after a number of years (without major breaches or interruptions to communications) the controlled flooding was, in the words of one expert, "such a boon to the country that the work is more in the nature of a public utility service" (UN, 1950, p. 46). This method is not basically different from some of the methods employed in the fluvial civilizations of anti-

quity. Indeed, traditional methods of adaptation to, instead of forceful control of, the environment received an unusual accolade from a technical expert, who wrote concerning the Cambodian section of the Mekong (UN, 1950, p. 89):

> The people of this region have adapted themselves very well to the flood conditions. In Cambodia . . . houses are built on the strips of higher land along the river banks, usually on tall piles. They are thus well above the highest flood level. Behind the land side is another strip which, being situated on the slope of the ridge, is not subjected to normal flooding . . . Still further back is a considerable area of paddy fields usually cultivated after floods. Behind this area lie the depressions in which fish-rearing is carried on. In fact, floods, except those of extraordinary magnitude, are considered beneficial . . .

In the Soviet Union a considerable body of information has accumulated (through the researches of ecologists, geographers, and others) on the environmental impact of existing water development works and the expected impact of those now proposed, including the huge Siberian diversion schemes. One situation which caused great concern in the 1960s was the 30-year drop in level of the Caspian Sea. Although due in part to climatic changes, the problem has been aggravated by man's activities in the drainage basins of the rivers that feed this sea, including the filling of seven great reservoirs and several smaller ones (all part of the Greater Volga project mentioned above), and the loss of streamflow through consumptive uses, especially irrigation, as well as through filtration and evaporation from the reservoir surfaces.

The economic losses were serious enough in themselves. Navigation was badly affected by the retreat of the shoreline and the shoaling of approach channels, which required constant dredging to maintain ports such as Baku. The oil industry was affected by disruption of the coastal pumping stations that supplied water for industrial and firefighting needs to oil wells and refineries. Along the coast and in the Volga delta, orchards were abandoned, swamp areas with valuable reed growths dried out, the cost of irrigation went up as the supply diminished, and livestock farms had to build their own pasture watering systems. Worst of all was the effect on the fisheries. Before 1929 the Caspian had yielded some 40 percent of the Soviet fish catch. Within the next thirty years its share dropped from 510,000 tons to 190,000 tons per year. Hatcheries and feeding grounds in the Volga and Ural deltas and the northern part of the sea were laid dry, and the construction of dams upstream deprived anadromous fish of their spawning routes. Cumulatively, the construction of water development projects is estimated to have caused the loss of all the natural spawning grounds of the beluga sturgeon and the Caspian whitefish and severe injury to other fish populations (Bobrov, 1961).

Similar damaging effects have resulted from irrigation projects in the Aral Sea region and other parts of central Asia (*New York Times*, 1969). The level of this 26,000-square-mile inland sea dropped nearly 6 feet between 1961 and 1967 and it is feared that it may become a dried-out salt waste by the end of the century. Here, as in the Caspian, reduced fresh water inflow and increasing salinity have upset the ecological balance, and the fish catch within the same period was exactly halved.

The engineers' and planners' answer to these problems has been large-scale trans-basin diversion, literally turning the north-flowing rivers around into central Asia. These diversion projects would all involve the construction of huge reservoirs in the swampy lowlands of western Siberia and northern European Russia, which are already described as "zones of optimal and excess moisture." Grave doubts have been expressed as to the wisdom of building such massive water development works (Vendrov, 1963, 1965). The Pechora-Kama scheme's three reservoirs, for example, would occupy a total area only

slightly smaller than Lake Ladoga, flooding a huge extent of cropland, meadow, pasture, and timber reserves. The similarly sited Rybinsk Reservoir is known to have brought about climatic changes felt 10 kilometers from its shores (as much as 30 km in some directions), as well as vegetation changes, with heavy damage to forest, due to a rise in the ground water level. Near another reservoir, a healthy pine wood died out within only a few years as a result of the raised water table. The effects on aquatic life are expected to be just as damaging here as they have been at the outlets of the central Asian streams as a result of changes in salt content and temperatures.

From the tropics to the zone of permafrost, in areas of excess and insufficient moisture alike, the deleterious effects of large-scale water development have been catalogued and noted and brought to the attention of governments and the public. Yet the construction of huge water works continues, without regard to the environmental consequences. One of the latest examples is the Bennett dam in British Columbia, which scientists, wildlife experts, and Indian trappers alike have characterized as a "catastrophe for wildlife" due to declining water levels in the delta of the Peace and Athabasca rivers. An area where muskrats, wood bison, ducks, and geese abound and provide the basis for a native trapping and fishing economy is, as a committee of scientists and engineers charged (*New York Times*, Dec. 9, 1970): ". . . fast becoming a succession of isolated mudflats whose communicating streams are drying up."

CONCLUSIONS

Both intensive and extensive water development have had great impact on the environment, but in different ways. The impact of intensive development is direct and all-embracing; that of extensive development is sporadic and indirect—it sets the stage and draws the lines along which future interaction between water development and the environment proceeds. As a general proposition, it may be true that for a particular region or community under investigation, an intensive stage usually follows an extensive stage in water development, but much depends on the span of time involved and the overall level of economic development before the transition, which in turn depend on the availability of water for the needs of the economy. Obviously there are disparities, for the fluvial civilizations attained an intensive utilization of water at a level of technology based on human and animal muscle-power, whereas western Europe, in an era of space technology, is still at a transitional stage in intensity of water utilization.

In the conditions—climatic and hydrologic—in which the fluvial civilizations arose at the dawn of recorded history, the water needed for crops had to be brought artificially to the fields. This required cooperative effort. Once the rudiments of cooperation were achieved, it became obvious that further cooperative effort would produce more available water, and hence bigger crops. Since machinery was not yet well developed, further effort could be achieved only by bringing together a great many people, if necessary by compulsion. Thus, more people bound together in a political or administrative unit meant more water for food for still more people who would produce still more water—truly an unending progression. But pushing water exploitation to the limits permitted by the existing technology, so as to produce the wealth necessary to maintain larger populations, led to the creation of powerful, populous, and despotic states. Perhaps the great and sustained effort necessary to build and maintain the waterworks on which the fluvial civilizations were based could be mustered only under the constant threat of the whip. In any case, though water development contributed to the power of the state, it did not contribute to the well-being of the individual. It is doubtful whether

the lot of the corvée laborer was any improvement on that of the small farmers, who are thought to have initiated the processes of water development that preceded the fluvial civilizations.

Although there may be no direct link between the impact of the fluvial civilizations on their environment and the present quality of life in the regions in which they thrived, some of those regions still teem with people, even if they are today considered underdeveloped areas. It was of these that Kipling wrote: "Out of the spent and unconsidered Earth The Cities rise again." Was it their low level of energy output that saved them from destroying utterly the environmental base that supported them? Other regions of fluvial civilization had begun to deteriorate long before external causes, such as war and invasion, brought about the final collapse. Their eventual failure—and it must be emphasized that this was a process of centuries and even millenia—lay not so much in the exhaustion of the physical environment, but in imposing a greater strain on the human element than it could safely give under the technological level then existing. Under such conditions, the quality of human life deteriorated even if the total amount of wealth increased—with the same result as if the environment itself were being destroyed.

Whereas the fluvial civilizations of antiquity tried to develop water resources beyond their technological capacity, western Europe did not even fully apply the technology it possessed to water development until the advent of hydroelectric power toward the end of the nineteenth century. On the whole, it had enough rainfall for its agriculture, and irrigation was not widely practiced. Its rivers were mainly highways of commerce and communication, but little work for this purpose, too, was done before the nineteenth century. The attitude toward water development is best exemplified in the customary water law which prevailed over most of Europe and which prescribed that flowing water should be left undisturbed and should flow as it always had done from time immemorial. These precepts were taken over by the riparian rights doctrine as it developed in England and the United States.

It is not surprising that the impact of water development on the environment of western Europe was generally small and localized in character. In contrast to the fluvial civilizations, water development had little influence on political structure except insofar as rivers, being highways of communication, contributed in the early Middle Ages to the consolidation of some of today's states. The lack of this influence may be one reason why European absolutism at its height looks like laissez-faire liberalism when compared with the fluvial despotism of antiquity.

But because water was abundant and could be had in sufficient quantity without much effort, it was used freely and without regard for its impact on the environment or on other users, building on the one hand indifference and on the other the expectancy that water should be free for any use whatever, or if not free, then at someone else's expense (see Fox, this volume). This attitude is well illustrated in the landowner's absolute right to use groundwater beneath his land, which prevailed in English common law and, until recently, in France. It is even better illustrated in the use of rivers and streams as sewers for municipal and industrial waste, a use which was shielded, at least in the United States, by the built-in common law protection of industrial and municipal interests.

From the middle of the nineteenth century onward, however, under the impact of increased population and of rapid industrialization, the demand for water began to grow at such a pace that it is expected to outgrow the existing supply in many regions before the present century is over. From being water surplus regions, Europe and the eastern United States are turning into water-deficient areas. The situation becomes not dissimilar to that which faced the engineers and administrators of the fluvial civilizations. And the answer, too, has been much the same—more and bigger dams, more and bigger reservoirs, more transfers of water over greater distances, and more centralization of administrative control over water disposition. Even water-rich England finally abandoned its riparian rights doctrine in 1963. It is true that this doctrine still lingers in most of the eastern United States, but a growing centralization is reflected in the role of the federal government, which has complete power over the development of navigable waters, based on the commerce clause of the federal Constitution.

Perhaps we are traveling the path of the fluvial civilizations. Even if there are parallels in water demand and water development, the occidental economies are so much more complex that their ultimate structure cannot be predicated on possible solutions to the growing water shortage. If, however, trends in water development and management reflect a general overtaxing of the limited environmental base of ever-expanding economies, then the inadequate quality of individual life of the fluvial civilizations may be in store for us.

ARE WE GOING THE WAY OF THE FLUVIAL CIVILIZATIONS?

The main factors which might tend to propel us in the direction taken by the fluvial civilizations already exist, namely: (1) shrinking water resources; (2) an expanding economy highly dependent on water; (3) a developmental outlook; and (4) the means to build large projects. The ancient water managers in a similar situation strove relentlessly to match the available water to the expanding needs of the economy, regardless of cost to the social and, sometimes, to the physical environment. Yet they showed an understanding of the environmental perils of intensive water development and some of their precepts have universal validity. Among them are:

1. Where an ecologically sound water management system has evolved over a long period of time, it should neither be tampered with nor allowed to deteriorate through neglect and apathy.
2. Water resources should be administered in harmony with the total environment.
3. Emphasis should be laid on the personal responsibility of the administration for all matters connected with water use and development, including environmental deterioration.
4. The potential harm should be weighed against the potential benefit of a project (in contrast to the modern benefit-cost criterion).
5. The concept of public duty extends to the entire population.

The concept of public duty, carried to the extreme of corvée labor, is certainly not palatable—in fact, it is irrelevant—to modern society . But popular involvement with water management problems is largely lacking today. Water resources development is not observed at first hand by the city dweller. He has attitudes toward the deterioration of his urban environment through water pollution, but no large dams are built in cities, and so he has no real conception of the developmental aspects of water management. In a predominantly urban and still rapidly urbanizing society, this could be a serious defect, for the conservation-minded water manager needs to win popular support and to draw upon a larger constituency than that immediately affected by a water project.

The most significant lesson of history is that without a technological breakthrough which would provide new sources of water or permit reduced consumption in many of the tasks which water now performs, sufficient water for the needs of a growing economy

can be provided only at ever increasing cost to the physical environment, or to the social environment, or both. There is a point in water resource development when water can no longer be matched to the economy, but the economy must be matched to the water available. This may be a bitter pill to swallow for a development-minded modern society, but history teaches that when such time arrives, water development must be controlled with utmost thoroughness.

Unbalanced water development in the past stemmed probably from lack of the necessary information to weigh short-term benefits against long-term detriment. We may decide, or be compelled, to go the same way as the fluvial civilizations, but if such a course be taken, it should be carried through with full awareness of the consequences. We have vastly superior means of gathering and evaluating data, and these should be improved and used to the utmost. In the light of past experience, one thing above all should be asked of modern, scientific water management—that major projects be undertaken only when all their potential effects on the totality of the environment have been assessed by all available means.

Although current water development may eventually have less political and social influence than its counterpart in antiquity, it has already had a greater and more widespread impact on the environment, as has been shown above in the effect of dams and diversions on the ecology of estuaries and in the existing and potential effect of large-scale water transfers on climate, vegetation, aquatic life, and human health.

Present-day technology, wedded to the developmental outlook bequeathed by a water-rich European past, may and can at last do what the low energy output of the fluvial civilizations could not do, namely irreversible damage to the environment, not just on a local but on a global scale. The injury to the aquatic environment of Lake Erie through overuse may still be viewed as local; the threat of a similar fate for the

Mediterranean Sea is on such a scale that it can properly be termed global.

The greater the front, the greater the back. The greater the power and capacity for development, the greater the obligation to use restraint and consider the consequences. A Chinese commentator of the Ming period wrote (Legge, 1969) that the wise ruler:

> in his single person, sustains the burden of all under the sky. People depend on him for their rest and enjoyment. Birds and beasts and creeping things, and the tribes of the vegetable kingdom, depend on him for the fulfillment of their destined being.

For "ruler" read "government." But persistence of the developmental outlook, based on a deeply ingrained belief in an inexhaustible environment, has been actually bolstered by a legally sanctioned lack of concern over environmental impact on the part of governmental agencies dealing with water development that has persisted almost to the close of the 'sixties. The lesson of the past is clear. The fluvial civilizations send a warning across the ages that there is a limit to which water development can be pushed without impairing the quality of life. And in the much more recent European and United States history, a message can be read that attitudes acquired in periods of water plenty dare not be carried over to periods of scarcity. Expansion at the expense of the environment and of the individual can be avoided if the growth of technology and the economy is geared to a pace concomitant with maintenance of the environment as a whole fit for what is considered to be the "good life."

References*

Berber, F. J. 1959. *Rivers in International Law.* (Batstone, R. K., transl.). New York, Oceana.

Beuscher, J. H. 1967. *Water Rights.* Madison, Wisconsin: College Print. & Typing Co.

Bobrov, S. N. 1961. The transformation of the Caspian Sea. 2 *Soviet Geography*, No. 7, 47 (Sept. 1961). Transl. from *Geografiya v. shkole*, 1961, No. 2, P. 5.

Briggs, J. C. 1969. The sea level Panama Canal: potential biological catastrophe. Reproduced in *Congressional Record* (daily), July 31, 1969, S. 8898.

Burch, W. R., Jr. 1970. Resources and social structure: some conditions of stability and change, 389 *Ann. Amer. Acad. Polit. & Soc. Sci.*, 27 (1970).

Chi, Ch'ao-Ting. 1936. *Key Economic Areas in Chinese History as Revealed in the Development of Public Works for Water-Control.* London: Allen & Unwin.

Conference of Governors, 1909. White House, Washington, D.C., May 13–15, 1908. *Proceedings.*

Congressional Record (daily), Sept. 12, 1968, H. 8599.

Congressional Record (daily), March 20, 1969, H. 1966.

Congressional Record (daily), Sept. 30, 1969, H. 8635.

Congressional Record (daily), Nov. 25, 1969, H. 11418–11426.

Cressey, G. B. 1958. Qanats, karez, and foggaras. 48 *Geog. Rev.* 27.

Darby, H. C. 1936. *The Draining of the Fens, A.D. 1600–1800.* Cambridge: Cambridge U. Press.

Darby, H. C. 1936. *An Historical Geography of England Before A.D. 1800.* Cambridge: Cambridge U. Press.

Derry, T. K., and Williams, T. 1960. *A Short History of Technology.* London: Oxford U. Press.

Dobkins, B. E. 1959. *The Spanish Element in Texas Water Law.* Austin, U. Texas Press.

Fair, G. 1961. Pollution abatement in the Ruhr district. In *Comparisons in Resource*

*Cases and treaties are listed by number in the following section.

Management 156 (Jarrett, H., ed.). Baltimore, Johns Hopkins.

Gottschalk, L. C. 1945. Effects of soil erosion on navigation in upper Chesapeake Bay. 35 *Geog. Rev.* 219.

Gregor, H. F. 1952. The Southern California water problem in the Oxnard area. 42 *Geog. Rev.* 16.

Gurber, J. W. 1948. Irrigation and land use in ancient Mesopotamia. 22 *Agr. History* 69.

Grund, F. J. 1837. *The Americans in Their Moral, Social and Political Relations.* London: Longman.

Hamdan, G. 1961. Evolution of irrigation agriculture in Egypt. In *A History of Land Use in Arid Regions* 119 (Stamp, L. D., ed.). Paris: UNESCO.

Hays, S. P. 1958. The mythology of conservation. In *Perspectives on Conservation* 40 (Jarrett, H., ed.). Baltimore, Johns Hopkins.

Helfrich, H. W., Jr., ed. 1970. *The Environmental Crisis.* New Haven, Yale U. Press.

Hirsch, A. M. 1959. Water legislation in the Middle East. 8 *Am. J. Comp. L.* 168; quoting Talmud Bavli, Nedarim, 80b.

Issawi, C. 1963. *Egypt in Revolution.* London, Oxford U. Press.

Jones, F. C. 1954. Tukiangyien: China's ancient irrigation system. 44 *Geog. Rev.* 543.

Legge, J. transl. 1969. *I Ching, Book of Changes* (vol. XVI of *The Sacred Books of the East*). New York, Bantam (paperbound edition).

Lilienthal, D. 1953. *T.V.A.: Democracy on the March.* New York: Harper.

McConnell, G. 1970. Prologue: environment and the quality of political life. In *Congress and the Environment* (Cooley, R. A., & Wandesforde-Smith, G., eds.). Seattle, Wash., U. Washington Press.

Marsh, G. P. 1965. *Man and Nature* (Lowenthal, D. ed.). Cambridge, Mass.: Harvard U. Press.

Nash, R. 1969. *Wilderness and the American Mind.* New Haven: Yale U. Press. (paperbound ed.).

New York Times, Feb. 16, 1969, p. 15, col. 1.

New York Times, Mar. 22, 1970, p. 14, col. 1.

New York Times, Nov. 1, 1970, Sec. 10, p. 41, col. 1.

New York Times, Dec. 9, 1970, p. 31, col. 3.

Nicholson, M. 1970 *The Environmental Revolution.* New York: McGraw-Hill.

Parsons, R. L. 1964. *Conserving American Resources.* Englewood Cliffs, N.J.: Prentice-Hall.

Teclaff, L. A. 1967. *The River Basin in History and Law.* The Hague, Nijhoff.

Teclaff, L. A. 1968. The river basin and beyond—changing concepts in U.S. water resources planning. (CF. 1/68-E/F.18) In *Proceedings,* 1st International Conference on Water Law, Mendoza, Arg., Aug. 28–Sept. 2, 1968.

Teclaff, L. A. 1970. The coastal zone—control over encroachments onto the tidewater. 1 *J. Mar. L. & Comm.* 241.

Teclaff, L. A. 1972. *Abstraction and Use of Water: A Comparison of Legal Regimes.* (ST/ECA/154) New York: United Nations.

Thoreau, H. D. 1950. A week on the Concord and Merrimack Rivers. In *Walden and Other Writings of Henry David Thoreau* (Atkinson, B., ed.). New York: Random House (paperbound ed.).

Thorner. 1962. *Land and Labour in India.* New York: Asia Publ. House.

Tocqueville, A. de. 1945. *Democracy in America.* Vol. 2 (Bradley, P. ed.). New York: Knopf.

Todd, D. K. 1959. *Ground Water Hydrology.* New York: Wiley.

Udall, S. 1963. *The Quiet Crisis.* New York: Holt, Rinehart &Winston.

United Nations. Department of Economic and Social Affairs. 1970. *Integrated River Basin Development: Report of a Panel of Experts.* (U.N. Doc. No. E/3066/Rev. 1) New York.

United Nations. Department of Economic and Social Affairs. Council Office. 1956. *Rec. 21st Sess., Annexes* (E/2827). New York.

United Nations. Economic Commission for Asia and the Far East. 1950. *Flood Damage and Flood Control Activities in Asia and the Far East.* (Flood Control Series No. 1.) Bangkok.

United Nations. Economic Commission for Asia and the Far East. 1952. *Proceedings of the Regional Conference on Flood Control in Asia and the Far East.* (Flood Control Series No. 3) Bangkok.

U.S. Congress. House of Representatives. 1949. *Message from the President of the United States Requesting the Establishment of Columbia Valley Administration,* H.R. Doc. No. 158, 81st Congress, 1st Sess. 3-4.

U.S. Congress. Senate. 1967. *Wetlands for Waterfowl Conservation.* Hearing before the Subcommittee on Merchant Marine & Fisheries of the Committee on Commerce, 90th Congress, 1st Sess.

U.S. Geological Survey. 1970. *A Preliminary Study of the Effects of Water Circulation in the San Francisco Bay Estuary.*

Vendrov, S. L. 1965. A forecast of changes in natural conditions in the northern Ob' Basin in case of construction of the lower Ob' hydro project. 6 *Sov. Geog.,* No. 10, P. 3, Dec. 1965. Transl. from *Izv. Akad. Nauk SSSR,* ser. geogr. 1965, No. 5, P. 37.

Vendrov, S. L. 1963. geographical aspects of the problem of diverting part of the flow of the Pechora and Vychegda rivers to the Volga Basin. 4 *Sov. Geogr.* No. 6, P. 29 (June 1963). Transl. from *Izv. Akad. Nauk SSSR,* ser. geogr., 1963, No. 2, P. 35.

Willcocks, W. 1914. *River Regulation and Control in Antiquity.* H. Doc. No. 18, 63rd Congress, 2nd Session.

Willcocks, W. 1903. *The Restoration of the Ancient Irrigation Works on the Tigris.* Cairo: Nat'l Printing Dep't.

Williams, W. D. 1938. Irrigation law in Colorado. 10 *Rocky Mt. L. Rev.* 87, 178, 190-191.

Wittfogel, K. A. 1963. *Oriental Despotism: A Comparative Study of Total Power.* New Haven: Yale U. Press (paperbound ed.).

Wright, J. 1966. *The Coming Water Famine.* New York: Coward-McCann.

CASES

1. Antioch v. Williams Irr. Dist., 188 Cal. 451, 205 P. 688 (1922)
2. Arizona v. California, 373 U.S. 546 (1963)
3. Blaine County Inv. Co. v. Mays, 49 Idaho 776, 291 P. 1055 (1930)
4. Carlyon v. Lovering, (1857) 1 H. & N. 784.
5. Clark v. Peckham, 10 R.I. 35 (1871)
6. Clark v. Syracuse, 13 Barb. 32 (1852)
7. Doherty v. Pratt, 34 Nev. 343, 124 P. 574 (1912)
8. Duncombe v. Randall, Het. 32, 124 Eng. 320 (C.P. 1628)
9. Economy Light Co. v. United States, 256 U.S. 113 (1921)
10. Empire Water & Power Co. v. Cascade Town Co., 105 F. 123 (Cir. Ct. of Appeals, 8th Cir., 1913)
11. Enterprise Irr. Dist. v. Willis, 135 Nebr. 827, 284 N.W. 326 (1939)
12. Gibbons v. Ogden, 22 U.S. (9 Wheat.) 1 (1824)
13. Green Bay & Miss. Canal Co. v. Patten Paper Co., 172 U.S. 58 (1898)
14. Hudson County Wateer Co. v. McCarter, 209 U.S. 349 (1908)
15. Hudson River R. Co. v. Loeb, 7 Robt 418 (1868)
16. La Countee de Rutland v. Bowler, Palm. 290, 81 Eng. Rep. 1087 (K.B. 1622)
17. Lamprey v. Metcalf, 52 Minn. 181, 53 N.W. 1139 (1893)
18. Lea Conservancy Board v. Hertford Corpn., (1884) 48 J.P. 628
19. McKeesport Gas Co. et. al. v. Carnegie Steel Co., Ltd., 189 Pa. 509 (1899)
20. Michelson v. Leskower, 155 N.Y.S. 2d 831 (1945)
21. Missouri v. Illinois. 200 U.S. 496 (1906)
22. The Montello, 87 U.S. (20 Wall.) 430 (1874)
23. Muench v. Public Service Comm'n., 261 Wis. 492, 53 N.W. 2d 514 (1952)
24. Namekagon Hydro Co. v. Federal Power Comm'n, 216 F. 2d 509 (1954)
25. New Hampshire v. A.E.C., 402 F. 2d 170 (1969)

26. New York v. Baumberger, 7 Robt. 219 (1867)
27. Oklahoma v. Atkinson, 313 U.S. 508 (1941)
28. Parker v. Cutler Milldam Co., 20 Me. 353 (1841)
29. City of Pasadena v. City of Alhambra et. al., 33 Cal. 2d 908, 207 P. 2d 17 (1949)
30. Pennsylvania Coal Co. v. Sanderson, 110 Pa. St. 126, 6 A. 453 (1886)
31. Prince v. Moulton, 1 Raym. Ld. 248. 91 Eng Rep. 1062 (K.B. 1697)
32. R. V. Medley, (1834) 6 Car. & P. 292.
33. Russell v. Handfords, 1 Leon 273, 74 Eng. Rep. 248 (K.B. 1583)
34. Sands v. Trefuses, Cro. Car. 575, 79 Eng. Rep. 1094 (K.B. 1639)
35. Somerset Drainage Comrs. v. Bridgwater Corpn., (1899) 81 L.T. 729
36. State ex rel. Cary v. Cochrane, 138 Neb. 163, 292 N.W. 234 (1940)
37. State v. Elk Island Boom Co., 41 W. Va. 796, 24 S.E. 590 (1896)
38. Udall v. Federal Power Comm'n, 387 U.S. 428 (1967) [quoting letter of Nov. 21, 1960 from the Secretary of the Interior to the F.P.C.]
39. United States v. Rio Grande Dam & Irrigation Co., 174 U.S. 690 (1899)
40. United States v. The Sadie, 41 F. 396 (S.D.N.Y. 1890)
41. Woodruff v. North Bloomfield Gravel Mining Co., 18 F. 753 (C.C. Cal. 1884)
42. Wright v. Williams, (1836) 1 M. & W. 77.
43. Zabel v. Tabb, 296 F. Supp. 764 (1969) [reversed in 1970 by Circuit Court under the impact of the National Environmental Policy Act of 1970; 443 F. 2d 199 (5th Cir. 1970)]

TREATIES

44. Acte Additionnel du 26 Mai, 1866, au Traités de Délimitation Conclus le 2 Decembre, 1856, 14 Avril, 1862, et 26 Mai, 1866, Entre la France et l'Espagne, 9 Clerq, *Recueil des Traités de la France* 544.
45. Convention Entre la Suisse at le Grand-Duché de Bade au Sujet de la Navigation sur le Rhin de Neuhausen Jusqu'en Aval de Bâle, 10 Mai, 1879, (1878–1879) 4 *Recueil Officiel des Lois et Ordonnances de la Confédération Suisse* (N. sér.) 339
46. Convention Entre Sa Majesté l'Impératrice-Reine et S.A.S. Electorale Palatine, May 13, 1779, 2 *Martens R. I.* (2e. éd.) 671
47. Traité de Limites Entre Leurs Majestés le Roi de Prusse et le Roi des Pays-Bas, Oct. 7, 1816, 3 *Martens N.R.* 54–55
48. Traité pour Régler le Régime de Prise d'Eau à la Meuse Entre la Belgique et les Pays-Bas, May 12, 1863, 1 *Marten N.R.G.* (2e sér.) 120

CHAPTER 4

Early preservationists who believed in the intrinsic importance of wilderness, and a rising public concern for the vanishing frontier prompted the formation at the turn of this century of a national policy to establish natural parks and reserves. From 1905 to 1913, a controversy raged as to whether the Hetch Hetchy Valley in Yosemite should be used as a water supply reservoir, or remain inviolate as a national park. Preservationists lost this battle; but in the ensuing fifty years, wilderness protection became a national concern.

After reviewing the Hetch Hetchy controversy, this chapter describes the recent conflicts between water development and park preservation in Dinosaur National Monument (Echo Park Dam) and in Grand Canyon National Park (Marble and Bridge Canyon dams). A commitment to leaving a few free-flowing streams intact was made with the decisions not to build these dams, and was reinforced with passage of the 1968 National Wild and Scenic Rivers Act.

However, the constant pressure of construction and development has not lessened. If wild rivers are not to become extinct, it is time to change our priorities from development to conservation, in keeping with the needs and values of today's and tomorrow's citizens.

RIVERS AND AMERICANS: A CENTURY OF CONFLICTING PRIORITIES

Roderick Nash

America's conservation movement has long swirled turbulently around its rivers. Since 1607, when the *Vanguard* of the Virginia Company dropped anchor in the lower James River, people have disputed the purposes of waterways. For some they were (and are), in Ralph Waldo Emerson's phrase, "commodity"—sources of transportation, power, irrigation, sanitation, and the morning coffee water. For others they were "the symbol of the spirit" (again Emerson) and as such the providers of beauty, inspiration, recreation, and religion. In rare instances these two sets of values coexisted in relative peace on the same river, such as the Niagara in the vicinity of the Falls which since the 1850s has managed to delight both technicians and aestheticians. But often these interests have conflicted sharply. Indeed, the nation's rivers have been the objects of some of the most bitter struggles in American environmental history. In 1913 and 1968 conflicts over dams in California's Hetch Hetchy Valley and Arizona's Grand Canyon made nationwide headlines. An examination of these controversies reveals much about American expectations with regard to rivers. It is also apparent that in the interval between the 1910s and 1960s the burden of proof shifted from the preservationists to the developers. The issue, however, is far from settled, and a look into the past can help inform those presently charged with shaping the American environment of the future.

I

I vanquished this wilderness and made the chaos pregnant with order and civilization, alone I did it.
Pioneer settlers' guidebook (1849)

In Wildness is the preservation of the World.
Henry David Thoreau (1851)

The roots of conflicting motivations for river development (or nondevelopment) reach far back in the history of man's relation to his natural environment. From his beginnings in the early Pleistocene until only yesterday, geologically speaking, man directed his energies to conquering, not conserving, the environment. Such behavior was highly appropriate for a people whose very survival depended on breaking nature to their will. With the saber-toothed tiger only a jump behind, conservation was inconceivable. In the first place, natural resources seemed inexhaustible—the problem was too many rather than too few trees, an overabundance of wild rivers rather than a scarcity. Moreover, the Judeo-Christian tradition taught that God had given the natural world to man for his exploitation. *Genesis* 1:28 commanded the first couple

to "be fruitful, and multiply, and replenish the earth, and subdue it: and have dominion over the fish of the sea, and over the fowl of the air, and over every living thing that moveth upon the earth." The environment existed solely for the satisfaction of man's immediate desires.

The first white Americans followed squarely in this tradition. Their transatlantic migration to a wilderness recreated the fears and drives of primitive man, and later generations of frontiersmen continued the pattern. A massive assault was directed at the virgin land in the name of civilization and Christianity. Progress became synonymous with exploitation. The strength of individualism and competitiveness in the American value system supported the pioneer's insistence that the land he owned could be used as he willed. The long-term interest of society made little difference; considerations of immediate profit directed relationships with the land. A scarcity of natural resources? Absurd! Over the next ridge was a cornucopia of wood, soil, game, and water. Up to the late nineteenth century, Americans experienced a population density unconducive to the conservation idea. But as man gained control over nature and his needs pressed against the natural limits of the New World, conservation began to make sense.

In this unpromising context early prophets of environmental stewardship, such as Henry David Thoreau and George Perkins Marsh, attempted to gain an audience. They challenged the prevailing conception of the land's purpose, exposed inexhaustibility as a myth, and even made so bold as to question the dogma of free enterprise when land health was concerned. Their contemporaries paid scant attention, but time was on the side of ideas such as these.

Several developments around the turn of the century help explain conservation's coming of age. Mounting evidence that the nation could exhaust—and, in fact, was exhausting—many of its vital resources proved highly important. Another precondition for conservation was an increasing public apprehension over the effects of concentrated wealth, which came to a head in the era of Progressivism, a political philosophy that held that the federal government should take an active, positive role in American life.

Finally, the early American conservation movement benefited enormously from the growth of widespread uneasiness over the psychological and physical consequences of the passing of the frontier. For two-and-a-half centuries the frontier had been almost synonymous with abundance and opportunity in the New World. As a consequence, few could regard the 1890 Census' announcement of the end of the frontier without regret. Suddenly, the nation seemed middle-aged, and conservation acquired new appeal. In a sense, conservation would be the new frontier. It would keep the nation prosperous, vigorous, democratic, and beautiful. For a civilization that had begun to notice its first gray hairs, conservation was a welcome tonic.

The conviction that natural resources could be scientifically managed in the long-term interest of the general public provided the mainspring of Progressive conservation, which envisioned, as Gifford Pinchot put it, "the complete and orderly development of all our resources for the benefit of all the people." The means to this end was efficient planning, devised by scientists, implemented by engineers, and guided by an understanding of the interrelationships of resources. Progressives expected the returns of conservation to be nothing less than the perpetuation of national greatness. W J (he insisted on this punctuation) McGee, a disciple of Powell and colleague of Pinchot, regarded the conservation movement as the capstone to the crusade for human rights that began with the American Revolution. Little wonder President Theodore Roosevelt opened the famous White House Conservation Conference in May 1908 with an allusion to conservation as "the chief material question that confronts us."

America's rivers were well suited to the kind of comprehensive, multiple-purpose planning Progressive conservationists advocated. Indeed, western water development, along with eastern forestry, formed the heart of the early movement. John Wesley Powell broke the trail. His 1878 *Report on the Lands of the Arid Region of the United States* broached the reclamation idea: with federal financial and technical support, land normally too arid for agriculture could be fructified by irrigation. Having run much of the rampaging Colorado by boat, however, he knew well that water in rivers was unique among natural resources; what happened at one place on a river could affect areas hundreds of miles downstream, possibly an entire watershed. In the Colorado's case, this drainage area amounted to over 240,000 square miles, or one-twelfth of the continental United States. Consequently, Powell thought of conservation in regional rather than local terms. This marked a breakthrough of major importance in American conservation history and heralded the concept of regional planning.

Powell succeeded in igniting the enthusiasm of several young colleagues in the U.S. Geological Survey who would help bring his ideals to realization. W J McGee, the champion of multiple-purpose river development, was one, but more important for reclamation was Frederick H. Newell. A Pennsylvania-born engineer who trained at the Massachusetts Institute of Technology, Newell joined the Geological Survey in 1888 and immediately began a national water resources inventory. Hydrologists measured the flow of the Colorado River in 1894 and 1895. At the same time, Newell joined forces with Representative Francis G. Newlands of Nevada and George H. Maxwell, a California lawyer, in a campaign to publicize the advantages of federally financed irrigation. The campaign culminated in the Reclamation (or Newlands) Act of June 17, 1902, which established a mechanism for applying the proceeds from the sale of public lands in the West to federal reclamation projects, and created the Reclamation Service (later known as the Bureau of Reclamation). Powell died the same year, but his ideas now had official sanction. Within five years the Reclamation Service under Newell had twenty-five major projects underway. Other water projects fell into the province of the Corps of Engineers, active in this area since the 1820s.

After the epoch-making reclamation act, conservationists pressed on in their campaign to control and develop the nation's water resources. The "Conquest of Water," W J McGee grandly declared, was as crucial to human progress as the "Conquest over Fire, Knife, Spring, and Wheel" and, indeed, "the single step remaining to be taken before Man becomes master over Nature." Before his untimely death from cancer in 1912, McGee labored ceaselessly for comprehensive river development. For Gifford Pinchot, Chief Forester and close friend of President Theodore Roosevelt, the single most important aspect of water conservation was the prevention of prime dam sites from falling into the hands of private developers. Multiple-purpose management would be precluded, and the lucky entrepreneurs, Pinchot feared, could quickly extend their control from hydropower to all of industry. Eventually, civil liberty itself might be threatened. Consequently, Pinchot believed that if permission to build dams was granted to private parties at all, it should be in the form of a revokable lease. The power to regulate the operation of the facility should reside with the government.

While the utilitarian motivation for conservation was growing under the leadership of Powell and Pinchot, an aesthetic or preservationist motivation also staked a claim to the definition of "conservation." The preservationists had made important gains before Progressivism with the creation of state parks in California's Yosemite Valley and New York's Adirondack Mountains in 1864 and 1885, respectively. The first national parks

protected spectacular wilderness in Wyoming's Yellowstone region (1872) and California's Sierra (1890). Theodore Roosevelt designated part of the Grand Canyon a national monument in 1908. But the catalyst of aesthetic conservation was John Muir, a self-styled "poetico-trampo-geologist-bot. and ornith-natural, etc.!–!–!," who believed that nature, especially in its wilder forms, reflected God and refreshed man. Combining this transcendentalism with glowing descriptions of California's Sierra Nevada, Muir gained a nationwide reputation as a nature writer. In 1892 he took the lead in founding the Sierra Club, which would come to play an important and highly controversial role in the history of river management.

Inevitably the utilitarian and aesthetic interpretations of conservation clashed. In fact, the conflict between opposing wings of the conservation movement, rather than between it and "exploiters," has furnished the main dynamic in twentieth century environmental history in the United States. The problem, simplified, was whether "conservation" meant planned, efficient development of resources or the preservation of nature for its nonutilitarian values. The answer, that it meant both (the multiple-use formula), might work in a regional plan but was meaningless for a small area. A given stretch of river, for instance, could be either wilderness or a reservoir—not both simultaneously. Recognition of this impelled the first great conservation controversy in American history—the battle over the Hetch Hetchy Valley, 1908 to 1913.

II

As to my attitude regarding the proposed use of Hetch Hetchy by the city of San Francisco . . . I am fully persuaded that . . . the injury . . . by substituting a lake for the present swampy floor of the valley . . . is altogether unimportant compared with the benefits to be derived from its use as a reservoir.

Gifford Pinchot, 1913

These temple destroyers, devotees of ravaging commercialism, seem to have a perfect contempt for Nature, and instead of lifting their eyes to the God of the Mountains, lift them to the Almighty Dollar .

John Muir, 1912

Situated on a dry, sandy peninsula, the city of San Francisco faced a chronic freshwater shortage. In the Sierra, about 150 miles distant, the erosive action of glaciers and the Tuolumne River had scooped out the spectacular, high-walled Hetch Hetchy Valley. As early as 1882, city engineers pointed out the possibility of damming its narrow, lower end to make a reservoir. They also recognized the opportunity of using the fall of the impounded water for the generation of hydroelectric power. In 1890, however, the act creating Yosemite National Park designated Hetch Hetchy and its environs as a wilderness preserve. Undaunted, San Francisco's Mayor James D. Phelan made application to use the valley as a reservoir site shortly after the turn of the century. Secretary of the Interior Ethan A. Hitchcock's refusal to violate the sanctity of a national park was only a temporary setback, because on April 8, 1906, an earthquake and fire devastated San Francisco and added urgency and public sympathy to its search for an adequate water supply. The city immediately reapplied for Hetch Hetchy, and on May 11, 1908, Secretary James R. Garfield approved the new application. "Domestic use," he declared in the Pinchot school of utilitarian conservation "is the highest use to which water and available storage basins . . . can be put."

John Muir did not agree. He feared that the whole national park concept would crumble if Hetch Hetchy was turned over to the dam builders. But Muir knew that resistance to a project both Pinchot and Theodore Roosevelt had blessed would be immensely difficult. "Conservation" seemed to be on the side of efficiently using Sierra water in San Francisco's mains. Muir realized that his first task was to create an alternative

definition and rally public opinion behind it. Telling arguments against the reservoir were needed. As the basis of their protest, friends of wilderness turned to the old romantic case against "Mammon." They made Hetch Hetchy into a symbol of ethical and aesthetic qualities, while disparaging San Francisco's proposal as tragically typical of American indifference toward them. This line of defense criticized the commercialism and sordidness of American civilization, while defending wilderness.

John Muir opened the argument for the Valley on aesthetic grounds with an article in *Outlook*. After describing its beauties, he declared that its maintenance as a wilderness was essential, "for everybody needs beauty as well as bread, places to play in and pray in where Nature may heal and cheer and give strength to body and soul alike." Others took up the same theme in the national press. Writing in *Century*, which he edited, Robert Underwood Johnson charged that only those who had not advanced beyond the "pseudo-'practical' stage" could favor San Francisco's proposal. The presence of these individuals in the nation, he added, "is one of the retarding influences of American civilization and brings us back to the materialistic declaration that 'Good is only good to eat'." As a self-appointed spokesman for culture and refinement, Johnson took it upon himself to defend intangibles. In a brief submitted at the first Congressional hearing on the Hetch Hetchy question in December 1908, he made his protest "in the name of all lovers of beauty . . . against the materialistic idea that there must be something wrong about a man who finds one of the highest uses of nature in the fact that it is made to be looked at."

As president of the American Civic Association, J. Horace McFarland took every opportunity to preach the desirability, indeed the necessity, of maintaining some element of beauty in man's environment. He believed the aesthetic should have a place in the conservation movement, and in 1909 expressed his displeasure at its concentration on utilitarian aims. In the same year he told Pinchot that "the conservation movement is now weak, because it has failed to join hands with the preservation of scenery." For McFarland, Hetch Hetchy was a test case, and he spoke and wrote widely in defense of the valley's preservation, taking the stand that if even national parks could be given over to utilitarian purposes, there was no guarantee that ultimately all the beauty of unspoiled nature would be destroyed. Speaking before the Secretary of the Interior on the Hetch Hetchy question, McFarland contended that such undeveloped places would become increasingly valuable for recreation as more and more Americans lived in cities. Yet when the preservation of wilderness conflicted with "material interests," those financially affected cried: "that is sentimentalism; that is aestheticism; that is pleasure-loving; that is unnecessary; that is not practical'." Usually such resistance carried the day and wilderness was sacrificed. McFarland objected because "it is not sentimentalism, Mr. Secretary; it is living." Elsewhere he elaborated on his ideas: "the primary function of the national forests is to supply lumber. The primary function of the national parks is to maintain in healthful efficiency the lives of the people who must use that lumber . . . . The true ideal of their maintenance does not run parallel to the making of the most timber, or the most pasturage, or the most water power."

Lyman Abbott, the editor of *Outlook*, also felt it was a mistake "to turn every tree and waterfall into dollars and cents." His magazine found most of its readers among a class of people concerned over what they thought was the eclipse of morality, refinement, and idealism by urbanization, industrialization, and an emphasis on business values. The defense of wilderness attracted them because it permitted making a positive case—they could be *for* something (wilderness) rather than merely against amorphous forces. Protecting the wild from an exploita-

tive civilization, in short, represented the broader struggle to maintain intangibles against the pressure of utilitarian demands. Sensing this, Abbott made *Outlook* one of the chief organs of the Hetch Hetchy campaign. He explained his stand in an editorial in 1909: "if this country were in danger of habitually ignoring utilitarian practice for the sake of running after sentimental dreams and aesthetic visions we should advise it . . . to dam the Tuolumne River in order to instruct its citizens in the use of the bathtub. But the danger is all the other way. The national habit is to waste the beauty of Nature and save the dollars of business."

The same disparaging reference to American tastes and values appeared in the statements of preservationists in early 1909 at the House and Senate hearings in regard to Hetch Hetchy. One man, who had camped in the valley, pointedly asked: "Is it never ceasing; is there nothing to be held sacred by this nation; is it to be dollars only; are we to be cramped in soul and mind by the lust after filthy lucre only; shall we be left some of the more glorious places?" Others joined him in pleading that "loftier motives" than saving money for San Francisco be taken into consideration. "May we live down our national reputation for commercialism," one letter concluded.

In the Senate hearings, Henry E. Gregory of the American Scenic and Historic Preservation Society appeared in person and spoke of the need to counteract "business and utilitarian motives" that seemed to him to dominate the age. He pointed out that wildernesses such as Hetch Hetchy had value beyond computation in monetary terms "as an educator of the people and as a restorer and liberator of the spirit enslaved by Mammon." Arguments along these lines struck home, especially at a time when many Americans squirmed uncomfortably at charges that their nation's aesthetic sense was stunted and deformed.

Another tactic of the preservationists emphasized the spiritual significance of wild places and the tendency of money-minded America to ignore religion. Hetch Hetchy became a sanctuary or temple in the eyes of the defenders. John Muir, for one, believed so strongly in the divinity of wild nature that he was convinced he was doing the Lord's battle in resisting the reservoir. The preservationists' innumerable puns about "damning" Hetch Hetchy were only partly in jest. John Muir and his colleagues believed they were preaching "the Tuolumne gospel." San Francisco became "the Prince of the powers of Darkness" and "Satan and Co." Muir wrote: "We may lose this particular fight but truth and right must prevail at last. Anyhow we must be true to ourselves and the Lord." This conviction that they were engaged in a battle between right and wrong prompted the preservationists to vituperative outbursts against their opponents. In a popular book published in 1912, Muir labeled his foes "temple destroyers" who scorned the "God of the Mountains" in pursuit of the "Almighty Dollar." A ringing and widely quoted denunciation followed: "Dam Hetch Hetchy! As well dam for watertanks the people's cathedrals and churches, for no holier temple has ever been consecrated by the heart of man."

Using these arguments, and the especially effective one that the valley as part of Yosemite National Park was a "public playground" which should not be turned over to any special interest, the preservationists were able to arouse considerable opposition to San Francisco's plans. Members of the Sierra and Appalachian Mountain Clubs took the lead in preparing pamphlet literature for mass distribution. *Let ALL the People Speak and Prevent the Destruction of the Yosemite Park* of 1909 for example, contained a history of the issue, reprints of articles and statements opposing the dam, a discussion of alternative sources of water, and photographs of Hetch Hetchy. Preservationists also obtained the sympathies of numerous newspaper and magazine editors in all parts of the nation. Even Theodore

Roosevelt retreated from his earlier endorsement of the reservoir and declared in his eighth annual message of December 8, 1908, that Yellowstone and Yosemite "should be kept as a great national playground. In both, all wild things should be protected and the scenery kept wholly unmarred."

Evidence of the effectiveness of the protest appeared in the action of the House after its 1909 hearings. Although the Committee on the Public Lands had approved the grant in a close vote, a strong minority report dissented on the grounds that such action would deny the public's right to the valley for recreational purposes. Testifying to the amount of popular opposition, the report observed that "there has been an exceedingly widespread, earnest, and vigorous protest voiced by scientists, naturalists, mountain climbers, travelers, and others in person, by letters, and telegrams, and in newspaper and magazine articles." In the face of this expression of public opinion, the House pigeonholed and killed San Francisco's application in the Sixtieth Congress.

San Francisco was bewildered and incensed at the public unwillingness that it should have Hetch Hetchy as a reservoir. Was not supplying water to a large city a worthy cause, one that certainly took priority over preserving wilderness? The San Francisco *Chronicle* referred to the preservationists as "hoggish and mushy esthetes," while the city's engineer, Marsden Manson, wrote in 1910 that the opposition was largely composed of "short-haired women and long-haired men." San Francisco argued that the beauties of wilderness were admirable, but in this case human health, comfort, and even human life were the alternatives. Phrased in these terms, even some of the members of the Appalachian Mountain Club and the Sierra Club felt compelled to place the needs of civilization ahead of protecting wild country. In the Sierra Club, Warren Olney, one of the founders, led a faction which supported the city. In 1910 the Club held a referendum in which preservation won 589 to 161, but in order to prosecute the defense of Hetch Hetchy, the preservationists were obliged to act in a separate organization: the California Branch of the Society for the Preservation of National Parks. The wilderness enthusiasts in the Appalachian group formed an Eastern Branch of the Society.

At every opportunity the proponents of the dam expressed their belief that a lake in Hetch Hetchy would not spoil its beauty but rather enhance it. A prominent engineer reported on the city's behalf that roads and walks could be built which would open the region for public recreation in the manner of European mountain-lake resorts. Since the preservationists frequently based their opposition on the need to maintain a "scenic wonder" or "beauty spot," and on the desirability of maintaining a public playground, the claims of San Francisco were difficult to dismiss. If, instead, more attention had been paid specifically to the wilderness qualities of Hetch Hetchy—which any man-made construction would have eliminated—San Francisco's point about the scenic attraction of an artificial lake could have been more easily answered. As it was, this tactical error cost the preservationists considerable support.

The Hetch Hetchy controversy entered its climatic stage on March 4, 1913, when the Woodrow Wilson administration took office. San Francisco's hopes soared, because the new Secretary of the Interior, Franklin K. Lane, was a native, a former attorney for the city, and a proponent of the reservoir. But Lane upheld the policy of previous Secretaries that in cases involving national parks Congress must make the final decision. On behalf of San Francisco, Representative John E. Raker immediately introduced a bill to the Sixty-third Congress approving the grant. The preservationists prepared to send protest literature to 1,418 newspapers and to make known their views before Congress. Robert Underwood Johnson distributed an *Open Letter to the American People* in which he declared Hetch Hetchy to be "a

veritable temple of the living God" and warned that "again the money-changers are in the temple." The stage was set for a showdown.

On the basis of the June 1913 hearings, the Committee submitted a report unanimously endorsing the reservoir plans. When the bill reached the floor of the House in late August, strong support immediately developed for its passage. Representative John E. Raker of California was typical in his assertion that the "old barren rocks" of the valley have a "cash value" of less than $300,000, whereas a reservoir would be worth millions. Muir and Johnson could only shudder at this logic and watch sadly as the House passed the Hetch Hetchy bill on September 3, 183 to 43 with 203 Representatives not voting. No Congressman from a western state voted against it. Most of its support came from southern and middle western Democrats. In fact, the bill was rumored to be an administration measure connected, in some minds, with the votes California had given to Woodrow Wilson in the recent election.

The Senate still had to decide on San Francisco's application, and in preparation the preservationists worked frantically. Their plan was "to flood the Senate with letters from influential people." In addition, the Society for the Preservation of National Parks and the newly organized National Committee for the Preservation of the Yosemite National Park published several pamphlets which called on Americans to write or wire their President and Congressmen and suggested arguments against the dam. Thousands of copies were circulated, and the public responded. Between the time of the House passage and early December when the Senate began its debate, the destruction of the wilderness qualities of Hetch Hetchy Valley became a major national issue. Hundreds of newspapers throughout the country, including such opinion leaders as the *New York Times*, published editorials on the question, most of which took the side of preservation. Leading magazines, such as

Outlook, Nation Independent, and *Collier's,* carried articles protesting the reservoir. A mass meeting on behalf of Hetch Hetchy took place at the museum of Natural History in New York City. Mail poured into the offices of key Senators: Reed Smoot of Utah estimated late in November that he had received 5,000 letters in opposition to the bill, and other Senators were likewise besieged. The protests came from women's groups, outing and sportmen's clubs, scientific societies, and the faculties of colleges and universities, as well as from individuals. The American wilderness had never been so popular before.

Meanwhile, San Francisco was not idle. The representatives of its cause lobbied quietly in Washington and prepared a special Washington edition of the San Francisco *Examiner* on Hetch Hetchy. Skillful drawings showed how the valley might appear as a man-made lake with scenic drives for automobiles and boating facilities for happy family groups. Also included was testimony from experts justifying the grant of the valley to the city on economic and engineering grounds. In comparison, the preservationists' campaign literature was considerably less impressive. The difference, and the strength of party whips, was evident on December 6, 1913, when 43 Senators favored the Hetch Hetchy grant, 25 opposed it, and 29 did not vote. The decisive factor was 18 votes from Southern Democrats, suggesting, as in the case of the House, that the Wilson administration was behind San Francisco. Only nine of the "yeas" came from Republicans. When President Wilson signed the bill December 19, Hetch Hetchy's future was determined. In due time the O'Shaughnessy dam impeded the flow of the Tuolumne and a reservoir rose in the valley. It did not fulfill the promises held forth in the *Examiner,* but the Hetch Hetchy episode did contain some benefits for preservationists. They had lost the fight for the valley, but they had gained much ground in the larger war for the existence of wilderness. A deeply disappointed John Muir took some consolation from the fact that "the conscience of the whole country has been aroused from sleep." Scattered sentiment for wilderness preservation had, in truth, become a national movement in the course of the Hetch Hetchy controversy. Moreover, the defenders of wilderness discovered their political muscles and how to flex them by arousing an expression of public opinion, and in Hetch Hetchy they had a symbol which, like the *Maine,* would not easily be forgotten. In fact, immediately after the Hetch Hetchy defeat the fortunes of wilderness preservation took an abrupt turn for the better. Early in 1915 Stephen T. Mather, a highly successful businessman and outdoor enthusiast, became director of the national parks and generated a campaign that resulted in the enactment in 1916 of the National Park Service Act. The publicity that accompanied its passage did much to increase the national interest in preserving wilderness that the Hetch Hetchy fight had aroused.

Near the close of the Senate debate on Hetch Hetchy, James A. Reed of Missouri arose to confess his incredulity at the entire controversy. How could it be, he wondered, that over the future of a piece of wilderness "the Senate goes into profound debate, the country is thrown into a condition of hysteria." Observing, accurately, that the intensity of resistance to the dam increased with the distance from Yosemite, he remarked that "when we get as far east as New England the opposition has become a frenzy." In Senator Reed's opinion this was clearly "much ado about little." He might have said the same about other manifestations of the growing American enthusiasm for nature (the rise of the Boy Scouts and the popularity of nature stories are examples) that occurred simultaneously with the Hetch Hetchy battle. But the point, as Reed himself suggested, was that a great many of his contemporaries *did* regard aesthetic conservation as something worth getting excited about.

Indeed the most significant thing about the controversy over Hetch Hetchy was that it occurred at all. A hundred or even fifty years earlier a similar proposal to dam a wilderness river would not have occasioned the slightest ripple of public protest. Traditional American assumptions about the use of undeveloped country did not include reserving it in national parks for its recreational, aesthetic, and inspirational values. The emphasis was all the other way—on civilizing it in the name of progress and prosperity. Older generations conceived of the thrust of civilization into the wilderness as the beneficent working out of divine intentions, but in the twentieth century a handful of preservationists generated widespread resistance against this very process. What had formerly been the subject of national celebration was made to appear a national tragedy.

Muir, Johnson, and their colleagues were able to create a protest because the American people were ready to be aroused. Appreciation of wild country and the desire for its preservation had spread in the closing decades of the nineteenth century from a small number of literati to a sizeable segment of the population. The extent and vigor of the resistance to San Francisco's plans for Hetch Hetchy constituted tangible evidence for the existence of a wilderness cult. Equally revealing was the fact that very few favored the dam *because* they opposed wilderness. Even the partisans of San Francisco phrased the issue as not between a good (civilization) and an evil (wilderness) but between two goods. While placing material needs first, they still proclaimed their love of unspoiled nature. Previously most Americans had not felt compelled to rationalize the conquest of wild country in this manner. For three centuries they had chosen civilization without any hesitation. By 1913 they were no longer so sure.

III

Representative Morris K. Udall [Arizona]: Mr. Brower, maybe we can start out by compromising . . . I had thought that maybe if we took Marble Canyon [dam] out as I am willing to do . . . and give you 158 miles of living river instead of 104 which wasn't sufficient last year, that maybe we had the grounds of compromise.

Mr. David Brower [Executive Director, Sierra Club]: Mr. Udall, you are not giving us anything that God didn't put there in the first place . . . [The Grand Canyon] is the primary scenic resource of this country. If there are no other ways to go about getting your water, I would still say that the compromise should not be made—that Arizona should be subsidized with something other than the world's Grand Canyon, or any part of it.

Representative Udall: You won't agree or compromise on any point regardless of . . . how high [the dam is], how low, how little damage or anything else.

Mr. Brower: We have no choice. There have to be groups who will hold for these things that are not replaceable. If we stop doing that, we might as well stop being an organization, and conservation organizations might as well throw in the towel.

Representative Udall: I know the strength and sincerity of your feelings, and I respect them.

Testimony before the House Committee on Interior and Insular Affairs, Subcommittee on Irrigation and Reclamation, March, 1967

In the interval between the Hetch Hetchy controversy and that occasioned by the proposal in the 1960s to build dams in the Grand Canyon, the American conservation movement underwent important changes. The aesthetic or preservation viewpoint had grown strikingly in sophistication and effectiveness. Persuasive exponents of the importance of wild country in modern America extended the early intellectual explorations of Henry David Thoreau and John Muir. The ecologist and wildlife manager, Aldo Leopold, argued in the 1930s that modern man's power to shape his environment should entail a sense of responsibility for the other life-forms sharing the planet. This responsibility was not a matter of economics or even aesthetics, Leopold insisted, but of simple ethics. It followed that conservation should not mean development of nature so much as maintaining its balance. In these terms wild places had significance as land in ecological harmony against which man could measure the effects of his violence, and hopefully "learn an intelligent humility toward [his] place in nature." Other twentieth-century champions of preservation, men such as Robert Marshall and Sigurd Olson, stressed the psychological importance of unmodified nature. Some men found wilderness essential, they pointed out, either as an alternative to the drabness of civilization or as a means of regaining serenity and perspective. Still others linked the continued existence of wild country to the maintenance of the sanctity of the individual in a mass society. "If we ever let the remaining wilderness be destroyed," Wallace Stegner warned, "we are committed . . . to a headlong drive into our technological termite-life, the Brave New World of a completely man-controlled environment."

The Preservation movement had also grown in size. When John Muir led the Hetch Hetchy protest, he could have called on only seven national and two regional conservation organizations. Fifty years later the figures had jumped to 78 and 236. The political effectiveness of private conservation efforts likewise had increased enormously. The Hetch Hetchy controversy revealed the disadvantage of not having professional lobbyists in Washington to conduct the infighting that could translate public opinion into political decision. After 1918 the National Parks Association helped remedy this defect, and in 1935 Robert

Marshall organized the Wilderness Society. With headquarters in Washington, it defined its purpose as "fighting off the invasion of wilderness and . . . stimulating . . . an appreciation of its multiform emotional, intellectual, and scientific values." The Isaak Walton League and the National Wildlife Federation also became towers of preservation strength on a national level.

Unquestionably, the most important asset of the preservationists on the eve of the Grand Canyon controversy was the support of a large and growing number of Americans. As the amount of wilderness in the country decreased, desire for protecting what remained increased. It was the familiar story of not appreciating something until threatened with its deprivation. Publicizers like Stephen T. Mather of the National Park Service labored to make Americans aware of the irreplaceable value of their parks. Serving as a sort of chamber of commerce for wilderness, Mather and his colleagues produced an astonishing volume of illustrated publicity and stimulated periodicals to carry articles on the nation's natural wonders. Over two million persons saw Emerson Hough's 1922 plea in *The Saturday Evening Post* for the preservation of the Kaibab Plateau, including the North Rim of the Grand Canyon, as a "typical portion of the American wilderness." If such a place was to be saved in its natural condition, Hough maintained, future generations could learn "what the old America once was, how beautiful, how splendid," The railroads' "See America First" campaign also attracted public attention to places like the Colorado's canyons, by pointing out that they were unmatched in Europe. And, ironically, the availability and vogue of the automobile, the nemesis of preservationists today, was highly important to the growth of the wilderness movement. With a car or two in many garages, the national parks and monuments were not merely names on pictures but realistic targets for the family vacation. This possibility of personal contact did much to broaden the social base on which the preservation movement rested.

The status of reclamation, and utilitarian conservation generally, also changed in the half century between the Hetch Hetchy and Grand Canyon controversies. Technological breakthroughs eased the fears about resource exhaustion which had impelled early conservation. In addition, many Americans came to realize that an environment conducive to survival was not enough. The land had to do more than just keep people alive; it must bring them joy. This was the basis for the emphasis in American conservation since World War II on *quality* of the environment. Beauty and recreational opportunity, rather than productivity, became the new yardstick for measuring the success of land management. Utilitarianism was partially eclipsed. Reclamation, in particular, seemed to many to have passed its zenith. The choice sites such as Boulder Canyon (Hoover Dam) and the Tennessee Valley had been developed and had unquestionably proved of great value. Many of those that remained were difficult to build, expensive, and at greater distances from the areas their water and power might serve. Some critics of reclamation contended that bananas *could* be grown on the top of Pike's Peak if the nation were willing to commit the necessary dollars and effort. Even without considering expense, others noted that the development of *new* cropland through irrigation made little sense when land already under cultivation produced more than the economy could absorb.

The Echo Park Dam controversy of the 1950s provided an indication of the new climate of opinion regarding river development. At stake in this battle were the wild canyons of the Green and Yampa rivers in northeastern Utah and western Colorado, which comprised part of the Dinosaur National Monument. A Bureau of Reclamation dam, part of the Colorado River Storage Project, would have innundated the canyons for a total of more than 100 miles. Moreover,

opponents of the dam contended, integrity of the national park system would have been breached, thus opening the doors to other "invasions." The reclamationists replied with the standard arguments about the importance of water and hydropower in the arid, undeveloped West. At first they carried the day, winning the approval of the Department of the Interior in 1950. But preservationists, convinced they faced a showdown situation, marshalled a large, vigorous, well-financed, and effective resistance. David R. Brower, executive director of the Sierra Club, and Howard C. Zahniser, who served the Wilderness Society in a similar capacity, led the crusade for Dinosaur. With unprecedented vigor and skill, they launched a national campaign against the dam. Hard-hitting illustrated pamphlets, flyers, and direct mailings asked the public: *Will you DAM the Scenic Wild Canyons of Our National Park System?* and *What is Your Stake in Dinosaur?* A professional motion picture, in color, had hundreds of showings throughout the country. Wallace Stegner edited a book-length collection of essays and photographs showing the importance of keeping Dinosaur wild. Conservation periodicals featured numerous articles on the monument. More important from the standpoint of national opinion was the extensive coverage the controversy received in *Life, Collier's, Newsweek,* and the *Reader's Digest,* as well as in newspapers all over the country.

The success of this effort was evident in the mail that poured into Washington, D.C. In the spring of 1954 the House received thousands of communications with a ratio of 80 to 1 against the Echo Park Dam. As a result Congress postponed consideration of the entire Colorado River Storage Project. Preservationists made it clear, moreover, that they would continue to block the whole package unless the controversial dam was deleted. Ultimately this strategy succeeded, and the Echo Park project was dropped. "We hated to lose it," Representative William A. Dawson of Utah commented in 1955, but "the opposition from conservation organizations has been such as to convince us . . . that authorizing legislation could not be passed unless this dam was taken out."

In the Echo Park controversy American conservation turned a significant corner. For the first time preservation had prevailed over utilitarian conservation in a major confrontation. The Echo Park affair revealed that henceforth the private, citizen-action group with a talent for arousing public opinion would be a strong candidate for the leadership of American conservation. The legacy of the conflict was widespread suspicion of the government's purposes with regard to the environment. Finally, the showdown at Echo Park left little doubt that in the future partisan conflict would unfortunately be the mechanism for environmental decision-making. This fear was confirmed when preservationists learned that the price of their victory at Echo Park was a dam at Glen Canyon and the transformation of 186 miles of the Colorado River into Lake Powell. As a requiem for the lost beauty of this central Utah wilderness, the Sierra Club published a new volume in its spectacularly illustrated Exhibit Format Series, *The Place No One Knew*. In truth, few were even aware of what was at stake in Glen Canyon. The lesson was clear. The existence of wild rivers in the continental United States depended on eternal vigilance and also on the ability to arouse a massive public protest. If Echo Park and Glen Canyon represented a stalemate between different interpretations of conservation on the Colorado, then the next decision would break the tie, and could not but be climatic. The Grand Canyon dams idea was not new with the 1960s. Two sites in particular had long attracted the attention of engineers: Bridge and Marble canyons. A bill authorizing the construction of a dam at Bridge Canyon had actually passed the Senate in 1950 only to be summarily defeated in the House. Hydrol-ogists had also long discussed an elaborate plan to bring water from a reservoir in Marble Canyon through a 40-mile tunnel under the Kaibab Plateau to hydropower facilities in Kanab Creek—91 percent of the Colorado's water would have been diverted from its normal course through the Grand Canyon.

According to the National Park Service Act of 1916, the alteration of natural conditions by hydropower projects in Grand Canyon National Park or Grand Canyon National Monument, immediately downstream, was clearly illegal. The legislation stated that "the fundamental purpose of the . . . parks . . . is to conserve the scenery and natural and historic objects and the wildlife therein, and to provide for the enjoyment of the same in such manner and by such means as will leave them unimpaired for the enjoyment of future generations." But reclamationists took heart from a provision in the act of February 26, 1919, establishing Grand Canyon National Park. "Whenever consistent with the primary purposes of said park," it declared, "the Secretary of the Interior is authorized to permit the utilization of areas therein which may be necessary for the development and maintenance of government reclamation projects." This obvious inconsistency left the way open for widely varying interpretations of the legality of Grand Canyon dams.

The Grand Canyon controversy began to gather momentum in 1963 when the Bureau of Reclamation made public its multibillion-dollar Pacific Southwest Water Plan. To solve the Southwest's growing water shortage, engineers proposed diverting water from the Columbia River and transporting it in a series of tunnels, ducts, and canals into the Colorado. The increased flow would be utilized with the aid of a series of dams and diversion facilities. One of them, the Central Arizona Project, called for hydropower dams at Marble and Bridge canyons. The sale of the electricity they produced would be used to pay for transporting water from Lake Havasu on the lower Colorado to the Phoenix-Tucson area.

The Bureau of Reclamation anticipated preservationist opposition: Marble Canyon Dam would flood 53 miles of Redwall Gorge, considered the scenic equal of the now inundated Glen Canyon. The proposed high dam at Bridge Canyon would back water up for 93 miles into a portion of Grand Canyon National Monument and along the northwestern edge of the national park. In preparation for the inevitable protests, Commissioner of Reclamation Floyd Dominy ordered the construction of a scale model of the Grand Canyon and used it to argue that the dams and reservoirs he proposed would not impair scenic values. Indeed, he argued, the lakes would permit millions to enjoy the little-seen beauties of the inner canyon with unprecedented safety. On this basis Secretary of the Interior Stewart Udall initially supported the dams and ordered the National Park Service to cease its opposition in the interests of department unity. Such official backing and the tenor of congressional hearings in 1965 and 1966 led many to expect that the dams would be approved by the Eighty-ninth Congress. But on June 9, 1966, a now-famous full-page advertisement appeared in the *New York Times* and the *Washington Post.* "Now Only You Can Save Grand Canyon From Being Flooded—For Profit," its headline blared. The ad cost the Sierra Club $15,000, but it paid remarkable dividends, as mail deploring the dams poured into key Washington offices. Senator Thomas Kuchel of California termed it "one of the largest letter-writing campaigns which I have ever seen." But the greatest success of the ad was unexpected: on June 10 the Internal Revenue Service warned the Sierra Club that henceforth any donations it received might be ruled nondeductible under a ruling forbidding organizations in its tax status from engaging "substantially" in efforts to influence legislation.

If the warning of the IRS was designed to help the cause of the dam builders, it was a backfire of colossal proportions, for it appeared that the Sierra Club was being punished for altruistic efforts on behalf of Grand Canyon. The issue became front page news all over the country, multiplying the effect of the ad many times. People who did not care in the slightest about wilderness now rose to support the Sierra Club in the name of civil liberties. Could bureaucracies intimidate citizen protest? Were only the well-heeled lobbies to be tolerated? The tax action made the issue of the dams transcend conservation and prompted protest letters from thousands who might never have written otherwise.

The simple reminder that the *Grand Canyon* was at stake headed preservationist agruments. If we can't protect this place, they asked Americans, what *can* we save? In answer to Commissioner Dominy's contention that the dams would not alter much of the canyon and their reservoirs would not even be visible from most places on the rims, the preservationists replied that it was important on emotional grounds to *know* that the free-flowing, living river that had cut the chasm was cutting it still, even if it could not be seen. Dams, furthermore, would eliminate the possibility of a supreme adventure: running the Colorado by boat through the Grand Canyon.

Supporting these points were charges that the dams served no purpose other than to make money to finance other parts of the Central Arizona Project. Was the nation so poor it had to use the Grand Canyon as a "cash register," preservationists wondered? Then they pointed out that coal-fired thermal plants or nuclear generators could perform the dams' functions equally well and at less cost to the taxpayer. Another criticism stemmed from the preservationists' belief that the dams would actually *waste* the Colorado's limited water supply through evaporation and seepage into the reservoir walls. In this way the dams were represented as working against the very purpose of the Pacific Southwest Water Plan and the Central Arizona Project.

As a result of the previous summer's furor over the Grand Canyon dams, reclamationists brought revised proposals to the opening of the Ninetieth Congress in January, 1967. They would abandon Marble Canyon dam entirely and extend Grand Canyon National Park 60 miles upstream as added protection for this part of the Colorado. Downstream from the park, however, the new plan called for the abolition of Grand Canyon National Monument so that Hualapai Dam (as Bridge Canyon Dam had been renamed) would not inundate any area in the national park system. Preservationists remained adamant. One bullet in the heart, they maintained, was just as deadly as two. And changing names on a map did not alter the fact that there would no longer be a live river in Grand Canyon. A nationwide advertising canpaign did much to drive these points home "and alert the public." Adding greatly to the preservation cause at this time were two potent weapons. Francois Leydet's *Time and the River Flowing* appeared in the Sierra Club's Exhibit Format Series to strengthen the point that the mistake made in Glen Canyon should not be repeated downstream in the Grand. The Club also produced two sound-and-color motion pictures on Glen and Grand Canyons. And slowly the resistance began to take effect.

On February 1, 1967, the dam builders' hopes plunged when Secretary of the Interior Stewart Udall announced that the administration had changed its mind about the Grand Canyon dams. Udall had been a major factor in that change. After a river trip through the Grand he became convinced that the highest use of this stretch of the Colorado was to leave it as it is. In June the Senate Interior and Insular Affairs Committee voted to authorize the Central

Arizona Project without either of the controversial dams. The Committee also took steps to preclude the possibility that either the state of Arizona or the city of Los Angeles would build a dam in the Grand Canyon on its own initiative. On August 8, 1967, the Senate followed its Committee's recommendations and passed a damless Central Arizona Project.

In the House, however, Representative Wayne Aspinall of Colorado, powerful chairman of the Interior and Insular Affairs Committee and a pro-dam stalwart, vowed to continue the fight. But by early 1968 even men of his persuasion saw the writing on the wall. On July 31 House and Senate conferees rang the death knell on Grand Canyon dams when they included in the Central Arizona Project Act the statement that "nothing in . . . this Act contained shall be construed to authorize the study or construction of any dams on the main stream of the Colorado River between Hoover Dam and Glen Canyon Dam."

American attitude toward rivers passed a significant milestone on September 30, 1968, when President Lyndon Johnson signed a damless Central Arizona Project bill into law. Dams that at one point seemed certainties, that had enjoyed the full backing of the White House, the Interior Department, most western Congressmen, and numerous water and power-users associations plus their lobbies, were blocked. The preventative force was a citizenry united only by a determination to *SAVE GRAND CANYON*, as their bumper stickers declared. Yet clearly this was no minor power. "Hell," remarked one disappointed Congressman, "has no fury like a conservationist aroused." He might have added that aesthetic conservation had finally come of age in the United States.

Additional evidence came in the form of acts creating the National Wilderness Preservation System (September 3, 1964) and a National Wild and Scenic Rivers System (October 2, 1968). The latter did not include any portion of the Colorado in its initial designations, but it did create a framework of protection into which portions of that river might one day be placed. More importantly, it demonstrated a commitment on the part of the American people and their government to perpetuate a representative sample of free-flowing, unpolluted, and undeveloped waterways.

In retrospect it would appear that American policy with respect to the Colorado River has been an accurate reflection of the ambivalence in the American mind. There is enthusiasm, almost a passion, for wild nature that currently rides the crest of the conservation wave. But for many , even for those who like the outdoors, total wilderness is too much. They demand mechanized access and some conveniences in their recreational pursuits. From their perspectives, reservoirs such as Lake Mead and Lake Powell have created recreational values, and they feel that Lake Powell in particular is beautiful, regardless of what lies beneath its surface. The reservoirs permit power boating, water-skiing, fishing, and camping to thrive, and for those who lack either the taste, the ability, or the money for wilderness river trips, the man-made lakes are valuable. The consumers of water for irrigation and of hydropower also have legitimate claims to the nation's rivers, and flood control has proved a blessing to millions of citizens.

In view of this division of interests, perhaps the compromise that occurred on the Colorado was unconsciously well designed. Glen Canyon Dam, Hoover Dam, and the lower dams represent one set of priorities; the free-flowing river in Dinosaur and the Grand Canyon another. Surely not every river can or should be kept undeveloped. But just as surely some rivers or portions of them should be left wild. Perhaps Boulder Canyon and Glen Canyon should have been included in this category. But in that case would preservationists have been willing to sacrifice Dinosaur and the Grand? The great-est challenge facing water policy makers is the sensitive weighing and balancing of the environments that make life possible and those that make it worthwhile.

POLICY RECOMMENDATIONS

The history of American attitude toward the environment in general and rivers in particular dramatizes the rise of enthusiasm for wilderness over the last century. We are currently on the crest of an onrushing wave of wilderness appreciation. There is widespread and increasing disenchantment with machines, technology, and a quantified (as opposed to qualitative) conception of progress. Many have come to understand that "civilization" is not exempt from the suggestion that there can be too much of a good thing.

At one stage in our national development we needed to give the first priority to river development; now the need is for preservation. Wild rivers are among our rarest environmental possessions. *There are fewer undeveloped rivers of meaningful length left in continental United States than there are condors or whooping cranes.* River management policy should reflect an awareness of this fact and of the growing national need and desire for wilderness experiences. All the nation's wild rivers that might qualify for permanent preservation should be placed in the National Wild and Scenic River System now. Let them start with protected status, and thereby *place the burden of proof on the developer.* For too long it has been on the preservationist. The mood of the 1970s and of the foreseeable future demands a change.

Water resource planners should be alert to the fact that they are in a real sense planning for the future—for *future* needs and tastes, not those of the present or the past. Dams, to be specific, take decades to plan, finance, and construct. Those responsible for their authorization must ask themselves if the rationale for a project can survive the erosive force of time and change. And they must have the courage to change their minds if the need arises. The recent demise of the Cross Florida Barge Canal, which involved the destruction of the wild Oklawaha River, is encouraging in this respect. But it required a nationwide expression of public opinion and ultimately the authority of the President himself, to stop the Corps of Engineers. In the case of the little-known Stanislaus River in California's Sierra, however, the Corps faces less resistance and is proceeding to construct the New Melones Dam which was authorized in the 1940s. Of questionable value even by the standards of that decade, the new dam (which replaces an entirely adequate smaller structure) is now environmental idiocy. The Stanislaus is one of the last, challenging whitewater rivers left in California. Thousands "run" it each season. Surely the rationale behind the dam authorization should be reviewed, perhaps as part of an "environmental impact" study under the auspices of the Council of Environmental Quality. Indeed, every river development project over three years old should be made to stand the test of such a review. Otherwise we plan for the future with criteria a half-century old.

References

Roderick Nash, *Wilderness and the American Mind* (1967) traces changes in attitude toward wild country over the entire course of American history and places the Hetch Hetchy and Echo Park controversies in their broader intellectual and institutional contexts. Other references on Hetch Hetchy include Holway R. Jones, *John Muir and the Sierra Club: The Battle for Yosemite* (1965) and Elmo R. Richardson, *The Politics of Conservation: Crusades and Controversies, 1897–1913* (1962). Richardson has also published "The Struggle for the Valley: California's Hetch Hetchy Controversy, 1905–1913," *California Historical Society Quarterly*, 38 (1959), 249–58. John Ise, *Our National Park Policy: A Critical History* (1961) discusses Hetch Hetchy in telling the national park story.

A review of American conservation history in the words of those who made it may be obtained in the author's *The American Environment: Readings in Conservation History* (1968). The bibliography in this volume will lead to most of the major secondary works in the field. For the Grand Canyon dam controversy see Francois Leydet, *Time and the River Flowing: Grand Canyon* (1964), the author's *Grand Canyon of the Living Colorado* (1970) particularly page 99 ff. and T . H. Watkins, ed., *The Grand Colorado: The Story of a River and its Canyons* (1969).

CHAPTER 5

Alterations of the natural environment may produce serious psychological effects on human beings. Little is known, however , about the psychological and physiological impact of man-made environments.

Contemporary controversy over the environmental effects of development is due partly to the failure of our regulatory laws to reflect popular definitions of pollution, which change as public values change. Among the general public there appears to be little relationship between environmental "concern" (based on social-psychological factors) and technical knowledge of a problem; personal impact is the motivating factor. Man's ability to adapt psychologically to conditions that may cause physiological harm (for example, to a "normal" level of smog) indicates that some natural areas must be preserved intact as a baseline for judging environmental quality.

Dr. Swan discusses possible explanations for increases in outdoor recreation and wilderness use. Other areas of behavior that are important to environmental planning yet little understood are: the varying degrees of importance that people attach to environmental conditions; their capacity to recognize future consequences of their actions and the collective impact of individual actions; and the measurement of environmental attitudes and motivating factors.

PSYCHOLOGICAL RESPONSE TO THE ENVIRONMENT

James A. Swan

INTRODUCTION

The term "environment" is commonly defined as all those things, conditions, and processes that surround an individual and are capable of affecting him. As this definition implies, environmental conditions have consequences for human behavior, just as human behavior may affect environmental conditions. The exact importance of the environment to behavior is a controversial issue among psychologists, but none would disagree that the role of the environment is important.

Recognizing the importance of environmental conditions in influencing human behavior, one might expect to find a wealth of literature dealing with behavior-environment interaction. This, however, is not the case. Most research has dealt only with the social environment—typically, interactions with other people—rather than with the physical environment. This condition is at least partially attributable to the professional training of people in both the behavioral and the environmental sciences, which is generally not integrative. The result is a rather uneasy, uncooperative relationship between the two professions, with only a few brave souls venturing into the middle (Winkel, 1970). It is essential that in the future we integrate the behavioral and environmental sciences and study man-environment interaction as a dynamic system.

The field of environmental psychology is new and has not been extensively studied, but we do already know many things that can be useful to environmental planning. The intent of this paper is to review aspects of environmental psychology that seem especially pertinent to water resources planning, with the attempt to be integrative and conceptual rather than exhaustive and specific.

Research in environmental psychology has generally not used the systems perspective. Rather, the research is largely focused on one of two perspectives: the impact of various environments upon behavior; and the behavioral responses to various environmental conditions. Because of the nature of the existing research, rather than the preference of the author, this dichotomy will largely be followed in this review. Hopefully, research in the next few years will give more attention to the study of man and his environment as an integrated system.

THE IMPACT OF ENVIRONMENTAL CONDITIONS ON MAN

Every living thing is totally immersed in its environmental surroundings. To survive, each organism must develop mechanisms for deciphering information coming from the environment and be able to respond to this information to satisfy its needs for survival. In this respect man is no different from an earthworm.

Man does differ from other living things, however, in his capacity to respond to environmental conditions. We are all too aware today that man is a powerful manipulator of his environment, surpassing all other species in his ability to restructure his physical surroundings. Man also has an unusual capacity to change himself or his culture to cope with environmental conditions. This tremendous power of adaptability is undoubtedly responsible for man's success in restructuring the face of the earth and supporting his ever-increasing numbers.

This "success," however, has not been without undesirable consequences. The environmental pollution that surrounds us is the by-product of human decisions that have shaped modern society. Man can also suffer personally from environmental conditions. Certain environmental conditions, termed "stressors," to which man is exposed can create a condition within man termed "stress."

The concept of stress has received considerable attention in research and numerous theories have been formulated. Reviewing the literature, Carson and Driver (1968) note several features common to all stress theories. First, stress is thought to be a state or condition that is evoked by many particular stimuli, called stressors. These stimuli may be either perceptually obvious to a person, such as noise or a bright light, or perceptually unobtrusive, such as the presence of mercury or DDT in foods.

Second, the sympathetic nervous system appears to participate in all stressful situations. Activity in this system can result in such consequences as increases in pulse rate, blood pressure, and palmar sweating, dilation of pupils, constriction of blood vessels, and inhibition of peristaltic movement of the gastrointestinal tract. Associated with the increased activity of the sympathetic nervous system is the stimulation of the reticular activating system of the brain, which serves to arouse the individual.

In the short run, stress can be useful. Athletes, for example, capitalize upon stress built up in expectation of competition to increase performance. If a stressful state is maintained over the long run, however, it can be harmful to an individual. Selye (1956) has described a three-stage process of individual response to a stressful situation that endures. The General Adaptation Syndrome, as Selye terms it, consists of an initial reaction of alarm followed by a stage of resistance that eventually leads to a stage of exhaustion. Each specific stressor has unique effects upon an individual, but the nonspecific effects are common to all: enlargement of the adrenal cortex; shrinking of the thymus; and the development of deep bleeding ulcers.

As we have noted, stressors can be both physiological and psychological. Physiological stressors may be further subdivided into those that can be readily perceived, such as loud noises, congested traffic, and visual blight, and those that cannot be readily perceived, such as mercury, asbestos, or radiation. Many of these perceptually unobtrusive stressors are best discussed under the topic of environmental toxicology and therefore will not be covered here. In passing, however, it is important to note that certain chemical stressors can reduce an organism's overall ability to withstand stress. Ludwig and Ludwig (1969), for example, have found that herring gulls from Lake Michigan with high concentrations of persistent pesticides in their bodies have a lowered ability to withstand stress induced by adverse weather conditions. As more research is carried out upon the effects of substances such as mercury and persistent pesticides upon humans, it is likely that we may find similar results.

One specific physical environmental stressor that has been studied and is pertinent to this discussion is sound. Initially, it is useful to distinguish between noise, which is a negatively valued sound, and sound that carries no evaluation. Some sounds that may produce physiological damage such as hearing loss may not be considered noise. Loud rock music, for example, may cause hearing loss to those who stand close enough to the amplifier to be able to "feel" the music, but they may, nevertheless, "enjoy" the experience.

The process of adaptation may be described as a response decrement to a constant stimulus over time (Helson, 1964). It is possible to adapt to some sounds that are constant, such as the hum (approximating or random noise) of the air conditioner in a bedroom. (It is perhaps a sad documentation of modern society that some people cannot sleep without this humming noise, and when the air conditioner is not in use they must install devices to simulate that sound in order to sleep.) Most sounds in our lives, however, are sporadic, thus making adaptation more difficult. Studies of public response to sonic booms, for example, have shown that the percentage of the population finding booms annoying increases as time passes during which they are exposed to periodic booms (Green, 1968).

A sound may not have to cause physical damage to health or property to create stress. In fact, some relatively weak sounds in certain environments may cause stress. Wilderness travelers, for example, may become very disturbed by the overhead flight of an airplane or the passing of a snowmobile, because it disturbs the serenity that they have worked so hard to find. As this example suggests, the stressful qualities of some noises are purely cultural. However, this makes them no less adversive. Those interested in the control of noise pollution should be as aware of those sounds that are psychologically undesirable as of those that can cause physiological damage.

The social environment may also produce stress. Perhaps the condition most relevant to this discussion is population density. As our population has grown, more and more people have settled in our cities, creating congestion, crowding, and confusion. Studies of the relationship between population density and the social behavior of rats in Norway have clearly documented the development of unusual antisocial behaviors as population increases (Calhoun, 1966). Similar studies of Sika deer have shown swelling of adrenal glands to be associated with increasing population density (Christian and Davis, 1964). One might (inappropriately) conclude from these studies that cities are driving people crazy from the stress produced by crowding them into small areas. A study of mental illness in midtown Manhattan seemingly confirms this conclusion (Srole, et. al. 1962). In a study of more than 2,000 persons, roughly one-half were found to be neurotic, one-fourth psychotic, and slightly less than one-fourth healthy. Before any conclusions can be drawn from this study, however, it must be pointed out that we do not have enough data on the incidence of mental illness in the general population with which to compare these findings. It should also be noted that the particular community studied was a transitional neighborhood with a relatively high population turnover and therefore more apt to have higher stress associated with its residents.

Nevertheless, it is likely that crowding does produce some stress in humans; but its nature is poorly defined and is influenced by cultural differences (Hall, 1966). Visitors to New York and other large cities are often struck by the coldness and impersonality of social interaction in these areas. Milgram (1970) attributes a good deal of this coldness to the necessity for urban dwellers to construct filtering mechanisms to keep themselves from being overloaded by the high-stimulus situations they live in. For example, within a 10-minute walking radius in midtown Manhattan it is theoretically possible to interact with more than 200,000 people. It is not unusual, therefore, for city residents not to bother to look every approaching person in the eye, say "excuse me," or pay attention to every person that may need help. If they did so, they would never get where they wanted to go. It is still questionable whether crowded urban conditions produce mental illness, but there is little question that they decrease interpersonal interaction and in some ways alter it radically.

Whether it is desirable or not, the United States population will continue to grow over the next few decades. This growth will require the planning and construction of well over two million dwelling units per year for quite some time. The implications of this expected growth for individual and social behavior are very important, yet comparatively little is known about the behavioral consequences of environmental design. It is well known, for example, that there are higher rates of mortality and morbidity in slums (Schorr, 1963); yet it is also known that people of lower socioeconomic status (who live in these areas) generally suffer more from sickness and have shorter life spans. Further, Fried and Gleicher (1961) report that moving slum dwellers from their old neighborhoods to facilitate urban renewal produces considerable social stress, even though the persons may be moved into much better (physically speaking) dwelling units. Reviewing the literature on site planning and social behavior, Gutman (1966) concludes that there is little question that site planning affects group life and social organization, household life and family organization, and the mental health of the individual, but data are not available from which to make many generalizations about the interrelationships involved. Concluding his review, Gutman states: "It is difficult to accept the conclusion that it makes no difference how these houses are built (referring to the expected millions of new houses to be constructed), where they are located, and how they are arranged in space. Surely, there must be better and worse methods of planning a site, and hopefully the social sciences will be able to guide us in deciding what these methods are."

One area of research that can provide insight into the impact of the physical environment on our lives is the study of psychological or cognitive mapping. Hans Blumenthal (1969) has pointed out that the perceptual structure of a modern city can be expressed by the silhouette of several skyscrapers or other clusters of buildings, but because of their vast size urban areas can no longer be expressed as fully articulated sets of streets, squares, and space. Lynch (1960), for example, has found that Bostonians are familiar with landmarks such as the Boston Common and Paul Revere's house, but vast areas of the city are simply unknown to the average citizen. Milgram (1970) proposes that the "ghettoization" to which the urban poor are subjected may hamper their perception of the possibilities for functioning in the larger society of the city. This conclusion is only speculation, yet it does suggest the need for us to learn more about the impact of our surroundings upon us. Some research exists, but it is largely concerned with indoor environments such as psychiatric wards (Ittleson, Proshansky, and Rivlin, 1970) and other unusual environmental situations (Burns and others, 1963). This research leaves us with the interesting situation of knowing much more about the impact of rare and esoteric environments upon human behavior than we know about the impact of customary human environments upon our lives (Sommer, 1966).

SATISFACTION WITH RESIDENTIAL ENVIRONMENTS

The environment affects us, and we in turn respond to the environment in which we live. Satisfaction with one's community is related to a number of social and physical environmental factors. Freid and Gleicher (1961), for example, found that in some of Boston's slums residents with low socioeconomic status derive considerable satisfaction from their community, despite the serious state of physical deterioration. They note an extremely strong sense of territoriality in the working-class people studied—both in recognition of ownership of spatial areas and in identification with areas. The satisfaction and sense of territoriality observed appeared to be largely based on social relationships rather than on physical amenities.

In contrast, Lansing and others (1970) found that physical environmental factors are of greater importance in middle-class suburban communities. Of particular significance in the ten communities they studied were density (and its correlates of noise and congestion) and the aesthetic physical appearance of the neighborhood. These factors were both rated above compatibility with neighbors as a source of satisfaction with the neighborhood.

The work of Lansing, Marans, and Zehner is also of interest because they attempted to determine the impact of community planning upon residents' satisfaction with their neighborhood. They found that overall satisfaction with one's community was greatest in the two totally planned communities studied—Reston, Virginia, and Columbia, Maryland. This study documents the point that planning cannot solve all our problems, but if properly carried out it can certainly increase the satisfaction of residents with their communities. Comparing all ten communities studied, the researchers note the following characteristics of planned environments: strong zoning regulations to prevent "undesirable" land uses; provision for a variety of housing types; relatively homogenous neighborhood housing types; harmonious appearance of contiguous buildings; proximity of neighborhood outdoor recreation facilities to housing; housing units surrounded by open land; separation of pedestrian and vehicular traffic; various modes of vehicular movement; preservation of trees and enhancement of natural greenery;

creation or preservation of bodies of water; provision of landmarks and visual symbols; absence of visible utility wires; provision of community information exchanges such as newspapers; provision of local employment; and plans for the harmonious integration of expected growth into the community. Since these factors, which seem to provide satisfaction for residents of the areas studied, are partially or totally absent from many existing communities, planners should be able to integrate them into future community designs in order to increase the satisfaction of residents.

RESPONSE TO ENVIRONMENTAL PROBLEMS

People often ask, "Why don't we do something about pollution?" The answer to this question is not at all simple. The condition called "environmental pollution" exists because of a present-day evaluation of an environmental condition that is the product of a number of past decisions, each of which was based upon unique information, emotions, and motives. Many theorists have developed explanations for the complex set of economic, political, technological, ecological, and social factors that produce pollution. Rather than examine these explanations, I will discuss why we consider certain contemporary environmental conditions to be undesirable and how we respond to them.

Perceptual Recognition of a Problem

For an environmental problem to exist one must recognize the existence of an environmental state that has a dimension of quality. The word "pollution" is used to describe environmental conditions that are viewed as having an unfavorable quality. For a pollution problem to exist, therefore, there must be a common set of personal values that consider a condition unfavorable.

The word "pollution" arises from the Latin noun *pollutinem*, which means defilement. Because of the lack of scientific environmental monitoring equipment, it is likely that the earliest forms of pollution were determined by gross sensory evaluations, such as smell and taste. For example, if many people had regarded a condition like rotten garbage as undesirable, it would have been considered a pollutant and disposed of. Gradually, we have expanded our definition of pollution to include those conditions that could be scientifically proven to cause damage to human health or property. To insure that we are protected from undesirable conditions, we have formalized our protections in laws. Thus, today some aspects of "pollution" are legal problems that have been formally defined by our attitudes and values regarding the desirability of certain environmental conditions.

One of the current problems of pollution control is that existing laws may not adequately reflect popular definitions of pollution. An excellent example is illustrated by a recent study of attitudes toward the quality of water in San Francisco Bay (Willeke, 1968). Citizens living along the bay were surveyed and asked if they considered the bay polluted. A majority said they did. Local public health officials also were asked to evaluate the quality of water in the bay. Their response was that the water was fine. The disparity in the responses of the two groups can be attributed to their differing definitions of pollution. Public health officials based their evaluation of quality upon scientific criteria, such as coliform bacteria counts, while citizens based their evaluations on readily perceivable conditions like the presence of garbage or dead fish. If the citizens' definitions, although not based upon scientific fact, affect behavior just as significantly as such scientific criteria as bacteria counts, then they should also be included in the definition of pollution used by the local regulatory agency.

As this example suggests, our attitudes and values shape our concept of pollution. It is logical, therefore, that as our attitudes and values change, so will our definitions of pollution. For example, several decades ago communities liked to advertise their economic prosperity and job opportunities with pictures of smoking industries. Today, in an age when comparatively fewer people are deprived of economic subsistence, the unappealing aspects of smoke are receiving more attention. It is likely that in the years ahead our concept of what constitutes environmental quality will change. It will be advantageous for regulatory agencies, therefore, to feel the pulse of these changes, lest they should fail to represent the public interest by employing an outdated definition of environmental quality.

To be aware of pollution, a person must be able to consciously perceive a condition. Many forms of environmental pollution, such as oil spills, black smoke, and loud noises, are readily perceptible to almost anyone in the immediate area and are likely to arouse public ire as social valuation of aesthetic aspects of the environment increases, a point documented elsewhere in this volume by McEvoy. In turn, it is likely that our regulatory efforts may become overly concerned with control of these forms of "cosmetic" pollution at the expense of controlling those substances that are less perceptually obtrusive but may be much more physiologically harmful. Mercury is a good example of the latter, as is DDT.

The average person can become aware of DDT or mercury as a pollutant but usually not through personal experience. Rather, he will have to listen to others more knowledgeable about the problem. Aside from some public mistrust of scientists in general, a serious issue that has already arisen is who will the public

trust, since "scientific" information can be presented to prove almost any point (Michael, 1969). In many environmental areas, such as nuclear power, toxicology, and eutrophication, the issues are very complex and beyond the comprehension of the average citizen. One of the most crucial needs in the years ahead will be to provide the public with a scientific basis for evaluating new environmental information.

The potential impact of mass media in forming public perceptions of environmental problems is almost unknown but could be very important. Auliciems and Burton (1970), for example, report that extensive media coverage of environmental problems in the Toronto, Ontario, area was largely responsible for generating considerable public concern for air pollution in Toronto, when in fact air in Toronto is comparatively clean. As these researchers point out, concern for environmental problems is desirable, but if concern is derived from secondary sources it is likely to quickly diminish when the coverage ceases. As we eliminate the most immediately obvious sources of pollution, the media must continue to keep the public aware of the more subtle, but often more dangerous, forms of pollution. McEvoy's discussion of the growth of environmental awareness and concern (in this volume) also stresses the role of the media in mobilization of opinion.

As I suggest later, there are social and political reasons for varying responses to pollution, but there also are psychological ones. Rene Dubos (1965, 1968) has eloquently spoken of man's ability to adapt psychologically to conditions that may cause physiological harm. My own research supports this observation (Swan, 1970). High school students in Detroit, Michigan, were shown a series of projected color slides of urban scenes and asked to identify problems seen in the slides. Not only did the students vary considerably in their awareness of visible smog in the slides, but in general those students who were from lower socioeconomic levels were significantly less aware of visible smog. One important factor producing this difference may be that students of low socioeconomic status are less able to travel away from Detroit, which receives from 8 to 16 percent less sunlight than surroundings areas (International Joint Commission, 1960). Consequently, they have come to accept blue-gray as a normal sky color. As Dubos has observed, many environmental problems do not manifest themselves dramatically and it is easy, therefore, for subsequent generations to accept environmental conditions that are of lower quality than those observed by their parents. For this reason alone, we will require the preservation of relatively large areas of wild land untouched by man's hand so that we will have a baseline from which to judge the quality of future environments.

One important factor related to the perception of many environmental problems, such as floods and coastal storms, is the perceived frequency of occurrence (Burton and others, 1970). There are approximately 2,000 cities built on flood plains in the United States and there are about 125,000 structures on the outer eastern coastal shore between Maine and North Carolina less than 10 feet above sea level. The damage to these structures exceeds one billion dollars annually. While there are many factors affecting location in such high-risk areas, these researchers found that the perceived frequency of occurrence of future events is an important determinant of locating behavior. If the probability of a flood occurring in an area is once every hundred years, for example, people are less likely to be concerned about flooding than people who are endangered by floods with a probability of occurrence every five years. Eventually of course, all the "players" in this game of flood plain location will lose their bets and society will be faced with

massive relocation and reconstruction costs resulting from decisions of this kind. The flooding in Pakistan in 1970, which took thousands of lives, is an excellent, though extreme, example of the social consequences of such decisions.

Behavioral Response to a Problem
Situation Once Perceived

Having recognized that a problem exists, a person's behavioral response will be one of three types: situation-alteration, situation-redefinition, or withdrawal. The particular behavioral response chosen is determined by the interplay of at least three major factors: one's concern for the problem; the relative priority of the concern; and one's personal perception of the role he can play in resolving the problem.

The concept of "concern" is important to clarify as there is little consistency in the many ways it is used in relation to the appraisal of problems. According to Lane and Sears (1964), "concern implies some gain in a preferred outcome; it is future-oriented, while an interest may apply to measures of the moment." If we accept this definition of concern, then we must conclude that we know very little about the degree of concern that the public holds for environmental quality. It is true that a May 1970 national Gallup poll (Gallup, 1970) found that citizens considered fighting environmental pollution second only to fighting crime as the major priority of the next decade. This finding, however, is difficult to interpret because the social desirability of being against pollution is very high, and the poll was taken immediately after Earth Day. Before any major conclusions can be reached about public concern for pollution, more research is needed that more clearly defines the degree of one's preference for a certain outcome. One of the few pieces of research we have in this area today is a national poll commissioned by the National Wildlife Federation, which found, among other things, that three-fourths of the population would pay more taxes if they were specifically earmarked for pollution control. This and other findings from the study are discussed in detail by McEvoy in this volume.

The creation of "concern" for a problem is related to many factors, but one of the most important is the perception of the impact of the problem on a person's life. In a study of public response to air pollution in three heavily polluted Detroit suburbs, those citizens who were aware of the relationship between air pollution and its effects on personal health were more likely to complain about air pollution than those who were not aware of it (Swan, 1971). The fact that there was no significant difference in the frequency of reported health problems related to air pollution between those who complained and those who did not confirms the importance of this perceptual dimension in activating concern.

Studies by the author have consistently shown that for the general population there appears to be little relationship between awareness or knowledge of a problem like air pollution and concern for the problem (Swan, 1970, 1971). These findings may be explained by the fact that neither technical knowledge of a problem nor perceptual recognition of its existence may have any relationship to an individual's perception of the impact of that specific problem upon his life. It is likely that once a person becomes concerned about a problem, perceptual awareness and technical knowledge may be reinforced by his concern, but it appears these factors have little role in initiating concern.

These findings have important implications for traditional public education programs, for most are based upon providing technical information and very few actually describe the personal results of

a problem. In fact, if people are presented technical information and its importance to their immediate lives is not readily apparent, they may pay very little attention to it or even ignore the message. For example, in Detroit an air pollution index called the MURC Index is only presented as a numerical figure accompanied by an interpretation of that number as being either light, moderate, or heavy pollution. What "light," "moderate," and "heavy" pollution mean in terms of personal damage is never discussed, so it is little wonder that local residents are not very familiar with the MURC Index (Swan, 1971). It should be noted that the reluctance of the media to relate problems like air pollution to personal health has been documented in other parts of the country (Brightman and others, 1962). It is likely, therefore, that this is why Crowe (1968) has found that people seldom define air pollution in health-related terms, but rather in perceptual terms like "smoke" or "smog." One of the most important contributions the media and educational efforts in general can make toward solving environmental problems will be to inform the public of the impact of environmental problems on their personal lives.

An important aspect of public information programs is that they can increase public acceptance of resource management programs simply by removing the apparent secrecy that sometimes surrounds a program. The secrecy may simply be due to a lack of communication, but if people think that they are not being adequately informed, they may distrust the best-conceived program. Hass (1970), for example, has documented increasing public acceptance of weather modification projects based upon public information efforts to explain the project clearly.

A person may be very concerned about a problem and yet not act to resolve it because of the relative priority of the issue. Most people do not have the time to become active in fighting many different problems. They therefore must choose those that are most meaningful to them. The criteria for establishing priorities vary among individuals and do not necessarily have to be based upon logic. According to Maslow's (1943) hierarchy of human needs, there are progressive changes in the relative importance of needs as other needs are satisfied. He has proposed that wants are ordered in the following sequence: (1) physiological needs; (2) safety needs; (3) belongingness needs and love needs; (4) esteem needs; and (5) self-actualization. To move to a higher need, a lower need must first be fulfilled.

Maslow's hierarchy of needs is useful in explaining the ordering of priorities of concern for the environment. In general, the worst pollution problems occur in those areas where people are poorest and are, therefore, living at the lower end of Maslow's hierarchy. Poor people may be concerned about smog and polluted water, but they must satisfy basic needs for food, shelter, and clothing before pollution can become an issue. This fact is significant in that too often our pollution-control regulatory agencies base their actions upon the level of public concern expressed for a problem. If this criterion is used to justify antipollution efforts, the prospects for cleaning up our cities are not bright. McEvoy's analysis (in this volume) of the positive relationship between higher socioeconomic status and concern for the environment tends to confirm this ordering.

Assigning a high priority of concern to the environment will still not be enough to motivate action unless a person perceives that he has a role to play in resolving the problem (White, 1966). Developing a perception of a personal role is a function of several factors. An important one is finding an appropriate course of action. If people do not know what they can do about a problem they are likely to repress their concern, rather than face the con-

tinued anxiety associated with not knowing what to do.

Perception of a role is also related to socioeconomic status. In general, the higher one's socioeconomic status, the more likely he is to have a positive sense of personal efficacy (Milbrath, 1965). As one might suspect, therefore, based upon relative priorities and personal perception of a role, environmental issues are more likely to be acted upon by people of higher socioeconomic status. The results of survey research support this conclusion. In a study of public sentiments about water problems, it was found that young, better educated, wealthier persons were the most concerned about water problems. This tendency for concern to predominate among people of higher socioeconomic status has also been observed in most air pollution surveys (Swan, 1970) and in surveys of the membership of the Sierra Club (Devall, 1970), as well as in McEvoy's analysis of public opinion reported elsewhere in this volume.

Two prevalent attitudes may be utilized to justify nonaggressive responses to pollution. One of them is what Stewart Udall has termed the "Myth of Scientific Supremacy" (Udall, 1965). In this country we have been immensely successful in resolving problems through technological advances and this success has led many to believe that we will continue to resolve problems in this manner. As already suggested in this discussion, environmental problems ultimately arise from human behavior and it will only be through changes in values and behavior that we ultimately resolve them.

The other somewhat related attitude is what Thibaut and Kelley call "fate control" (1959). Fate control means that what one does has little effect on the outcome of large issues, but may have significant effects upon one's own situation. In contemporary society many individuals have the economic and technological resources to dramatically affect their personal lives, but when confronted with larger issues that are discussed daily in the mass media, such as pollution or war, the individual can do very little. In such situations it is not unusual that some people resign the fate of society to someone else and focus their concerns upon more personal matters.

RECREATION

Increased leisure time, population growth, affluence, and mobility have all contributed to the current recreation "boom" in this country. Demographic factors alone, however, cannot account for the tremendous increased popularity of outdoor recreation. Human attitudes, values, and motivations must also be considered as important determinants of recreational demands.

Centuries ago, when this country was founded, its social values were somewhat different than they are today. The "Protestant ethic" was quite strong and it placed a high priority on the importance of hard work. Recreation was seen as something that should only occur after all work was completed. It is little wonder, therefore, that few recreation areas were built or even planned at that time.

Only recently has recreation gained widespread social acceptance. One indication of the increasingly important role of recreation in modern society is that the National Advisory Commission on Civil Disorders has recently reported that inadequate recreational facilities and services was the fourth most frequently mentioned grievance in a list of possible causal factors leading to the civil disorders during 1967.

Increased interest in recreation is also partially attributable to the fast pace of modern urban American society. Increased population densities, noise levels, congestion, and social problems place a considerable amount of tension upon the average American. There is no question that a major motivation of many recreationists is escape. Recreational opportunities provide choices for disengagement, locomotion, variety, change, diversion, isolation, and withdrawal—all related concepts that frequently appear in stress literature within the context of temporary escape. The stress mediating value of outdoor recreation is further documented by responses of users to the survey question "Why are you visiting this area?" in several recent national recreation surveys (Driver, 1970). Depending upon how the question is worded and how the answers are recorded, 50 to 70 percent of the users respond with "peace and tranquility," "get away from the city," and a "change from the routine." McEvoy's review of the supporters of the conservation movement (in this volume) also shows a strong antiurban influence on the recreational behavior of conservationists-preservationists.

Another interesting aspect of current taste in recreation is the increasing interest in forms of recreation that include taking risks Michael (1963) has suggested that recreational activities such as skydiving, snow skiing, snowmobiling, water-skiing, and mountain climbing are popular because the average daily routine of the urban American has little challenge. As machines take over more jobs of manual labor, interest in active high-risk sports is likely to increase. Also, these sports provide stressful situations in which the stress is built up and released in a more or less natural manner, rather than becoming chronic and repressed as in modern urban living.

While outdoor recreation is more popular than ever before and is a useful function in modern society, there is no research to substantiate the claim that outdoor recreation is essential for every man. The importance of change to alleviate stress is well documented, but there is nothing magic about the out-of-doors as a place for reducing stress. For some people, for example, indoor activities such as dancing, bowling, drinking, or reading may have as much stress-reducing value. Many people choose to use drugs and alcohol to change their perceptions of life. This argument should not, however, be construed as justification for lessening the importance of outdoor recreation in contemporary society. On the contrary, attitudes and values are a major determinant of human decision-making, and if a major segment of the public derives satisfaction from certain types of outdoor recreational experiences, then this alone should justify economic and space allocations for outdoor recreation.

There is no question that water strongly affects a person's choice of recreational site (O.R.R.R.C. Study Report 10, 1962). Water is used for recreational purposes in physical interactions, such as swimming or boating, and for visually enhancing the aesthetic aspects of the recreational experience. While water may provide both of these sources of satisfaction, conflicts may arise from trying to satisfy both demands simultaneously. High-density use of water for physical-contact recreation such as boating or swimming, for example, may conflict with the aesthetic use of the water by others. This conflict has necessitated in some cases the restriction of certain water sports (the use of power boats, for example), to specific zones of lakes or times of the day.

It should be noted that the aesthetic use of water has much lower requirements for quality, for some parameters of quality at least. If water is free from visible pollutants, such as garbage or oil slicks, and yet is not safe for water-contact sports, people may still highly value visual access to water. Residential riverfront property values along Michigan's Lower Detroit River, for example, are much higher than any surrounding property, despite the fact that the river is considered unsafe for water-contact sports (Swan, 1967).

The diversity of motivations for someone seeking out a particular environment for recreation is illustrated by Bultena and Taves (1961) in a study of the motivations for wilderness visitation. They asked campers

and canoeists to define their images of the wilderness they were visiting, according to the satisfactions they derived from it. The respondents reported five classes of images: wilderness as a locale for sport and play; wilderness as a place of fascination; wilderness as a sanctury; wilderness as a heritage; and wilderness as a source of personal gratification. Using such interview techniques to form his conclusions, Lucas (1966) proposes the possibility of developing recreational-area-land-management plans by trying to group compatible uses in specific sections of a recreactional area. Such a practice is, of course, easiest in a large recreational area, where land is abundant. The separation of conflicting activities is much more difficult in a small area with high visitation. With increased leisure time, mobility, and interest in wilderness recreation, however, even the modern wilderness is not free from conflicts and, in fact, conditions that may not be considered to be conflicting in smaller high-use areas may be very undesirable in wilderness places. Wilderness visitors dislike most other people and the signs of their presence, yet with the prediction of a tenfold increase in wilderness visitation in the years to come, the presence and impact of humans upon wilderness areas will become more common unless access is limited and controlled (O.R.R.R.C. Study Report 3, 1962).

One of the biggest problems in recreation planning today is that we understand very little about motivations for outdoor recreation. Studies of the characteristics of water-recreation visitors for example, show very different populations seeking out different areas (Myles, 1967). Without a firm understanding of why such patterns occur and what satisfactions people derive from recreational experiences, areas will be designed according to the values of the recreational planner, which may be quite different from those of the area's visitors. Myles (1967), for example, reports that visitors to several recreational areas in Nevada disliked concessions and did not care if parking lots were paved or not. Instead, they thought that the money for concessions and paved parking should be spent on planting more trees and enlarging parking areas. In a similar vein, interviews with wilderness hikers (conducted by Shafer and Mietz, 1969) suggest that hiking trails should be designed to provide maximum scenic enjoyment, rather than a supreme test of one's physical capabilities. If such questionnaires are administered to users before recreational areas are planned, it might be possible to satisfy the public's needs more closely.

We must also recognize that the desires for recreation in general, and certainly specific types of recreational activities, are not constant. Witt and Bishop (1970) give five theories of leisure-seeking behavior—an outlet for surplus energy, a need for relaxation, an opportunity to release emotions, a means of personal compensation for work, and a learned social behavior—and note that several of these theories may be useful to explain why a person selects a certain time and place for recreation, and that the importance of each reason may change with time and place.

Because of the present tremendous demand for outdoor recreation and its relationship to human attitudes and values, we must attempt to discover a great deal more about why people presently find outdoor recreation so important and the actual purposes it serves. Some relevant questions are: (1) Are most campgrounds crowded because many people like to camp, or because camping is a cheap and mobile way to travel? (2) Do people really like the "wilderness type" experience we try to simulate in many national recreational areas, or would people prefer other plans if they were available? and (3) Does outdoor recreation provide an experience for most people that could not be duplicated indoors? In short, a great deal of outdoor recreation planning today is based upon the assumption that we know what people want, when in fact we do not.

SOME CONCLUDING QUESTIONS

This analysis of our knowledge of the relationship between human behavior and environmental conditions has stressed the importance of environmental psychology to successful planning, as well as pointing out the lack of knowledge in this area. In conclusion, it is useful to note briefly four additional areas of environmental psychology that are extremely important and yet poorly understood.

Our sudden appreciation of the importance of ecology raises a question about the ability of the average human to comprehend his total surroundings in terms of complex systems. In a systems approach there are no absolute answers, only degrees of importance associated with elements of the system. Such cognitive processes as tolerance for ambiguity and simultaneous consideration of multiple objects will greatly affect ecological thinking. At present we know very little about these factors, much less how to teach them.

A second important aspect of human behavior is our capacity to consider the future consequences of present actions. Toffler's recent work, *Future Shock* (1970), examines some of the difficulties of future thinking, and Don Michael's *The Unprepared Society* (1969) discusses a wide variety of likely dilemmas to be faced if we do not begin to give the future more serious consideration. Here also the implications for educational programs are very important.

Another aspect of human behavior that will have very important implications for the future is our ability as individuals to recognize the collective importance of individual actions. Recent research has shown that while many Americans acknowledge the problem of overpopulation, very few can relate it to the determination of family size (Barnett, 1970). Population size is one contributing factor to our problems of air, water, and land pollution. As population increases, the likelihood of serious pollution problems occurring will likewise increase, simply because of the collective· actions of increasingly larger numbers of people. Here again there are important implications for environmental education programs.

Finally, we are learning more about how to measure environmental attitudes (although research is still in the beginning stages), but we know very little about how environmental attitudes are formed and changed. There is no question that mass media, schools, contemporary life styles, and many other factors affect our attitudes toward the environment, but how they affect them is virtually unknown. In view of the present state of the environment, it should be clear that we cannot afford to continue not knowing. It is likely that education can play a major role in coping with environmental problems in the long run, but the chances of realizing its potential are not great unless we can learn a great deal more about environmental psychology and translate this knowledge into educational programs.

References

The Impact of the Environment on Behavior and Environmental Perception

Blumenthal, Hans. 1969. *The Quality of Urban Life*. Sage Press.

Burns, N. H., R. M. Chambers, and R. Hendler. 1963. *Unusual Environments and Human Behavior*, Free Press of Glencoe.

Calhoun, John. 1966. The role of space in animal sociology. *Journal of Social Issues*, 22(4): 46-58.

Carson, Dan and Beverly Driver. 1968. An environmental approach to human stress and well-being: with implications for planning. University of Michigan Mental Health Research Institute, Reprint #194.

Christian, John J. and David E. Davis. 1964. Social and endocrine factors are integrated in the regulation of growth of mammalian populations. *Science*, 146:1550-60.

Freid, Marc and Peggy Gleicher. 1961. Some sources of residential satisfaction in an urban slum. *Journal of the American Institute of Planners*, 27(4):305-15.

Green, David. 1968. Sonic booms. *Psychology Today*, 2(6).

Gutman, Robert. 1966. Site planning and social behavior. *Journal of Social Issues*, 22(4): 103-15.

Hall, Edward. 1966. *The Hidden Dimension*, Doubleday & Co.

Helson, Harry. 1964. *Adaptation Level Theory: An Experimental and Systematic Approach to Behavior*, Harper & Row, Inc.

Ittleson, W. H., H. Proshansky, and L. Rivlin. 1970. Bedroom size and social interaction in a psychiatric ward. *Environment and Behavior*, 2(3):1255-70.

Lansing, John B., Robert W. Marans, and Robert B. Zehner. 1970. *Planned Residential Environments*. Institute for Social Research Survey Research Center, University of Michigan.

Ludwig. J. P. and C. F. Ludwig. 1969. The effects of starvation on insecticide contaminated herring gulls removed from a Lake Erie colony. Proceedings of the 12th Conference on Great Lakes Research, pp. 53-60.

Lynch, Kevin. 1960. *The Image of the City*, M. I. T. Press.

Milgram, Stanley. 1970. The experience of living in cities. *Science, 167*:1461-68

Schorr, Alvin L. 1963. *Slums and Social Insecurity*. U.S. Department of Health, Education and Welfare, Social Security Administration, Division of Statistics, Research Report No. 1, Washington, D.C.

Selye, Hans. 1956. *The Stress of Life*, McGraw-Hill.

Sommer, Robert. 1966. Man's proximate environment. *Journal of Social Issues*, 22(4):59-70.

Srole, Leo, et. al. 1962. *Mental Health in the Metropolis*, McGraw-Hill.

Winkel, Gary. 1970. The nervous affair between behavior scientists and designers. *Psychology Today*, 3(10).

Response to Environmental Problems

Auliciems, A. and Ian Burton. 1970. Perception and awareness of air pollution. Natural Hazard Research Working Paper No. 13, University of Toronto.

Brightman, Jay, Alexander Rihm, and Sheldon Samuels. 1962. Air pollution and health. *Journal of the Air Pollution Control Association*, 12:225-31.

Burton, Ian, Robert Kates, and Gilbert White. 1970. The human ecology of extreme geophysical events. Natural Hazard Research Working Paper No. 1, University of Toronto.

Crowe, Jay. 1968. Toward a 'definitional model' of public preceptions of air pollution. *Journal of the Air Pollution Control Association*, 17:29-37.

Devall, W. G. 1970. Conservation: an upper-middle class social movement. *Journal of Leisure Research*, 2:123-126.

Dubos, Rene. 1965. *Man Adapting*, Yale University Press.

Dubos, Rene. 1968. *So Human an Animal*, Charles Scribners Sons.

The Gallup Reporter. 1970.

Hass, Eugene. 1970. Response to weather modification: implications for urban resource management. *Urban Demands on Natural Resources*. Western Resources Conference Proceedings, University of Denver, pp. 251-57.

International Joint Commission. 1960. *Pollution of the Atmosphere in the Detroit River Area*. Washington-Ottawa.

Lane, Robert and D. O. Sears. 1964. *Public Opinion*, Prentice-Hall.

Maslow, Abraham. 1943. A theory of human motivation. *Psychological Review*, 50:370-96.

Michael, Donald. 1969. *The Unprepared Society*, Basic Books Inc.

Milbrath, Lester. 1965. *Political Participation*, Rand-McNally.

National Wildlife Federation. 1969. A study of the attitudes of the American public toward improvement of the natural environment.

Smith, W. S., J. J. Schueneman, L. D. Zeidberg. Public reaction to air pollution in Nashville, Tennessee. *Journal of the Air Pollution Control Association*, 14(10).

Swan, James. 1970. Results of the Downriver Environmental Inventory. University of Michigan School of Natural Resources.

Swan, James. 1971 (In Press). Public response to air pollution. *Psychology and the Environment*, edit. by D. Carson and J. Wohlwill. American Psychological Association.

Thibaut, J. W. and H. H. Kelley. 1959. *The Social Psychology of Groups*, John Wiley.

Udall, Stewart. 1965. *The Quiet Crisis*, Holt, Rinehart and Winston.

White, Gilbert. 1966. The role and formation of public attitudes. *Environmental Quality in a Growing Economy*, edit. H. Jarrett, Johns Hopkins Press. pp. 105-27.

Willeke, Gene. 1968. Effects of water pollution in San Francisco Bay. Report EEP-29, Project on Economic-Engineering Planning, Stanford University.

Winkel, Gary. 1970. The nervous affair between behavior scientists and designers. *Psychology Today*, 3(10).

Recreation

Bultena, Gordon L. and Marvin J. Taves. 1961. Changing wilderness images and forestry policy. *Journal of Forestry*, 59:167-70.

Driver, B. L. 1970. Potential contributions of psychology to recreation resource management. University of Michigan School of Natural Resources, unpublished paper.

Lucas, Robert C. 1966. The contribution of environmental research to wilderness policy decisions. *Journal of Social Issues*, 22(4):166-26.

Michael, Donald. 1963. *The Next Generation*, Alfred Knopf, Inc.

Myles, George A. 1967. Effect of quality factors on water based recreation in western Nevada. University of Nevada, Reno Agricultural Experiment Station.

National Advisory Commission on Civil Disorders Report 1968. E. P. Dutton & Co.

Outdoor Recreation Resources Review Commission. 1962. Water for recreation—values and opportunities. *Study Report 10,* U.S. Government Supt. of Documents, Washington, D.C.

Outdoor Recreation Resources Review Commission. 1962. Wilderness and recreation—a report on resources, values, and problems. *Study Report 3,* U.S. Government Supt. of Documents, Washington, D.C.

Witt, Peter A., and Doyle W. Bishop. 1970. Situational antecedents to leisure behavior. *Journal of Leisure Research,* 2(1):64-77.

Conclusion

Barnett, Larry D. 1970. U.S. population growth as an abstractly perceived problem. *Demography,* 7(1).

Michael, Donald. 1969. *The Unprepared Society,* Basic Books.

Toffler, A. 1970. *Future Shock,* Random House.

CHAPTER 6

The complexity of ecosystems and the value-laden attitudes of the public toward environmental quality make definitive interpretations difficult. This paper describes the dynamics of ecosystems in general and the ways in which they can be disrupted by human influence. We have included a lengthy discussion of the problems encountered in measuring human and ecosystem values, and describe some measurement techniques currently available. We have reached the conclusion that the major difficulty in evaluating environmental quality is not in measuring particular aspects of natural or human systems, but in integrating such measurement into a comprehensive scheme. No simple, rigorous, scientific devices exist that can compensate for wise judgment on the part of decision-makers, and public involvement in water resources development.

However, several types of formal planning methods have been developed which are useful for incorporating diverse measurement data, economic parameters, and human value judgments into planning and decision-making. Such useful techniques include impact analysis, map-overlay planning, and resource inventory-land use zoning methods. Each of these methods can incorporate diverse kinds of data from a variety of relevant disciplines. Scenic quality indices should be available in the near future; rapid progress is being made in other difficult areas of measurement, notably aesthetics.

THE MEASUREMENT OF ENVIRONMENTAL QUALITY AND ITS INCORPORATION INTO THE PLANNING PROCESS

Peter Richerson and James McEvoy III

INTRODUCTION

The management of environmental quality is one of that class of paradoxical human problems for which solutions seem simultaneously both essential and impossible. While admitting no final answers, this problem must be faced in planning and developing water resources. This paper describes the process of incorporating environmental and environmental quality measurements into systems of planning and management.

There are three basic problems in measuring the environment. First, the environment itself is a complex set of phenomena. For the most part, technical means to measure chemical, physical, and biological parameters are adequately developed, but our ability to predict the response of whole ecosystems, including their human elements, to manipulation is poor. Our ability to describe is not matched by an ability to predict. The second problem is an outgrowth of the complexity of human perceptions and attitudes toward environmental quality. Useful measures of aesthetic and other value-related qualities of the environment are very difficult to develop. Finally, there remains the problem of incorporating conceptions and measurements of environmental quality into formal planning methods which are useful within the political framework of water development.

Beginning with a discussion of how aquatic ecosystems work, we will attempt to show how the measurable phenomena of natural and modified ecosystems relate to human conceptions of environmental quality. Finally, we will identify the conceptual and practical difficulties involved in measuring environmental quality and suggest ways of dealing with them.

AQUATIC ECOLOGY

Aquatic ecosystems, whether they be lakes, reservoirs, streams, estuaries, or oceans are composed of broadly similar components. Most derive their basic energy from the activities of plants, the primary producers which convert solar energy into chemical food energy through photosynthesis. These may be free-floating plankton (insignificant in streams), forms attached to rocks or other fixed substrates (periphyton), or rooted waterweeds. Significant amounts of chemical energy may also be obtained from outside the aquatic ecosystem itself. Debris from land is one source and sewage, food processing, and other industrial wastes contribute large quantities of chemical energy to aquatic systems.

The energy from plants or other basic organic energy sources is used by a hierarchy of grazers and predators which typically pass about 10 percent of the food energy they consume on to the next level. The other 90 percent of the energy consumed by a population of organisms is either metabolized or passed on to decomposer organisms, mainly bacteria and fungi. The decomposers form an important part of biotic communities not only because they use the portion of its energy otherwise lost to the community by death, but also because they recycle inorganic nutrient salts contained in the bodies of dead organisms and allow them to be reincorporated into the primary producers (green plants). While this recycling is not perfect it is often remarkably efficient. Thus, chemical energy fixed from sunlight by the primary producers passes through ecosystems and is dissipated while the nutrient materials mobilized by bacteria are returned to the base of the food chain. The simple model of an aquatic ecosystem in Figure 1 can be used to illustrate the major ways in which alterations in the system can be occasioned by water development.

MODIFICATION OF ECOSYSTEMS

The most dramatic alteration of an ecosystem is through its total replacement. For example, a reservoir replaces a stream and its associated terrestrial systems with a drastically different, lake-like system. New systems resembling streams may be created in the canals of the reservoir's distribution system. Not all of the changes associated with massive manipulation of water are so thorough; for example, the character of the ecosystems in the stream below a reservoir will change, but the stream will still exist.

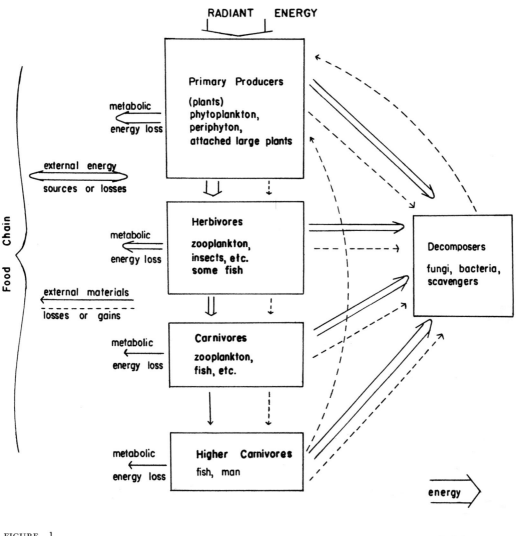

FIGURE 1
A model of an aquatic ecosystem.

No law-like generalizations can be applied to such ecological modifications, since at least a portion of each ecosystem will react uniquely to any given situation. Usually, however, changes will be most detrimental if they are drastic (that is, from terrestrial to aquatic) and if subsequent conditions are variable. If extreme changes in water or temperature regime are imposed upon an ecosystem, the types of organisms which can exist are altered, recycling is less likely to be complete and the utility of the system to man is likely to be impaired (Margalef, 1968). Rapidly fluctuating temperatures, for example, are likely to prevent the establishment of game fish since few of them can tolerate large, unpredictable variations in this parameter of their environment.

Manipulation of water itself is not the

114

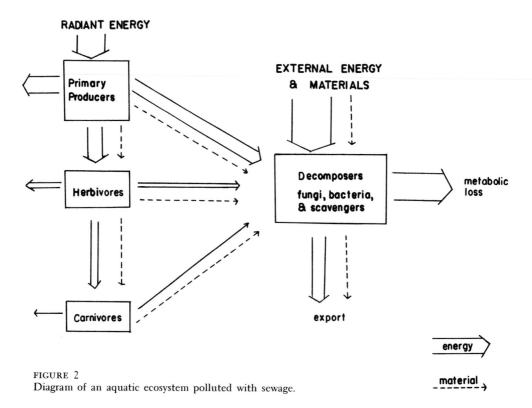

FIGURE 2
Diagram of an aquatic ecosystem polluted with sewage.

only way in which aquatic systems can be physically changed. Excessive siltation, alteration of streambeds, and dredging of estuaries are examples of manipulations which can have negative effects upon aquatic ecosystems.

Another common means of disruption of aquatic ecosystems is through the input of large amounts of external chemical energy in the form of domestic sewage or other organic materials. These inputs permit vast increases in the amount (biomass) of bacterial and fungal decomposer organisms which then may consume all available oxygen in metabolizing the newly introduced organic matter, making life impossible for most primary producers, herbivores and carnivores. Again, the consequences of such external energy inputs can range from subtle to drastic, depending upon degree. Figure 2 is a

diagrammatic representation of a polluted ecosystem, showing in contrast to Figure 1 a larger decomposer component subsisting on the larger input of chemical energy.

In contrast to sewage pollution the related problem of eutrophication is caused not by the input of energy, but by the input of nutrient materials which stimulate the growth of algae. These materials may already be mineralized by sewage treatment processes, or they may be released from their organic source by decomposers in the aquatic system itself. If conditions are suitable for the growth of primary producers, such nutrients may be rapidly converted back to organic matter. At low levels of input, this stimulation of growth may not be especially harmful and its effects may be seen higher in the food chain as increases in the productivity of fish. The ecosystem, however, may change in undesirable ways. Beeton (this volume) describes the change from an abundance of lake trout to less desirable species in the Great Lakes as a result of eutrophication. Since untreated sewage contains both large amounts of chemical energy and nutrients, both problems may occur sequentially in a lake or stream.

In extreme cases, expansion of the upper levels of the food chain cannot keep pace with the increase in primary producers. The plant biomass then has effects much like direct sewage pollution: dead algae are utilized directly by decomposers in large quantities and dissolved oxygen declines to very low levels. Moreover, highly eutrophic ecosystems, especially lakes, are often dominated by blue-green algae which tend to float and develop unsightly mats and scums. The "death" of Lake Erie might better be described as excessive life, brought about by eutrophication. Ordinary primary and secondary sewage treatment is ineffective in coping with this problem, since most of the nutrient materials present in sewage are mineralized but not removed and thus are passed directly into the aquatic ecosystem. The two principal nutrients present in mineralized form in treated sewage, nitrogen and phosphorus, can be removed from waste streams by tertiary treatment (Rohlich and Uttormark, 1972). The costs are substantial, but not necessarily prohibitive.

Active discussion is now occurring in the literature regarding the importance of inorganic carbon as a eutrophicating influence. See Likens (1972) for an extensive treatment of this controversy. There is evidence that in very eutrophic situations low levels of carbon (the material needed in greatest quantity by any organism) may actually limit productivity. Under most circumstances, however, it is clear that nitrogen and especially phosphorus are limiting, that is, that their concentrations deter-

mine the rate of productivity (Mackenthun, 1965; Vallentyne, 1970; Kuentzel, 1969; Lange, 1967). Occasionally, micronutrients such as molybdenum (Goldman, 1960) are important eutrophicating elements.

The direct poisoning of ecosystems may result from mining, industrial, or agricultural wastes. Acid mine drainage, for example, can reduce the biota of a stream to a few bacteria (Lackey, 1938, 1939). Wastes from pesticide manufacture have been known to produce large fish kills (United States Federal Water Quality Administration, 1970). Of course, due to the interlocking relationships among the components of an ecosystem, the destruction of even one population will have effects on all others. Even when toxic substances are present in low concentrations organisms may, due to peculiarities in their metabolism, concentrate certain poisons and pass them on up to the highest levels of the food chain. These materials are especially dangerous since lag time between their introduction into the food chain and the appearance of effects may be long, and the route of the poison difficult to detect. Classic cases include bioconcentration of mercury (Malling and others, 1970), radionuclides (Davis and Foster, 1958) and DDT (Hunt and Bischoff, 1960; Woodwell and others, 1967). The birds now threatened with serious population attrition or even extinction due to the effects of DDT in their environment are mostly carnivorous marine birds such as pelicans and ospreys, or those which feed on other birds already high in food chains, such as the peregrine falcon. In part, their great distance from the source of the pesticides delayed recognition of the pernicious effects of the DDT and similar agents.

An important comparative measure of all ecosystems is their *diversity*, on the numbers of different kinds of organisms present adjusted for balanced population numbers. This measurement has attracted attention recently as an important indicator of change in an ecosystem (Margalef, 1968; Odum, 1969; Hutchinson, 1967; the Brookhaven Symposium, 1969, also offers reviews of this work). Natural ecosystems can be arranged on a scale of increasing diversity related to the fundamental environmental factors to which they are exposed. Aquatic systems with the lowest diversity include such rigorous habitats as saline lakes, hot springs, and permanently frozen antarctic lakes, all of which have just a few kinds of primary producers and decomposers and perhaps an herbivore or two (Goldman and others, 1967). An example of an aquatic ecosystem with high diversity is a tropical coral reef. Such a highly diverse system occurs when environmental factors rarely approach critical values for the existence of life itself and when major, irregular fluctuations in the environment are rare. It seems, therefore, that one of the most fundamental properties of ecosystems is that they increase their diversity up to some limit imposed by the nature of the habitat in which they exist.

A common illustration of this property is the behavior of organisms in colonizing an empty habitat such as a newly plowed field or a new lake—a process ecologists term "succession." MacArthur and Wilson (1967) have developed an extensive theoretical framework for understanding these processes, based upon the consideration of oceanic islands.

A newly formed reservoir at first is limited to a few kinds of algae and herbivores which establish themselves during the first flooding. Succeeding years will bring the establishment of other kinds of algae and herbivores, fish populations, bottom organisms, and perhaps attached aquatic plants of various kinds near shore. Some of the newly established organisms will displace the original pioneers, but on the average there will be more successful introductions than extinctions, and diversity will rise. Eventually the reservoir becomes "full"—successful introductions are balanced by extinctions—and diversity stabilizes at a level dependent upon the particular characteristics of the site. An ordinary example of nature's abhorrence of low diversity is the way in which gardens and fields, upon which man has imposed an artificial simplicity, tend to fill up with weeds and thereby begin a succession which, if allowed to proceed, would eventually result in higher diversity.

Diversity can be used as an index of the "health" of ecosystems. More important, changes in diversity are useful measures of the disruption of an ecosystem because they summarize the state of the entire, complex, integrated system, and because they can be measured with relative ease. Patrick (1964) has described the use of diatom diversity as an index of stream pollution. In general, the activities of man tend to reduce the diversity of aquatic ecosystems (Odum, 1969; Woodwell, 1970). The reduction may be caused by imposing extremely adverse conditions (such as acid mine drainage) or introducing fluctuations of great intensity and irregular period into the system.

One final property of ecosystems which must be taken into account is their openness. Few ecosystems more than approximate completely closed cycles of material and energy. Indeed, all are dependent ultimately upon energy from the sun, and upon other processes which take place outside the system itself. Margalef (1968) postulates that diverse ecosystems tend to exploit less diverse ones for matter and energy. It follows that human disruption of ecosystems, by lowering diversity, will tend to "open" them and produce a large export of chemical energy and nutrients to adjacent systems. This effect of disruption can be seen in the output of nutrients from a badly disturbed watershed (Likens and others, 1970), as well as in other examples which show that the levels of disturbance associated with normal management practices in such fields as agriculture, forestry and urbanization also open nutrient cycles, increase erosion, and may have substantial long-term negative effects on the areas subject to these human influences.

COMPONENTS OF ENVIRONMENTAL QUALITY

Before we can measure "environmental quality" we need to define the term. Of several concepts involved, the broadest is what we have called *holistic environmental quality*. This term stands for the conception of man and nature as a functioning whole and it is shared by many preservationists, conservationists, and ecologists. Another concept is *aesthetic quality*, the evocation of feelings of beauty or ugliness on the part of an observer of an environment. *Recreational quality*, a closely related concept, is the relative value of an environment for enjoyment and leisure. *Economic quality* is the measure of an environment's value in producing goods and services for human users. It is this quality which most water development seeks to enhance. *Health quality* reflects the degree to which an environment is free of disease-producing agents. In this section we will discuss each of these concepts from the point of view of their relationships to water development.

Holistic Environmental Quality

This quality concerns the dynamics of the man-nature interaction, and is related to the ecosystem concept which has had a strong influence on ecological thought in the past thirty years. An ecosystem is defined as the complex of plants, animals, and people, together with all the physical factors of a given site—soils, water, and air—interacting with one another. Although holistic environmental quality includes all other aspects of environmental quality, it implies that the whole is greater than the sum of its parts, that synergistic effects occur in each ecosystem. While it is certainly the least technical and the most difficult aspect of the environment to describe, it is in many cases the most important one for a full evaluation of the relationships between development and environmental quality.

The development of a holistic attitude toward environmental quality is important to scientists, technicians, and managers. It demands a certain humility—a recognition that phenomena exist of which one is ignorant and which may even be unsuited to scientific and managerial understanding. In its most extreme form this concept is frankly religious or mystical. Everson's contribution to this volume explores and illustrates this aspect of environmental quality. The human values and preferences included in holistic environmental quality are also the subject of several other contributions to this volume from the social sciences and the humanities.

Many scientifically trained conservationists and ecologists have underscored the concern of poets and preservationists for the intrinsically important qualities of the environment. Leopold's (1949) discussion of a "land ethic" was a landmark in this regard, although his arguments are based more on ethical than on scientific reasoning. Recently several professional ecologists have given scientific arguments in support of Thoreau's dictum "in Wildness is the preservation of the World" to complement its earlier philosophical, aesthetic and spiritual appeal.

Ecologists such as E. P. Odum (1969), Margalef (1968), H. T. Odum (1971), and Woodwell (1970) have stressed the dependence of man upon the as yet poorly understood ecological systems for the maintenance of climatic and biotic stability, without which he cannot survive. They have emphasized that man's activities have the potential to disrupt catastrophically not only local ecosystems, but even global ones. A cumulative interaction of local effects which in themselves are not totally disruptive may produce large-scale disaster, and deterioration of the environment on a global scale is now a widely discussed possibility. Lamb (1970), for example, reviews the large-scale climatic effects which are likely to result if massive southward diversions of northward-flowing rivers were to be made in the Soviet Union.

Beyond the debate over any particular model of catastrophe the indisputable fact remains that maintenance of healthy ecosystems is essential to human welfare. Failure to consider the impacts of development commonly has adverse and costly results. Degradation of environmental quality on a regional scale by water developments which are poorly planned is too common to need special documentation. However, planning which fails to give sufficient weight to the complex, integrated character of the environment may have effects fully as serious as no planning at all. The ambitious California Water Plan, for example, did not give adequate attention to the effects of diverting most of the freshwater inflow away from the huge Sacramento-San Francisco Bay estuarine system (Goldman, in press; Hagan and Roberts, this volume). As Hollis and McEvoy point out (this volume), this particular project may degrade the environment further by increasing the population density of the Los Angeles area.

Since man's life on earth is made possible only by a healthy, smoothly functioning global ecosystem, any reduction of diversity through large-scale water development and pollution may make the earth susceptible to large fluctuations from its natural equilibrium. As we have seen earlier, such fluctuations often have serious negative consequences for the continuation of life. For example, consider the bioconcentration in food chains of toxic substances such as DDT, mentioned earlier. Top carnivores such as predatory birds represent only a small component of the biomass in communities of which they are a part, but they are important regulators of the lower trophic levels. Without them, major changes may occur such as excess productivity of species beneath them on the food chain.

Still another aspect of holistic environmental quality which deserves close attention by planners is the foreclosing of future options caused by irreversible water development (see Teclaff and Teclaff, this volume).

For example, most reservoirs fill with sediment in relatively short periods of time. For reservoirs in the Colorado River Basin the range appears to be from about 2,000 years for the Flaming Gorge Reservoir to about 300 years for Lake Powell (Gessel, 1963). Of course, major impairment of reservoir function will occur long before the reservoir is actually full of sediment. The construction of reservoirs, then, is analogous to the exploitation of a non-renewable resource.

Aesthetic Quality

A number of papers in this volume—as well as our common sense—point to the fact that aesthetic factors are highly significant in determining the quality of an environment for human beings. What then are the aesthetic values to be considered in evaluating impacts of water-related development?

Before attempting to answer this question, it is important to identify the two principal components of aesthetic judgments—subject and object, or observer and scene. While we think of the scene or object as constant, we know that it changes with time and in response to development, and we know that human response to the scene varies with the particular observer. This two-dimensional, rather subjective character of aesthetic judgments poses serious problems for the development of generalized metrics to assess aesthetic values objectively. However, as we will point out later in the chapter this is a difficulty, not an insoluble problem.

Aesthetic factors of an environment are those aspects which are seen, smelled, heard, or felt by an observer and to which he reacts according to their degree of beauty or pleasantness. R. Burton Litton and his colleagues at Berkeley have devised an elaborate categorical system for isolating the spatial elements of a water-related environment included in aesthetic judgments (Litton and others, personal commun.). We believe that their scheme is comprehensive and isolates most of the relevant dimensions. Briefly, they distinguish the following elements as important in the determination of an environment's aesthetic quality: water setting (for example, type of enclosure), features (peaks, rock outcrops), vegetative cover, evidence of human impact, vertical pattern of water edge, lateral pattern of water edge, conformity of edge with setting, water movement, water pattern, water appearance, temperature, and sound. However, it is not enough merely to assess the character of a single landscape through application of measurements like Litton's. Whatever method is used for measurement, its categories must be site-independent, that is, must be usable at any place chosen for evaluation, to permit calculation of differences between various sites so that objective comparisons of their aesthetic qualities can be made. We will consider Litton's contributions in solving these problems in some detail later in this chapter.

In addition to the elements suggested by Litton, a number of measurements employed by scientists and engineers to assess physical and biological characteristics of water have some application to the evaluation of aesthetics. Principally, these are the standard measurements of water color, temperature, odor, and velocity, all of which are variables that could easily be integrated into a measurement scheme like that proposed by Litton et al.

Recreational Quality

Recreational quality, like aesthetic quality, is a combination of the objective character of the environment in which recreation takes place—for example, whether or not the environment is suited to a particular activity, and the subjective experience of the people engaging in the activity at that site—or whether or not they are satisfied with it.

American society has a pluralistic and complex organization and contains many social groups with dramatically different orientations to recreation. Thus, some people find hunting and fishing the most desirable outdoor experience, others like backpacking, others off-road vehicle travel, and still others find car camping or golf most suited to their needs. There has been a large increase in outdoor recreational activities in the past fifteen years. Sports such as snow skiing are growing by 20 to 25 percent per year, sales of backpacking equipment are increasing by about 50 percent per year (San Francisco *Chronicle*, July 20, 1971), recreational vehicle sales are booming, and rates of visitation to natural areas, especially the national parks, are expanding rapidly. Due to both the rapid growth of outdoor recreation and the concentration of population in urban areas, numerous conflicts between different recreational use patterns have occurred. Furthermore, recreational activities of all types are placing an increasing strain on natural environments and in some cases altering them seriously.

The resource manager concerned with recreation has four basic problems: (1) he needs extensive financial resources; (2) he needs thorough data on recreational demand so he can plan for the society's future needs; (3) he needs to provide facilities in such a way that conflicting uses do not occur in the same areas; and (4) he must devise means of protecting the environment from overuse or damage by recreationists. Recreational planners are at present constrained in fulfilling their responsibilities as more and more streams, lakes, rivers, reservoirs, and estuaries become polluted and unfit for swimming, fishing, boating, or drinking. Therefore, measurements of environmental quality must also assess effects on recreational behavior associated with changes in water quality.

Economic Quality

The definition of the economic quality of an environment is restricted in this discussion to direct monetary effects. Although some economists (for example, Gaffney, 1965) have argued that economics in the broadest sense should measure all benefits (and costs) of the environment to man, in fact economic techniques are presently of limited value beyond market-oriented or willingness-to-pay methods (Allee, this volume). Recreation can sometimes be realistically valued in dollars, as can those aspects of pollution, for example, which result in increased production or treatment costs downstream. In economic efficiency terms, however, pollution control can seldom be justified by economic effects on recreation, fish and wildlife, and aesthetic benefits, which are difficult to measure. Since aesthetic and health qualities and some aspects of recreation have so far escaped meaningful monetary evaluation, we have chosen to include most aspects of environmental quality in other categories and to reserve for economic quality only those which can be measured easily and convincingly in dollar values.

The absolute necessity of water for life itself and for most of the industrial processes of modern civilization has placed a high economic value upon an environment rich in water. As noted in this volume, most major American cities have grown up on the shores of rivers, lakes, or oceans, in large part for economic reasons. The benefits of water for manufacture, irrigation, transportation, and waste disposal are readily appreciated. The costs of uncontrolled flooding are equally obvious. Most water development is undertaken to increase the economic benefits of water (water supply systems) or decrease its damage costs (flood control works). Water development is also often viewed as a general stimulus to regional economic growth, (Hollis and McEvoy, this volume) but this theory has recently been subjected to question by studies of the actual effects of local projects on the rural economy (Cox and others, 1971).

Economic environmental values often conflict with other values, and it is especially important to formal decision-making that they be evaluated as accurately as possible.

The tendency of construction-oriented resource development agencies to abuse cost-benefit analysis techniques is documented in several papers in this volume and elsewhere; the tendency for profit motivated private enterprise to neglect pollution control through externalizing pollution costs has also been widely discussed (see, for example, Allee and others, in this volume).

Health Quality

Water quality has profound effects upon human well-being. The health aspects of environmental quality were among the first to receive scientific consideration through recognition of waterborne disease during the nineteenth century, and this knowledge soon led to the development of water supply and treatment works in Europe and North America. The carriers of such diseases as malaria and schistomitosis are associated at some point in their life cycle with water. Others, such as typhoid, dysentery, poliomyelitis, infectious hepatitis, and cholera, result from the use of water as a human waste receptacle, which is still a problem in the United States. The U.S. Water Resources Council (1968) lists 228 outbreaks of waterborne diseases causing 25,984 cases of illness from 1946 to 1960, many of which came from contaminated, untreated water. There are indications that these figures are far too low (Drewry and Eliassen, 1968). However, due to efficient and widespread treatment, the direct health hazards associated with sewage disposal in water will likely remain small in the United States. Aside from diseases contracted from contaminated water the provision of clean water in sufficient quantities to maintain personal hygiene at a high level can prevent several diseases such as diarrhea, shigella, and Ascaris infections (Taylor and others, 1967).

A second major source of health problems due to water development is the use of bodies of water to dilute potentially poisonous industrial and agricultural wastes.

A broad spectrum of organic and inorganic chemicals falls into this category, though only a few are likely to be important on a large scale. They include heavy metals, pesticides, radionuclides, and groundwater contamination with nitrates. The most dramatic case of human fatalities due directly to pollution of water with such poisonous wastes is the notorious Minimata Bay episode in Japan, where industrial mercury pollution resulted in 111 deaths or cases of severe disability from 1953 to 1960. In Niigata, Japan, 26 cases of mercury poisoning and 5 deaths have been recorded, while 120 persons have reported one or more of its clinical symptoms (Lofroth, 1969; Malling and others, 1970; Irukayama, 1966).

MEASURES OF ENVIRONMENTAL QUALITY

Technical measures of environmental quality have long been used to evaluate and enhance man's control of his relationship with nature. In the past, these measures have been constrained on the one hand by a limited interest in the environment and on the other by limited technical and ecological sophistication. Such limits are rapidly disappearing. Progress in measurement techniques is rapid, and measurement of some components of environmental quality is now perfectly adequate. However, in other areas present techniques are not so advanced. Major limitations exist especially in the development of evaluation systems which are useful for planning and management decisions affecting environmental quality. The purpose of this discussion is to assess briefly the specific measurement techniques now available and their relevance to the categories of environmental quality defined above. In a later section we will examine the problem of evaluation systems.

The major measure of water contamination historically has been the fecal coliform test, supplemented by various chemical tests for toxic materials. Fecal coliforms are used as an index of sewage contamination because simple incubation techniques can be used to measure their numbers. However, there is no direct correlation between coliform counts and pathogenic organisms. New techniques have been developed to measure directly populations of pathogenic organisms but these measurements are generally not undertaken on a routine basis because they are costly and laborious. As larger waste loads are imposed upon our water and as more recycling of water is contemplated, the need to conduct routine assays for viruses will grow, since viruses are relatively resistant to disinfection.

Various kinds of population sampling programs are often undertaken in conjunction with efforts to suppress annoying or disease-carrying insects. To our knowledge, in this area measurement techniques are adequate for the problems encountered. Oysters and other filter-feeding organisms concentrate pathogenic organisms such as hepatitis viruses to dangerous levels. At present, initial detection of such diseases is left to epidemiological investigation (Wilber, 1969). Perhaps a routine use of direct surveys for such conditions is indicated.

Potentially more serious than microbial disease problems are the increases in amount and variety of industrial pollutants. To measure all of the organic, inorganic, and radioactive wastes commonly dumped in our waters requires elaborate, costly monitoring programs. Organic materials are especially difficult to detect. Moreover, merely testing water samples may not be sufficient when the bioaccumulation of poisons (mentioned above) is taken into account. However, a program for monitoring the various effects of pollutants, including health hazards, is described in an N.A.S.–N.R.C. report (1970, Chapter 2), and the cost of an adequate monitoring program for all aspects of water quality, including health parameters, would probably be only a few percent of total waste treatment costs.

Measurements can be used to evaluate environmental quality either directly or indirectly. For example, algal biomass, a measure of the amount of algae in the water, may be used indirectly as a measure of aesthetic quality if nuisance levels are approached through eutrophication. The same index is used in conjunction with measures of productivity, diversity, and bioassays to delineate an ecosystem's response to disruptive influences upon various components of environmental quality.

Table 1 outlines the major kinds of measurements used to evaluate environmental quality within physical, chemical, biological, and social categories. It indicates the way in which the measures are used and which kinds of environmental quality they are likely to be helpful in describing.

The Evaluation Program

The quantification of environmental quality is difficult for several reasons. First, natural ecosystems themselves are exceedingly complex. Some feeling for this complexity was, hopefully, communicated in the preceding pages. Second, to determine and then measure what people mean by environmental quality is a serious difficulty. Finally, even if we understood perfectly both ecosystems and human values, there would remain the problems of integrating the two into a comprehensive evaluation scheme. No comprehensive method strictly comparable to cost-benefit analysis is available now or is likely to be in the foreseeable future. We are certainly far from being able to propose an environmental quality calculus that can formally rationalize the balance between water development and environmental quality.

With regard to the problem of ecosystem complexity, measurement and measurement systems have progressed rapidly in the past decade and present levels of sophistication allow measurement of many parameters of ecosystem change in response to specific manipulations. The gross form of many kinds of changes is well known from experience, and only a minimum of measurement may be necessary to describe or predict them. With the rise of systems ecology, prediction of even quite complex responses to change are often possible (Watt, 1968). However, where detailed answers are sought, ecosystem complexity tends to make investigation very expensive; also, agency planning staffs usually lack the expert personnel to conduct such studies. Thus, estimations of the effects of developments either planned or operating are seldom available. However, while difficulties are numerous, major advances in the quality of present evaluations are certainly feasible with present methodologies, *if* human and financial resources are committed to applying them. The proposals of the Water Resources Council for an environmental quality objective (U.S.W.R.C., 1970a) and the National Environmental Policy Act's (42 U.S.C. 4321) requirement for reports on the environmental impacts of federal development have raised the expectation that evaluations of better quality are forthcoming, although to date real efforts have been weak. The initial tests of the W.R.C. procedures (1970b) were notable for their lack of environmental sophistication, and none of the N.E.P.A. reports which have come to the authors' attention make adequate use of available techniques.

Human, Aesthetic, and Economic Values

The problem of measuring human values and incorporating them into formal decision-making procedures is indeed a perplexing one. Professor William Marshall Urban (1958), in a discussion of the nature of values, points out that:

> Neither Plato nor Aristotle developed this line of reflection fully, nor did succeeding

philosophers investigate the subtle and perplexing problems involved in it. Plato himself called this the most difficult question of all science.

It would be naive to assume that no progress at all has been made in value theory since Plato, but it is true that the area is one of great theoretical and empirical complexity. At present, attention to aesthetic and non-economic values is by no means standard procedure in water planning; thus decision-makers are left struggling in the dark in attempting to balance these factors with others such as need and demand for water, hydroelectric power, or recreation.

Economic values are usually defined as exchange ratios and the price system in conjunction with monetary systems permits the application of uniform, numerical measurement of the values of all goods and services that are exchanged. Under this definition nothing is defined as morally or aesthetically better or worse than another. Semantic confusion can easily arise when attempts are made to introduce what Boulding (1967) terms "absolute values" into economic calculus. Absolute values are different from economic, that is, price-related values, and aesthetic values are usually, though not always, classified as absolute values. Absolute values are, in fact, preferences. For example, an individual with preference for the aesthetic value of the Grand Canyon ignores all other considerations in making a decision about its appropriate use. His choice is to leave the Canyon alone.

Let us briefly examine the role that measurement of aesthetic characteristics of the environment and the assessment of individual response to an environment might play in decision-making. As a first step, consider the model (Figure 3) of the interrelationships between the observer and the environment developed by R. Burton Litton's group at Berkeley. This figure depicts the joint interaction of psychological (broadly speaking) and environmental phenomena within an individual which is necessary for an "aesthetic visual experience."

Assessment of the aesthetic quality of an experience rests upon two entirely different kinds of measurement: one, an example of which we have mentioned earlier, consists of objective measurements of the features of an environment that impinge upon sensory receptors; the other concerns human response to these sensory inputs. We must be careful to enforce this distinction in developing both types of measurement in order to satisfy the requirements of independence; that is, measures of the environment must not rely entirely upon subjective judgments because of the bias that such judgments can introduce into the measurement process.

There are a number of current research efforts directed at the development of these measurements. Leopold (1969), Litton and others (this volume), Craik (1971), Steinitz and others (1969), McEvoy (1971), McHarg (this volume), Fines (1968), and Zube and others (1970) are only a few of the investigators who have developed, reviewed, or proposed various quantitative or map-overlay methods for assessing environments and individual response to them. While no particular method has yet emerged as distinctly preferable to the others, progress seems rapid in the area of environmental assessment. We anticipate that a number of generally applicable quantitative or overlay methods will be available to the resource manager within the next few years.

Of what actual utility will such methods be to the resource manager? It seems likely that their principal employment will be in assessing alternative site locations for proposed developments. They certainly will not offer a panacea in the form of outputs of magic numbers which will determine whether or not development should or should not occur in a particular area. They may enlighten such decisions, but without a series of value judgments concerning the "worth" of the numbers these indicators

TABLE 1
Environmental Quality Measures

Environmental quality measures	Applicable habitats or situations	Measure of what process or condition	Causes of condition or process	Implications for environmental quality
Physical Temperature	All habitats, waste streams.	Used relatively to compare pristine condition with the effects of certain management or use procedures.	Temperature is raised by uses of many kinds, but especially cooling of power plants. Generally a severe disruptive factor. Hypolimnetic reservoir releases will cool water.	May affect recreation (fishing, swimming) especially and has a serious effect upon all biological processes. Both enhancement and degradation are possible. Extreme fluctuations of temperature are most likely to have serious negative effects.
Transparency	All habitats, especially lakes, reservoirs and estuaries.	Clarity of water.	Increased sediment or increases in biomass of organisms decrease transparency.	Various and considerable. Scenic values. May damage biota, including fish. High biomass of organisms may be unsightly and be accompanied by undesirable changes in composition of flora or fauna.
Sediment load	Usually streams and estuaries.	Amount of nonliving particulate material.	Waste disposal, erosion.	Usually undesirable as described under transparency. In certain situations may limit PPR and prevent algal nuisances and bind toxic chemicals.
Settable Solids	Usually waste streams but also polluted habitats.	Amount of suspended solids which fall to the bottom of a container in a given period of time (usually one hour).	Any source of relatively large suspended solid will contribute. Often used to measure quality of waste water before and after treatment.	Similar to suspended solids except that this component may sink and have adverse effects upon DO and conditions for bottom dwelling organisms including some baby fish, eggs, and food.
Flow rates	Streams, canals, and reservoirs, waste streams.	Amount (water level) and rate of flow of water.	Describes the water budget of aquatic systems.	The flow rate and timing of flow has many effects upon water bodies. Altered releases due to management may have serious effects upon biota and scenic qualities. Timing of release from reservoirs alters stream conditions and may leave unsightly bare banks, for example.

Chemical				
Dissolved oxygen content (DO)	All aquatic habitats, especially rivers, estuaries and lake hypolimnia.	Amount of oxygen often expressed as a percent of saturation at existing temperature.	Consumption of oxygen to degrade materials responsible for BOD. Thermal pollution reduced DO at saturation.	Low DO usually reduces the diversity and quality of biota; i.e., trout are replaced by warm-water then rough fish. With complete absence of DO, odors become a nuisance.
Total dissolved solids (TDS)	All aquatic habitats, especially rivers.	Content of mineral salts.	Consumptive uses for agriculture, domestic water storage, and waste disposal.	Degrades quality for agricultural, domestic, and some industrial uses. May change biota and harm recreational uses, such as fishing.
Toxic substances, organic and in-organic chemicals	All habitats.	Amounts of substances potentially harmful to humans or aquatic organisms.	Sources of toxic substances may be natural or result from human activities of various kinds.	May be directly hazardous to human health. May destroy useful or otherwise desirable biota.
Organic matter	All habitats.	Amounts of specific kinds of chemical constituents.	Character of drainage basins, including human influences, have complex effects upon the concentrations of these ions.	Variable. May have no effects or considerable effects, depending upon specific habitat and substance.
Various inorganic ions	All habitats.	Similar to above.	Similar to above.	Similar to above.
Biological				
Biological oxygen demand (BOD)	Usually rivers and estuaries.	Content of heterotrophically degradable (organic) material.	Input of sewage, pulp wastes, food processing wastes, or other organic material.	If extreme, total destruction of recreational and aesthetic quality. Serious degradation of water quality for many economic, especially consumptive, uses.
Coliform count	All aquatic habitats, waste streams.	Number of bacteria of the type associated with sewage.	Degree of contamination by sewage of human or animal fecal origin.	Public health measure. Standard by which beaches and other contact water sports areas are judged for health.
Primary productivity (PPR)	Usually lakes, reservoirs, and estuaries.	Rate of photosynthetic activity of plants, usually planktonic algae.	Increases caused by eutrophication, increased supply of nutrient salts (N, P especially).	Various. Slight to moderate increases improve fisheries. Water clarity declines so scenic values often are affected negatively. Extreme levels cause unsightly and biologically harmful blooms.

(continued)

TABLE 1
Continued.

Environmental quality measures	Applicable habitats or situations	Measure of what process or condition	Causes of condition or process	Implications for environmental quality
Diversity	All situations in which a biota occurs.	The number of different kinds of organisms present.	Disruption of habitats lowers diversity.	General measure of biological quality, scenic, recreational (fishing) and aesthetic quality should be positively associated with diversity.
Biomass	All habitats.	Amount of living organisms, often broken down into complex submeasures.	Eutrophication and often pollution with organic matter increases biomass.	Important biotic measure. Increases in biomass generally are accompanied by changes in composition that may be undesirable.
Toxicity	All habitats, especially streams and estuaries used for waste disposal, or effluent itself.	Tendency to kill living organisms, usually an indicator fish.	A wide variety of chemicals (organic chemicals like phenols, pesticides, heavy metals).	Lowers quality of biota. May pose health hazards. Extreme cases like fish kills are unsightly and odiferous.
Biomass composition Fish biota	All habitats.	Kinds and numbers of fish present.	Often adversely affected by eutrophication, high sediment load, toxicity, TDS, BOD, and low DO.	Recreational quality in many habitats is related to quality of fish biota.
Indicator Organisms	All habitats.	Kinds and numbers of organisms found to accompany certain conditions.	Important to describe many quality factors bearing directly on the biology of the habitat.	General measure of biological quality, scenic, recreational and aesthetic quality should be positively associated with diversity.
Bioassays	All habitats.	Usually the toxicity with respect to some indicator organism, although various kinds of more sophisticated bioassays are also used.	Pollution with toxic or other materials that have an adverse effect on living organisms.	Toxicity and other conditions detrimental to living organisms often reduce fishing quality, may indicate hazards to human health, and may be associated with visual degradation.
Social Scenic indices	All habitats.	Aesthetic quality of site.	The degree and aesthetic sensitivity of development and the intrinsic nature of the site.	Intends to measure directly one of the most important aspects of perceived quality.

Attitude surveys and opinion polls	Any situation where human judgment is important.	Attitude and opinion of surveyed population toward a particular situation development proposal, etc.	Various development or preservation alternatives may elicit quite different sets of attitude and opinions on this part of the public.	Human values are a dominant element in many aspects of environmental quality and such measures help define such values.
Taste and odor	All habitats.	Tastes and odors detectable by man.	Inorganic ions from natural and human sources may cause objectionable taste. Odors are more likely to be associated with organic materials from pollution or blooms of certain algae.	Objectionable in water supplies, recreation waters, or around human habitations.
Economic Economic analysis Benefit-cost ratios regional multiplier effects	All development situations.	The projected economic costs and benefits of a project alternative.	The economic effect of the mobilization of water for domestic, industrial, agricultural, or recreational uses.	The measure of one important aspect of environmental quality.

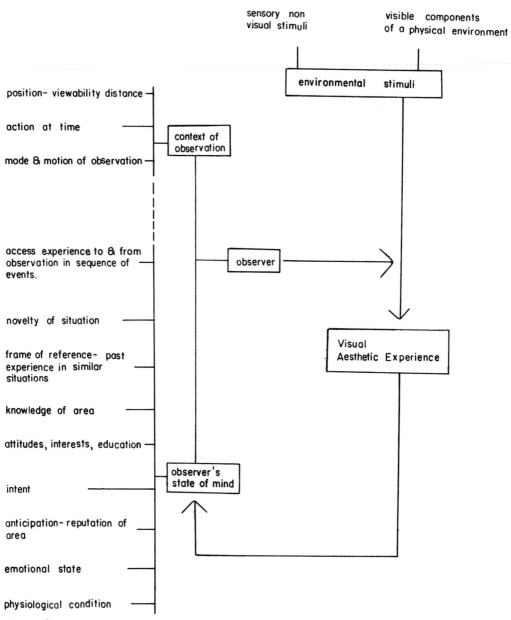

FIGURE 3
Diagram of joint interaction of psychological and environmental phenomena.

will not be directly compatible with economic quality measures. Nevertheless, skillful quantitication of variables of this kind will prove worthwhile and should be encouraged.

The second area of measurement—psy-

chological response to the environment, especially to its aesthetic qualities—is much more advanced than the assessment of aesthetic qualities of the environment itself, as a result of extensive theoretical and applied work by psychologists in the study of attitudes generally. Thus, fairly straightforward applications of already existing "technology" to this problem should be quite fruitful. These probably will take the form of explanations of varying responses to a constant environment through the assessment and ordering of psychological variables such as those indicated on the left side of Figure 3; that is, "access experience," "intent," "emotional state," and so on. Craik (1970, 1971), in particular, has greatly expanded our knowledge of these processes.

Whether or not a particular individual finds a particular environment attractive—or at least what that person says are his reasons for like or dislike—is much easier to assess, and the latter type of information seems to be what many resource managers think they would like to have about people. With this information in hand, presumably the manager could follow the dictates of public opinion, implementing the principle of majority rule. As White points out (this volume), the unidimensional conception of the public implied in such a crude model is fallacious. When surveys simply collect responses from people who have no information about or no interest in a particular issue, but who are perfectly willing to offer their opinion of it, the results are meaningless. On the other hand, opinion research can be a useful tool for the decision-maker if he designs his research and analyzes his data from a sophisticated point of view. While research on environmental attitudes, opinions, and response always results in quantitative outputs, these must be buffered by value judgments as to their worth and appropriate role in decision-making.

Economic Measurement

It is also clear that exchange ratios or prices are useful in some cases as indicators of aesthetic values. A simple example of relevant economic behavior is found in the price differential existing between single family residences which possess a special aesthetic amenity, a view for example, and those which lack this amenity but are in all other respects similar. In general, however, it is not private property which commands the attention of the resource manager. By moving from the area of private to public goods, we substantially complicate the economic assessment of aesthetic value.

There appear to be two keys to proper use of economic measurement of environmental quality. First, the true monetary costs and benefits of a given alternative must be accurately calculated. Cost-benefit analysis should include more comprehensive measurements of economic values than they do at present, particularly avoiding false externalization of costs, and the assessment of values should be related to the time horizon used by the decision-maker. Furthermore, economic techniques should not attempt to evaluate all components of environmental quality, but be restricted to those areas in which they are actually valid (Allee, this volume).

We do not mean to imply that cost-benefit analysis should not be expanded or modified to conform more closely to reality, nor that no attempt be made to extend it to the measurement of aesthetics, recreation, or other difficult areas. In fact, one method of value measurement that has been given too little attention is to incorporate economic variables associated with the consumption of aesthetic amenities into an assessment of aesthetic value. Knetsch and Davis (1966) and Lerner (1963) review several such methods that could be applied to outdoor recreation and perhaps to aesthetic amenities as well. Their suggestions include ascertaining hypothetical prices users would pay to use an area for recreation, and the determination of user access costs. They review the GNP method, the Consumers' Surplus Method, the market value, and the monopoly revenue methods of determining economic values, among others. Added to these could be factors such as those based upon economic "sacrifices" made by visitors to particular areas; for example, the loss of wages if users are professionals or inclusion of an hourly wage rate factor if users are salaried or hourly employees. Here we assume that users could maximize their economic utility by converting their vacations into work for wages. Obviously, more sophisticated measures (and assumptions) may be needed but the general idea should be clear: if we acquire accurate data about absolute values in many situations we will have a far clearer picture of the "cash value" of a particular area than we do at present.

If these measurements are introduced into cost-benefit computations they will encounter the problem of the appropriate time horizons within which benefits should be computed and discount rates applied. While a hydroelectric plant is expected to justify its construction in 50 years or so of operation, it is not at all clear that a wilderness or recreation area could (employing cost-benefit assessments of the type suggested above) be as "productive" as the hydro installation in the same time period. Clearly, alternative models with varying time horizons should be computed as a first step toward determining the feasibility of using cost-benefit analysis as an indicator of aesthetic, recreational, and other "intangible" values.

As White suggests elsewhere in this volume, in-depth studies should be made of contemporary cost-benefit planning projections to detect errors and place confidence limits upon further projections. We note that replicated studies of individual projects conducted by the U.S. Water Resources Council (1970b) often showed gross discrepancies between the cost-benefit ratios of different planning teams. The work of Cox and others (1971) has opened another avenue of research on the true economic effects of water development. Despite these

difficulties, there is little doubt that the measurement of economic qualities through cost-benefit analysis is highly advanced. Conscientious and honest economic evaluations provide valuable information about many of the effects of environmental manipulations and human response to them; they are an important aspect of the measurement of environmental quality. Given these existing techniques, we encourage their proper use and independent review, while recognizing their limitations. Increased accuracy and objectivity in economic measurement will probably be achieved only with separate, unbiased governmental planning units as suggested by McCloskey (this volume), or at least through separate, extended review by an environmentally committed agency.

Three kinds of planning and evaluation methods that can coordinate specific measures, systems evaluations, and value judgments of the various kinds of environmental quality we have defined are discussed in this volume. First, impact analysis, as described by Henwood and Coop involves procedures by which the full range of environmental effects of water development can be assessed and presented to decision-makers. Second, the paper by McHarg and Clarke sets forth the methods and application of the map-overlay technique, which is designed to synthesize data on a variety of environmental and human effects of alternative developments, and to project capacities of an area for development. The third method is the resource inventory and land use zoning procedure described by Yanggen.

All of these methods, whether merely inventories or analytic and predictive models, have attractive features. First, they are quite flexible. Data can be used which is of varying precision and in different units of measurement. Second, such methods are amenable to computer storage, and to manipulation and graphical display of the quantities of information gathered. Third, the use of data from diverse fields is possible. For example, McHarg and Clarke's case study employed information from such disciplines as history, ecology, and engineering.

A fourth appealing feature of these methods for displaying and predicting the effects of water development is their conceptual simplicity. While the problem of measuring and predicting environmental effects is complex and often highly technical, the ideal planning method to involve laymen (and even the most sophisticated planner is a layman with respect to many of the disciplines which contribute to comprehensive studies) is one in which inputs can easily be evaluated for quality, and in which the integrative procedures are clearly understandable. Several other authors in this volume (McCloskey, Fox, Ross, White, and Luken and Langlois, among others) comment on the need to involve the lay public and public-oriented interest groups in the planning process. Efficient methods of evaluating environmental quality can provide a formal vehicle around which to develop such public participation. Hedgpeth remarks on the success of McHarg's procedures in this regard in the case of the Yaquina Bay, Oregon, plan.

SYSTEMS ANALYSIS

Steinitz and many others of his persuasion (unpub. ms.) urges that increased use be made of full-scale systems analysis techniques in the evaluation of natural resource problems. In some respects, systems analysis satisfies the criteria we find necessary to make proper use of the information needed to balance water development and environment quality. Models of sufficient complexity may be formulated to avoid reducing complex variables to dollar values or introducing other invalid commensurating procedures. If the model is sophisticated enough, a variety of data from divergent disciplines can be incorporated into it.

Several objections to the use of systems analysis must be raised, however. Such methods are still experimental and are subject to severe operational difficulties. We may not assume that applying them to environmental problems, with their mixture of technical, value-oriented, and political components, will result in understandable solutions or even assist in refining the concept of the problem. Systems analysis is dependent upon highly formal and technical procedures for completion. On one hand this dependence is the power of the method: it provides the ability to formulate specific hypotheses and rigorously test them. On the other hand, it introduces clear disadvantages. The analysts are provided with ample opportunities to conceal their prejudices through technical smoke screens. Such prejudices have certainly influenced the calculation of benefit-cost studies in past water developments, and there is no doubt that the temptation (conscious or otherwise) to do so will continue to exist. Furthermore, the use of elaborate mathematical procedures can give an air of bogus precision to evaluations of complex phenomena while, in fact, understanding of the natural and human systems involved and the data representing them are relatively weak.

Certainly systems analysis will be less useful than the simpler map-overlay methods of impact analysis in involving the public in decision-making. However, none of the preceding discussion ought to be taken as discouraging the development of systems techniques for application to water resources planning. We merely wish to illuminate their weaknesses, especially in the area of public involvement, as compared to other methods. Perhaps in the short term the most effective use of systems analysis will be to provide models of the limited sets of problems for which it can provide definitive information.

CONCLUSIONS AND RECOMMENDATIONS

We conclude from our discussion that while significant problems still exist, major advances in the quality of environmental measurement for planning are possible with present techniques. Measurements of ecological phenomena—the backbone of any measurement program—are available for all relevant parameters. Due to the inherent complexity of ecosystems, some skill is necessary to understand such methods, but this difficulty for the decision-maker can be alleviated by hiring competent personnel and making careful use of outside experts. The measurement of aesthetic, recreational, and holistic qualities of the environment often presents serious technical difficulties. However, the use of planning and evaluation techniques we have suggested for incorporating public values should reduce such problems. In any case, progress in the quantitative estimation of some components of aesthetic and other values is rapid at this time. No doubt further research is desirable in many areas, but the real impediment to improvement in today's evaluation and decision-making is the lack of money, manpower, the commitment to make the best use of available techniques, and the dominance of economic values in decision making.

While quantitative measurement of aesthetic characteristics of an environment and more realistic application of classical economic value theory to the problem of aesthetic measurement may help the resource manager to balance environmental quality with development, there is no quantitative means of incorporating absolute values into the decision process other than through recourse to the political system. For this reason the proposals in this volume for restructuring current procedures for public involvement in resource development decisions are essential. Only through the political process can aesthetic and human values be given certain priorities in decisions. If this happens, of course, the political process itself will have made a value judgment, that is, that aesthetic and human values are to be measured, introduced into the decision-making process and given a certain weight in relation to other variables.

In some respects the process of formalizing values may have contradictory side-effects. There is certainly no guarantee that quantitative measurements of aesthetic and other value preferences will not be abused in the same way as have personality inventories or I.Q. tests when applied to the prediction of individual behavior, or cost-benefit analysis has when used to assess economic values. Despite these possible pitfalls, and the lack of any comprehensive value theory which would permit mathematical comparison of price-related values and absolute values, their measurement can increase our understanding of the role that values play in resource policy, and consequently the quality of decisions attempting to balance water development with environmental quality.

References

Boulding, Kenneth. 1967. The basis of value judgments in economics, in S. Hook, ed., *Human Values and Economic Policy*. New York University Press, New York.

Brookhaven Symposium. 1969. *Diversity and stability in ecological systems*. Biology Department, Brookhaven National Laboratory, Upton, N.Y.

Cox, P. T., Grover, C. W., and Siskin, B. 1971. Effect of water resource investment on economic growth. *Water Resources Res.* 7(1), 32–38.

Craik, Kenneth. 1970. *Landscape appraisal.* University of California, Berkeley, Dept. of Psychology (mimeo.).

Craik, Kenneth. 1971. *Assessing the objectivity of landscape dimensions.* Paper prepared for Resources for the Future Multi-Disciplinary Workshop on Research on Wildlands, Wildlife and Scenic Resources.

Davis, J. J., and Foster, R. F. 1958. Bioaccumulation of radioisotopes through aquatic food chains. Ecology 39, 530–535.

Drewry, William and Eliassen, R. 1968. Virus movement in groundwater. *Water Pollution Control Fed. J.* 40, R257–R271.

Fines, K. D. 1968. Landscape evaluations: a research project in East Sussex. *Regional Studies*, pp. 41–55.

Gaffney, M. Mason. 1965. Applying economic controls. *Bull. Atom. Sci.* 21, 20–25.

Gessell, Clyde E. 1963. Sediment storage and measurement in the upper Colorado basin. *U.S.D.A. Misc. Pub. 970*, 78, 778–784.

Goldman, C. R. 1960. Molybdenum as a factor limiting primary productivity in Castle Lake, California. *Science* 132, 1016–1017.

Goldman, C. R. in press. Reduced flows and the future ecology of the San Francisco Bay Delta System. *Am. Water Res. Assn. Journal.*

Goldman, C. R., Mason, D. T., and Hobbie, J. E. 1967. Two antarctic desert lakes. *Limnol. Oceanogr.* 12, 295–309.

Hunt, Eldridge, and Bischoff, A. 1960. Inimical effects on wildlife of periodic DDD applications to Clear Lake, *California Fish and Game.* 46, 91–106.

Hutchinson, G. E. 1967. *A Treatise on Limnology.* Vol II: Introduction to lake biology and the limnoplankton. John Wiley & Sons, New York.

Irukayama, Katsuro. 1966. The pollution of Minimata Bay and Minimata Disease. *Adv. Water Pollution Res.* 3, 153–180.

Knetsch, J. L., and Davis, R. 1966. Comparisons of methods for recreation evalua-tion. In Kneese and Smith, eds., *Water Research.* Johns Hopkins Press, Baltimore.

Kuentzel, L. E. 1969. Bacteria, carbon dioxide and algal bloom. *W ater Pollution Control Fed. J.* 41(5), 1737–1747.

Lackey, J. B. 1938. The flora and fauna of surface waters polluted by acid mine drainage. *Pub. Health Repts.* 53. 1499–1507.

Lackey, J. B. 1939. Aquatic life in waters polluted by acid mine waste. *Pub. Health Repts.* 54, 740–746.

Lamb, H. H. 1970. Climatic variation and our environment today and in the coming years. *Weather* 25, 447–455.

Lange, W. 1967. Effects of carbohydrates on the symbiotic growth of planktonic blue-green algae with bacteria. *Nature* 215, 1277–1278.

Leopold, Aldo. 1949. *Sand County Almanac.* Oxford University Press, New York.

Leopold, Luna B. 1969. Quantitative comparison of some aesthetic factors among rivers. *U.S.G.S. Circular 620.* 16 pp.

Lerner, Lionel J. 1963. Quantitative indices of recreational values. In *Water Resources & Economic Development of the West*, Report No. 11, Economics and outdoor recreational policy.

Likens, G. E. (ed.). 1972. *Nutrients and Eutrophication: the limiting-nutrient controversy.* Special sumposia, Vol. I, American Society of Limnology and Oceanography. Allen Press, Inc. Lawrence, Kansas. 328p.

Likens, G. E., Bormann, F. H., Johnson, N. M., Fisher, D. W., and Pierce, R. S. 1970. Effects of forest cutting and herbicide treatment on nutrient budgets in the Hubbard Brook watershed-ecosystem. *Ecol. Monographs* 40:23–47.

Lofroth, Goran. 1969. Methylmercury: a review of health hazards and side effects associated with the emission of mercury compounds into natural systems. In U.S. Senate, Pub. Wks. Comm., Hearings. *Water Pollution—1970*, pt. II, pp. 676–716.

MacArthur, R. H. and Wilson, E. O. 1967. *The Theory of Island Biogeography*. Princeton University Press.

Mackenthun, Kenneth M. 1965. Nitrogen and phosphorus in water: an annotated selected bibliography of their biological effects. *Pub. Health Serv. Pub. no. 1305*. Washington, D.C.

McEvoy, James. 1971. Visual pollution in the Lake Tahoe Basin. University of California, Davis, Institute of Governmental Affairs.

Malling, H. V., Wassom, J. S. and Epstein, S. S. 1970. Mercury in our environment. In U.S. Senate, Pub. Works Comm., Hearings. *Water Pollution—1970*. Part II, pp. 717–726.

Margalef, Ramon. 1968. *Perspectives in Ecological Theory*. U. Chi. Press.

National Academy of Sciences and National Academy of Engineering. 1970. *Waste Management Concepts for the Coastal Zone*. Washington, D.C.

Odum, E. P. 1969. The strategy of ecosystem development. *Science* 164:262–270.

Odum, H. T. 1971. *Environment, Power and Society*. John Wiley & Sons, New York.

Patrick, Ruth. 1964. A discussion of natural and abnormal diatom communities. In D. F. Jackson, ed., *Algae and Man*.

Rohlich, G. A. and P. D. Utthormark. 1972. W astewater Treatment and Euthrophication. In G. E. Likens (ed.) *Nutrients and Eutrohpication: the limiting–nutrient controversy*. Special Symposia, Vol. I, American Society of Limnology and Oceanography. Allen Press, Inc. Lawrence, Kansas. pp. 231–243.

Steinitz, Carl, Murray, T., Sitton, D., Way, D. 1969. *A Comparative Study of Resource Analysis Methods*. Harvard Univ. Grad. School of Design, Dept. Landscape Arch. Res. Office. (Mimeo.)

Taylor, F. B., Long, W. N., Maddox, F. D., Hughes, P., 1967. Economic and social benefits from improving health by provision of safe drinking water supplies. In Internatl. Conf. on Water for Peace. *Water for Peace*. Washington, D.C., pp. 107–116.

U.S. Federal Water Quality Administration. 1970. *1969 Fish Kills Caused by Pollution*. Washington, D.C.

U.S. Water Resources Council. 1968. *The Nation's Water Resources, First National Assessment*. Washington, D.C.

U.S. Water Resources Council. 1970a. *Standards for planning water and land resources*. Special Task Force Report. Washington, D.C.

U.S. Water Resources Council. 1970b. *Summary analysis of nineteen tests of proposed evaluation procedures on selected water and land resource projects*. Special Task Force Report. Washington, D.C.

Urban, W. M. 1971. Values. *Encyclopedia Brittanica*, Vol. 22. p. 866.

Vallentyne, J. R. 1970. Phosphorus and the control of eutrophication. *Canadian Research and Development* 3:30 ff.

Watt, K. E. F. 1968. *Ecology and Resource Management*. McGraw-Hill Book Co., New York.

Wilber, Charles G. 1969. *The Biological Aspects of Water Pollution*. Charles C Thomas.

Woodwell, G. M. 1970. Effects of pollution on the structure and physiology of ecosystems. *Science* 168:429–433.

Woodwell, G. M., Wurster, C. F. Jr., and Isaacson, P. A., 1967. DDT residues in an east coast estuary. *Science* 156:821–824.

Zube, E. H., et al. 1970. *Regional Water Resources Study*. Appendix N: Visual and cultural environment. Research Planning and Design Associates, Amherst, Mass.

CHAPTER 7

There have been few reliable studies made of the attitudes of the American public toward environmental quality that could assist decision-makers in planning for national water development. One recent major study, performed by the Gallup Organization, is described in this paper, and the author is able to draw from his analysis some useful conclusions about the environmental values of Americans.

Americans are strongly concerned about their environment, and support technological, legal, and financial solutions to problems with environmental quality. The public tends to respond most strongly to matters which affect it directly, such as air and water pollution. However, there is broad support for the preservation of open space and wildlife, as well as for eventual control of population growth. The demographic characteristics of concerned citizens indicate that this segment of society possesses a relatively great degree of political power, and that its size and effectiveness will grow in the future. However, presently available sample survey data is quite inadequate for more sophisticated knowledge of public attitudes and policy preferences. Much more extensive research is required before resource managers are provided with adequate information for planning water development in accord with public goals.

THE AMERICAN PUBLIC'S CONCERN WITH THE ENVIRONMENT

James McEvoy III

INTRODUCTION

It seems fairly certain that a large segment of the American public has held a varied series of attitudes and opinions toward the natural environment since the founding of the colonies. However, except for a small body of historical evidence and anecdotal data there is little basis for attempting an assessment of the public's views on environmental ques-tions over the entire span of American history. It is, however, possible to derive from this limited evidence some broad conclu-sions about the public's orientation to the environment, and to isolate the major points of conflict within the society over questions of alteration and exploitation of the environ-ment during the past 300 years. Clarence Glacken (1967) and Roderick Nash (1967) have explored in detail the role that the natural environment and wilderness have played in Western and American culture, and Nash's review of the Hetch Hetchy and Grand Canyon controversies in this volume provides important additional information on the influence of preservationist thought on development policy. Other writers have also discussed the meaning of nature, wilderness, and environment to Americans throughout the history of the country (Huth, 1967; McCloskey, 1966).

No brief summary of these scholars' analyses of elite and (in some cases) mass opinion can do more than isolate some of the important organizing concepts around which Americans' attitudes and behaviors toward their environment have been directed. However, it will be useful in our studies of contemporary public opinion to have in mind two of the prominent orientations that Americans have shared so that current empirical data—at both the mass and elite levels—can be organized and interpreted.

Historical evidence suggests that one early and prominent orientation to the natural environment was fear, and with this fear was eventually associated a desire to conquer and control the environment for man's ends. Nash, for example, points to the Puritans who, he says, gave "transcendent importance . . . to conquering wilderness." This view did not end with the decline of puritanism, but persisted throughout the seventeenth and eighteenth centuries during the westward expansion of the country (Nash 1967, pp. 38-43). Indeed, it is still common today. This orientation to the environment might be termed transformational and it includes not only the appreciation of agrarian pastoralism which motivated the Puritan settlers and their westward-migrating descendents, but also a view of the natural environment which supports obtaining maximum economic return from the exploitation of natural resources. This dimension of environmental orientation was isolated by Kluckhohn and Strodtbeck (1961) in their studies of the values of five different, but geographically contiguous, communities in the American Southwest. These authors identified control and mastery over nature and the environment as one of three important orientations of individuals and collectivities to their surroundings.

The contemporary significance of this orientation should be obvious. If we have a population whose beliefs about the environment are governed by a transformational orientation to it, we can then expect little resistance to large-scale environmental alterations such as those produced by massive water storage and diversion projects, electrical transmission systems, extensive forest utilization, and mining. Indeed, Kluckhohn and Strodtbeck identify "mastery-over-nature . . [as] the dominant orientation of most Americans. Natural forces of all kinds are to be overcome and put to the use of human beings . . . The view in general is that it is a part of man's duty to overcome obstacles; hence there is the great emphasis upon technology" (1961, p. 13).

Transformationists argue over the aesthetic consequences of environmental development and, more importantly within this tradition, have debated policies of outright exploitation versus "wise" and multiple use of renewable and nonrenewable natural resources. Nevertheless, although this grouping greatly simplifies and glosses over differences in emphasis and direction among its "members," it makes sense concerning public opinion, because we can often detect only the grossest and broadest conceptualizations of issue areas among much of the mass public. This is particularly true of the assessment of values and value orientations among the public.

Arrayed against the dominant transformational orientation to the environment in the United States is an opposing view, often termed preservationist, which developed in the early part of the nineteenth century (Nash, 1967, pp. 96–107). Arising out of fundamental changes in man's conception of nature, the promulgation of this view became the goal of the American wilderness movement. Its spokesmen, Audubon, James Fenimore Cooper, Thomas Cole, Francis Parkman, and John Muir, were responding to the destruction of America's forests and wild areas by an unplanned and sprawling civilization which, after 1850, was to be dominantly urban and industrial. The ideology of this early movement was organized around the goal of preserving, in their natural state, tracts of wilderness for the spiritual, aesthetic, tradition-evoking, and scientific values inherent in undisturbed nature. Formally embodied within voluntary organizations such as the Sierra Club, the ideology of preservationism—with its implications for restriction and cessation of industrial expansion—has gradually gathered support among the elite and the general public and is now a major element in the ideology of the ecology movement of the late 1960s and early 1970s. In some cases, however, preservationism has gone far beyond the wilderness-saving goals of its founders, and in its more radical forms urges the abolition of growth economics in particular and capitalism in general (Lee, 1970).

Finally, a position which attempts to harmonize development with natural land forms and environmental quality has recently found support in the planning professions and among some developers. To what extent this view is simply an evolutionary modification of traditional transformational thinking remains to be seen.

The tracing of these and similar themes through American intellectual and social history is, however, not the task of this paper. These positions are outlined merely to suggest that an analysis of the environmental values held by the public should be sensitive to the presence of the conflicting value structures which have historically divided Americans' thinking on environmental issues. They will continue as an important aspect of the debate over the means of maintaining the environmental and ecological integrity of American society in the next thirty years.

RISING CONCERN

During the past 100 years there have been surges and declines in the public's concern about America's natural environment. A previous high point of interest occurred during the Pinchot-Muir era (1898-1913) when events such as the conflict over Hetch Hetchy, the expansion of the national forest reserves, and the White House Governor's Conference attracted and were in part a function of public concern for the environment. Two world wars and the Depression deflected public interest to the point where McConnel (1964, p. 463) could say that the organized conservation movement was "small, divided and frequently uncertain," and attracted little public attention. However, a dramatic change in the posture of the public toward the environment and conservation has occurred in the years since McConnell's review.

AN AROUSED CITIZENRY

While it is a truism to remark that the processes whereby an individual or a public becomes aware of and responds to an "issue" are complicated in the extreme, it should nevertheless be recognized that behavioral research in psychology, sociology, and politics has only recently begun to explore and identify the components of these processes. We are not at a stage of certainty and our best studies are merely statistical. Why you or I become aware, aroused, and react to a particular issue is a joint function of, among other things, our education, our peer group's values, our exposure to various types of media, our occupations, our reference groups, our socioeconomic status, our belief systems and those of our parents, our political party identifications and the institutional structure of our society and its political processes—to name only a few of the most obvious variables.

The data available for this paper, however, will do little more than touch on a few of these mediating factors and furthermore require that we adopt a highly simplified model of the process of the development of public concern.

To assess the recent apparent change in this level of concern, I will briefly examine evidence of growth drawn from periodical circulation figures, consider some probable causes of the rates of growth of this concern, then move to a discussion and analysis of a national cross section sample survey dealing with the American public's present levels of concern for the environment, and finally give some brief consideration to the environmental values of the American public and the adequacy of data on the mass public's views toward the natural environment.

One index of public interest in an issue can be derived from studies of periodical content. While a measure of this type does not reflect an entire population's behavior with respect to issue concerns, it is a rough index of what the media-attentive segment of the mass public is consuming and it may be considered to have an interactive effect on public opinion. That is, it not only reflects the media-attentive public's interests but also serves to activate concern about an issue among this segment and very possibly other segments of the population.

Figure 1 is a graph depicting patterns of periodical content during the period 1953 to 1969. The graph is a compilation of the content of nonresource and resource periodicals which occasionally carry articles about environmental issues. The data are grouped by two-year blocks and are based on an examination of 133 periodicals in 1954, and 160 in 1969. The categories selected for environmental articles appear in the *Guide to Periodical Literature* and include "National Resources," "Smog," "Sewage," "Air Pollution," Water Pollution," "Oil Pollution," and "Noise Pollution."

As this figure clearly demonstrates, there has been a striking increase in the number of environmentally oriented articles appearing in American periodicals during the years examined (1953-1969). The most obvious characteristic of the curve is its nearly linear progression from the period 1959 to 1961 when 68 articles appeared, to the most current period, 1967 to 1969, when 226 articles were published, an increase of more than 330 percent. The overall increase for the 16-year period was slightly greater than 470 percent, from 48 to 226 articles.

An interesting question that emerges from these data is: What environmental values are of particular importance in this expansion of media attention to these problems? Unfortunately, the scope of our research does not permit an extensive content analysis of all of this literature, but the study by Russell (1970), from which these figures are drawn, reviews some of the themes of environmental concern expressed within three resource-oriented periodicals in the period 1953 to 1969.

Russell selected her three publications on the basis of ratings by professionals in the fields of conservation education and forestry. From an original list of nine, the publications selected for their "breadth of subject matter and degree of influence" included *Outdoor America*, *National Audubon*, and *American Forests*. A total of 371 articles randomly sampled from a time-stratified universe of all articles in the period 1953 to 1969 formed the basis for a thematic analysis of types and changes in environmental values, issues, and concerns, as reflected in these three publications during this period.

What is most interesting in this analysis is a review of the specific content of articles which advanced and declined in importance in these periodicals between the two comparison periods, 1954 to 1960 and 1963 to 1969. Most prominent among these shifts in emphasis was the emerging concern with problems of the urban environment. Twelve times as many articles on this problem occurred in the seven-year period 1963 to

1969 as occurred in the seven years from 1954 to 1960. Typically, urban environmental problems involve specific issues such as open space, smog, and other forms of air pollution, population growth and density, planning, and the like. There was also a substantial (65 percent) increase in concern with outdoor recreation, particularly centered on the need for more outdoor recreation facilities. Another area with a very large (1:4) increase in media attention was environmental problems created by industrialization. Other issues which attracted more attention in the recent period included legislation (5:8), conservation education (5:8), and threatened animal species. (The ratios refer to rates of appearance by type of article between the two time periods examined. The first number refers to the early period, the latter to the years 1963-1969.)

Declining in importance in the same time frames were natural history (2:1), rural environmental problems (5:4), research (7:5), general news (7:5), and biographical-personal tribute types of articles, according to Russell's work.

The general trend of these data is obvious. These media reflect and are anticipating the environmental problems introduced into the society through the joint effects of large-scale urbanization, population growth, and industrialization. They are transmitting to their readers information and opinion about both general and specific instances of these problems. As we shall see in our survey analyses, many of these problems are now of direct concern to the public generally, not merely to the small segment reached by these particular periodicals.

Two other types of analysis of these articles were also employed by Russell—thematic analysis and a comparative study of authors between the two time clusters. The articles' themes suggested a growing concern with the total environment; that is, they reflected more ecosystem awareness, and in the latter period far more frequently advocated federal intervention to solve environmental

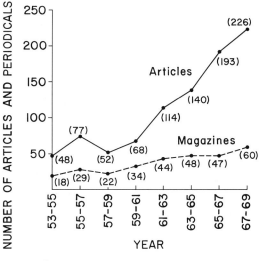

FIGURE 1
Growth rates (in frequency) of articles concerning environmental issues in selected periodicals and number of periodicals containing environmental articles from 1953 to 1969 in the United States.

problems. As I noted, the later period also produced more emphasis on conservation education, and this theme was manifested as a concern for the extension of this mode of education—both in quality and in quantity—to a greater proportion of the American public. Finally, Russell observed that the professional and occupational roles of contributors to these three journals had shifted markedly. In the period 1954 to 1960 less than 3 percent of the identified authors were from business, government, or education. By the end of 1969, these three categories of authorship accounted for almost 25 percent of the articles in which it was possible to identify authorship. This finding is significant because it suggests not only that environmental problems are of growing concern to the public at large, but also that there is a growing dispersion of environmental awareness and concern among professionals outside of the resource and environmental sciences.

In addition to this growth in media attention, some limited time-series survey data on two specific environmental problems—air pollution and water pollution—show that public concern over these two environmental quality issues is rising sharply. In 1965, 13 percent of the public indicated that they felt the water pollution problem was "very serious." By 1968, this percentage had increased to 27 percent, and by 1970 the figure rose to 30 percent (Gallup, 1970). The same general trend over concern with air pollution is evident; 10 percent classifying it as a "very serious" problem in 1965, and 25 percent giving the same response only three years later (Davies, 1970). By 1970 (February), the percentage of the public giving the same response had risen to 43 percent (Gallup, 1970).

Before turning to a discussion of factors which may be responsible for this increasing attention to environmental problems, we shall consider briefly another index of public concern about the environment—membership growth rates in conservation and environmental preservation organizations. Figure 2 depicts the growth rates of four of these groups, two predominantly western in their membership bases and two predominantly eastern. As this figure shows, growth in membership in these organizations has been spectacular. In the past twenty years, the Sierra Club went from a small, San Francisco Bay Area based organization of less than 8,000 people, to a national organization of more than 140,000 members as of this writing. (Figure 2 shows the membership for 1969.) Other groups have done almost as well, and the bulk of their growth has come in the five-year period 1965 to 1969. The obvious point, and the reason for presenting these data here, is that they are an additional indicator of public concern, and show that the organized environmental "issue public" is rapidly gaining strength in the United States today.

In the fall of 1968, the Survey Research Center at the University of Michigan conducted a national cross section sample survey as part of its series of studies of Americans' political and economic behavior. Respondents were asked to indicate what they be-

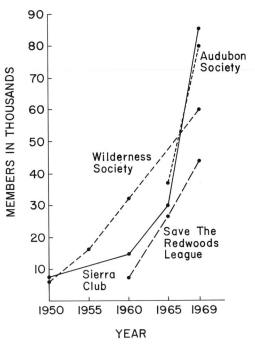

FIGURE 2
Membership of four conservation organizations from 1950 to 1969. The Sierra Club, Wilderness Society, Audubon Society, and Save the Redwoods League (in absolute numbers of members).

lieved to be the three most important problems facing the United States today. General concern with the environment ranked far below other problems in the public's mind at that time. In fact, only 25 or more than 1,500 respondents gave answers which could be interpreted as expressive of environmental concern. Issues such as the war in Vietnam, race relations, and student unrest were at that time far more salient for the public than the problems of the environment. Less than a year later the Gallup survey mentioned earlier found some 51 percent of the adult public expressing "deep concern" over the problems of destruction of the natural environment. It is unfortunate that we cannot directly compare these two surveys. Presenting an individual with an open-ended question is a far better method of tapping his concern than asking him how concerned he is about x or y when x or y have been selected by the researcher as problems he thinks ought to concern a respondent. Nevertheless, this finding in conjunction with the Gallup data from a year later suggests that there was a broad shift in primary issue concerns among the public from 1968 to 1969. A survey conducted for the President's Commission on Obscenity and Pornography by Abelson (1970) also showed that this shift evidently had occurred. Employing an open-ended major problems question very similar to that used by the Survey Research Center, Abelson found that "pollution and misuse of resources" was mentioned by 19 percent of the respondents as a major problem "facing the country today." It was exceeded in concern by the war (54 percent), race (36 percent), the national economy (32 percent), youth rebellion (23 percent), breakdown of law and order (20 percent), and drugs (20 percent). Due to sampling error inherent in such surveys it is probably appropriate to treat the latter three problem areas as equivalent in concern to the public's views on pollution and misuse of resources. An additional 4 percent of this sample mentioned overpopulation as a major problem.

These data indicate a rise in primary public concern over problems of the environment from a point where less than 2 percent of the population expressed concern, to a point where at least 23 percent and probably more of the public now volunteers the environmental or population control issues as major problems facing the country—an increase by a factor of 11 since 1968.

Let us digress briefly from the main discussion and consider the relationship of these three types of indicators of change to the more general questions of diffusion or transmission of concern throughout the public.

The three elements of this model are displayed in Figure 3. The first curve (A) represents the percentage of change between the indicated time periods and the number of environmental articles appearing in the sample of American periodicals studied by Russell from the period 1953 to 1969. For

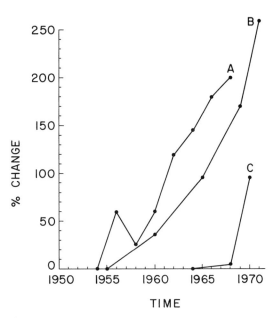

FIGURE 3
Percentage change in three indicators of environmental awareness: media, voluntary associations and public opinion.

example, between 1966 and 1968 the publications in her sample showed a 20 percent increase in the number of environmentally oriented articles they printed. I take these data as an (admittedly rough and generalized) indicator of the rate of change (increase) in media attention to the environment in the United States for the period covered.

The second curve (B) simply shows the rate (computed as above) of change in the membership of the Sierra Club for approximately the same time period. Similar data from any of the national environment-conservation groups would serve as well since all of them show almost precisely the same rate of change (growth) as the Sierra Club (see Figure 2).

The final curve (C) is unfortunately based on only the three national sample surveys just discussed and shows the rate of change in the public's identification of environmental problems as the primary social problem facing the country. The rates are computed from a base year for A and B but, in fact, appear to be computed from a true zero point in the case of curve C.

Obviously, the slopes of the curves are very much alike (the correlation using interpolated data points of A with B, for example, is 0.94). The two most interesting questions raised by these data concern (1) the time lags between them, and (2) the magnitude of the changes occurring between them over time. Making the assumption (most likely partly invalid)[1] that the ordering of the three curves implies an addative causal sequence, with change in A yielding change in B and A + B = C, we can at least speculate about the role that the media and voluntary organizations actually play in the creation of a major social and political issue[2] among the mass public. If these data are representative, the time lag between A, B, and C in terms of the point when the three curves exhibit approximately the same slope is roughly nine years. Second, the extremely close relationship between media attention (A) and growth in voluntary organizations (B) affirms, as I argue below and as we expect from other social research, that the media attentive segment of the public is far more likely to translate its interest in an issue to action. These data suggest that the written media had no substantial effect at the *mass* level for at least ten years and possibly fifteen years after publication although, of course, when the issue actually becomes salient it is coupled with a flood of additional media attention. Further and considerably more comprehensive research employing content analysis and other measures of media behavior, voluntary association activity, and surveys of public opinion, to name only three important variable complexes, would expand

our knowledge of the responsiveness of this political and social system to new information. In the case of environmental issues many biologists believe that this lag time may be a critical factor in the survival of life itself.

If public concern for the environment has increased, it is appropriate to review two possible causes of this rising level of public attention to environmental problems. In addition to the effect of the media and the activities of voluntary associations in increasing the public's level of attention to the environment, the existence of two distinct trends in the society may also have had an impact. The first of these trends is the apparent increase in personal exposure to the natural environment. The second is the deterioration of many aspects of the natural, rural (but especially the urban) environment.

TABLE 1
Visits to national and state parks
1950–1968, all areas (in thousands)

	National parks	State parks
1950	33,253	114,291
1955	56,573	183,188
1960	79,229	259,001
1965	121,312	*
1967	139,676	291,063
1968	150,836	*

Source: *Statistical Abstract*, 1969.
*Not supplied

Table 1 displays total visit rates for national and state parks for the period 1950 to 1968. In the case of state parks, the rate of visitation in the eighteen-year period shown in the table increased almost 350 percent. The national parks had an even greater visit increase from 33.2 million visits in 1950 to 150.8 million in 1968, or a gain of more than 450 percent. At the same time, land areas and the number of facilities in these areas has not expanded at all like the rate of use. National park land areas increased by almost

---

[1]This is so because of the certain effects of variables not measured but influencing C (for example, television), and because of interactive effects between A, B, and C.

[2]As the earlier discussion of the survey data pointed out, only 19 percent of the public gave environmental problems major priority in the 1971 survey by Abelson, but this ranks the problem in the top six.

6 million acres—from 22.9 million acres to 29.1 million acres, or almost 30 percent. State park areas had more substantial increases— from 4.7 million acres to 7.4 million acres in 1967, or about 75 percent. There was also a substantial increase in the absolute number of state park facilities in the same period, from 1,725 in 1950 to 3,202 in 1967.

These events may have had two general effects on the public. First, those persons coming for the first time to the parks and forests, encountering in many instances a crowded and semi-urbanized environment, may have contrasted the potential beauty of these areas with the localized squalor, and concluded that America was running out of open space and parkland and that what was left was overcrowded.

Furthermore, these rates of visitation, in conjunction with increases in the general mobility of the population, have provided an opportunity to contrast one environment with another directly. As in all such cases, judgments—favorable and unfavorable—are more readily made and the increasing opportunity for environmental contrast implied by these data may well have resulted in both increased environmental awareness and increased concern.

Secondly, America's physical environment is changing—many feel for the worse. One simple indicator of this change is the density of the population, which rose from 44.2 persons per square mile in 1940 to 60.1 in 1960 to an estimated 70 per square mile in 1970. Other indicators, such as increasing rates of urbanization, air pollution (which is now evidently stabilized or declining), water pollution, increasing automobile density and traffic volume, growing urban crime, electrical failures and higher noise levels, are but a few of the objective environmental problems which may have stimulated public concern. These factors and changes in the society are of grave concern to conservationists, preservationists, and ecologists. The problems, if not their basic sources, are also of substantial concern to the American public.

WHO IS CONCERNED ABOUT THE ENVIRONMENT?

In January 1969, the Gallup Organization asked a national cross section sample of 1,503 American adults a series of questions concerning their opinions about problems of the natural environment. This survey, sponsored by the National Wildlife Federation, was the first and, as far as I know, the only national survey, to assess public concern for a comprehensive set of environmental problems (Gallup, 1969). The survey began with the following question:

> You may have heard or read claims that our natural surroundings are being spoiled by air pollution, water pollution, soil erosion, destruction of wildlife and so forth. How concerned are you about this—deeply concerned, somewhat concerned, or not very concerned?

The distribution of responses to this question stratified over six demographic variables is reported in Table 2.

Surprisingly, given the high rate of participation by youth in such events as Earth Day, there is little substantial difference in level of concern by age, with the exception of a 9 percentage point difference between the 21-34 age group and the over-50 age group in the proportion of these groups that are "not very concerned" about the problems raised in the question. The younger group has a smaller proportion of unconcerned members than the older group.

However, data from a nation-wide survey conducted by *Seventeen* magazine (1971) a year later suggest that the problems of the environment are, in general, of great concern to this age group. For example, 96 percent of this sample stated they were in favor of "stricter laws to prevent further pollution by industry," and 84 percent rejected the assertion that "industry for the most part is doing everything it can to control pollution and clean up the environment." Finally, 95 percent stated they believed that the government was spending too little money

TABLE 2
Level of environmental concern (Gallup 1969).

	Deeply Concerned %	Somewhat Concerned %	Not Very Concerned %	No Opinion %	Total %	Number of Interviews
National results	51	35	12	2	100	1,503
By Sex						
Men	56	31	10	3	100	744
Women	46	38	14	2	100	759
By Age						
21–34 years	51	41	7	1	100	403
35–49 years	50	38	10	2	100	476
50 years +	52	28	16	4	100	605
Undesignated: 19						
By Education						
College	62	32	6	*	100	395
High school	52	37	10	1	100	748
Grade school	39	34	20	7	100	352
Undesignated: 8						
By Annual Family Income						
$10,000 and over	58	34	8	0	100	449
$7,000–$9,999	53	38	8	1	100	336
$5,000–$6,999	55	35	8	2	100	237
Under $5,000	41	34	20	5	100	463
Undesignated: 18						
By Size of Community						
1,000,000 +	51	36	8	5	100	277
250,000–999,999	52	35	11	2	100	296
50,000–249,000	55	35	9	1	100	235
2,500–49,999	52	31	16	1	100	233
Under 2,500	46	37	14	3	100	462
By Region of Country						
East	46	38	12	4	100	425
Midwest	56	34	9	1	100	400
South	44	36	16	4	100	428
West	59	31	10	*	100	250

*Less than half of one percent

for pollution control. The discrepancy between the Gallup and the *Seventeen* data are probably the result of time differences between data collection, question wording and, perhaps, the representativeness of the *Seventeen* sample.

In addition, the April 19, 1971 *Water Newsletter* (Gillies, 1971), reports, "Dirty water and air were rated the nation's most important problem by junior and senior high school students polled by *Scholastic* magazine. The quiz went to 57,000 students who were asked to select the three most important issues facing the nation: 57 percent cited

pollution; the Vietnam war and drug abuse rated 51 percent each; next in order were crime, inflation, race relations, hunger and poverty, and communism.

Returning to the Gallup data, education and family income, as we would expect, both show an effect on the level of expressed concern. College educated respondents were more likely to be concerned than any other group; 62 percent of them saying that they were "deeply concerned" and only 6 percent expressing little concern. The same general effect is observed in the data on the family income, but it is by no means as strong a predictor of environmental concern as education, with only the lowest income group differing importantly from the other three in the proportion of its members at the highest level of concern.

In general, the higher the socioeconomic status of the respondent, the more likely he is to express high concern and, conversely, the lower his socioeconomic status, the more likely he is to be unconcerned about these matters. This finding confirms our common sense expectations and findings from previous social research. There is, however, one important implication that may be drawn: unlike many contemporary social issues such as race, welfare and poverty and, to some extent, the continuing war in Vietnam, the environmentally concerned segment of the society is relatively powerful in terms of its access to the economic and political resources of our society. Thus, if this segment's disproportionate level of concern continues to increase, there is a greater probability of its values and preferences being reflected in political decisions, which in turn will affect the environment.

The two other variables in Table 2 are also of interest. Environmental concern is substantially greater in urban areas, and it is markedly greater in the western United States. This is a confusing result because if the concern is generated by urbanization (as it appears in part to be), we ought to find high levels of concern in areas of high urbanization, particularly the East. Further tabulations will hopefully clarify this confusion.

SPECIFIC ENVIRONMENTAL CONCERNS OF THE PUBLIC

The respondents were presented with a list of seven environmental problems and asked to indicate which one of them they felt was most important. Table 3 presents the results of this question for the total sample.

TABLE 3
Public concern for specific environmental problems (Gallup, 1969).

Air pollution	36%
Water pollution	32
Pesticides (chemicals used to kill insects)	7
Preservation of open green spaces	6
Wildlife preservation (birds and mammals)	5
Soil erosion	4
Don't know	10
Total	100%

Clearly two problems—air and water pollution—were of principal concern to the public at the time of this survey. Each of these was at least four times as likely to be named as any of the remaining four problem areas. However, it should be stressed that simply because pesticides, open space, wildlife preservation, and soil erosion did not receive as much attention as air and water pollution, that they are therefore unimportant to the public. This question is merely a measure of primary concern and it is possible that many respondents who are most sensitive to water pollution may be nearly as disturbed by air pollution, erosion, and the preservation of open space.

Some differences in concern emerge when responses to this question are stratified over various demographic variables. Women are more likely to be concerned with air pollution and its associated effects than are men and this may be the result of their being differentially affected by it. For example, in Los Angeles, during "smog alerts," young children are often kept inside and this may be an added burden to their mothers. In Detroit, Swan (1970) has studied a residential area in which 22 *tons* per square mile of particulate matter settle to the ground *each month*, or more than 250 tons of such material each year. The problem such a vast quantity of particulate matter causes for the average urban housewife may easily be imagined.

There is also a substantial effect of age on the type of environmental concern expressed by this sample. Young people are more concerned about air pollution than are older persons, and are 10 percentage points higher in concern over air than water pollution. Older people, on the other hand, are four times as likely as the younger group to express primary concern over pesticides. Among the older group (over 50) concern for air and water pollution as the primary environmental problem is equal (31 percent). These data are presented in Table 4.

Controls for educational level and income show few important differences other than the generally higher level of concern expressed among persons with more money and education. However, it is somewhat surprising that the college-educated segment of the society fails often to locate its concerns in areas of pollution such as pesticides, erosion, and open space preservation? These are problems for which technological and political solutions (such as those available for air and water pollution) are by no means well developed, and which will have a greater long-term effect on the biosphere than the more readily solved problems of air and water pollution. It is also interesting that only 7 percent of the group primarily concerned with pesticides as the major environmental problem thought we should stop using pesticides, while 26 percent felt that "new and improved" pesticides were the answer. Ecosystem awareness seems somewhat deficient in both the best-educated subset of our sample and among those most concerned about pesticide pollution. The tabulations displaying the results of these breakdowns appear in Table 5.

Table 6 presents the responses to specific environmental concerns of the sample stratified by size of community of residence. There is a generally linear increase in concern for air pollution as the size of the respondent's community of residence increases. Concern in metropolitan areas of 1,000,000 or more persons is more than twice as great as it is in areas of less than 2,500 persons. The opposite is true of water pollution, but the curve is not linear. Persons in areas of less than 1,000,000 population are, on the average, about 11 percentage points above those in the largest areas in their level of concern over water pollution. These findings are typical of what we expect from other surveys of air pollution. As exposure to air pollution increases (as it does in the U.S. with growing urbanization), opposition to it increases. A number of local studies by de .

TABLE 4
Importance of specific environmental problems by sex and age (Gallup 1969).

Problem	Men %	Women %	21–34 years %	35–49 years %	50 years and older %
Air pollution	33	40	42	39	31
Water pollution	36	27	32	32	31
Pesticides	6	8	3	6	11
Preservation of open green spaces	4	7	7	7	4
Wildlife preservation	6	3	6	4	5
Soil erosion	6	3	2	3	6
Don't know	9	11	8	9	12
Total	100	100	100	100	100
Number of interviews	744	759	403	476	605

Groot and Samuels (1962), Smith et al. (1964), and Medalia and Finkner (1965) all support this basic and obvious finding. It seems appropriate to suggest that rural residents' greater relative concern with water pollution is found both in their relative freedom from air pollution and in their greater exposure to polluted rivers, lakes, and streams.

Finally, there are some distinct regional differences in the distribution of Americans' concern about their environment (Table 7).

The problem we encountered in our discussion of the public's basic level of concern, and the apparent discrepancy between concern and community size, seems clearer. Concern over air pollution is strongest in the two areas of the country with especially serious problems of this type (excepting Chicago which has very high rates of all types of air pollution)—the West (essentially, the Los Angeles and San Francisco Bay Area Standard Metropolitan Statistical Areas), and the East (Boston, New York, Philadelphia and

TABLE 5
Importance of specific environmental problems by family income and education (Gallup 1969).

Problem	By Education			By Annual Family Income			
	College	High School	Grade School	$10,000 and over	$7,000-$9,999	$5,000-$6,999	Under $5,000
	%	%	%	%	%	%	%
Air pollution	40	39	29	42	42	36	28
Water pollution	34	31	31	32	32	33	30
Pesticides	5	8	7	6	7	6	8
Preservation of open green spaces	8	5	4	9	5	5	3
Wildlife preservation	4	5	7	3	5	7	7
Soil erosion	3	4	5	3	1	5	7
Don't know	6	8	17	5	8	8	17
Total	100	100	100	100	100	100	100
Number of interviews	395	748	352	449	336	237	463

TABLE 6
Importance of specific environmental problems by size of community (Gallup 1969).

	1,000,000 and over	250,000-999,999	50,000-249,000	2,500-49,999	Under 2,500
	%	%	%	%	%
Air pollution	55	41	41	29	23
Water pollution	22	33	34	34	34
Pesticides	6	5	5	8	10
Preservation of open green spaces	6	5	5	8	6
Wildlife preservation	1	3	3	6	10
Soil erosion	2	4	4	4	5
Don't know	8	9	10	11	12
Total	100	100	100	100	100
Number of interviews	277	296	235	233	462

TABLE 7
Importance of specific environmental problems by region of
country (Gallup, 1969).

	East %	Midwest %	South %	West %
Air pollution	43	34	26	47
Water pollution	31	38	30	24
Pesticides	5	6	10	6
Preservation of open green spaces	6	5	6	6
Wildlife preservation	3	5	7	6
Soil erosion	2	4	6	5
Don't know	10	8	15	6
Total	100	100	100	100
Number of interviews	425	400	428	250

Washington, D.C. SMSA). But westerners are somewhat less concerned than others about water pollution, most likely because they have not yet been exposed to this problem on a scale comparable to that in other regions of the country.

In the next section we will move to a discussion of what solutions—technological or political—the public believes to be appropriate to solve two of the six problem areas we have discussed above.

SOLUTIONS FAVORED BY THE AMERICAN PUBLIC TO TWO MAJOR ENVIRONMENTAL PROBLEMS

After each respondent indicated what environmental problem he felt was most pressing he was asked, in open-ended format, "In your opinion what can be done to correct this problem?" He could give as many solutions as he wished. Tables 8 and 9

TABLE 8
Solutions favored to air pollution by persons designating air
pollution as the most important environmental problem
(Gallup, 1969).

	Percent
1. Find way to controll auto exhaust	24
2. Control of chemical and industrial wastes	17
3. Provide filters, smog control devices	16
4. Enforce present laws or pass new legislation	10
5. Careful study, research	7
6. Do away with gasoline engine	6
7. Control burning of rubbish or garbage	3
8. Move industry to suburbs	2
9. Educate the public	1
10. Other answers	3
Don't know	31
Total (exceeds 100% due to multiple responses)	120
Number of interviews	538

TABLE 9

Solutions favored to water pollution by persons designating water pollution as the most important environmental problem (Gallup, 1969).

	Percent
1. Stop industrial pollution	26
2. Enforce present laws, pass new legislation	23
3. Keep sewage out of water	12
4. Individuals should be more careful	8
5. Careful study, research	5
6. Sewage conversion plants	5
7. Educate the public	3
8. Chemically purify the water	3
9. Use filters	2
10. Other answers	2
Don't know	27
Total (exceeds 100% due to multiple responses)	116
Number of interviews	475

present the results of this inquiry for air pollution and water pollution, the only two problems with a sufficiently large response to make analysis appropriate.

These responses are worth brief examination because they point to the relative importance of technological, political, and value change solutions in the public's thinking and suggest which kinds of solutions may or may not be well received.

In the case of air pollution, industrial emissions and their control rank first in importance to the public with a total of 35 percent of the subset of the sample giving responses (in the three separate categories 2, 3, and 8) which indicated a focus on industry. Auto exhaust emission control was next with 30 percent (categories 1 and 6) of this group favoring this as the most efficacious means of eliminating air pollution. Only 10 percent of the responses focused on legislation directly although the solutions posed to this problem by the public appear to require legal sanction before they could be implemented.

Water pollution is seen as much more of an industrial problem than is air pollution, and legislation and legal solutions are also more attractive to the public most concerned

with this particular problem. Only 17 percent (categories 3 and 6) of this group recognized the need to keep sewage out of the water, a major source of water pollution, which is largely the result of inadequate and overloaded sewage treatment systems owned by municipalities.

One result that did *not* appear in response to either of these queries was particularly significant. Very few or none of the respondents suggested reducing air pollution by introducing economies of scale such as mass transit or by reducing industrial production. In the case of water pollution, few if any of the respondents suggested that population control or limitation of industrial output might be partial solutions to this problem. Technical and legal solutions are seen as sufficient to these difficulties. In short, there is little indication in these free responses that the American public is seriously entertaining changes in its expansionist, growth-oriented value system—a topic to which we will turn our attention in the concluding section of this chapter.

Two other areas of inquiry in this survey provide us with some additional information about the public's attitudes and values with respect to the environment. The first of these concerns setting aside more public land for conservation purposes. The question was:

Are you in favor of setting aside more public land for conservation purposes such as national parks, wildlife refuges, bird sanctuaries, and so forth, or not?

Table 10 presents the responses to this question stratified by a series of demographic variables. Essentially, the patterns which we observed in our previous discussion of the public's general concern for the environment apply here as well. A desire to set aside land for conservation purposes is positively associated with education and income, and

in this case there is a relatively strong effect of age—the younger group substantially (14 percentage points) higher in support of land preservation than the older group. There is no systematic increase in a desire for land reserve as size of community increases—only a rather sharp dropoff in support in areas of less than 2,500 residents. This result is what we might expect given the probable availability of open space lands in these rural or quasi-rural communities. Regional differences reflect similar differences, that is, the South, with the greatest number of small towns, is less likely to produce residents favoring land reserve than

TABLE 10
Attitude Toward Reserving Public Lands For Conservation Purposes
(Gallup, 1969).

	Yes %	No %	Don't know %	Total %	Number of Interviews
National Results	75	19	6	100	1,503
By Sex					
Men	76	19	5	100	744
Women	74	19	7	100	759
By Age					
21–34 years	83	13	4	100	403
35–49 years	76	18	6	100	476
50 years and older	69	24	7	100	605
Undesignated: 19%					
By Education					
College	82	15	3	100	395
High School	78	18	4	100	748
Grade School	64	26	10	100	352
Undesignated: 8%					
By Annual Family Income					
$10,000 and over	81	16	3	100	449
$7,000–$9,999	81	15	4	100	336
$5,000–$6,999	75	18	7	100	237
Under $5,000	66	25	9	100	463
Undesignated: 18%					
By Size of Community					
1,000,000 and over	79	15	6	100	277
250,000–999,999	78	17	5	100	296
50,000–249,999	80	16	4	100	235
2,500–49,999	78	19	3	100	233
Under 2,500	66	25	9	100	462
By Region of Country					
East	82	12	6	100	425
Midwest	76	20	4	100	400
South	68	24	8	100	428
West	75	21	4	100	250

the East with the greatest percentage of large metropolitan areas.

One fact that should be stressed, however, is the generally strong support that exists for the issue raised in this question. The younger segment of the population is, in particular, anxious to reserve public lands for the purposes specified in the question. With three-fourths of the public in favor of such measures and only one-fifth of the public opposed, there is a near consensus on this issue—one which might well be exploited by state and federal legislators in their current search for ecologically sound legislation with broad public appeal.

The final issue, and one with great potential impact on the American environment, is population control. The question asked by Gallup is not a particularly good one because it is diffuse and unspecific in time horizon but, on the other hand, this diffuseness may be an advantage in tapping the general orientation of the public to this matter. The results are not, in the face of current population projections, very encouraging. Respondents were asked.

> It has been said that it will, at some time, be necessary to limit the human population (number of people) if our present living standards are to be maintained. Do you think this will be necessary or not?

The results of this question are presented in Table 11, stratified by the same set of demographic factors employed in the previous analyses.

Support for population limitation, like other measures of environmental preservation, comes from the young, well-educated, and relatively high-income segment of the population. In addition there is a substantial increase in support as the size of a respondent's community increases, but even in the areas of greatest population density in the United States (places of more than 1,000,000 persons) the proportion of respondents favoring such limitation is only 50 percent.

Education and age appear to have the greatest effects, and in this respect these data

argue for increasing support for population limitation among those in the society with the most potential for reproduction. Rates of acquisition of higher education are, of course, increasing. In 1947, for example, only 5.4 percent of the population over 25 years of age completed four years or more of college; by 1967 the percentage had increased to 14.6, a three-fold increase in twenty years. In addition, the median age distribution of the population is declining in the U.S., from 30.7 years in 1950 to 28.8 years in 1967 (Statistical Abstract, 1969).

A number of other national surveys have also focused on factors likely to influence population size and growth. Judith Blake (1967), for example, has focused her attention on the causes of the recent decline in the U.S. crude birth rate. Her discussion (of fifteen national surveys) suggests that at the aggregate level there was essentially no change in the desired family size between 1963 and 1966. However, she found that one of the trends revealed in the Gallup data reviewed here was also present in her data— that younger men and women are very slightly more likely to have lower family size goals than older persons. This effect was particularly strong among Catholics, where the mean ideal family size of females declined from 4.3 in 1961 (based on an age range of 14 to 23) to 3.7 in 1966 (based on an age range of 21 or older). Her data are substantially older than the ones we have been discussing and, unfortunately, she does not report tabulations of her surveys by educational and income levels. Nevertheless, if we assume that one substantial behavioral response to environmental problems is the voluntary natural reduction of population growth, there are indications in both survey data and vital statistics that suggest that inhibiting growth mechanisms are now forming in the American public. These tendencies now appear to be definite trends as shown by fertility data from the 1970 census. Unfortunately, due to the absolute size and absolute rate of increase of the population at this time, far more immediate and large-

TABLE 11
Attitude Toward Limitation of the Population (Gallup, 1969)

	Necessary %	Not Necessary %	Don't Know %	Total %	Number of Interviews
National Results	44	43	13	100	1,503
By Sex					
Men	47	42	11	100	744
Women	41	45	14	100	759
By Age					
21–34 years	55	37	8	100	403
35–49 years	44	43	13	100	476
50 years and older	36	48	16	100	605
Undesignated: 19%					
By Education					
College	60	34	6	100	395
High School	45	44	11	100	748
Grade School	29	51	20	100	352
Undesignated: 8%					
By Annual Family Income					
$10,000 and over	53	38	9	100	449
$7,000–$9,999	52	39	9	100	336
$5,000–$6,999	41	45	14	100	237
Under $5,000	32	50	18	100	463
Undesignated: 18%					
By Size of Community					
1,000,000 and over	50	36	14	100	277
250,000–999,999	48	40	12	100	296
50,000–249,000	43	46	11	100	235
2,500–49,999	42	47	11	100	233
Under 2,500	38	47	15	100	462
By Region of Country					
East	45	39	16	100	425
Midwest	44	47	6	100	400
South	36	47	17	100	428
West	54	39	7	100	250

scale means of population control must be established and implemented in the United States if population control is to become a reality.

BEHAVIORAL CORRELATES OF ENVIRONMENTAL CONCERN: TAXATION

A final question from the survey concerns the public's willingness to pay taxes to improve its natural surroundings. While this is a hypothetical situation posed to the respondents in the sample, data on water bond issue voting patterns (League of Women Voters, 1966) suggests that the public is, in fact, often willing to pay for increased environmental quality and this finding parallels the result that emerges from the survey, and is reported in Table 12.

A very large majority (73 percent) of the population appears willing to pay additional sums in taxes each year for the specific purpose of "improv[ing] our natural surroundings." Only 9 percent rejected the idea totally, and 18 percent said they were undecided.

The general effects originating from the demographic variables we have examined thus far are also present in this measure.

TABLE 12
Distribution of responses to the following question: How much would you be willing to pay each year in additional taxes earmarked to improve our natural surroundings—a small amount as $10.00 or less, a moderate amount such as $50.00, or a large amount such as $100.00 or more? (Gallup, 1969).

	Small amount %	Moderate amount %	Large amount %	None %	Don't know %	Total %	Number of interviews
National Results	51	18	4	9	18	100	1,503
By Sex							
Men	49	21	6	9	15	100	744
Women	53	16	2	9	20	100	759
By Age							
21–34 years	53	25	5	5	12	100	403
35–49 years	52	20	3	8	17	100	476
50 years and older	49	13	4	12	22	100	605
Undesignated: 19							
By Education							
College	45	30	12	5	8	100	395
High School	52	20	2	9	8	100	748
Grade School	49	6	1	12	27	100	352
Undesignated: 8							
By Annual Family Income							
$10,000 and over	45	28	10	6	11	100	449
$7,000–$9,999	52	20	3	10	15	100	336
$5,000–$6,999	59	15	2	8	16	100	237
Under $5,000	52	10	1	11	26	100	463
Undesignated: 18							
By Size of Community							
1,000,000 and over	52	19	5	4	20	100	277
250,000–999,999	43	28	6	8	15	100	296
50,000–249,999	53	16	2	12	17	100	235
2,500–49,999	49	18	4	12	17	100	233
Under 2,500	56	13	2	9	20	100	462
By Region of Country							
East	49	17	6	9	19	100	425
Midwest	56	19	3	11	11	100	400
South	51	15	3	6	25	100	428
West	47	24	3	9	17	100	250

There is, however, a very strong effect of income on this variable with a positive relationship between ability to pay and willingness to pay for this particular public good. Persons with incomes of $10,000 or more are ten times as likely as those with $5,000 or less income to express a willingness to pay "a large amount such as $100.00 or more" for environmental improvement. They are almost three times as willing to pay "a moderate amount such as $50.00" than the lower income group. Again, however, we see the relatively strong effect of education, with a college education being the strongest predictor of the willingness to pay a relatively large amount in additional taxes.

Earlier we saw that 86 percent of the population (Table 1) expressed strong or some concern over the environment. It is quite clear that there is a positive association between concern and willingness to pay for improvement, but that the relationship is by no means perfect. While 51 percent of the public expressed strong concern about environmental problems only 4 percent are willing to pay $100 or more in taxes, and only 18 percent are willing to pay $50 to improve the environment. Thus, while

aroused and willing to increase its taxes somewhat, the public has clearly not reached the
point where it is willing to make substantial
financial sacrifices in order to insure improvement of the natural environment. Nevertheless, if this expressed willingness were translated into tax dollars, approximately two
billion dollars could be provided to increase
the government's efforts at protecting and
improving the environment.

In part, the public's views in this matter
may be influenced by its evident expectations that enforcement and anti-pollution
laws against industrial polluters, and the
prospect of technological solutions (see
Tables 8 and 9) to many (in particular, air
and water pollution) environmental problems may not necessitate substantial tax
increases.

Finally, in March 1971, the Gallup organization conducted another national survey
that suggests that concern about the environment was at that time still prominent among
the public, and distributed in much the same
way that we have reported here. Of more
interest, however, are data from this survey
concerning the personal sacrifices and economic sanctions against polluters that the
public appears willing to accept in order to
improve the quality of their environment.
With respect to the level of concern, for
example, 60 percent of the public in 1971
agreed that "Americans are using up too
much of our country's natural resources, and
that *now is the time* to cut back on buying
things and conserve our resources for future
generations." Furthermore, 70 percent of the
public saw clean air and pure water as becoming "relatively more scarce" in the next ten
years or so. At the same time, three quarters
(75 percent) of the population agreed that
they would do "without some modern conveniences, meaning such things as a dish-
washer or a large automobile . . . ." rather
than put up with "severe pollution." What
seems rather striking is the fact that only
22 percent of the adult population said they
would put up with the pollution of a local
plant which could not be altered to stop

polluting the environment, while 45 percent
said they were for closing it down even if
"many of [their] neighbors worked in that
plant." These results, collected fourteen
months after the survey analyzed above, suggest that environmental issues are still
prominent public concerns and that the
public appears willing to make some personal
sacrifices to improve the environment.

ENVIRONMENTAL VALUES,
AND A COMMENT ON THE
ADEQUACY OF DATA
AVAILABLE TO
DECISION-MAKERS

From this limited analysis, some information
about the environmental values of Americans
can be drawn.

First of all, Americans *are* concerned about
the quality of their environment. This fact
is underlined by the rapid rate of growth
of environment and conservation organizations, accompanied by the willingness to
increase tax loads that we have seen expressed
in the survey data. Americans want their environmental problems solved, and they support technological, legal, and financial
solutions to these problems.

Foremost among the problems of concern
to the public is air pollution, followed
closely by water pollution.

The public tends to respond most strongly
to those specific environmental problems
which affect it most directly. Regional location and city size have a substantial effect
on the distribution of opinion about matters
such as open space, air and water pollution,
and the acquisition of land for purposes of
conservation.

There is very broad public support for
increasing the amount of public land devoted
to conservation in the form of national parks,
wildlife refuges, and the like.

Substantial minorities of the population
are seriously concerned about the preservation of open space, the use of pesticides,
wildlife preservation, and soil erosion.

A near majority of the population sees eventual control of population growth as a necessity.

In general, the more affluent, better educated, and younger segment of the population is the most concerned about problems of the environment—although this group by no means has a monopoly on concern.

On the other hand, the data we have examined tell us very little about possible value and attitude changes in the general orientations to the environment with which we began our discussion—transformationalism and preservationism. Nor do they indicate directly the degree to which the public believes that environmental preservation can be realized in a society with unchecked population and industrial growth. They tell us nothing about the linkage of political beliefs with attitudes toward the environment and, because the analysis was necessarily conducted with a small number of variables from tables supplied to the author, I have been unable to discern anything but gross surface relationships between the variables examined.

ACKNOWLEDGMENTS

I would like to thank Thomas Kimball, Director of the National Wildlife Federation, for his permission to analyze the Gallup survey data presented herein.

References

Blake, Judith. 1967. Family size in the 1960's—a baffling fad? *Eugenics Quarterly 14*, 1, 60–74.

Campbell, Angus, Converse, P. E., Miller, W. E., Stokes, D. E. 1960. *The American Voter.* John Wiley & Sons, Inc., New York.

Davies, J. C. 1970. *The Politics of Pollution.* Pegasus Press, New York.

deGroot, I. and Samuels, S. 1962. *People and air pollution: a study of attitudes in Buffalo, New York.* N.Y. State Dept. of Health, Air Pollution Control Board, Buffalo.

Gallup Organization, Inc. 1969, 1970. (I would like to thank Thomas Kimball, Director of the National Wildlife Federation, for his permission to analyze the Gallup survey data reported here.)

Gillies, Paulette, ed. 1971. *Water Newsletter 13*(8):3. Water Information Center, Inc. Port Washington, N.Y.

Glacken, Clarence. 1967. *Traces on the Rhodian shore.* University of California Press, Berkeley.

Huth, Hans. 1967. *Nature and the American: three centuries of changing attitudes.* University of California Press, Berkeley.

Kluckhohn, Florence, and Strodtbeck, Fred. 1961. *Variations in value orientations.* Row, Peterson & Co., Evanston, Illinois.

League of Women Voters Education Fund. 1966. *The Big water fight.* The Stephen Greene Press, Brattleboro, Vermont.

Lee, Robert. G. 1970. *World Savers or Realm Savers.* University of California, Berkeley, School of Forestry and Conservation.

McCloskey, Michael. 1966. The Wilderness Act of 1964: its background and meaning. *Oregon Law Review 45*, 288–321.

McConnell, Grant. 1964. The conservation movement—past and present. *Western Political Science Quarterly 7*, 463.

Medalia, and Finkner. 1965. Community perception of air quality: an opinion study in Clarkston, Washington. *U.S.P.H.S. Publication* 99–10, Cincinnati, Ohio.

Nash, Roderick. 1967. *Wilderness and the American mind.* Yale University Press, New Haven, Connecticut.

National Commission on Obscenity and Pornography. 1970. *Report.* U.S. Government Printing Office.

Ogden, Daniel M., Jr. 1970. Environmental values and water project planning. Arkansas-White-Red Inter-Agency Committee Meeting.

Robinson, Ray, ed. 1971. Special survey: you tell what's right and wrong with America. *Seventeen*, Feb. 1971, 116–127.

Russell, Cynthia. 1970. The evolution of the nature magazine: a case study of three publications: *Outdoor America, National Audubon, American Forests*, 1954-1969. M.A. thesis, University of Michigan, Ann Arbor.

Smith, W. S., Scheuneman, J. J., and Zeidberg, L. 1964. Public reaction to air pollution in Nashville, Tennessee. *Journal of the Air Pollution Control Association, XIV*, 445–448.

Swan, James A. 1970. *Response to air pollution: a study of attitudes and coping strategies of high school youth.* University of Michigan School of Natural Resources.

University of Michigan Survey Research Center. 1968 election study. (Interim version, 1971. Tables computed from interim tapes.)

U.S. Department of Commerce, Bureau of the Census. 1969. *Statistical Abstract of the United States.* 90th ed. U.S. Government Printing Office, Washington, D.C.

White, Gilbert F. 1966. The formation and role of public attitudes, in Garrett, H., ed., *Environmental quality in a growing economy: essays from the sixth Resources for the Future forum*, pp. 105–127. The Johns Hopkins Press, Balitmore, Md.

CHAPTER 8

A radical reordering of priorities and decision-making devices is required to cope with the major changes in public attitudes which are in evidence today. This paper examines the structure of the decision-making network, the interest groups involved in water development planning, and existing impediments to changes in policy.

The weaknesses in present assumptions about public values are discussed and the points in the planning process where values are significant are identified. Methods of discovering the preferences of interest groups and their likely responses to proposals for water resources development are examined critically, and attempts by agencies to respond to these new challenges are described.

Suggestions for improvement in decision-making include a careful assessment of the impacts of past water developments, a clear definition of national goals by governmental agencies, and experimentation with public participation in decision-making.

PUBLIC OPINION IN PLANNING WATER DEVELOPMENT

Gilbert F. White

INTRODUCTION

Public opinion about environmental quality is both a determinant and a product of planning water development. Water policies and plans reflect sets of public values and preferences about the hydrologic, aquatic, and terrestrial systems that are manipulated when man intervenes in the natural movements of water on the land, underground, and in the stream. At the same time, the manner in which the planning takes place and in which the results are submitted for decision has a powerful influence upon opinion formation. The interaction is as frequent as the drafting of revised plans. If the configuration of values changes slowly, as during the 1950s when increased emphasis was placed on water-based recreation by consumers, there is only modest tension in the readjustment of the planning activity to take account of the new emphasis. However, when the values change rapidly the method of preparing for water development is placed under severe strain, new institutions are demanded, and the technical folk who draw up plans become confused, defensive, and insecure. This was the case during the late 1960s and early 1970s.

Water development was caught up in profound shifts among articulate sectors of the citizenry in the value placed upon environmental quality and in the value assigned to community participation in public choice. Within half a dozen years the old and comfortable formulations were challenged and conventional means of channeling the interaction proved inadequate. By early 1971 it seemed likely that radically different devices would be required to respond to the new and dynamic ordering of the nation's priorities in resource management.

The points at which change is in progress and may be expected to be most far-reaching are revealed by examining the network of decisions in water management as it responds to expressions of value.

DECISION NETWORKS AND INTEREST GROUPS

Decisions as to how, where, and when water is manipulated in the United States are chiefly the result of the working and interaction of twelve major networks of decision-makers. These are: (1) farmers and suburbanites who develop their own domestic supplies; (2) ranchers and Bureau of Land Management offices who improve stock water on grazing lands; (3) farmers, irrigation districts, Bureau of Reclamation offices, and legislators; (4) farmers and drainage districts who drain agricultural lands; (5) freight carriers, TVA, and Corps of Engineers offices and legislators who improve waterway transport; (6) municipalities and franchised companies providing municipal water; (7) municipalities disposing of urban waste; (8) private companies supplying their own

water and disposing of their own waste; (9) municipalities, levee districts, TVA, and Corps of Engineers offices and legislators controlling flood flows; (10) private and public hydroelectric power producers; (11) municipal, state, and federal operators of water-based recreation; and (12) farmers, Forest Service and Soil Conservation Service offices carrying out watershed management.

Each of these networks involves individuals or offices having primary responsibility for making decisions about water management. Each is limited in some degree by state or federal regulations prepared by legislative bodies, for example, state surveillance of waste disposal and federal licensing of water power sites. Each is affected by the supporting activities of other people or agencies, such as pump manufacturers who sell the equipment for individual domestic water supply, and state extension services that advise farmers on land drainage or cropping practices. For each network there is a well defined set of people directly involved in making choices about projects for altering the water cycle. They, in turn, are loosely associated with others who are aware of the effects of such alteration upon their own welfare. Thus, shopkeepers in agricultural service towns feel closely identified with nearby irrigation development, and railroad executives feel threatened by competing waterway development.

Each of the decision networks and its associated individuals who perceive themselves as affected by those decisions may be regarded as an interest group. The interest group may span a wide spectrum of opinion but it has in common its perception of some relation to the particular water development. An interest group may exclude people who are directly concerned but who are not aware that public investment is made in water-based recreation that is available only to people who can drive their own cars 20 miles to enjoy it; the dwellers in central city slums may be unaware that they suffer by default. Contrariwise, the size of an interest group may expand in response to recognition of an environmental linkage which has gone unperceived: when schoolboys realize that phosphates contribute to eutrophication of a recreational lake they may become involved in agitation to control detergent use. When multipurpose projects are posed, the number of interest groups expands accordingly.

In theory, if people were fully aware of the effect upon their lives and their children's lives of manipulations of the water cycle, they would all be members of an all-embracing interest group. But the relationships are so diverse and complex that there would have to be a sorting out of relative priorities according to expected effects and the particular values that different people place upon them. Even if a central city resident is aware of the contribution of phosphates to a distant lake, he may feel that rat control and employment problems render detergent ordinances superficial. At any given time the public opinion about an environmental intervention is the aggregate of what each interest group regards as directly affecting them. There is no one public, no one public opinion. Each interest group shares in the decisions about its selected aspect of water development, and its array of opinion is an expression of its awareness and its value systems.

WHAT IS THE EVIDENCE?

Each of the interest groups is handicapped in its assessment of water development by the lack of what is essential to sound judgment: evidence as to what actually happens after a project is in operation. The overwhelming proportion of studies of water development are normative. Needs are presented, and plans are outlined and found to be economically feasible. Rarely is there any comprehensive analysis of the full set of consequences of development—physical, biological, and social. Although annual statistics accumulate on power generation,

agricultural production from irrigated lands, and river-borne freight, only a few scattered and incomplete appraisals have been made of all of the effects of a given project. Any such attempt is certain to be incomplete; the techniques for appraisal are crude at best in certain instances. Yet, a candid, searching appraisal by revealing weaknesses in method and gaps in knowledge would spur efforts to improve the process. In the absence of appraisal, no matter how incomplete, the reactions of interest groups to Grand Canyon dams, cross-Florida barge canals, and Long Island power plants must be largely speculative. The few studies which have been made of project effects, such as economic analysis of public investment (Haveman, 1965), and geographic analysis of specific irrigations and flood-control projects (Beyer, 1957; White et al., 1957; Macinko, 1963; Day, 1970) throw serious doubts on the extent to which project objectives were realized and side-effects anticipated.

The handicap of lack of evidence is no impediment to confident judgment. Without data, it is easier to make sweeping assertions about the economic feasibility or absurdity of a project, and to charge that its side effects are insignificant or determinative in calculating its social desirability.

The reasons for this remarkable discontinuity between normative plans and scientific validation need not be reviewed here. What is especially significant about it is that notwithstanding the mounting concern over environmental matters, the effort to find out what has happened as a result of previous projects is still pitifully small.

WHO TAKES PART IN WATER DECISIONS

In the more complex networks we may distinguish three types of participants: (1) the planners who are responsible for preparing and carrying out water development works; (2) individuals affected by such works either directly or indirectly; and (3) the administrative-political officers who act as mediators between the planners and the affected groups as public opinion develops with regard to any particular action or its consequences.

In the simpler networks, such as household water supply, the principal participant may be the individual homeowner, and he may plan the new work with no surveillance by others and without others feeling they are affected. The role of public opinion in each of these networks is quite different. We shall point this out after reviewing the decision process and the points in that process where values are especially influential.

THE MYTH OF OPTIMIZING

At no important point in the whole process is the decision an optimizing activity. Although it is common and convenient to think of any individual or group as arriving at public decision with respect to resources management in terms of maximizing marginal returns, there is little evidence to suggest that the decisions in fact are made on such criteria. The process is more clearly one of rationalization. Certain minimum goals are sought, but rarely if ever do those responsible for the final choice set up guidelines to select what could be considered an optimal result.

Neither the large-scale and long-term international negotiations over water development (Krutilla, 1967; Day, 1970) nor the highly individualized and decentralized decisions made by industries (Wong, 1968) or by individual drawers of water for domestic purposes suggest that the economically efficient choice is sought or achieved. Benefit-cost calculations often are made and published, but usually help to justify a particular choice rather than to determine it. The process is more intricate than would be indicated by an ordinary optimization model. For that reason it lends itself less to generalization.

It cannot be described accurately as a careful search for expected utility. Nor can it be recognized in practice as a careful effort to optimize what are the subjectively defined expected outcomes.

NEEDS, ALTERNATIVES, AND VALUES

We seem to be dealing with a process in which there are parallel subjective views of reality. These are: (1) the perceived needs; (2) perceived coping actions; and (3) the judgment of the values at stake in the perceived needs and actions.

One reason that much water resources management has gone so far astray in the United States and in countries powerfully influenced by similar methods of project evaluation and benefit-cost analysis is that the planners have ignored the facts of the decision process and have chosen to act as though people would select the efficient alternatives, or failing to do so would drop out of the productive system. Thus, both soil conservation and reclamation programs have assumed that farmers would adopt farming methods that yield maximum returns and preserve the soil heritage. Only as people have seen that the consequences of public actions were quite different than those anticipated in the elegant benefit-cost findings have they begun to rebel against the methods and underlying assumptions.

The perceived need usually is different from and more vague than that stated by the project analyst. For example, in the Colorado Basin there were explicit economic and engineering analyses for a long time which were directed primarily at the attainment of some kind of economic efficiency objective within the constraints of political allocations of water and of providing family-size farms. Although much of the basic appraisal was grounded on the attainment of these aims, the response from the responsible legislative and interest groups was in terms of a different mix of objectives. They included objectives not explicitly contained in the initial analysis, such as the management of the stream for satisfaction of human sense of mastery of nature, and the promotion of the economic development interests of the central Arizona area (NAS-NRC, 1968).

Even more restraining in analysis is the tendency for both planning personnel and affected groups to consider the range of possible coping actions in terms of a very limited number of alternatives. When confronted with flood, drought, power shortage, or polluted streams, it is easy to ignore unconventional solutions which might or might not be acceptable according to the information people have about them or according to the values used in assessing their suitability.

For a long time it was out of the question for a planning officer to study any way of dealing with flood losses other than by constructing engineering works or by providing public relief (U.S. House of Representatives, 1966). It was no less uncommon for citizen's groups dealing directly with the engineering agencies because they were bound by the availability of federal dollars under the Flood Control Act of 1936. Yet, many citizens were carrying on individual types of adjustments to flood losses calling for less modification of the environment, such as the flood-proofing of their structures or the arrangement of special insurance or damage funds to deal with losses when incurred. While these other possibilities were theoretically available they were perceived neither by the planners nor by the affected groups. Similarly, the traditional view of possible means of coping with water shortage for irrigation is to provide more water rather than to increase efficiency of water use or to insure against droughts and thus distribute losses over longer time or wider space.

The value systems upon which new projects or the results of old ones are appraised likewise differ greatly from group to group and place to place. Inherently there are deep conflicts, as between the relative value placed by farmers and hunters on the use of wetland for crop production versus waterfowl nesting. If the values do not change and if the activities they reflect do not expand rapidly the interest groups tend to work out accommodations of policy and method. The conflict over use of wetlands first became acute in the 1930s when automobile travel and reduced working hours made hunting possible over large new areas and when that demand coincided with federal financial support of farm drainage of wetlands of the upper Middle West. Valuation of waterfowl was enhanced and a great new constituency of hunters was added to the interest group concerned with drainage. Agricultural workers were trained to increase crop production, and wildlife management experts were trained to increase nesting areas. The conflict was over both purpose and method. On the other hand, in the same region the proposed construction of navigation dams in the Upper Mississippi met with eventual approval from both farmers and hunters, for the planned inundations promised better farm prices along with improved feeding areas on the migratory waterfowl flyway.

One of the very early and probably the first of organized attempts in federal water planning to take account of environmental impacts was the Executive Memorandum of 1936 which required all agencies planning water storage and land drainage projects to report them in advance of initiation so that wildlife management and public health groups might have an opportunity to register complaints where appropriate (U.S. National Resources Subcommittee, 1936). That gave rise to the Executive Order requiring review of departmental recommendations on water resources to the Congress. In turn, the Coordination Act specified the clearance that should be obtained from state and other federal agencies before submitting such reports.

All of these efforts were based upon the propositions that the responsible agencies would correctly mirror the preferences and judgments of interest groups and that differences among them could be reduced by review and discussion prior to presenting final plans for Congressional action. Full reconciliation of differing value systems was never contemplated and it certainly was not attained, but a good deal of co-operation and mutual accommodation was encouraged, and the agencies found it comfortable to work out mutual arrangements for examination of each other's proposals. That sort of adjustment was acceptable as long as the agencies were in tune with their respective interest groups and so long as among them they represented the chief groups having articulate concerns.

Sometime in the mid-1960s that situation began to change. By 1970 it was clear that none of the agencies were fully expressive of the interest groups concerned with its activities. The Bureau of Reclamation had misjudged southwestern valuation of the Grand Canyon, the Corps of Engineers had run into opposition to large dams, and water pollution control agencies found themselves confronted by groups who were dissatisfied with chief reliance on waste disposal plants. Large constituencies interested in preservation of landscape had joined the groups concerned primarily with hunting and fishing. The preferences and composition of the interest groups were changing much more rapidly than the orientation of their associated agencies in reaching decisions about water manipulation.

SIGNIFICANCE OF VALUES

Values play a vital role in the way in which community need is perceived and defined. The definition customarily is by administrative-political personnel who initiate investigations in reaction to what they consider to be the needs and preferences of interest groups. Means of defining the preceived need, as, for example, in the policy statement for the Flood Control Act of 1936 or in the Environmental Quality Act, commonly are given by the administrative-political group to the planning personnel and are very rapidly absorbed by and diffused among affected groups who fasten upon them as firm criteria with which they can deal readily with the planning personnel.

In the course of the planning studies it is the planner himself who in subtle and diverse ways defines values which will be employed in the studies. In this, he brings to bear two sets of values. First are his own values. These reflect not only his accumulated experience and personal traits but the training of a professional sort which he has received and the pressures and sense of role which attaches to his professional position. The second set of values is that which he believes to be held by other members of the interest group of which he is a part.

Until recent years he rarely made any systematic attempt to assess either set of values. He assumes he is objective and will not let his own preferences prevail. As for the preferences of others he relies upon curbstone judgment and upon one very practical test. The test is whether or not what he produces receives favorable response when his plan is subjected to the critical gaze of superior officers and of legislative committees. In his effort to assess the values held by others, he reasonably asks at which points there is difficulty in public hearings, or at which other administrative officers raise embarrassing questions, or at which Congressional committees and, often more significantly, members of their technical staffs challenge the judgments in his report. The legislative groups pride themselves on being close to the electorate. Their approval then becomes a kind of validation of the planner's judgment.

When the values held by one sector of the group change rapidly the planner may be caught with his misjudgments. Legislators may be quick to sense the shift, and find it easier to readjust their positions: they need not be tied to the authorship of a project. The planner may then become sensitive to a change in the interest group's values without understanding the circumstances contributing to it.

FACTORS AFFECTING VALUE SYSTEMS

When the planner asks why value systems change from place to place and from time to time, he must examine at least five sets of factors influencing in some way an individual expression of value in a decision situation. It is important at once to draw a distinction between articulated attitudes and behavior. One of the most difficult of all problems faced in social science is that of understanding the relationship between an expressed attitude and explicit behavior. It is well known that an individual who pleads for water purity may be one of those who most threatens it by his use of chemicals or fertilizers. An articulated expression of attitude is not necessarily associated with consistent performance. The better measure of a value is in behavior. Rather than in polls, the opinion that counts is the opinion that shows in action.

Precisely how those values are related to other conditions is far from clear. However, a few observations may be helpful in trying to identify what would account for changes in the values placed upon environmental conditions and in estimating what effects government activity might have on them.

Direct experience and information often are regarded as major determinants, and government administrators like to think that their publications and utterances will sway the positions of people affected. The evidence is that experience—either direct or vicarious—rarely has a marked effect upon value orientation and decision. It may support positions already arrived at. It may encourage change to which the individual is predisposed. There is little evidence that information in reports, brochures, movies, and radio is linked with value shifts. Television does have an element of immediacy that strengthens preferences and judgments developed from other sources. These always need to be considered in conjunction with personal experience and information.

A second set of factors has to do with the decision situation. The extent to which the individual feels obliged to make a choice and the conditions in which he interacts with others may at times dominate his behavior. The record of community response to drinking water fluoridation proposals is illuminating in this regard, for it shows that information about fluoridation risks and benefits may be less significant in the decision to adopt or reject than are circumstances of the municipal government's centralized control and its position toward citizen participation (Crain and others, 1969). As environmental issues become more complex and as the interaction of different interest groups increases with greater leisure and income, people may be drawn to take positions they would not have assumed in simpler situations.

The third set relates to what may be called world views and a sense of efficacy. It is likely that individuals perceive environmental needs differently according to their sense of capacity to deal effectively with such needs. In studies carried out by Strodtbeck and Bezdek (1970) it appeared that individuals who feel there is little they can do about water pollution see exactly the same phenomena as being less severe than do individuals who have the conviction that they may be able to influence the results.

There is some reason to think that part of the current concern about environmental deterioration is a displacement phenomenon that reflects frustration with the inability to resolve the Vietnam situation, urban poverty, and nuclear destruction. Seeking a course in which he can feel effectual, the individual turns to immediate problems of the environment. Legal adversary actions and Earth Day demonstrations build a sense of efficacy.

Fourth is the sense of role of individual participants in decision. Engineers seem to view their own responsibilities in a different light than do officers of the public health department, the Isaac Walton League, or the League of Women Voters (Sewell, 1971). Their sense of the individual's role in relation to the group around them reflects training and professional norms and colors powerfully the way in which they perceive needs and possible course of action (Craik, 1970). One example of this is the way in which the engineer who usually is the water planner underestimates the willingness of consumers to experiment with new techniques such as waste water renovation (Johnson, 1971). With the widening range of alternatives considered in water management, new professional orientations are introduced.

The personality traits of individuals may be expected to influence the kind of decisions they make, but the evidence on this is very restricted. Personality may become significant primarily in conditions of extreme stress and tension imposed by other factors. Thus, two planners preparing a flood control project in a situation in which there was little difference of opinion among administrators and interest groups might be expected to be alike in the nature of their response to perceived needs and alternatives. However, if severe controversy were to arise about the values at stake, individual judgments might be expected to diverge.

No one yet has an adequate explanation for the profound shifts in assessment of environmental values over recent years. It represents some convergency of information about environmental deterioration, direct exposure of previously uninvolved interest groups to environmental manipulation, increasing sharpness of value conflicts among alternative uses, frustration with inability to handle other aspects of the human scene, and the entry of new professional groups on the management stage. There probably is a substantial strain of religious movement in the shift (as McEvoy suggests in his review in this volume).

It has been suggested that there are two major conditions which affect an individual's disposition to act upon a generally accepted value (Schwartz, 1970). One of these is his awareness of consequences of his activity. The other is his sense of personal responsibility for those consequences. Norms which had lip service for a long time may become tenets of action when their holder is convinced that he can correct injuries he has caused. As Heberlein (in press) has pointed out, a change in public information and personal experience with respect to both the likely consequences of disturbing the natural systems and to individual responsibility for bringing them about may have a profound change upon individual behavior even though the values themselves have not changed. Whatever the precise combination of circumstances, the behavior toward the environment represents response to a complex set of factors including but not limited to scientific evidence concerning environmental threats to human well being.

Because of the intricacy of these relationships it would be a mistake to treat the value systems of the different interest groups concerned with water development as uniform or as responding similarly to changed government policy. The water planner needs to deal with the several interest groups separately in trying to discover their actual preferences and in estimating their reactions to the great variety of goals and methods which he must canvass (White, 1966; O'Riordan, 1971; Sewell, 1971).

DISCOVERING THE PREFERENCES OF INTEREST GROUPS

Customarily the water planner sounds out the value judgments of the interest groups for whom he is planning by the unsystematic but oftentimes sensitive methods noted above. When those fail, as they have repeatedly in recent years, he may turn to opinion polling, the favorite device of political forecasters and market analysts. Often these polls attempt to find out what the consumer thinks are his problems and his capacity to cope with them (Ibsen and Bollweg, 1969).

Polls are at best a crude device for soliciting preferences. When applied to water management they have the handicap of having to deal with large numbers of alternatives in contrast to the yes-no answer for political candidates and household products. They cannot give the respondent a feeling for the efficacy of his possible action, and they cannot take account of interaction with other persons in their professional roles. Asking a man how he will vote between two candidates is quite different from finding out how he will choose among a broad range of alternatives after being exposed to new sets of information about them. Surveys of public opinion in water matters may reveal a good deal about voiced attitudes without assuring any insight into likely behavior when concrete decisions are required.

Federal and state agencies have only begun to experiment with these and other devices. At present, there is proper caution as to the effectiveness of such measures. There should not be any doubt, however, as to the need for perfecting them.

HOW TO ESTIMATE RESPONSE TO PLANS

A hackneyed, popular, and generally sterile method of eliciting response from interest groups to tentative and final plans is the public hearing. Although it may in favorable circumstances bring to light fresh judgments, the hearing procedure tends to reflect only the known views of well identified members of interest groups. Thus, it airs the obvious without significant effect upon either the speaker or the listener. If there is unexpected demonstration of approval or opposition to a given plan the water planner may be moved, and in doing so he regrets that he had not been aware of the preferences earlier. But, as Wengert (1971) has noted, there is nothing magically good in community participation for its own sake.

The most careful effort thus far to improve the hearing procedure is that in the Susquehanna Basin where the Corps of Engineers set out to try a variety of workshop procedures (Borton and others, 1970). Supported by a research team from the University of Michigan, the Corps sought to establish more congruent perceptions of water resource problems, to build up mechanisms for disseminating information, and to involve local groups in final plan review. The early results were favorable, but more searching trials will be desirable. Several models of community-agency interaction have been suggested but none has been explored in depth (Bishop, 1970). Practical experiments will be troublesome but are essential to finding improved techniques for presenting and appraising the issues.

The form of consultation needs to be tried earlier in the review process. Instead of being limited to the reputedly influential community leaders, it should be extended to influentials in groups not currently aware of their relation to water development. The whole process of presenting genuine alternatives of purpose in water development is immensely demanding of technical synthesis as well as of communication skills. It cannot be expected that community leaders, however bright, can in a mysterious way ferret out the strengths and weaknesses of massive proposals presented for prompt review. Time is required. Even more, aid must be given so that the responses are deliberate and will be in a form likely to affect the types of program that then will be produced. There is need for an interactive device that would identify issues and values, give information on acceptable alternatives, and clarify conflicts and choices. Beyond the hearing and the community conference lies a series of new ventures: group discussions, extended consultations with selected leaders, and analysis of judgments using computer graphics. Each of these devices offers hope for more accurate sounding of preferences.

Observation of consumer behavior is practical where the utilities from water management are for sale in relatively open markets, as with some water-based recreation. For the most part the public character of and restricted market for water itself, navigation, flood control, and waste disposal inhibits pricing practices which would reveal consumer preferences. So few aspects of environment are subject to pricing, and so few past decisions have been made without heavy social constraints that clear preferences are hard to identify. Pricing in accord with direct cost or social cost is to be sought. In its absence, other means are required.

Content analysis of published materials can reveal something of the value systems of authors and approving readers. It suffers most of the deficiencies of opinion polls, yet it may offer insights that would escape the routine kind of polling. This requires rigorous analysis of the printed, broadcast, or televised communications about an issue or problem. Each statement is classified according to characteristics of form direction, authority, and value, and the results show much that is not apparent from casual reading (Berelson, 1952).

A device that has not been utilized extensively but that offers promise is the programmed discussion in which representative members of interest groups are exposed to the range of technical information and peer judgment that might accompany a sustained, thoughtful community debate on a water project. They receive the same information and are encouraged to exchange initial reactions. The grounds for disagreement are aired, and then the respondents move toward a judgment after reviewing the basic data, considering the apparently practical solutions, and responding to the arguments and feelings of colleagues in situations resembling a community discussion. Their behavior is significant not only in the decision reached but in the direction of change, if any, that takes place.

MEASURES FOR IMPROVEMENT

One sane response to a situation in which government water planning machinery and the perceptions of its operators has failed to keep pace with the value placed on environmental impacts by influential sectors of the public is to let affairs run their course without studied manipulation. Adversary action and vocal discontent with the conventional agency procedures might then be expected to lead in time either to a revision of agency procedures or to new agencies better suited to the needs. The agencies already are trying to revise their methods. Impact reports are being prepared, ecologists have been hired to work alongside engineers, and new hearing formats have been devised. The immediate question is whether or not there are constructive measures which might be taken beyond those now in motion. No special encouragement seems required to continue those efforts. However, there are persuasive reasons for considering three additional sorts of ventures in the same direction.

1. An obvious but persistently neglected step to assist in public evaluation of water development is the careful appraisal of impacts of past projects. It is important because as long as discussion of the social and environmental impacts of water investment is based upon speculation rather than hard evidence, the judgments are bound to be ambiguous and likely to be distorted.

The major federal agencies have been slow to carry out post-audits. Academic groups have lacked incentive and financial support for what necessarily are interdisciplinary ventures. Much of the mounting debate about the wisdom of either the purposes or methods of water development could be clarified by providing balanced, incisive appraisal of selected development projects.

Ideally, those appraisals should be carried out by teams of scientists independent of the planning and operating agencies. They might well be commissioned by the agencies working through the Water Resources Council. They should be based in academic institutions and private research organizations and should be supplemented by one or more centers, such as the proposed Environmental Institute, giving systematic attention to problems of method and interpretation. The projects would be selected to include horrible examples as well as bureaucratic show pieces. From the outset it would be known that no completely satisfactory appraisal would result, but the reports would be seen as interim documents which would specify the solid findings and the remaining questions. The reports would be prepared in two forms: one to help the technicians involved in further planning, the second to guide public discussion of similar projects elsewhere. Out of the latter should come not only a more precise understanding of consequences but a sense of the degree to which prior actions can shape them.

2. The most ambiguous of the elements involved in evaluation of water development by interest groups has to do with national and regional goals. When a local citizens association challenges a bond issue for water supply extension because population expansion planning is inadequate, it is questioning in inchoate fashion the aim of economic growth as well as the municipality's specific land-use plans. While no early resolution can be expected of the broad problem of how much growth, if any, is desirable, government agencies are under heavy obligation to

help clarify the issues involved. The White House report on national goals in 1970 was a first, very cautious step in that direction (U.S. Goals National Research Staff, 1970). It gave little or no attention to several of the issues most troubling the American people and thereby related to the stance taken on environmental action, but it did define the broad problem of quantity versus quality. Moreover, it sought to provoke wider examination of the problem.

A further, more searching inquiry into the quantity-quality problem as it affects views of manipulation of the environment would help outline the frameworks in which regional discussions may take place. Both the agencies and their interest groups are at sea in grappling with the definition of social goals. Through some kind of arrangement between the Domestic Council and the Water Resources Council, the inquiry and resulting public statement should be initiated.

3. Experimentation with methods of refining public participation in decisions about water development should be encouraged. The field efforts already under way by the Corps of Engineers and the studies supported by other agencies hold promise for finding new ways of reaching interest groups in circumstances permitting interaction. However, they merit extension and more systematic appraisal in terms of how the innovations would affect the Congress, the agencies, and the interest groups. In particular, attention should be given to ways of reaching groups that may be affected but are not yet aware of their interest or feel powerless to affect the course of events. Emphasis should be on means of clarifying understanding of development impacts and the values placed upon them rather than on pursuit of the mystique of community participation in its own right.

The Water Resources Council should initiate a vigorous program of experimentation, building on the current efforts, inducing others to join in it, and drawing in the collaboration of social scientists from the universities. What it would yield is difficult to predict. However, it could not help but stir some new modes of communicating with interest groups, of presenting project plans for review, and of both strengthening and benefiting from the expression of public opinion on the social values involved in water development.

References

Berelson, Bernard. 1952. *Content Analysis in Communications Research*, Glencoe: Free Press.

Beyer, Jacquelyn. 1957. *Integration of Grazing and Crop Agriculture: Resources Management Problems in the Uncompahgre Valley Irrigation Project*, Geography Research Paper, Chicago: University of Chicago Department of Geography.

Bishop, A. Bruce. 1970. *Public Participation in Water Resources Planning*, Institute for Water Resources, Springfield, Virginia: FSTI.

Borton, Thomas E., Katherine P. Warner, and J. William Wenrich. 1970. *The Susquehanna Communication-Participation Study*, Institute for Water Resources, Springfield, Virginia: FSTI.

Çraik, Kenneth. 1970. "The Environmental Dispositions of Environmental Decision-Makers," *Annals of the American Academy of Political and Social Science*, 389: 87–94.

Crain, Robert L., *et al.* 1969. *The Politics of Community Conflicts; The Fluoridation Decision*, Indianapolis: Bobbs-Merrill.

Day, John Chadwick. 1970. *Managing the Lower Rio Grande*, Geography Research Paper, Chicago: University of Chicago Department of Geography.

Haveman, Robert H. 1965. *Water Resource Investment in the Public Interest*, Nashville: Vanderbilt Press.

Heberlein, Thomas. 1971. *Moral Norms, Threatened Sanctions and Littering Behavior*. University of Wisconsin: unpublished Ph.D. dissertation.

Isben, Charles A. and John A. Bollweg. 1969. *Public Perception of Water Resource Problems*, Blacksburg: Virginia Polytechnic Institute.

Johnson, James F. 1971. *Renovated Waste Water*, Geography Research Paper, Chicago: University of Chicago, Department of Geography.

Krutilla, John V. 1967. *The Columbia River Treaty: The Economics of an International River Basin Development*, Baltimore: Johns Hopkins Press.

Macinko, George. 1963. "The Columbia Basin Project: Expectations, Realizations, Implications," *Geographical Review*, 53:185–199.

National Academy of Sciences—National Research Council. 1968. *Water Choice in the Colorado Basin*, Publication No. 1689, Washington.

O'Riordan, Timothy. 1971. "Public Opinion and Environmental Quality: A Reappraisal," *Environment and Behavior*, 3:191–214.

Schwartz, S. H. 1970. "Moral Decision Making and Behavior," in *Altruism and Helping Behavior*, Macauley and Berkowitz (eds.), New York: Academic Press. pp. 127–141.

Sewell, W. R. Derrick. 1971. "Environmental Perceptions of Engineers and Public Health Officials," *Environment and Behavior*, 3:491–502.

Strodtbeck, Fred L. and William Bezdek. 1970. "Sex-Role Identity and Pragmatic Action," *American Sociological Review*, 25:491–502.

U.S. National Goals Research Staff. 1970. *Toward Balanced Growth: Quantity with Quality*. Washington, D.C.: White House.

U.S. House of Representatives (89th Congress). 1966. *Report of the Task Force on Federal Flood Control Policy*, House Document 465, Washington, D.C.: Government Printing Office.

U.S. National Resources Committee, Special Sub-Committee of the Water Resources Committee. 1936. *Drainage Policy and Projects*. Washington, D.C.

Wengert, Norman. 1971. "Public Participation in Water Planning: A Critique of Theory, Doctrine, and Practice," *Water Resources Bulletin*, 7:26–32.

White, Gilbert F. 1966. "Formation and Role of Public Attitudes," in *Environmental Quality in a Growing Economy*, Henry Jarrett (ed.), Baltimore: Johns Hopkins Press.

White, Gilbert F., *et al.* 1957. *Changes in Urban Occupance of Flood Plains in the United States*, Geography Research Paper, Chicago: University of Chicago, Department of Geography.

Wong, Shue Tuck. 1968. *Perception of Choice and Factors Affecting Industrial Water Supply Decisions in Northeastern Illinois*, Geography Research Paper, Chicago: University of Chicago Department of Geography.

CHAPTER 9

The requirement in the National Environmental Policy Act of 1969 (NEPA), that environmental impact statements be made for major federal projects, reflects the growing concern of Americans for their environment. Sophisticated impact studies will aid the discovery of potentially irreversible effects, help evaluate planning alternatives, and provide a definition of the public interest in water resources development. They will also allow independent evaluation of project alternatives to be made by all interested parties. The formulation of impact studies requires an interdisciplinary team which is well-trained and is as free as possible from prejudice and pressures from vested interest groups.

The categories of water development impacts which should be assessed are physical, chemical, biological, economic, aesthetic, and social. Secondary or higher order impacts due to interactions between components of these categories require special consideration, as do long-term effects. Many impacts, especially higher order interactions, are likely to be peculiar to the individual project; generalities must be drawn with caution. An open, research-oriented strategy is called for. We will discuss alternative organizational structures for an environmental study group, some methods of training the group's personnel, and the place of impact analysis in environmental planning.

IMPACT ANALYSIS AND THE PLANNING PROCESS

Kenneth Henwood and Carole Coop

INTRODUCTION

Water development will always entail impacts on the environment. Some impacts are judged beneficial while others are detrimental, and in many cases the nature of this judgment depends upon the values of the person evaluating the change. In the past, environmental quality took a back seat to "economics" and "progress" in the decision-making process. Today, however, alterations in the natural system are more frequently being viewed by the public as deleterious, and with this change in values those doing planning for future development, including future use of water resources, are being forced to evaluate more fully the total environmental consequences of their planning decisions.

One result of this change in environmental values was the passage of the National Environmental Policy Act (P.L. 91–190, 42 U.S.C. 4321 et. seq.) in 1969. A major provision of the act is the requirement in section 102(2)(c) for preparation of environmental impact studies by federal agencies proposing legislation and/or contemplating development that could significantly affect the environment. Each such agency is required to submit its impact studies for review to other concerned agencies, both local and federal, to the public, and to the new Council on Environmental Quality. Unfortunately, there is no requirement in the act that the implementing agency or Congress actually take the impact statement for a particular project into account in deciding whether to go ahead with the project. That is, the NEPA requirements are procedural, not substantive. Still, members of Congress will have to give careful thought to the political consequences of a vote in favor of a project which has been publicly exposed as entailing significant danger to the environment.

The changes in public opinion and law discussed above are not the only reasons that we can look forward to a more thorough evaluation of the environmental effects of our actions in the future. Scientific advances will also facilitate this evaluation. Traditionally, many environmentally significant effects of development have been unrecognized and therefore ignored in the planning of water projects. But, as the science of ecology grows more sophisticated, we are beginning to understand some of the more complex effects of environmental alterations and are able to take them into account in decision-making. Advances in computer technology and systems analysis have facilitated the projection of effects to be expected from development, and the temporal, spatial, ecological, and social extent of these effects.

VALUE OF IMPACT ANALYSIS TO DECISION-MAKERS AND THE GENERAL PUBLIC

The aim of the impact analyst should be to produce an environmental impact study which is so sufficiently comprehensive and technically persuasive as to be weighed at least as seriously in the planning and evaluation process as the traditional benefit-cost ratio, which is essentially a purely economic impact statement.

The availability of environmental impact statements can be of great value to decision-makers. Advantages accruing to decision-makers through such analysis include the discovery of potentially irreversible effects, the facilitation of evaluation of alternatives, and a comprehensive definition of where the public interest lies. In addition, the impact study can supply critical information to decision makers and the public for the identification of irreversible environmental effects and other aspects of what Richerson and McEvoy (in this volume) term "intrinsic environmental quality."

As has been briefly mentioned above, the decision-maker's job is greatly simplified once a complete impact study is available, since favorable alternatives can be more readily discerned when complete information is available on the potential effects of different forms of a project. Any one of the proposed alternatives will have similar information requirements, thus the impact analysis of the primary project may, in many cases, satisfy most of the data requirements for the alternatives as well.

Potential advantages of comprehensive impact analysis to members of the general public are also numerous. Foremost among these, of course, is the advantage accruing from more informed decision making on the part of its representatives, both legislative and administrative. In addition, public input into the impact study itself may become a vehicle through which public values and interests are integrated into the planning process. In fact, administrative agencies responsible for project evaluation are already beginning to understand the new value placed on the environment by the public and to devise methods for incorporating these values into the planning process (see Petersen, in this volume). However, at present, such an approach has not been widely adopted, and until it is agency development proposals will continue to be forced to run the gauntlet of legal delays and reviews which is currently the principal means of public input into the planning process.

Another advantage accruing to the general public from the impact study requirement embodied in NEPA is that the bases of federal administrators' decisions will now be more fully documented. Whereas in the past decisions as to which of a number of alternative courses of action to take may have been made on the basis of internal memoranda or mere verbal communication (making the basic assumptions underlying decision making difficult to determine and therefore difficult to challenge), now the bases of such decisions must be explicitly set forth in the impact statement.

Further, the preparation of impact studies for all major governmental projects will facilitate periodic re-evaluation of the basic assumptions used by governmental agencies in planning. A periodic comparison of actual project characteristics (for example, recreation days actually spent at the project per year, actual economic development stimulated by the project, real ecological effects of the project, actual flood control benefits of the project, and the like) with the predictions for these characteristics contained in the impact statements will be of great benefit to government project planners and to the general public in evaluating the accuracy of their prediction techniques and, hence, will facilitate more accurate predictions in future project planning.

One further major benefit of impact analysis, if it is rigorously done, will be the "spin off" of basic information from the applied research that will surely be necessary in some cases to accurately evaluate the potential impacts of proposed projects.

IMPACT CATEGORIES FOR EVALUATION

Satisfactory impact analysis requires recognition of all major primary and secondary effects of development on the environment. The first step in this process is, of course, to thoroughly describe the present condition of the ecosystem to be affected.

Next, to supply the broad spectrum of information required for complete impact analysis, the analyst must exhaustively specify all possible environmental impacts of the proposed project. Five broad categories of impacts can be used to organize and define the various areas in which effects can be expected from water development projects. This arrangement of categories is not, of course, the only possible one, and significant overlapping is likely to be present.

These five categories for impact assessment include physical, biological, economic, aesthetic, and social aspects of the environment. The physical and biological categories contain most ecological impacts and the broad range of socioeconomic effects is covered in the other three. Each category should be weighted as equally as possible in the formal decision regarding which of a series of alternatives best suits the long- and short-range public welfare.

The physical portion of the analysis should measure site characteristics such as geology, topography, soils, climate, and hydrology. Biological impacts can be assessed by classifying the members, locations, and diversity of the plant and animal communities established in the area of, or otherwise affected by, the development. Evaluations of predator-prey relationships and other dynamic species interactions will also be necessary in many cases. Many of these biological impacts are related to the physical impacts and will have to be assessed in conjunction with them.

The economic portion of the impact study should include comprehensive benefit-cost analyses, as well as identification of the recipients of the beneficial and detrimental effects of each proposed development. Allee (this volume) points out that the political system often does not adjust the losses suffered by various groups as a result of development. This lack of compensation is frequently a result of the fact that certain losses were unknown to the groups that would assume them at the time a given development was being planned. Identification of both losers and gainers in advance of project implementation would allow both groups to represent themselves in the planning and decision-making process and should result in closer adherence to the tenets of welfare economics upon which the rationale for large-scale public resource development is based.

The aesthetic impacts to be studied should include the objective project alterations (for example, visual impacts) as well as less tangible aesthetic changes. Impacts that are perceived visually and/or by smell or hearing should be thoroughly chronicled, especially if an irreplaceable resource (such as a wild river) is to be materially changed. Impacts appreciated in more abstract terms such as the loss of ecosystem diversity along a river due to impoundment (see McCloskey, in this volume), or the changes in fish species due to effluent discharge are also aesthetic to a large degree and should appear in the aesthetic analysis as well as in the biological.

Social impacts can encompass a wide range of effects. Important among these are the project's influences on urbanization, flood plain utilization, agricultural crops, markets and subsidies; the regional tax base, local service costs, and recreational opportunities. Different alternatives to the project are likely to cause wide variations in social impacts, since regional systems are very sensitive to changes in the forms and amounts of national subsidies for resource development. There-

fore, this phase of the impact study will be of great interest to the area to be directly affected by any given development and will enable local representatives to provide support for, or make objections to, the various alternatives based on more factual material than has been available to them in the past. Equal study and consideration must be given to both the social advantages and disadvantages of a particular project for a particular region.

Leopold and others (1971), in developing a procedure for impact analysis to be used by federal agencies, have specified a fairly detailed set of environmental parameters for study, suggesting that they be expanded where necessary for a specific project. However, their "check list" approach can be an invitation to assume that the list provided covers all parameters in all cases and may tempt agency personnel to ignore the need for meticulous on-site analysis by the study team. A broad set of parameters is necessary if the impact analysis is to cover all the important potential effects of a given project. For this reason, the five categories delineated above are general in scope, with the study expected to cover each area in greater detail. A detailed procedure such as Leopold and others provide can be useful as a minimum standard if it is recognized as such and is conscientiously expanded according to the project and the specific area for which it is proposed.

SECONDARY, HIGHER ORDER, AND LONG TERM IMPACTS

Impacts resulting from the interaction of other impacts are termed higher order (or secondary) impacts. They are more difficult to assess and often an experimental or systems analysis approach is required to estimate the impacts of the more complex interactions.

Secondary environmental costs present an especially difficult problem for those interested in economic impact analysis in that they are frequently long-term and may persist long after the economic benefits of a project have terminated. Consideration of long-range environmental impacts of this sort in the planning process is often at odds with the economic time horizon imposed by the discount rate. In spite of the fact that environmental costs from development may continue indefinitely, and may even increase with time, traditionally the economic evaluation of these costs is progressively reduced due to the imposition of the discount rate. For this reason, long-term or irreversible environmental impacts are beyond the scope of traditional cost-benefit analysis as an aid to rational decision making. Such impacts ought to be subject to special consideration and discussion beyond the usual benefit-cost analysis. An example may serve to better illustrate this point.

The expected life for a typical reservoir development (including flood control, irrigation, and power generation benefits) is usually in the neighborhood of 100 to 300 years. During this period significant development may occur in reliance on the flood control and/or irrigation water provided by the project. As a consequence, a problem arises when the reservoir silts-in to such an extent that its functioning is seriously impaired. Since the economic life dictated by the discount rates used for most major federal projects is generally much shorter than 100 to 300 years, this impairment in the operation of the dam is not taken into account in determining costs for purposes of the benefit-cost ratio. At the point where project operation is seriously impaired, the economic benefits which originally justified the project are no longer present. If development has occurred in reliance upon the provision of flood control and irrigation water, an entire socioeconomic system based on the benefits supplied by the project is placed in jeopardy as the project's effectiveness declines. These long-term costs of the project to the environment and the society as a whole continue

even though the project is no longer providing any benefits. But they are effectively ignored because they are outside the time horizon imposed by the discount rate used. Currently, "planning" for such long-term costs seems to consist of simply assuming that another project will be built above or below the old, or that some form of technological advance will obviate the problem. This reasoning does not recognize that good dam sites are a non-renewable resource, nor does it recognize that a "technological quick-fix" (Odum, 1971) may not always be available.

The National Environmental Policy Act, requires (section 102(2)(c)(iv)) "a detailed statement by the responsible official on the relationship between local short-term uses of man's environment and the maintenance and enhancement of long-term productivity." In other words, the relationships and interactions discussed above must, by law, be explored before development can proceed. No easy solutions can be expected, but as these possible long-term costs are brought to the surface for critical appraisal and judgment, the political and decision-making processes can better attempt to maximize the public's environmental interests.

THE ENVIRONMENTAL STUDY GROUP

Insuring an Impartial Consideration of Impacts

The information needs of a comprehensive impact analysis require an impact staff, review board, or technical group to collect and review data. Some administrative structures are much more likely than others to ensure collection of good data, resistance to political and agency pressures, and representation of the public interest. One of the key problems of any intra-agency arrangement for impact analysis is the "insider perspective" described by Sax (1971). Essentially, the insider perspective is the tendency of bureaucrats to develop a sense of identity of interest with the bureaucracy they represent. The prevalence of this type of attitude—a desire to work for the good of the agency itself rather than the public as a whole—has led to the administrative tendency to adopt courses of action which cause a minimum of public controversy. In the past, this strategy has resulted in decisions desired by the regulated industry or client interest groups, and inevitably the agencies have become heavily influenced by such interests.

The insider perspective seems to have caused agencies to fail in fulfilling their legal and political mandates, particularly the mandate to impartially determine, and act consistent with, the public interest. In the future, the extent to which an agency's structure for impact analysis is resistant to the insider phenomenon will determine the success of the impact study in influencing decision making. In addition, due to increased public concern with environmental matters, and the recent growth of the right of private citizens to challenge agency decisions in court (see, for example, Landau and Rheingold 1971, p. 56-63, 325-326) there may come a time in the future when the desire to avoid controversy—the insider perspective—will dictate careful consideration of environmental impacts in order to avoid a court room challenge.

Possible Alternative Organizational Structures

Four examples will be discussed to illustrate the possible range of evaluation structures through which impact analysis might be implemented.

The least independent structural framework for analysis is one in which the agency responsible for a project's implementation also does the impact study for that project. This structure is the one most susceptible to pressure both by outside interests working through the agency and by the agency's own construction and development staff. Traditionally, benefit-cost analyses for the Corps of Engineers and the Bureau of Reclamation have been done under this type of administrative structure, and in some cases such analyses have been manipulated to justify predetermined goals. (See, for example, Morgan, 1971, p. 387-396.) Unfortunately, the impact studies now required by section 102 of the National Environmental Policy Act are being approached in this same manner. It is the least satisfactory method available and should be terminated at once through Congressional action.

A specific example of this environmentally unfortunate organizational structure may be seen in the Army Corps of Engineers, Sacramento, California, District Office (see Figure 1). The organizational framework for most other Corps District Offices in the United States is similar, except that in some cases the Environmental Resources Section is elevated to a level equal to that of the Sacramento District's Project Planning Branch.

An administrative arrangement such as the one revealed in these diagrams cannot undertake an impartial, independent scrutiny of the potential environmental effects of construction projects. As the figure indicates, the Environmental Resources Section, which is responsible for a substantial majority of this District's environmental impact statements for civilian construction projects is in a position of subordinance both to the Engineering Division and the Project Planning staff.

Any opinion of Environmental Resources Section personnel as to potential adverse environmental effects of a project is subjected to scrutiny and possible modification or omission by the Engineering Division before it proceeds through administrative channels.

This is unfortunate for several reasons, First, the Engineering Division is the group with responsibility for conceiving, planning, justifying to Congress, and designing civilian construction projects. Its personnel can

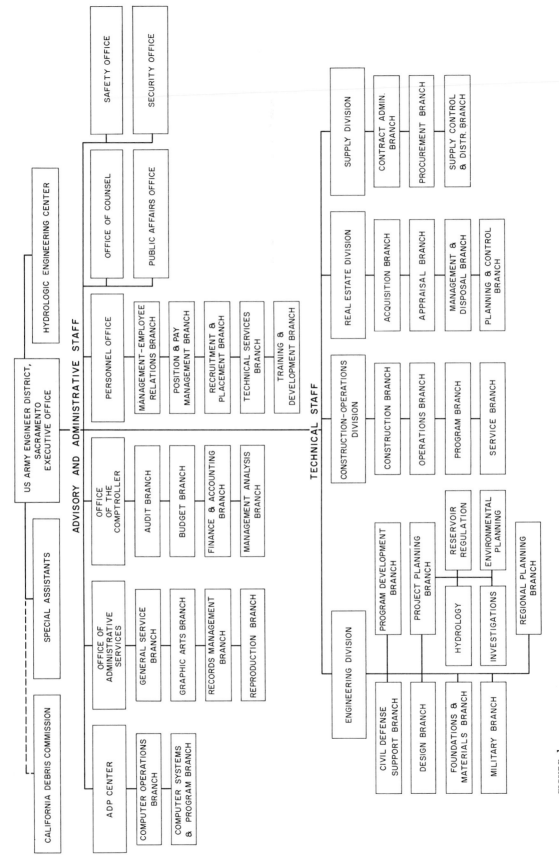

FIGURE 1
Organizational chart for U.S. Army Engineers Sacramento Office.

hardly be expected to look favorably or open-mindedly upon criticism of projects which they look forward to (or in many cases are already engaged in) planning and designing, particularly criticism which is so severe that it may result in cancellation of the project altogether.

Second, Engineering Division supervisory personnel are, appropriately enough, chiefly engineers with little or no training in any natural or social sciences (other than economics). For the most part, their training and background has left them "construction oriented." Such personnel cannot be expected to easily adapt to the NEPA mandate, which has been interpreted by one Federal appeals court as "extraordinarily broad, compelling consideration of any and all types of environmental impacts of federal action." (*Calvert Cliffs Coordinating Committee v. United States Atomic Energy Commission.*)

In summary then, both the primary mission and the educational background of most Engineering Division personnel leaves them particularly unsuited to supervise the thoughtful, thorough consideration of environmental impacts which the National Environmental Policy Act requires.

To the extent that similar organizational arrangements occur in other federal agencies, environmental impacts of federal projects are not likely to receive adequate consideration in the absence of litigation (or the threat of it) on the part of public interest groups.

A more adequate administrative arrangement for impact statement preparation would involve the creation of an impact analysis unit still within the project-implementing agency itself but on a par with its development and construction staffs. Going back to our Corps of Engineers example (see Figure 1), such a result could be accomplished by the creation of a fifth division—the Environmental Resources Division—on a par with the extant Engineering, Construction-Operations, Real Estate, and Supply Divisions.

Assuming the people in this environmental resources division were competent and conscientious and were allotted sufficient time and funds, such an arrangement would facilitate more thorough consideration of the potential environmental effects of any given project. It would also allow unimpeded communication between the Executive Officer, the supervisor of the entire District Office, and the Environmental Resources Division. This is important because whereas the people in the lower echelons of the agency are somewhat insulated from public pressure for sound environmental policy, the executive officer feels it directly. He is responsible for public relations at the local level. He gives speeches and attends public meetings, and he is the one who must bear the brunt of criticism from environmental interests should a project prove to have unforeseen environmental consequences. Thus, unlike Engineering Division personnel, he has reason to apply positive pressure for the production of impact statements which are honest revelations of the potential environmental consequences of the Corps' projects.

Still, the dangers of a less than thorough investigation of potential environmental effects in allowing any element of the project-implementing organization (no matter at what level in the organization structure) to do the evaluation of a proposed project's environmental impacts should be obvious. Were private profit to be gained by Corps employees under either of the organizational arrangements discussed above, a conflict of interest would clearly be involved.

A recent California Court of Appeals decision, *Bayside Timber v. Board of Supervisors of San Mateo County*, recognized the danger of inadequate protection of the interests of the general public when the personnel of an agency charged with protection of environmental interests have a personal stake in belittling environmental concern. This judicial decision struck down, as an improper delegation of the authority of the legislature, sections of the California

Forest Practices Act. These sections left the supervision of the California logging industry, including protection of environmental and other public interests, to a board of five which included by statutory mandate three lumber company representatives. In the court's opinion, leaving supervision of the lumbering industry to such a board would insure that whenever the interests of the public and the lumbering industry conflicted the forest industry's representatives on the Board would be inclined to vote in favor of the latter. Of course, under the Forest Practices Act, direct monetary gain to the forest industry's representatives due to their position on the Board was a distinct possibility. Whereas it may not be true that Corps employees are tempted with personal monetary gain in exchange for inadequately revealing the potential environmental impacts of Corps projects, their personal prestige, position, and power may be at stake if too many projects are disclosed to be environmentally unsound.

An impact statement which revealed too many adverse effects on the environment might lead Congress to decide that the project in question should not be built. This would result in a "wasting" of all the effort already expended in project investigation and planning, a diminishing of monetary appropriations for the Corps, and a decline in its staff size, hence a decrease in authority and respect for its supervisory personnel. So, even though the second intra-agency impact review scheme discussed above may be considerably better than the first, it is still not designed to give truly adequate, impartial consideration to environmental values because the executive officer at the District level and the personnel who supervise him can never be free of a predilection toward construction. After all, this is what they as engineers were specifically trained to do; this is what the organization is "tooled up" to do and, in fact, this is, by and large, the primary mission which Congress has directed them and pays them to undertake.

Further improvement would result if the impact assessment was prepared by the development agency itself under a structure similar to the two already mentioned, but if, in addition, these studies were subject to detailed review by a staff under the supervision of the Council on Environmental Quality. It would be essential that the staff of the Council be enlarged to permit thorough review of the impact studies, and that it be empowered to reinvestigate any questionable analyses. Studies poorly or improperly done would be sent back to the originating agency for required revision before being allowed to go on to the decision makers. (At present, the CEQ can only *suggest* revision.)

The fourth and final suggestion for environmental impact analysis entails the formation of an independent agency for the assessment of government activity impacts throughout the nation. This agency would make all impact studies after being furnished with the plans for a resource project and its alternatives as proposed by the developing agency. Recommendations as to which of these alternatives would best fit national environmental goals would be made before the studies were returned to the originating agency for public evaluation and legislative review. If, in the opinion of the evaluating agency, the range of alternatives proposed by the project implementing agency was too narrow, the implementing agency could be instructed to investigate other specified alternatives. Or, the evaluating agency might feel that the problem in question was susceptible to a more environmentally sound alternative solution within the competence of a completely different implementing agency. In this case the evaluating agency would ask the second implementing agency to investigate and report upon these other alternatives. This arrangement is similar to that suggested by McCloskey and Fox in this volume.

The latter proposal would require substantial changes in national environmental policy and legislation, but biasing the impact analysis to justify a prior decision through selective information gathering, which would be a danger even under the third system discussed above, must be avoided. Special interest groups benefiting from construction, and the resource development agencies themselves, will undoubtedly attempt to stop formation of an environmental protection agency with a powerful, independent voice in resource development. On the other hand, the current structure, including an inadequate system for review, impact studies overwhelmed by the "insider perspective," and insufficient technical staffing to even approach complete analysis, is unacceptable to one seriously interested in thorough consideration of projects' environmental impacts. The result has been the filing of an increasing number of lawsuits under section 102 of the National Environmental Policy Act. It is obvious that analysis and evaluation structures must be established with a clear mandate to develop studies as completely as possible, and to maintain open channels for public participation.

Other Elements Influencing the
Adequacy of the Impact Statement

The adequacy of the administrative structure chosen is not the only factor which will affect the breadth and depth of impact studies. They will also be affected by variables such as cooperation with other agencies, funding, the speed the planning process forces upon the impact assessment group, the procedures for self-analysis (that is, quality control) by the impact study group, and the quality and training of the personnel that comprise the impact study section.

Coordination with other agencies includes consideration of environmental interactions on a regional level as well as acquisition of data, generation of alternatives, and anticipation of impacts unforeseen by the impact study group itself. Interagency cooperation allows effects outside the geographic locale of the project to be more fully anticipated, as well as those outside the experience of the primary agency.

If impact analysis is to be carried out properly, sufficient funds must be made available to gather a wide range of background material for the study. In some cases, systems simulations or a series of long-term experiments at the site may be necessary to identify and predict environmental responses. Obviously, the effects which take longer to assess or require extra funding will go unstudied if too little money or (more importantly) too little time is allocated for this phase of the planning process. Quite clearly, impacts which are not considered because of a lack of time or money cannot enter the alternative evaluation process, and it is the lack of consideration of just these environmental effects which has caused much of the recent loss of public confidence in development agencies. It is important to note that many of the costs of an exhaustive study are one-time costs. If natural resource inventories used by planners like McHarg (McHarg and Clarke, this volume) or the land use zoning program described by Yanggen (this volume) are made, much of the information required for subsequent impact analyses will be available.

The adequacy of an agency to plan for and avoid deleterious environmental effects depends upon its ability to evaluate its own performance and to control the quality of its work. Such evaluation can be accomplished through periodic comparison of actual project impacts with the impacts predicted by the study group before the project was built.

Equally important is the provision of a mechanism for enforcement of the impact study group's proposals for preventing or mitigating adverse environmental impacts. Elaborate plans to ameliorate impacts are ineffective if they are not followed up by site visits, inspections, performance bonds, and a willingness to halt development if unacceptable impacts develop. The public is often the best judge of whether national and agency goals are being met and must be allowed to aid in setting standards, reviewing impact assessment, and checking the real project impacts.

The personnel who develop the impact study will be instrumental in determining its content and depth. With growing knowledge of the complex interrelationships within and between physical, biological, and human systems, it is clear that a thorough assessment of those relationships and, more importantly, the effects of large changes in the subsystems, cannot be accomplished without a technical staff competent in a wide range of fields. Staff for the physical analysis should include hydrologists, climatologists, geologists, and soil scientists. A biological analysis requires limnologists, zoologists, botanists, animal and plant ecologists, wildlife biologists, and entomologists. The economic assessment should be made by economists, resource economists, engineers, geographers, and political scientists. Aesthetics should be analyzed by architects, landscape architects, environmental psychologists, conservationists, and the public. Personnel skilled in systems analysis techniques should be utilized to insure proper consideration of secondary and long-term impacts.

Finally, a proper social impact study should use the skills of political scientists, economists, sociologists, historians, archaeologists, and social planners. With interagency consideration and a multidisciplinary analysis team, a comprehensive impact analysis would be likely. The group approach to assessment would also allow extensive individual research on especially difficult problems.

Training the Impact Study Groups

With increasing legal and public pressure to require environmental impact assessment as an aid in making resource decisions, agencies are bound to evolve a specialized staff for the preparation of these studies either along guidelines similar to those presented here or according to some other structural scheme. The temptation to begin using such groups immediately should be avoided. Rather, considerable effort should be devoted to their proper training.

The complex and diverse nature of an impact study team makes it liable to all of the problems in administration and coordination of interdisciplinary study groups. Since large amounts of money, years of planning, legal action, and commitments to extensive environmental changes are likely to be based upon the impact studies, an extended training period for both the administrative and technical staffs is advisable. Coordination between personnel skilled in the different areas of impact analysis should be stressed.

A valuable training method would entail having the impact staff analyze several different types of existing developments on which considerable impact information is available. Ideally, a series of examples could be selected and used to train study groups in each agency involved in water resources development. The groups would be given the parameters for each example project and asked to predict its environmental effects using theoretical analysis techniques. Afterward, the actual environmental impacts of each of these extant projects would be revealed to the study group. The value in this method lies in the group's ability to see how closely their trial impact analyses conform to the project's actual effects. The follow-up studies would also serve to identify weaknesses in the analysis procedure which could then be reinforced before studies of new proposals were begun.

In order to maintain a high level of competence on the study staff, certain important projects should have periodic follow-up studies. Reassessments during construction for short-term impacts and at five, ten, fifteen, and twenty-five year intervals for long-term effects would serve two purposes. They would provide repeated tests of the group's effectiveness as well as retrospective studies of the worth of the projects themselves. If impacts were observed which would have precluded development in the first place, and were found to be irreversible, serious consideration could be given to ameliorating these impacts or, in extreme cases, to removing the project.

THE PLACE FOR IMPACT ANALYSIS IN ENVIRONMENTAL PLANNING

One of the characteristics of the planning techniques developed by McHarg (see McHarg and Clarke, this volume) and those described by Yanggen and Scott (this volume) is their requirement for large amounts of environmental information. Before planning is begun, primary data are collected on physical, biological, aesthetic, and cultural aspects of the site to define the resource base of the area. The plan is then developed from these data.

The planner uses information derived from these primary data, the judgment of technical consultants, and his intuition about man's relation to the land to determine the capability of the site to withstand different types of use and degrees of development. The "resource utilization matrix" (McHarg and Clarke, this volume) is used to graphically display the resources of the site and determine their capabilities.

The difference between McHarg's method and the one now used in water resources planning is in the value placed on environmental quality and the point at which it enters the planning process. In McHarg's method the planner considers the integrated physical, biological, cultural, and aesthetic attributes of a site in determining probable impacts of different types and levels of development. Then, using his own value judgments or those derived from public involvement, he decides on acceptable levels of environmental impacts and arranges the desired development on the land accord-

ingly. On the other hand, in current water resources development, engineers and hydrologists first propose a project, and then make a study of its probable environmental effects. The decision makers must then judge the relative merits of the different values represented in the case. Both methods use a data base generated by an impact analysis, but in the former method environmental effects are considered the primary constraint on the development, while in the latter environmental effects are considered in proportion to the public pressure put on the decision makers to do so, and secondary to engineering and economic constraints.

The basic difference, then, is philosophical. The point where environmental limitations enter the planning process will determine whether development is accomplished with maintenance of a high-quality environment, or in spite of the limitations imposed by the environment.

Zoning on the basis of a resource inventory, such as in the method described by Yanggen (this volume), is an attempt to minimize negative environmental impacts of development. The resource inventory, as the first phase of any complete impact study, is used to identify areas particularly sensitive to these pressures. For sensitive areas, environmental planning attempts to reduce deleterious impacts by preventing or severely limiting development through restrictive zoning. Again, in this form of planning the limits imposed by intrinsic qualities of the environment are the primary constraint on development. Zoning methods are often complementary to impact analysis, since zones are delineated according to anticipated impacts of (usually) small-scale private developments not normally subject to individual impact studies.

CONCLUSION

The changing context for water development decision making has been prompted by the public's desire for greater emphasis on environmental values and its desire to play a more central role in incorporating such values into resource policy. The National Environmental Policy Act of 1969 allows for limited but significant public access to the decision-making process. The major provision of the Act is to require impact studies (which become public information) for all federally funded projects affecting the environment. These studies, if they are to fulfill the spirit of the Act and aid decision makers and the public in evaluating resource development projects, must broadly cover all environmental impacts and analyze in depth impacts which are irreversible or which entail severe environmental degradation. A mere checklist approach to impact analysis is inadequate and original research is a necessary adjunct to thorough analysis.

To undertake this sort of impact study, interdisciplinary teams will have to be formed within either the development agencies themselves, or an agency set up exclusively for environmental control. For a complete, unbiased assessment of environmental effects it is essential that these groups be as independent as possible from the engineering and development staff of the resource agency. As the study groups are formed, a training period should be alloted to permit the development of an interdisciplinary framework for staff analysis as well as the administrative structure for the control and application of the efforts of such a diverse group. Continued in-service training of such groups should be a goal to be accomplished by reanalysis at various intervals after construction of the originally-projected impacts. Unforeseen impacts discovered in the reassessment process which would have precluded the original development will indicate the need for developing methods to avoid such oversights in the future. Also, if such effects are discovered to be severe, a new study should examine the possibilities of removing the project and restoring the local environment. Projects cannot be considered sacred if they are accruing large, long-term environmental costs.

References

Landau, N. J. and P. D. Rheingold, 1971. *The Environmental Law Handbook*. Ballentine Books Inc. New York.

Leopold, L. B. and F. Clarke, B. Hanshaw, J. Balsley. 1971. A procedure for evaluating environmental impact. U.S.G.S. Circular 645.

Morgan, A. E. 1971. *Dams and Other Disasters*. Porter Sargent, Boston, Ma.

Odum, E. P. 1971. *Fundamentals of Ecology*. W. B. Saunders Company, Philadelphia, Penn.

Sax J. L. 1971. *Defending the environment: a strategy for citizen action*. Alfred A. Knopf, New York.

CHAPTER 10

Comprehensive planning for small watershed conservation has had strong support from resource managers, but two decades of experience with Public Law 566 has clearly demonstrated that a balance between protection and development has not been achieved. Extensive drainage and channelization destroy ecological systems, environmental quality, and public values. Downstream areas often are subjected to increased flooding and eutrophication. Changing policies and terminology, and human prejudice, cause confusion and abuse. For example, all channelized streams are called "improved," and drastic biological upsets are not compared to flood control benefits. Cost-benefit analyses are grossly miscalculated. Fish, wildlife, and recreation benefits lost to development are inadequately represented, while more subtle damages are not assessed at all and benefits are exaggerated, promoting unwise floodplain development. Planning draws almost entirely upon engineering and economic data.

Ecological dimensions should be incorporated into planning, and administrative structures should be improved to reflect it. In future, the stress should be on conservation to protect present cropland, rather than in bringing marginal land into production. In order to accomplish these goals, the author proposes specific measures for comprehensive, ecologically sensitive evaluation of management practices.

WATERSHED PROGRAM LACKS ECOLOGICAL DIMENSIONS

Laurence R. Jahn

INTRODUCTION

The federal government has advocated and sponsored management of small watersheds for more than a quarter of a century. The Flood Control Act of 1944, Public Law 534, authorized the U.S. Department of Agriculture to carry out exploratory flood prevention work in eleven selected upstream watersheds. This included planning and installing measures to reduce runoff, erosion, and downstream flows in parts of California, Georgia, Iowa, Maryland, Minnesota, Mississippi, New York, Oklahoma, Pennsylvania, Tennessee, Texas, Virginia, and West Virginia.

Initial gratifying experiences with those projects emphasized the feasibility of resolving soil and water management problems through the watershed approach. Therefore, an additional sixty-two pilot watersheds were authorized in the Agricultural Appropriations Act of 1953, of which fifty-four have received attention. And in 1954 the Watershed Protection and Flood Prevention Act, Public Law 566, was enacted. In the subsequent sixteen years, through 30 June 1970, planning assistance was authorized for 1,561 watersheds, with developments being completed in 273, construction in progress on 728, and planning terminated for various reasons in 192. Planning was in progress on 368 projects. An unserviced backlog of 1,300 applications had accumulated, and 8,904 of the 19,195 watersheds of less than 250,000 acres in the United States were reported needing attention before the year 2000 (U.S. Department of Agriculture, 1970a).

The founding concept of the small watershed program—planning for the management of soils, waters, and vegetation on a comprehensive basis—was and still is supported generally by resource managers. The small watershed act originally was visualized as the authority required to develop the one program needed to promote orderly development and wise use of the country's soil and water resources.

The objective of comprehensive planning and management is to blend landscape manipulations proposed by individual landowners and local groups with protection of designated features of the resource base that yield a desired complex of public values. A balance is sought between development and protection of the different ecological units of the landscape, for example, streams, rivers, marshes, shorelands, flood plains, ground water recharge areas, woodlots, forests, upland fields.

Over two decades, experiences with the small watershed program clearly demonstrate that the balance sought between protection and development of the resource base is not being achieved in many cases (Jahn, 1966; Martin, 1969; Poole, 1968; Wharton, 1970; White, 1970). Increasing problems are being encountered in many states with watershed projects, but the two most serious involve maintaining valuable wetlands and streams and their associated shore lands and flood

plains from inappropriate physical developments planned and installed in watershed projects with taxpayers' funds.

Vast amounts of drainage, including channelization, have been applied in a detrimental manner and lead to the degradation and destruction of ecological systems, environmental quality, and public values. The purposes of this article are to identify phases of the program which promote excessive developments and to offer suggestions for corrections. New approaches are needed to help establish a better balance between development and protection, thereby making the watershed program more beneficial and more ecologically sound.

PROGRAM WEAKNESSES

The increasing volume of adverse reaction to small watershed projects focuses in large part on shortcomings resulting from outdated Congressional directives, misleading terminology, inadequate benefit-cost calculations, and incomplete planning.

Outdated Congressional Directives

Two policies established by the Congress for small watersheds have combined to keep project planning and development from being truly comprehensive. One statement offered in a Senate debate in 1956 actually authorized the invasion of flood plains and the degradation and destruction of stream channels (*U.S. Congressional Record*, 1956).

> It is the intention of the Committee that the term flood prevention shall be construed to mean not only land treatment and structures, such as detention reservoirs, but also drainage channels and related improvements to remove excess water caused by precipitation for overflow on flatlands.

In 1967, flood prevention, including drainage, was given top priority in proposed watershed projects (Poole, 1968). In a letter to the Speaker of the House of Representatives, the chairman of the House Committee on Agriculture wrote that since passage of P. L. 566 the committee "has felt, and still feels, that a project must first be justified on the grounds of flood prevention . . ."

He continued:

> As in the past, the committee will welcome incidental benefits such as recreation, irrigation, and municipal water supply which are consistent with good soil and water management; however, such benefits must be secondary to flood prevention . . . The committee respectfully urges the Department of Agriculture to carefully consider this policy in order that no further projects whose primary purpose is not flood prevention will be submitted to the committee.

This mandate makes the small watershed program largely single-purpose rather than fully multipurpose, as originally intended. Subsequently, the Soil Conservation Service, the administering agency of P. L. 566, has carried out these two Congressional directives without objection. Planners have been urged to maximize flood control through drainage, including channelization, in small watersheds. Some alternatives for preventing and controlling flood losses, such as flood plain management, have not received adequate attention.

The immediate need is for the Congress to replace these ecologically unsound directives with more meaningful new policies called for by the National Environmental Policy Act signed by the President on New Year's Day 1970. New policies should be aimed at maintaining and restoring environmental quality in the public interest, as well as meeting the needs of local landowners.

Misleading Terminology

Changing policies and terminology used in watershed planning and development have caused confusion, misunderstanding, and at times have been grossly misleading from an ecological standpoint. The following three examples illustrate how different terminology recognizes man's use of the land rather than the basic ecological systems or relations involved.

Wetlands, woodlands, and other similar areas grazed by livestock have been classified as poor pastures requiring treatment to upgrade them or convert them to croplands. In watersheds planned prior to 1967 such tracts could be converted to intensive agricultural uses through flood prevention measures installed at taxpayer expense. This constituted bringing new or additional land into agricultural production.

This same historical policy on "bringing new or additional land into crop production" has permitted and encouraged the loss of wetlands. For example, if the natural basin of a shallow marsh, deep marsh, or open water area (wetland types 3, 4, 5) was cropped or had a crop on it for three out of five years prior to 1963, the tract was considered cropland with an excess water problem. The solution was to remove the water with federal assistance (100 percent technical and 50 percent cost sharing) to permit cultivation every year. Such action was not considered bringing new or additional land into production. This improvised definition of cropland failed to recognize the ecological relationships involved. The basins must remain intact to benefit from periodic natural flooding and drawdown. But under these guidelines drought favored conversion of wetlands to croplands.

Under those policies, definitions, and previously described legislative directives, use of land for agricultural purposes was given priority over almost all other uses. Fortunately, Soil Conservation Service policies currently are more restrictive. Lands not presently used for growing cultivated crops or crops normally seeded for hay or pasture are considered additional lands ineligible for P. L. 566 financial and technical assistance. This policy and the new memoranda on ecological values issued in 1970 need

FIGURE 1
A stream with variable depths, clean water, vegetated shore lands, and unobstructed flood plains is an essential ecosystem that indicates proper adjustment of man's activities to the land. (Photograph courtesy of Georgia Game and Fish Commission.)

clarification and testing in field application. Restoration of overgrazed wetlands and woodlands, for example, should be given attention equal to converting them to intensive agricultural uses.

The third example of recognizing man's use of the land involved streams. Stream channels are "improved," according to Soil Conservation Service specifications, when they are cleared through snagging, or widened, deepened, and straightened by excavation to accelerate the flow of waters from specified sites within watershed projects. Labeling such physical disruptions of streams as "improvements" is misleading in most cases.

FIGURE 2

Channel construction commonly results in uniform stream depths, silted waters, and cleared shore lands. Although vegetation will over time become reestablished on undisturbed soils, biological productivity usually is lowered significantly and hydrological and ecological relationships are seriously disrupted. (Photograph courtesy of Georgia Game and Fish Commission.)

Reductions of height, extent, duration, and frequency of overflows, as achieved through channelization, often drastically reduce biological productivity of the stream channels treated, threaten the survival of plants and animals requiring periodic overflows of flood plains, and promote more intensive use of flood plains. All of these results degrade and destroy the bottomland ecosystems which depend upon periodic overflows for sediment and nutrient influx and deposition.

Downstream areas also are degraded. Nutrients that have accumulated in lowland sites over geological time are released through drainage and accelerate eutrophication and lower quality of surface waters (Amundson, 1970). The increase in volume and velocity of water flows in excavated channels maxi-

mize their erosive force and permit them to carry a higher silt load, as well as the more abundant nutrients, downstream to community lakes, reservoirs, and other streams. And, in some cases, channelization in one small watershed upstream may stimulate need for more downstream flood-control measures to offset higher or prolonged flood peaks induced by the new drainage. The volume of drainage must be reduced to an absolute minimum to control these undesirable and unwanted side effects.

Rather than consider channelization as stream "improvement," it should be regarded as a technique which, when used in an ecologically insensitive manner, degrades and destroys ecological relations, environmental quality, and public values. With few exceptions, every stream period-

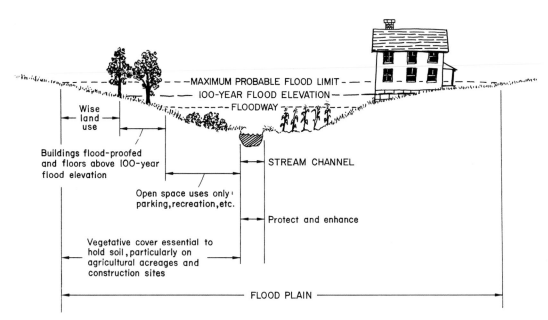

MAXIMUM PROBABLE FLOOD LIMIT

100-YEAR FLOOD ELEVATION

FLOODWAY

Wise land use

Buildings flood-proofed and floors above 100-year flood elevation

Open space uses only: parking, recreation, etc.

Vegetative cover essential to hold soil, particularly on agricultural acreages and construction sites

STREAM CHANNEL

Protect and enhance

FLOOD PLAIN

FIGURE 3

The primary alternative for destructive channelization of streams is flood plain zoning and management. Delineated channels, shore lands, and flood plains are maintained for nature's use, with man's activities adjusted to flood hazards. This approach promotes ecological soundness. Model flood plain zoning statutes will soon be available through the Water Resources Council. (Illustration courtesy of C. D. Trefethen.)

ically overflows its banks onto its flood plain to accommodate the flows it cannot carry in its channel. Areas adjacent to streams are natural flood storage sites and should not be protected completely from overflowing. The extent and frequency of flooding should serve as the basis for adjusting human activities (Hine, 1969; Lee, 1970). Only those encroachments which are compatible with maintaining stream channels, shorelands, water quality, open space, recreational opportunities, and fish and wildlife habitat should be permitted on flood plains. Obviously, channelization should be used much less frequently and more discreetly than at present. Nonstructural flood plain management should be used in every possible situation as an alternative for channelization in small watersheds.

Inadequate Benefit-Cost Calculations

Procedures currently used by economists and planners in small watershed projects to accumulate agricultural and nonagricultural benefits are (1) promoting conversion of wetlands, flood plains, woodlands, and other tracts to intensive agricultural uses; and (2) encouraging business, industrial, and residential developments in flood plains. Soil classifications, predicted changes in land use, economic calculations, and technical and financial aids available through the small watershed program combine to encourage landowners to develop soils and waters at the expense of ecological relations, environmental quality, and public values.

Lands that never have been cultivated in the past are classified on the basis of soil capabilities for a number of potential uses, but primarily for agricultural purposes. Benefits from drainage, including channel construction, are predicated on assumed changes of using lands more intensively. No values are assigned to lowlands for flood, sediment, and nutrient storage. Drainage assessments are based on the potential value of the lands as croplands or pasturelands, not on their existing condition.

With free technical assistance, 50 percent cost-sharing for drainage, 100 percent tax-payer payments for channels associated with flood control (= drainage), and 100 percent payments for administering construction contracts, landowners have plural incentives that discourage them from maintaining wetlands, woodlands, and other similar areas. These taxpayer-funded services and incentives promote converting ecologically useful areas to agricultural and other uses.

Dollar benefits also are accumulated from predicted business, industrial, and residential developments in flood plains to justify flood control expenditures. This is inconsistent with the best flood plain management programs being advanced by the Water Resources Council, Executive Order 11296 of the President of the United States, and laws of progressive states, such as Wisconsin, Minnesota, and Nebraska.

Even fish, wildlife, and recreation benefits are measured incompletely. Only estimates of the value of a visitor-day and the total man-days of anticipated use enter calculations. Thus, only a few recreational values of valuable ecosystems, such as wetlands and woodlands, supporting fish and wildlife, and associated recreational activities, are considered. No dollar values are assigned to water quality and quantity, nutrient exchange, biotic productivity, existing flora and fauna, esthetic values, and the like.

This complex of existing economic evaluation procedures is leading to degradation and destruction of ecological relationships and to man dominating the landscape rather than adjusting to it. No consideration is given to ecological values of woodlands, wetlands, streams, and flood plains. This is a serious void in procedure and in the program. These ecological oversights must be corrected immediately. New procedures must be developed and utilized to maintain valuable ecological relations, promote environmental quality, and enhance public values. We should not sacrifice them, knowingly or unknowingly, merely to enhance dollar values. This approach also would assist in voiding

production of crops that are under acreage allotments, marketing quotas, or in surplus. Ecological considerations simply must receive greater emphasis than economic procedures in all small watershed projects to reduce and avoid justifiable criticisms of the program and to expand total human benefits.

Incomplete Planning

Outmoded Congressional directives, misleading terminology, inadequate benefit-cost calculations, and lack of independent ecological review have resulted in biased and incomplete planning of small watershed projects, primarily by engineers and economists. Ecologists and biologists of all agencies involved have minor responsibilities due largely to administrative shortcomings. They have been permitted to conduct primarily reconnaissance-type evaluations of proposed watershed projects and to provide recommendations of a secondary nature for enhancing and mitigating fish and wildlife habitat. Approaches for maintaining important aquatic areas, woodlands, and other ecologically valuable areas have been lacking in the small watershed program.

The immediate pressing need is to develop and incorporate an ecological dimension in watershed planning, plans, and developments. This could be achieved, in part, by requiring that ecologists and biologists have primary responsibilities for initial project design, not secondary advisory roles in predominantly engineering-economic developments. Inappropriate technical services and financial aids must also be realigned to encourage local project sponsors and citizens to promote maintenance of ecological relations, environmental quality, and public values, instead of continuing to degrade and destroy them.

Since each small watershed project must be approved by the Governor, or a state agency designated by him, these authorities should insure that plans for developing the resource base in their state are ecologically sound and in the public interest. Insensitive and inappropriate developments of the land, largely at taxpayer expense to benefit relatively few people, no longer should be tolerated.

Personnel of Soil and Water Conservation Districts, usually the local sponsors of watershed projects, and the Soil Conservation Service can contribute significantly by aggressively aiding in realigning and establishing authorities and procedures to advance comprehensive watershed management. The overall objective should be to build more effective federal-state-local partnerships for managing resources for long-term as well as short-term benefits.

CORRECTIVE MEASURES

Considerable effort will be required to reorient planning and development of small watersheds to make them truly comprehensive resource management projects. Opinions not supported by facts and misleading entrenched views must be suppressed to maintain ecological soundness as soils and waters are developed. This will require incorporating an ecological dimension in watershed planning and development, as is being done by a few regional planning commissions (Southeastern Wisconsin Regional Planning Commission, 1969, 1970; also see McHarg and Clarke, this volume). Without this new dimension many projects will fail to optimize human and social benefits.

Expand Project Evaluations

Bringing about needed realignments will require full use of existing knowledge and findings from in-depth investigations of small watersheds that have received attention in the past twenty-five years. Unfortunately, intensive investigations have been completed on only a few small watershed projects. More evaluations are needed immediately on three groups of watersheds.

1. *Post-construction investigations of the 273 P. L. 566 watersheds completed as of July 1970 and the upstream watershed projects authorized through earlier enacted laws.*

Gains and losses in ecological relations and changes in land use resulting from projects should be identified. Effectiveness of executing project plans and attaining planned objectives would be determined. Insight would be gained for realigning and strengthening institutional arrangements, technical services, financial incentives, objectives, plans, and developments in watershed projects. They must combine to help resolve pressing land and water management problems, while simultaneously maintaining important units of the landscape, such as aquatic areas.

2. *Re-examination of the 1,288 watersheds approved for federal planning assistance, including the 728 in some phase of construction and the 368 now in some stage of planning.*

These projects have been evaluated and planned without benefit of full ecological considerations. Alternatives for drainage and channel construction should be incorporated. This need is critical. At least 38 percent of more than $19 million for small watershed construction in fiscal year 1971 is for channelization (U.S. Soil Conservation Service, personal communication).

3. *Pre-authorization evaluations of the 8,904 small watersheds are identified in the National Soil and Water Conservation Needs Inventory have problems requiring resolution.*

Inventory procedures used in defining watershed problems do not fully encompass ecological relations. They must be given primary attention when identifying problems and suggesting solutions through land treatments. Misleading terms, definitions, and procedures used for determining needs for land treatments should be replaced and avoided in the future.

Special efforts will be needed to guard against being misled by soil capability classifications used to alter, for the benefit of a relatively few individuals, wetlands, streams, shore lands, and flood plains which should be maintained—regardless of soil type—to yield a complex of public values. These important ecological areas do not have to and should not be converted to agricultural production, especially at taxpayer expense.

According to the recent National Inventory of Soil and Water Conservation Needs, the nation's agricultural land is feeding and clothing our expanding human population from reduced acreages of cultivated crops and grazing lands (U.S. Department of Agriculture, 1970b). Increasing food and fiber needs are being and can continue to be met substantially through proper use of existing agricultural acreages.

About two-thirds of our present cropland is not being handled in a manner that avoids deterioration and assures sustained production in the future. Similarly, 67 percent of privately owned pastures and ranges and 62 percent of private forests are not adequately managed. Some 16 million acres of land not generally suitable for cropland, but presently in cultivation, should be converted to permanent cover.

These great needs for better management of existing agricultural lands should receive primary attention in each of the 19,195 watersheds of less than 250,000 acres in the United States. Likewise, maintenance of wetlands, shorelands, and flood plains should receive top priority consideration. New approaches must be developed to meet these twin goals through comprehensive watershed planning and development.

Strengthen Procedures and Authorities

The immediate need is to realign existing procedures, incorporate new approaches, and broaden federal and state authorities to permit, encourage, or require small watershed projects to be planned and developed on a truly comprehensive resource management basis. This will entail a change in attitudes of many people, particularly watershed planners and local sponsors, as well as of procedures and authorities.

Wetlands and streams with their associated shorelands and flood plains must be recognized as unique ecological systems. Wetlands can no longer be looked upon as wastelands. They are important features of the landscape which provide unique diversity and are of inestimable public value.

To maintain these essential areas state and federal resource agencies should inventory the land and water resources in each proposed watershed project in sufficient detail to permit designation of important features of the landscape for maintenance and ecological management.

1. Streams or sections of streams should be delineated in each watershed that are not to be impounded, channeled, or altered in any way. Every stream of local, state, regional and national significance should be included. Degraded streams should be restored, whenever feasible, through ecologically sound modifications and management that reduce erosion, sedimentation, and pollution and improve their biological productivity.

2. Flood plains of all streams should be delineated using boundaries of the regional flood, which, on the average, may be expected once in a hundred years. Within this defined area man's activities should be planned and carried out according to standard development criteria based on flooding hazards. They should be designed to prevent and minimize damages, expenses, and inconveniences to citizens. Only that development consistent with nature's requirements for conveying flood waters should be permitted. Planners and engineers must protect the bottomland environments from man's inappropriate degrading and destructive activities.

State authorities having responsibilities for safeguarding the soil, water, plant, and animal resources for their respective areas should make sure that all streams are inventoried and flood plains delineated in each watershed. In some states efforts are being made to protect streams and rivers from unwarranted physical modifications. Louisianna, for example, in 1970 enacted a law making it illegal to modify in any way thirty-seven streams or sections of streams having important ecological, recreational, and esthetic values. Other states, such as Montana and Michigan, also protect stream channels. Nebraska, Minnesota, and Wisconsin laws extend protection to all shorelands and flood plains (for example, see Yanggen, in this volume).

In all of these states the public trust doctrine of law is used to maintain ecological relations, environmental quality, and values in the public interest. Every state should establish similar statutes to maintain all surface waters and their associated shorelands and flood plains, prohibit incompatible physical developments, and allow other physical developments only after careful interagency review and through a permit system.

Public Law 566 should be amended to require protection for streams or sections of streams delineated in each watershed project by an interagency task force. Minimal standards, such as those being advanced by the Water Resources Council, should be used in planning and approving watershed projects (U.S. Water Resources Council, 1969). Applications for planning assistance should be approved only if they meet the minimal federal standards in states lacking appropriate statutes or equivalent standards in those states having adequate laws and regulations. State standards could, however, be more restrictive but not more liberal than federal standards.

Currently three federal orders are available to help states maintain their streams, shorelands, and flood plains from insensitive, inappropriate, and degrading developments: the President's Executive Orders 11296 and 11514 issued in August 1966 and March 1970, respectively, and the Office of Management and Budget's Circular A-95 issued in July 1969. The President's orders require all executive agencies responsible for land-use planning to protect and enhance the environment, to take flood hazards into account when evaluating plans, and to encourage land use appropriate to the degree of flooding hazard involved. Circular A-95 encourages establishment of review procedures in each state to insure that all federal aid for local projects comply with state laws and plans. Applications for watershed planning assistance are covered, since watersheds are regarded as federally assisted local projects. Nebraska is using this procedure to insure that watershed applications involving flood plain developments comply with its Flood Plain Regulation Act (Fairchild, 1970).

In Wisconsin a policy signed in June 1970 by the State Soil Conservation Board specifically brings proposed small watershed projects in line with the state's 1965 shoreland and flood plain law. Applications for watershed planning assistance will be approved only if they meet state specifications. This is a commendable advance in authority and procedure which should strengthen the position of watershed planners to incorporate greater ecological considerations in watershed projects.

All state and federal administrators and planners dealing with watersheds should use these orders and seek other essential authorities to deny consideration of watershed applications and to withhold planning assistance and technical services from existing projects lacking stream, shore land, and flood plain maintenance and management features.

3. *Wetlands that must be preserved or mitigated should be delineated. By knowing in advance the wetlands requiring preservation, the need for and expense of mitigation can be minimized through appropriate project design. Specific needs for mitigation can be determined as planning proceeds.*

Federal, state, and local programs for

FIGURE 4
A secondary alternative to avoid channelizing a
stream involves installing an auxiliary floodway to
convey excess flows above a minimal level in the
main channel. Channels and shore lands are
maintained. But reduction in height, extent, duration,
and frequency of floods adversely alters hydrological
and ecological relationships in flood plains. This
alternative is being used in the Tennessee Valley
Authority's Bear Creek Watershed in Alabama and
Mississippi. (Illustration courtesy of TVA.)

acquiring wetlands in fee title and through easements should be used wherever available. In addition, the Water Bank Act, Public Law 91–559, enacted in December 1970, authorizes the U.S. Department of Agriculture to provide a financial incentive to landowners for maintaining designated wetlands that yield a broad spectrum of public values. These payments constitute an alternative for drainage whereby the general public shares in the cost of maintaining important wetlands. In many watersheds, wetland areas comprise much of what remains of historical plant and animal communities in an otherwise man-dominated and ecologically simplified environment.

In most cases it is impossible to replace streams and wetlands degraded and destroyed by excavated channels. Complaints of mitigation center on this critical point. Mitigation measures usually are unsatisfactory, have not always been installed as planned, and are costly to taxpayers. Current procedures call for using taxpayer funds totally or partially to replace important ecological areas degraded or destroyed by government technical assistance and financial aids paid for with other taxpayer dollars. Mitigation must be held at an absolute minimum to avoid (1) its use as an excuse to accomplish undesirable watershed development, (2) inadequate replacement of essential areas, and (3) double payments by taxpayers. Important ecological areas must be maintained.

4. *Sites that can hold excess runoff waters should be designated and maintained or developed to minimize flooding downstream within and outside a watershed and, when feasible, to enhance fish and wildlife habitat and public recreational opportunities.*

The prevailing philosophy of getting rid of excess water by draining and channeling it from each watershed must be replaced with the objective of helping to hold runoff water within each watershed by concentrating it in delineated natural and man-made basins. This means emphasizing application of land management practices throughout a watershed, not merely in those portions of watersheds above flood control structures. Holding water where it falls on the land is one of the founding principles of both the Soil Conservation Service and the watershed program. It should be the guiding principle in project design now and in the future. It means using a combined ecological-engineering approach, rather than solely engineering, for soil and moisture management.

5. *Other unique features of the landscape should be delineated, such as ground water recharge areas and outstanding or rare plant communities.*

All available federal, state, and local approaches should be used to maintain these unique designated areas. Information from hydrologists, botanists, and other knowledgeable persons should be sought and used. University and college personnel and local citizens could contribute much valuable information. Existing U.S. Department of Agriculture long-term land conversion and retirement programs should be modified to help accomplish maintenance and management of all delineated units of watersheds. Project funds should be available for acquiring key tracts in fee title or through easements. Acquired acreages could be turned over to state and federal land managing agencies.

Watershed planners having information on all five foregoing types of designated areas should design realistic and practical plans for meeting more than agricultural objectives. No assumed benefits or drainage assessments should be permitted on these delineated units of the landscape. Arrangements for maintaining them should be incorporated directly into each project together with flood prevention and flood control designs. This will require greater ecological-engineering-political imagination and skill than now evidenced in watershed planning and development. Effective teamwork will be required to bring about constructive changes (Grant, 1970).

The approaches recommended here would be consistent with the proposed National Land Use Policy Act (S. 3354, 91st Congress). It would authorize federal grants to stimulate preparation and implementation of state land use plans. Ecologically sound resource planning and management on a watershed basis would constitute one important vehicle for implementing that act. Properly designed projects could integrate developments with constraints required to promote ecological soundness.

References

Amundson, R. W. 1970. Nutrient availability of a marsh soil. M. S. Thesis, University of Wisconsin, Madison. 56 pp.

Fairchild, W. D. 1970. Unwilling host to an unwanted guest. *Water Spectrum* 2(4): 24-29.

Grant, K. E. 1970. Watershed action: resources and teamwork. *Proc. Natl. Watershed Congress* 17:134-140.

Hine, R. L. (Editor). 1969. Water use principles and guidelines for planning and management in Wisconsin. Wis. Chapt. Soil Conserv. Society of American, Madison, Wisconsin. 96 pp.

Jahn, L. R. 1966. A wildlife organization's views of P. L. 566. Presented at U.S. Soil. Conserv. Service, Midwest Biology Workshop, Madison, Wisconsin, 25-29 July. 24 pp (multilith).

Lee, T. M. 1970. Flood plain management in Wisconsin: a local-state effort. Presented at Flood Damage Abatement Seminar, Virginia Polytechnic Institute, Blacksburg, Va., 19-20 May. (Multilith)

Martin, E. C. 1969. Stream alteration and its effects on fish and wildlife. Presented at Annual Meeting, Southern Div. Amer. Fisheries Soc., Mobile, Ala., 20 Oct. 19 pp (multilith).

Poole, D. A. 1968. Weaknesses in the Public Law 566 watershed program. *Proc. of Natl. Watershed Congress* 15:42-51.

Southeastern Wisconsin Regional Planning Commission. 1969. A comprehensive plan for the Fox River watershed: inventory, findings and forecasts. *Vol. 1, Planning Report No. 12,* 445 pp. S. E. Wis. Reg. Pl. Comm., Old Courthouse, Waukesha, Wisconsin.

Southeastern Wisconsin Regional Planning Commission. 1970. A comprehensive plan for the Fox River Watershed: alternative plans and recommended plan. *Vol. II, Planning Report No. 12.* 497 pp. S. E. Wis. Reg. Pl. Comm., Waukesha, Wisconsin.

U.S. Congressional Record. 1956. Procedings and debates of the 82nd Congress. *Vol. 102, Part 10*:13642-13648. 20 July.

U.S. Department of Agriculture. 1970a. Status of watershed protection (P. L. 566) program. Soil Conserv., Washington, D.C. 43 pp.

U.S. Department of Agriculture. 1970b. America has enough farmland, but needs to take better care of it. Release of 14 August. 2 pp.

U.S. Water Resources Council. 1969. Proposed flood hazard evaluation guidelines for federal executive agencies. Water Resources Council, Washington, D.C. 45 pp.

Wharton, C. H. 1970. The southern river swamp: a multiple-use environment. Georgia State University, Atlanta. 48 pp.

White, Gilbert F. 1970. Flood-loss reduction: the integrated approach. *J. Soil and Water Conservation* 25(5):172-176.

CHAPTER 11

The environmental impacts of water development projects have recently become the source of considerable concern by various groups. On the one hand there exists a continuing need to satisfy man's water requirements and on the other there is a recognition that projects to accomplish these ends may cause very serious adverse impacts.

The outcry raised by organizations and individuals who are concerned with environmental impacts has resulted in the establishment of federal and state (California) policies and procedures for evaluating them. A framework for assessing the social desirability of a project still needs devising, but a careful assessment of all the effects of water development is a step in the right direction.

Several general kinds of ecological impacts associated with water development encompass the many concerns expressed by various groups. These include effects in the area of impoundment, downstream effects, effects along the conveyance route, and effects in the area of project use.

ECOLOGICAL IMPACTS
OF WATER STORAGE
AND DIVERSION PROJECTS

Robert M. Hagan and Edwin B. Roberts

Ecologists and environmentalists are increasingly concerned about man's lack of complete understanding of possible ecological impacts of water projects. Some cause for worry is to be found in statements by leading scientists. Referring to Soviet plans for diverting southward three large Siberian rivers now flowing into the Arctic Sea to irrigate desert areas in central Asia, Hubert Lamb of the British Meteorological Office was reported in a February 1970 interview (Mauthner, 1970) as fearing such projects could cause worldwide climatic changes. By depriving the Arctic of freshwater, the world's climatic belts would be shifted northward and possibly even cause greater deserts in the United States (see also Teclaff, in this volume). Raymond L. Nace of the U.S. Geological Survey is reported to have suggested during the 1970 Conference of the International Hydrological Decade at UNESCO in Paris that the proposed diversion to the south of great rivers in Siberia and North America, by moving weight from the north pole toward the equator, might slow the earth's rotation and make it wobble more on its axis. Dr. Nace's comments, which were disputed by other hydrologists in attendance, were intended to dramatize how little thought has been given in some cases to the consequences of great water projects. Similar concerns are expressed about smaller water projects in the United States.

Those concerned about ecological impacts, or those prepared to make use of these concerns, now argue that water projects in California should be deferred until such impacts are thoroughly explored and understood even if such delays might force some hardships as a result of temporary inadequacy of water supplies pending completion of new projects. The authors' experience with students enrolled in Resource Science courses during the past year indicates that a number of them are strongly supportive of preservationist ideas. They say that it is of priceless importance to them to leave an area the way it was before man appeared. Whether these students and others would really be willing to alter substantially their personal use of water or power is less certain. It is perhaps understandable that one who has been made comfortable and prosperous by the availability of resources provided under previously constructed projects can be outspokenly critical about further water developments.

VIEWPOINTS ON ECOLOGICAL IMPACTS

The introduction to the book *Water, Earth, and Man* (Chorley and Kates, 1969) reports estimates that 10 percent of the national wealth of the United States is found in capital expenditures for structures designed to alter the hydrologic cycle; that is, to collect, divert, and store about one-fourth of the available surface water, distribute it where it is needed, cleanse it, carry it away, and return it to the natural system. In California numerous works exist to carry out these objectives and many more are planned to meet the needs of its growing population.

Water is becoming increasingly recognized as a vital resource. Water projects affect all the people in some way or another. They often have substantial effects on man's way of life and especially on quality of life and economic conditions. Water projects are viewed increasingly by some as vehicles for initiating or controlling development and industry and also useful in altering the distribution of wealth and effecting social change. Water projects can induce, directly or indirectly, a vast array of changes in environment, some of which, many feel, cannot be adequately predicted. These projects also require long lead times for planning and construction, involve large capital expenditures, and are often essentially irreversible and produce permanent changes. Thus, there are growing concerns today about our environment and its preservation for future generations. Ecological issues often provide more acceptable grounds for opposition to water projects than arguments that arise from personal gains or losses. For these and other reasons water has become an emotionally charged issue.

We are now experiencing a great outpouring of statements by public officials, special interest organizations, business groups, voters associations, conservationists and environmentalists, and alarmed but sometimes confused citizens who call attention to ecologic issues. This crescendo of public concern about ecological impacts will certainly affect the planning, construction, and operation of major water projects. It has already led to adoption of federal standards for planning projects involving water and land resources and to parallel action by California to require evaluation of the ecological impacts of such projects. The major federal and state agencies involved have now established special sections to deal with environmental aspects of water project planning.

The Sierra Club and other organizations are increasingly urging that further water development be critically reviewed. In its statement to the House Committee on Science and Astronautics at the hearing in San Francisco on March 17, 1970, the Club states that

> Future water development in California, as outlined in the California Water Plan, will have devastating effects on the environment and quality of life enjoyed by Californians. This Plan, produced in an era when public concerns were far different than today, is no longer valid in the light of 1970 knowledge, experience, and technology. It is now apparent that the cost of implementing the Plan in dollars and in environmental damage is too high a price to pay for illogical encouragement of growth in our already crowded urban areas . . . The California Water Plan rests on three assumptions that are inconsistent with present environmental concerns and technology. First, the California Water Plan assumes that there is no loss of value when a wild, free-flowing river is tamed, that the river valleys of Northern California may be drowned with no concern for the land, scenic and recreation resources destroyed. Second, the California Water Plan assumes that the diverse estuarine biological communities of the Sacramento-San Joaquin Delta can survive the alterations in water quality that will accompany the many-fold reduction in the quantity of water flowing to the Delta, to San Francisco Bay, and to the ocean, or that the destruction of this living resource will have no effect on the recreation and enjoyment experienced by millions on the Bay and Delta each year. And third, the California Water Plan assumes that population growth in California will continue at a high rate and be localized around present urban centers, disregarding the resultant urban crowding, transportation problems, noise and air pollution.

In a series of resolutions adopted by the Board of Directors in February 1970 the Sierra Club called for a

> complete re-examination of the entire California Water Plan and its implementation, particularly with regard to the underlying assumptions and value judgments. This re-examination must emphasize studies of environmental effects throughout the state including the effects of the construction, and of storage and transport facilities, of water withdrawals from source and downstream areas, and of the stimulation of growth in the areas supplied. During the period of this re-examination there must be a halt to further design and construction of any major local, state or federal division or project of the Water Plan. With regard to California's State Water Project, there should be no further construction contracts awarded until this re-examination is complete; authorization for new projects or divisions on the Central Valley Project should be deferred until this re-examination is complete. Furthermore, during this re-examination period. the sale of water by the Department of Water Resources through the State Water Project and by the United States Bureau of Reclamation through the Central Valley Project should be limited to those minimal amounts actually contracted for. The sale of "excess" water should be halted, and pumping from the Delta should be limited to the winter months as far as practical.

As might be expected, other interest groups attacked the Sierra Club statement. The California Water Resources Association in its April 1970 newsletter referred to the Sierra Club position as "killer conservation." The *Newsletter* states:

> We are surprised that an organization dedicated to protecting the environment would take this meat-ax approach toward water projects whose major goal is enhancement of man's environment. The Sierra Club resolution adopted last year contains no guidelines or criteria for determining when a water project is good or bad for the environment. Water developers have historically used the rule that unless a water project put the environment to a higher use for benefit of man, it was not a

feasible project. Historically water projects have utilized the environment for man's health, welfare and enjoyment. They have made California green, agriculturally productive, free in large measure from disastrous floods and provided recreation for millions.

The *Newsletter* takes exception to the Sierra Club charge that the States Water Plan was "narrowly conceived and unresponsive to the new goals and values society is fast adopting to ensure its own survival."

Several other agencies, including the Colorado River Association and the Irrigation District's Association of California, have gone on record as supportive of the State Water Project plans. The Colorado River Association in its September 1970 *Newsletter* refers to a report made by the California Field Offices of the Federal Water Quality Administration and the Bureau of Reclamation which indicates that by 2020 the population in the Central Valley of California will increase three- to five-fold, irrigated acres by 50 percent or about 3 million acres, and net water use by over 50 percent. It is estimated that federal and state construction funds will be needed between 1970 and 1990 in the amount of more than 3 billion dollars to meet the water needs of this valley area. Former Interior Secretary Hickel commented:

> A large investment in water quality management systems must accompany economic development if environmental quality is to be preserved. Such an investment can likely be supported by an economic use.

Opposition to California Water Projects is not limited to environmentalist groups and to segments of the general public attracted by the statements of such groups. In October 1970 the California Council of the American Institute of Architects wrote to the Governor of California asking him to

> immediately appoint a special governor's committee of professionals skilled in planning to re-evaluate the State Water Plan . . .

This request for a re-study was not lightly reached. It is founded on the conviction that the [State] Water Plan cannot help but have a significant effect on the environment and the very real fear that such an effect may be diastrous.

The Institute's request cited seven reasons including the following: (1) Pollution of San Francisco Bay has become critical, and any diminution of water flow in the Sacramento River System can only make matters worse; (2) Construction of the San Luis Drain and the Peripheral Canal could cause virtual destruction of both San Francisco Bay and the Delta; (3) Construction of dams on virtually all of the wild rivers of Northern California may constitute excessive manipulation of the environment; (5) There is serious question as to the wisdom of stimulating unlimited population growth in the Los Angeles basin.

This statement continues by calling attention to the escalation of construction and operating costs and to recent population figures which indicate that growth throughout California has slackened and that there is time to reflect and reconsider future water needs. The California State Department of Water Resources in a *Summary Report* issued December 1970 confirms that, because of decreased population projections for the state,

> sufficient water is developed by completed water projects, or will be developed by those under construction, to satisfy most urban and irrigation needs for about two decades . . . The favorable status of developed water supplies affords time to evaluate potential alternative sources of water and devote more attention to the emerging environmental problems associated with water conservation projects and the evolvement of definite public policies on such problems.

The foregoing quotations support the conclusion of Chorley and Kates (1969) that there appears to be a growing recognition that much of what may be socially important (to some) in assessing the desirability of water-resource developments will escape our present techniques of feasibility analyses for much time to come. The need for a wider basis of choice to account for the social desirability of water-resource development persists and deepens as a number of water-related values increase and the means for achieving them multiply. A framework for assessing social desirability still needs devising, but it could be hastened by a careful assessment of what actually follows water-resource development. There is much to be learned from the extensive developments planned or already constructed. (See Teclaff, in this volume.)

White (1969) called attention to the problem of contrasts between the perception of environment by scientists and by others who make practical decisions in managing resources of land and water. Studies of environmental perception have grown rapidly in number, method, and content, but it is evident from reading the statements by concerned groups and involved agencies that much more detailed investigations need to be carried out. It is also obvious that technical and economic feasibility studies, which were formerly considered quite independently, are now seen as closely related questions. To these analyses we must also add social impacts or costs of water projects. It is possible that the methodology for making such determinations has outrun our understanding of the actual relationships involved. Those who promote water projects need to recognize the erosion of their political base and to try to make peace with conservation groups and urban interests (McCloskey and others, this volume).

KINDS OF ECOLOGICAL IMPACTS ASSOCIATED WITH WATER PROJECTS

In order to appreciate fully the great breadth and diversity of ecological concerns expressed by various individuals and groups, an effort has been made in Tables 1 through 5 to outline the many kinds of impacts which are

TABLE 1
Areas Possibly Experiencing Ecological Impacts From Water Storage and Diversion Projects

Area of impoundment (see Table 2 for details)
Downstream from impoundment and/or diversion River channel and flood plain (see Table 3, part A) Delta, bay, or ocean (see Table 3, part B)
Along conveyance route for project water (see Table 4)
Areas of project water use Agricultural (see Table 5, part A) Urban (see Table 5, part B)

specifically included or implied in their statements. As indicated in Table 1, different types of ecological impacts may be found in areas of impoundment, downstream from impoundment and/or diversion, along conveyance routes for project water, and in areas of project water use. The subsequent tables outline the kinds of impacts which may occur in the different areas. The tables are intended to list the large array of possible impacts, not all of which may be important in a given project. The tables do include some replication between areas because certain kinds of impacts are to be found in all of the areas from impoundment to the service area.

Illustrations are presented for only a few items. Additional cases are to be found in the sections of this report prepared by McCloskey, Teclaff, Beeton, Edmondson, Hedgpeth, and Henwood. Detailed analyses of the ecological impacts of water projects requires substantial expertise in a great diversity of professional fields (see McEvoy, Henwood, Hollis, Luken and Langlois, Scott, and White, in this volume). Scientifically acceptable studies reported with detail necessary for adequate understanding are difficult to find. Very little is reported in professional journals or other generally available publications. Much comment, often quite emotional, is found in newspapers, magazines, and books on ecology. In some cases, the impact is recognized by knowledgeable people although no data appear to have been collected or published. It appears that the best available information may be contained in special reports of state and local agencies and those of consultants, but these are unavailable or of very limited distribution. Ecological impacts are now often discussed at meetings of many types of organizations which do not issue proceedings. For this reason, we have quoted from sources of limited availability and included newsletters and other publications not generally cited in bibliographies.

ECOLOGICAL IMPACTS IN AREA OF IMPOUNDMENT

Many people concerned with the environment view any change in the natural state of the area as environmental damage. The Committee on Water of the National Research Council (1968) states, "These people feel a sense of stewardship over the remaining primitive, wild or 'natural' sectors of the earth's surface, and they believe that no market analysis can assay properly the ethical aspects of preserving these sectors for later generations." This attitude has contributed to great controversy over plans to dam the Eel River and the other few remaining "wild" rivers of Northern California. Table 2 summarizes the many ecological impacts which may occur in the area of impoundment.

There appears to be only limited evidence of significant changes in microclimate as a result of water impoundment. Waddy (1966) suggests that a lake such as that above the Aswan High Dam in the United Arab Republic will provide such a tremendous surface area for evaporation that the climate of the region may be affected. Worthington (1966) reports that Lake Victoria in Africa and some other natural lakes create their own climatic system with daily sea breezes and nightly land breezes, influencing rainfall and vegetation. Cutting down surrounding hills during construction of the San Luis Project in California is said by residents to have increased winds locally. However, Thornthwaite (1956) reports that the creation of the Salton Sea and Lake Mead have resulted in scarcely any change in climate, even in the immediate vicinity.

Reservoirs can substantially increase evaporation from river systems. In 1963 there were 1,562 reservoirs in the U.S. larger than 5,000 acre-feet of usable capacity. These reservoirs had a total usable storage of about 360,000,000 acre-feet and covered an area of nearly 15,000,000 acres (Todd, 1970). In California alone there were 205 reservoirs with a usable capacity of 28,000,000 acre-feet covering 650,000 acres. If the annual evaporation in the central Pacific area averages about 2.5 feet, the total evaporation loss exceeds 1,600,000 acre-feet per year. Evaporation from impoundments in the 17 western states is estimated to range from 15,600,000 to 21,000,000 acre-feet per year (Symons and others, 1964).

Thermal stratification in reservoirs is discussed by Kittrell (1965) and by Symons and others (1964). Although release of cold lower layers may have profound effects downstream, the temperature change most noticeable at the impoundment is the warming of the surface layer, which encourages recreational use and may alter aquatic life. It has been reported (Harvey, 1969) that increased temperatures in the Columbia River due to dams and nuclear reactors have aided a formerly rare, but deadly, bacterial fish disease to flourish and threaten the salmon runs. Furthermore, the anticipated future development of the Columbia could raise the temperature above maximum levels that may be tolerated by salmon and steelhead. The California Department of Fish and Game (1970) refers to an unpublished report by Weidlein who predicted that operation of a projected Shasta-Trinity complex would result in water with a temperature of 60° F or more being released from Keswick Dam in 20 percent of the years prior to 2020. Since the maximum

TABLE 2
Ecological Impacts In Area of Impoundment

Disturbs natural state of area

Desire to preserve natural conditions for present and future generations: "wild" rivers versus controlled rivers.

Changes scenic values: conversion of rivers to lakes.

Modifies micro-climate: temperature, humidity, wind.

Alters land form, vegetation, wildlife, etc. (through construction and subsequent activities) and thus affects ecological diversity.

Increases evaporation loss

Reduces water supply.

Degrades water quality.

Changes water temperature

Altered aquatic life.

Effects on some water uses, primarily water sports.

Alters erosion and sedimentation

Erodes reservoir banks, causes land slides.

Deposits sediments in reservioirs: delta formation, loss of reservoir capacity.

Submerges land areas

Affects scenic values: submerges scenic treasures; creates new scenic values; causes visual "pollution" from exposed banks during drawdown.

Loss of historic sites.

Displaces people (see economic and social effects).

Loss of farm land (see economic and social effects).

Alters habitat for fish and wildlife (see below): mitigation enhancement.

Creates environments for new life forms: plants, insects, fish, and other wildlife.

Possibly influences earthquake frequency.

Modifies fish production

Substitution of lake for stream fishing: changes in fish species.

Dam creates barrier for anadromous fish migrating to spawning grounds: fish ladders.

Still water and deeply submerged spawning beds affect reproduction and return of young fish to sea: fish hatcheries.

Alters wildlife production

Submerges feeding areas.

Substitutes other areas or more intensively managed areas.

Provides new nesting and feeding areas for migrating birds.

Denuded zone exposed during drawdown restricts access to water by timid animals.

Reservoir brings "people pressures" which may upset delicate environmental balances, adversely affecting rare species.

Modifies recreation potential of area

Alters opportunities for swimming, skiing, and boating.

Modifies fishing and hunting.

Creates or expands sites for camping and other recreational facilities.

Increases people pressures on life of area with resultant ecological impacts.

Increases penetration of adjacent and remote wilderness areas by hikers.

Intensifies traffic, noise, and air pollution.

Expands needs for pollution control and waste removal.

Increases development of surrounding lands for urban or vacation housing

Destroys native plant cover.

Increases erosion from construction and loss of plant cover.

Increases people pressure on surrounding areas.

Intensifies pollution and waste disposal problems.

Alters economic, social, and political life of area with resultant secondary ecological impacts

---

temperature tolerance of salmon eggs is 57° F, a detrimental effect on salmon propagation in the river can be expected.

Siltation of reservoirs may be a serious problem in some sites. It is said that the new Bhakhra Nangal Dam in India will be filled up with silt within 40 years, and 100 million tons of silt a year are estimated to be trapped behind the Aswan Dam. Near Santa Barbara, California, a reservoir built on the Santa Ynez River soon began to fill with silt. The city of Santa Barbara then built a second dam with the same results, and now a third

dam has been built (Marine, 1968). A desilting works constructed at Imperial Dam returned over 455,000 tons of silt to the Colorado River in 1968 (Colorado River Association, 1969).

Construction of the Glen Canyon Dam on the Colorado River provides a prime example of controversy over dams and scenic values (see also Nash, in this volume). Conservationists decry submergence of beautiful canyons while the Bureau of Reclamation stresses the values of new Lake Powell. Dams have been proposed which could back water into a portion of the Grand Canyon where one of the world's most spectacular gorges is yet essentially undisturbed. Opponents of further dam construction on the Colorado River gorge argue that the principal social value of the Grand Canyon is its unique aesthetic quality which should not be traded for a different and less unique aesthetic value were dams constructed and reservoirs created (National Research Council, 1968).

In reservoirs with greatly fluctuating water levels, vegetation is killed along the edges by a high water level and an ugly scar is exposed when the water level is drawn down. However, due to differences in local conditions, there are important exceptions. For example, in operating Folsom Reservoir east of Sacramento, California, drawdown of the water level causes the worst of the scar to appear after peak recreational use, and the exposed slopes normally re-seed naturally.

It is not widely recognized how extensive the displacement of people and inundation of farm land may be when reservoirs are constructed in populated areas. The reservoirs supplying water for New York City alone displaced 6,000 people from more than twenty villages and hundreds of farms (Highsmith and others, 1969). Much controversy has surrounded recent plans for a Dos Rios Dam in Northern California, partly because of the effect flooding Round Valley would have on the Yuki Indians who inhabit the valley. Proposals to trade the Indians two acres of hill land for each acre of flatland lost to the reservoir were called unthinkable by a group of anthropologists and archeologists (Treganza and others, 1968). They pointed out that the Indians are flatland dwellers not hill dwellers, and that the hills are not suitable for any type of habitation. Furthermore, the farmers whose fathers settled the fertile valley were not going to adapt to "renting rowboats and selling hotdogs."

The inundation of a free-flowing stream, replacing it with a vast body of still water, may greatly alter the types of life forms

present. Little (1966) discusses the invasion of man-made lakes by plants. Vincent (1965) has shown that trapping of water in reservoirs helps create a homogenous environment in which only a reduced variety of organisms can survive. Also, if water quality is degraded the variety of surviving organisms and the variety of possible uses for the water are reduced (see also McCloskey, this volume).

It has been reported that the weight of water held in surface water reservoirs may actually cause earthquakes in the surrounding area (Saines, 1969). While on the subject of earthquakes, it has been suggested (Marine, 1968) that water from the California Water Project, applied through irrigation and reservoir seepage, may make clay deposits underlying large areas unstable and increase landslides during earthquakes.

For convenience, effects on fish and wildlife occurring in the area of impoundment (Table 2) will be discussed together with effects on fish and wildlife occurring in the river channel (Table 3). Gottschalk (1967) of the U.S. Bureau of Sport Fisheries and Wildlife, states that fish and wildlife provide a unique recreational base which contributes substantial money to the economy and provide a source of high protein food. There are also unmeasured values associated with the maintenance of an ecological orderliness, and the recognition that man, himself, is a part of a large whole whose total integrity must be assured (see Everson and others, this volume). He explains why water is absolutely essential for fish and wildlife and states that "it must be available in dependable quantities and qualities and present at the critical time and place." As a result of building dams on most major rivers, the rivers no longer meet the requirements for many species.

Damage to fish and wildlife resources of California resulting from the Trinity River Project have been documented by the California Department of Fish and Game (1970). Not only has Lewiston Dam on the Trinity blocked access of salmon and steel-

TABLE 3
Ecological Impacts Downstream From Impoundment and/or Diversion

A. In river channel and flood plain

Disturbs natural state of area

Modifies downstream hydrograph
  Reduces peak flows.
    Minimizes flood damage along channel and in flood plain.
    Reduces channel scouring and increases sedimentation (affecting channel capacity, fish spawning grounds).
    Reduces opportunities for water spreading for ground water recharge.
    Reduces capacity for flushing, diluting, and transporting wastes.
  Increases minimum flows.
    May weaken stream banks and levees, causing slumping.
    May increase severity and duration of seepage and raise water table along channel and river basin.
    Permits more adequate year-round waste dilution and transport.
    Benefits navigation and power generation.
    Increases water supply for expansion of agricultural, domestic, and industrial uses along river with resulting secondary impacts.
  Introduces abnormal and variable flows caused by project operation.
    High flows to create flood control space in reservoir.
    Periodic discharges for peak power generation.
    Mitigating effects and impacts of regulating reservoir.

Alters quality of river waters
  Evaporation can increase salinity of stored waters.
  Maintenance of higher minimum flows can reduce salinity of rivers affected by salty tributaries or return irrigation water.
  Alters content of nitrogen and oxygen in discharged waters.

Alters river water temperature
  Typically, lowers temperature during summer flow period.
  Affects agricultural and industrial uses, types of fish and their production, and water sports.

Modifies sediment transport
  Reduces peak flows lessening channel scouring, increasing sedimentation.
  Traps sediment in reservoir.
    Lowers downstream sediment load, affecting agricultural and other uses; increases channel scouring at given flows.
    Muddy discharges can extend over greater portion of year where sediment remains in suspension in reservoir.

Changes aquatic and riparian vegetation
  Increases encroachment on channels.
  Influences ecological diversity.
  Affects scenic values and recreation uses.

Modifies fish production
  Changes water temperature altering fish production: may prevent survival of uniquely adapted species.
  Dam interferes with migrating fish: mitigation by substitution of hatcheries and additional artificial spawning areas.
  Dam reduces length of channel for stream fishing; increases people pressures on environment along shortened stream channel.

Changes recreational potential of river
  Shortens channel available for river boating; may improve or worsen boating in remaining part.
  Regulated flow: allows boating and navigation over greater part of year; affects other water sports; alters fishing.

Alters economic, social, and political life of area with resultant secondary ecological impacts

B. In delta, bay or ocean

Disturbs natural state of area

Alters pattern of water flows and possible effects
  Reduces peak flows or reduces total flow due to diversion.
    Decreases flood hazard to agriculture and cities in delta.
    Reduces flooded areas available for bird resting and feeding.
    Alters channel scouring and sedimentation in delta.
    Affects commercial and recreational navigation in delta.
    May alter salinity of inflow water.
    Reduces capacity to flush pollutants and salts from delta and bay.
    May reduce turbidity or receiving waters affecting light transmission and, in turn, algae production and estuarine life.
    Affects land and estuarine plants and wildlife.
    Reduces sediment supply to maintain beaches of ocean, and possibly increases wave erosion on beach-front lands.
    Alters off-shore sandbars.
  Increases minimum flows.
    Alters sediment transport and delta formation.
    May decrease salinity and pollutants in inflow water.
    Increases capacity to dilute and transport pollutants from delta and bay.
    Increases capacity to repel salt intrusion.
    Improves navigation and water sports in delta.
    Increases water supply for expansion of agricultural, domestic, and industrial uses in surrounding areas, with resulting secondary impacts.
    Alters fish and wildlife potential of area.

Altered economic, social, and political life of area with resultant secondary ecological impacts head to 109 miles of spawning grounds upstream from the dam but also has interfered with downstream spawning by reducing the annual flow by 88 percent and peak discharges from over 70,000 to 250 cfs. Annual King Salmon runs at one point on the river have been reduced from 7,250 fish in 1959-1960 to 4,772 in 1968-1969. In the same period steelhead have been reduced from 2,071 to 554. Deer numbers have declined about 27 percent due to project-caused losses of habitat and lack of satisfactory alternate ranges in the immediate area. The measures which have been undertaken to mitigate these losses at the existing Trinity Project have been generally ineffective. Conservationists are critical of continued investigations by water agencies of possible means to develop additional supplies from the Trinity River for export to central and southern California.

Gottschalk (1967) states that although most reservoir projects flood vital fish and wildlife habitat, new water areas suitable for fish and wildfowl are provided. Losses to wildlife can be reduced, and new and important fish and wildlife habitat developed, but, conservationists claim these measures are often unsatisfactory. Although new fisheries can be developed in the still water of the lake behind dams with different species, the angling opportunity provided is not considered by many as adequate compensation for the loss of salmon and steelhead (California Department of Fish and Game, 1970). In an unpublished report prepared for the National Symposium on Fish and Wildlife Protection and Enhancement at Water Resource Projects, held in Washington, D.C., in October 1970, the California Department of Fish and Game points out that anadromous fish and waterfowl supplies in California do not meet damands, while there is an oversupply of warm water reservoir fisheries. Mitigation measures for wildlife have been relatively ineffective, in part because alternate sites have been limited to marginal lands while competitive land uses

such as timber production have pre-empted the better sites (California Department of Fish and Game, 1970). The Trinity River Salmon and Steelhead Hatchery has been constructed to replace the fish which would have been spawned in the area above Lewiston Dam. Unfortunately, the temperature and quality of the water supplied to the hatchery are unfavorable for satisfactory fish growth. Only about 15 percent of the juvenile steelhead attain satisfactory growth each year. In 1968, low water temperatures at the Feather River Fish Hatchery resulted in 12,000,000 salmon fry being killed by a cold water virus. Another disease contaminating the river water killed all but 500 steelhead out of the 378,000 hatched (California Department of Water Resources, 1970).

The California Department of Fish and Game in its October 1970 report (see above) feels that mitigation of losses is not an acceptable policy and that full resource preservation should be the objective. The Department declares that appreciable, unreported losses of wildlife have occurred because the federal construction agencies have evaluated fish and wildlife losses in strictly monetary terms, such as income from hunting and fishing use, disregarding the values of both game and nongame species which are not taken by sportsmen and remain to preserve and maintain the diversity of the ecosystem. Such evaluations are used to limit expenditures for preservation measures. The Department further states that "proposed federal projects that could actually enhance the highly-valued resources are few and far between in California."

Important ecological impacts arise from recreational and urban developments which often follow reservoir construction. Existing and new reservoirs are increasingly drawing land developers who recognize the growing attractiveness of water and water-related activities especially in semi-arid and hot climates. Aggressive developers have bought up land areas surrounding proposed reservoirs often years in advance of construction with the result that water agencies or other public agencies are unable to acquire sufficient land to provide adequate setback from the shoreline of the reservoir when developed. Home sites are clustered around the reservoir where water-view lots bring premium prices. These developments often make no provision for sewage other than septic tanks. Often these have been permitted by local authorities who are subjected to great pressures and apparently unwilling to look into future consequences of such decisions. Since most developments around reservoirs are on hill or mountain land with a shallow soil mantle over bedrock or relatively impervious subsoils, much of the drainline effluent will soon find its way into the reservoir, leading to eutrophication with resultant effects on fish habitat in reservoir and also in downstream waters. Several lakes east of Sacramento, California, have recently been the scene of such controversies over ownership of land along shorelines and provisions for sewage disposal. In Lassen County consulting firms have reported that the development of suitable sewage disposal systems is the number one priority in developing areas around reservoirs. The consultants point out that these reservoirs become the focal point for people and that the lakes will soon become "cesspools" unless precautions are taken to prevent sewage from seeping into the lake. The report goes on to say that many of the facilities either existing or planned for reservoir areas are in direct conflict with each other and in many cases with more desirable uses. Particularly serious is the fact that decisions are being made now which often preclude long-term possibilities for sound future developments. Once zoning regulations governing the use of private land have been set and facilities put in place there are often few opportunities to undo the damage which may have resulted. Certainly the development which precedes and follows new reservoirs can have serious ecological impacts. Prebble's (1969) study of land use change around a reservoir attempts to provide a basis for planning to avoid some of these problems.

ECOLOGICAL IMPACTS DOWNSTREAM FROM IMPOUNDMENT AND/OR DIVERSION

Modifications in the downstream hydrograph due to construction of dams (Table 3, Part 1) are discussed by Jones (1967) for the Sacramento River, by the California Department of Fish and Game (1970) for the Trinity River, and by Gervais (1970) for the American River. Jones reports that the low flows on the Sacramento River during the summer months prior to construction of Shasta Dam allowed river banks to drain. Grass, weeds, and willows grew upon the steep banks and stabilized them. Since the operation of Shasta Reservoir has begun, summer flow water levels are within a few feet of natural ground elevation. The banks never dry out, and there has been considerable damage to them from erosion and caving in. Drastic variations in river flow in May 1958 caused by reservoir operations at Shasta Dam resulted in practically all of the steep, saturated banks slipping into the river along a 56-mile stretch.

Evaporation of water from reservoirs has been discussed above. Not only does evaporation reduce the total amount of water available to downstream users but concentrates the salts in the remaining water. For example, dissolved solids in the Colorado River increased from 200-300 parts per million (ppm) a generation ago to 700-800 ppm at Hoover Dam in 1968 (McGauhey, 1969). By the time the river reaches Mexico, the salt content approximates 1,100 ppm making the water marginal for further use. The Colorado River Board of California (Colorado River Association, 1970) recently warned that increasing salinity of the Colorado River may cause annual damage in California exceeding $40 million by the year 2000. The salinity of the river at Imperial Dam where irrigation water is diverted for the Imperial and Coachella Valleys is projected to reach 1,340 ppm by the year 2000. As McGauhey (1969) suggests, "In many localities the long-term result of large-scale transfers could be a buildup of saline ground waters to such levels as to reach the root zone and destroy agriculture."

The effect of return irrigation water on the salinity of downstream river water is certainly an important consideration in project planning. Maintenance of higher minimum flows in the summer may serve to dilute the salt added to the river at points downstream, whereas diverting water out of a river basin, as some projects do, may have the opposite effect by reducing total downstream flow. Over 128,000,000 acre-feet of water are used annually for irrigation in the seventeen western states. Eldridge (1960) estimates that only approximately one-third is returned to surface or ground sources as return irrigation water, the rest being lost by evaporation and transportation. It is also estimated that salt concentration in return flows can become five to ten times greater than in irrigation water with the proportion of sodium being increased. Hardness (calcium and magnesium) may increase 400 to 700 percent.

Deep reservoirs, such as the one behind California's new Oroville Dam, retain water from melting snow and winter floods which does not warm up. Thermal stratification, the layering of water based on temperature-induced density differences, prevents the deeper water from warming by mixing with the surface water warmed by solar radiation and contact with the atmosphere. Thermal stratification is discussed by Kittrell (1965) and Symons and others (1964). Churchill, in a speech presented in 1963 at the Symposium on Streamflow Regulation for Quality Control (Symons and others, 1964), reported an abrupt drop in river water temperature from 75° F to 45° F when large discharges were made from lower depths of a reservoir. Release of such cold water can place great stress on aquatic life in the river, adversely affect recreational use of the river, and damage irrigated crops. A brochure given out by the California State Department of Water Resources titled, "Temperature Control of Water From Oroville Reservoir" describes special features of the Oroville Dam Project, including movable shutter intakes capable of taking water from different depths and the Thermalito Afterbay in which water is warmed by the sun, which enable the project to meet the diverse temperature requirements of both cold-water and warm-water fisheries, rice and other crops, and water-based recreation.

The storage and transbasin diversion of water in the Trinity River Project has changed a highly fluctuating river into a relatively small and stable stream (California Department of Fish and Game, 1970). High flows no longer occur to flush out the accumulated sediments and renew the gravel-bed spawning grounds. Tributaries such as Grass Valley Creek pour sediment into the river where it buries fish eggs, fills the deep pools, and compacts the gravel beds.

Lewiston Reservoir also causes muddy water to flow down the Trinity River over a longer period of time than under natural conditions. Formerly the turbid water which followed heavy rains cleared rapidly as the river receded, but now turbid water is held by the reservoir and released gradually over a longer period of time creating conditions which may be unsuitable for fishing or fisheries preservation. Similarly, Lake Mendocino on the Russian River causes muddy discharges to extend over several months.

Under other conditions the sediment load of downstream water may be reduced by dams. When silt settles to the bottom of a reservoir, the clear water released can scour the river channel causing damage to the banks while it picks up a new load of silt to deposit in another area. Thomas (1956) describes such a situation as occuring following the construction of Hoover Dam on the Colorado River when clear water released from the dam eroded the channel below the dam and deposited the sediment at Needles, California, partially filling the channel and causing relatively small flows to become local floods. He points out that not enough is known about river mechanics and related subjects to make adequate forecasts of possible downstream effects.

Removal of silt from a river by a reservoir is sometimes said to be detrimental to agriculture. Many dire predictions have been made concerning the effect of Egypt's Aswan Project on the fertility of agricultural areas along the Nile River. However, the value of silt to the maintenance of a productive agriculture may be overplayed, especially where soils of desirable physical characteristics exist and fertilizers can be applied. In some cases the removal of silt is considered essential to the maintenance of the canal and water distribution system. As an example, the Imperial Irrigation District operates extensive desilting works to reduce silt content of waters diverted from the Colorado River to the Imperial Valley.

Heavy sediment loads and low flows encourage encroachment by riparian vegetation into the stream channel along the Trinity River, but a different effect has been reported on the Missouri River where the sediment load has been decreased as the result of dam construction. Here the resulting clear water allows light to penetrate to greater depths, encouraging the dense growth of aquatic vegetation which obstructs river passage by boats.

Biological and chemical quality of river water can be affected by the existence of a dam and by reservoir operations, as reviewed by Symons and others (1964) and by Kittrell (1965), with resultant implications for aquatic life downstream. The lower, cold layer of a reservoir in which thermal stratification has taken place may become low in dissolved oxygen concentration and various chemical reactions may occur. It is usually

this layer, the hypolimnion, from which reservoir releases are made. Ingols (1959) reported downstream stress on aquatic life as a result of discharging hypolimnion water with a low dissolved oxygen concentration and high manganese content during peaking power operations. The absence of fish life was observed in stretches of river below peaking power dams. Churchill, in a 1963 speech at the National Council for Stream Improvements' Annual Meeting (Symons and others, 1964), reported one situation in which an extremely high manganese concentration developed in the bottom waters of an impoundment which was so detrimental to downstream water quality that bottom water could not be drawn from the reservoir.

The California Department of Fish and Game report on the Trinity River Project (1970) states that 165 miles of the stream are now used by fishermen for some of the best salmon and steelhead fishing in the state. If the proposed additional development of the Trinity Project is constructed, 90 miles will be inundated, leaving only 75 miles. The 90 miles which would be lost presently support about 50,000 angler days of use, and projected future use for the section (without inundation) is 300,000 angler days.

Dams have often spared downstream areas from serious flooding, yet their role in relation to flood damage has some contradictory aspects. Although tremendous amounts of money are being spent building dams to hold back flood waters and levees to confine rivers, reported flood damage continues to increase. The Corps of Engineers estimated in 1960 that the current annual rate of expenditures for flood control, $300 million, could only keep up with the increasing flood damage (U.S. Senate, 1960). Building large flood control projects only encourages more development of the newly protected flood plains. Often this flood protection is not as complete as the people who build in the flood plains are led to believe, since it is usually not economically feasible to provide complete protection against the really catastrophic floods which occur only rarely. Thus the flood damage protection afforded by dams may be offset by failure to control development in downstream flood plain areas. The problems of development of flood plains were studied in great detail by Sewell (1965) using the example of the Fraser River in British Columbia.

Direct and secondary ecological impacts of water projects on delta, bay and ocean areas (Table 3, Part 2) are described fully by Chapman (1970). The organisms that inhabit estuaries live in a delicate balance between freshwater from rivers and streams and saltwater from the sea. In many cases they require different concentrations of salt and nutrients during different parts of their life cycles, having adapted to seasonal fluctuating flows of water from tributary streams. Seemingly minor changes in the estuarine environment can have far-reaching effects on the organisms that inhabit the estuaries and on fish, waterfowl, and mammals which feed on them.

In 1969 about 3.3 billion pounds of fish and shellfish caught by commercial fishermen in the U.S., worth about $370 million, were from 70 species dependent on estuaries (Chapman, 1970). In addition, about 4.1 million anglers fished in estuaries in 1965 and another 4.2 million fished in the ocean, mostly on fish dependent on estuaries. This recreational fishing added greatly to the economy of the adjacent areas.

Much concern is now being expressed in California about the impacts of water projects in modifying estuaries and contributing to water pollution in these areas. Chapman (1970) lists the problems arising from diversion of freshwater from estuaries as (1) reduced tributary runoff, (2) changes in seasonal runoff cycles, and (3) poorer water quality. Lively controversy presently surrounds the proposal to construct a peripheral canal around the Sacramento-San Joaquin River Delta to convey water from the Sacramento River to state and federal pumping stations located on a forebay south of the Delta. Proponents claim the peripheral canal is necessary to convey water to the aqueduct pumping stations without degrading its quality through mixing with Delta waters, and to minimize damage to water quality and fish life within the Delta caused by reverse flows in waterways leading to the forebay, which now occur under certain conditions of flow and pumping. Opponents fear serious damage to estuarine life by diverting freshwater flow around the Delta. Proponents claim such damage can be overcome by planned releases along the peripheral canal into Delta waterways. Also, major considerations in the controversy are the expected effects in San Francisco Bay of reducing the freshwater inflow from the Delta. Complex technical, environmental, social, economic, and legal issues are involved in this controversy.

Another problem of concern in coastal areas is the possible eroding away of beaches following the damming of streams flowing to the sea with subsequent reduction in the supply of sand that otherwise would replenish the beaches (see Hedgpeth, this volume).

ECOLOGICAL IMPACTS ALONG CONVEYANCE ROUTE

The area through which project water passes from its area of origin to the service area will generally be less affected. However, altering the pattern and volume of flow in river channels used for conveyance can lead to substantial changes as outlined in Table 4.

ECOLOGICAL IMPACTS IN AREAS OF PROJECT WATER USE

Only brief mention can be made here of the ecological impacts in the service area (see Table 5). Aspects of this subject have been discussed by participants in the 1968 Symposium on Water Importation Into Arid

210

TABLE 4
Ecological Impacts Along Conveyance Route

A. Using river channels

Disturbs natural state of river

Increased flow results in:
  Changed water temperature.
  Altered erosion and sedimentation.
  Seepage and raised water tables along channel.
  Modified riparian vegetation.
  Modified fish production.
  Modified recreation potential.
  Improved navigation.
  Increased capacity to dilute and transport pollutants.
  Increased attractiveness for homesites.

B. Using canals

Interferes with land access along right-of-way

May transport and introduce plant, insect, and animal pests along route

Results in loss of fish at intakes and along canal

Results in loss of wildlife

Creates safety hazard for children

Provides opportunities for parks and recreation where developed

Lands (Bagley and Smiley, 1969). Clyma and Young in a speech at the 1968 ASCE National Meeting on Environmental Engineering, summarizing the environmental impacts of water in the service area, pointed out that irrigation has modified the environment of the Central Valley of Arizona over a period of 2,500 years beginning with the irrigation systems of the Hohokam Indians. Modification of the physical environment is reported to have included changes in climate, ground water, surface water, and vegetation. The social environment has been changed from a rural economy to an urban industrial economic system.

Development of irrigation can lead to numerous secondary ecological impacts. For example, Thomas and Box (1969) point out that irrigated farming usually results in large acreages of single crops. Such monoculture can lead to great changes in insect population. This may then require widespread application of chemicals for control of crop pests with resultant further ecological impacts. In California, increases in irrigated area and more frequent irrigation, often aggravated by careless water management, have left many places where vast numbers of mosquitoes can breed. This problem will likely become much worse because of the growing resistance of mosquitoes to insecticides and increasing restrictions on their use.

Irrigation return flows may carry salt leached out of soil, fertilizer and pesticide residues, and plant and animal wastes and deposit them into both surface and ground water. The Utah State University Foundation (1969) has recently summarized the characteristics and pollution problems of irrigation return flows. Very great concern is now being shown by water quality and pollution control authorities, and numerous reports by control agencies and research workers are appearing.

More intensive cultivation of certain high value crops in areas newly supplied with water as a result of a water project can have serious economic effects on other agricultural areas. Dean and others (1970) indicate a danger of overdevelopment of irrigated acreage in California in the next decade or more with the result that prices of high value specialty crops may be depressed below recent levels. The relatively high price charged farmers for water supplied to the west side of the San Joaquin Valley by the State Water Project will force the increased planting of high value crops, some of which are already in overproduction (Dean and King, 1970). The west side will then be in competition with older, established agricultural areas that do not benefit from the project development and may actually have to bear some of the cost due to certain nonreimbursable benefits not completely charge to water users in the project area.

In the western states water is frequently the most obviously limiting resource for urban and industrial development (Table 5, part 2). When water is provided to an area such as the Los Angeles Basin in Southern

TABLE 5
Ecological Impacts in Areas of Project Water Use

A. Agricultural and rural areas

Provides potential for changing natural state of area

Allows development of irrigated farming
  Causes visual changes in landscape.
  Alters environment for plants: native plants, crop plants and introduced weed species.
  Alters environment for wildlife.
    Area flooded during irrigation and leaching offers resting and feeding areas for birds.
    Replacement of natural vegetation by irrigated crops under intensive farming may restrict or encourage certain species of wildlife.
  Changes insect population.
    Allows breeding of insects in canals, ponds, poorly drained areas, and in wet fields.
    Allows breeding and development of insects on introduced crops and weeds.
  Alters incidence of plant, animal, and human diseases.
  Modifies local climate: increases humidity, moderates temperatures, and changes rainfall patterns (where large dry areas are under irrigation).
  Increased ground water recharge and high water tables create poorly drained and salinized areas.
  Increases pollution of surface and groundwater from return irrigation water, use of agricultural chemicals, and plant and animal wastes.

Supports increased population and altered economic, social, and political life of area, with resultant secondary ecological effects

B. In urban areas

Permits drastic changes in natural state of area

Permits expansion of cities to become vast urban areas

Provides water, permitting populations to exceed other physical or social resources of area.
Allows large industrial development including high water-use industries.
Need for flood control leads to channelization and levee construction along streams with changes in flow patterns, ground water recharge, and riparian vegetation.
Concentrates people, vehicles, and industry, leading to air and noise pollution.
Creates vast water pollution and waste disposal requirements.
  Results in pollution of ground water and surface waters, including bays and ocean shorelines.
  Affects recreation.
  Affects wildlife and especially growth of fish and shellfish and their suitability as food.
Increases power requirements in area, often leading to atmospheric and thermal pollution.
Increases people pressure on surrounding areas, particularly for recreation.
Increases social problems.
Increases availability of water which can be used to improve environment with parks, fountains, artificial ponds and gardened areas, and to develop water-based recreational facilities.

Permits introduction of urban areas into deserts and other water-deficient locations
  Disturbs natural environment.
  Can spread populations over larger areas, reducing problems associated with urban crowding.

Affects land development, industry, and population, resulting in drastically altered economic, social, and political life, with resultant secondary ecological impacts

California, the population may exceed the other physical and social resources of the area. In the absence of any overall planning, development may occur simply on the expectation that when more water becomes necessary, it will be provided. The problems of such urban sprawl are illustrated by Highsmith and others (1969).

Water projects that can store large amounts of water and transport it great distances may make possible socially, culturally, and economically desirable population shifts into new areas to avoid adding to the problems of existing cities. McGauhey (1969) provides an interesting discussion of possible implications of water transfers on a large scale. While there is little doubt that water projects will continue to bring people into arid areas, the specific implications of water transfers, particularly as regards local situations and microclimates, must remain speculative. He suggests that the potentials of water projects are such that they might serve as an instrument of public policy with which "government, for good or evil, may come to guide land use planning and economic growth [and] to control the pattern of urbanization."

TABLE 6

Some Factors Affecting Individual Recognition and Degree of Concern Over Ecological Impacts of Water Projects

A. Persons living in area of water impoundment and/or diversion (area of origin)

Land owners directly affected by project—concern depends on whether:
    land area is submerged,
    land provided with new vista or shoreline frontage,
    land is subjected to increased seepage or higher water table,
    land receives better flood protection.

Area residents—concerned about:
    Effects on general economy of area:
        loss in agricultural production from submerged areas,
        payroll arising from project construction and operation,
        development of adjacent areas for housing and industry,
        altered recreational opportunities and travel.
    Effects on tax base.
    Effects on local government costs for public services (police, fire, roads), schools, and social programs.
    Anticipated effects on future development and economy of area.

Sensitivities to ecological issues: may be secondary to above considerations for many individuals.

B. Persons living in area served by water project

Land owners, farmers, and residents of rural areas
    Increased land values and crop income.
    Improved economic conditions for rural communities.
    Higher tax base for local governments.

Urban areas: augmented water supply may:
    Eliminate or lessen periodic water shortages for present populations.

Improve water quality.
Allow increased land development, new industry, increased construction and higher population with economic benefits to some residents.
Permit expansions of industry and population unwanted by some residents.

Undeveloped areas: new water supply permits settlement and urbanization of previously unoccupied or sparsely settled districts.

Sensitivities to ecological issues: for many individuals, these are secondary to above considerations.

C. Persons living outside of areas of origin or service

Farmers and rural communities already adequately supplied with water may suffer economically from production of new irrigated areas.

Rural and urban dwellers:
    May be concerned about possible future costs to them for water projects through taxation.
    May deplore disturbance of natural conditions of wild rivers.
    May be concerned about maintenance of beaches along sea coast.
    May desire to boat, fish, and hunt in undisturbed areas.
    May be concerned about effects of project on commercial fishing and continued availability of sea food.
    May welcome new opportunities for fishing and water-based recreation on newly-created lakes.
    May be concerned about continued opportunities for dilution and transport of wastes from their communities.

Sensitivities to ecological issues: many individuals consider these of compelling importance.

FACTORS AFFECTING RECOGNITION AND DEGREE OF CONCERN

The types of ecological impacts recognized by people and the degree of concern generated by given conditions will vary greatly among individuals within regions and between regions (see McEvoy and White, in this volume). Table 6 summarizes some factors which determine whether individuals recognize certain possible ecological impacts and also their degree of concern about these impacts. The factors listed explain why persons residing in the area of impoundment and/or diversion often have very opposing views on the desirability of a water project depending upon whether their land, business, or social condition is adversely or beneficially affected by the proposed project. Thus, we have seen in California associations formed to promote a new water project while another association arises to fight the project. Increasingly both associations may employ ecological arguments to support their positions. Persons living outside the areas of origin or service, expecially those in areas or communities now enjoying an adequate supply of water, are likely to be much more concerned about the ecological impacts of proposed projects. It is apparently easy for one to forget that, in many cases, his own water supply is dependent upon water development projects such as he now criticizes on ecological grounds. A proposed new dam, although it may have substantial benefits in the service area, may thus be vigorously opposed by such persons on ecological grounds because it interferes with their enjoyment of the wild river with its fishing and boating or with their honest desire, at this stage in the development of our country, to preserve the remaining undeveloped areas.

Unfortunately, in our opinion it appears that some persons and organizations whose primary concern about a water project stems from economic or political advantages now tend to use individuals and groups which have genuine ecological concerns as fronts to cover their special interests and legitimize their position with respect to a water development. In view of the factors summarized in Table 6, it is not surprising that strong differences arise over water projects and that numerous statements are made about ecological impacts—some real and some exaggerated.

A report to the U.S. Water Resources Council (1970) summarizes principles for planning water and land resource projects and gives findings, recommendations, and standards. These principles, with the standards and procedures to be established subsequently by the Water Resources Council, provide the basis for federal participation with states and others in the preparation, formulation, evaluation, review, revision, and transmission to the Congress of plans, regions, river basins, and federal and federally assisted water and land resource programs and projects. It states that plans for the use of the nation's water and land resources will emphasize improved contributions to the multi-objectives of national economic devel-opment, environmental quality, social well-being, and regional development. Planning for the use of water and land resources in terms of these multi-objectives will aid in identifying alternative courses of action and will provide the type of information needed to improve the public decision-making process.

CONCLUSIONS

We conclude that the chorus of outcries about ecological impact will have lasting effects on water project planning, construction, and operations, and that such impacts will be given much greater attention by all concerned. To avoid stagnating future projects, much greater effort must be given to studies which will allow separation of the unreal from real ecological concerns. Methods are needed which will adequately mitigate undesired ecological impacts and, to the extent possible, achieve the overall enhancement of man's environment.

We do not agree with the extreme preservationists who would stop *all* further development of water resources. Also we do not agree with planners and water project users who tend to label and discredit those questioning water project plans as "do-gooder obstructionists." There is an unfortunate tendency among both the environmentalists and the water project planners to focus on only one aspect of the environment or to look at benefits or "costs" (in a broad sense) in only one part of the complex system from the area of origin to the area of use. A much broader and more thorough review of all aspects of water projects, including direct and indirect effects, is now needed. More detailed reviews of environmental impacts of water projects are now specified by recent actions of federal land state governments.

Intensive research will be required if man is to have the detailed information necessary as he attempts to constructively modify the complex and finely balanced ecosystem. Only with such information can realistic alternatives be arrayed and evaluated. Fortunately, in California the extensive water projects constructed in past years appear to allow time for research and more comprehensive analysis of possible ecological impacts from future projects.

Some say that man must choose between water development projects and protection of the environment. Others believe that man, in most cases, can have both development and protection. Here is a challenge which certainly calls for increased cooperation among engineers, ecologists, scientists in many other fields, economists, sociologists, political scientists and responsible leaders in government, interest groups, and associations concerned with man's environment. It seems to us that solutions to many of the problems we face will require much greater objectivity and willingness to deal with complex issues. This will call for public understanding of the real issues and a willingness on the part of all to deal with these issues in harmony and with a minimum of economically and politically induced confusion.

References

Bagley, J. M., and Smiley, T. L., eds. 1969. Symposium on water importation into arid lands. In *Arid Lands in Perspective*, W. L. McGinnies and B. J. Goldman, eds., A.A.A.S. and University of Arizona Press, Tucson, pp. 339-421.

California State Department of Fish and Game. July 1970. Preliminary report on impact of Trinity River water development on fish and wildlife resources. *Environmental Services Administrative Report 70-2.*

California. State Department of Water Resources. June 1970. The California State Water Project in 1970. *Bulletin No. 132-70.*

California. State Department of Water Resources December 1970. Water for California—the California Water Plan,

outlook in 1970. Summary report. *Bulletin 160-70.*

California Water Resources Association. 1970. *Newsletter. 14*(4):2, April 23, 1970.

Chapman, C. R. 1970. Estuaries need freshwater. Speech before A.S.C.E. Specialty Conference, *Ecological Aspects of Water Deficiencies,* Miami.

Chorley, R. J. and Kates, R. W. 1969. Introduction. *Water, Earth, and Man.* R. J. Chorley, ed., Metheun & Co., London.

Colorado River Association. 1969. *Newsletter.* April–May, 1969.

Colorado River Association. 1970. *Newsletter.* September, 1970.

Dean, G. W. and G. A. King. 1970. Projection of California agriculture to 1980 and 2000: potential impact of San Joaquin Valley West Side development. *Giannini Foundation Research Report No. 312,* Ag. Exper. Sta., University of California.

Dean, G. W., G. King, H. Carter, C. Shumway. 1970. Projections of California agriculture to 1980 and 2000. *Bulletin 847,* Agricultural Experiment Station, University of California.

Eldridge, E. F. 1960. *Return Irrigation Water— Characteristics and Effects.* U.S. Public Health Service, Region 9, Portland.

Gervais, R. 1970. Effects on fish and wildlife resources of the El Dorado hydroelectric project, Federal Power Commission Project 184. *Water Projects Branch Administrative Report 70-1.* California State Department of Fish and Game, Sacramento.

Gottschalk, J. S. 1967. Fish and wildlife and water resources. *International Conference on Water For Peace,* Washington, D.C. Vol. 6, pp. 409-413.

Harvey, H. T., 1969. Is there an ecological crisis? In *Man and His Environment: Interaction and Interdependence.* J. Y. Yang, ed., Environmental Sciences Institute, San Jose, California. Pp. 1-11.

Highsmith, R. M., Jr., J. G. Jensen, R. D. Rudd. 1969. *Conservation in the United States.* 2nd ed. Rand McNally and Co., Chicago.

Ingols, R. S. 1959. Effect of impoundment on downstream water quality, Catawba River. *Journal,* American Water Works Association, Vol. 51, pp. 42–46.

Jones, G. H. 1967. *Alteration of the Regimen of Sacramento River and Tributary Streams Attributable to Engineering Activities During the Past 116 Years.* American Society of Civil Engineers, Sacramento Section.

Kittrell, F. W. 1965. Thermal stratification in reservoirs. *Symposium on Streamflow Regulation for Quality Control.* Pub. 999–WP–30, U.S. Public Health Service.

Little, E.C.S. 1966. The invasion of man-made lakes by plants. *Man-Made Lakes.* R. H. Lowe-McConnell, ed., Academic Press, New York. Pp. 75-86.

McGauhey, P. H. 1969. Physical implications of large-scale water transfers. In *Arid Lands in Perspective,* W. R. McGinnies and B. J. Goldman, eds., A.A.A.S. and U. of Arizona Press, Tucson. Pp. 358–363.

Marine, Gene. 1968. America the Raped. Simon & Schuster, Inc., New York.

Mauthner, G. 1970. How the Soviet Union will change the earth's climate. *Atlas,* July 1970, pp. 47–48.

National Research Council, Committee on Water. 1968. Water and choice in the Colorado Basin. *Publication 1689,* National Academy of Sciences, Washington, D.C.

Prebble, B. R. 1969. Patterns of land use change around a large reservoir. *Research Report No. 22,* Water Resources Institute, University of Kentucky, Lexington.

Saines, M. 1969. Surface water reservoirs—a possible cause of earthquakes! *Ground Water,* 7(2):41.

Sewell, W. R. D. 1965. Water management and floods in the Frazer River Basin. *Department of Geography Research Paper No. 100,* University of Chicago.

Symons, J. M., S. R. Weibel, and G. G. Robeck. 1964. Influence of impounds on water quality. *Publication No. 999–WP–18,* U.S. Public Health Service.

Thomas, W. L., Jr., ed. 1956. *Man's Role in Changing the Face of the Earth.* University of Chicago Press.

Thomas, G. W. and T. W. Box. 1969. Social and ecological implications of water importation into arid lands. In *Arid Lands in Perspective,* W. L. McGinnies and B. J. Goldman, eds., A.A.A.S. and U. of Arizona Press, Tucson.

Thornthwaite, C. W. 1956. Modification of rural microclimate. In *Man's Role in Changing the Face of the Earth,* W. L. Thomas, ed., U. of Chicago Press.

Todd, D. K., ed. 1970. *The Water Encyclopedia.* Water Information Center, Inc., Port Washington, N. Y.

Treganza, A., et. al. 1968. Dos Rios Dam. *Indian Historian,* 1(2):14,16.

U.S. Senate. Select Committee on National Water Resources. 1960. *Water Resource Activities in the United States, Floods and Flood Control.* Committee Print No. 15, 86th Cong., 2d Session.

U.S. Water Resources Council. Special Task Force. July 1970. *Report to the Water Resources Council.* Washington, D.C.

Utah. State University Foundation. 1969. *Characteristics and Pollution Problems of Irrigation Return Flow.* U.S.F.W.P.C.A., Robt. S. Kerr Research Center, Ada, Oklahoma.

Vincent. R. E. 1965. The ecology of water quality. *Water Resources and Economic Development of the West.* Report No. 14, Western Agricultural Economics Research Council, San Francisco, pp. 89–97.

Waddy, B. B. 1966. Medical problems arising from the making of lakes in the tropics. *Man-Made Lakes,* R. H. Lowe-McConnell, ed., Academic Press, New York, pp. 87–94.

White, Gilbert F. 1969. *Strategies of American Water Management.* University of Michigan Press, Ann Arbor.

Worthington, E. B. 1966. Introductory survey. *Man-Made Lakes,* R. H. Lowe-McConnell, ed., Academic Press, New York, pp. 3-6.

CHAPTER 12

From a demographic point of view, the crux of the water problem in the United States lies in the discrepancy between the natural distribution of the water supply and the distribution of the consumers. In addition, water users "consume" more per capita each year as incomes, spending, and leisure time increase. A major problem in water resources planning is the "self-fulfilling prophecy." Population and water demand projections for semi-arid lands (based only upon trends and as options) are taken as immutable fact, and the "threat" of future water famine prompts water managers to search always farther afield to serve a hypothetical population which might appear if more water were not made available.

The attempt to supply an area with unlimited quantities of water has serious environmental and social effects at both ends of the distribution system, and the magnitude of them will increase as our population continues to concentrate disproportionately in urbanized, semi-arid regions. As an example, Los Angeles' century-old quest for water is described. To encourage growth for its own sake is a questionable philosophy in view of the decreasing quality of life it portends. A national policy should be established to reassess all long-term demographic projections used to justify large-scale water development.

DEMOGRAPHIC EFFECTS OF WATER DEVELOPMENT

John Hollis and James McEvoy III

INTRODUCTION

A good, dependable supply of water has always been of paramount importance in determining where man has settled, and where he could pursue agricultural and industrial activities. In some countries water is in good supply in all regions the year around. The United States is not so fortunate. Even though the average stream runoff over the conterminous states (1,200 billion gallons daily) is more than enough to meet the country's needs (about 400 billion gallons per day in 1970), the distribution of runoff is uneven, and when one area is in drought another may be suffering from floods.

Spatially and temporally uneven distribution is not a serious problem in itself, but man makes it one by settling in areas where the water supply is not dependable. Many natural factors other than water supply

TABLE 1
Conterminous U.S. Census Population, 1900–1970,
with Projection to 1980 (thousands)

	Total Population	Percentage Increase In Decade	Annual Average Growth Rate (%)	Urban Population	Urban Percentage
1900	75,995	21.02	1.91	30,160	39.7
1910	91,972	14.94	1.39	41,999	45.7
1920	105,711	16.14	1.50	54,158	51.2
1930	122,755	7.24	0.70	68,955	56.2
1940	131,669	14.45	1.44	74,424	56.5
1950	150,697	18.43	1.69	96,468[b]	64.0[b]
1960	178,464	13.19	1.24	124,699	69.9
1970	202,113	(14.26)	(1.33)	152,000	75.2[c]
1980	230,800[a]				

[a]Assumption used in projected water use in 1980 (see Table 3).
[b]Definition changed.
[c]Estimate of Kingsley Davis in *World Urbanization, 1950–1970*, Vol. 1, Berkeley, Institute of International Studies, 1969.

Sources: U.S. Vital Statistics, 1969; U.S. Bureau of the Census

influence the growth of a local population, but the determining characteristic is usually economic. If there is money to be made in a place then people will come there, even if other factors are undesirable. If water is made available in sufficient quantity, the population can grow by leaps and bounds even in arid and semi-arid areas, and in the United States the phenomenal growth of some of the southwestern states in recent years shows this only too well (Table 1, and Figure 1).

Many millions of dollars must be spent for water supply to support population growth in arid or semi-arid regions; individual projects are often immense. Projects are usually planned to meet the needs of the area in the "foreseeable future," that is, to support the population "projected" to be in the receiving area in about 30 years time. Yet the very act of constructing such projects usually insures that the projected population becomes a reality, so projects become both self-fulfilling and self-perpetuating.

From a demographic point of view, the crux of the water problem in the United States lies in the discrepancy between the natural distribution of the water supply and the distribution of the consumers. Furthermore, a population of over 202 million individuals, each of whom needs one gallon of water per day but is using (directly or indirectly) over 2,000 gallons per day, means that due to population growth alone total water use is rising at an annual rate of about 2 percent, or about 8 billion gallons per day per year. At this rate, in less than 60 years water use will match the stream runoff over the conterminous states, although some local areas will reach such levels much sooner.

POPULATION CHANGE IN THE UNITED STATES, 1900–1970

The demographic history of the conterminous United States has been dominated by three major phenomena, all pertinent to the demand for water, and all particularly marked in the twentieth century. These are: absolute growth of population, the movement of population to the West, and increasing urbanization. In 1900 the popula-

218

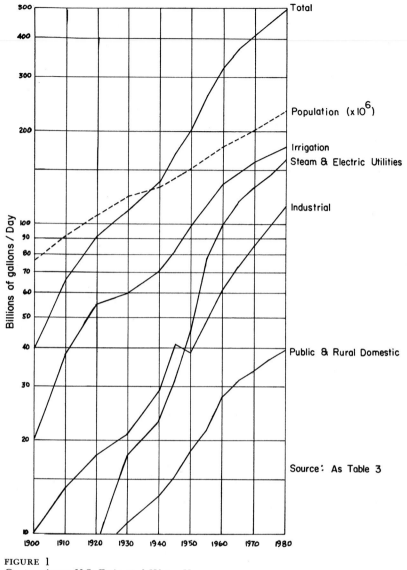

FIGURE 1
Conterminous U.S. Estimated Water Use.

tion of the conterminous United States was nearly 76 million persons; by 1970 this figure had grown to more than 202 million, an increase of more than 126 million (or 165 percent) at an average annual rate of growth of 1.4 percent. Growth has not been constant during these 70 years; the Depression of the 1930s effected a brake on both in-migration and also on fertility, since many marriages and births were delayed due to the lack of money. The population in 1940 was not quite 9 million more than it had been in 1930, an increase of only 7.24 percent, and the annual average growth rate (0.7 percent) was less than half what it had been between 1900 and 1930.

Between 1940 and 1960 the growth rate returned to the levels experienced before

1930. Conditions were more favorable to in-migration, with the economic boom brought about by the war in Europe, and almost all the births delayed in the 1930s had been added to the population by about 1948. A trend toward younger age at marriage after the war also contributed to this "baby boom." The net effect was to make 1947 the year with the highest crude birth rate since 1921. Birthrates remained high through most of the 1950s, but fell during the 1960s, a reflection of the small cohorts born during the 1930s. Birthrates have now begun to fall, but it can be expected that, with no apparent change in individual fertility preferences, the United States will go on experiencing peaks and troughs in its birthrate as a reflection of the upheavals of the 1930s and 1940s, but the oscillations in the rate will dampen.

The overall effect has been a population rise during the 1940s of over 19 million, and during the 1950s of an unprecedented 27.8 million, or 18.43 percent, at an annual average growth rate of 1.69 percent. By 1970 the population had grown another 23.7 million, but at a lower annual growth rate of 1.24 percent. It is not certain that the low growth of the 1960s will prevail in the 1970s because of the current age structure of the population; neither is there expected to be particularly rapid growth, although in absolute terms the current decade may see the greatest increase ever in the population of the conterminous United States of perhaps 30 million persons. The effect of the recent down-turn in the birthrate and its stability over time is difficult to assess at this point.

Since records began in 1790, "The point marking the centre of the (conterminous) United States population has moved steadily westward along the 39th parallel at the rate of four or five miles per year" (Peterson, 1969). This means that more and more people have been moving out of the humid, well-watered East into the relatively dry, and even arid, West. Of course not all of the

West is dry; in fact, the Pacific Northwest is the wettest part of the country, with over 170 inches of precipitation per year on the Olympic Peninsula. However, in the entire western drainage area the average runoff is only 2.3 inches per year , or 16 percent of the total volume in the country, in an area containing more than half the land area and about 23 percent of the population. In 1900 only 4.2 million persons lived in the West, a little over 5 percent of the total population, but by 1970 over 33.7 million (over 16 percent) lived there. Eleven states make up the West region used by the U.S. Bureau of the Census. The increase in the last decade in California alone was greater than the entire population of the West in 1900. The total 1960-1970 increase of the West was over 6.5 million, second only to the 7.8 million increase in the South. Expressed as a percentage, the West increased by 24 percent, compared to the South's 14 percent.

Throughout this century California has been the most populous state in the West. In 1900 its population was about 1,485,000, or approximately 35 percent of the total in the region; in 1970 19,953,000 people lived in California, and accounted for nearly 60 percent of the West's total population.

Washington, Oregon, and Colorado have been the next most populous western states in this century. As is shown in Table 2, however, it is Arizona and Nevada that have joined California in the last 30 years as the fastest growing western states, on the basis of percentage increase. These states are not only the fastest growing, but also the most arid—large tracts of each state have an extremely variable annual precipitation.

There is an increasing tendency for population to increase in those parts of the country with the most meager water resources. As a result, in the more arid parts of the West the value of water is rising and these states are prepared to spend more to ensure a dependable supply. That pressure on natural water supply systems can result in the abuse,

TABLE 2
Percentage Increase in Population, 1940 to 1970, for the ten fastest growing states
in each decade, and the conterminous U.S.

1940–1950	%	1950–1960	%	1960–1970	%	1940–1970	%
California	53.3	Florida	78.7	Nevada	71.3	Nevada	344.6
Arizona	50.1	Nevada	78.2	Florida	37.1	Florida	257.9
Florida	46.1	Arizona	73.7	Arizona	36.1	Arizona	255.1
Nevada	45.2	California	48.5	California	37.0	California	188.9
Oregon	39.6	Delaware	40.3	Maryland	36.5	Maryland	115.4
Washington	37.0	New Mexico	39.6	Colorado	25.8	Delaware	105.2
Maryland	28.6	Colorado	32.4	Delaware	22.8	Colorado	96.6
New Mexico	28.1	Maryland	32.3	New Hampshire	21.5	Washington	96.4
Utah	25.6	Utah	29.3	Connecticut	19.6	Utah	92.5
Virginia	23.9	Connecticut	26.3	Washington	19.5	Oregon	91.8
U.S.	14.5	U.S.	18.4	U.S.	13.2	U.S.	53.5

Sources: 1940–1960, U.S. Vital Statistics, 1969; 1970, U.S. Bureau of the Census

and eventually the destruction, of these systems is documented by several other authors in this volume.

The third important demographic variable affected by water supply is urbanization. In 1900 the percentage of the population living in urban areas in the conterminous states was a little under 40 percent, today it is estimated to be more than 75 percent (Davis, 1969). California, although it was a late starter in urbanization, was 52 percent urban in 1900 and 86 percent in 1960; only New Jersey had a higher percentage of urban population in 1960.

The role of urbanization in water supply is unique in that it creates a massive, almost constant demand for water of the highest quality to be supplied to a small land area. This demand must be met either by adjacent fresh water rivers, streams, and lakes, or by importing water via aqueducts and storage reservoirs from other sources. The use of ground water is not a viable proposition for most large cities since the demand is so great that the sustainable yield of the aquifers would soon be exceeded, and in coastal areas this can lead to salt water intrusion of over-pumped aquifers, destroying them for future use. This has occurred at several localities on

the Atlantic Coast (Wright, 1966), in California, and in Mexico.

Landsberg (1964) estimated that the average resident of an urban area in the United States was personally drawing about 60 gallons per day for domestic uses, including washing, cooking, drinking, laundering, garden watering, and air conditioning. On top of this, 26 gallons per capita were supplied to commercial establishments, and the municipality itself drew 25 gallons per capita for cleaning streets and fire fighting; thus a total of 110 gallons per resident per day were used in 1960 for domestic and municipal needs. Since then the number of urban residents has increased by 27.3 million persons, a disproportionately greater increase than that of the absolute population in the last decade, and there is little prospect in the near future of reversing the trend toward larger urban populations. We shall discuss below the implications of increasing urbanization and agglomeration of the population.

CHANGING DEMAND FOR WATER, 1900-1970

If per capita water use were a simple linear function of population size, then water

TABLE 3
Estimated Conterminous U.S. Water Use, 1900 to 1968,
with Projection to 1980 (Billions of Gallons Per Day)

	Total	Irrigation	Public	Rural, domestic	Industrial	Steam, electric utilities
1900	40.19	20.19	3.00	2.00	10.00	5.00
1910	66.44	39.04	4.70	2.20	14.00	6.50
1920	91.54	55.94	6.00	2.40	18.00	9.20
1930	110.50	60.20	8.00	2.90	21.00	18.40
1940	136.43	71.03	10.10	3.10	29.00	23.20
1945	170.46	83.06	12.00	3.20	41.00	31.20
1950	202.70	100.00	14.10	4.60	38.10	45.90
1955	263.80	116.30	16.30	5.40	49.20	76.60
1960	322.90	135.00	22.00	6.00	61.20	98.70
1963	352.18	142.86	23.80	6.30	68.40	110.82
1964	361.94	145.48	24.40	6.40	70.80	114.86
1965	371.70	148.10	25.00	6.50	73.20	118.90
1966	379.70	150.28	25.40	6.58	75.76	121.58
1967	387.50	152.46	25.80	6.66	78.32	124.26
1968	395.40	154.64	26.20	6.74	80.88	126.94
1970	411.20	159.00	27.00	6.90	86.00	132.30
1975	449.70	169.70	29.80	7.20	98.40	144.60
1980	494.10	178.00	32.00	7.40	115.00	161.70

Source: U.S. Vital Statistics, 1965–1969.
Projection based upon population of 230.8 million in 1980, and the Index of Industrial
Production being 330 in 1980.

demand would have increased 165 percent (or 106.5 billion gallons per day) from 1900 to 1970, or at the same rate as the population. (The actual demand was 4.2 billions of gallons per day.) Thus, in 70 years, the per capita demand for water has risen by 285 percent. As can be seen from Table 3, in 1970 demand was a little more than ten times the demand of 1900, but the increases were not of similar magnitude in each sector. Steam electric utilities now use over 26 times that used in 1900, and irrigation, public, and industrial uses have risen to between eight and nine times their earlier levels.

Table 4 and Figure 2 show the changing per capita use levels in each sector. With the exception of the decade 1920 to 1930 in the irrigation sector, demand has risen steadily on all fronts. Industry and steam electric utilities are the areas where per capita demand still shows significant increases, but the public and irrigation sectors appear to have reached plateaus, with slow growth for public use and a projected decline for irrigation use in the next decade.

The ever-increasing per capita demand by expanding industry and steam electric utilities reflects the tastes of a consumer society with increasing wage levels and an increasing capacity to buy goods and services.

Since there is not a large reserve of land suitable for or in need of irrigation to bring it into production, the potential for growth is small in this sector. With anticipated advancements in irrigation technology it is expected that the annual figure of 2.5 acre-feet of water distributed per acre may be reduced to near 2 acre-feet per acre by the end of the century (Landsberg, 1964). However, the method of application used may be directly related to the cost of the water supplied, and at current prices much of the water used for irrigation purposes is highly subsidized. To encourage more frugal use of irrigation water may require drastic revisions of present pricing policy. The general

TABLE 4
Estimated Conterminous U.S. Water Use Per Capita Per Day,
1900 to 1970, with Projections to 1980 (Gallons)

	Total	Irrigation	Public, rural, domestic	Industrial	Steam, electric utilities
1900	529	266	66	132	66
1910	722	424	75	152	71
1920	866	529	79	170	87
1930	900	490	89	171	150
1940	1036	539	108	220	176
1950	1345	664	124	253	305
1960	1809	756	157	343	553
1970	2036	787	168	426	655
1980	2141	771	171	498	701

Sources: U.S. Vital Statistics, 1965-1969; U.S. Vital Statistics, 1969;
U.S. Bureau of the Census.

public's use of water is also lavish and Landsberg's projections were based upon the premise that although rising incomes seemed incompatible with lower per capita use, the tendency toward increased water use would be largely offset by lower per capita use in urban areas with a trend back to apartments and multifamily dwellings. Thus, nationwide per capita use may remain largely at its present level. Again, alterations in the cost structure might significantly affect use patterns among certain segments of the public.

Recreational use, as opposed to physiological needs for other major uses of water (see Swan, McEvoy, and Richerson and others, in this volume), is an increasingly significant aspect of the value of water for intangibles. It is a use that has many separate (and sometimes incompatible) facets; boating, skiing, swimming, fishing, and duck hunting to name but a few. Perhaps most vital of all, bodies of water are beautiful to behold and have a fundamental spiritual value for man (Everson, and McCloskey, in this volume).

. Figure 3 shows that several indices of water-oriented recreation use are currently growing far more rapidly than is the population. Increasing income and leisure time are making it possible for Americans to take to the outdoors in increasing numbers. Although it is obvious that the part played by water in outdoor activities is substantial it is nearly impossible to judge how much water is "needed." (The terms "used," "withdrawn," or "depleted" in this context are not as accurate as "needed.") Recreational demand has not gone unnoticed by water resources development planners and any increased recreational opportunities offered by a proposal are used as strong arguments for the project, not only from the point of view of amenities provided (or supposedly provided) but also because of the added income that such facilities generate.

One question that cannot be adequately answered is: To what extent are population pressure and urbanization responsible for the increased demand for water-related outdoor recreation? McEvoy's review of research on conservationists and public opinion elsewhere in this volume suggests that dissatisfaction with urbanization is definitely an important factor in producing this demand. It is entirely possible that the growth rates in recreational use are step functions derived from population/urbanization growth and their associated psychological effects. If this is so, then projections of demand based on

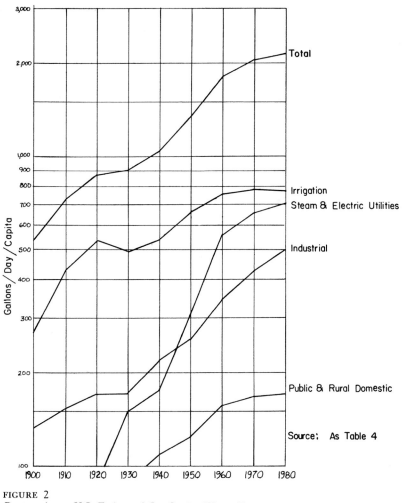

FIGURE 2
Conterminous U.S. Estimated Per Capita Water Use.

simple extrapolation are bound to err. Regardless of the mathematics of the case, the point is that synergistic effects of population growth may result in rates of demand now unforeseen by planners and decision-makers.

THE SELF-FULFILLING PROPHECY

One of the arts of the demographer is to make projections about the size of future populations. Given a set of assumptions about the death rate, birthrate, and migration, the demographer can turn them into future population estimates. There is considerable sophistication in this art, and over the past three decades projection methods have been refined by John Hajnal (1947), Pascal Whelpton (1954), and others. However, demographers are still brought to task for wayward projections. They usually answer that their calculations were not infallible predictions but reasonable projections of present trends under a set of given assumptions, not all of which may turn out to be accurate. Projections cannot take account of major intervening events which upset trends in fertility, such as the Depression

224

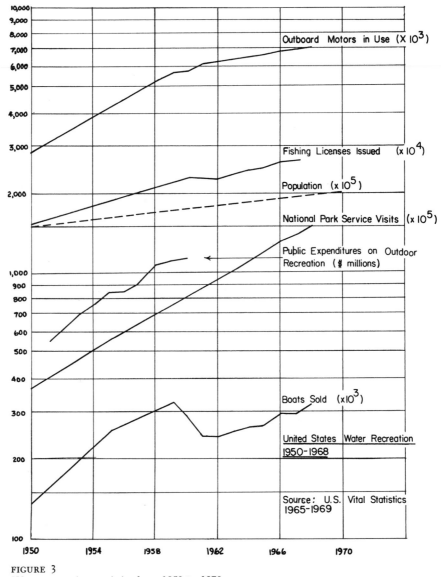

FIGURE 3
Water recreation statistics from 1950 to 1970.

and World War II. It is also difficult to predict changes in peoples' tastes which may effect corresponding changes in fertility or migration.

A set of population projections for the affected area is usually produced to back up water development schemes. In such cases it may be better to work on a basis of overestimates rather than underestimates of future populations, and projections are usually made with the most generous (but still reasonable) assumptions possible. A high degree of faith is placed in population projections by most people, and the underlying, and most important, assumptions are rarely questioned—projections are taken to be sacrosanct, inevitable. Once published, projections are assured of immortality.

Writing of the California Water Project, for example, Senator Frank E. Moss (1967) states that the population of the state *will* be 56 million in 55 years. This was the figure projected for California for the year 2020 by the project's planners when the plan was introduced in 1959. At that time the population was a little less than 15 million and the projection was for 61 years into the future. The chance of any projection's accuracy diminishes in proportion to the square of elapsed time, and most demographers put little faith in projections for more than 20 years into the future. In fact, as the 1970 census has shown, these projections for California were substantial overestimates. The detailed projections developed in connection with the California Water Project were as follows (Hirschleifer and others, 1960):

1970	21.7 million
1980	28.2 million
1990	35.0 million
2000	42.0 million
2010	49.0 million
2020	56.0 million

The census of 1970 shows a California population of 19.95 million; that is, the water project projections overshot the actual figures by 1.75 million at their first test. How inaccurate will they be by 2020?

In a short paper, Luten (1963) outlined the processes involved in the making of a self-fulfilling projection. When someone, or some organization, with influence and respect makes a prediction, such as has been made for the California Water Project, wheels are set in motion to attempt to make sure that the prediction is realized. Luten notes that the capital construction necessary to supply housing and services for such a predicted population may make the local labor market so attractive that in itself it helps to generate the projected population that it is supposed to serve. In California, one of the vital services is water, so that the supply of 4 million acre-feet per year to Southern California (if the water plan is fully implemented) will stimulate the development of industry, population growth, and in-migration. How closely the population approaches the projections will be a measure of the success of the public relations of those involved in the project (see Fox, in this volume). With stimulated growth the Metropolitan Water District of Southern California will then have more ammunition to use in its unrelenting search farther and farther afield, particularly into Northern California and the Pacific Northwest, for increased supplies of water.

URBAN LIVING AND POPULATION DISTRIBUTION

As Scott notes (this volume), cities historically grew up adjacent to a body of water, either on the coast or the banks of a river or lake. The reasons for this location were to enable trade to be carried on with cheap water transportation and for defensive purposes. All of the old European cities were built upon this pattern. European settlers continued this tradition in America and built the first American cities on the great natural harbors, rivers, and lakes of the North and East. Today all the great American cities are close to water, either fresh or salt. Where the water is fresh it is often used as the municipal supply, being drawn off upstream of the community, and released in some condition of degradation farther downstream. This method is adequate when communities along the river course are well spaced and not too large, and also where the returned water is in a good condition, but along the larger rivers of the East towns have grown up into cities and even merged to form linear cities along the river banks. Where there is a city, industry is inevitably present, demanding a massive flow of water for various processes. The end result is that the river gets dirtier and dirtier with the passage of time as more people put greater demands upon it. Without suitable treatment of the returned water, a degree of pollution results which overloads the self-purifying properties of the river ecosystem and makes downstream use of the water costly, if not impossible.

Coastal cities pose a different kind of problem, since the adjacent water is saline and nonpotable even though it is useful for many processes in industry and power plants, especially for cooling. The common solution for coastal cities, and for others sited on rivers that have become too polluted for use, is to import water directly from mountain sources, or at least from rivers that have not already been tapped upstream for municipal and industrial use. In California, the three largest urban areas (San Francisco-Oakland, Los Angeles-Long Beach, and San Diego) are on the coast, and each imports its water supplies: San Francisco from Hetch-Hetchy Reservoir on the Tuolumne River in Yosemite National Park; Oakland from the Sacramento River Delta and the Mokelumne River; Los Angeles from both the Owens Valley and the Colorado River; and San Diego also from the Colorado. In 1960 over two-thirds of the state's population lived in these cities, and on the coastal belt as a whole 78 percent of the population lived in counties that drained their effluents directly into the Pacific Ocean or San Francisco Bay.

The implications of such a coastal-urban distribution are that considerable sums must be spent to find distant water supplies and bring them to the cities, perhaps hundreds of miles away. Systems of dams, aqueducts, and storage reservoirs are essential to meet the demand, and their effect is to short-circuit the natural routes of the water from the mountain streams and rivers to the ocean. The natural flow of rivers is severely reduced, and in one instance, in the Owens Valley, where the entire valley's water rights were purchased by the city of Los Angeles in 1913, the once-large Owens Lake is now dry. Such large-scale water projects with their intensive reservoir and distribution systems have serious environmental impacts (see Hagan and Roberts, this volume).

A distinct negative benefit of the water projects needed for coastal cities is in the reservoirs that are built for storage both at the headwaters and near the users. Standing water evaporates much faster than does flowing water, and evaporating rates can be high. Moss (1967) has reported that such losses amount to 24 million acre-feet daily in the western United States (which is over 20 billion gallons, or 5 percent of the country's withdrawal use in 1970), and the storage reservoirs for New York City alone lose 25 billion gallons every year. As urban demand increases and pressure on the nation's water resources builds, every effort must be made to stem the evaporation losses from such reservoirs. It is doubly wasteful to short-circuit many uses of a river by storage and diversion, and then not be able to use such a large proportion of this water as is currently being lost through evaporation.

Wright (1966) pointed out several other effects of urbanization on water. When natural vegetation is replaced by asphalt and concrete, the natural water storage capacity of the landscape is reduced, leading to quicker runoff and evaporation (and thus greater waste) of any precipitation. Another salient point is that "introduced" types of suburban vegetation, particularly lawn grasses, are notoriously thirsty and demand up to five times the amount of water required by their native cousins.

Hand in hand with increasing urbanization and affluence goes the trend in urban living to own more and more gadgets, many of which are heavy users of water, for example, washing machines, dishwashers, garbage disposals, and swimming pools. All of these require a large amount of water, and this water, after use, carries away not only organic household garbage but also detergents, which are a perpetual nuisance in sewage systems, and if treatment is inadequate, cause major visual pollution and nutrient enrichment in

TABLE 5
Population Growth in Los Angeles and Orange Counties (thousands)

	Los Angeles	Long Beach	Central cities	Outside	S.M.S.A.	Urbanized Area
1900	102	2	105	85	190	–
1910	319	18	337	202	539	–
1920	577	56	632	366	998	–
1930	1,238	142	1,380	947	2,327	–
1940	1,504	164	1,669	1,248	2,916	–
1950	1,970	251	2,221	2,147	4,368	3,997
1960	2,479	344	2,823	3,920	6,743	6,489
1970*	2,816	359	3,175	5,278	8,452	8,183

*In 1970 the Los Angeles-Long Beach S.M.S.A., that had been the sum of the two counties, was split into two, forming the new Los Angeles-Long Beach S.M.S.A. (Los Angeles County) and the Anaheim-Santa Ana-Garden Grove S.M.S.A. (Orange County). The Urbanized Area was similarly split.

open waters. As population increases, incomes rise, and leisure time grows, one can only expect to see more water-using gadgets in use, more beautiful lawns and more garden pools, all adding to the heavy absolute demand for clean water in the urban and suburban areas.

LOS ANGELES

Of all the cities in the United States, Los Angeles is the best example of one that owes its growth, both demographically and economically, to the skillful management of its water supply and the foresight of its water planners. The maximum sustainable water yield from the Los Angeles basin, that is, what is available from the Los Angeles River and wells in the San Fernando Valley, is only about 100 cubic ft/sec, or about 65 million gallons per day. At present rates of consumption this is sufficient to sustain a population of about 280,000 persons. In 1970 the population in the urbanized areas of Los Angeles and Orange counties was 8,183,000, and the city of Los Angeles itself was home to 2,816,000 persons (see Table 5).

Cyclical dry years are typical of the Los Angeles area. The importance of these cycles has been in acting as a catalyst, forcing the city to continually expand its supply system.

The dry spell of 1893 to 1904 resulted in the construction of the Los Angeles Aqueduct and the importation, in 1913, of water from Owens Valley. During the 1920s a drought hastened the construction of the Colorado Aqueduct, and another drought in the 1940s brought about significant changes in the structure of the Metropolitan Water District of Southern California, making it an areal supplier of water (Ostrom, 1953).

Los Angeles can trace its roots to a Spanish pueblo built in 1781 on the banks of the Los Angeles River, on the site that is now downtown Los Angeles. In this coastal desert the river was essential for supplying irrigation water to crops grown by the small community. Under Spain (and Mexico) pueblo rights gave Los Angeles, with prior use, permanent dominion over the waters of the Los Angeles River, and it was legally able to prevent the water being used to its own disadvantage upstream in the San Fernando Valley. Thus, until the advent of American rule with its English riparian rights system so unsuitable to arid lands (see Teclaff, in this volume), the pueblo was able to expand both physically and technologically, developing a sophisticated irrigation system without fear of losing its water. After California joined the United States, and development and settlement in the area increased, the city had to fight a long legal battle through the 1870s

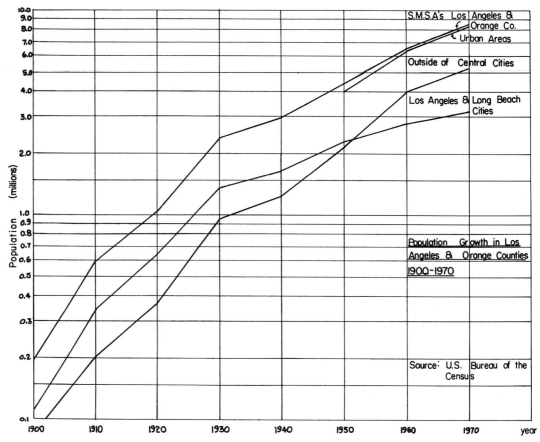

FIGURE 4
Population growth in Los Angeles County and Orange County from 1900 to 1970.

and 1880s to keep its historical water rights. Court decisions did not always favor the city, and in some instances it was forced to buy out upstream users. However, in 1909, a further court decision gave the city the rights to the underground supplies as well as the surface water. Thus the city could legally develop a hitherto untapped resource which could be used to meet the expanding requirements of its growing population.

The uncertainty of the local water supply was brought home to the city during the 1893 to 1904 dry cycle. The population was growing fast and wells had to be dug in order to supplement the river's depleted flow. Even with the wells, however, the city had a supply of only about 46 million gallons per day, and in 1905 the population passed 250,000. It was clear that this rate of population growth could not be sustained with existing local supplies, whether during dry cycles or in the best of circumstances. Not only was the supply cyclical, but the demand was seasonal. Ostrom (1953) reports that for a 10-day period in July 1904, the daily flow into the reservoirs was 35.8 million gallons, and the consumption was 39.3 million gallons. The reservoirs, of course, fell and only rose again when temperatures fell. The city was forced to look farther afield to supplement its local supplies. It was perhaps fortunate for the city that research into this problem had been undertaken by a former engineer with the Los Angeles City Water Company during his vacations over a period going back to 1890. The man was Frederick B. Eaton, and his research had focused on the Owens Valley, 250 miles across the Sierra Nevada from the city. Eaton's investigations convinced him that it would be possible to bring Owens Valley water to Los Angeles.

Eaton showed considerable foresight. Even before he presented his findings to the city, he posed as a cattle rancher and began to buy out water rights in the valley, with the intention of turning the water over to Los Angeles and turning a handsome (if ill-gotten) profit. Los Angeles made a quick and favorable reaction to Eaton's scheme and little more than a year elapsed before the city had voted a bond issue to begin work on the Los Angeles Aqueduct, which was opened in 1913, just over nine years after Eaton had first approached the City Water Department.

The Aqueduct was capable of delivering about 440 cubic ft/sec, or 285 million gallons per day, an amount far in excess of the city's needs. The excess water became no embarassment of riches, however, because much of the area around Los Angeles was annexed and put under irrigation. But the population continued to grow and the dry spell of the early 1920s also affected the Owens Valley.

Los Angeles next tried to extend northward up the Owens Valley to the Mono Basin, and then to the Colorado River. Water from Mono first arrived via the Los Angeles Aqueduct in 1936, and the city finally began to learn the full capacity of the Aqueduct, which had previously been limited by the flow in the Owens River and the amount of pumping that was allowed in the Owens Valley. The first Colorado River water arrived in 1941, but in supplies adequate only for particular local needs. The city's major supply still came via the Aqueduct, which together with the local supplies had a potential of about 540 cubic ft/sec, or 350 million gallons per day, enough to support a population of about 1,525,000 at current rates of consumption (230 gallons/day per person).

The pueblo water rights held by Los Angeles gave it a trump card to play in decisions for growth in the entire Los Angeles River Basin. Since the city had prior rights to water use it was able to physically expand into the area around the old pueblo, as well as to sell its surplus water to surrounding communities. Its prior rights also gave it the option of refusing further sales to any community if it chose to do so, the option being that these areas become annexed to the city. In 1895, following a Supreme Court ruling on the purchase of the excess water, annexation began, which by 1900 added 50 percent to the city's area. Further court rulings in favor of the city brought more communities into Los Angeles via annexation as a result of the long dry cycle, and even before Owens Valley water arrived. By 1913 Los Angeles was a city of 74.5 square miles; only 18 years before it had been 29.2 square miles. Annexation continued apace with the arrival of the surplus Owens Valley water and it was made a condition of water sale that the area become annexed. The rush to annex was halted in 1927, when a decision was made that no more land could be incorporated until the current water supply could be bolstered. However, by that time Los Angeles stretched over nearly 450 square miles, in a highly irregular pattern.

Los Angeles began as an area of great agricultural potential, with a long growing season and plenty of water for irrigation. Much of the water imported from the Owens Valley was used to open up more land for agriculture, but it was not agriculture that enabled the city's population to make its staggering increases. The availability of so much water at a reasonable cost, and also of abundant power generated by the water on its way down the Los Angeles Aqueduct, made the area extremely attractive to modern industry.

In 1919 a precedent was set when the

Goodyear Rubber Company decided to set up its western plant in Los Angeles. Water and power supplies were evidently the most important considerations in its decision. It had considered San Francisco and San Diego, but Los Angeles held a great advantage. In fact, the company estimated that it would need nearly twice as much water as the whole city of San Diego was then using. Goodyear was the first national company to be drawn to Los Angeles, but in the 1920s it was followed by many more. The city actively campaigned for industry and the combination of abundant water and the coastal desert climate made the city into an industrial Mecca. In the 20 years following completion of the Los Angeles Aqueduct, the city grew into one of the country's top ten industrial producers and its population was well on the way toward 1.5 million (Ostrom, 1953).

In summary, one can point directly to water when looking for a reason for Los Angeles' spectacular early growth and, more specifically, to the water from Owens Valley in opening up the area to industry. William Mulholland, Superintendent of the Los Angeles City Water District, recognized this perfectly when he said, "If we don't get the water, we won't need it" (Ostrom, 1953). He was aware of the concept of the "self-fulfilling prophecy," and knew that Los Angeles could not grow without a growing water supply system.

Growth continued during the Depression, although the pace was checked, and was further stimulated by the Second World War. As Los Angeles began to fill up, the surrounding communities grew to take up the overflow, although this was achieved without further annexation. As recently as 1940, more than half the population of both Los Angeles County and Orange County lived within the Los Angeles city limits, but now the outside regions, particularly in Orange County, are the fastest growing. Today the city of Los Angeles has only one-third of the total population in the two counties.

In 1960 the urban areas of Los Angeles and Orange counties, where the water supply was largely under the auspices of the Metropolitan Water District of Southern California, were estimated to consume about 1,308,700 acre-feet per year, while irrigated lands in the rest of coastal Los Angeles County and Orange County used about 197,000 acre-feet. Of this total demand of 1,505,700 acre-feet, only about 576,000 acre-feet could be supplied locally, with another 320,000 acre-feet coming from Owens Valley. The deficit, 610,700 acre-feet, had to be brought in from the Colorado River (Main, 1960). At this time the population of the area was about 6,500,000. If we assume that local water supplies were used at the same per capita rate, then fewer than 2,500,000 could have been supported by the local supply, implying that the importation of water accounted for the extra 4,000,000 inhabitants. In 1970 the same area held about 8,200,000 people, an increase that must be accounted for by water from the Colorado, less than that made available by the reduction of irrigated acreage. Between the two dates about 50,000 acres were taken out of agricultural production for subdivisions. The water-use equivalent is about 100,000 acre-feet, enough for about 500,000 people for a year; thus the Colorado had to cater to 1,200,000 more than these and supply an extra 240,000 acre-feet.

Using the Colorado water to support growth cannot be continued, since its supply is used by several other areas, including Arizona, Nevada, and Mexico. Future demand is now expected to be met by Northern California's ample supply, at least until 1990, via the State Water Project. Should such growth continue (and there are many signs that it will not, setting aside the question of whether or not it should) then the target for Los Angeles' appetite becomes the Pacific Northwest and especially the Columbia River.

The disadvantage of growth which breeds more growth is that ever more money must be put into ever-larger projects such as the State Water Project, reducing money that would be available to other services which might more equally benefit all of the state's residents rather than only those living in the receiving area. The California Project will cost at least $2 billion and very probably more. Some of the increase will come from state funds, some from federal funds, and the largest proportion from the sale of bonds. Pricing of the imported water is scheduled to return to the state its outlay and to pay off the bonds, so after all is done it is probable that the state will be the beneficiary of a water system at no expense to itself. This expected outcome, of course, is a projection based upon cost-benefit analysis which, as many of the contributors to this volume and numerous economists point out, may well be biased either intentionally or unintentionally. In terms of the total benefit of the project compared with its irreversible commitments of resources and closing of future options, northerners can indeed express concern over subsidizing the growth of the southern giant, as they witness the degradation or possible destruction of California's last wild rivers, the Sacramento-San Joaquin Delta, San Francisco Bay, and other aquatic amenities.

CONCLUSIONS AND RECOMMENDATIONS

We have argued that water project planning is commonly justified on the basis of population projections which are frequently over-optimistic and, in the nature of things, prove to be inaccurate. More serious, however, is the fact that water projects themselves spur population growth, particularly urban growth, through the operation of the self-fulfilling prophecy, a scenario sketched above and described in detail for Los Angeles. While much of this growth is in the form of in-migration to the region opened for resi-

dential and economic development, we believe that long-term net gains in population size are also inevitably encouraged as the result of both the economic stimulation from such projects and their expansion of area available for human habitation under the conditions of an industrial society.

It is our opinion that the Federal Government should establish a policy of carefully evaluating all population projections used as background to proposals for water projects. These investigations should be made in the light of prevailing demographic and economic criteria for the particular area involved and the country as a whole. Merely projecting past trends into the future, with no concern for the underlying demographic and economic situations, has serious shortcomings. Attempts should be made to determine to what extent a project would create, and not merely serve, the projected population. The population growth potential of the area should be considered in the light of available local supplies of water, raw materials and jobs, and with regard to the area's geographic importance. The effect on future growth of not building a project, as well as the effect of buildup, should be assessed. How would the residents of the area benefit most? Would the project benefit all of the affected parties, or only a select few?

References

Davis, Kingsley. 1969. *World Urbanization, 1950–1970, Vol. 1.* Institute of International Studies, Berkeley, California.

Hajnal, John. 1947. Tha analysis of birth statistics in the light of the recent international recovery of the birth-rate. *Population Studies*, 1(2).

Hirshleifer, J., *et al.* 1960. *Water Supply*, University of Chicago, Chicago, Illinois.

Landsberg, Hans H. 1964. *Natural Resources for U.S. Growth,* Johns Hopkins, Baltimore, Maryland.

Luten, Daniel B. 1963. How dense can people be? *Sierra Club Bulletin,* 48:10, (December 1963).

Main, Charles T. Inc. 1960. *Appendix to the Final Report: General Evaluation of the Proposed Program for Financing and Constructing the State Water Resources Development System of the State of California Department of Water Resources,* Boston, Mass.

Moss, Frank E. 1967. *The Water Crisis,* Praeger, New York.

Ostrom, Vincent. 1953. *Water and Politics,* Haynes Foundation, Los Angeles, California.

Peterson, William. 1969. *Population* (2nd edition), *Macmillan,* New York.

Whelpton, Pascal. 1954. *Cohort Fertility,* Princeton University Press, Princeton, New Jersey.

Wright, Jim. 1966. *The Coming Water Famine,* Coward-McCann, New York.

CHAPTER 13

Wherever a river runs into a sea, a special combination of physical, chemical, and biological processes results from the mixing of fresh and sea water; this, then, is an estuary. In this paper the dynamics and biology of estuaries are delineated to provide a basis for understanding the effects of man's activities on them.

Estuarine ecosystems are biologically rich, being the habitat for all or part of the lives of fish and shellfish, waterfowl, and many other important organisms. However, technological man has been slow to recognize and correct the negative effects on estuaries of direct pollution and destruction, and of upstream development and poor land management as well.

The irreplaceable economic and aesthetic value of our vanishing estuaries is now well documented, as are the many factors which endanger them. A national policy which recognizes the value of our estuaries has been established, and it is time to act and utilize knowledge of how to protect them. Neither complex and fragmented political powers, nor systems analysis on a national scale, nor ecologically insensitive exploitation will maintain them in a viable, productive condition. Scientific monitoring, management, and protection should be tailored to the unique and specific qualities of each estuary and must unify all political entities concerned with estuarine management.

PROTECTION OF ENVIRONMENTAL QUALITY IN ESTUARIES

Joel W. Hedgpeth

INTRODUCTION

An estuary is that part of the hydrologic system where the waters that have flowed over the earth's surface mix with the waters of the sea under the influence of tidal action. This, at least, is the restricted definition which is further restricted by the general idea that estuaries are shallow, low-lying aquatic systems bordered by marshes and flats of mud and sand. Such estuaries, more technically termed coastal plain estuaries, are characteristic of the Atlantic and Gulf seaboards of the United States. A few small coastal plain estuaries of this type and San Francisco Bay occur on the Pacific seaboard.

Another type of estuary, whose deeper waters are often somewhat isolated from tidal exchange by a shoaling near the mouth, is characteristic of the coastal regions of Washington, British Columbia, and Alaska. The controlling morphology of such fjord-type estuaries is mountainous terrain with deep, narrow valleys penetrated by the sea. The inland water regions of Puget Sound and the Straits of Georgia are in a sense one large estuarine system (Waldichuk, 1968). The waters of large rivers, such as the Amazon and the Columbia, maintain their identity for many miles to sea, and the mixing process is affected by large scale variations in the oceanic regime and occurs many miles at sea. Somewhat similar conditions are being duplicated, on a smaller scale, artificially in the Hyperion and White's Point outfalls of used water from the Los Angeles megalopolis.

In all estuarine systems the essential process is that of mixing, or the interchange between waters of terrigenous derivation and water of oceanic origin. In a "true" estuary this exchange is affected primarily by tidal action, not by the stirring up of outflowing water from the surrounding lands. The tide acts essentially against the stream gradient—that is, "uphill"—and at times of heavy runoff, its effect may sometimes be increased rather than decreased. The essential fact that tidal action in an estuary works like a pump and may produce tides on the fresh water reaches of a stream system well above the actual region of mixing, is well known to hydrographers (there is still tidal action at Sacramento, California, for example, although somewhat reduced in the last 150 years because of man's interference). The alteration of river water in an estuary to something more saline than rainwater, but less saline than the water of the ocean, indicates the degree of incursion of water from the ocean. Whenever there is water with a greater salt content in a tidal estuary (as opposed to a partly closed lagoon) than that of the incoming stream, it is an indication that the tide has moved water into the system.

In the simple condition, the incoming water from the sea forms a "salt wedge" of underlying, denser water than mixes with the outgoing river water along shear surfaces (Figure 1). During relatively stable periods this layering of water of different densities is well marked, but in many small estuaries the salinity wedge is, during the winter runoff period, a transitory phenomenon of a few days' duration. In those parts of the world where precipitation and runoff exceed evaporation in coastal regions, salinity progressively decreases upstream, and the greatest concentration is nearest the ocean. Such an estuary is termed a "positive estuary" (Figure 2). In regions where evaporation exceeds fresh water input, the salinity of the enclosed waters may exceed that of the ocean by two or three times; such "negative estuaries" occur in southern Texas and northern Mexico, the Sivash adjoining the Sea of Azov, and in certain South American and Australian lagoons (Figure 2). Thus, in a positive estuary there is fresh surface water in the upper reaches, whereas in a negative estuary the lighter, less dense water is at the surface nearer the mouth of the system. In both kinds of estuaries, however, there are regions of mixing along interfaces. The important thing to remember about estuaries is that mixing is rarely completely homogenous, except possibly during periods of very heavy storms, monsoons, hurricanes, or winter gales in which turbulence may stir the system to the bottom. In deep fjord-type estuaries this may never happen, because mixing depends on the amount of denser water brought in by the tidal prism to replace the deeper water behind the sill (Duxbury, 1971).

Even in the simplest example all the water from the land does not mix completely with the sea water and go out to sea with the next outgoing tide, but some of it lags behind to be carried out on subsequent tides. Similarly, the water that enters an estuary with the incoming tide, the "tidal prism," does not all go out with the same tide, but remains behind, so that the time required to flush an

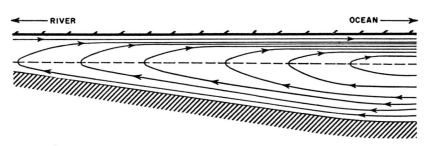

FIGURE 1
Schematic presentation of streamlines in a longitudinal section down the central axis of an estuary. (Emery and Stevenson, 1957, after Pritchard).

estuary completely is usually greater than the time required for a single cycle of the tide to come and go. In large, complicated estuaries this flushing may take several days—or perhaps weeks or months.

Waters of terrigenous origin characteristically carry with them some part of the land as sediment. The sediment load depends on the type of terrain; it may consist of "glacial flour" in some Alaskan fjord-type estuaries or pure flocculent clay as in certain lowland estuaries. These sediments tend to be suspended in fresh water, but flocculate, agglutinate, and precipitate as the water meets the saline water from the ocean. Thus, an estuary is a region of active deposition of sediments, in which the process of sedimentation is also a process of adsorption of other materials onto the sediment particles—nutrients, heavy metals, and other matter in suspension. Obviously, the residence time of materials adsorbed to sediment particles on the bottom is greater than that of such materials suspended in the water. Because of the combination of delayed exchange between fresh and salt waters and the retention of materials by the sediments, estuaries are often referred to as "nutrient traps." They are usually, in their undisturbed condition, biologically productive regions with abundant populations of bottom-dwelling organisms, young stages of fishes, and crustaceans. This productivity depends not only on the retention and regeneration of nutrients on the bottom sediments, but on the chemical exchanges caused by the flushing action of the tides over the contiguous shallows and marshlands. The success of colonization of the Atlantic seaboard by European immigrants in the seventeenth century was largely due to the rich, easily harvested resources of the estuaries, although we usually think of the sheltered harbors they provided for the colonists.

Surprisingly little understanding of the significance of estuaries and their resources to the maritime economy has been evidenced in our history; indeed, our awareness of the significance of marshes and mud flats and our concern for the maintenance of estuaries is very recent. It is distressing to realize that a person otherwise so aware of natural processes and the severe limit of our planetary resources as Nathaniel Southgate Shaler could state in 1906,

> Although the basis for computation is imperfect, it may fairly be reckoned that in this debatable ground of the shore zone now occupied by mud flats, marshes, and mangrove swamps, there is a reserve of land awaiting such work of improvement as has been done in Holland, amounting to an aggregate area of not less than 200,000 square miles of land (which) with a fully peopled earth will be brought to tillage.

Yet in the same book, a few pages farther on, Shaler concluded his discussion of the resources of the sea by stating that

> in the regions far from the shores, the life is commonly small in amount and consists

236

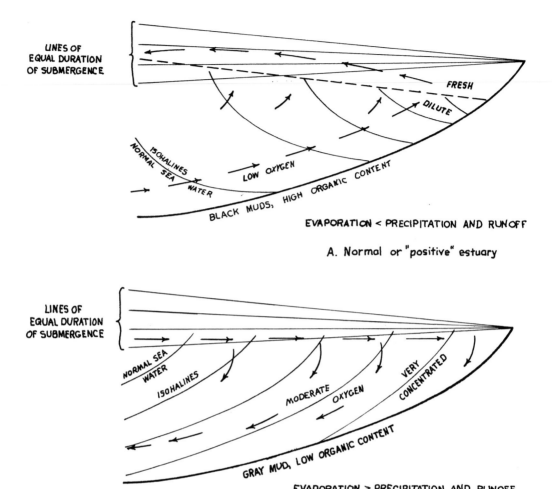

LINES OF
EQUAL DURATION
OF SUBMERGENCE

FRESH

DILUTE

ISOHALINES

NORMAL SEA
WATER

LOW OXYGEN

BLACK MUDS, HIGH ORGANIC CONTENT

EVAPORATION < PRECIPITATION AND RUNOFF

A. Normal or "positive" estuary

LINES OF
EQUAL DURATION
OF SUBMERGENCE

NORMAL SEA
WATER

ISOHALINES

MODERATE OXYGEN

VERY
CONCENTRATED

GRAY MUD, LOW ORGANIC CONTENT

EVAPORATION > PRECIPITATION AND RUNOFF

B. Hypersaline or "negative" estuary

FIGURE 2
Schematic sections of two basic types of estuaries. (From Emery and Stevenson, 1957).

mostly of the lower forms. But in the shallower water, near the shores, are the fields to which we may look for help in the ages when the world is to be taxed to meet the needs of our kind.

Since it is precisely the nearest shore areas, the estuaries, that man has the best prospect of controlling for cultivation of useful organisms, the attitude that the principal resource of mud flats and marshes is their potential for obliteration by filling is of utmost concern. Along with this lack of respect for the borders of estuaries is the equally

repellant attitude that one of the prime uses of an estuary is as a sewer. Insofar as the attitudes of Americans, from Point Barrow on the Arctic to Punta Arenas on the Straits of Magellan, are concerned, we came by our estuaries too easily. They were such rich resources for so many of our needs and activities that they were taken for granted.

THE PHYSICAL DESTRUCTION OF ESTUARIES

The simplest way to destroy an estuary is to obliterate it, either by damning it off from

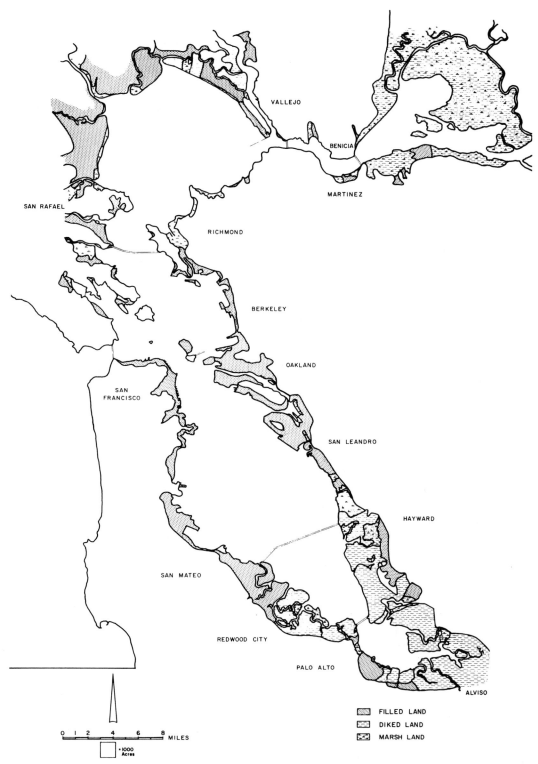

VALLEJO

BENICIA

MARTINEZ

SAN RAFAEL

RICHMOND

BERKELEY

OAKLAND

SAN
FRANCISCO

SAN LEANDRO

HAYWARD

SAN MATEO

REDWOOD CITY

PALO ALTO

ALVISO

FILLED LAND

DIKED LAND

MARSH LAND

0 1 2   4   6   8 MILES

☐ = 1000 Acres

FIGURE 3
Filling and diking in San Francisco Bay since 1850. (San Francisco Bay Conservation and Development Commission).

the sea or by filling it. The Dutch are now completing the obliteration of the Zuider Zee and have started on the Oosterschelde, with the resultant extirpation of the mussel and oyster culture for which that region has been famous for generations. Such reclamation does not, however, solve or alleviate the dilemma of supplying food to an overpopulated nation; Holland still requires the annual importation of 170 pounds of protein per person (Borgstrom, 1969).

The reclamation of tidal areas in Holland is a national policy; but without any policy or awareness of the ultimate effect on the environment, some 280 square miles of shallows and marshlands of San Francisco Bay were filled in the course of about a hundred years (Figure 3). The prospect of an almost completely filled bay, which would have produced a smog-generating basin without the ameliorating influence of the surface area of bay waters, brought the San Francisco Bay Conservation and Development Commission into being.

In other parts of the country deliberate filling and reconstruction of estuaries is carried out as intensively as if it were actually an established policy. The surface area of Boca Ciega Bay in Florida has been reduced by 20 percent since 1950, with the resultant estimated loss of fisheries worth about $1.4 million annually (Figure 4). This loss is related to the reduced volume of the bay from filling, the disturbance of the bottom by dredging, bulkheading that separates marshes and mud flats from tidal action, and the impairment of the tidal regime and its flushing. Such dredging and consequent filling also seriously impair the capacity of the estuary to handle industrial and municipal waste. Most of the filling in Florida and along the Gulf Coast is done to increase facilities for private boats. The astronomical increase in boat ownership has become a significant factor in the degradation of estuaries, comparable to the environmental effects on land that are associated with the numbers of automobiles. Two significant differences, however, are that automobiles do not have toilets

adding untreated waste to the environment, and that the custom of throwing garbage from automobiles is not socially acceptable, although dumping it from boats appears to be. We are reminded of the days of open toilets on passenger trains; they were locked while the train was standing in the station, a courtesy to outsiders not observed by even the most expensive yachts at anchor in crowded, public harbors or, for that matter, by the United States Navy.

Filling resulting from bad land practices in the drainage area of an estuary may have serious effects on the productivity and general economy of the estuary. The most notorious example of this was the increased sediment load in the Sacramento River drainage during the years of hydraulic mining in the Mother Lode, which resulted in a shoaling of Suisun Bay—the upper part of San Francisco Bay—by 3.3 feet, and of San Francisco Bay itself by about .7 foot as a result of the deposition of more than a billion cubic yards of sediment in a period of about forty years (Gilbert, 1917). Although hydraulic mining was stopped in 1884, not because of the shoaling of the bay but because of the deterioration of agricultural lands, the effects of this sediment endured for many years thereafter.

Indeed, it is not certain even now how much of the rapid decline of salmon stocks at the turn of the century can be attributed to such shoaling. It is also impossible to be certain of the extent to which the natural distribution of bottom organisms in San Francisco Bay was affected by this disturbance; studies of the ecology of the bottom organisms must consequently be carried out without a "base line."

An unseasonal and transitory deposition of sediment may cause more than just the disruption of visibility and impairment of navigation. In many small estuaries of the Pacific Northwest increased sedimentation has resulted from logging operations or highway construction. Often such disruptions occur in the summer, when waters are warmer and the effect on stocks of young fish

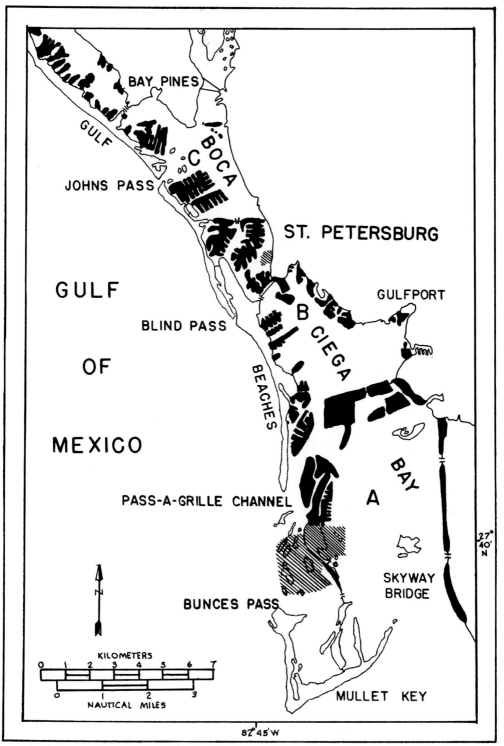

FIGURE 4
Filling in Boca Ciega Bay, Florida (most of this has occurred since 1951). (From Taylor and Saloman, 1968).

may be more severe. Bivalves such as oysters may suffer from sediment overloads that are due to channel dredging during the summer (usually it is not possible to move the maintenance dredges during the winter).

Even more serious to the natural balance of an estuarine system may be the opposite effect of mechanical intervention by man— reduction of sediment load. This is brought about either by the construction of dams which trap the sediments or by diversions of large amounts of water. After diversion not only may the sediment load be reduced, but the deposition pattern of sediments will be altered with the upstream migration of the salinity wedge. The most famous example is the Delta of the Nile. With the construction of the first Aswan barriers in the 1860s, recession of the Nile Delta shoreline began because of the reduced sediment load. This recession has exposed the estuarine areas of the Delta to the saline waters of the Mediterranean, and has also effected the transfer of sediments of the Delta to the northeast. Eventually the remaining fertile sediments of the delta region will be carried to the waters off the coast of Israel. All these processes will be greatly accelerated by the entrapment of sediments and the regularization of stream flow induced by the Aswan Dam. It is also expected that the lake behind the dam, Lake Nasser, will be an excellent culture medium for the trematodes that cause schistosomiasis, a severe, endemic tropical disease. The fisheries of the deltaic lakes of the Nile have been greatly reduced, and the retreat of the shoreline is so marked that the lighthouse has had to be moved back almost a mile.

Reduction of sediment load will also induce eutrophication because of the greater transparency of the water and resultant increase of phytoplankton. This has apparently happened in the lower Don River because of the hydroelectric and diversion projects, and may be expected in the upper San Francisco Bay system if the scheduled program of diversions take place. A fresh water analogy of the sort of effects to be anticipated from regularization of stream flow and reduction of sedimentation and nutrient loss is now available in the delta of the Peace River in Lake Athabasca (*New York Times*, December 9, 1970).

The most devastating result of dams and diversions upstream of an estuary has been the reduction of runs of anadromous fishes. Salmon, once so common as to be almost despised as food, have disappeared from many northern Atlantic streams, have been almost extirpated from the rivers of central California, and are now disappearing from the Columbia River.

Less spectacular, but ecologically more significant to the health of the estuary and its inhabitants, are the combinations of effects associated with the reduction of sediment load and the diversion of fresh waters. Not only does the reduction of fresh-water input change the ecological milieu from that of reduced or fluctuating salinity, but it may also change the effect of additives. Some pesticides and possibly other substances act differently in salt water than in fresh water. Eisler (1969) found that the toxicity of some pesticides to crustacea increased directly with an increase in salinity whereas that of others decreased, but that the toxicity of all compounds tested increased directly with temperature. It is possible that increased toxicity of some agricultural pesticides in salinity is related to the reduced reproductive success in recent years of commercial crabs in the ocean near San Francisco Bay. We are not aware of any studies of the possible relationship of reduced sediment load to the toxicity of pesticides and herbicides in estuaries.

THE CHEMICAL DESTRUCTION OF ESTUARIES

Destruction of estuaries by the addition of chemicals or foreign substances is a less noticeable process than that of the reduction of physical dimensions by filling. As Odum

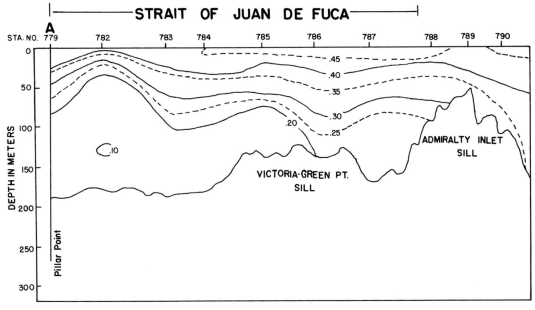

FIGURE 5
Dissolved oxygen content in the Strait of Juan de Fuca, July 1953. (Duxbury, 1971).

(1970) has pointed out, "all of the factors which enable an estuary to concentrate and recycle nutrients also allow the estuary to become a pollution sink." This process becomes particularly dangerous when, as in the fjord estuaries of northwestern America, deep water may be renewed only during periods of intense upwelling in summer. Such deep water, dense enough to replace water behind the sill, is also low in oxygen (Figure 5). As yet the Puget Sound region does not seem to be in the sort of trouble that is reducing the Baltic (a large estuary) to a dying sea (Fonselius, 1970), but time will undoubtedly demonstrate that cleaning up Lake Washington by transferring the deposition of nutrient-rich sewage to the deeper waters of Puget Sound has many hidden costs.

The very low natural oxygen content of upwelling water has prompted industrial representatives to suggest that such low concentrations might be used as a standard for waste releases, but they do not mention that upwelling water is also cold water and that the warming of oxygen-poor water in an estuary could result in an even lower oxygen content. This aspect could be particularly significant where industrial activities lead to thermal alteration or "calefaction."

In such a complex, interrelated system as an estuary, the alteration of one factor may be associated with changes in many properties, some of them acting against each other. In his interesting series of diagrams of the effects of the addition of fertilizers to the Chesapeake Bay system, Mansueti (1961) does not consider alteration of such properties as temperature and sediment. However, he does caution against unrestricted or uncontrolled addition of materials to the environment, and some of the inherent complexities are indicated in the diagram reprinted here as Figure 6. Since 1961, studies in Chesapeake Bay and elsewhere have indicated that the phytoplankton crop of a region could be seriously reduced by passage of water through a cooling system (Morgan and Stross, 1969). If this is done, it could place an extra burden upon the endemic phytoplankton of the receiving water, and could

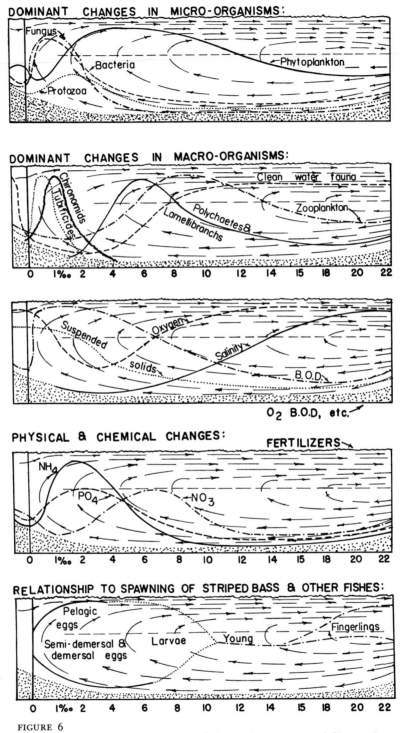

FIGURE 6

Schematic representation of hypothetical changes in an estuary of Chesapeake Bay brought about by addition of fertilizers. (From Mansueti, 1961, modified by Hedgpeth, 1966).

possibly cause changes that could be ecologically damaging.

As we increase our industrialization and our demands for energy, we increase the heat load in the environment, especially in waters. At best, the efficiency of our conversion of heat to electrical energy seems to be fixed around 40 percent, and is even somewhat lower if we use nuclear fuel. In a controversial popular article on calefaction of the lower Connecticut River by the Haddam Neck power plant, Merriman (1970a) observes that there has been "no significant deleterious effect on the biology of the river." This conclusion is based in part on the finding that the thermal discharge of the plant did not cause a "thermal block" of the river, but this provides no basis for generalization, since in the part of the river that was studied tidal action prevents "thermal blockage." Temporary disruptions of the phytoplankton production near the effluent source and replacement by blue-green algae were observed, and catfish were not doing well in the river, but on the whole the article was so reassuring that it was favorably received by engineers as an indication that raising the temperature of a river a few degrees will not cause much damage, and that such an alteration of temperature "is not pollution in the true sense"— to use the words of the late Theos J. Thompson, a member of the Atomic Energy Commission.

In a more detailed discussion, Merriman (1971) does suggest that the "thermal carrying capacity of the Connecticut River as presently planned is, to all intents and purposes, approaching its upper limits." The alteration of estuarine systems by the addition of large volumes of water with higher temperatures than that of its own environment is manifest, and it is generally conceded that large-scale power generating plants ought not to be built on estuaries. It is misleading to repeat the old observation that "fishing is best around power plant outfalls" without attempting to separate three variables: the increased temperature, the steady current, and the supply of food brought by the current (possibly cooked or concentrated because of the trip through the condenser tubes).

The effect of temperature on a biological system will also vary with the natural regime. Where there is already a wide annual temperature range, or in estuaries with a well-developed eurythermal biota, small changes in the temperature regime will have less immediate effect than in localities with a restricted temperature range. In tropical or other warm waters, where most of the organisms may already be living near the top of their natural temperature tolerances, a slight increase in the environmental temperature will have more serious effects than in northern latitudes. The temperature relation in nature is the dependence, in regions of wide temperature ranges, of the organisms on that range. Thus a stabilization or leveling off of temperature by a steady effluent of increased temperature would be expected to upset the natural cycles of organisms in that environment (Hedgpeth and Gonor, 1969). The increased temperature in Biscayne Bay at the Turkey Point power plant, for example, is much more critical to the biota than the increased temperature in the Connecticut River.

In a somewhat speculative article, Weinberg and Hammond (1970) suggest that it may be possible, with improved reactor technology, to supply the power demands of 20 billion people. This might be done by about 4,000 "nuclear parks" located "on the seashore." The amount of heated water generated by such an activity, whether the plants are on the seashore or comfortably away from shore, would be an appreciable fraction of the surface layers of the near-shore ocean. Yet the exchange patterns of many large estuary systems depend on the waters of the ocean to an extent that may not be clearly appreciated by promulgators of such speculations (Figure 7). This figure, incidentally, also indicates the manner in which waters from the Columbia River are part of the

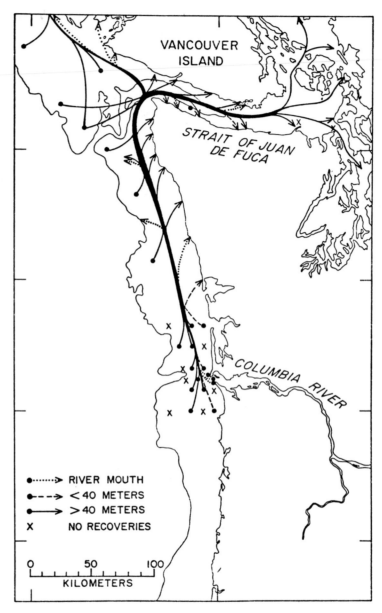

FIGURE 7
Release points and hypothetical paths of seabed drifters along the
Washington coast. (Duxbury, 1971).

estuary system of Puget Sound and coastal waters of British Columbia. Similar water movement patterns have been demonstrated for the coastal waters of the estuary system of San Francisco Bay. Such circulation patterns indicate that simply bypassing an estuary with ocean outfalls for undesirable effluents or heated waters may not be enough for the entire coastal system must be taken into consideration.

NATIONAL POLICY
ON ESTUARIES

Although it seems many more years than it has been, national awareness of the plight of our estuaries dates from the symposium on estuaries held at Jekyll Island, Georgia, from March 31 to April 3, 1964. This symposium was arranged under the auspices of the American Society of Limnology and Oceanography, and was originally intended to be an informal, restricted meeting. More than eighty-five papers were accepted for presentation, of which seventy were ultimately published. Several federal, private, and state agencies provided support, and the proceedings were published as a symposium volume of the American Association for the Advancement of Science in 1967. In the interlude between the Jekyll Island meeting and publication of its proceedings, the American Fisheries Society held a short symposium on estuarine fisheries in September 1964, which issued a report in 1966. In August of 1967 a "National Symposium in Estuarine Pollution" was held at Stanford University; the proceedings of this symposium, primarily by and for engineers, was subsequently reproduced in a soft paper format.

In the five or six years since the results of these symposia became available there have been several national reappraisals of the problems of estuaries, both by congressional committees and by departmental "line" agencies, and the end is not in sight. The governmental reports have been prepared in response to Public Law 89–454, the Marine Resources Engineering and Development Act of 1956, Public Law 89–753, the Clean Water Restoration Act of 1966, and Public Law 90–454, the Estuary Protection Act of 1968. Certainly one cannot say that Congress is unaware of the need to do something about estuaries, even if the concept of environmental management is given little attention by many of our most eminent and influential national politicians.

During the first session of the 91st Congress hearings were held by the Conservation and Natural Resources Subcommittee of the House Committee on Government Operations on the problems of San Francisco Bay, first in Washington in May 1969, and later in San Francisco in August. Two comprehensive reports were made to the second session of the 91st Congress in response to legislation. One of these is a seven volume report by the Fish and Wildlife Service of the Department of the Interior (then consisting of the Bureau of Sport Fisheries and Wildlife and the Bureau of Commercial Fisheries). Entitled *National Estuary Study*, it provides a comprehensive summary of the major estuarine regions of the United States (including Alaska and Hawaii), the status of many individual estuaries, and the manner in which the various state and local jurisdictions have carried on estuary maintenance and conservation. The other report is that of the Federal Water Pollution Control Administration (then of the Department of the Interior; now the Water Quality Office of the Environmental Protection Agency), "The National Estuarine Pollution Study" (Senate Document 91-58) in a single volume. This report is concerned primarily with the effects of man on estuaries, the types of studies needed to establish baselines for water quality standards, and recommendations for a national management program. There are other reports and hearing documents, of which the proceedings of the Coastal Zone Management Conference held in Washington on October 28 and 29, 1969, should be mentioned (House Document 91-14). This was a congressionally sponsored conference which met to discuss the proposition that "the problems of our coastal zones can only be solved by the people most directly affected. The states and the municipalities, through their normal political processes, must remain the focus for coastal planning."

This ultimate responsibility of state and local governments is reiterated in the conclusion of all the federal agency reports on the state of our estuaries; the general content of these reports has been summarized in the *National Estuary Study* (Vol. 7, Appendix K, p. 7):

> The bulk of the values currently realized from the oceans are either taken directly from within the territorial seas of the United States or are heavily dependent on these same waters and adjoining uplands.
>
> The land and water resources of the coastal zone are so linked biologically and physically that they can and should be considered as parts of a single system.
>
> There is presently a national interest in several aspects of coastal resource use, but the extent of that interest in other spheres of interest is in need of re-examination.
>
> The present system of management of coastal resources—particularly the estuarine portions—is hampered by a multitude of *faits accomplis* which are in disagreement with the basic nature of the resource system, by a limited knowledge about the resource system, and by a diversity of agencies having responsibility and jurisdiction over different aspects of the system.
>
> The states, by law and accepted practice, represent the key managerial units for coastal resources.
>
> The buildup of population, affluence, and urbanization will increase the number and intensity of competing demands made for the finite resources.

The concept that coastal zone planning and administration should reside with the states and municipalities simply will not work in the apolitical system of the environment is most obvious in the Chesapeake Bay, where three states and numerous local jurisdictions are involved. Only if all the political and industrial jurisdictions whose futures are predicated on the continued existence of the Chesapeake Bay as a viable environment surrender their individual sovereignty to a single cause, will there be hope for this region.

At present there is an impasse, even in determining who is to investigate what (see *Science,* 21 May 1971, p. 825–830). San Francisco Bay is somewhat better off since it lies entirely within the jurisdiction of a single state; yet even in planning for San Francisco Bay there is conflict, since some political jurisdictions and economic interests are impatient with long-term goals.

It would appear that by this time we should know what to investigate and how it should be done, yet there seems to be no end in sight to studies of studies, proposals for monitoring schemes, and appraisals of the state of the art. Our federal structure has become obsessed with computers and data banks and storage of information in central depositories. At the same time it is realized that national data systems cannot adequately handle diverse information from individual estuaries; no two estuaries are quite alike, and attempts to codify information in a uniform manner would bury or distort information. It is of no advantage to store data in a central bank, like the gold at Fort Knox, from two such diverse systems as the San Francisco and Chesapeake bays. Each major estuarine system should have its own nerve center for information, consultation, and planning that is capable of responding to changing environmental needs.

Yet even for the estuarine planning most frequently held up as an ideal (or at least the beginning of an ideal)—San Francisco Bay—there is a confusing and uncoordinated complexity of jurisdictions and activities. Not only is there a Bay Conservation and Development Commission (BCDC), but there is also the Association of Bay Area Governments (ABAG), the San Francisco Bay Delta section of the California Water Resources Control Board, federal agencies, and so on. The BCDC and ABAG are concerned primarily with problems of land and air, filling, open space, and planning for the periphery of the bay; the well-being of the water itself has been left to the state pollution agency, the Water Quality Control Board. This is the agency that contracted with a private engineering firm to produce a water quality program for San Francisco predicated on the assumption that the people of the area would not accept recycled water. This, then turned out to be a model of a vast sewer system. At the same time another branch of the agency was considering a schedule of water diversion that might make such a plumbing system inoperable. So, even in San Francisco with its model BCDC, there seems to be no one in charge of the estuary system.

The Corps of Engineers has often been regarded as the villain in our estuaries because they have the jurisdiction over dredging, filling, revetment, and all other improvements to navigation, and all permits for such activity must be reviewed by them. Too often the military attitude and protocol of the Engineers have provided an opportunity for local interests to carry out unwise and extravagant alterations of estuaries and navigable streams. The Corps has no policy other than to carry out the will of Congress in public works projects; recently, however, it has been placed under obligation to refer all permits for projects to state and local agencies, as well as to other federal agencies so that the Corps itself takes no initiative and in large part defers to other agencies in the matter of environmental impact. It is my impression that while there are good and earnest men in the Corps of Engineers, they function like a military branch and have not adopted a popular concern for the environment.

If we are interested in maintaining the environment of an estuary in a reasonably viable and productive condition it would seem that the environment must be considered first, and jurisdictional problems second. There must be a sense of responsibility, an orientation toward the estuary rather than toward what man can get out of it, or whose economic interests should take precedence. Although while a broad national policy and federal guidelines for conduct

may be indispensable for estuaries, it is impractical to administer each separate estuary system from a central command post. Once the basic guideline is determined (perhaps along the lines being considered by the Oregon State Land Board that filling estuary land is itself a form of permanent pollution), some regional organization for the maintenance and operation of large estuaries or groups of smaller ones is essential.

Such regional or estuary centers would accumulate all information and coordinate all the activities related to the natural system or systems. Having a physical locus for studying, monitoring, and managing a given estuary does not mean that all political, governmental, and economic units concerned should be physically under the same roof, but that at some central or common location all the necessary information is available, like the yard control center of a railroad; and that all key personnel representing the different entities should go there regularly not only for formal meetings and hearings but for individual briefings. Since, under our present system, decision-making is often in the hands of people who do not have the background to follow intricate computer analysis or grasp the significance of a change in parts per million of some obscure chemical, a command center in which the events could be graphically represented and demonstrated by simulation models would be of incalculable aid in gaining and continuing support for maintenance of the environment. I have been impressed by the manner in which a group of people in the communities of Toledo and Newport, Oregon have utilized a master plan for Yaquina Bay based on the planning concepts presented by the multiple chart methods developed by Ian McHarg (see McHarg and Clarke, in this volume). Systems of this kind, are needed to carry on the continuous, never-ending process of environmental management.

Management of any kind presumes a manager—someone or some delegated authority—

must be in charge. Although it may be difficult to gather together even a small commission that will always agree that environmental concerns should take precedence over economic harassment of the environment and the hunger for public works dollars, the attempt must be made. There will always be objections to limitation of jurisdiction and decision making from those who fear that their economic oxen may be gored, but without some common dedication to a mutually agreed course of action, there can be no hope for our estuaries. This is especially true for the Chesapeake Bay, where three separate state agencies are losing the fight to keep the estuary as more than a barren *cloaca maxima* of the eastern megalopolis.

SUMMARY

Maintenance of estuaries as viable, ecologically healthy entities requires, first of all, a sense of obligation and dedication to the management of estuaries as environmental entities; the "estuarine conscience," as in Aldo Leopold's "ecological conscience," is the prime requisite.

Not all governmental and economic entities involved in an estuary can be equally sovereign; jurisdiction and decision-making power must be entrusted to some central management for each major estuary.

Delegation of permit and hearing procedures to the managing commission from the Corps of Engineers should be given serious consideration to maintain the two agencies' separateness.

Filling should be considered basically a form of pollution: the most permanent and irreversible kind.

The environment of an estuary includes the watershed of streams flowing into it, and the entire drainage basin of an estuary must be dealt with during some phase of the management process.

Management, data storage, interpretation, research, education, and meeting and hearing procedures should be conducted in a permanent center for each estuary or group of estuaries.

The continued reliance on consultants and other advisers to produce development plans, management studies, and proposals for monitoring programs diverting funds from needed activities. The broad national policy is that estuaries must be preserved and maintained, and it is time that we begin to do just that.

References

Borgstrom, Georg. 1969. *Too Many: A Study of Earth's Biological Limitations.* The Macmillan Company, New York. xiii + 368 pp.

Duxbury, Alyn C. 1971. Coastal zone processes and their influence on estuarine conditions. *Proceedings* of the Northwest Estuarine and Coastal Zone Symposium. (in press)

Eisler, Ronald. 1969. Acute toxicities of insecticides to marine decapod crustaceans. *Crustaceana, 16*(3): 302–310.

Emery, K. O. and Stevenson, R. E. 1957. Estuaries and lagoons, I. Physical and chemical characteristics. In *Treatise on Marine Ecology and Paleontology,* Joel Hedgpeth, ed. Geol. Soc. America, Memoir 67, pp. 673–693, 11 figs.

Fonselius, Stig H. 1970. Stagnant sea. *Environment, 12*(6): 2–11, 40–48.

Gilbert, Grove Karl. 1917. Hydraulic mining debris in the Sierra Nevada. U.S. Geol. Survey *Professional Paper* 105:154 pp.

Hedgpeth, Joel W. 1966. Aspects of the estuarine ecosystem. Amer. Fish. Soc., *Spec. Publ.* 3:3–11, 5 figs.

Hedgpeth, Joel W. and Gonor, Jefferson J. 1969. Aspects of the potential effect of thermal alteration on marine and estuarine benthos. In *Biological Aspects of Thermal Pollution,* Peter A. Krenkel and Frank L. Parker, eds. Vanderbilt University Press, pp. 80–118, 7 figs.

Mansueti, Romeo J. 1961. Effects of civilization on striped bass and other estuarine biota in Chesapeake Bay and tributaries. *Proceedings*, Gulf & Carib. Fish. Inst., *14*: 110–136, 5 figs.

Merriman, Daniel, 1970. The calefaction of a river. *Sci. Amer.*, 222(5):42–52. Available as Offprint No. 1177 from W. H. Freeman and Company.

Merriman, Daniel. 1971. Does calefaction jeopardize the ecosystem of a long tidal river? Environmental Aspects of Nuclear Power Stations, *Proceedings of a Symposium*, New York, August 1970. International Atomic Energy Agency, Vienna.

Morgan, P. R. and Stross, R. G. 1969. Destruction of phytoplankton in the cooling supply of a steam electric station. *Chesapeake Science*, *10*(3–4):165–171.

Newman, W. A. 1967. On physiology and behaviour of estuarine barnacles. *Proceed-ings*, Symposium on Crustacea held at Ernuklam, Jan. 12–15, 1965. Marine Biol. Assoc. India, pp. 1038–1066, 9 figs.

Odum, William E. 1970. Insidious alteration of the estuarine environment. *Trans. Amer. Fish. Soc.* 1970 (4):836–847.

Shaler, Nathaniel Southgate. 1906. *Man and the Earth*. Fox, Duffield & Co., New York. vi + 240 pp.

Taylor, John L. and Saloman, Carl H. 1968. Some effects of hydraulic dredging and coastal development in Boca Ciega Bay, Florida. *Fishery Bull.*, U.S. Fish & Wildl. Serv., 67(2):213–241, 13 figs.

Waldichuk, Michael. 1968. Waste disposal in relation to the physical environment—oceanographic aspects. *Syesis*, 1:4–27, 21 figs.

Weinberg, Alvin M. and Hammond, R. Philip. 1970. Limits to the use of energy. *Amer. Scientist*, 58:412–418, 3 figs.

CHAPTER 14

The Great Lakes rank among the largest bodies of fresh water in the world. For many years they have been centers for great fisheries, industry, navigation, and varied water-based recreation. Once it was believed that huge bodies of water such as these could not be affected by man. But now, especially near shore, in bays, and in the shallower lakes, the impacts of overuse are changing and often destroying the ecological character of the lakes. The commercial fish catch has declined drastically, in some cases accompanied by radical changes in species composition, due to the impacts of pollution, over-fishing, navigation, and competition from the sports fishery. The rivers that feed the lakes bring excess nutrients and poisons from industrial wastes, and dredging spoils from harbors spread toxic effects. The shores are filled in and built upon almost at random; power plants are being designed to use lake water as a coolant. Meanwhile a multiplicity of uncoordinated jurisdictions, from municipal to international, attempt to regulate use of the lakes.

My recommendations are aimed at enforcing present quality control laws, coordinating the programs of all governmental agencies, establishing environmental monitoring systems, and studying other ways to encourage ecologically sensitive use of the shorelands and waters of the Great Lakes.

MAN'S EFFECTS ON THE GREAT LAKES

Alfred M. Beeton

INTRODUCTION

The changes that have occurred in the Great Lakes are striking results of the misuse of one of the major resources of North America. Dramatic changes in the biota and the increased chemical and biological activity of Lake Erie, often erroneously referred to as the "death of Lake Erie," are cited repeatedly as the dire consequences of pollution. Yet as recently as the early 1950s most people, including the scientific community, believed that the Great Lakes were too large to be seriously affected by man's activities. Pollution of tributaries, bays, harbors, and some inshore waters was evident, but the possibility that a body of water covering almost 10,000 square miles, such as Lake Erie, could be undergoing measureable changes was not recognized until late in the 1950s. Nevertheless, it has been well documented that all of the Great Lakes, except Lake Superior, have undergone significant changes in quality of their environments and nature of their biota. Furthermore, present use of Lake Superior for disposal of taconite

TABLE 1
Great Lakes Dimensions and Discharge

Lake	Water surface (sq. km)	Volume (cub. km)	Max. depth	Mean depth (meters)	Drainage basin (sq. km)	Average Outflow 1860-1968, m³/sec	Average surface level above sea
Superior	82,102	12,154	405.4	149.0	207,458	2,110	183.0
Michigan	57,757	4,839	281.3	85.0	175,860	1,586	176.0
Huron	59,570	3,447	222.8	59.4	193,731	5,296	176.0
Erie	25,667	484	64.0	18.9	103,600	5,806	173.8
Ontario	19,011	1,638	244.4	86.3	82,880	6,768	74.6
Totals	244,107	22,562	—	—	763,529	—	—

iron ore waste has generated concern that this lake may also undergo irreversible changes unless preventive steps are taken.

The lakes are a major resource of North America and of inestimable value to Canada and the United States (Figure 1). With their connecting waters and the St. Lawrence River they provide a waterway of almost 2,000 miles extending into the heartland of the continent from the northern Atlantic Ocean. The region is rich in extensive forests and farmlands, and along the shoreline of the lakes are vast coal, iron, copper, limestone, and other mineral deposits. The combination of a ready transportation route, vast resources, and an abundance of high-quality water favored early settlement of the region and the development of huge industries and large metropolitan areas.

MORPHOLOGY AND MORPHOMETRY

The Great Lakes and their connecting waters lie in a drainage basin with a total area of almost 295,000 square miles (246,049 km²), shared by Canada and the United States. Their total volume constitutes one of the largest reservoirs of fresh water in the world and the combined shoreline (9,400 miles or 15,040 km) is considerably more extensive than the length of the U.S. Atlantic coast (6,400 miles or 10,300 km). Various dimen-

sions of the lakes are compared in Table 1 (Beeton, 1971).

Lake Erie's physical characteristics differ considerably from those of the other lakes, and this has made Lake Erie subject to more accelerated eutrophication. It is smaller than the other lakes, but of greater significance is its shallowness, with a mean depth of only 62 feet. Although it ranks eleventh among the world's lakes in surface area, it is only fifteenth in volume. The western basin is very shallow (mean depth 24 feet), the central basin has depths of 50 to 80 feet, and the eastern basin is up to 210 feet deep—the maximum.

The water levels of the lakes vary from one to two feet annually, with the highest levels occuring in summer and the lowest in early spring, although there are periods of extreme low or high levels. Suggestions that these are cyclic fluctuations have not been substantiated. Fluctuations in water level in Lake Erie are of special concern because of the shallowness of the basin and the magnitude of the fluctuations; differences in level of as much as 13.5 feet (4.1 m) between Buffalo and Toledo have been recorded. Such fluctuations affect hydroelectric power generation on the Niagara River, and may leave ships temporarily stranded in the shallow west end.

The lakes modify the climate of the region, for as huge heat sinks they take up thermal energy in the warm months and release it in the winter, thus slowing down warming in the

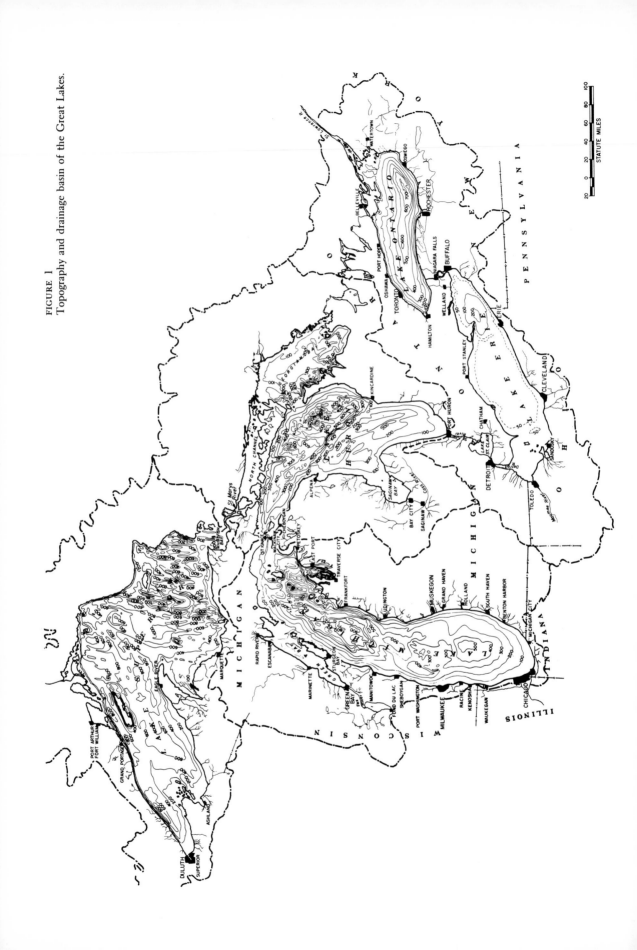

FIGURE 1
Topography and drainage basin of the Great Lakes.

spring and cooling in the fall. As a consequence, the Door Peninsula and the eastern shores of Lake Michigan are excellent fruit growing areas. Precipitation patterns are also affected by the lakes, and as a result there are zones of heavy precipitation along the eastern shores. The increase in average annual water temperatures for Lake Erie—2° F, as recorded since 1918—has, until recently, coincided with a general climatic warming documented for southwestern Ontario (Beeton, 1961).

PRESENT USES AND PROBLEMS

More than 32 million people live in the Great Lakes basin, where the population has increased from about 2.3 million people in 1860 to about 31.8 million in 1960, an increase of 1,282 percent (Figure 2). However, some of the northern counties of Michigan and Wisconsin, as well as areas of Ontario, have not shown any major change in population, and in some areas there has even been a slight decrease. The major population increase has been in urban areas in the basins of Lake Erie and Lake Michigan, where along with Lake Ontario, pollution has been most severe.

The population of the Lake Erie basin increased from one million to more than 10 million from 1860 to 1960. By 1900 some 4 million people lived in the Lake Michigan basin. In that year the Chicago Sanitary and Ship Canal was opened and sewage from Chicago was diverted away from the lake, so that there was slight relief to the drainage basin after 1900. Nevertheless, population pressure on the lake has increased to almost 6 million from 1900 to 1960. The Lake Ontario basin was settled early in the history of the region, but population growth was gradual until the 1940s; almost 4 million people lived in the Lake Ontario basin by 1960.

Population growth will continue, since the reasons for the settlement and rapid growth will be valid for some time. At present growth rates, an estimated 40 million people will live in the basin by the year 2000. It is expected that within the next 50 years a megalopolis will stretch continuously from Milwaukee to Montreal (Beeton and Rosenberg, 1968).

Much of the land in the northern lakes' area is reforested land, because the virgin forests were logged by 1900, and it is still valued for its timber and recreational resources. The southern half of the basin is agricultural, owing to the more favorable climate and richer soils.

Shoreline property has long been among the most desirable sites for private dwellings, and shoreland prices have risen accordingly in response to heavy demands. This makes obtaining additional park lands difficult and expensive, and prohibits recreational use by the public. Frequently, building sites have been developed when water levels were low; subsequent high levels, accompanied by accelerated shore erosion, have led to substantial property losses. In some areas shorelines have receded as much as 200 feet during the past 100 years, and proper zoning of property close to each lake appears necessary to protect the lakes and the public.

The abundance of limestone, iron ore, copper, salt, sand and gravel, and clay are important to the economy of the basin. Production of iron ore has been of major importance for many years in the Lake Superior basin; approximately 100 million tons were produced during the peak year of 1953. Supplies of iron rich ores have been exhausted, but processes have been developed to enrich the taconite ores efficiently.

The major population centers and industrial areas are in the southern half of the Great Lakes' basin. Many kinds of industry, are present, including about one-third of the industries and one-half of the steel-producing capacity of the U.S. The importance of the automobile industry to Detroit and southeastern Michigan is well known.

The value of the lakes and their connect-

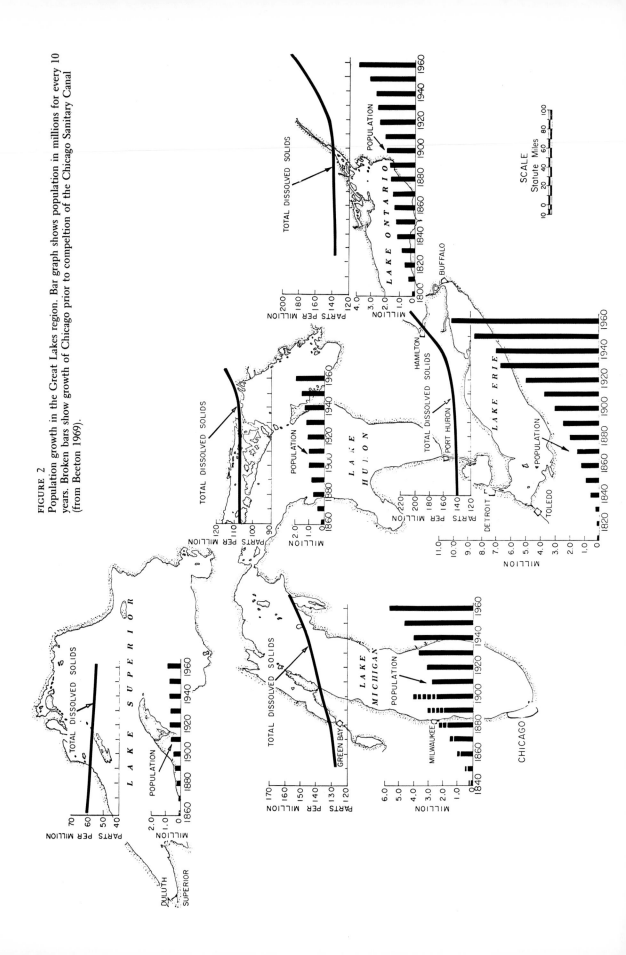

FIGURE 2
Population growth in the Great Lakes region. Bar graph shows population in millions for every 10 years. Broken bars show growth of Chicago prior to completion of the Chicago Sanitary Canal (from Beeton 1969).

ing waterways as a transportation route into the heartland of the continent was recognized very early in the history of North America. The importance of the lakes to shipping has continued to the present. Over the years various canals have been built to make the lakes accessible (MacNish and Lawhead, 1968). Small ocean vessels have been entering the lakes for years, but the completion of the St. Lawrence Seaway in 1959 allowed "deep draft" ocean-going vessels, up to 735 feet in length, to enter the lakes. Shipping through the Seaway has been around 5 million tons per year, although total shipping on the lakes in 1966 was about 246 million net tons (Brockel, 1970).

The most important use of the lakes is as a source of water for municipalities and industry. Approximately 16,000 million gallons are used daily by some 240 communities and the industries. It is estimated that the industrial pumpage from the lakes is three times that supplied to the municipalities (Great Lakes Basin Commission, 1969). Regardless of the uses of water, it is never returned to the lakes in its original condition. Unfortunately, the expansion in waste treatment facilities has not kept pace with the ever-increasing use of the waters and the lakes for waste disposal.

Electric power generation is primarily from fossil fuel and hydroelectric plants, although a number of nuclear power plants are being constructed along the lakes to utilize the lake waters as coolants. There are approximately 160 hydroelectric stations in the basin, the major ones, on the St. Marys, Niagara, and St. Lawrence rivers, having a total capacity of about 8 million kilowatts. The thermal power plants have a total capacity of about 20 million kilowatts.

Commercial fishing was important in the Great Lakes until recently, when populations of the more highly valued species drastically declined. Although total production has fluctuated around 100 million pounds annually, the value of the catch has decreased.

Even in Lake Erie, production has remained at about 50 million pounds per year. However, in 1969 the catch consisted of yellow perch, smelt, carp, sheepshead, and white bass, instead of lake herring, blue pike, sauger, whitefish, and walleye caught some seventy years before.

During the late 1960s, sports fishing in Lake Erie gained greater importance as a result of the successful introduction of coho, kokanee, and chinook salmon. Protective legislation for the sports fishery, further declines in stocks of commercial species, and the detection of potentially harmful levels of DDT and mercury in fish have all helped to accelerate the demise of commercial fishing in the lakes.

The Great Lakes are of inestimable value for recreational activities. Many miles of sandy beaches are found along the shorelines. Sailing and power boating have become popular, and miles of lake-front park lands provide sites for camping, picnicking, and a variety of sports. The tourist industry is of major importance to the economy of many communities as evidenced by a recent study of Door County, Wisconsin—the 491 square mile Door Peninsula which extends into Green Bay and Lake Michigan—where tourism generates more than $28 million in annual economic activity (Strang, 1970).

Though the uses of the Great Lakes for the shipping and hydroelectric power industries and recreation often come in to conflict and require controls, the main problem is that waters withdrawn from the lakes are returned at lower quality. Treatment removes many pathogens and toxic materials, but often does not remove nutrients such as nitrogen and phosphorus, and other chemicals, such as DDT and mercury. Consequently, the water re-enters the lakes as a solution of new chemicals, and this daily, continuous process throughout the basin results in progressive degradation of the water resource. This is a subtle and gradual alteration of the total ecosystem—certainly not as obvious to the

TABLE 2
Average chemical characteristics of the St. Lawrence Great Lakes

Lake	Calcium (ppm)	Mag-nesium (ppm)	Potas-sium (ppm)	Sodium (ppm)	Total alka-linity (ppm) (CaCo₃)	Chloride (ppm)	Sulfate (ppm)	Silica (ppm)	Total phos-phorus (ppb)	Nitrate (ppm)
Superior	12.4	2.8	0.6	1.1	46	1.9	3.2	2.1	5	0.52
Michigan	33	11	1.1	3.9	110	6.5	20	2.5	13	0.13
Huron	26.7	6.3	0.9	2.5	82	5.9	13	1.9	10	—
Erie	37.9	9.6	1.4	10.6	95	23.4	21.1	0.8	61	0.10
Ontario	38.2	8.2	1.3	12.0	102	26.7	27.1	0.3	9.6-28	—

casual observer as the closed bathing beaches of western Lake Erie and southern Green Bay.

The conflict in water use between navigation and fisheries is not immediately apparent, but the long-term consequences of constructing aids to navigation have been disastrous. Garbage is dumped overboard, and sewage and engine oil are pumped into the lakes from ships. The Great Lakes' states sought to overcome this misuse by passing stringent legislation, but unfortunately more lenient federal regulations will supersede those of the states. Of greater importance, however, are the drastic ecological changes attributed indirectly to shipping (Beeton and Mraz, 1969).

The canals built to provide access to all the Great Lakes also provide migration routes for predatory marine fishes. The sea lamprey invaded the upper lakes, wiping out the lake trout and other species. More recently the alewife migrated into the upper lakes and became the dominant species in Lakes Huron and Michigan.

Maintenance of suitable harbor depths has also become a critical problem in the lakes. Most harbors have been developed at river mouths and provide good settling basins for the sediments and pollutants carried by the rivers—a problem further aggravated by the absence of tidal flushing action. The U.S. Army Corps of Engineers dredges about 10 million cubic yards of sediments yearly and commercial interests dredge another 2 million cubic yards from over 120 harbors, so that dredged materials have been dumped in the lakes. Unfortunately, most of the dredged sediments were polluted and as a result are frequently toxic to aquatic life owing to a high oxygen requirement. Although the Corps has developed an interim plan of diked disposal for polluted sediments, the ultimate solution to the problem must be pollution abatement in the rivers.

PRESENT ENVIRONMENTAL QUALITY OF THE GREAT LAKES

The waters of the lakes are bicarbonate, and the pH ranges from 8.0 to 8.5, except for Lake Superior which has a pH of 7.4. Dissolved oxygen content of even the deepest waters remains near saturation throughout the year except in Lake Erie and southern Green Bay in Lake Michigan. Silica, an important nutrient for diatoms, is about 2 ppm (parts per million) in open waters of the upper lakes, but may decrease to trace amounts in Lake Erie and Lake Ontario or in especially productive waters of other lakes. Other chemical characteristics of the lakes are summarized in Table 2.

The coliform content is usually low in most open-lake waters, and the 5-day biochemical oxygen demand is usually less than 1 ppm. In general, the open waters of all the lakes are of good to excellent quality.

The suspended microscopic plants and

animals of the planktonic community are the same species found in other large deep lakes, and many are cosmopolitan in distribution. Diatoms are probably the most important components of the algal communities, although green and blue-green algae become very abundant at times, especially in the more productive nearshore waters, in bays and harbors, and throughout Lake Erie. The peak abundance of plankton usually occurs once a year in spring or early summer in the less productive waters, however the plankton seem to be abundant twice a year in such nutrient-rich warm waters as Lake Erie, Green Bay, and southern Lake Michigan.

Animals living in or on the sediments in deep waters are primarily pollution-intolerant organisms, such as the opossum shrimp, *Mysis relicta*; the deep-water amphipod, *Pontoporeia affinis*; midges of the genus *Heterotrissocladius*; some sphaeriid clams; and oligochaetes of the genera *Euilyodrilus* and *Stylodrilus*. The shallow-water fauna includes most of those organisms common in smaller inland lakes, such as some species of oligochaetes, various midge larvae, leeches, clams, snails, mayfly nymphs, and caddisfly larvae. Only the more pollution-tolerant oligochaetes and midge larvae, are abundant in areas of heavy organic pollution, although even these species cannot survive in the badly polluted harbors and rivers.

Most families of North American fishes are found in the Great Lakes and tributaries. The salmonids, which include the whitefish, have been major species in all the lakes until very recently. Species associated with warmer waters—carp, freshwater drum, yellow perch, sauger, walleye, white bass, and smelt—are or have recently been abundant in Green Bay, Saginaw Bay, and Lake Erie. The white perch is a recent immigrant into the lower lakes from the Atlantic Coast via the Erie Canal, and it has become a major species in some areas of Lake Ontario. The establishment of sea lamprey and alewife populations in the upper lakes has been previously mentioned.

Large numbers of coho, chinook, and kokanee salmon have been introduced to provide a sports fishery and possibly control the alewife. Previous attempts to introduce salmon were not successful, but evidently the presence of large schools of alewife for food have made the recent introductions a success. The salmon, rainbow trout, and lake trout provide excellent sports fisheries, especially in Lake Michigan.

Most areas of Lakes Huron and Superior are considerd as oligotrophic (nutrient poor) waters because of the high transparency, high dissolved-oxygen content, low total dissolved solids content, and nature of the biota (Beeton, 1965). The offshore waters (more than 10 miles from shore) of Lake Michigan also have a high dissolved-oxygen content and relatively high transparency, but the concentrations of several chemicals approximate those of Lake Erie (Table 2). Nevertheless, phosphorus concentrations are much lower than those of Lake Erie and the biota is similar to that of Lake Superior, although more abundant. These waters probably can be considered somewhat less oligotrophic than Lake Huron. Lake Erie is classified as eutrophic because of high phosphorus concentrations, low transparency, an annual oxygen depletion in the bottom waters, very abundant plankton, and high productivity (Beeton, 1969). Lake Ontario is probably best described as mesotrophic. It receives nutrient-rich waters from Lake Erie, but its great depth probably does not permit full utilization of the nutrients by the algae. Such lakes have been called morphometrically oligotrophic (Rawson, 1960). Lake Ontario has a greater chemical content than Lake Erie, but much of the biota consists of those organisms which are also important in Lakes Huron and Superior.

Many of the changes in the Great Lakes are similar to those which have been observed during the accelerated nutrient enrichment (eutrophication) of smaller lakes. It would be erroneous, however, to expect these large bodies of water to respond to nutrient loading like small lakes do. In small lakes increased nutrient input stimulates the growth of algae, favoring those species requiring high nutrient levels. The increased productivity is reflected eventually in the reduced dissolved-oxygen content of the bottom waters and, subsequently, in changes in the sediments. The large lakes of the world simply cannot respond to nutrient loading in this manner, because their size and diversity of habitats preclude any such overall response. The shallow-water environments—bays, harbors, and inshore waters—receive the nutrients and may undergo significant changes. Although changes eventually may affect the open lake, it is the shallow-water environments that are first altered by pollution, as they are utilized for a water supply, waste disposal, fish production, and recreation.

The major problem areas, those which have undergone or are undergoing serious degradation from pollution, are southern Green Bay and the inshore waters of Lake Michigan, Saginaw Bay in Lake Huron, the west end of Lake Erie and its southern shore, and the shore near metropolitan centers on Lake Ontario. These areas, of course, are not isolated from the rest of the lake environments and added pollution is undoubtedly affecting the entire ecosystem. Efforts to correct these conditions will benefit all of the Great Lakes.

CHANGES IN THE ENVIRONMENT AND BIOTA— MAN'S IMPACT ON THE ENVIRONMENT

More than 100 years ago there was concern over the decreased catch of commercially important fish, such as the lake trout and the whitefish, in addition to the reduced size of the fish being caught and the decreased abundance of certain other fish in some areas (Smiley, 1882).

The decreased abundance of many fish can be attributed to over-fishing. In the early years the lake sturgeon, which is a primitive,

slow-growing fish attaining lengths of 9 feet and weighing over 300 pounds, was abundant in the shoal waters of the Great Lakes and in some of the large rivers. It is a good food fish, and its roe is made into caviar. Nevertheless, these fish were caught and purposely destroyed to eliminate them from fishing grounds, since their large size damaged gear used to capture other species (Smith, 1968). According to commercial records over 8 million pounds were caught in 1879, 5 million pounds in 1890, and there are indications that in the early years many more pounds of sturgeon were piled on the beaches to rot. Only 41,000 pounds were taken throughout the Great Lakes in 1969 (U.S. Department of Commerce, 1970). The early decline in abundance of this species is a good example of man's misuse of the resource through overfishing. The sturgeon has been protected since 1929, but its numbers have not increased, since many of the rivers and suitable shallow areas are now severely polluted.

Pollution was of concern over 100 years ago. In the 1840s, whitefish used to migrate 20 miles up the Oconto River from Green Bay to spawn. But the great pine forest of the lake states was being cut during this period, and by 1880 sawdust covered the bottom of the Oconto River and extended for 2 miles out into the Bay. Spawning runs had ceased by 1880, and the 90 percent decrease in the whitefish catch in that part of Green Bay was attributable to sawdust pollution.

Many of the activities in the Great Lakes region during the last century led to the problems we are faced with today. Niagara Falls, which is between Lakes Erie and Ontario, presented a formidable barrier to migration of aquatic life as well as to the transportation necessary for development of the region. The Erie Canal between Buffalo and Albany was completed in 1825 and freight rates dropped from $120 to $4 per ton. Construction of the Welland Canal between Lakes Erie and Ontario was started the same year, and the canal was opened in 1829. Not only did these canals provide an inexpensive transportation route, but they also opened the upper lakes to the predatory sea lamprey and the alewife. In addition, drainage basins of the lakes were being transformed. The forests were being logged, marsh lands were being drained, and dams were built across streams (see Teclaff, in this volume). In a little more than 200 years, the drainage basin of Lake Erie was transformed from a near wilderness, populated by about 100,000 people, to a watershed used extensively for agriculture and industry, and with a population of approximately 12 million in 1970.

Changes in the drainage basin of Lake Ontario, by damming and siltation of streams made streams unsuitable for stream spawning fish, such as the Atlantic salmon. This salmon ascended various streams tributary to Lake Ontario in the pioneer days, but rapidly declined in abundance and had almost disappeared by 1880 (International Board of Inquiry, 1943).

Some consequences of man's alteration and use of the environment were apparent before the turn of the century, but there is no evidence that widespread and long-term implications were recognized. By 1900 the sea lamprey had already made its way through the Welland Canal and had established spawning populations in the upper lakes. Several developments between 1900 and 1950 were especially important to later changes in the Great Lakes. Pesticides such as DDT, and detergents came into wide use after the Second World War. Attempts at uniform fishing regulations were unsuccessful, and over-fishing of many stocks continued. The large population build-up in the region was of major importance to later developments. Major urban centers were rapidly developing and sewerage systems were being expanded to carry waste to the lakes, under the assumption that the plentiful supply of water in the lakes would dilute any pollutants to harmless concentrations. However, it was soon discovered, at least in some areas such as southern Lake Michigan, that this assumption

was not correct, especially since typhoid fever was related to contamination of domestic water supplies. Consequently, because of combined public health and transportation interests, the Chicago Sanitary Canal was built and put into operation in 1900 to divert sewage away from Lake Michigan into the Mississippi River drainage system, a fortunate development that retarded the rate of change of Lake Michigan (though it was disastrous for the Illinois River below).

Some significant changes were taking place in Lake Erie. Lake trout production had been almost 100,000 pounds per year before 1900 but the catch progressively declined until only a few hundred pounds were being taken in the late 1930s (Figure 3). Lake herring, called cisco in Lake Erie, and whitefish were being caught throughout the lake and in the Detroit River before 1900, but the fishery for these species in the Detroit River collapsed at the turn of the century and shortly thereafter the Michigan fishery in the far western end of the lake declined. The commercial catch increased for a time in the Ohio waters of Lake Erie and then declined, and although the eastern waters of Pennsylvania and New York continued to provide many cisco and whitefish, there was a progressive reduction from west to east in the lake. The cisco fishery had been a very productive one, with a peak production of almost 49 million pounds in 1918, but in 1925 it collapsed and less than 6 million pounds were taken. The commercial catch continued to decline, and by 1929 less than 1 million pounds were being caught annually. Finally the fishing industry and government agencies became concerned. Lake Erie was studied intensively during 1928, 1929, and 1930 (Wright, 1955; Fish, 1960), and it was concluded that no environmental changes of significance had taken place. The commercial catch of cisco has continued to decline, however, except for a catch of over 16 million pounds in 1946, which demonstrates that if conditions were suitable the population could recover. In 1967 the commercial catch of cisco was less than 500

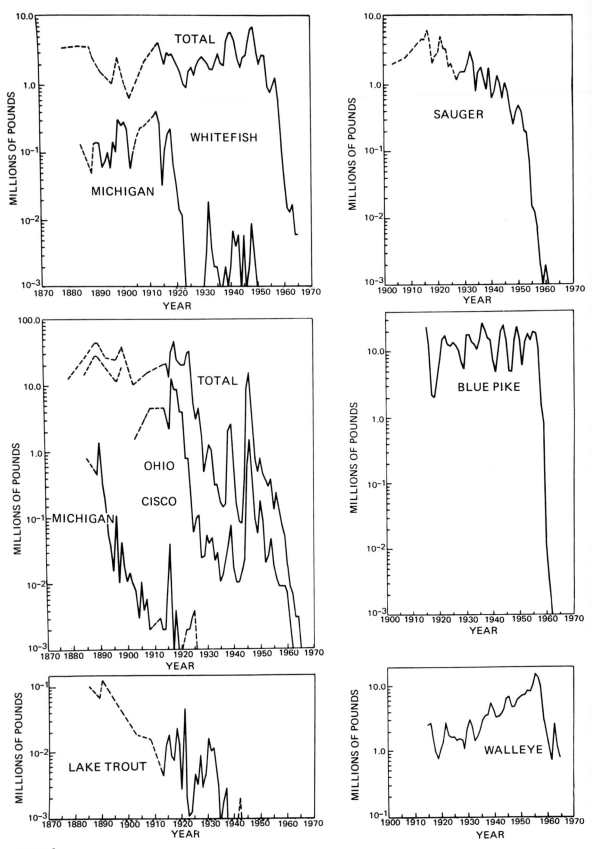

FIGURE 3
Commercial production of certain fishes in Lake Erie (from Beeton 1969).

pounds and the whitefish production was only 3,000 pounds, compared to an annual catch of more than 2 million pounds before 1954 (Figure 3). Over-fishing and pollution have taken their toll.

The migration of the predatory sea lamprey into the lakes above Niagara Falls spelled the doom of the once thriving commercial fishery (Baldwin, 1964). The sea lamprey, *Petromyzon marinus,* is native to the Atlantic Ocean, whence it migrates up streams to spawn. This predatory fish attaches itself to other fish with its sucker-like mouth and feeds on the blood of its victims. A lamprey destroys at least 20 pounds of fish during its life, lake trout being especially vulnerable to them. Sea lampreys have been in Lake Ontario for many years, but Niagara Falls was a natural barrier to further migration until construction of the Welland Canal in 1829 provided access to Lake Erie, and although the first catch of a lamprey in Lake Erie was not recorded until 1921, they probably had been moving through the Canal since its construction. By the 1930s lampreys were in Lakes Huron and Michigan, where conditions were ideal for spawning and survival (Applegate and Moffett, 1955); in 1946 they were found in Lake Superior. Once spawning populations of the lamprey were established it was only a short time before the lake trout fishery collapsed. During the 1930s the annual lake trout catch was around 10 million pounds in Lakes Huron and Michigan; by 1949 less than 1 million pounds were being caught annually in these lakes. The Lake Superior trout catch dropped from more than 4 million pounds in 1952 to less than 1 million pounds in 1960. Lake trout populations almost disappeared except for a reduced population in Lake Superior and a small population in Georgian Bay, Lake Huron, and now the lampreys have preyed on other species, such as the whitefish and deep-water chubs.

Several other fish have migrated into the lakes or have been introduced. Carp were introduced in the 1880s as a highly desirable species and rapidly became so abundant that over 13 million pounds were taken in Lake Erie by 1914 (International Board of Inquiry, 1943). The effect of this species on native fish populations remains unknown, although it is considered undesirable. Smelt were introduced into the Great Lakes in 1912 and subsequently established large populations in Lakes Erie, Huron, and Michigan (Van Oosten, 1937). Some people believe that the smelt were a factor in the decline of some native species. Alewife resemble shad and they were probably accidentally introduced into Lake Ontario with some shad, which were planted there in 1870. Alewife had migrated into Lake Erie in 1931 and Lake Huron by 1933. They had moved into Lake Michigan by 1949 and Lake Superior by 1954. The alewife migration into the upper lakes came at an opportune time since their predators, such as the lake trout and burbot (a freshwater codfish), were already declining because of the sea lamprey. Consequently, no predators remained to control the population explosion of the alewife. Alewives are a serious problem when the beaches become littered with tons of dead fish during their periodic die-offs. Furthermore, evidence is being accumulated to indicate that these fish have upset the ecological balance of the lakes and have adversely affected native fish and fish food organisms.

Despite the early declines in population of various fish and evidence of increased pollution, the consequences of pollution were not recognized until the late 1950s. Data on the major changes are reviewed in the following sections.

Lake Erie

The amount of total dissolved solids, as well as that of calcium, chlorides, sodium-plus-potassium, and sulfate in Lake Erie has increased significantly during the period from 1819 to 1970 as summarized in Figure 4. The amount of magnesium has not changed. Data

262

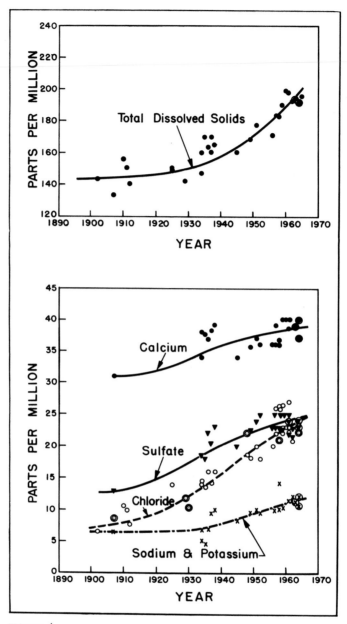

Changes in the chemical characteristics of Lake Erie (from Beeton 1969).

from the few open lake studies of the western basin indicate that ammoniac-nitrogen increased five-fold and total nitrogen about three-fold between 1930 and 1958. Total phosphorus concentrations appear to have doubled between 1942 and 1958.

Recent studies of seasonal and local changes in dissolved oxygen indicate a much greater oxygen demand in the lake today than in the past. Synoptic surveys conducted jointly by a number of organizations in 1959 and 1960 demonstrated the extent and severity of oxygen depletion when the lake is thermally stratified, especially in the central basin (Figure 5). Other studies have since substantiated the conclusion that low dissolved oxygen concentrations probably affect a similar area each year after the lake is thermally stratified. The degree of depletion and the area affected have recently become greater. Only five days of calm weather and subsequent stratification were necessary for dissolved oxygen to drop below 3 ppm in the western basin in 1963, whereas 28 days were required in 1953 (Carr *et al.*, 1965). Oxygen depletion in the hypolimnetic waters is probably caused by the high oxygen demand of the sediments. All of the surveys show that the severest oxygen depletion develops in the western part of the central basin where oxygen demand of the sediments is greatest, and that conditions improve toward the east. The western basin is usually homothermous, and consequently oxygen depletion is not detected as frequently there as in the deeper central basin, although the high oxygen demand of the sediments removes oxygen rapidly when stratification occurs.

Some major changes have occurred in the benthos of the western basin of Lake Erie. Nymphs of the mayfly, *Hexagenia*, a "clean-water" organism that formerly dominated the benthic community of western Lake Erie, have almost disappeared because of severe oxygen depletion (Britt, 1955), and since 1930 pollution-tolerant oligochaetes have become the dominant organism. Pollution-tolerant species of fingernail clams, midges, and snails also have increased considerably (Carr and Hiltunen, 1965). The number of oligochaetes per square meter has been used by several scientists to indicate the degree of pollution. On this basis the zones of heavy and moderate pollution had moved 5.5 and 8 miles lakeward from Maumee Bay between 1930 and 1951 (Brown, 1953). The area of western Lake Erie affected by heavy pollution was ten times greater in 1961 than in 1930. The benthos of most of the central basin consists of animals considered to be pollution-tolerant, although organisms such as *Hexagenia* may have been abundant in the past. Some other "clean-water" organisms, such as *Mysis relicta* and *Pontoporeia affinis*, which were found throughout the lake forty years ago, are now confined to the eastern part of the central basin and the eastern basin.

In recent years blooms of blue-green algae have appeared in Lake Erie. Between 1919 and 1963 the abundance of algae increased three-fold, spring and fall maxima became greater and lasted longer, and different diatom genera became dominant (Davis, 1964). *Melosira binderana*, a diatom favored by nutrient-rich waters and unreported in the United States until recently, has become a major species that at times makes up as much as 90 percent of the phytoplankton. Microscopic animals, such as copepods and cladocerans, increased in abundance between 1939 and 1958. *Dioptomus siciloides*, a copepod which was found occasionally in 1929 and 1930 and usually inhabits eutrophic waters, has become a dominant zooplankter. Recently, a brackish water copepod, *Eurytemora affinis*, has been noted in the lake.

In recent years great changes in the fish populations have caused the virtual disappearance of blue pike, lake herring, sauger, and whitefish from the lake (Figure 3). The dramatic reduction of the blue pike population owing to conditions unsuitable for reproduction has been especially alarming, as the blue pike population has not been replenished since the mid-1950s. The decline in the whitefish population also started at about the same time and occurred at approximately the same rate. The number of lake herring continued to decline after the fishery ceased to exist in the 1920s. Beginning in 1920 the sauger population continued a downward trend until 1950, when it almost disappeared completely.

No single factor has been responsible for bringing about the changes in the fish populations of Lake Erie. The sea lamprey has never been as important there as in the upper

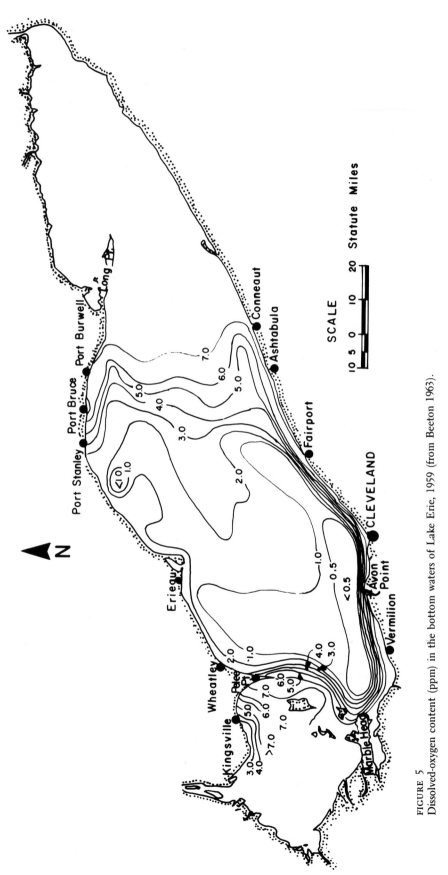

FIGURE 5
Dissolved-oxygen content (ppm) in the bottom waters of Lake Erie, 1959 (from Beeton 1963).

lakes, since only a few of the lake's tributary streams are suitable for lamprey spawning. Fishing has obviously decreased the numbers of some species, but its effect is difficult to determine, especially since the combined commercial and sports fishing catch is not known. The marked changes in the environment must have affected most species. The lake trout fishery was never especially important, but the long-term decline and eventual disappearance of this species indicates development of an unsuitable environment. When the areas of the lake inhabited by lake herring and whitefish became unsuitable, these species were restricted to the eastern part of the lake. Reduction of the blue pike and sauger populations took place during the period when extensive oxygen depletion and changes in the benthos were first reported.

Lake Ontario

Increases in total dissolved solids and in the major ions in Lake Ontario (Figure 6) closely parallel the increases in Lake Erie, as could be expected, since the main flow into Lake Ontario is from Lake Erie. The close agreement among the few early analyses (made in 1854, 1884, and 1907) indicates that increases in the chemical content of Lake Ontario, as well as Lake Erie, started around 1910.

The mean annual amount of plankton almost doubled at the Toronto water intake between 1923 and 1954, and a shift in dominant general occurred (Schenk and Thompson, 1965). This observation may be applied to the entire lake because the dominant genera are the same ones which were important in the open lake.

The commercial fishery of Lake Ontario never has been as important as those of the other lakes, and there has been great fluctuation in the catch of the major species (Figure 7). Consequently, the relative importance of certain species in the commercial catch frequently has changed during the period of record, although some long-term trends are

apparent. Lake herring and chubs, catfish and bullheads, yellow perch, whitefish, northern pike, suckers, and sturgeon (in order of importance) dominated the catch in 1899. The 1940 production consisted of lake herring and chubs, carp, whitefish, blue pike, lake trout, catfish and bullheads, and yellow perch. The 1969 catch reflected the major declines in abundance of lake herring, lake trout, whitefish, and blue pike (Figure 7), and consisted of carp, yellow perch, white perch, bullheads, eel, and sunfish. Total production was about 2.5 million pounds, a substantial decrease from the 4.3 million pound catch of 1940 and the 7.5 million pounds of 1890.

The major changes of importance are in the lake herring, lake trout, and blue pike fisheries (Figure 7), which indicate the development of an environment unsuitable for these species. The destruction of the lake herring population is similar to that which occurred in Lake Erie, although the major decline started 15 years after that of the Lake Erie population. The decline of the lake trout population, which started around 1930, was more gradual than in the other lakes, and although the sea lamprey has been in Lake Ontario for many years, it does not appear to be the only cause of the lake trout decline. The destruction of the blue pike population in Lake Ontario was concurrent and remarkably similar to that in Lake Erie.

Lake Huron

The site for the slightly increased concentrations in chloride, sulfate, and total dissolved solids (Figure 8) is mainly in the Lake Huron basin. Much of the increased chemical content can be attributed to recent urbanization and industrial growth in the Saginaw Valley.

Little information is available on past biological conditions, except for data from the commercial fishery. What information we do have indicates that the same mayfly (*Hexagenia*) that was replaced by pollution-tolerant worms in Lake Erie has become much

266

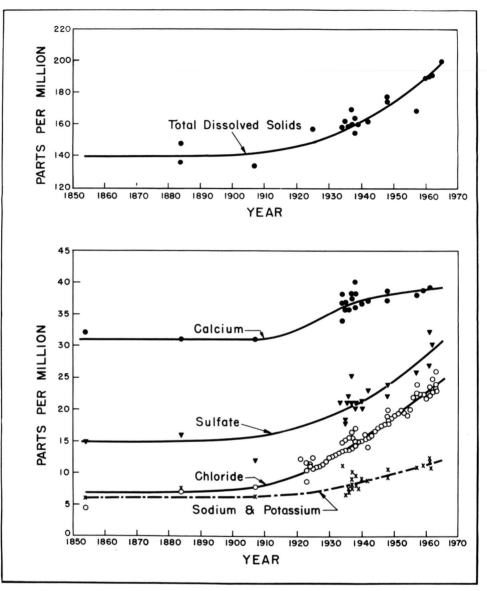

FIGURE 6
Changes in the chemical characteristics of Lake Ontario (from Beeton 1969).

less abundant in Saginaw Bay (Schneider *et al.*, 1970).

The commercial catch indicates that several significant changes have taken place in the fish population. Lake trout, lake herring, yellow perch, walleye, whitefish, and suckers were important in the fishery at the turn of the century. By 1940, the relative importance

of species had not changed much, although the catch of yellow perch had declined and carp had become important commercially. A period of dramatic change began in 1943, and by 1968 carp, whitefish, yellow perch, walleye, and suckers, in that order, constituted the greater part of the catch. The chub populations have seriously declined since the

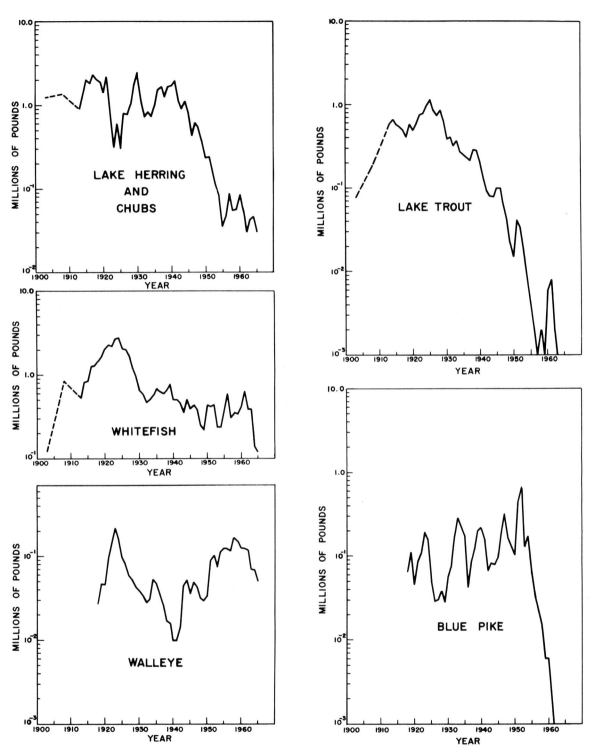

FIGURE 7
Commercial production of certain fishes in Lake Ontario (from Beeton 1969).

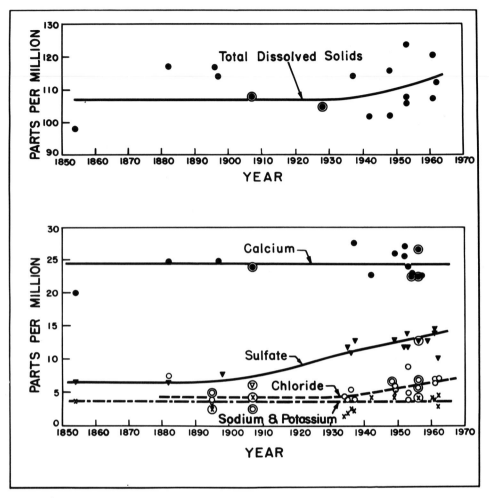

FIGURE 8
Changes in the chemical characteristics of Lake Huron (from Beeton 1969).

mid-1960s: total production for the lake was only 5.2 million pounds in 1969 compared to 14.6 million in 1940 and 21.6 million pounds in 1900.

Lamprey predation is considered the major cause of the decline of the lake trout. Before 1940 the fishery produced 4 to 6 million pounds annually without major fluctuations (Figure 9), but in the 1960s it produced only a few thousand. Decline of the whitefish in the 1930s is attributed to excessive exploitation by deep trap nets. The whitefish continued to decline, however, after the use of trap nets was restricted to water less than 80 feet deep, a decline that was probably caused by heavy sea lamprey predation. In the 1940s production of lake herring began to decrease in Saginaw Bay, where the lake herring catch was greatest (Figure 9), and production has declined significantly in all areas of the lake, especially in Saginaw Bay, since 1954. Walleye production has declined primarily because of the demise of the fishery in Saginaw Bay (Figure 9). Overfishing apparently was not a significant factor but pollution has been considered important (Hile, 1954). The sauger has not been an important commercial species in Lake Huron. Production data are

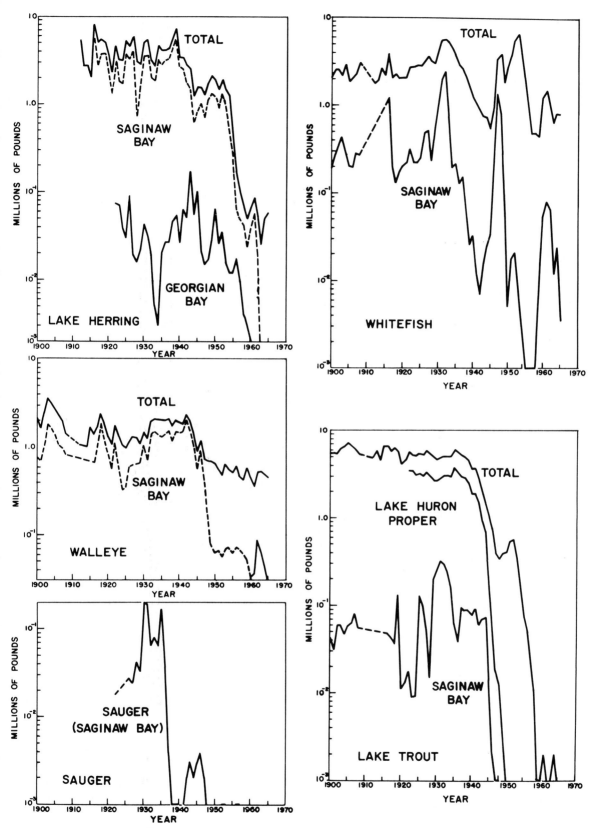

FIGURE 9
Commercial production of certain fishes in Lake Huron (from Beeton 1969).

included here because of the significant decline in catch after 1935. The catch has been less than 500 pounds in most recent years, and none were recorded in the commercial statistics for 1969.

Lake Michigan

Chemical concentrations in the water of Lake Michigan have increased substantially since the 1980s (Figure 10). Dissolved oxygen in southern Green Bay is probably more depleted in recent years than it has been in the past. The main tributary, the Fox River, has a severe oxygen deficiency as it enters the Bay during the summer, and in the winter oxygen concentrations of less than 1 ppm, are found in the southern part of the Bay under ice cover.

A number of changes have been observed in the plankton. The abundance of large zooplankters appears to have an inverse relationship to the size of the alewife population, presumably because of size-selective predation by the alewife (Wells, 1970).

Two diatoms, *Stephanodiscus hantzschii* and *S. binderanus* (probably *Melosira binderana* Kutz) not previously reported from Lake Michigan, have become abundant enough at the Chicago water intake to cause filtration problems. Blooms of the blue-green algae, such as *Anabaena* and *Aphanizomenon*, have been observed more frequently in recent years. Growths of *Cladophora* seem to have increased substantially, since floating mats of detached *Cladophora* have become a serious problem on the beaches in recent years.

The major changes in species composition and abundance of benthic organisms in southern Green Bay are closely similar to those observed in Lake Erie. Nymphs of the mayfly, *Hexagenia*, which were once an important component of the benthic community, being found in 31 percent of the samples from a survey made in 1938–1939, had disappeared by 1966 (Howmiller and Beeton, 1971). The number of midge larvae increased substantially between 1939 and 1966, and both the distribution and the abundance of oligochaetes changed in the same period. More oligochaetes are found today, but the zone of maximum abundance is farther out in Green Bay from the mouth of the Fox River. Evidently conditions near the river mouth have become unsuitable for even the more pollution-tolerant organisms.

Fish populations have changed substantially in recent years, with the most apparent changes being those in the commercial catch of lake trout, whitefish, lake herring, and alewife (Figure 11). The present fishery (1969) consists of alewife, chub, smelt, carp, whitefish, and coho salmon.

The lake trout catch dropped from 5.4 million pounds in 1945 to less than 500 pounds in 1953. Before 1945 this species had provided a stable fishery without major fluctuations. The decline of the lake trout in Lake Michigan was rather sudden and began when the sea lamprey population was relatively small. If the trout were being exploited at the optimum rate, the additional mortality caused by the lamprey may have been sufficient to bring about the destruction in the lake trout population (Smith, 1968). Although other changes were taking place in the environment which probably placed an additional stress on the lake trout, the evidence to date indicates that sea lamprey predation triggered their decline.

The whitefish catch declined rapidly from 1949 to 1957 (Figure 11), primarily because of lamprey predation. The present upward trend in the commercial catch may be among the first indications of successful control of the lamprey in Lake Michigan.

The decrease in catch of lake herring from 1954 to 1962 took place when the alewife was becoming abundant in the Lake. The lamprey and the alewife have probably contributed to the decline of the lake herring, but it should be noted that the major lake herring fishery was in Green Bay where accelerated eutrophication undoubtedly played

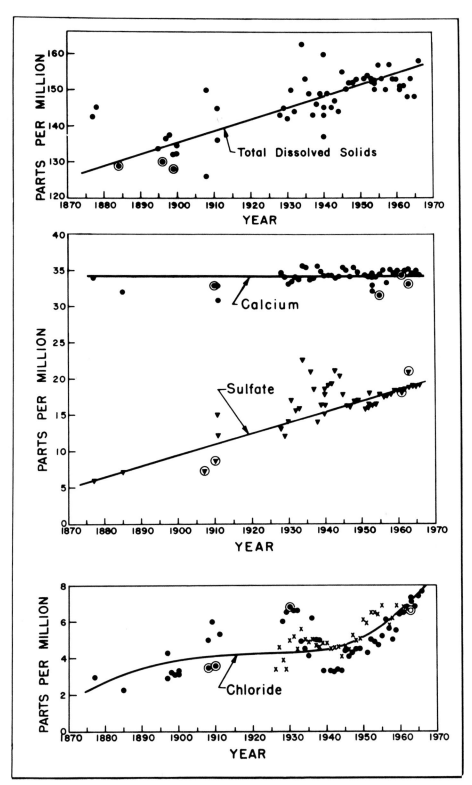

FIGURE 10
Changes in the chemical characteristics of Lake Michigan (from Beeton 1969).

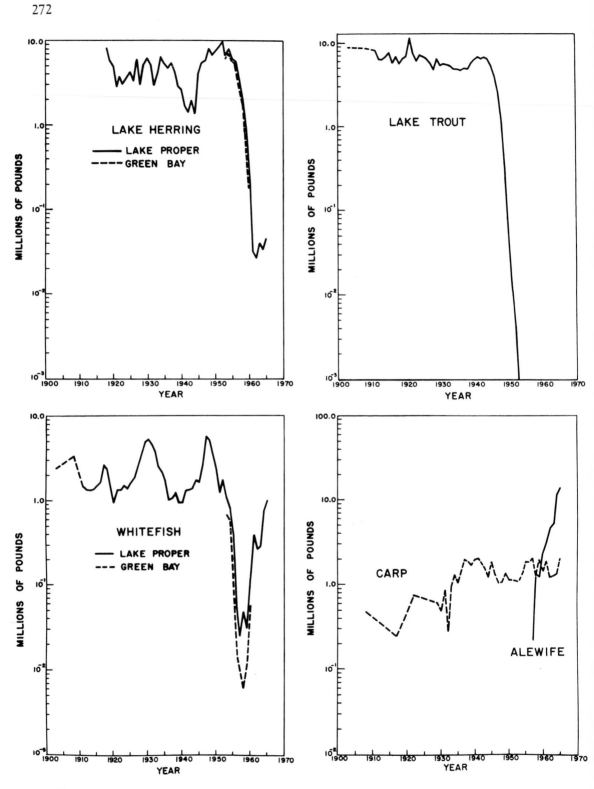

FIGURE 11
Commercial production of certain fishes in Lake Michigan (from Beeton 1969).

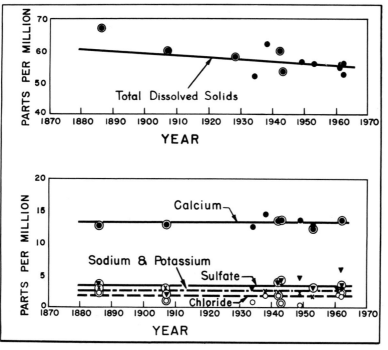

FIGURE 12
Changes in the chemical characteristics of Lake Superior (from Beeton 1969).

a part in the collapse of the lake herring population.

Chub populations have changed significantly, although this is not obvious from the commercial catch records. The chub fishery became important after the end of the Lake Erie cisco fishery in 1925. By 1932 the larger chubs (*Coregonus johannae* and *C. nigripinnis*) were becoming scarce so that mesh size of the nets was gradually reduced to capture the smaller species. Increased commercial fishing and sea lamprey predation resulted in such substantial changes in the chub population that medium sized chubs (*C. alpenae, kiyi, reighardi,* and *zenithicus*), which made up about 66 percent of the population in the 1930s, had declined to about 24 percent in 1955 and to about 6 percent in 1960. The smallest species, *C. hoyi,* an important food of lake trout and too small for lamprey predation, made up less than a third of the population in 1930, but about 94 percent in 1960. This species has responded to its changed environment as shown by an increase of 2

inches in mean length and an increased growth rate (Smith, 1968).

Lake Superior

No long-term changes have been detected in Lake Superior except for some localized pollution harbors, bays, or tributaries (Figure 12). A littoral current, which flows from west to east above the south shore and then into the open lake, receives the outflow from various tributaries and urbanized areas and carries it to Whitefish Bay and the outflow of Lake Superior: it may divert some pollution from the open lake.

Some major changes in the fish populations of Lake Superior have resulted from man's activities. The early fisheries, circa 1900, consisted of lake trout, whitefish, lake herring, chubs, and walleyes, respectively. Lake herring became the major species in the commercial catch commencing about 1900, and by 1940, the catch, on order of importance,

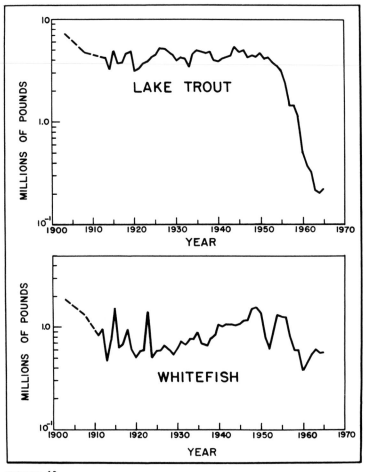

FIGURE 13
Commercial production of certain fishes in Lake Superior (from Beeton
1969).

consisted of lake herring, lake trout, white-fish, chubs, and walleye. Chubs have not attained major importance until recently. The recent decline in the lake trout and whitefish populations (Figure 13) and the successful establishment of the smelt have resulted in the present (1969) fishery of lake herring, smelt, chubs, whitefish, and lake trout. The decline in lake trout and white-fish coincides with the establishment of the sea lamprey. The total commercial catch has been declining since 1964, the result of a sharp decline in lake herring production. The successful control of the sea lamprey has led to rapid recovery of the lake trout, and its re-establishment as a major predator; this and the introduction of salmon will undoubtedly result in yet additional changes in the fish population.

THE EUTROPHICATION PROBLEM

Many of the changes that have taken place in lakes Erie, Michigan, and Ontario indicate accelerated eutrophication, that is, nutrient enrichment. Increases in nitrogen and phosphorus and decreases in dissolved oxygen content are accepted indices of eutrophication. Increases in the major ions may indicate environmental change not necessarily associated with eutrophication, but such increases also reflect nutrient changes. Most of the alterations in the biota have considerable significance as indices of eutrophication. Changes in species composition of plankton and its increased abundance, and the decline and disappearance of salmonid fishes, have been found in a number of small lakes undergoing eutrophication.

It appears, however, that the important changes in the Great Lakes are those taking place in the sediments owing to the entrance of tremendous amounts of pollutants. Major changes in the benthos and extensive depletion of dissolved oxygen offer evidence of change in the sediments. Present information suggests that depletion of dissolved oxygen in the hypolimnetic waters of western and central Lake Erie is greater than can be accounted for by organic synthesis in the epilimnion. The oxygen demand of Lake Erie sediments is about three times that of Lake Michigan sediments and at least ten times as great as that of Lake Huron sediments. Changes in the fish population of Lake Erie also may be closely related to changes in the sediments, since all Great Lakes fishes, except sheepshead, have eggs that settle to the bottom, which means that most fish are part of the benthos during a critical period in their life histories. Elsewhere in the Great Lakes there is also evidence of change in the sediments. Oligochaete species, which are associated with eutrophic conditions, are important in the benthic communities of southern Green Bay—an area of significant benthic change—southern Lake Michigan, Saginaw Bay, Lake Erie, and in the inshore zone of Lake Ontario.

Recent studies have demonstrated significant differences between inshore and open lake waters. The results of these studies indicate that inshore environments are deteriorating at a much faster rate than the offshore ones. These findings make it unrealistic to assume that the entire volume of a lake is available for dispersion and dilution of domestic, industrial, and thermal wastes.

Inshore (less than ten miles from shore) and offshore waters of Lake Michigan have pronounced differences in concentrations of major nutrients, especially in the vicinity of urban centers and along the east shore where most of the major tributaries enter the lake (Federal Water Pollution Control Administration, 1968). Inshore concentrations of ammonia, nitrate, organic-nitrogen, and soluble phosphate were 0.13, 0.14, 0.21, and 0.04 mg/liter, respectively, whereas offshore concentrations of ammonia, nitrate, organic-nitrogen, and soluble phosphate were 0.06, 0.13, 0.19, and 0.02 mg/liter, respectively, in 1962-1963. The abundance of algae reflected the inshore-offshore differences in nutrients, with low densities of 100 to 300 organisms per milliliter offshore and over 500 organisms per milliliter inshore. Diatoms were the major phytoplankters and had an obvious influence on silica concentrations—2.5 mg/liter offshore and 1.7 mg/liter inshore.

A continuous input of large quantities of nitrogen and phosphorus compounds is necessary to maintain high concentrations of these nutrients inshore. The greater abundance of algae inshore in Lake Michigan indicates the biological response to this input, but the response is not limited to an increased abundance of algae. The inshore and bay composition of species is different from that offshore, with eutrophic species inshore in many areas. Similar inshore-offshore differences have been demonstrated for Lakes Erie and Ontario.

Future Prospects

Changes in the Great Lakes, such as increases in chemical content, increased abundance of plankton, and changes in the benthos, have been subtle, and were not recognized until lake conditions were substantially altered. It is not coincidental that the major changes have taken place in the lakes with large metropolitan areas in their basins. Population growth has been greatest in the Lake Erie Basin, and this lake has shown the greatest changes in environment and biota. Increases in the chemical content and abundance of plankton in Lake Ontario closely parallel changes in Lake Erie, and do not indicate changes just within the Lake Ontario basin. The effect of a rapidly increasing plankton population is beginning to show in Lake Michigan, although changes have been more gradual than in Lake Erie and probably will continue to be more gradual, because the volume of Lake Michigan is much greater than that of Lake Erie. The extent of change in Lake Michigan undoubtedly would have been much greater if the Chicago Sanitary Canal had not been constructed to divert wastes from Chicago away from Lake Michigan. The long-term outlook for Lake Michigan is not encouraging, since the net addition and flow-through of water is small and most of the major tributaries are seriously polluted. The possibility of improving conditions in Lake Erie is somewhat better, since high-quality Lake Huron water enters it through the St. Clair and Detroit Rivers. Abatement of pollution of the rivers should eventually lead to the improvement of conditions in Lake Erie, since it is theoretically possible to exchange the entire volume of the lake in about three years, because of the short residence time of the water and the shallowness of the lake.

Municipalities contribute the major phosphorus input to the lakes, as shown by data from the International Joint Commission report (1970) on pollution of Lakes Erie and Ontario—10 percent of the total phosphorus is from direct input to Lake Erie. The municipalities also contribute about 55 percent of the phosphorus input from tributaries to Lake Erie, and municipal and industrial wastes account for about 75 percent of the estimated total: it is estimated that up to 70 percent of the phosphorus comes from detergents. This ever-increasing discharge of nutrients is a major factor in accelerated eutrophication of the lakes. The input of nitrogen and phosphorus stimulates the growth of algae, leading to large blooms of blue-green algae and *Cladophora*. The problem is compounded because these nutrients are retained or stored in the lake, especially in the sediments: 80 percent of the phosphorus is retained in Lake Erie.

The recent discovery of high mercury concentrations in the sediments and fish of Lake St. Clair illustrates the industrial waste problem and our serious lack of knowledge about many environmental pollutants. A wide variety of new pollutants are being discharged into the lakes. For example, plasticizer compounds show up as DDT in analyses, and it is possible that these compounds may be as harmful as DDT itself.

As pointed out previously, pollution flows directly into inshore areas, bays, and harbors. The critical areas now adversely affected are Green Bay, southern Lake Michigan, Saginaw Bay, Detroit River, western Lake Erie, southern shore of Lake Erie, and western Lake Ontario. Intensive pollution abatement programs in these seven critical areas will undoubtedly be a major step toward improving conditions throughout the Great Lakes.

CONCLUSIONS AND RECOMMENDATIONS

The plight of Lake Erie and the increasing evidence of parallel or similar changes elsewhere in the Great Lakes have resulted in greater concern and increased activity toward solving these problems on the part of governmental agencies, public institutions, and private citizens. Some progress has been and is being made toward solving pollution problems as well as such water-use problems as regulation of lake levels and extending the shipping season into the winter, but the return has been small in relation to the number of organizations and people involved. Perhaps it is not surprising that missions overlap and activities are uncoordinated: agencies of two nations, eight states, one province, 191 United States counties, and thousands of municipalities and other governmental units make decisions and engage in activities that affect components of the Great Lakes system.

Various institutions have been established to deal with problems in the Great Lakes system; some deal with fairly broad aspects of management, but most only with specific problems, and all are restricted by limited funding, staff, and other resources. The International Joint Commission was originally established by treaty between Canada and the United States to deal with pollution of boundary waters and water level regulation. The disastrous consequences of the invasion of the sea lamprey led to establishment of the Great Lakes Fishery Commission, also by treaty. The Great Lakes Basin Commission and the Upper Great Lakes Regional Commission were established by agreement between the federal and state governments. The Great Lakes Commission was established by the Great Lakes states to deal with water resource developments, programs, and problems related to use of the lakes.

The Canadian government recently established the Canada Centre for Inland Waters, and major studies of the Great Lakes are being handled through the Centre.

United States agencies with major responsibilities for the Great Lakes have been the U.S. Army Corps of Engineers; U.S. Lake Survey, formerly part of the Corps of Engineers, but now administered through the National Oceanographic and Atmospheric Agency; Federal Water Quality Administration; Bureau of Sports Fisheries and Wildlife; Coast Guard; and St. Lawrence Seaway Development Corporation.

Each of the states and Ontario have one or more agencies concerned with the lakes. In addition, several universities have major research programs on the Great Lakes; for example, the University of Michigan, the University of Wisconsin, and the University of Toronto.

It is obvious that attempts to manage the resources of the Great Lakes region are futile within the present framework of uncoordinated and often conflicting programs. It is generally agreed, however, that management will not be possible without a comprehensive water resources plan for the region. Development of such planning is a formidable task. The best approach may be through the development of plans for subregions (such as Green Bay), metropolitan areas, and small harbors. At present (1972), problems to be dealt with fall into three major categories: (1) water quality, (2) regulation of lake levels, and (3) demand for water-based recreation.

Some progress toward coordination, at least at the planning level, was made by establishment of the Great Lakes Basin Commission, which is charged with coordination of federal, state, interstate, local, and nongovernmental plans for the development of water and related land resources of the Great Lakes. A major responsibility is the development of a comprehensive framework study that will provide more information on which to base the plan that is now being considered. It is expected that the plan will do the following:

1. Provide economic projections.
2. Translate economic projections into demands for water and land resources.
3. Project water supply in terms of quantity and quality.
4. Project availability of land resources.
5. Indicate possible water and land resource problems.
6. Indicate the best approaches toward dealing with these problems.

Although numerous studies have been made, few have had the impact they should on decision-making at the political level. This probably will be true of the planning now underway. The missing link is that no one organization has a mandate for management and therefore our goals are not clearly defined.

The following recommendations are offered to assist management in dealing with some critical problems:

1. Establish an organization of representatives of diverse interests and institutions to serve as a central clearing house for developing a priority list of unsolved problems and for channeling projects to those individuals, agencies, and institutions most capable of working on them.
2. Coordinate efforts and goals of all governmental agencies, from local townships through the federal governments of Canada and the United States.
3. Disseminate information among all people concerned with use, conservation, and management of the Great Lakes.
4. Enforce all water laws now in effect.
5. Improve basic authority for management through constructive legislation as understanding of the dynamics of the Great Lakes system develops.
6. Establish environmental monitoring systems to detect any improvement or additional degradation in the Great Lakes. Data obtained through this approach are essential to evaluate present management efforts and to plan new procedures.
7. Conduct a socioeconomic study to determine the costs and benefits of improving water quality through pollution control. Some of the benefits would be increased land values, reduced cost of operating water treatment plants, minimization of public health hazards, augmented aesthetic appeal, growth of the tourist industry, and enhancement of water-based recreational activities such as swimming, water-skiing, boating, and fishing.
8. Develop water quality models for subregions of the Great Lakes. A comprehensive systems-analysis model would aid in examining and interrelating a wide variety of diverse variables. As there is no one goal that can be optimized for the Great Lakes region, a mixture of objectives must be considered: some are complementary, others are incompatible. A simulation model would allow the planner to observe the effects of different policies over time, make comparisons, and select the most reasonable alternatives.
9. Determine whether it is feasible to construct a large interception sewer system along the west and south shore of Lake Michigan and another along the south shore of Lake Erie to carry treated wastes away from the lakes into neighboring watersheds.
10. Study further the possibility of using dredging spoil to develop recreational lands close to large metropolitan centers.
11. Consider development of deep water harbors, which would eliminate many dredging problems.
12. Develop land-use planning for the region with emphasis on the relationship between land-use and water quantity and quality.

References

Applegate, V. C. and J. W. Moffett. 1955. The sea lamprey. *Sci. Amer.*

Baldwin, N. S. 1964. Sea lamprey in the Great Lakes. *Canadian Audubon Mag.* 7p.

Beeton, A. M. 1961. Environmental changes in Lake Erie. *Trans. Amer. Fish. Soc.* 90:153–159.

_____. 1965. Eutrophication of the St. Lawrence Great Lakes. *Limnol. Oceanogr.* 10:240–254.

———. 1969. Changes in the environment and biota of the Great Lakes. *In*: Eutrophication: Causes, consequences, correctives. Nat. Acad. Sci., Washington, D. C.:150–187.

———. 1971. Chemical characteristics of the Laurentian Great Lakes. Proc. Conf. on Changes in the Chemistry of Lakes Erie and Ontario. *Bull. Buffalo Soc. Nat. Sci.*, vol. 25:1–20.

——— and D. Mraz. 1969. Great Lakes. *In*: Water Use: Principles and guidelines for planning and management in Wisconsin. Wis. Chapter, Soil Conserv. Soc. Amer., Madison, Wis.:36–49.

——— and H. B. Rosenberg. 1968. Studies and research needed in regulation of the Great Lakes. Proc. Great Lakes Water Resources Conf., Amer. Soc. Civil Engr., Toronto:311–342.

Britt, N. W. 1955. Stratification in western Lake Erie in summer of 1953; effects on the *Hexagenia* (Ephemeroptera) population. Ecol. 36:239–244.

Brockel, H. C. 1970. Great Lakes ports face formidable challenges. *Seaway Rev.* 1(1).

Brown, E. G., Jr. 1953. Survey of the bottom fauna at the mouths of ten Lake Erie, south shore rivers. *In*: Lake Erie Pollution Survey. Ohio Dept. Nat. Res., Final Rept.:156–170.

Carr, J. F., V. C. Applegate, and M. Keller. 1965. A recent occurence of thermal stratification and low dissolved oxygen in western Lake Erie. *Ohio J. Sci.* 65:319–327.

Carr, J. F. and J. K. Hiltunen. 1965. Changes in the bottom fauna of western Lake Erie from 1930–1961. *Limnol. Oceanogr.* 10:551–569.

Davis, C. C. 1964. Evidence for the eutrophication of Lake Erie from phytoplankton records. *Limnol. Oceanogr.* 9:275–283.

Federal Water Pollution Control Administration. 1968. Lake Michigan basin, physical and chemical conditions. FWPCA, Chicago Region. 81 pp.

Fish, C. J. 1960. Limnological survey of eastern and central Lake Erie, 1928–29. U.S. Fish and Wildl. Serv., Spec. Sci. Rept.—Fish. No. 334.

Great Lakes Basin Commission. 1969. Comprehensive framework study (Type I). Plan of Study. G.L.B.C., Ann Arbor, Mich. 317 p.

———. 1969. Great Lakes Institutions. G.L.B.C., Ann Arbor, Mich. 58 p.

Hile, R. 1954. Fluctuations in growth and year-class strength of the walleye in Saginaw Bay. U.S. Fish Wildl. Serv., Fish. Bull. 56:7–59.

Howmiller, R. and A. M. Beeton. 1971. Biological evaluation of environmental quality, Green Bay, Lake Michigan. *J. Water Pollution Control Fed.* 43:123–133.

International Board of Inquiry for the Great Lakes Fisheries. 1943. Report and supplement. U.S. Govt. Printing Off., Washington. 213 p.

International Joint Commission. 1970. Pollution of Lake Erie, Lake Ontario and the international Section of the St. Lawrence River.

MacNish, C. F. and H. F. Lawhead. 1968. History of the development and use of the Great Lakes and present problems. Proc. Great Lakes Water Resources Conf., Amer. Soc. Civil Engr.:1–48.

Rawson, D. C. 1960. A limnological comparison of twelve large lakes in northern Saskatchewan. *Limnol. Oceanogr.* 5:195–211.

Schenk, C. F. and R. E. Thompson. 1965. Long-term changes in water chemistry and abundance of plankton at a single sampling location in Lake Ontario. Univ. Mich., Great Lakes Res. Div. Publ. 13:197–208.

Schneider, J. C., F. F. Hooper and A. M. Beeton. 1970. The distribution and abundance of benthic fauna in Saginaw Bay, Lake Huron. Proc. 12th Conf. Great Lakes Res.:80–90.

Smiley, C. W. 1882. Changes in the fisheries of the Great Lakes during the decade 1870–1880. Trans. Amer. Fish. Cultural Assoc. (Trans. Amer. Fish. Soc.) 11:28–37.

Smith, S. H. 1968. Species succession and fishery exploitation in the Great Lakes. *J. Fish. Res. Bd. Canada.* 25:667–693.

Strang, W. A. 1970. Recreation and the local economy. Univ. Wis. Sea Grant Prog. Tech. Rept. No. 4. 68 p.

United States Department of Commerce. 1970. Great Lakes fisheries 1969. Annual Summary, C.F.S. No. 5474.

Van Oosten, J. 1937. The dispersal of smelt, *Osmerus mordax* (Mitchell), in the Great Lakes region. Trans. Amer. Fish. Soc. 66:160–171.

Wells, L. 1970. Effects of alewife predation on zooplankton populations in Lake Michigan. *Limnol. Oceanogr.* 15:556–565.

Wright, S. 1955. Limnological survey of western Lake Erie. U.S. Fish. Wildl. Serv., Spec. Sci. Rept. Fish. No. 139. 341 p.

CHAPTER 15

This paper discusses both the scientific and the political aspects of a water pollution problem in Lake Washington and Puget Sound.

The history of Lake Washington's eutrophication and the changes in the lake in response to increasing nutrient levels as a result of increasing sewage volume are noted. Changes caused by the shift of the sewage outfall to Puget Sound and the subsequent response of Lake Washington are also studied.

This paper describes the participation of the public in the cleanup of Lake Washington, and shows how a concerned and motivated citizenry can accomplish a major improvement on its own initiative.

LAKE WASHINGTON

W. T. Edmondson

INTRODUCTION

A discussion of the deterioration and recovery of Lake Washington from pollution could best be presented in two parallel columns to be read together, because two different series of events that influenced each other took place simultaneously and resulted in concerted public action to protect the lake. Even this would be considerable simplification of the participation of individuals, governmental agencies, and citizens' groups in defining the problems, and then finding solutions. Since it is impractical to publish a discussion in such a form, the following material is primarily organized around the limnological work on the eutrophication of the lake, the response of the lake to increasing amounts of sewage, and the final diversion of sewage. The character of the public action is then described and some generalizations are made about the potential use of the knowledge gained to evaluate other cases of eutrophication.

In recent years Lake Washington has been valued primarily for its beauty and for its recreational uses, such as swimming, boating, and water-skiing. It has not been used for drinking water since 1965. The lake is fished, but its use for that purpose until recently has been secondary. About 1964 a very large population of sockeye salmon developed from eggs planted in the Cedar River and in the lake more than three decades before.

In 1955 the lake showed unmistakable signs of deterioration, and by 1962 had such a dense population of algae as to attract widespread public notice. In the meantime, public action had been taken to protect the lake, and in 1963 diversion of sewage effluent commenced.

Much public concern has been expressed about the cost of programs for curing environmental deterioration. It is worth pointing out that the program that was adopted for Lake Washington and Puget Sound not only improved them but was done at a considerable savings, because the old treatment facilities were rapidly becoming obsolete, and large expenditures would have been necessary to replace or repair them anyway. The development of a centralized, efficient treatment system by the Municipality of Metropolitan Seattle actually reduced the costs below what would have been required to maintain and enlarge eleven different treatment plants. Had the latter been the choice, the lake and Puget Sound would have deteriorated further.

HISTORY OF SEWAGE DISPOSAL IN LAKE WASHINGTON

The city of Seattle lies between Puget Sound and the west side of Lake Washington. It was founded on the shores of Puget Sound, but in the late 1880s significant amounts of forest clearing had begun on the lake side of the city, and small communities were being developed on the east side of the lake. Early in the 1900s the lake began to be used for disposal of raw sewage, first from individual houses and then from small sewage collection systems. By 1926, 30 raw sewage outfalls serving a population of 50,000 people

were putting sewage into Lake Washington. This situation was obviously unsatisfactory for public health, and after much study most of the sewage was diverted to Puget Sound by way of large interceptors and tunnels. Thus, most of the raw sewage generated by the city of Seattle has gone into Puget Sound at sea level until very recently. Unfortunately, there appears to have been no limnological study of the lake during the early period of pollution, and little is known of the limnological effects of the sewage.

The diversion project was completed about 1936, and for a few years the pollution of the lake was considerably reduced. However, Seattle was expanding north and south, and the smaller towns around the lake were growing. In 1941 a secondary biological sewage treatment plant was established on the lake, and by 1954 ten such plants had been built. In 1959 another one was built on the Sammamish River; the construction of this plant had been planned and started years earlier, but it was not finished until after the vote had been taken that permitted the removal of sewage from Lake Washington. Thus, during the 1940s and 1950s the input of treated sewage to the lake increased as the number of sewage treatment plants and the amount of sewage being processed by them increased. Some of the smaller streams were contaminated with drainage from septic tanks, and there were storm water overflows from the combined sewer system.

Beaches on Puget Sound were closed because of the influx of large volumes of raw sewage and some of the swimming beaches on Lake Washington were closed from time to time. Lake Washington was in much better condition than the littoral of Puget Sound, since the sewage going into the lake was given secondary treatment. Some treatment plants became overloaded at times, and some of the creeks entering the lake received seepage from badly located septic tanks. One such creek entered a few meters away from one of the public swimming beaches that was closed because of high bacterial counts. Seattle had a combined sewerage system, and diluted raw sewage could enter the lake through storm water overflows. However, about 80 percent of the sewage entering the lake had been through secondary treatment.

CHANGES OF LAKE WASHINGTON IN RESPONSE TO ENRICHMENT

Although the deterioration of the lake in the 1920s is not documented by limnological data, the changes brought about by the second period of sewage enrichment are reasonably well known. A full year of study in 1933 included repeated measurements of nitrogen, phosphorus, and carbon dioxide, among other things (Scheffer and Robinson, 1939). Most of the raw sewage outfalls had been diverted by then. In 1950 a similar study was made, not as detailed in chemistry, but with the addition of quantitative studies of phytoplankton and zooplankton (Comita and Anderson, 1959). These two studies showed increases in the content of nutrients and decreases in the amount of dissolved oxygen in the deep water in the summer.

Because of concern about the condition of the lake and awareness that a eutrophication problem was developing, the Washington State Pollution Control Commission made another study in 1952 of the nitrate, phosphate, and chlorophyll in surface waters at many locations in the lake (Peterson, 1955). There were further changes, notably the appearance of *Oscillatoria rubescens* in 1955, and so the lake was sampled several times in 1955 and 1956 (Edmondson, and others, 1956). In 1957 an intensive study was started that has continued ever since (Edmondson, 1961, 1963, 1966, 1968a, 1969a, b, 1970, 1972a, 1972b).

The effect of the pollution on the supply of nutrients to the plankton was considerable (Edmondson, 1971, 1972a). Although it is difficult to get actual measurements of rate of supply, one can use measurements that give indirect information. In Lake Washington, the dissolved nutrients (phosphate, nitrate, and carbon dioxide) reach maximum concentrations during the winter because uptake by photosynthetic organisms is at a minimum, and nutrients can accumulate. During this time the inflow from tributaries is at a maximum, and there must be some dilution, but the lake is in full circulation all winter with the incoming water being dispersed through the entire lake. Presumably the concentrations would be even higher without this dilution. During the spring, these substances are absorbed by the growing phytoplankton population and are reduced to low concentrations. Meanwhile, a corresponding increase in the amount of the elements contained in the plankton takes place. Thus, we can use the wintertime concentration as an index of the supply and the way it changed with pollution. For example, in 1933 the maximum concentration of phosphate phosphorus observed in the surface water was 8 μg/liter, while in 1963, the richest year, it was 62. Averages for the entire winter period are lower, but are of the same order of difference.

The biological changes in the lake were also great. The abundance of planktonic algae during the summer increased several fold. In 1955 a conspicuous qualitative change took place in the phytoplankton that was a signal of coming deterioration; that is, a relatively dense growth of the blue-green alga *Oscillatoria rubescens* developed (Edmondson and others, 1956). This change attracted attention because this species of alga had occurred early in the process of deterioration of a number of European lakes. Thus, it seemed to be a reliable vanguard of deterioration by pollution, and indicated that Lake Washington could be expected to develop unsatisfactory conditions because of dense algal populations and exhaustion of dissolved oxygen from the deep water. This event then showed that the lake required intensive observation and led

284

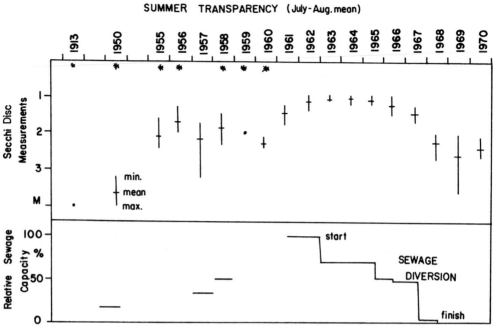

SUMMER TRANSPARENCY (July-Aug.mean)

FIGURE 1
Sewage diversion in Lake Washington.

to the study that has continued to the present with the assistance and cooperation of many colleagues (Edmondson, 1972a).

RESPONSE OF LAKE WASHINGTON TO DECREASE IN NUTRIENTS

Because of the magnitude of the project, the diversion of sewage took place over a five-year period. The first diversion of about one-third of the sewage was made in March 1963 (see Figure 1), and the final diversion in April 1968; with 99 percent of the sewage having been diverted by March 1967 (Edmondson, 1970).

The lake showed a very prompt and sensitive response to the changes in the input of sewage. The winter phosphate concentrations that had been increasing rapidly fell off and, after some irregular variations, began a sharp decrease in 1965. Nitrate and carbon dioxide showed a lesser decrease, which is reasonable in view of the fact that treated sewage is richer in phosphorus than the other elements, relative to natural drainage. Biological changes were considerable also. The summer abundance of phytoplankton as measured by its chlorophyll dropped in 1970 to about 22 percent of its 1963 value, and in 1971 to 18 percent. The volume of phytoplankton material in 1970 was still about 30 percent of its 1963 value. The transparency of the lake (Figure 1), as measured by the depth to which a white Secchi disc can be seen, increased from a summer mean of 1.0 meter in 1963 to 2.5 meters in 1969; it had been 3.7 in 1950. In the summer of 1971 the maximum transparency was 4.5 m, greater than had been observed in 1950; the mean was 3.5 (Figure 1). Many of the chemical and biological changes are well recorded in the sediments (Shapiro et al., 1971; Griffiths et al., 1969; Stockner and Benson, 1967).

The changes in plankton have been quite noticeable, and considerable public satisfaction about the progress of the lake has been expressed in the newspapers and in discussions with people who are in contact with the lake. One element of the change is not entirely desirable. Although data on rooted plants are very scanty, it appears that plants may be growing more abundantly in certain protected areas now that the water is clearer. The areas where this condition could be a nuisance are relatively limited.

Lake Washington has shown an ability to absorb a large load of concentrated nutrients without serious deterioration, and there is reason to believe that it can maintain a satisfactory condition in its present circumstances. At the moment of writing, Lake Washington has improved greatly and rapidly, but probably has not completed the changes that will bring it into equilibrium with its new nutrient conditions. Of course it cannot be expected to be immune to the influences of the human activities in the watershed. If it turns out that important changes have taken place or will take place in the watershed, the lake can be expected to react. The Cedar River, an important source of low-phosphorus water to the lake, may become a focus of attention. At present the nitrate concentrations are almost double those reported in 1957, perhaps the result of clearing and building in the lower reaches of the river (Edmondson, 1972a). The river is also a major source of drinking water for Seattle, and increasing amounts have been taken out, thereby reducing the amount available to dilute the nutrients in Lake Washington.

Of course it was important to ascertain that diversion of the Lake Washington sewage to Puget Sound would not generate equally serious problems there. The nutrients added to Puget Sound by the diversion were not expected to cause a problem because Puget Sound is so richly provided with nutrients from the water upwelled from deep in the Pacific. During the summer, at times of low tides, phytoplankton blooms start to develop, but usually the period of high tides comes before nutrients are exhausted and the water is mixed to great depths, diluting and stopping the growth of the population (George C. Anderson, personal commun.).

Thus the diversion of sewage to Puget Sound was not a matter of moving an alga problem from one place to another. In fact, one could wish that the diverted nutrients would increase the useful fisheries of Puget Sound. Nevertheless, one cannot be complacent about these matters because sewage contains more than nutrients. Vigilance must be maintained about the effects of toxic materials that are disposed of in sewage. Any system could be overloaded, even one with as great a capacity for dilution as Puget Sound.

Another aspect of sewage in Puget Sound was of considerable concern, however. The early diversion of raw sewage from Lake Washington was made into Puget Sound, until recently, 70 million gallons per day of raw sewage has been entering Puget Sound at sea level. It was decided, therefore, to make a comprehensive improvement in the sewerage of the watershed that would not simply divert effluent from Lake Washington, but would also give primary treatment to the raw sewage from Seattle and deposit it at a depth of 240 feet, 3,600 feet offshore instead of at sea level along the shore. Under these conditions, the sewage is rapidly diluted and dispersed, as most of Puget Sound has a short retention time with the water being replaced by tidal action several times a year (Clifford A. Barnes, personal communication, Friebertshauser and Duxbury, 1972).

CHARACTER OF THE STUDY OF LAKE WASHINGTON

Since the study of Lake Washington reported here has attracted a certain amount of attention, it may be worthwhile to say something about the motivation to initiate the study and the circumstances in which it was carried out.

My own primary motivation in carrying out a detailed study of Lake Washington came from my interest in the mechanism of control of productivity and population abundance in lakes. Fertilization of lakes and other bodies of water is a well recognized technique for studying the role of the nutrient income and concentration of nutrients in affecting productivity, and I have been previously associated with such studies (Nelson and Edmondson, 1955; Edmondson and Edmondson, 1947; Edmondson, 1955). The trouble with this technique is that with ordinary resources it is practicable only for relatively small lakes, which means that one rarely has a chance to study the effects of fertilization on a large, thermally stratified lake. Heavy pollution with the effluent from biological treatment plants does provide fertilization, and the Lake Washington situation therefore could be treated as a large-scale experiment in lake fertilization. The intention of the study was to define the changes in the entire lake system in response to the increasing input of concentrated nutrients. Although there was a temptation to cover the entire range of limnology in the study, practical considerations made necessary a rather rigorous selection of properties relevant to the evaluation of the relationship between nutrient income and productivity and the abundance of organisms.

Thus, it was decided to measure a number of chemical, physical, and biological properties that give information about the conditions affecting the production of organisms or about the activities of the organisms. Among the chemical and physical measurements are total phosphorus, dissolved inorganic phosphate, particulate phosphorus, nitrate, nitrite, ammonia, total Kjeldahl nitrogen, particulate Kjeldahl nitrogen, free carbon dioxide (by titration), alkalinity, pH, oxygen, temperature, and transparency. These measurements are made at a central station about every two weeks, and at other stations less frequently. The number of depths sampled varies according to the thermal stratification of the water. In the summer, more than a dozen depths are usually sampled.

The abundance of planktonic organisms, both phytoplankton and zooplankton, is determined by counting, and chlorophyll is measured in acetone extracts. Photosynthetic activity of the phytoplankton is measured by the rate of oxygen production and radiocarbon uptake in clear and opaque bottles suspended at various depths. The reproductive rate of the animals is measured by a technique that uses the abundance of the eggs. The benthic invertebrates are sampled several times a year, and the rate of growth of periphyton on glass slides is measured continuously. Sediment traps are used to catch material that is sinking to the bottom, and cores of sediments are sliced and analyzed for nitrogen, phosphorus, and other substances.

The work was supported for the first two years (1956–1958) by the National Institutes of Health, and since then by the National Science Foundation. Support by NSF is appropriate since the work is basic limnological research and is not directed specifically at pollution control. Nevertheless, the aims and material of the two different kinds of study are largely congruent in that they require in part the samke kind of data, and include prediction of lake conditions. Some of the data we have been obtaining might not have been taken if the main emphasis had been on pollution and what the engineers call water quality—for example, the reproductive rate of zooplankton, and sinking material are two features of importance only to a limnological study. Conversely, we have not measured some properties that might have been prominent in a pollution study, such as chemical oxygen demand.

The work has been carried out, largely as a part of the normal research activity of a professor in a university department who had additional research interests (Edmondson, 1965, 1968b, 1969c) and who was carrying a normal teaching load. The only unusual feature was perhaps the degree of communication of the results to the public (see following section on Public Action). Of course the project has depended on the work of many people, and while it needed considerable funding to maintain the technicians, student helpers, and post-doctoral associates, it was not carried out in a full-scale research insititute. I mention this because many interesting research opportunities must be developing in polluted lakes, and in many cases study of some well-defined restricted problems on a modest scale could be very useful.

PUBLIC ACTION

Public concern had been growing about the sewerage situation in the entire metropolitan area for a long time. City and state agencies had made many studies, some with help from university engineers, of the sources of pollution in Lake Washington and Puget Sound (Sylvester and Jones, 1955). Many counts were made of *Escherichia coli*, an organism that is an indicator of fecal pollution. It was well recognized that a health problem existed.

In 1956 the Mayor of Seattle, Gordon S. Clinton, appointed a Metropolitan Problems Advisory Committee under the chairmanship of James R. Ellis to study, among other things, these sewerage conditions. It became clear to the committee that expanding and improving the conventional sewage treatment plants would not prevent the deterioration of the lake by eutrophication, and that with the techniques then available the only certain solution would be diversion of sewage from Lake Washington. The committee made use of the limnological information that was being developed at the University of Washington.

It was not a simple matter to carry out the diversion (Clark, 1967; Chasan, 1971). Under existing legislation the action would have been so difficult that many people doubted that it could be done, and it was therefore necessary first to prepare appropriate legislation and get it adopted by the state legislature. The law, as adopted by the legislature,

permits communities to join together and form a municipality to finance and carry out certain functions jointly. Forming the Municipality of Metropolitan Seattle (called Metro) required a majority of votes in Seattle as one unit and the smaller towns as another unit. The purpose of this qualification was to prevent a large city from dominating smaller ones. The first measure submitted covered a large area and included functions other than sewage control, such as transportation and comprehensive planning. Although in the first vote early in 1958 a majority of the total votes favored the measure, it failed because the smaller towns did not give it a majority. A revised version reduced the area, omitting some towns that had been opposed, and limited the function of Metro to sewage disposal. This measure passed in the fall of 1958. Although it did not cover the entire drainage basin, it did include all major divertible effluents. Later, some of the communities that had been excluded in the revised measure asked to be included, and they were admitted with a somewhat higher charge being made, although this qualification was dropped in 1971.

It is important to distinguish between the operation of improving the sewage arrangements and the governmental mechanism that was selected to carry out the operation. Conceivably the legislation could have taken a different form, but the execution would always depend on the competence of the people in the organization.

To present a detailed and accurate account of the formation of Metro is beyond the scope of my personal knowledge, but it is possible to outline the part that I was aware of and participated in. The major basis of the action as I saw it was the initiative and outstanding leadership of the concerned citizens who followed up the work of the Mayor's committee. Such organizations as the League of Women Voters and the Municipal League participated actively. I think a very important feature of the campaign was that it was not carried out by a unit of government. Specifically, a volunteer group of citizens, the Metro Action Committee, conducted a vigorous campaign to distribute informational bulletins and to present lectures and debates in community clubs and on TV and radio. The debates were particularly important, because they assured that the full range of viewpoints was set forth, and that voters were informed of arguments both for and against Metro.

In the campaign, a prominent part of the information concerned what would happen to Lake Washington if pollution continued, and how the lake would respond to diversion of sewage. My participation consisted of giving lectures in public, on TV, and radio about the principles of limnology as they applied to our situation; writing many letters giving the results of the work and predictions; and having long telephone conversations about the same matters with many people, both proponents and opponents of Metro. From my point of view, these activities were simply the normal work of a university professor in disseminating the results of his studies. My research interests until then had not had a particular application and were not being carried out for purposes of pollution control, but in this situation they were pertinent to a very practical matter .

The campaign for Metro did have some vigorous opposition, largely by people who worried about the possible costs and feared governmental excess ("supergovernment," or "creeping socialism"). In view of this kind of objection, it is interesting that the form proposed for Metro was an association of communities operated by a council that is composed of already elected officials; that is, mayors and councilmen. Thus, Metro did not add another layer of officials to the governmental structure, but added yet another task to those already being performed by these same elected officials.

Some of the opponents of Metro went far beyond a discussion of their fears of the proposed system, and expressed doubts about the scientific findings. One man, a lawyer, told me that he doubted that sewage could have the effect I described, and that if it could it was too late to do anything about the damage. More than that, attempts were made to discredit the source of the scientific information. Some of the anti-Metro debaters tried to deny the validity of simple and well-understood limnological principles, or presented distorted and falsified accounts of limnological studies and then knocked them down (the straw man technique). People who did not want Metro tried to discredit the reasons that caused other people to want it. In some of the debates it was pointed out that algae are plants; I was a zoologist, and zoology was defined as the study of animals confined in cages in zoos. This seemed to mean that I did not know what I was talking about. Many of the arguments against the diversion program were simply irrelevant. For example, some people pointed out that algae need light as well as nutrients, and asked what good it would do, therefore, to divert sewage. This is worth comment as many people are involved in similar educational activities about pollution problems elsewhere in the country, and I suspect that they will have similar experiences.

It is important in dealing with this kind of controversy to distinguish between honest doubt or honest ignorance and a desire to win an argument by any means, including discrediting the opposition. The first can best be met by clear explanation of scientific data, whereas the second is harder to deal with because it is often based on intangibles.

DEVELOPMENT AND ENVIRONMENTAL QUALITY OF LAKE WASHINGTON

The major effect of the Metro program on Lake Washington has been to improve those qualities that preserve its beauty and make it suitable for various kinds of recreation, such as swimming, boating, and fishing. Several other uses of the lake are to some extent incompatible with its recreational use, but at present there is no major conflict.

The ship canal connecting Lake Washington with Puget Sound opened in 1916 and was developed primarily for commercial purposes. Today it is used for transportation of rafted logs and of ships and barges into Lake Washington. The logs are brought in from Puget Sound and stored in two places in the lake on their way to sawmills. The effect on salinity must be trivial, but there has been some concern about the local effect of decaying bark on the lake. The areas affected are small, and the amount of storage is now being reduced. Commercial traffic to industries in the southern part of the lake offers some hazards, but the density is small enough that it appears not to be a major problem. A steam power plant near the southern end uses lake water for cooling.

The Naval Air Station at Sand Point for many years operated an active fleet of airplanes. When sea planes were practicing landing, part of the lake was barred to other traffic, and this constituted a distinct restriction on the use of the northern part of the lake. The station's activities were a major source of noise pollution that annoyed many residents along much of the northern part of the lake. In 1970 the station was placed on inactive status, and practically no flying is being done from it now. The future use of the property has not been decided. Some interest has been expressed in developing it as a field for small private airplanes, but this plan has received vigorous opposition. The alternative seems to be a combination of public park and educational and research facilities.

A commercial flying service at the northern end of the lake does an active business, which includes the use of float planes. On a good day, about seventy take-offs and landings are made. In addition, about thirty privately owned planes are moored on the lake, and airplanes from flying services elsewhere use the lake for training.

A remarkable feature of Lake Washington is the two multilane highways carried across the lake on floating bridges. In 1971, the two bridges carried 31,397,327 vehicles. The first, opened in 1946, was a very important factor in the development of small towns on the eastern shore of the lake that later contributed important amounts of sewage effluent. Although the bridge offered some hindrance to water traffic, ships were able to pass through an opening section in the middle, and small boats could go under elevated approachways at both ends. The opening of the second bridge in 1963 greatly facilitated an increase in commuter automobile traffic, but also generated considerable opposition from people who resented the additional interference with water use.

An additional bridge that will parallel the first bridge has been planned, but such plans have met with increasing opposition, as another bridge would clearly degrade recreational use of the lake. The effect on the beauty of the lake might be judged differently by different people, for at night the colored lights of the bridges are rather attractive.

A major potential conflict of uses centers on the Cedar River, the southern inlet of the lake, which is the primary source of drinking water for Seattle and adjacent communities. Thus, Seattle and Lake Washington are in competition for good water—one for drinking, one for dilution—and the water of the Cedar River has very small concentrations of phosphate. As the demand for drinking water increases with population growth, it is conceivable that enough water would be diverted that the condition of the lake would be affected. This could involve some degree of deterioration, although serious algal nuisances would not be expected again unless some other major change took place in the input of material to the lake.

The recent development of an important sockeye salmon fishery based largely on spawning beds in the Cedar River has given strong motivation for maintaining a high flow of the river during spawning and when eggs are in the gravel on its bed. The drinking water inlet is upstream from the salmon spawning beds, so no deterioration of drinking water is caused by decaying salmon.

In summary, the present uses of the lake appear to be in reasonable harmony with each other, with recreational use dominating the others, although the traffic across the bridges is an important feature of suburban life in the area. As for Puget Sound, the conversion of 70 million gallons per day of raw sewage entering near the shore at sea level to primary effluent entering 240 feet deep, 3,600 feet offshore, can be regarded only as an improvement for the waterfront of Seattle and adjoining communities on Puget Sound.

APPLICATION OF THE LAKE WASHINGTON EXPERIENCE TO OTHER SITUATIONS

The examples outlined in the preceding sections can be used in several ways. First, the limnological data can be used to help understand and predict the consequences of changes in nutrient supply of other lakes of similar character. Several experienced limnologists doubted that Lake Washington would recover as rapidly as it did (Edmondson, 1972b). Thus the data provide information about quantities and rates of important processes that will improve our ability to predict limnological conditions. Nutrient income is only one of the properties that affects the productivity of lakes and the abundance of organisms in them. Lake morphometry and the climate will affect the way a lake uses its nutrient supply. Further, the nuisance properties of eutrophicated lakes are not based on productivity as such, but on the way the productivity is expressed in population density of particular kinds of organisms and its consequences. That is, cloudiness ("dirty" water), odor, and taste are the main properties that affect use of a lake for recreation and drinking. Thus the Secchi disc trans-

parancy may be a more useful measure for some purposes of public information than a plankton count. Problems arising from undesirably dense growths of rooted plants may not necessarily be associated with heavy artificial eutrophication; in any case they must be handled differently from problems involving the plankton.

With Lake Washington, it was possible to improve conditions by total diversion of sewage without transferring the problem somewhere else, an option not open to most communities. Nevertheless, the data can be used elsewhere because options that are open to other communities may involve partial diversion or removal of nutrients from effluent, or other methods such as controlling the kinds of materials permitted to be put into sewers. It is desirable to know which nutrients have to be limited and by how much. The changes in sewage effluent affected the phosphorus content of Lake Washington much more than that of nitrogen or carbon dioxide, and this gives a chance to evaluate the relative effects. One should not be misled into thinking that the results from Lake Washington can be used for evaluating only total diversion.

A second way in which the Lake Washington experience can be used is an example of how volunteer citizen action can lead to major accomplishments in protecting the environment. Many events that took place during the Metro campaign are likely to be repeated in any similar effort elsewhere, and it might be useful to anticipate them.

I shall therefore review the experience with Lake Washington to develop a basis for suggesting procedures in other areas with problems of eutrophication and related conditions. It is impossible to extend these comments to a detailed formula for use by other communities in solving their water quality problems. Just as each lake is different, each community has its own individuality. Nevertheless, all lakes have certain properties in common, and some of the elements of the Lake Washington experience will be found in other places. These elements may appear in varying proportions, and each place will have unique characteristics, but in general, the following sequence of events might occur.

First, it is necessary to identify the problem in enough detail to find the causes and possible solutions, and the engineering possibilities for implementing any corrective plan. At this stage, many people will want to propose prolonged, expensive research, or even monitoring projects to "get the facts." Undoubtedly studies will have to be made and a factual background developed, but it is not necessary to recapitulate the entire development of limnological knowledge in each lake. Full use must be made of existing principles and relationships. For many polluted waterways there is already a large background of facts, although in some cases it may consist of the wrong kind of facts. A key kind of information will concern the limnological condition of the lake before it was influenced by human activity. Secure predictions about Lake Washington were made possible by the fact that two limnological studies had been made before deterioration set in and while the pollution problem was relatively simple and clear-cut. Such information is not available for many important deteriorated lakes. Nevertheless, there is some hope that effective information can be obtained by paleolimnological techniques (Stockner and Benson, 1967; Shapiro and others, 1971; Edmondson and Allison, 1970). It will, in fact, be necessary to show that deterioration has taken place. Some lakes that are considered to generate nuisance conditions are basically productive for natural reasons, or are producing masses of rooted plants because they are in an advanced stage of normal ecological succession.

In general, nutrient budgets and water budgets will be required for eutrophicated waters, but even here some corners may be cut. Some situations are obviously dominated by sewage, others are dominated by toxic wastes, and it would not require many years of study to decide what to eliminate. Perhaps

the greatest difficulties will arise in places where diversion of effluents is not practicable, and decisions have to be made about the kind and degree of treatment to be given wastes.

Second, having identified the problems, it is necessary to make predictions about the effects of various alternative actions. The predictability of the behavior of lakes should improve steadily as basic work on productivity and population growth continues, and full advantage should be taken of each new development in pollution control. For instance, Lake Washington should not be regarded as unique when we are talking about lakes that have deteriorated under the influence of human activity, largely by sewage disposal. Of course, the effectiveness with which a lake will use its nutrient supply is affected by its size, shape, rate of flushing, and other properties, but these effects are subject to study and prediction.

The response to diversion of sewage can ordinarily be expected to reverse the changes that took place during the period of increasing enrichment with sewage, but the rate of recovery may be strongly affected by hydrological and morphological factors. Experience with diversion is now accumulating to the point where some generalizations are beginning to emerge, although some diversions are so recent that it is too early to define the rate of recovery. So far, the outstanding examples of reluctance to recover have been shown by shallow lakes or lakes with a relatively small rate of replenishment of water. For example, Lake Trummen is only 1.1 meters in mean depth, and during the period of enrichment developed dense growths of vegetation (Björk, 1972), and Stone Lake, Indiana, is reported not to have shown an immediate improvement during the first five years after diversion of sewage. However this lake has such a relatively small inflow that the retention time of water is eleven years, and about half of the lake is less than three meters deep. It has maintained very high phosphorus concentrations. (Tenney and others, 1970). Both lakes were heavily enriched for many years. Techniques other than simple nutrient diversion may be needed for speedier recovery of such lakes.

Some confusion in evaluating changes in lakes has been generated by using outdated concepts of lake succession and trophic conditions, and by applying the concept *eutrophic* to cover both the idea of a rich nutrient supply and a high productivity. Much more realistic is Hutchinson's concept of trophic equilibrium. An oligotrophic lake may become more productive and maintain denser stands of aquatic vegetation during ecological succession without having a major increase in the rate of nutrient input from the watershed. Eutrophication concerns an increase in the rate of supply of nutrients but no case of a slow, steady increase by natural causes has been documented. These matters are discussed by Hutchinson (1967), Hutchinson and Cowgill (1970), Edmondson (1971), and Beeton and Edmondson (1972).

In some existing situations, enough limnological knowledge may already be available to serve as a basis for effective predictions, but judgments about the significance of the findings and predictions of the effects of alternatives can be made only by experienced scientists who are not afraid to extrapolate beyond the border of present knowledge, using scientific imagination and a reasonable amount of intuition.

The prompt public protective action toward Lake Washington was doubtless facilitated by the fact that detailed knowledge of the lake was being developed as the lake deteriorated. Further, it was not necessary for the local community to finance the purely limnological part of the study, although the city of Seattle did contribute a great deal in making chemical analyses of the inflows to the lake, the city, county, and state financed an elaborate engineering report that was the basis for the Metro plan (Brown and Caldwell, 1958).

After making predictions about the ecological future of a lake, the next step is to propose a plan of action and carry it out.

This is probably the most difficult part of the process. Some of the most well-known cases of lake pollution are of such magnitude that they cannot be solved by local action of the Seattle Metro type, although Metro might well serve as a model for some interstate or even international operations (for example, see Hedgpeth, "Estuaries," in this volume). The major problems will probably require initiation of plans and action by appropriate governmental agencies.

Scientific advisers might worry about their responsibility for predictions that turn out to be erroneous. "Suppose I am wrong; do I go to jail?" Here the community needs to take an enlightened view of how to investigate problems, and to decide to support continued limnological experiments, as with the Lake Washington experiment. Some programs may not be as successful as had been hoped, but carrying them out will provide information upon which more effective programs can be based.

It would be easy to conclude that no cleanup is worth attempting unless it can be shown to bring the concentrations of some pollutant down to a particular level. This is probably not a productive view. The Lake Washington experience documents what many people already knew: lakes are sensitive and responsive to changes in their watershed and, in general, they change in proportion to changes in their watershed—up to a point. There may be some critical points of inflection, but as a rule partial amelioration will have a proportional beneficial effect on the lake. Perhaps the key to solving Lake Erie's problem is to start all technically possible improvements now, and improve its condition step by step. One does not have to work hard to prove that the crimson plume of the Cuyahoga River represents damage to the lake in terms of conditions that are valued by people. Obviously, the sewage effluent from a large city is damaging, and the damage could be lessened by installing a process to remove phosphorus. To wait for action until a complete plan has been developed in detail will result in no improvement at all.

This country has already spent enormous sums on weapons systems that were expected to become obsolete in a few years. We can adopt the same attitude toward expensive pollution control measures: carry them out until something better comes along, then scrap the old. (Professor Arthur D. Hasler, a University of Wisconsin limnologist, has suggested this analogy.)

In those cases where local public action is possible or required, it is necessary to develop and provide some motivation for public involvement and to give the public the information it needs to understand the situation and to assign priorities. (Also see Luken and Langlois, this volume.) The motivation will probably center on public use of the water in question. A dominating factor in the formation of Metro was Lake Washington itself. Although the Metro action was designed to clean up the beaches of Puget Sound as well as the lake, public attention was focused on the lake as a unique community asset, and some sense of community pride was involved. Newspaper advertisements for Metro contained such words as "shameful" and "disgraceful"; apparently the community felt that to permit the lake to deteriorate would indeed be a matter for shame. Cynics have commented that many of the most active proponents were owners of lakeshore property, but the landowners were, of course, too few to swing the vote alone. On the other hand, to the extent that issues are decided by contention between special interest groups, people interested in maintaining or restoring environmental quality have to make their views known.

An essential part is the public information campaign, which must be tailored to fit each situation. In Seattle the newspapers and television and radio stations were of great service in providing opportunities for informative lectures and debates. The State Pollution Control Commission issued simple leaflets explaining sewage treatment, lake eutrophication, and related matters. An important element is to avoid perpetuation of erroneous ideas and to avoid exaggerated

scare tactics. Any deliberate attempt to mislead people into doing the "right" thing is likely to misfire because it will be easy to expose, and this will generate a lack of confidence in the campaign.

The key to a successful campaign is probably the public spirit and quality of the civic leaders; somebody has to take initiative and do a great deal of work. A vital event in the development of Metro was the appointment of James Ellis by the Mayor of Seattle to head the Metropolitan Problems Advisory Committee. Ellis' character and activity dominated the campaigns, and if any one person is to be credited with Metro it is he. But one must recognize that in doing what he did he had the help of literally hundreds of people (Chasan, 1971). The volunteer Metro Action Committee was a remarkable organization, a sort of glorified debating team composed of people of very diverse backgrounds and occupations, united by their concern for environmental quality (and this in 1958!). One of the participants, an engineer named Daniel J. Evans, is now Governor of the State of Washington.

Next, some points about the use of scientific evidence and predictions should be made. Such decisions as to form a Metropolitan Municipality always involve more than simply the validity of a set of scientific facts and predictions. One has to make value judgments and choices of priority even if there is no argument about the facts. It is conceivable that the people of the Lake Washington basin could have decided that deterioration of the lake was more acceptable than the commitment to spend more than $120 million. It would have been most unfortunate if such a decision had been made on the basis of false claims by the opponents of Metro, but had such a decision been made on the basis of a rational evaluation of options and conscious establishment of priorities, we would have to accept the public choice of priority, though many people would deplore the quality of the judgment that would lead to such a choice. It is clear that, as far as possible, all people involved in deciding these issues should be presented with a fair and unbiased picture of the situation and the possible courses of action.

The people concerned with making the scientific studies and with preparing proposals for action should also prepare for public action themselves. Any plan for extensive improvement of the environment will meet opposition from someone, and sometimes it will be massive opposition. As in the Lake Washington case, opponents to improvement may try to show that the scientific work is inadequate and the scientists incompetent. The opponents may object to any reliance on general principles or theory, and assert that the entire investigation is useless if it does not include measurements of every imaginable property of the lake. One tactic that is sure to generate confusion is to cite a great deal of information that is true, but irrelevant to the particular situation. (See the previous section on public action for examples).

Some of this kind of opposition will be based on genuine misunderstanding, but some will be an unprincipled attempt to prevent by any means the success of the proposal. It may be very difficult to distinguish those people who oppose a particular action on the basis of a reasoned choice of priority from those who are doing so for extraneous reasons or who are simply mistaken, but it seems inevitable that the question will have to be raised. For example, some participants in the debate about phosphorus-containing detergents have presented documents so biased or factually incorrect that they can be regarded only as interfering with sound decision. It apparently became important to certain people to show that phosphorus is not important in deteriorated lakes, and some of the writing goes far beyond the bounds of scientific incompetence, closely approaching the borders of dishonesty.

THE DETERGENT QUESTION

This is not the place for a full review of the controversy about the use of phosphorus-containing detergents, and the related controversy about the relative importance of phosphorus and carbon in eutrophication, but they are highly relevant to the subject of this chapter and illustrate very well some of the points made above.

The question can be simplified to: Is it worthwhile to stop using detergents that contain large amounts of phosphate? To answer this question obviously requires a judgment of the advantages and disadvantages of each course of action and a selection according to some scale of values or priorities. To judge the advantages and disadvantages requires knowledge of the participation of phosphorus in lake productivity, the characteristics and effects of possible substitutes, and many other matters. A very large volume of material has been presented in scientific and engineering journals, magazines, newspaper articles and advertisements, trade bulletins, and testimony before the Federal Trade Commission, Congress, and other governmental agencies. Much misinformation and misinterpretation of correct information about the importance of phosphorus has been included. The following paragraphs summarize some of the main points, but no attempt is made here to give a full review of this extensive and diversified material, much of which has not been formally published. A dominating feature of the material is that much of it has been written by people who understand neither how lakes work nor how to interpret data on limnological conditions. For instance, it has been pointed out that since algae contain about 50 percent carbon and only about 1 percent phosphorus, carbon dioxide is more important than phosphate in lakes. Of course the importance in limiting the size of algal populations depends not on the composition of the algae but on the supply of the two elements relative to the demand, and because publications in this field have generated misunderstanding, even among scientists, I will give a brief explanation of the problem as I see it.

It is understood that carbon dioxide, nitrate, phosphate, and many other substances are important for the growth of phytoplankton. But the question arises as to what kinds of corrective measures can be taken to restore lakes that have deteriorated as a result of sewage pollution. This limitation to a particular group of lakes is important, but is frequently ignored. No one proposes to control lakes that are productive for natural reasons by changing detergents. The main idea behind detergent control is that many lakes, in their natural state, are limited primarily by phosphorus, meaning that at times of rapid phytoplankton growth, the supply of phosphate becomes effectively exhausted before that of nitrate or carbon dioxide. Such a lake would respond to added phosphate by an increase in algae up to the point where another element becomes limiting. Sewage is so rich in phosphate that a lake heavily enriched with sewage may have excess phosphate, and nitrate or carbon dioxide may become exhausted first. If the enrichment is heavy enough, such a lake may not respond to added phosphate, but in an intermediate state of enrichment, the ability of the lake to produce algae will be proportional to the amount of phosphorus (see Figure 3 of Edmondson, 1972a). Since detergents contribute about half the phosphorus content of modern sewage, a big difference could be made in the phosphorus input to a lake by eliminating phosphorus in detergents. If a lake were on the verge of becoming a nuisance, a decided improvement could be made by a change in detergents. If the lake were more heavily enriched, the degree of response would depend on the quantities involved. A large enough human population can produce enough phosphate physiologically to cause deterioration of a lake of given size; Lake Zürich began its deterioration in 1898, long before detergents came into use.

Lake Washington started to improve noticeably when only half the sewage was gone. The same difference in phosphorus income would have been made by eliminating phosphate detergents from all the sewage. Lake Washington was responding to diversion of whole sewage, not partial control of individual elements, but measurements of materials dissolved in the water show that the diversion was followed by a large change in phosphorus content, but relatively little in that of nitrate or carbon dioxide (Edmondson, 1970).

Detergent control would not be the only technique required to help eutrophication in general, and it would not benefit lakes that are nuisances because of natural reasons, or any that have been eutrophicated from drainage without detergents. It would reduce the phosphate income of some lakes that could be difficult to manage otherwise.

Many people have misunderstood the position of those who think that control of phosphorus can be important in the control of eutrophication. To say that phosphorus is a key element in control of eutrophication is not to say that it is the only element important to algae. Representations have been made that the importance of sewage lies in its carbon, not its phosphorus. Many statements seem to imply that "organic matter" contains only carbon compounds, but decomposing organisms and excreta liberate phosphate as well as carbon dioxide. In fact, secondary effluent contains a much higher proportion of phosphorus relative to nitrogen and carbon dioxide than do most natural lake waters. Further, the statements made in defense of phosphate detergents almost never refer to the large limnological literature in which it is shown that unproductive lakes have produced large increases in algae in response to the addition of phosphate or phosphate and nitrate compounds without an addition of carbon dioxide or organic materials (for example, see Einsele, 1941; Thomas, 1967, 1968; Nelson and Edmondson, 1955). Correspondingly, failure to respond to an addition of phosphate has sometimes been shown in lakes known to be rich in phosphorus (see Allen, 1972).

Various arguments, based on a variety of reasons, have been raised against the banning of phosphate detergents: the cost of changing over would be great, adequate substitutes do not exist at present because they either do not clean as well, have bad biological effects, are hazardous to have around the house, or would eutrophicate coastal waters of the ocean. It is proposed that it would be better to install tertiary treatment for removal of phosphate from sewage, even if the cost of treatment would be higher with detergents in the sewage. Improvement of sewage treatment facilities is, of course, highly desirable and is an essential part of a full program of eutrophication control, but it will take a long time and considerable public expense to carry it out.

It is easy to state that nutrient removal from effluent will be required as part of a program of full control of eutrophication, but the matter is not simple, and a number of implications must be examined carefully. For one thing, the need for nutrient removal has been vastly exaggerated. An unnecessarily elaborate program of nutrient control would waste a lot of money and natural resources that could be used to better effect. I am convinced that much could be done on the basis of even partial removal of phosphorus, but some people seem to believe that it will be generally necessary to remove nitrogen, a much more difficult problem.

Even the removal of phosphorus is not as simple as it may seem. With some of the chemical methods of precipitation, the amount of chemicals, or complexity and cost of treatment vary with the concentration of phosphate, and they remove only a fraction of the phosphate. Thus, even if phosphorus is to be removed in a treatment process, it is advantageous to limit the amount of phosphorus that gets into the sewage in the first place. This would be a reason for changing from phosphorus detergents, quite apart from the eutrophication problem, providing the substitute detergents do not introduce more difficulty than did phosphate.

Even broader issues are involved. It has been pointed out that to remove phosphate from sewage in only the Washington, D.C., area by an alum process would require 8 percent of the current U.S. production of

alum (Clair N. Sawyer, personal commun.). To increase alum production or importation to and meet the additional demands of sewage treatment would put significant demands on transportation and the production of electrical power with a ramifying set of environmental consequences. This is not to say that sewage should not be treated, but that the consequences of various methods of treatment be evaluated.

It would be attractive to think of using the precipitated phosphate for agricultural fertilizer, but most precipitation processes will carry down a variety of materials, and the possibility of concentrating toxic metals and other substances may limit the use of sewage nutrients. Again, it would be better not to let the material into the sewage in the first place, if possible, than to have to remove it later.

Certainly nutrient removal will be a necessary part of a general program to control eutrophication; the degree is uncertain, but surely it should be adjusted to the requirements. I think that control programs should be established in a series of selected lakes on an experimental basis, with the expectation that some programs will not make the required amount of improvement in the lake, and that they will then have to be amplified to do so.

One important difference between the Lake Washington problem and the detergent problem, aside from general magnitude, was that there was no enormous financial stake in maintaining the status quo of Lake Washington. Whatever is done about detergents, large financial interests will be affected.

Nevertheless, just as with Lake Washington, choices have to be made, balancing a complex of advantages and disadvantages. I think it would be most unfortunate if the choice that is finally made about detergents were to be made on the basis of not understanding the critical role of phosphorus in eutrophication. If there are better ways to control eutrophication than changing detergents, the decision should be made on that basis, not on the false evaluations of phosphorus and carbon dioxide that are being promulgated currently.

SUMMARY

Lake Washington responded sensitively in a graded way to increases and decreases in the input of treated sewage effluent. Of the major nutrients, the largest changes were made in phosphorus because secondary effluent is much richer in phosphorus than are natural water supplies.

The decision to divert sewage from Lake Washington and to improve the manner of disposal into Puget Sound involved much activity by a volunteer citizens' committee.

The Lake Washington situation can be regarded as a model on a small scale of many kinds of environmental problems that remain to be solved in various parts of the country.

References

Abelson, P. H. 1970. Excessive emotion about detergents. *Science.* 169: 1033.

Allen, H. L. 1972. Phytoplankton photosynthesis, micronutrient interactions, and inorganic carbon availability in a soft-water Vermont Lake. *Amer. Soc. Limnol. Oceanogr. Special Symposia* I: 63–83. (see also discussion p. 81 and 106–107).

Beeton, A. M. and W. T. Edmondson. 1972. The eutrophication problem, *Jour. Fish Res. Bd. Canada,* 29: 673–682.

Björk, S. 1972. Ecosystem studies in connection with the restoration of lakes. *Verh. Internal Verein Limnol.* 18: (in press).

Brown and Caldwell, Civil and Chemical Engineers. 1958. Metropolitan Seattle sewerage and drainage survey; a report for the City of Seattle, King County, and the State of Washington.

Chasan, D. J. 1971. The Seattle area wouldn't allow death of its lake. *Smithsonian.* 2(4): 6–13 (July, 1971).

Clark, E. 1967. How Seattle is beating water pollution. *Harper's Magazine,* 234: 91–95 (June, 1967).

Comita, G. W., and G. C. Anderson. 1959. The seasonal development of a population of *Diaptomus ashlandi* Marsh, and related phytoplankton cycles in Lake Washington. *Limnol. Oceanogr.* 4: 37–52.

Edmondson, W. T. 1955. Factors affecting productivity in fertilized salt water. *Deep Sea Research.* Suppl. 3: 451–464.

Edmondson, W. T. 1961. Changes in Lake Washington following an increase in the nutrient income. *Verh. Internat. Verein Limnol.* 14: 1167–1175.

Edmondson, W. T. 1963. Pacific Coast and Great Basin, pp. 371–392. IN: *Limnology in North America* D. G. Frey (ed.) University of Wisconsin Press, Madison, Wisconsin.

Edmondson, W. T. 1965. Reproductive rate of planktonic rotifers as related to food and temperature in nature. *Ecol. Monogr.* 35: 61–111.

Edmondson, W. T. 1966. Changes in the oxygen deficit of Lake Washington *Verh. Internat. Verein. Limnol.* 16: 153–158.

Edmondson, W. T. 1968a. Water quality management and lake eutrophication: The Lake Washington case. IN: *Water Resources Management and Public Policy.* pp. 139–178. T. H. Campbell and R. O. Sylvester (eds.). University of Washington Press, Seattle.

Edmondson, W. T. 1968b. A graphical model for evaluating the use of the egg ratio for measuring birth and death rates. *Oecologica* 1: 1–37.

Edmondson, W. T. 1969a. Eutrophication in North America. IN: *Eutrophication: Causes, Consequences, Correctives.* pp. 124–149. National Academy of Sciences Publications 1700.

Edmondson, W. T. 1969b. Cultural eutrophication with special reference to Lake Washington. *Mitt Internat. Verein. Limnol.* 17: 19-32.

Edmondson, W. T. 1969c. The present condition of the saline lakes in the Lower Grand Coulee, Washington. *Verh. Internat. Verein. Limnol.* 17: 447-448.

Edmondson, W. T. 1970. Phosphorus, nitrogen and algae in Lake Washington after diversion of sewage. *Science,* 169: 690-691.

Edmondson, W. T. 1971. Freshwater pollution. pp. 213-229. IN: Environment: Resources, Pollution & Society. W. W. Murdoch (ed.) Sinauer Associates, Stanford, Connecticut.

Edmondson, W. T. 1972a. Nutrients and phytoplankton in Lake Washington. American Society of Limnology and Oceanography. Special Symposia. I: 172-193.

Edmondson, W. T. 1972b. The present condition of Lake Washington. *Verh. Internat. Verein Limnol.* 18: (in press).

Edmondson, W. T. And D. E. Allison. 1970. Recording densitometry of X-radiographs for the study of cryptic laminations in the sediment of Lake Washington. *Limnol. Oceanogr.* 14: 317-326.

Edmondson, W. T., G. C. Anderson, and D. R. Peterson. 1956. Artificial eutrophication of Lake Washington. *Limnol. Oceanogr.* 1: 47-53.

Edmondson, W. T. and Yvette H. Edmondson. 1947. Measurement of production in fertilized salt-water. *Sears Foundation Journal of Marine Research.* 6: 228-246.

Einsele, W. 1941. Die Umsetzung von zugeführtem anorganischen Phosphat im eutrophen See und ihre Rückwirkung auf seinen Gesamtaushalt. Zeits. für Fischerei und deren Hilfswissenschaften. 39: 407-488.

Friebertshauser, M. A. and A. C. Duxbury. 1972. A water budget study of Puget Sound and its subregions. *Limnol. Oceangr.* 17: 237-247.

Griffiths, M., P. S. Perrott and W. T. Edmondson. 1969. Oscillaxanthin in the sediment of Lake Washington. Limnol. Oceanogr. 14: 317-326.

Hutchinson, G. E. 1967. A Treatise on Limnology. Vol. II. John Wiley and son, New York.

Hutchinson, G. E., and U. Cowgill. 1970. The history of the lake: A synthesis. IN: Ianula: an account of the history and development of the Lago di Monterosi, Latium, Italy. *Trans. Amer. Philos. Soc. N. S.* 60 (4): 163-170.

Leauge of Woman Voters. Education Fund. 1966. *The Big Water Fight.* Stephen Greene Press, Brattleboro, Vermont. 246 pp.

Nelson, P. R., and W. T. Edmondson. 1955. Limnological effects of fertilizing Bare Lake, Alaska. *U.S. Fish and Wildlife Service Fishery Bulletin.* 102: 414-436.

Peterson, D. R. 1955. An investigation of pollution effects in Lake Washington. Washington Pollution Control Commission. *Tech. Bull.* No. 18.

Scheffer, V. B., and R. J. Robinson. 1939. A limnological study of Lake Washington. *Ecol. Monogr.* 9: 95-143.

Shapiro, J., W. T. Edmondson, and D. E. Allison. 1971. Changes in the chemical composition of sediments of Lake Washington, 1958-1970. *Limnol. Oceanogr.* 16: 437-452.

Stockner, J. G. and W. Benson, 1967. The succession of diatom assemblages in the recent sediments of Lake Washington. *Limnol. Oceanogr.* 12: 513-532.

Sylvester, R. O. and K. R. Jones. 1955. The sewerage problem in the Everett-Seattle Interurban area. Washington Pollution Control Commission. *Tech. Bull.* No. 17.

Tenney, M. W., W. F. Echelberger, Jr. and T. C. Griffing. 1970. Effects of domestic pollution abatement on a eutrophic lake. (Progress Report, Environmental Health Engineering Laboratories, University of Notre Dame, Indiana 46556).

Thomas, E. A. 1967. Die Phosphate-hypertrophie der Gewässer. *Chemish Weekblad.* 26: 305-312; 27: 313-319.

Thomas, E. A. 1968. Die Phosphattrophierung des Zürichsees und anderer Schweizer Seen. *Mitt. Internat. Verein. Limnol.* 14: 231-242.

CHAPTER 16

This paper describes an ecological approach to planning developed by Ian McHarg, and illustrates its use in a case study of Skippack Watershed in Pennsylvania where a proposed development of the area's water resources stimulated public concern over its economic, social, and aesthetic effects.

Water resources planning in the past has lacked an ecological viewpoint. This method provides a way to incorporate nonmonetary costs and benefits into a plan as a complement to standard socioeconomic techniques. In McHarg's method, called "ecological determinism," the physical, biological, and social processes operating on a landscape are assessed and varying propensities for use are evaluated accordingly. Natural processes are visualized to underlie social values, acting as attractions for or constraints on different uses of the land.

SKIPPACK WATERSHED AND THE EVANSBURG PROJECT: A CASE STUDY FOR WATER RESOURCES PLANNING

Ian L. McHarg and Michael G. Clarke

The ecological approach to planning that is detailed here was developed in the course of a study of Skippack Watershed in Montgomery County, Pennsylvania, where a controversy emerged over a proposed reservoir project scheduled for construction by the Commonwealth in 1976. Although few readers will have special interest in the local data concerning the project, the insights gained from the study depended entirely upon the quality of evidence gathered and its acceptance by all parties involved in the controversy. Moreover, because the strength of the ecological approach rests upon the planner's perception of biophysical processes, local data are included in the paper to illustrate fully the planning method employed.

AN ECOLOGICAL APPROACH TO PLANNING

Water Resources Planning

In the Comprehensive Survey of the Delaware Basin, of which the Evansburg Project is a part, project evaluation by the Corps of Engineers was predicated upon the engineering and real estate costs of providing benefits from flood control, water supply, and outdoor recreation. As evidenced from the Evansburg experience, those values do not cover the total spectrum of social costs and benefits actually associated with each project. Other considerations, such as water quality, watershed management, destruction of historical sites, traffic congestion, and effects on local communities, can become important. Even if such costs cannot be translated into dollars, they obviously may be real social costs which, if ignored, can produce the kind of controversy which evolved over Evansburg.

The Evansburg controversy reaffirms that water resources planning has generally lacked an ecological viewpoint. Too often, water resources planners have perceived dams and similar projects as both means and ends—a myopic view exacerbating efforts toward environmental quality.

Clearly, water resources planning must be changed. It must be seen as part of an infinitely larger perception of man and the world he lives in.

Planning and Environment

Planning must consist of the presentation of alternative courses of social action related to the costs and benefits of such action. Increas-

ingly, costs have been at the expense of the environment, reflected in environmental degradation, and these operate in the realm of non-price costs and benefits. It is for this reason that ecological planning has become prominent. Based upon the natural sciences, integrated through ecology, it represents a competence to perceive the environment as an interacting biophysical process. Yet ecological planning is not an alternative but a complement to socioeconomic planning. Both are essential. The case for the latter is assured. It represents the orthodoxy of planning. Ecological planning is still sufficiently novel that it requires both explication and justification.

In the field of ecological planning one of the most distressing yet promising circumstances is that the bulk of necessary data is likely to be already available in reports and studies by the Weather Bureau, the Geological Survey, the Soil Conservation Service, the Fish and Wildlife Service, their state counterparts, and studies conducted by universities. These data are available, but are not being employed. The ecological view promises that these data can be collected, integrated, and interpreted for their relevance to the planning process.

In socioeconomic planning, available information is likely to be employed, but the disparity in planning competence in different units of government tends to vitiate its value. Furthermore, ecological data have rarely been employed with socioeconomic information to produce a comprehensive planning process. Yet one without the other represents a profoundly inadequate basis for planning.

Analysis of Natural Processes

The Place is the Sum of Interacting Natural Processes

To understand a place sufficiently to diagnose and prescribe, it is necessary to investigate the major physical and biological processes that have occured in the past and are operative today.

The surficial expression of a region is a consequence of its geological history and subsequent modification by climatic and hydrologic processes. The climatic processes over time have modified the geology, which accounts for current physiography, drainage, and distribution of soils. Varying plant associations are present, making it possible for a myriad of animal species to exist. Human occupation responds to those same processes and modifies them by its own contribution.

The place is a result of the dynamism which is inherent in all natural processes. Glaciers have advanced and retreated, leaving their signatures in hills, kames, kettles, and a myriad of lakes. But the seasons of the year, the hydrologic cycle, and the recycling of vital nutrients are still going on. Hills are eroded, sediments follow gravitational paths, and rivers change their courses over time. Most important, the dynamism of physical and biological processes affect man and are affected by his intervention.

Natural Processes Represent Social Values

An ecological inventory reveals natural processes. These constitute social values. Geological data may be reflected in foundation savings or in scenic value. Climatic factors may explain population migrations or successful agriculture. Physiography and hydrology help explain the distribution of population and the value of land, and the characteristics of soils make clearer the patterns of agriculture. Plant and animal ecology can be viewed as scenic, scientific, and recreational values. All of these processes are interacting. A single drop of water may occur in clouds, rivers, lakes, rain, snow, dew, frost or fog. It may participate in plant or animal metabolism, in respiration, combustion, as sweat or tears, in industry, commerce, urbanization, agriculture, forestry, mining, or recreation. It may be considered in problems of flood, drought, water supply, erosion control, navigation, hydroelectric power, food processing, and manufacturing.

Thus, the elements of nature can be seen first as phenomena, and then as processes. Next, it is seen that these processes are interacting. Finally, they are seen as social values consituting intrinsic opportunities and constraints for all human uses.

Each Area has Intrinsic Suitability for Human Use

Once it has been accepted that the place is a sum of natural processes which constitute social values, inferences can be drawn regarding its utilization to ensure optimum use and enhancement. It is possible to identify those attributes of land, water, air, and life most propitious for every prospective land use. When these are found, the intrinsic uses and values of the land are revealed.

Natural processes more often than not are inherently suitable for a multiplicity of human uses. Flat, well-drained land with deep soils is intrinsically suitable for active recreation as well as for commercial and industrial development. These apparent conflicts may be resolved in a number of ways. Certain resources, because of their scarcity and vulnerability, may represent such high value that other uses should be excluded, although in other areas multiple uses may be permitted if the representative social values are not compromised.

How does one proceed with this task? It must be emphasized that nature is process and value, exhibiting both opportunities and limitations to human use. Therefore, we must identify the major physical and biological processes which caused the region to be and which operate there now. Data must be compiled, interpreted, and evaluated. For instance, general data on climate are of little significance, but the probability of floods and the resultant inundation are vital. By identifying gradients of susceptibility to inundation, the basic data are interpreted and reconstituted as a value system.

These data must then be related to the major prospective land use groups: (1) production—including agriculture, forestry, wildlife, and extractive minerals; (2) protection —including unique, scarce, or vulnerable resources; (3) recreation—both active and passive; and (4) various categories of urbanization—including residential, industrial, institutional, and commercial.

Absolute economic values cover only a small range of social values. By employing a relative system for evaluation of most to least, it is possible to include all of the important social values and circumvent the economist's narrow pricing system. While this denies the illusory precision of traditional cost-benefit analysis, it does show the maximum concurrence of positive factors or their relative absence. Although it is difficult to assign precise monetary values to natural processes, it is safe to assume that in the absence of any supervening value, the concurrence of a majority of positive factors in a location indicates its intrinsic suitability for the land use or uses considered.

Analysis of Socioeconomic Processes

Human Ecology

To match public policy with intrinsic opportunities for a plan, it is necessary to understand the social processes at work in the region, and present and future demands on the region's resources. It requires an inventory of the present society through historical perspective, and projections into the future. These projections can then be matched to the opportunities represented by the region's resources.

Inventory of Social Phenomena

The first step is to determine the scope of man's present activity in the region—who he is, where he lives, what his institutions are, how he uses the land. This is the base line for planning, from which projected changes in demography and land use can be measured.

Interpretation of Social Phenomena as Processes and Values

Without knowledge of historical processes, the present is incomprehensible, and the future unpredictable. What types of people came to the region, and why? What attitudes did they bring to the land, society, institutions? What variability in attitudes exists and how is it reflected in location, employment, ethos? What values do people attribute to family, education, religion, government? These values will be reflected in homes, neighborhoods, schools, churches, city halls, and state houses. Of all buildings, places, and spaces, which are most cherished, which least? Using the perceptions of anthropology, sociology, and ethology, the underlying motives and aspirations generating the growth and development of the region may be understood.

A Regional Growth Model

Because growth can be understood as an orderly process, it is predictable. Within certain geographic limits, use and development become established in locations for specific reasons. With knowledge of demand projections, the real estate and development market, and the impact of public "agents of change" (for example, investment policy), an accurate forecast can be made of the future character of a region, assuming status quo planning. Such a model will serve as a benchmark from which all other alternative futures can be compared.

Formulation and Implementation of a Plan

The next step of the planning process is to identify alternative futures. The region's proclivity for all prospective land uses is analyzed for locations most fitting for each type of anticipated demand. A synthesis results wherein all development is located in the most propitious locations. This procedure can be accomplished for alternative assumptions of public goals and policies, thus permitting comparisons of social benefits and costs generated by each of the alternatives. Ultimately, a plan may be formulated and adopted which best achieves selected objectives.

The final task is to implement the plan, an undertaking requiring both public and private policies and action. It will employ fiscal and legislative tools, and capital investments in highways and utilities. It will include planning and regulatory powers. Only when the social objectives are identified, and the means to achieve them have been allocated, is there a planning process. This is a dynamic and continuous process of action and feedback, responsive to ecosystems and social aspirations, its success revealed in the health of the environment and society.

Merits of the Ecological Viewpoint

Although the majority of orthodox planning studies emphasize socioeconomic determinants, the planning process described here differs in certain fundamental respects. A major distinction is that economic opportunity is related to the opportunities and constraints inherent in the region's natural suitabilities. Further, the region is represented as a composite of social values, so that society can choose to accept or reject actions such as the transformation of a bog to land fill. The most important difference lies in the criteria used to measure performance. Money is the measure of socioeconomic planning. In ecological planning the criteria used to assess natural ecosystems also include the presence of complexity, diversity, stability, the demonstration of creative fitting, and the presence of physiological, social, and mental health.

One further value is that the information so compiled and interpreted constitutes the data base required to subject any future planning proposal to the test of least cost-maximum benefit. The values of the region have been identified, so that the degree to which any proposal will destroy or enhance these can be quickly determined. Moreover, these data simplify the quest for least social cost locations. It is then possible for both individuals and society to insist that the development process, both public and private, respond to these values.

THE EMERGENCE
OF A CONTROVERSY

Genesis and Early History of the Proposal

The Evansburg reservoir site became a serious proposal in a report completed by the Corps of Engineers entitled, "Comprehensive Survey of the Water Resources of the Delaware River Basin." Authorized in 1950 by the Senate Committee on Public Works, the Corps' study was a multi-agency effort, one of the early comprehensive basin studies in the United States.

The Corps plan, made public in 1960, had three major components: (1) major impoundments to regulate flow in the principal watercourses and to provide pools for recreation, fish and wildlife habitat, and hydroelectric power production; (2) small impoundments to regulate flow in local streams and to provide pools for local recreation needs; and (3) measures to eliminate or ameliorate needs caused by environmental changes from land and water use.

The Evansburg site was one of 19 nonfederally funded projects (initially for recreation, with second stage multipurpose development after 2010), with a project area of about 3,200 acres and a reservoir with a long-term storage pool of about 1,120 acres. The project site is located on Skippack Watershed in Montgomery County, Pennsylvania, a 54-square-mile tributary of the

Schuylkill River which, in turn, is a tributary of the Delaware River.

Project Adoption (1972)

No decisive action was taken on the report's recommendations until 1962, when three decisions were made.

First, in January the Commonwealth of Pennsylvania adopted Evansburg as one of the elements of a proposed bond issue for acquiring outdoor recreation lands in the Commonwealth. This bond issue was eventually activated in June 1964 when the State Department of Forests and Waters assumed responsibility for the project.

Second, in March 1962 the new Delaware River Basin Commission held a public hearing on the Delaware Basin Report. Subsequently, the commission adopted the report and its recommended projects, including Evansburg.

Third, in October Congress adopted the Corps' report and its recommendations in the Flood Control Act of 1962. Although Evansburg was assigned to "non-federal interests," the U.S. Congress indirectly enhanced the project's status.

Opposition and Controversy (1967–1969)

From 1962 to 1967, little action was taken. However, in June 1967 the Department of Forests and Waters held its public hearing on the project in Montgomery County. A large number of local residents attended the hearing. A small group of persons in the Evansburg area were particularly upset by the hearing, and decided to form a group called "Citizens to Save Skippack Valley." Their principal complaint was not the proposed Evansburg State Park but the "high dam" which was to be its focus. They felt that the department had not really justified the high dam; the department had admitted that the reservoir would be unsuitable for

swimming because of water quality problems. The group was especially provoked after finding out that a recent limnological survey of Perkiomen Watershed (of which Skippack is a tributary) concluded that high dams should not be constructed because of the hazard of accelerated eutrophication. In addition, the department's description of the project's water supply function was vague. As conceived by the Corps, the project would not be needed until sometime after the year 2010. Yet at the hearing the department announced its plans to construct the dam in the early 1970s. Finally, the citizens felt that the department had ignored the presence of important historical sites and structures which would be inundated by the reservoir.

Shortly after holding their own public meeting, the citizens submitted a statement to the State Planning Board, endorsing the acquisition of land for a state park but recommending that the high dam be reexamined and compared with alternative smaller impoundments. At about the same time, the Department of Forests and Waters requested the Planning Board to approve land acquisition for Evansburg.

Shortly afterward, state legislators from the area and the County Commissioners notified the Governor and the Secretary of the Department of Forests and Waters that they opposed the project. The Delaware River Basin Commission endorsed early action by the Commonwealth.

In September, the citizens held another public meeting to discuss the project. Early in October, the Governor asked the State Planning Board to remove the project from its agenda until the problems were resolved.

In March 1968 numerous private citizens, groups, local, county, and Commonwealth officials presented statements to the board. "Citizens to Save the Skippack Valley" submitted recommendations similar to those it gave before: (1) that the land needed for the reservoir be acquired to protect the site, and (2) that an ecological study of Skippack Watershed be conducted.

The board recommended the project to the Governor for approval provided that construction of the project be deferred until 1977. The Governor approved the project; however, after meeting with county political leaders, he announced that he had instructed the state to make no further expenditures on the project until completion of ecological study.

The Governor's decision infuriated the Secretary of the Department of Forests and Waters, who threatened to resign. This led to a compromise agreement in December 1968 between the Governor, the Secretary, and the county that land acquisition and an ecological study would proceed concurrently (the study to be paid for by the county). The agreement also stated that the dam and reservoir would not be constructed until 1977, with the understanding that if the study recommended otherwise, its findings would be integrated into the final plan following local public hearing before construction.

Search For Evidence (1969–1970)

In the summer of 1968 Ian McHarg met with some Montgomery County Commissioners and they discussed the means by which the firm of Wallace, McHarg, Roberts, and Todd could undertake an ecological study of the Evansburg area. Skippack Watershed was agreed to be the acceptable study area because resolution of the controversy required an understanding of the intrinsic suitability of the region for demands other than water resources development, such as housing, commerce, industry, and recreation. Eastern Montgomery County was experiencing the strains of rapid urbanization in locations dictated by the whims of the real estate market, and the rural environment was disappearing quickly. Suburban immigrants seeking a quality environment with breathing space, recreational areas, and contact with nature were being denied these opportunities

by totally insensitive development, the sole benefactors of which were speculators and developers.

After some delay to acquire support, funds, and time, the Commissioners signed a contract with the firm in April 1969. The study had two purposes: to examine the consequences of constructing the project, and to recommend a county position. Further, it was to identify the watershed's resources and their tolerances for accomodating future land use demands.

A technical advisory committee was established early, composed of government representatives who had become involved in the controversy. Three public meetings were held to inform concerned citizens on the conduct of the study and its findings. For the major issues of history, water quality, and water resources engineering, the firm sought the insights of distinguished persons in those fields.

SEARCH FOR EVIDENCE:
AN ECOLOGICAL STUDY
OF SKIPPACK WATERSHED

The Study Approach

The study began with an hypotheses (McHarg, 1969),

> The pattern of indiscriminate metropolitan urbanization dramatizes the need for an objective and systematic way of identifying and preserving land most suitable for open space, diverting growth from it, and directing development to land more suitable for urbanization. The assumption is that not all land in an urban area needs to be, or even ever is, all developed. Therefore, choice is possible. The discrimination which is sought would select lands for open space which perform important work in their natural condition, are relatively unsuitable for development, and self-maintaining in the ecological sense, and occur in a desirable pattern of interfusion with the urban fabric. The optimum result would be a system of two intertwining webs, one com-

posed of developed land and the second consisting of open space in a natural or near natural state.

Planning that understands and properly values natural processes must start with identification of the processes at work in nature. It must then determine the value of subprocesses to man, both in the parts and in the aggregate, and finally establish principles of development and nondevelopment based on the tolerance and intolerance of the natural processes to various aspects of urbanization. It is presumed that when the operation of these processes is understood, and land use policies reflect this understanding, it will be evidence that the processes can often be perpetuated at little cost.

First, it was necessary to document existing and anticipated urban growth to understand the land-use demands being exerted on the Skippack Watershed. The development process was simulated through four uncontrolled growth models. With knowledge of expected population change, the real estate and development market, land use controls, and the impact of "public agents of change," it was possible to forecast accurately the future character of the watershed, assuming status quo planning.

Simultaneously, an inventory of natural and cultural processes was undertaken to reveal how the present character of the watershed had come to be. The next task was to review the inventory and select those characteristics important to prospective land uses. The attributes of each location in the watershed were reviewed to determine whether they were beneficial, detrimental, or neutral to prospective uses. Natural and cultural characteristics were then reconstructed into five resource categories: historical, scenic, water, agricultural, and developable. Where appropriate, each category was described in a gradient of values ranging from those most tolerant with the fewest limitations to those least tolerant with the most limitations for prospective use.

The final task in the analysis of the watershed's resources was to identify resource utilization alternatives, and to portray them on a synthesis map. With a knowledge of socioeconomic demands and the watershed's intrinsic suitabilities for all prospective land uses, it was then possible to evaluate the consequences of the project and make recommendations to the county.

Determining Opportunities and Constraints

The Specter of Uncontrolled Growth

The extent of urban development expected in Skippack Watershed in the next 15 years was quantified by preparing four uncontrolled growth models. The models were "handicraft" rather than mathematical because the latter would have been too crude for the grain of data available.

These models outline several probable futures for the watershed, each based on a different set of public policy decisions. They show the extent to which such decisions affect private development as well as other public decisions. The models were not intended to show how development should take place, but rather how it would occur, given the stated assumptions.

The models allocated expected growth by 5-year iterative periods and illustrated the continuous development process by accounting for the introduction of new land-use decisions at many points in time.

Model 1 described urban development in the watershed during the 1969–1984 period, assuming indefinite deferral of other planned projects, including three expressways, a major bridge crossing, and sewer and water system expansions. Model 2 described development during 1969–1984, assuming construction of the proposed project in the 1970s, in addition to all of the other assumptions of Model 1. Model 3 and Model 4 described development during 1969–1984, assuming construction of the proposed project *and* an adjacent expressway in the 1970s. Model 3 assumed that the expressway would be located along the edge of the project, whereas Model 4 assumed that it would be on the eastern edge. In Models 3 and 4, expressway interchanges became important nodes of high land value, attracting both industrial and commercial development. Multifamily residential development is attracted to areas easily accessible from interchanges.

In summary, the models of uncontrolled growth indicated that in the next 15 years the watershed will change from a rural area on the fringe of suburbia to a rapidly developing suburban area itself. Although over half of the watershed's acreage will remain undeveloped, the pattern of suburban sprawl will be set and the rural character of the countryside will be changed irrevocably. The park or park-and-expressway would accelerate growth and increase residential densities and commerical and industrial uses immediately around them. However, they would probably not significantly increase the Watershed's population.

Inventory of Natural and Cultural Processes

Skippack Watershed began to take shape almost 200 million years ago during the Late Triassic when torrential streams brought sediments into the area from the bordering highlands. Since that time, climatic, geologic, hydrologic, and biological processes have been operating as agents of change and form and, in large part, are responsible for the way that Skippack looks today. The other major influence has been man. Although a relative newcomer, he has brought distinct change to the watershed during the past 250 years.

Climate. The watershed has a humid continental climate, with warm summers and moderately cold winters. Average total annual precipitation is 44 inches, fairly evenly distributed throughout the year, with peaks occurring in July and August, and lows occurring in February and October. Snowfall varies from 20 to 30 inches a year, generally during the period between December and early March. The average growing season is 203 days.

Geology. Bedrock in the watershed is Triassic and part of a series of disconnected, downfaulted basins extending from Nova Scotia to North Carolina. It is part of the Newark Group, typically reddish in color, which is divided from oldest to youngest into the Stockton, Lockatong, and Brunswick formations. The Brunswick Formation underlies most of the watershed, consisting chiefly of red shale and siltstone; the Lockatong, principally a dark gray argillite, appears mainly in a single continuous belt along the southern edge of the Brunswick. A few thin tongues of Lockatong also occur within the Brunswick, two of which help to form a broad, open, westward-plunging syncline. The Brunswick has also been intruded by numerous diabase dikes and sills.

Physiography. In the southern part of the watershed the Lockatong Formation has produced a ridge rising 300 feet or more above the adjacent landscape. The Brunswick shale is more erodible and forms a lower, more gently rolling terrain with broad shallow valleys and low ridges. Except for streamside areas and parts of the Lockatong ridge, slopes are typically less than 8 percent.

Hydrology—Ground Water. The ground water table stands at or near the land surface in valleys and rises toward adjacent topographic divides. As the seasonal variation in precipitation is small, the dominant factor controlling water table fluctuation in areas remote from pumped wells is the seasonal variation in evaporation and transpiration. Thus the water table declines during summer and fall.

The Brunswick Formation is generally a reliable source of small to moderate supplies of ground water. However, the amount of ground water stored in the typical Brunswick shale and siltstone is low. Poor ground water yields are typical of the Lockatong Formation. Ground water in both formations is largely of the calcium bicarbonate type.

Hydrology—Surface Waters. Water budget calculations for the Delaware Basin indicate that of the 44 inches of average annual precipitation, approximately one-half becomes natural runoff in the basin's streams. The remainder goes into evapotranspiration, ground water storage, soil moisture, surface water storage, ground water flow out of the basin, and consumptive use by man.

There are high runoff periods in late winter and early spring, when snow melts and soil saturation is near field capacity. Low runoff periods occur in late summer and early fall when evaporation rates are high and vegetative cover is dense; at this time base flow may account for one-half of observed stream flow. Three-year gauge records for Skippack Creek in the vicinity of the proposed Evansburg Dam show that discharge is extremely variable, ranging from less than 1.0 cfs (cubic feet per second) in September 1966, to over 1,800 cfs in March 1967.

Pedology. The characteristics of soils depend upon the parent material, physiography, climate, plant and animal life in and on the soil, and the point in time.

A soil survey prepared by the U.S. Soil Conservation Service indicates that soils in the watershed are almost uniformly silt loams derived from the area's shales. The predominant series is a deep, moderately well-drained soil found on nearly level or moderately sloping uplands. Other series are moderately deep, well to poorly drained soils found on rolling uplands, which tend to be wet in spring and droughty during the summer.

Plant Ecology. Vegetation types were mapped using aerial photographs. Mapping units were selected to reveal the presence of major woody plant associations and to indicate the effects of man-caused and natural disturbances on successional trends.

Plant succession, if allowed to proceed without disturbance, will culminate with an uneven-aged mixed hardwood forest. The watershed has been dominated by agriculture for 200 years, until recently. On abandoned farm lands, a sequence of "old field," "even-aged pioneer forest," "uneven-aged forest," usually exists, each reflecting factors of time, site and conditions, and land-use practices. Owing to the watershed's agricultural history and increasing urbanization there is little forest land. In short, the forest is residual, allowed to remain in locations not being used for agriculture or urbanization. Its continued presence will depend primarily on the lag period between declining agriculture and increasing urbanization, and the degree to which the forest is valued in the suburban environment.

Limnology. The firm asked Dr. Ruth Patrick, Curator of the Limnology Department of the Academy of Natural Sciences of Philadelphia, to evaluate water quality in the watershed and to identify pollution sources.

The Academy gathered physical, chemical, and biological data from 70 stations located throughout the watershed. Every station showed signs of organic enrichment. Two of the four major tributaries in Skippack Watershed, which together comprise over one-third of the watershed's drainage area (East Branch and Towamencin), were found to have serious water quality problems, largely due to growing urban communities in their headwaters. Major waste discharge sources include two municpal secondary treatment plants, one of which is operating at less than one-third of its design capacity. However, the plant already causes heavy enrichment downstream. The other plant, operating at about 80 percent capacity, is located in headwaters, which, unfortunately, are where most reproduction of aquatic life occurs. In September 1969 approximately 90 percent of the water below that treatment plant was estimated to be sewage effluent. Other major offenders in those two tributaries are a pumping station which intermittently discharges raw sewage into the stream, and three industrial firms which release large amounts of organic and toxic wastes.

Water quality conditions in the other two major upstream tributaries (West Branch and Zacharias) are generally healthy except where septic tanks, runoff from urban settlements, croplands, dairy herds, and scattered industry have contributed organic loads exceeding the streams' assimilative capacities. Those sources pose a complicated and widespread quality control problem in the watershed.

In the lower third of Skippack Watershed, Skippack Creek begins to recover from upstream pollution. This is attributed to a high surface-to-volume ratio and a high gradient, and to the dilution of wastes from the two heavily enriched tributaries by the two healthier ones. In addition, major waste loads of the headwaters have already been partly assimilated before reaching the lower third of Skippack Creek.

The Pennsylvania Department of Health is responsible for enforcing water quality standards in the watershed. Until recently, and with the exception of one industrial firm, the major pollution sources have consistently met those standards. New abatement orders were issued by the Health Department in 1970, reflecting more stringent water quality standards adopted by the Pennsylvania Sanitary Water Board in 1968. The new orders will require compliance within a "reasonable" time, which in most cases is thought to be about two years. Effects of the new standards on stream health in the watershed have not been studied.

Cultural History. Dr. Anthony B. Garvan of the University of Pennsylvania's Department of American Civilization was hired to compile a history of the area, as it is reflected in buildings and places in the vicinity of the

proposed project and as it is preserved by and interpreted through structures and sites in the area. For his documentary study, Dr. Garvan gave priority to those sites located within the area to be inundated by Evansburg Reservoir.

Identification of Resources

Following the inventory, natural and cultural characteristics of Skippack Watershed were examined for social values. Five categories of prospective land uses were recognized: agricultural, developable, historical, scenic, and surface-water resources.

Agricultural Resources. For many years the U.S. Soil Conservation Service has categorized agricultural resources in terms of capability classes, that is, "the grouping of soils that shows, in a general way, their suitability for most kinds of farming" (U.S.S.C.S., 1967). SCS usually recognizes eight such classes. Class I soils have few limitations restricting their use. The succeeding classes have increasing limitations, the most restrictive being Class VIII whose soils are generally unsuitable for commercial agricultural production.

To supplement SCS capability *classes*, the firm examined SCS capability *units*, which are more detailed classifications, each representing a group of soils enough alike to be managed similarly for crops and pastures. To indicate necessary management practices for different parts of the watershed, the firm organized capability units into eight additional classes. Class I soils are those capable of sustaining a maximum intensive crop rotation. The succeeding classes have successively increasing limitations for management, the most limited being Class VIII, whose soils are generally unsuitable for cultivation.

Maps of agricultural resources in the watershed indicate that prime agricultural lands are scarce and confined to alluvial soils along Skippack Creek. Most of the watershed soils have moderate to severe limitations for cultivation.

Developable Resources. Although no area in the watershed is considered undevelopable, proclivities and tolerances for development vary from one location to the next with respect to the costs of development. Various kinds of costs must be considered: engineering, construction, and environmental costs. All of these represent social costs that various segments of society must pay either directly or indirectly.

Geology, soil, and slope data were the basis for estimating construction limitations in the watershed, which were then mapped.

A study of water resources in Mercer County, New Jersey, provided useful information relevant to ground water supply limitations in Skippack Watershed (Widmer, 1965). The study indicates that for red shale (the Brunswick Formation) smallest residential lot size should average two-thirds of an acre. Argillite (the Lockatong Formation) has a safe yield of about one-third that of shale, and a minimum lot size of two acres or more is recommended. Because of varying water demands, it is difficult to provide similar well-spacing guidelines for industry.

A number of areas in the watershed were identified as requiring protection measures if developed for urban purposes.

1. Within 300 feet of either side of a perennial stream. All development within this zone could have major deleterious effects on stream health, resulting from septic tank effluents, sedimentation, destruction of stream banks, and runoff from roofs, parking lots, and other structures.

2. Alluvial soils. In the absence of flood plain surveys, alluvial soils represent an accurate approximation of areas subject to flooding. Because floods may endanger life and property, such areas are not suitable locations for most kinds of development, particularly residences.

3. Erodible soils. Such soils within or contiguous to the 300-foot zone may become major sediment sources to nearby streams. Disturbance during construction should be minimized.

4. Slopes. Areas located within or contiguous to the stream buffer zone that have long slopes on impervious soils or slopes that exceed 15 percent are potentially serious sediment sources. Building on these slopes should be discouraged.

5. Erodible slopes. Erodible soils on these slopes that are within or contiguous to the stream buffer are particularly hazardous sediment sources on which building activity must be limited or rigorously controlled.

Historical Resources. Historical resources of the lower Skippack Valley were described by Garvan (1970) in his survey conducted for the study. In conclusion he remarked:

> The historical tradition of this area has been one of quiet, moderate independence from the mainstream of American life. This independence has dominated the religious, social, political and economic life of the area and preserved it largely free of the main currents of change which have so remolded urban America. Moreover, the nature of this variance has been surprisingly consistent. It has taken the form of careful adaptation to the natural and social environment. In consequence, an ecology of a modest remodel of the landscape, small farms, little machinery, modest waterworks, plain style churches, and simple graveyards has seemed the most fitting and proper solution to particular problems.
>
> This strong respect for the past and for natural environment also appears in most local building. The stone for the 1792 bridge was quarried nearby for a bridge built so conservative in design it suggests late medieval English structures yet it carries modern traffic. Outside the proposed Evansburg park area, but nearby, the Mennonites, in 1873, built a meetinghouse that in its interior arrangements presisely preserves Reformation traditions. Lime for whitewash, oak for mill machinery and floor frames, local stone for walls, shingles, and clapboards could still be supplied by the land which has been treated with respect and reverence for 250 years.

Scenic Resources. It is possible to identify the visually perceptible environment in distinctive categories indicating a range of desirable locations for different land uses. Broadly, two groups of landforms occur in the watershed—places having a strong sense of enclosure, and open places with long views visible from many areas.

Enclosed areas are visual bowls manifesting a sense of containment. Such areas may exist along major permanent streams and may be wholly contained in stream corridors, along the water's edge. Others are located in minor tributary valleys where the presence of water is now only incidental, but where small impoundments could be constructed. Woodlands within the visual bowls or on their edges become an integral component of the scenic experience.

The most notable scenic feature of the watershed occurs at a point where the diabase dike alters the direction of Skippack Creek by about 90 degrees. On the east side, the dike descends steeply to the edge of the creek; on the west side gentle slopes extend back to a minor ridge. This area is a natural amphitheater, in which the feeling of a theater is heightened by the presence of woodlands on all of its edges.

The second type of land form, affording long views, consists of pronounced continuous ridges or ledges with flat or generally sloping areas falling off on three sides. Ledges often occur at the edges of enclosed spaces, with complementary woodlands on scenic ridges and ledges.

In the overall distribution of scenic resources, the northern third of the watershed is characterized by relatively flat lands; narrow bands of forest frequently define stream sides which, in turn, blend into small areas of gently sloping land. the Lockatong ridge, occupying the southeastern edge of the watershed, may be characterized as a scenic unit. The top of the ridge is neatly defined by a line of loosely connected ledges offering scenic views of gently sloping lands, which, in turn, are interrupted frequently by smaller ledges. Skippack Creek and its tributaries offer another scenic unit in the southern portion of the watershed, constituting a spine

of water bordered by steep and often wooded streamsides occasionally broken by wide rooms within the stream corridor: the most unusual feature of the stream corridor system is the diabase theater. The remaining scenic unit occupies the central portion of the watershed between Skippack's headwaters and the Lockatong ridge. It consists of a conglomerate of numerous scenic land rooms and ledges. Streamsides in this belt are enclosed within broad corridors of generally sloping land that recedes into low flat plateaus.

Surface Water Resources. Evaluation of the watershed's surface water resources focused on identifying potential dam sites which could provide valuable water supplies and recreation benefits to the region.

Distinctions were made between "major," "intermediate," and "small" reservoir sites, which must be considered in relation to the watershed. That is, the proposed Evansburg Project site and other comparable multipurpose projects are *major* sites. *Intermediate* sites are capable of providing regional recreation opportunities but have limited water supply yields. *Small* impoundment sites have small pools capable of providing local public or private recreation opportunities.

A. Investigation of Major Reservoir Sites. Because the Delaware River Basin Report does not refer to major alternatives in the watershed, the firm and its engineering consultant reviewed available data to determine other possible sites. It concluded that the Evansburg site is the most propitious site for a major multiple-purpose project.

B. Investigation of Intermediate Reservoir Sites. The investigation of intermediate sites was undertaken in seven steps.

1. Sites investigated by government agencies. As part of the comprehensive survey completed in 1960 by the Corps and other federal agencies, 293 potential dams and reservoirs were investigated. Of these, 39 were

found to have sufficient economic value for inclusion in the overall plan for the basin. The remaining 254 potential projects, which include two sites in Skippack Watershed, were recognized as potentially worthwhile in groups as major control developments, as alternatives, or as augmentations of major control projects.

In response to requests from Montgomery County, the Pennsylvania Department of Forests and Waters investigated three intermediate reservoir sites, located nearly equidistant from one another on Skippack Creek between the Evansburg site and the confluence of Skippack's east and west branches, as alternatives to the Evansburg Project.

2. Wallace, McHarg, Roberts, and Todd survey of intermediate sites. To be assured that those sites investigated by government agencies represented all potential intermediate sites in the Watershed, the firm surveyed additional sites which might be feasible. Those with potentially serious engineering and storage problems, or with very small watershed drainage areas, were eliminated.

3. Analysis of tributary drainage areas. The longevity and performance of any reservoir project depend upon upstream conditions as they affect water quality. Thus, in determining the feasibility of any project, cognizance must be taken of such watershed conditions as existing and future land use patterns, waste disposal, ground and surface water withdrawals, potential soil loss, and stream health.

Skippack's four major tributary drainage areas were evaluated. Because of existing and anticipated urban growth, it was concluded that the East Branch and Towamencin drainage areas were unfavorable locations for intermediate impoundments, as both areas already have serious water quality problems. In contrast, the West Branch and Zacharias drainage areas are considerably more favorable for intermediate sites, although they have minor rural pollution problems and are also subject to increasing urban pressures.

4. First screening of all potential sites.

Decisions made in the first screening were to eliminate from further consideration all potential sites located in East Branch and Towamencin creeks, to eliminate all but two sites from West Branch and Zacharias creeks, and to accept prima facie all other sites on Skippack Watershed studied by government agencies.

5. Recreation potential analysis of intermediate sites. The remaining sites were evaluated for their recreation resources by examining all lands within one-quarter and one-half mile radius zones of reservoir areas. Particular attention was given to the quarter-mile zone, which was chosen because that is a reasonable maximum distance to expect most visitors to walk from their cars to the reservoir's edge. Lands within this zone of each site were examined for the following characteristics: slope, existing vegetative cover, acres in forest land, physiography, soil/slope suitability for construction of recreation facilities, and existing urban land use. All existing recreation facilities within a half-mile radius of each site were inventoried, as was potential project acreage. With a few exceptions, none of the sites were found to vary significantly from each other within the quarter-mile zone.

6. Limnological evaluation of intermediate sites. The quality of the water at all intermediate sites surviving the first screening was reviewed by Dr. Patrick, who concluded that

Because of the large number of pollution sources in the region, the Skippack and its tributaries do not appear to be well suited for impoundments from a biological standpoint. Any impoundments constructed prior to a significant improvement in water quality are very likely to become eutrophic. . . .

Impoundments that are extremely eutrophic are generally unsuitable for water supply and recreation. Blooms of some species of planktonic algae cause taste and odor problems that are difficult to eliminate. Algae may also clog filters of water supply systems. Mats of floating algae litter beaches, and rotting algae usually emit very strong odors. The bacteria, which decompose dead algae, exert a demand on the dissolved oxygen supply; lowered, dissolved oxygen may cause fish kills. Although fish productivity is high in eutrophic lakes, large populations of the less desirable but more tolerant fish species . . . would be expected to develop in all of the proposed Skippack impoundments. . . .

If an impoundment is to be used for water supply, recreation, or both, nutrient concentrations and bacteria counts in the tributary streams must be reduced significantly . . . .

Even if a very rigorous pollution control program is implemented, there may be sufficient nutrients in streams to cause nuisance growths of algae . . . potential sources of pollution should be located where nutrients can be assimilated easily. . . . Future development should be restricted from the headwater region of the Skippack and its tributaries if water of high quality is desired.

Potential sources of pollution should be spaced so that recovery in streams occurs before an additional pollutant enters the stream. This means that potential sources of pollution should not be located on small tributaries, but rather where there is adequate water for dilution. Also, it means that development should be spaced so as to permit streams to recover. . . . Buffering zones between future developments are strongly recommended. These zones could be carefully managed farms, wooded areas or meadows.

7. Second screening of sites. Of the eleven sites passing the first screening, five were eliminated in the second screening largely because of the character of existing urban land use within their one-quarter mile zones and/or exceptionally poor water quality.

The six remaining sites were divided into two groups. The first could possibly be constructed under water quality conditions revealed at the time of the limnological survey. The second group are those sites which should not be constructed at this time due to poor water quality conditions encountered during the survey.

C. Investigation of Small Reservoir Sites. Propitious locations for small reservoirs are in small watersheds where water quality can be managed efficiently and where flood problems are less severe. Therefore, this investigation focused on the small tributaries flowing into the branches and the main stem of Skippack Creek.

Identification of individual dam sites was beyond the scope of the study. Consequently, the investigation of small sites examined the qualifications of each small tributary watershed in its entirety, rather than the feasibility of any particular location within.

Certain small tributaries were observed to be more amenable than others to watershed management. Since longevity and performance of any impoundment will depend upon upstream conditions as they affect water quality and the stream regimen, the smaller the drainage area per given length of stream, the smaller the area of watershed that must be managed. Other things being equal, such a "hydrologically efficient" watershed might constitute a higher recreation resource than one of lower efficiency. (Conversely, if a location suitable for high density urban development is sought, a watershed having a low ratio may be preferred, assuming it was not to be used for disposal of wastes.)

Thirty-six small tributaries in the watershed were examined to determine the character of existing urban land use, expected future urban growth, development constraints of soils and slopes for recreation facilities, existing forest acreage, and scenic value. Each tributary was categorized as either a potential reigonal or local recreation resource. Both the regional and local designations were qualified according to whether they were "primary" or "secondary," the former having physical qualities lacking in the latter. Therefore, one of four ratings was given to each of the small tributary watersheds.

The results of the analysis of small tributary watersheds indicate that one tributary in Skippack Watershed may qualify as a primary regional resource, four are potential secondary regional resources, and sixteen are considered as secondary local resources. The major constraint on those rating was existing and projected urban land use. A number of tributaries categorized as local resources would have received higher ratings if existing urban land use had been less prominent or distributed differently.

Utilization of the Watershed's Resources

As described by Garvan, the cultural tradition of the Lower Skippack Valley has been "one of quiet moderate independence from the mainstream of American life [which has] preserved it largely free of the main currents of change which have so remolded urban America." The watershed's scenic resources reflect the physiography of the rural Triassic lowland landscape, one of gentle relief offering a composite ranging from intimate enclosures to exposed areas having expansive views. Its surface water resources have varying potentials for reservoirs of different sizes. Its agricultural resources are generally secondary in character, although it offers a number of areas of high value. Its developable resources are varied, rainging from those offering many opportunities to others having many constraints.

The watershed, then, was revealed to be a composite of diverse resources, derived from both natural and cultural processes. The next task, to employ that knowledge in prescribing future land use, consisted of reviewing all prospective land uses, constructing a matrix relating those uses to the watershed's resources, and finally, producing a synthesis of alternatives for resource utilization.

The Resource Utilization Matrix (Figure 1)

A resource utilization matrix was constructed to relate prospective land uses to the watershed's resources. The criteria used in assigning utilization ratings were judgmental, based upon estimates of the benefits to be derived from utilizing a given resource as compared to the costs likely to be incurred. The kinds of costs and benefits considered varied with the specific resource and land use being evaluated. However, wherever possible, all social costs and benefits were considered, both intangible and tangible.

Resource/land-use relationships suggesting high net benefits received a "primary" utilization rating. Those evaluations suggesting high benefits if certain management conditions were met, received "primary-qualified" ratings; those suggesting lower net benefits received "secondary" utilization ratings. Finally, those evaluations suggesting negative net benefits received "low" ratings. Certain evaluations, such as agricultural uses of streams and ponds, were considered irrelevant or "nonapplicable" in that none of the agricultural enterprises contemplated would require those kinds of resources.

The matrix can be read in two directions: horizontally, indicating how the watershed's resources can be used, or vertically, indicating where each prospective land use can be located. The vertical column for resource utilization, is described below.

Utilization of Agricultural Resources. Agricultural resources were identified as soils capable of supporting a rotation of two years in row crops, one year in small grains, and one or two years in legumes or grasses. Although such resources should be protected exclusively for agriculture, a secondary use would be the Outdoor Recreation Review Commission Class III (Natural Environment Areas) and possibly Class II (General Outdoor Recreation Areas) recreation.

Utilization of Developable Resources. Developable resources are utilized as described below.

1. Slopes. Slopes up to 8 percent are considered as excellent locations for all land uses. Slopes in the 8 to 15 percent class are adequate for O.R.R.R.C. Classes II and III, low density estates, and certain institutional uses. Slopes in the 15 to 25 percent class may be adequate for certain kinds of O.R.R.R.C.

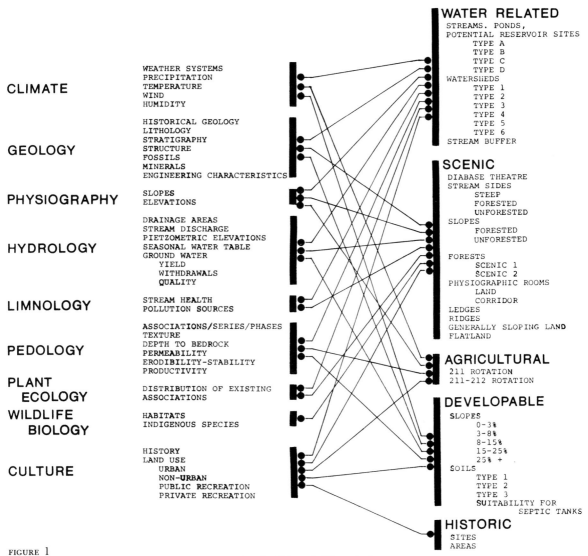

FIGURE 1

Resource Groups and Recommended Land Uses for the Skippack Watershed

Class II and III activities, such as hiking and natural history interpretation, but are poorly suited for all other uses. Slopes exceeding 25 percent are considered unsuited for all uses except O.R.R.R.C. Class III recreation.

2. Soils. The watershed has limited areas of soils well suited for construction, thus presenting theoretically a highly competitive situation among all land uses (theoretical because soils are not the only determinant of land use). Consequently, if all determinants were minor or equal, the best soils would be used first. When those soils were depleted, all land uses would then compete for the next best grades, and so on.

However, such a purely competitive situation would not serve as the basis for a land use plan for the watershed. Although "good

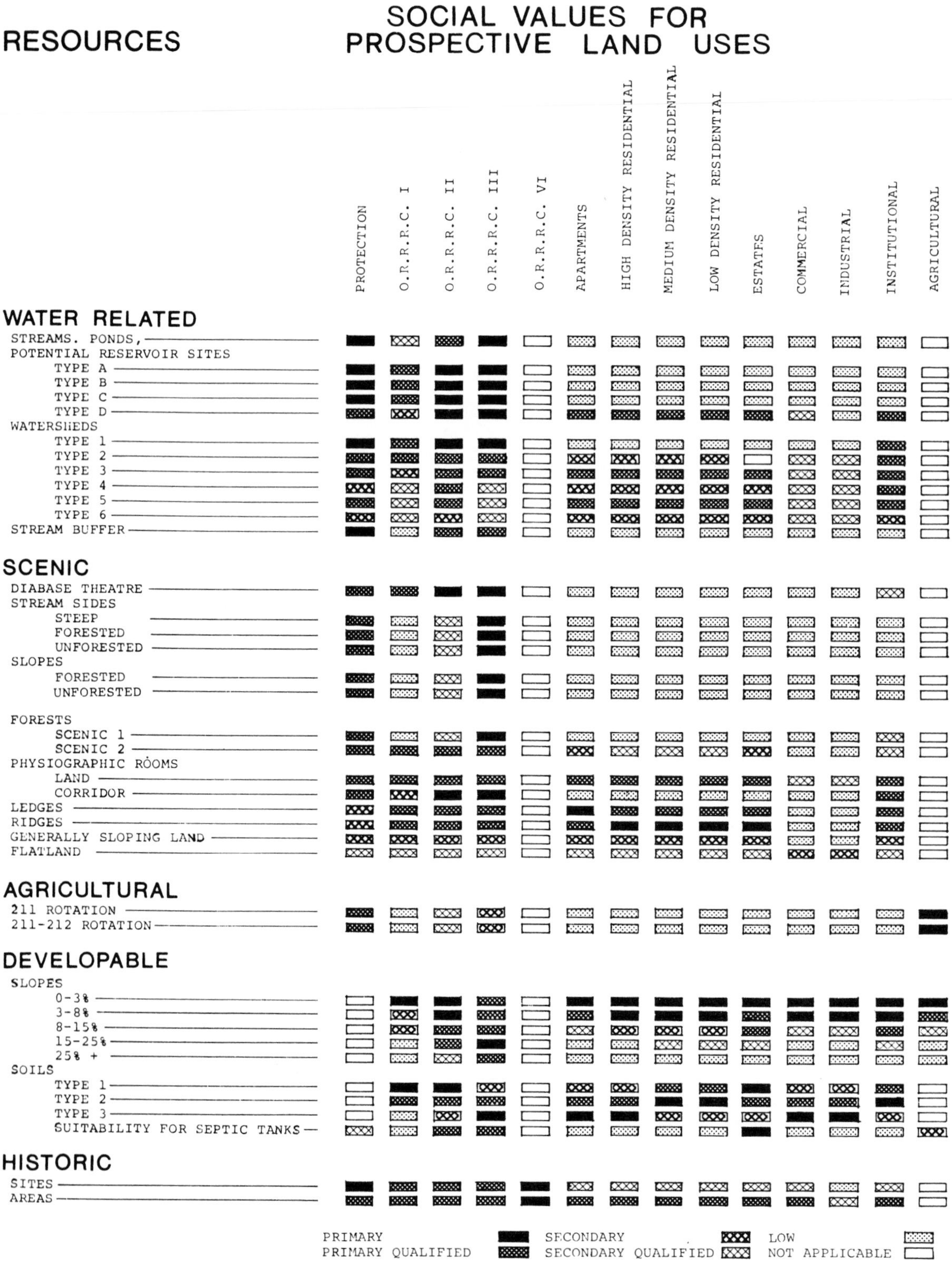
RESOURCES
SOCIAL VALUES FOR PROSPECTIVE LAND USES
PROTECTION
O.R.R.R.C. I
O.R.R.R.C. II
O.R.R.R.C. III
O.R.R.R.C. VI
APARTMENTS
HIGH DENSITY RESIDENTIAL
MEDIUM DENSITY RESIDENTIAL
LOW DENSITY RESIDENTIAL
ESTATES
COMMERCIAL
INDUSTRIAL
INSTITUTIONAL
AGRICULTURAL
WATER RELATED
STREAMS. PONDS,
POTENTIAL RESERVOIR SITES
TYPE A
TYPE B
TYPE C
TYPE D
WATERSHEDS
TYPE 1
TYPE 2
TYPE 3
TYPE 4
TYPE 5
TYPE 6
STREAM BUFFER
SCENIC
DIABASE THEATRE
STREAM SIDES
STEEP
FORESTED
UNFORESTED
SLOPES
FORESTED
UNFORESTED
FORESTS
SCENIC 1
SCENIC 2
PHYSIOGRAPHIC ROOMS
LAND
CORRIDOR
LEDGES
RIDGES
GENERALLY SLOPING LAND
FLATLAND
AGRICULTURAL
211 ROTATION
211-212 ROTATION
DEVELOPABLE
SLOPES
0-3%
3-8%
8-15%
15-25%
25% +
SOILS
TYPE 1
TYPE 2
TYPE 3
SUITABILITY FOR SEPTIC TANKS
HISTORIC
SITES
AREAS
PRIMARY
PRIMARY QUALIFIED
SECONDARY
SECONDARY QUALIFIED
LOW
NOT APPLICABLE

FIGURE 1 (continued)

RESOURCES	RESOURCE SUITABILITY GROUPS: PROTECTION, RECREATION	PROTECTION, RECREATION, AGRICULTURE	PROTECTION, RECREATION, INSTITUTIONAL	RECREATION, INSTITUTIONAL, RESIDENTIAL	PROTECTION, RECREATION, URBAN (EXCEPT INDUSTRY), AGRICULTURE	PROTECTION, RECREATION, URBAN, AGRICULTURE	RECREATION, URBAN, AGRICULTURE
WATER RELATED							
STREAMS. PONDS,	□						
POTENTIAL RESERVOIR SITES							
TYPE A		□					
TYPE B		□					
TYPE C		□					
TYPE D		□					
WATERSHEDS							
TYPE 1		□					
TYPE 2					□		
TYPE 3					□		
TYPE 4					□		
TYPE 5							
TYPE 6							□
STREAM BUFFER	□						
SCENIC							
DIABASE THEATRE			□				
STREAM SIDES							
STEEP	□						
FORESTED	□						
UNFORESTED	□						
SLOPES							
FORESTED				□			
UNFORESTED							
FORESTS							
SCENIC 1	□						
SCENIC 2				□			
PHYSIOGRAPHIC ROOMS							
LAND						□	
CORRIDOR			□				
LEDGES						□	
RIDGES						□	
GENERALLY SLOPING LAND					□		
FLATLAND							□
AGRICULTURAL							
211 ROTATION		□			□	□	□
211-212 ROTATION		□			□	□	□
DEVELOPABLE							
SLOPES							
0-3%	□	□	□	□	□	□	□
3-8%	□	□	□	□	□	□	□
8-15%	□	□	□	□	□	□	□
15-25%	□	□	□	□	□	□	□
25% +	□	□	□	□	□	□	□
SOILS							
TYPE 1	□	□	□	□	□	□	□
TYPE 2	□	□	□	□	□	□	□
TYPE 3	□	□	□	□	□	□	□
SUITABILITY FOR SEPTIC TANKS	□	□	□	□	□	□	□
HISTORIC							
SITES	□	□	□	□	□	□	□
AREAS					□		

FIGURE 1 (continued)

soils" are scarce, not all land uses have an equal need for them. Adverse soil conditions are likely to impose greater hardships on medium and lower intensity uses than on high intensity ones. Because it was felt that low intensity uses would benefit more from good soils, they were given priority on the matrix; that is, recreation areas, medium and low density residential areas, and institutions are shown as having primary use of Type 2 soils. High density urban uses are given primary use of Type 3 soils.

Soils suitable for septic tanks are a resource because they can accommodate sewage effluent without public investment in collection and treatment facilities. Estates and low density recreation areas are the most appropriate uses of such soils.

Utilization of Historical Resources. Garvan proposed an historical park or district for the Lower Skippack Valley. He suggested the following development concepts.

Historical dams and natural fords remain in great numbers. Rebuild these dams to form a series of pools suitable for fish and plant life, some even adaptable to rowboat and canoe. Reopen the neglected roads to walkers, horseback riders and bicyclists. Develop the large mill structures as buildings for folk arts, amateur studios, adult classes, group meetings and historical exhibits.

Lease one or two of the smaller farms as riding stables and model sheep or dairy farms. Open playing fields, tennis courts and other athletic facilities to schools, churches and individuals of the local community which will suffer tax loss by the establishment of this park. Develop within the park suitable sites for folk festivals, fairs, horse and animal shows.

To assure success of the historical park, Garvan gave three conditions:

First, the abandonment of high dam construction . . .

Second, no major construction should be planned for Evansburg. This town is a complete unit . . . built between 1740–1840 for the most part. To cut it up with even par-

tial demolition or additional traffic will commence its rapid decline and decay. It will be a necessary complement to the future park from which it can benefit and serve if it is a viable organic community . . .

[Third] necessary traffic flow increase should be directed along or near the Ridge Pike, a road which has already been partly modernized and rebuilt so historical damage would seem to be less. In addition such construction would not bisect the future park with a noisy artery and monumental scale engineering.

Utilization of Scenic Resources. Scenic resources are overlooked almost as often as they are abused; some prime scenic uses are described here.

1. Diabase "theater." This is one of the watershed's outstanding scenic resources. Its primary use should be for outdoor recreation. All urban land uses constitute a low utilization of this area.

2. Stream sides. These areas offer a pronounced sense of enclosure along with a continual stream environment. Their primary use would be for O.R.R.R.C. Class III recreation.

3. Scenic forests (scenic 1). The scenic forest is a prime resource for O.R.R.R.C. Class III recreation. Class II and possibly estates and certain institutional facilities may also occur, providing that the forest remains largely intact.

4. Other forests (scenic 2). Forested areas having moderate scenic qualities provide excellent locations for recreation facilities. Residential and institutional developments are secondary uses.

5. Steep slopes. Slopes exceeding 15 percent, whether forested or not, should be reserved primarily for O.R.R.R.C. Class III recreation.

6. Physiographic "rooms." These are desirable locations for most kinds of recreation development and for certain institutional uses. If land rooms are near tributaries suitable for small impoundments, they are particularly valuable. Such rooms are frequently not visible from other areas and can hide

development within. A high degree of developmental control is necessary.

7. Ledges and ridges. Ledges offer scenic views and are well suited for most recreation and residential uses, although they are vulnerable to insensitive development. Ledges are particularly suited for high density uses because they can remain intact and simultaneously offer a high scenic experience.

Ridges are similar in that they offer propitious sites for residences, institutions, and recreational developments, if they are protected from insensitive exploitation. They are less suitable for high-rise buildings than ledges when such structures are conspicuous from surrounding areas.

8. Generally sloping lands. Because they are visible from many other areas in the watershed, even minimal development can cause havoc to the landscape. Development must be nucleated or allowed to occur only in low densities.

Utilization of Water Resources. All streams and ponds should be protected by a buffer zone extending at least 300 feet from the waters' edge. O.R.R.R.C. Classes II and III recreation areas are recommended for the buffer. All other land uses are considered as low utilization of this zone. (See Water Resources Map.)

Potential water resources in Skippack Watershed consist of four kinds of impoundments: Type A—"large" water-supply/recreation sites (the Evansburg site); Type B—"intermediate" recreation sites having few water quality problems if constructed today; Type C—"intermediate" recreation sites having serious quality problems if constructed today; and Type D—"small" tributary impoundments.

1. Large and intermediate impoundment sites (Types A, B, and C). If these sites are to be preserved or developed, the decision to do so must be made soon, before new urban development pre-empts them. The sites should include not only the reservoir area, but surrounding lands within about one-

quarter mile of the reservoir, which would be used for outdoor recreation. At this time, recreation and agriculture are recommended as interim uses.

If any of these sites is used, a watershed management program will be necessary. In Type A and Type C sites, current water quality would have to be substantially improved prior to construction. Management programs for Type B sites would be less expensive and would consist primarily of stream buffer protection and improved agricultural practices.

2. Small tributary impoundment sites (Type D). Dam site locations for small impoundments were not identified in the study. However, the tributaries and their drainage areas were given recreation resource rankings according to character of existing land use, scenic qualities, and stream-length/drainage-area ratio. Except for Type 1 tributaries, which may be worthy of exclusive use for recreation, dam sites on most of these tributaries should also be considered for residential and institutional uses. None of these tributaries is desirable for location of waste treatment plants.

Resource Synthesis

In synthesizing the watershed's resource suitabilities, resources having similar utilization characteristics were combined into resource utilization groups. Resource groups, the recommended allowable uses, and the concept of land use priorities were based on developable resources. A synthesis map was prepared in which those resource groups most restrictive to land use were mapped first. Resource groups next most restrictive were mapped second, and so on. The mapping order of resource groups followed the sequence from one to seven.

In making the map, all of the watershed's resource groups were delineated in the order discussed above. This established groups of recommended land uses for all locations in the watershed. Next, land use priorities were mapped, based upon the character and distribution of the watershed's developable resources. This established a hierarchy of land uses within each of the previously identified resource groups.

The synthesis portrays land use alternatives for Shippack Watershed based upon recommended allowable land uses within each of the seven groups. Developable resources within each resource group vary with that group's occurrence throughout the watershed. Therefore, land use preferences for a given group vary with its location.

Because an examination of the watershed's recreation resources was an important mandate of the study, recreation impoundment sites (Resource Group 2) were pre-empted early in the synthesis so that they would not be excluded by other resource groups. The synthesis suggests that many other recreation experiences are available throughout the watershed, their locations depending upon the particular combination of resources desired.

Similarly, the synthesis shows that all of the prospective urban land uses may occur in a wide range of locations. These uses are restricted completely in only a few locations, namely, the stream buffers, the scenic forests, the corridor rooms, and the large and intermediate impoundment sites. However, in most locations various controls on urban land use are necessary to protect the watershed's resources.

Finally, the synthesis shows that the watershed contains a number of areas having prime agricultural lands. To use those lands for other purposes would mean a permanent loss of a resource which, in Skippack Watershed, is relatively scarce.

Evaluation of the Evansburg Project

Evaluation of the project (including both the reservoir and the state park) focused on four questions: (1) What was the project's expected performance in terms of water yields and water quality? (2) Was the project an economic solution to regional water supply needs? (3) How could the project contribute toward satisfying recreational demands? (4) What were the environmental consequences of building the project? These were the basic questions in dispute during the controversy over the project.

Expected Project Performance

Storage and Yields. As proposed by the Corps of Engineers, the project would have 23,500 acre-feet of active long-term storage and a net yield of 36 cfs. After adjusting for reservoir evaporation and downstream flow requirements, the Pennsylvania Department of Forests and Waters estimated net yields would be 12.9 and 27.6 million gallons daily for five and ten foot drawdowns, respectively.

Water Quality. From her limnological data, Dr. Patrick concluded that the reservoir could be extremely eutrophic if water quality were not significantly improved. In her words,

> The water in the vicinity of the dam site is of significantly better quality than the water near the tail of the proposed pool. However, since the upper reaches of Skippack Creek showed such definite signs of pollution, it is very likely that the pool would be extremely eutrophic if water quality is not improved . . . . Although retention time in any impoundment is often an important factor, the retention time of the Evansburg pool under various flow conditions is not known. Impoundments with long retention times act like nutrient traps. . .
>
> If the Evansburg project were developed at this time, numbers of bacteria and algae would probably limit its use for recreation. Its potential for water supply is very difficult to evaluate. However, algal blooms that cause taste and odor problems have been reported in other reservoirs with lower nutrient concentrations (Sawyer, 1952).

FIGURE 2
An ecological study of the Skippack Watershed

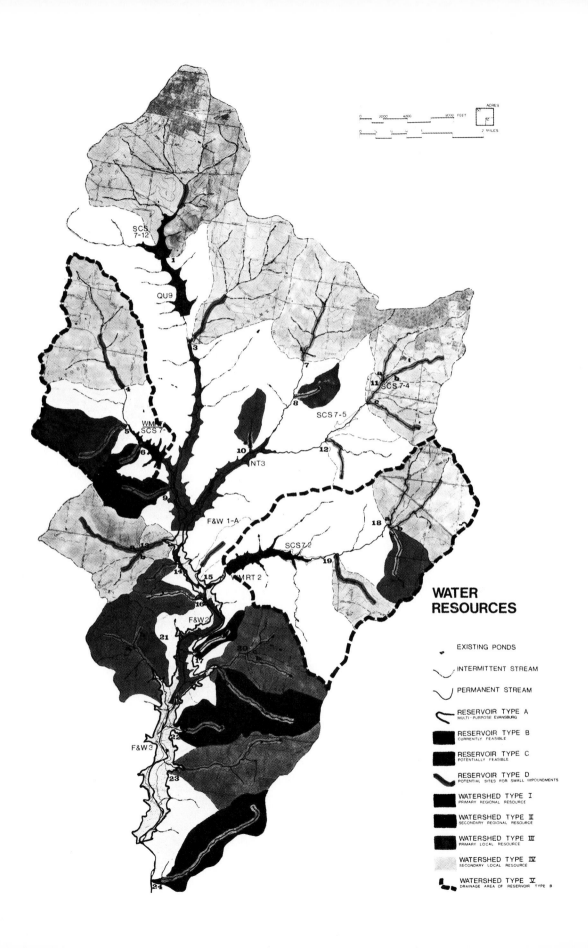

WATER
RESOURCES

EXISTING PONDS

INTERMITTENT STREAM

PERMANENT STREAM

RESERVOIR TYPE A
MULTI-PURPOSE EVANSBURG

RESERVOIR TYPE B
CURRENTLY FEASIBLE

RESERVOIR TYPE C
POTENTIALLY FEASIBLE

RESERVOIR TYPE D
POTENTIAL SITES FOR SMALL IMPOUNDMENTS

WATERSHED TYPE I
PRIMARY REGIONAL RESOURCE

WATERSHED TYPE II
SECONDARY REGIONAL RESOURCE

WATERSHED TYPE III
PRIMARY LOCAL RESOURCE

WATERSHED TYPE IV
SECONDARY LOCAL RESOURCE

WATERSHED TYPE V
DRAINAGE AREA OF RESERVOIR TYPE B

ACRES

0   2000   4000   8000 FEET

0   ½   ¾   1   2 MILES

Our study showed that organic enrichment of Skippack Creek is likely to increase in the future despite the Pennsylvania Health Department's efforts to impose more stringent controls on treatment plants. Consequently, the project's future water quality may deteriorate.

The Project as an Economic Solution to Water Supply Needs

The Corps of Engineers' Position. In its comprehensive plan the Corps divided the Delaware Basin into nine water problem areas, one being the Philadelphia-Trenton metropolitan region. Gross and net gound and surface water needs for the region, when compared with minimum surface flows of Schuylkill and Delaware rivers, indicate that in 1980 and 2010 the region would require additional flows of 317.6 mgd and 1,335.7 mgd, respectively. Although it is situated in the Philadelphia-Trenton region, the Evansburg project was not included by the Corps in its strategies for meeting water needs, as the project would not be needed until some time after 2010.

The Delaware River Basin Commission's Position. The Delaware River Basin Commission included Evansburg in its own comprehensive plan for the Delaware River Basin, and endorsed early action by the Commonwealth to develop the project because it felt that it would "provide storage or supplies of water to help meet long-term future needs in the immediate area, along the Lower Schuylkill and in the Delaware Estuary . . ."

The Department of Forests and Waters Position. In a water resources survey of the Schuylkill River, the Department of Forests and Waters studied future municipal and industrial water needs and projects proposed by other agencies. It concluded that natural stream flow of the Schuylkill River must be augmented to "assure water users along the main stream of an adequate supply of water for the future." The department also believes that the Evansburg project is itself currently needed "locally," in addition to meeting long-term "regional" needs. However, the department's position is not based on a substantive study other than the Corps report. Our firm's survey of fifteen potential major water users in the area suggests that local needs are increasing, but did not determine if Evansburg is the most economical solution to those needs.

Montgomery County Planning commission's Position. In 1960, the Planning Commission contracted a firm of consulting engineers to study central Montgomery County's water resources. Its conclusions were as follows (Albright and Friel, Inc., 1962):

> Water requirements for central Montgomery County will increase from 2.95 mgd, which is practically entirely furnished from wells, to an estimated 44.7 mgd by the year 2010.
> Ground water capacity can be increased to an estimated 16 mgd by drilling wells. . . Peak day demands are expected to amount to 16 mgd by 1970, indicating that a surface supply would be required by about that time.

The Evansburg site (Skippack Reservoir) was one of the seven alternate plans studied. Although utilizing the same site as Evansburg, Skippack Reservoir would have been larger (a dam 110 feet high and a reservoir with 16.5 million gallons of storage). Albright and Friel did not consider the Evansburg project, as conceived by the Corps, because it would not have met their storage requirements.

> The Skippack Reservoir . . . would be one of the most expensive water supply projects for the . . . area. On this basis, it was eliminated from further discussion in this report . . .
> There is . . . no firm policy within the Department of Forests and Waters as yet as to how water impounded for municipal use would be released and made available and what the allocation of costs would be for such

water. Nevertheless, the Secretary has indicated a desire to proceed with the development of the Skippack site as a State Park prior to 2010.

In view of the probability of the State constructing the Skippack project for water supply purposes so as to be of any benefit to the central Montgomery area, it does not appear to be practical for Montgomery County to expect that it could derive any water supply benefits from such a project (p. IV–11).

Evansburg as a Supplier of Recreation Opportunities. The Department of Forests and Waters policy is to assume responsibility for supplying approximately 30 percent of the outdoor recreation demand in Pennsylvania. Although insufficient data are available to indicate how Evansburg fits into the Department's demand and supply picture for the area, its facilities would still be far below its estimates of demands, with or without the project.

The Department's land use plan indicates that the project will provide the following: day-use activities, special activities, boating, nature study, golfing, and lakeside observation. In the absence of more detailed plans, it was difficult to evaluate the reacreational facilities that Evansburg is expected to offer. However, by projecting what the water quality in the reservoir will be and knowing the character of adjacent lands, certain conclusions can be reached about the project's potential.

1. Water-related Recreation. The limnological studies suggest that if the reservoir were constructed today, bacteria and algae would probably limit its use for recreation. This observation was accepted by both sides of the controversy. Since swimming is by far the most popular water-related activity in the region, the value of the proposed reservoir as a recreational resource was dramatically reduced.

2. Land related Recreation. The characteristics of lands within a one-quarter mile radius of Evansburg's long-term storage pool were inventoried. Geology, soils, and slopes in approximately 70 percent of the quarter mile zone have some limitations for state park types of recreational facilities. The remaining lands within that zone will impose numerous limitations on the construction of such facilities owing to steep slopes, and are better left as natural areas where recreational facilities are not available.

The characteristics of potential project lands suggest that the park would be representative of the landscape typifying the Piedmont country of southeastern Pennsylvania—gentle undulating topography occupied by rural-suburban settlement in a post-agricultural setting of abandoned fields and scattered woodlots. It is expected that the Evansburg project lands could offer a range of passive and active recreational opportunities, including such activities as hiking, bicycling, horseback riding, camping, picnicking, and natural and human history interpretation, although some existing woodland will not be easily developed.

Environmental Consequences of Building the Project

Alteration of Stream ecosystems. The project would alter the present "open" system of Skippack Creek by retaining runoff, sediments, nutrients, and industrial pollutants or inhibiting their passage downstream. The extent to which these constituents of runoff would build up in the impoundment will depend upon the project's design, retention times, reservoir management policies, and upstream conditions. In any case the reservoir may become extremely eutrophic.

Destruction of the Area's Cultural Heritage. Dr. Garvan estimated the effects of the dam and reservoir on the area's culture and its historical resources.

Out of roughly 200 [historical] sites and structures in the planned flood and park area, a

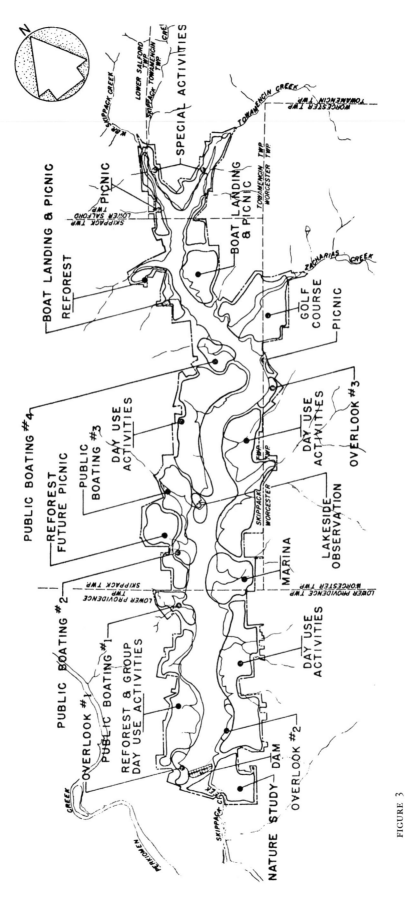

FIGURE 3
Diagrammatic Land Use Plan for the Evansburg Project

minimum of 70 sites predate 1870 or are at least a century old. Over 50 sites and structures date from or before 1830. More than 20 of these sites have substantial claim to either origin before 1800 or memorable association in the nineteenth century.

This report is limited to a survey of the foreseeable impact upon the historical heritage of the area. . . . Three apsects of that heritage would seem to be directly affected by the park and dam. First, since many structures may be inundated or destroyed, the material cultural inheritance of past structures may be reduced. Second, the introduction of a State park into this rural and residential area will substantially alter the traditional customs and ways of life in the area, and some attempt must be made to assess the extent of that alternation. Third . . . there is the possibility that the area's self-image and world-view will be altered by this project, and the implications of this change will reach beyond the boundaries of the park to adjoining towns and farms . . . three powerful enemies, highway construction, undirected real estate exploitation and large-scale public reservoir . . . will destroy many buildings, force the removal of the Mennonite folk and radically alter the natural ecology. In short, it will destroy the existing historical community and replace it with another, uniform in all respects to that which stretches along the Pennsylvania Turnpike from Levittown to Norristown.

Disruption of the Existing Highway System. From comprehensive studies, the firm concluded that major highways in the project's vicinity are already overcrowded during peak hours. The most succinct statement on highways and traffic volume came from the Pennsylvania Department of Highways (1971):

> Construction of a single large impoundment would disrupt traffic flow on no less than seven (7) state highways, the replacement of which would be extremely costly and likely the revised system would meet serious opposition from the residents of Central Montgomery County.

Rearrangement of Future Urbanization Patterns. In the near future, the watershed will experience a suburban boom, with or without Evansburg. Under normal conditions, development will follow the established order of past suburban growth. The park will accelerate growth slightly. Its effect will be greatest in its attraction and concentration in the immediate area of commercial and high density residential uses, which otherwise would occur elsewhere in the watershed.

Summary, Conclusions, and Recommendations

Skippack Watershed's Future. The models of uncontrolled growth indicate that in the next fifteen years, the watershed will change from a rural area on the fringe of suburbia to a rapidly developing suburban area. Although development will be far from complete, with over half of the watershed's acreage still undeveloped, the pattern of future development will be set and the rural character of the countryside will be irrevocably changed.

Under current zoning and subdivision controls, the watershed's future is bleak. Unless innovative and assertive programs are undertaken, its waters may soon be entirely polluted and hazardous to health. Its pleasant, rolling Piedmont landscape will be transformed into the dull and senseless homogeneity of suburban sprawl. The farms will be gone, and the prime agricultural lands will be lost forever. The rural lanes will be busy, overcrowded arterials linking shopping centers to homes and lined with gas stations, drive-in eating places, and other sundry establishments. Remnants of the area's cultural heritage will be mostly obliterated. The quality of life in the watershed will resemble, in all major respects, suburban life elsewhere in the Philadelphia metropolitan region. The watershed will have no distinction.

None of the current plans for jurisdictions within the watershed were predicated on knowledge of the proclivities and tolerances of the watershed's intrinsic resources. Those plans, which presume the area to be an undifferentiated entity, groom the watershed for its demise by a form of urban growth which is insensitive and inherently self-destructive. However, Skippack Watershed does not have to submit to the mediocrity so characteristic of current urban growth patterns. A choice lies in that planning process which directs the future, rather than responds to it.

The study described in this paper offers the beginning of such a planning process. Its proposition was that planning, consisting of the presentation of alternative courses of action, cannot proceed without an understanding of "how the place works." It revealed Shippack Watershed as a composite of resources, offering multiple gradations of opportunities and constraints for all prospective land uses. Those resources, reflecting both natural and cultural processes, have strong implications for the pattern of development. The study demonstrated that instead of being one of those bland areas with little character that are normally selected for urbanization, the watershed possesses a diversity suitable for various residential densities, a wide variety of recreational opportunities, a continuous structure of open space, and locations for industry and commerce. Resource maps and synthesis must be scanned not for single intrinsic land uses, but for mixes of uses which can lead to richness of the environment. The study, therefore, provides a foundation upon which the planning process may proceed toward a plan for the watershed offering maximum social benefits and minimum costs.

The Proposed Evansburg Project. Limnological data gathered during the study suggest that the reservoir would be quite eutrophic if the present water quality were not significantly improved, and that bacteria and algae would probably limit its use for recreation purposes. The quality of the water supply is difficult to evaluate; however, algal blooms causing unpleasant taste and odor have been reported in other reservoirs having lower nutrient concentrations than those expected to occur in Evansburg Reservoir.

There is no evidence that the project would be an economical solution to water supply needs in the county. The only noteworthy study, conducted by a consulting engineering firm in 1962 for the county, suggested that the Evansburg site would be one of the most expensive water supply projects for the area, and recommended another project in the Schuylkill River Basin as the most feasible water supply development.

In his historical survey of the Skippack Valley, Dr. Garvan identified the Town of Evansburg as "a northern, rural Williamsburg not of elite achievement but of minority adherence to traditional values, values which the national majority rejected once in the Revolutionary War for their pacifist content and again in the gilded age of Darwin, mass production, and conspicuous ostentation, for their seemingly over-simple and archaic way of life." Dr. Garvan concluded that the proposal for a park in the area is timely and valuable, but a park with a high dam as the chief feature is totally out of scale with landscape, history, and present future use, self-destructive, and may initiate the rapid and absolute decay of the neighborhood and region it seeks to enhance.

The Pennsylvania Department of Highways has stated that Evansburg Reservoir would disrupt traffic flow on at least seven state highways, the replacement of which would be extremely costly.

From its conclusions, our firm recommended that Montgomery County formally request the Commonwealth of Pennsylvania to abandon the construction of Evansburg Dam and reservoir because the project would destroy significant remnants of the county's cultural heritage, because the project would have substandard water quality, and because there is no evidence that the project is an economical solution to the region's water supply needs.

An analysis of how the project could contribute toward satisfying recreational needs in the region suggests that although demand has been poorly defined, public outdoor recreation facilities in the whole region are limited and far below standard. It is believed that lands adjacent to Evansburg Reservoir could offer a range of passive and active recreation opportunities.

The acquisition area for the state park, as proposed by the Department of Forests and Waters, contains two intermediate recreation impoundment sites studied as alternatives to Evansburg Reservoir. If both were built, shorelines and reservoir-related park lands which in length and acreage would be more than 60 percent greater than the lands provided by Evansburg Reservoir could be provided. These two sites seem more desirable than Evansburg in that they would inundate fewer historical sites and would probably be considerably less expensive. If current water quality problems are not mitigated, and recreational impoundments are considered indispensable to the state park, the Department has the option of developing such reservoirs on other tributaries of Skippack Creek with fewer water quality problems and adequate potential dam sites. In addition, the area being acquired for the state park contains small dam sites (as opposed to the intermediate sites). A number of the small sites described by Garvan in his report are historic mill dams that are no longer operative but that could be renovated to provide small recreation pools.

The firm therefore recommended that Montgomery County endorse and encourage the creation of an Evansburg State Park offering opportunities for diverse outdoor recreation activities, which would contain those historical-cultural features recommended by the historical survey of the Skippack Valley, and include the construction of impoundments only if such sites were approved by our consultant, Dr. Patrick, or another limnologist of equivalent reputation.

One recommendation of the study—to abandon construction of the proposed large reservoir—was presented to the Planning Board of the Commonwealth in March 1971. The Board reaffirmed its earlier position in favor of construction in the near future. The Governor, however, is personally reviewing the project and the study before making a decision.

ACKNOWLEDGMENTS

The director of the study was Ian L. McHarg. David. A. Wallace, partner of Wallace, McHarg, Roberts and Todd, directed that portion concerned with the specter of uncontrolled growth. Ian McHarg was assisted by Narendra Juneja, Associate, who assumed major responsibilities for the overall conduct of the study. The Study Manager was Michael Clarke, Associate. James Chappell, under the direction of David Wallace, developed the models of uncontrolled growth. Richard Nalbandian and Charles Meyers contributed large portions of the natural processes inventory.

References

Geology

Erickson, G. P., and J. L. Kulp. 1961. "Potassium-Argon Dates on the Palisades." *Geological Society of Americ Bulletin,* 72: 649–652.

Glaeser, J. D. 1963. "Lithostratigraphic Nomenclature of the Triassic Newark-Gettysburg Basin." *Proceedings, Pennsylvania Academy of Sciences,* 37: 179–188.

Glaeser, J. D. 1966. *Provence, Dispersal, and Depositional Environments of Triassic Sediments in the Newark-Gettysburg Basin.* Pennsylvania Geological Survey, 4th Series, Bulletin G-43.

Henry, F. D. C. 1956. *The Design and Construction of Engineering Foundations.* London: McGraw-Hill Book Company.

Institute of Civil Engineering. 1954. "Foundations." *Civil Engineering Code of Practice No. 4.* (As reported in Henry, 1956.)

Jumikis, A. R. "Engineering Geology in Newark Area." *Proceedings, American Society of Civil Engineers,* vol. 84, paper 1646.

Krynine, D. P., and W. R. Judd. 1957. *Principles of Engineering Geology and Geotechnics.* New York: McGraw-Hill Book Company.

McLaughlin, D. B., and B. Willard. 1949. "Triassic Facies in Delaware Valley." *Proceedings, Pennsylvania Academy of Sciences,* 23: 33–34.

Minard, J. P., W. W. Holman, and A. R. Jumikis. 1953. "Engineering Soil Survey of New Jersey, Report N. 9." *Morris County Engineering Research Bulletin No. 23.* New Brunswick, New Jersey: College of Engineering, Rutgers.

O'Neill, B. J., D. M. Lapham, N. G. Jarson. A. A. Socolow, R. D. Thomson, and H. P. Hamlin. 1965. *Properties and Uses of Pennsylvania Shales and Clays.* Pennsylvania Geological Survey, 4th Series, Bulletin N. M-51.

Van Houten, F. B. 1960. "Composition of Upper Triassic Lockatong Argillite, West-Central New Jersey." *Journal of Geology,* 68: 666–669.

Van Houten, F. B. 1962. "Cyclic Sedimentation and the Origin of the Analcime-Rich Upper Triassic Lockatong Formation, West-Central New Jersey and Adjacent Pennsylvania." *American Journal of Science,* 260: 561–576.

Van Houten, F. B. 1965. "Composition of the Triassic Lockatong and Associated Formations of the Newark Group, Central New Jersey and Adjacent Pennsylvania." *American Journal of Science,* 263: 825–863.

Willard, Bradford, et. al. 1959. *Geology and Mineral Deposits of Bucks County, Pennsylvania.* Pennsylvania Geological Survey, 4th Series, Bulletin No. C-9.

Ground Water

Bock, W. 1959. "The Ground Water Picture of the Triassic Southeastern Pennsylvania." *Proceedings, Pennsylvania Academy of Sciences,* 33: 162–184.

Greeman, D. W. 1955. *Ground Water Resources of Bucks County, Pennsylvania.* Pennsylvania Geological Survey, 4th Series, Bulletin N. W-11.

Longwill, S. W., and C. R. Wood. 1965. *Ground Water Resources of the Brunswick Formation in Montgomery and Berks Counties, Pennsylvania.* Pennsylvania Geological Survey, 4th Series, Bulletin W. 22.

Parker, G. G. 1965. *Water Resources of the Delaware River Basin.* U.S. Geological Survey, Professional Paper No. 381.

Rima, D. R., H. Meisler, and S. Longwill. 1962. *Geology and Hydrology of the Stockton Formation in Southeastern Pennsylvania.* Pennsylvania Geological Survey, 4th Series, Bulletin No. W-14.

Widmer, Kemble. 1965. *Geology of the Ground Water Resources of Mercer County.* Trenton: Bureau of Geology and Topography, New Jersey Department of Conservation and Economic Development.

Land Use Plans

Delaware Valley Regional Planning Commission. 1965. 1985 Interim Regional Open Space Plan. Plan Report No 3, Technical Supplement. Philadelphia.

McHarg, Ian. 1969. *Design with Nature.* New York: Natural History Press.

Montgomery County Planning Commission. 1969a. *Comprehensive Plan for Worcester Township.* 1969. *Land Use Plan Survey.* 1967. *Comprehensive Plan Report for North Penn Area,* Vol. II. 1969. *Comprehensive Plan Report for North Penn Area,* Vol. III. Norristown, Pennsylvania.

Montgomery County Planning Commission. 1969b. *Comprehensive Plan Report for Lower Perkiomen Valley Area.* Prepared by Kendree and Shepherd in conjuction with Montgomery County Planning Commission. Vol. 1, *Physical Features;* Vol. 2, *Population and Ecology;* Vol. 3, *The Plan;* Vol. 4, The Perkiomen Creek and Proposed Scenic Highway; Vol. 5, *The Proposed Evansburg Park Project.* Montgomery County, Pennsylvania.

Outdoor Recreation

Cesario, Frank J. and Larry E. Wolfe. 1968. *Report on Analysis of Recreation.* Prepared for Pennsylvania Department of Forests and Waters. Columbus, Ohio: Battelle Memorial Institute, Columbus Laboratories.

Chubb, Michael and Peter Ashton. 1969. *Park and Recreation Standards Research: The Creation of Environmental Quality Controls for Recreation.* A report to the National Recreation and Park Association. Technical Report No. 4. East Lansing: Michigan State University.

Cicchetti, Charles J., Joseph J. Seneca, and Paul Davidson. 1969. *The Demand and Supply of Outdoor Recreation.* New Brunswick, New Jersey: Bureau of Economic Research, Rutgers.

U.S. Outdoor Recreation Resources Review Commission. 1962a. *The Future of Outdoor Recreation in Metropolitan Regions of the United States.* Study Report 21. Washington, D. C.

U.S. Outdoor Recreation Resources Review Commission. 1962b. *Outdoor Recreation for America.* Washington, D. C.

U.S. Outdoor Recreation Resources Review Commission. 1962c. *Prospective Demand for Outdoor Recreation.* Study Report No. 26. Washington, D. C.

U.S. Outdoor Recreation Resources Review Commission. 1962d. *Trends in American Living and Outdoor Recreation.* Study Report No. 22. Washington, D. C.

Soils

U.S. Department of Agriculture Soil Conservation Service. 1967. *Soil Survey—Montgomery County, Pennsylvania.* Washington, D. C.

Water Resources Development

Delaware River Basin Commission. 1970. *Seventh Water Resources Program.* Trenton.

Montgomery County Planning Commission. 1962. *A Study of the Water Resources of Central Montgomery County.* Philadelphia: Albright and Friel, Inc.

Leopold, L. B. 1968. *Hydrology for Urban Planning—A Guidebook on the Hydrologic Effects of Urban Land Use.* U.S. Geological Survey: Circular No. 554. Washington, D.C.

Pennsylvania Department of Health. 1969. *Water Quality Report of Skippack Creek.* Open Files Report, Philadelphia Office.

Pennsylvania Department of Forests and Waters. 1966. *Report on Water Resources Study of Neshaminy Creek Basin and Vicinity, Bucks and Montgomery Counties.* Prepared by E. H. Bourguard and Associates, 1966.

Pennsylvania Department of Forests and Waters. 1968a. *Water Resources of Schuylkill River Basin.* Water Resources Bulletin, No. 3. Prepared in cooperation with U.S. Geological Survey, Department of the Interior.

Pennsylvania Department of Forests and Waters. 1968a. *Water Resources of Schuylkill River.* Water Resources Bulletin No. 4. Prepared by E. H. Bourguard and Associates.

Pennsylvania Sanitary Water Board. 1968a. *Rules and Regulations: Article 300, Treatment Requirements.* Harrisburg.

Pennsylvania Sanitary Water Board. 1968b. *Rules and Regulations: Article 301, Water Quality Criteria.* Harrisburg.

Sawyer. C. N. 1952. "Some New Aspects of Phosphates in Relation to Lake Fertilization." *Sewage and Industrial Wastes,* 24:6, 768-776.

Sylvester, R. O. and R. W. Seabloom. 1957. "Influence of Site Characteristics on Quality of Impoundment Water." *Journal of the American Water Works Association.* 57:1528-1545.

U.S. Army Engineers. Philadelphia District. 1960. *Comprehensive Plan for Development of the Water Resources of the Delaware River Basin*. "Fish and Wildlife Resources," Appendix J. "Gross and New Water Needs," Appendix P. "Hydrology," Appendix M. "Project Designs and Cost Estimates," Appendix U. "Recreation Needs and Appraisals," Appendix W. "Water Control at Intermediate Upstream Levels," Appendix R.

U.S. Federal Water Pollution Control Administration. 1968a. *Water Quality Criteria*. Report of the National Advisory Committee to the Secretary of the Interior. Washington, D.C.

U.S. Federal Water Pollution Control Administration. 1968b. *Water Supply and Water Quality Control Study, Blue Marsh Reservoir, Schuylkill River Basin, Pennsylvania*. Boston: U.S. Department of the Interior.

CHAPTER 17

The public is becoming acutely aware of the tradeoff between environmental quality and water development, but often feels powerless to affect the choices made. Project planners have abdicated their normative role of maximizing social benefits and have become partisans of particular development programs.

Instead, water resource planners should define alternatives, convey accurate information to the public as well as to the decision makers, and develop technically integrated planning procedures. Experts in the various disciplines involved in planning for water development must recognize their limitations and seek to accommodate their contributions to the interdisciplinary process, so that inherent biases can be corrected. The planning process must be able to inform affected citizens fully enough and soon enough so that it can provide the essential value judgment involved in development: environmental tradeoffs.

INNOVATIONS IN WATER RESOURCE PLANNING: CREATING AND COMMUNICATING DISCERNABLE ALTERNATIVES

Ralph Luken and Lucille Langlois

INTRODUCTION

During the past decade, segments of the American public have become increasingly aware of the adverse environmental consequences of unconstrained growth. Previously, our nation's water resources were viewed as the key to economic development; now the value of waterways as nongrowth-related resources is more evident and the tradeoffs between environmental quality and water-related development are perceived more sharply. The use of water to generate electricity or as a coolant in steam generating plants provides low-cost energy only at the price of destroying natural waterways and unique recreational areas and creating thermal, chemical, or radiological pollution (see Henwood, in this volume). Private entrepreneurs have been allowed to develop waterfront property for a few at the expense of curtailed access for many (see Scott, this volume). Sustained industrial growth around the Great Lakes is resulting in diminishing water-related environmental amenities and the slow demise of the lakes themselves (see Beeton, this volume).

Although the public is becoming more aware of these tradeoffs, it often feels powerless to control growth or effect any real choice between preservation and development. Power companies sometimes do not hold hearings, or they hold unpublicized hearings on the building of new plants, and often construction has begun before the public is aware of their activities. Or, perhaps, a private developer will secure wetlands from the state at nominal cost and obtain favorable zoning decisions from local "representative" authorities before informing the community of his plans to fill in and build on this shorefront land (Hedgpeth; Scott; Yanggen, this volume). Although environmentally concerned groups can succeed in obtaining marginal concessions to preservation, such as more effective pollution control devices or public easements across developed wetlands, they seldom succeed in efforts to constrain development or eliminate its more serious adverse effects.

Planning for water-related resource development should prevent or minimize many of these inefficiencies, and produce a rational program for water resource development and the resolution of some of the conflicts between preservation and development oriented groups in society. For particular regions or problem areas, water resource planning should identify and assess numerous discernible sets of alternative projects for maximizing social benefits (see McCloskey; McHarg and Clarke, this volume).

However, the present state of planning for water-related resource development is such that very few water resource planners view their role as normative, aimed at maximizing social benefit. Having abdicated this vital function, they become "project managers" for various individual development programs, and reinforce rather than redirect the patterns of uncontrolled growth that develop (see Fox, this volume).

Equally as important as defining discernible alternatives is the need for planners to convey such information to the general public in an intelligible fashion. This latter role is crucial to securing an indication of societal values regarding the most acceptable balance between preservation and development. This process is especially important for weighing preservation-related alternatives, which are not usually subject to market determined prices and hence are difficult to evaluate (see Allee and Chapman, this volume).

The role of a water resource planning agency is to effect the management of water resources to insure optimal configuration of development and preservation. Planners must first identify the possible alternatives which will achieve or contribute to this goal, analyze the tradeoffs between them, and describe the implications and consequences of each. They must then evaluate each alternative in the light of whatever constraints—if any—exist on their implementation (budgeting limitations, administrative difficulties, environmental or social considerations). Those alternatives which are not dismissed as unfeasible by this process finally become the nucleus of the plan which will be submitted for public approval as a means of satisfying public water needs. Such a plan may include sets of projects and guidelines, all of which further, in a coordinated fashion, the public interest (see Peterson, this volume).

Unfortunately, water resource planning—like other types of resource planning—has failed to implement public goals through water management. Instead, most water resource planning and management agencies tend to operate in reverse: rather than identifying a goal and a range of alternatives, and then devising a plan, they often begin with a project or group of projects related to certain interests, and then formulate a plan to justify its implementation. Because many water resource planners have rejected taking an active normative role, their plans consist largely of such responses to proposals by the interest groups who form their constituency. The major drawbacks of such a system are twofold. First, because planning becomes largely an endorsement procedure of individual projects, water resource development becomes a piecemeal, uncoordinated process over which no one has any real control (see Scott, this volume). Second, because such plans are constructed around specific projects or programs, they ignore the existence of a whole range of possible alternative actions, and at least implicitly deny the importance of any countervailing or opposing interests (see McCloskey, this volume).

If water resource planning is to play a role in directing the future use of our water resources, we argue that there must be a shift from the present "tyranny of small decisions" to more catholic and evaluative planning, and a serious effort on the part of planners and decision makers to communicate to the public the importance of attaining a planned balance between preservation and development.

PROVIDING TECHNICALLY INTEGRATED INFORMATION

To achieve more comprehensive planning, it is necessary to gather, integrate, and make known technical information regarding the possible alternatives associated with preservation and development. Ideally this should involve more than merely gathering reports from different academic disciplines or gov-

ernment agencies. Since each discipline or agency has biases and limitations, the effective planner must first identify, and then compensate for, these flaws in the information process (see McHarg and Clarke, this volume). Many planners, however, accept technical information uncritically, thus building into the planning system the limitations of each separate informational input.[1]

For example, the role of engineering in the planning process is the provision of technical alternatives which indicate cost-output functions. As the primary input into the formation of any plan it generates several structural alternatives for flood control, irrigation, water treatment plants, and the like, and indicates their feasibility.

The inherent limitation in engineering input is that not all relevant alternatives will be presented in the planning process. Within a relatively narrow frame of reference, alternatives will be discussed, but very often alternatives which represent a significant departure from traditional engineering thought, or which are contrary to vested interests, are omitted entirely from consideration. This particular limitation of the engineering mentality is presently being encountered in cases of power plant location. Proposed plans simply state that there are no feasible alternatives either to the location site or the type of generation unit; frequently they do not even question the described "need" for the proposed project. A specific example of this is the current controversy over sources of cooling water for power generation. The power industry continues to assert that once-through cooling systems are the only economically feasible ones, whereas others have indicated that wet cooling towers with mechanized or natural draft will increase generation costs by less than 5 percent, and that even dry cooling towers are feasible (Hauser, 1970).

---

[1] The disciplines discussed below and the associated examples are intended to be illustrative and do not comprise a comprehensive review of all sources of technical intelligence.

The role of ecology in the planning process is to indicate a range of possible changes in and damage to the environment resulting from human activity. Often emphasized are such factors as biomass yield, species essential to a productive cycle, and the effect of such factors as trophic web and spatial distribution on the stability and productivity of species populations (Watt, 1968; Richerson and others, this volume).

Two common biases found in ecological studies are the presentation of data as if they represented clearly defined causal relationships, and the absence of marginal analysis. In water resource planning, the first is exemplified by a tendency to say categorically that human interference will be destructive of marine life when in fact some species may gain as a result while others lose (see Hagan and Roberts, this volume). For example, in Sweden, construction of dams and regulation of impounded waters caused the grayling population to increase and the numbers of pike to decrease (Watt, 1968). Second, a failure to rank the significance or admit the separability of various impacts of a project precludes any basis for evaluating their relative importance. This frequently results in an exaggeration of the actual damage done by some human impacts, as evident in the issue of thermal pollution at Calvert Cliffs in Maryland. The surface area of the tidal segment adjacent to the power plant (that is, the segment which will be affected by the thermal discharge) is 37,000 acres. Of these 37,000 acres only 4,890 acres (or 13 percent) will have an excess temperature of $0.5°$ F and only 5.5 acres (or 0.015 percent) will have an excess temperature of $3°$ F (Seliger, 1971). Thus the significant impact of the project is limited to a very small area of Chesapeake Bay, although many concerned ecologists tend to imply the opposite.

Public adminstration ought to provide information about the processes and means of implementing alternative plans. It should also suggest modifications of institutional structures which might involve either resturc-turing the mandates of existing organizations or creating new ones.

One past limitation of public administration has been its tendency to assume that existing bureaucracies can change or can perform new tasks when in reality a new organization is necessary for effective and responsive implementation of a new plan. An existing organization often fails to implement a development plan for several reasons. First, if a plan adds to the costs of an autonomous agency without bringing in additional resources—or if it adds very little to the agency's resources—that agency will usually not engage in vigorous implementation of the plan. Second, agencies which are highly specialized, and which have been successful in procuring resources in the past on the basis of their functional specialities, will not strongly espouse programs which do not draw upon or enhance these specialities. Third, existing agencies must maintain at least three external relationships—with interest groups, with other organizations desiring to occupy the same behavior space, and with the appropriate legislative body (see Fox, this volume). If implementation of a plan interferes significantly with any of these relationships, then the agency will tend not to promote it.

Although most other disciplines primarily contribute an array of alternatives to the planning process, economics proposes to offer in addition a technique for evaluating and ordering these alternatives, and the relative tradeoffs between them. Obviously, the quality of such an evaluation will first depend on the sufficiency of the alternatives presented to economists by the various other disciplines. But the benefits to be gained from economic evaluation are also limited by the bias of the discipline toward an overriding concern for efficiency, as determined and expressed in a market system.

This leads first to an assumption that market values can be imputed to all goods and services related to an alternative that is being evaluated. If the market fails to establish a price, then alternative procedures are devised for determining a proxy for market value. The imputing of market values to recreation experiences by expenditure or imputed demand curves is the most common example in the water planning field. The values are interpreted as if they measure the worth of a recreation experience in the same manner as do actual prices. Their inclusion as a measure of efficiency is misleading since they are not equivalent to market prices and may be significant over- or under-estimates of the real values. This problem frequently arises when planners try to weigh the gains of preservation against those of development. Since most preservation-related activities, unlike development, have no market value, a traditional benefit cost analysis might well conclude that preservation is a cost to society rather than a benefit. The applicability of such analysis for evaluating and ranking alternatives is therefore limited (see also Allee and Chapman, this volume).

Second, economics is too often concerned with the efficient allocation of resources to the exclusion of a concern for equitable distribution. Asking who receives the benefits is quite often as important as how to increase the size of the benefits. Too often, water development plans as they are now formulated and implemented involve a regressive distribution of benefits away from low income farmers or urban residents.

Given the limitations of the disciplines from which it draws data, one of the prime functions of water resource planning should be to correct the biases of this technical intelligence and to place it in perspective, so that discernible alternatives and their associated consequences can be made available to decision-making bodies. Where necessary, planning should introduce equity considerations and relevant technical and institutional alternatives, and should limit the tendency of disciplines like economics and ecology to overstate their case. Quite often this type of evaluative intelligence is available, but the gains and losses as presented in plan formulations are so unclear as to render the information useless. Although this is seldom done, planning should structure and integrate technical intelligence so that the relevant range of impact is perceived by the decision-making body.

This crucial interdisciplinary synthesis is sometimes made more difficult in the water resource field because such planning has been dominated by several bureaucracies. Any coordination of information and effort thus involves political tradeoffs among the different interests, constituencies, objectives and values of the various agencies. In such instances, "interdisciplinary synthesis" takes the form of "interagency cooperation," and results only in a compromise of agency positions (Lyle Craine, personal commun.).

Two extreme cases, nuclear-fueled power plant siting and airport expansion, illustrate the necessity of integrating and structuring technical intelligence so that discernible alternatives between preservation and development emerge for public evaluation. The first concerns the siting of a nuclear-fueled power plant at Calvert Cliffs, Maryland on the Chesapeake Bay, a situation in which no discernible alternatives emerged or were were made clear in the controversy between preservation and development. During the planning stages of this project there was almost a total absence of information coordination, even among various state agencies responsible for providing such data to the decision makers. The Departments of Health and Natural Resources and the Public Service Commission each generated information about plant siting and its effects, but the findings of all the parties concerned were never structured or integrated until long after construction was underway and public controversy had grown vociferous.

The second case concerns expansion of Kennedy Airport into Jamaica Bay, where several feasible alternatives were presented to the public (National Academy of Science, 1971). In this instance, the National Academy of Science assembled specialists in several fields and focused their attention on one problem with the mandate to come up with a series of recommendations. The interaction of members of a multidisciplinary team upon one issue forced the integration of several different academic perspectives rather than allowing them to stand as independent reports. In this situation, there were obvious choices between preservation and expansion, and reasons were presented for preferring certain alternatives.

Although these examples are oversimplifications of the actual situations, they do indicate the importance of structuring and integrating the diverse technical intelligence so that discernible alternatives about the tradeoffs between development and preservation are perceived by decision makers. To achieve this in the future, planners should adopt the following strategies: invest more effort in generating alternatives outside of the organizational constraints of the information-generating disciplines (engineering, ecology, etc.); and evaluate alternatives more realistically, correcting for the disciplinary biases of informational input.

PUBLIC COMMUNICATION OF TECHNICAL INTELLIGENCE

Although evaluation of alternatives is an integral and vital part of plan formulation, the ultimate determination of the most acceptable configuration of preservation- and development-oriented alternatives lies with the general public. For this reason, the final step in the planning process involves communicating a plan to the public for evaluation and approval. Only thus can planners determine whether or not their proposals are truly responsive to societal objectives. It is, therefore, an important function of planning to maintain effective communications with decision makers and with the general public.

The strategy is often ignored, however, so that organizations such as federal or private agencies may develop and even implement plans for water resource projects with minimal consultation (particularly in the pre-

liminary stages) with state and local authorities (see Scott, this volume). Similarly, both the planners and decision makers frequently fail to inform the general public, or even those people directly affected by a proposed project, of its true nature and impact. Sometimes preliminary hearings are held during which the plan is described in a very general way and crude estimates—if any—are given of its potential impact. Such hearings, however, may only be held if the public is already sufficiently informed about the project to express vociferous concern over its impact, or to demand that hearings be held. Even if such hearings are held, the final plans can end up very different from the original proposal described to the public. But the general public is seldom explicitly made aware of any such changes, for example, by the reopening of hearings.

These problems in communications are largely a function of the fact, mentioned earlier, that the planning process presently works in reverse. Instead of sifting through alternatives for an optimal balance between preservation and development, planning agencies begin with the advocacy of a single project and work from there to provide proper justification for the plan and obtain social or authoritative approval for its implementation.

In the field of water resource management, there are two types of projects which typify these communication gaps in the planning process with their consequent problems. The first includes multipurpose flood control-recreation projects constructed by the army Corps of Engineers; the second are the dams and pump storage sites built by power companies to supply electricity for their consumers.

In the case of the Corps, each project is usually presented to the local populace and to local levels of government (that is, state, county, and municipal) with the usual advantages of flood control, recreation facilities, economic development, water supply and quality (low flow augmentation), and adjacent land management described in general and beneficent terms. Information such as unfavorable impacts or irreversible damages are seldom explained fully or are minimized in public presentation. These issues often may not even be fully investigated by the Corps, on the grounds that they involve matters outside its jurisdiction. Until recently, these included such considerations as environmental quality. But in a recent report by the House Committee on Government Operations, historical and legal documentation was described which makes clear that the Corps has a broad range of responsibilities to protect environmental quality in all areas under its jurisdiction (U. S. Congress, 1970).

More important, the relationship of a particular project in question to other projects in the area is seldom discussed by the Corps. The possible or even probably interrelation of nearby projects may not be disclosed, so that the ultimate impact of any one project is often greater or less than anticipated by the community. For example, in southeastern West Virginia, three dams were constructed in the New River-Kanahwa River Basin, each of which was to provide flood control, water quality, and recreational facilities to the area. However, not one of these projects fulfills the predictions of the planners. In fact, in dry periods, drawdowns in one reservoir may seriously impair the recreational and water supply capacities of the other sites; in rainy periods, entire stretches of the river are unprotected (U. S. Federal Power Commission, 1970). More coordinated dissemination of information and more complete disclosure of the limitations of the proposed projects might have resulted in less support for the projects as constructed, and greater pressure for a more effective and comprehensive project. But such actions were effectively prevented both by compartmentalized communications and by time lags in disclosure of the separate plans.

Another common problem is the tendency of planners in explaining a project to impute all benefits of the project to all affected areas. Often, only after the plan has been approved

and constructed do residents on the shores of a reservoir behind a dam designed to provide low flow augmentation find that their water supply at times dwindles significantly to provide water quality benefits downstream.

The second type of communications problem often results when interchanges between water project planners and interested federal agencies are far better than those between planners and their local constituents. While this might be expected in the case of an agency like the Corps, it is often true of private planning agencies as well. Bureaucrats relatively removed from a project area frequently have access to far more information about a proposed project than do the people to be affected. For example, consider the selection of dam sites. Except for those dams constructed by TVA, Bonneville, or the Bureau of Reclamation, most sites are planned and constructed by private companies with approval from the Federal Power Commission. The process of gaining this approval is a political one—the applicant not only must show the merits of the project itself, but also must garner support for the plan from "experts" who will testify on its behalf. Unfortunately, there are inherent drawbacks in this procedure, most of which can also be identified in the planning and constructing of other public projects. These problems usually are direct results of the narrow project-advocacy role which planners and public decision makers most frequently play, instead of exploring alternatives to implement broad public goals. The result is a limitation of communications at all levels of the decision-making process.

A typical example of this process is a recent case before the Federal Power Commission to grant a license to a private power company for a pumped storage site on the Virginia-North Carolina state line (U. S. Federal Power Commission, 1970). The plans for the project were initiated more than seven years ago and presented at that time to the residents of the affected counties. The original project design called for a simple pumped storage dam, and was approved by the three counties and the two states directly involved. In the process of gathering approval from successively higher layers of government, however, the plan was considerably modified. At the request of the Department of the Interior, the design was changed to include recreational facilities, economic development benefits and —most significantly—flood control and low flow augmentation for the downstream areas of the New and Kanahwa rivers. Thus did the state of West Virginia become affected by the proposed project, although the state's officials were not consulted, nor apprised of the impacts of the plan on their state until after the original hearings had been closed. Similarly, the counties originally affected had not been consulted regarding the expansion of the project. Furthermore, no disclosures whatever had been made concerning the possible environmental impacts of the proposed project. As a result, considerable confusion and resentment arose on several levels, and the subsequent controversy delayed construction of the dam, occasioning significant additional costs to the power company.

The political process of obtaining a license for a water project from the proper authorities sometimes leads not only to neglectful communications as described above, but also at times to deliberate exclusion of opponents to the proposal from participation in the planning process. The Corps of Engineers has admitted in Congressional testimony that they frequently tend to dismiss or discount known citizen opposition to proposed projects, and sometimes deny hearings to such groups (Boerger, 1969). Such incidents are even more serious than mere lack of communication between planners and decision-makers and the general public. They represent deliberate attempts to prevent such communication and to frustrate community involvement in the planning process in order to gain approval for a plan even though it may not be responsive to public policy or interest. Citizens should not be denied the opportunity to participate in the planning process when it directly affects them, on the grounds that they lack technical expertise, political credentials, or financial resources to commission expert studies, lawyers, etc. If their objections are based on misinformation, this also reflects a failure on the part of the planners. However, the questions of the public should be answered rather than stifled. Otherwise, such practices will effectively kill community support not only for the particular plan at issue, but also for planning and planners in general and seriously impede the effectiveness of the planning process (also see Ross, in this volume).

The importance of these case histories is not to cast aspersions on the parties involved, for they are, unfortunately, all too typical. Plans made by consulting some of the interested but not all of the affected parties cannot really be considered responsive to the public interest (see Fox, and McCloskey and Scott, this volume). Such a process rejects the planners' role of exploring alternatives and evaluating the tradeoffs and impacts of each. The failure to communicate whatever technical information is available regarding proposed plans compounds this abdication of public responsiveness and responsibility on the part of the planners. Moreover, such an approach does little to popularize implementation of the proposed plan. Whether or not a plan devised in the public interest is detrimental to some of the affected parties in a sense is not relevant. At times the best of plans may require compensation of private loss for a public benefit. What is crucial, however, if planning is to be effective, is that both the public and the local decision makers be kept fully aware of the true nature and full impact of the proposed plan as it is developed, and of the tradeoffs between alternative plans. This then, would give rise to public debate with the hope that practical and intelligent decisions could be made.

We suggest the adoption of three strategies which will improve communications between planners and their constitutents:

(1) full disclosure of information; (2) community involvement at all levels of the planning process; and (3) a commitment to comprehensive and active planning. Full disclosure of technical intelligence and community involvement in the planning process will increase public awareness of possible alternative projects and their impacts, and increase their commitment to plan implementation. In cases of power plant location, such as the Calvert Cliffs experience cited above, more frank and open communications by the planners before construction was begun might well have averted much of the vigorous opposition of those who believe that the public was given no alternative or voice in the matter. Similarly, a commitment to assertive planning on the part of the planning organization in behalf of the public interest will often result in better implementation. Too often the aim of planning is viewed merely as the presentation of technical alternatives and advocacy of special interest projects, rather than modification of the societal guidance system. The importance of such a commitment is evidenced in the successful implementation of the plan of the San Francisco Bay Conservation and Development Commission in 1969. An essential ingredient to its success "was the original commitment to the idea that the purpose of the plan was to bring effective control over future actions on the Bay's shoreline rather than planning for the sake of the plan only" (Schoop and Herten, 1971).

SUMMARY

Present planning practices in the water resource field tend to advocate narrowly focused or special interest projects, concentrating on gaining approval for their implementation. Ideally, planners should begin by exploring various means of implementing public goals and the tradeoffs between them, as presented by various technical experts, synthesizing this information into discernible alternatives which they communicate to the appropriate decision makers and the affected parties. We suggest that in the future, water resource planners concentrate on designing discrete alternative balances between preservation and development, and make serious efforts to improve evaluation of alternatives by planners themselves, by decision makers, and by the general public. These innovations should increase the possibility that concerned parties would grasp the implications of competing plans for preservation and development and would participate accordingly in an intelligent and positive manner. Water resource planning then would become—as it should be—effective, responsive, and actively normative.

References

Boerger, Col. F. C. 1969. Statement at Hearing before a Subcommittee of the Committee on Government Operations, "The Nation's Estuaries in San Francisco Bay and Delta, California," May 15, 1969, pp. 125–126.

Hauser, L. G. 1970. "Cooling Water Sources for Power Generation." ASCE National Water Resources Engineering Meeting, 1970. *Meeting Report 1102*.

National Academy of Sciences and National Academy of Engineers, *Jamaica Bay and Kennedy Airport*, Washington, D. C., 1971.

Schoop, E. Jack and John Herten. 1971. "The San Francisco Bay Plan: Combining Policy with Police Power," *Journal of the American Institute of Planners*, 37 (January, 1971): 6.

Seliger, H. H. 1971. "Nuclear Power: Panacea or Pandora's Box." *The Charles Street Journal*, 1 (1) (February-March, 1971).

U. S. Congress. 1970. House Committee on Government Operations, Conservation and Natural Resources Subcommittee. March 18, 1970. "Our Waters and Wetlands: How the Corps of Engineers Can Help Prevent Their Destruction and Pollution," *House Report* No. 91–917.

U. S. Federal Power Commission. 1970. Hearings on Project 2317.

Watt, K. E. F. 1968. *Ecology and Resource Management*. McGraw-Hill Book Company, New York.

CHAPTER 18

Most of America's larger cities are located on the shores of oceans, lakes, or rivers, which offer the residents of these cities many potential opportunities for recreation and aesthetic amenities. In many cases, however, no public access to these shorelands exists, their recreational and aesthetic potential has been destroyed, and their condition may actually detract from the quality of urban life.

For many reasons planners traditionally have been frustrated in their efforts to represent the public interest in the control of shoreline access and development. The most important factors in this have been the historical pattern of waterfront development for industry, and a lack of regional planning and effective, representative regional institutions. Fragmented political jurisdictions, private industrial ownership of waterfront sites, and conflicting, often outdated, land uses are other important limiting factors in realizing the potential of urban waterfronts for public use. The author concludes that coordination of development plans and laws, replacement of outmoded and unused waterfront development, and stronger control powers for zoning and subdivision are basic requirements for reform. Federal legislation is needed to strengthen existing programs and to create more regional planning and political authorities.

WATER DEVELOPMENT AND URBAN RECREATION

Lois H. Scott

INTRODUCTION

Most of the current problems associated with providing shoreline recreational facilities in urban areas have their roots in the historical pattern of American urban development. Many cities have inherited a patchwork of jurisdictions and agencies that regulate their shorelines along with a complex array of private owners with title to adjacent dry land. The problem of urban water pollution is a legacy of previous industrial development of shoreline areas.

Urban residents generally lack any direct elective control of governmental decision making on waterfront use. They also lack opportunities for visual and physical access to shoreline areas. Boating, fishing, or swimming opportunities are often strictly limited or nonexistent, and in many cases recreationists would face health hazards from direct contact with the water.

Because of the work urban planners and many other professional groups have done with local and regional agencies, they have developed a concern with the use of land along urban waterfronts. Their concern, broadly, is the public interest in the waterfront, as distinguished from various private or special interests. Their special task is to articulate this concern into policy objectives for waterfront use.

The objectives most planners would support in relation to waterfronts are: (1) to provide for public enjoyment of waterfronts, through facilities such as parks, roadways, trails, viewpoints, vistas; (2) to retain the economic benefits of shipping and industrial activities along waterfronts; (3) to encourage shifts away from these activities if they are no longer economic; (4) to encourage shifts away from other land uses which may no longer be functional—such as obsolete military or naval installations—and to supersede them with new public uses; (5) to preserve natural resources, for example, water quality and shore contour; (6) to take advantage of a city's location near water, by relating city design to the view of the water, and thus providing visual relief from dense urban development.

The articulation of such concerns ideally becomes part of an adopted plan which, through appropriate zoning or administrative regulations, influences both governmental and private decisions. Zoning, for example, specifies and limits various land uses, and administrative regulations require that development proposals be reviewed by a planning commission. Limitations on powers to implement both plans and regulations reduces the effectiveness of planning commissions at a local level. Professional planners generally advise these lay commissions, whose decisions in turn are subject to veto by elected city councils or county boards of supervisors. Further, the fragmentation of jurisdictions and the number of other nonelected agencies that have stakes in waterfront development and use hinder the consistent application of plans and regulations. There may be a con-

sensus on the design concepts and principles of the plan, but the governmental units which are to adopt the plan are usually hesitant to surrender any of their powers to other units, even though this is often required if the plan is to be achieved. Where there has been effective progress in waterfront planning, the effort has usually been regional rather than local in scope and has involved interagency governmental coordination. A concern for environmental quality, in fact, has been a salient motivation for the formation of regional governments or, if regional government has not been feasible, of regional special-purpose agencies.

It is also necessary to consider critically the tools other than zoning or administrative regulations which planners may use as part of their advice to decision makers. At a local level, planners and planning commissions may advise political bodies on the capital budget. This may include expenditures for acquisition and development of shoreline parks, for port development, or for roads along the shoreline. The planners, of course, will have to consider the relative priority of such shoreline expenditures against other needs in the jurisdiction.

When it comes to money, however, the federal government, with its wide variety of financial assistance programs, is likely to have a strong influence on the local selection of projects. Planners often have a hand in the processing of grant proposals for such programs as urban renewal, flood control, or economic development of ports. Again, they face a multiplicity of uncoordinated federal programs and jurisdictions, which in their turn may be locally administered by diverse agencies: port authorities, redevelopment agencies, or the Army Corps of Engineers. Tax policy is another tool with strong potential, but so far it has not been used as a means of improving environmental quality.

Recent public awareness of environmental issues and the support the public has shown for clean, attractive waterfronts encourages planners to make efforts toward solving such problems. However, public awareness seems to be focused mainly on visible, physical manifestations of the problems, rather than on one of the basic factors that sustains them; namely, governmental organization.

The main recommendations made in this paper address the problems of governmental organization: in brief, substantial incentives for the use of regional approaches to problems which are regional in scope, and maximum coordination between the goals and administration of federal programs.

PROBLEMS FACED BY PLANNERS

Fragmented Political Units

The two basic problems for planners is providing recreational opportunities on urban waterfronts both involve spatial organization, but on different scales. The first is that of fragmented political units and their powers and jurisdictions. The second is the conflicting and often obsolete pattern of land ownership and land use. Both of these problems should be seen in the context of the relatively long history of American cities. Once-practical unit sizes for government agencies and ownership parcels have now become impractical.

Ironically, the political fragmentation comes from the pragmatic genius of American government. Each time a particular problem arose, a governmental entity was created to solve it. At a local level, port authorities were created to facilitate bond financing separate from other financial liabilities of the city government. Sometimes port authorities were chartered by the state and thus became responsive to another level of government. Many urban waterfronts traverse the boundaries of several cities that once were separate enough to justify their individual jurisdictions, but now have grown together both economically and socially.

At a regional level, state-chartered agencies regulating air or water quality generally exist independently of whatever regional government may have evolved. County governments, if they have jurisdiction over unincorporated shorelines, also become involved in waterfront administration. State governments play a major role as the source of legislation which enables planners to create yet other regulatory bodies and to suggest new regulatory measures. States may also be important clearing houses for federal assistance (although it is worth noting, as an example of fragmentation, that most large cities deal directly with Washington and even have staffs of "grantsmen," usually located in the City Manager's office rather than in the Planning Department).

The federal government has from its beginning profoundly influenced the shaping of waterfronts with its mandate to advance interstate commerce—first on water, then on rails, and now in air and on freeways. It has also regulated navigation, created national seashores and wildlife preserves, and funded hydroelectric and flood control projects, among others.

The complexity of the many governmental entities involved, together with the fact that most planners work for a city department which is only advisory to the city council or manager, compounds the problem of planning. But it remains the planner's responsibility to determine what action should be taken and to recommend, given the array of political units, how it can be done. It is safe to predict that the planner will advocate regional government as a means to rationalize and coordinate waterfront development, but he often has only limited power to generate such proposals if his base is in a municipal agency.

The second major problem for planning, land ownership along the shoreline, is also related to governmental structure. Originally the beds of navigable waterways were federal, but some of this area has been turned over to the states. For example, in California submerged parcels were often sold into private ownership, and adjacent dry land was usually allowed to become privately owned as well.

Conflicting or Obsolete Land Uses on Waterfronts: Historical Perspective

During the growth of American cities there also arose problems of patterns of ownership, land and water use, and development of industry and trade on the waterfront. All of these problems antedate the growth of city planning, as this is a profession that is only about fifty years old. With the possible exception of federal hydroelectric projects—whose setting is seldom an urban one—professional city planners have had little opportunity to allocate waterfront land "in the public interest," with fair shares for enterprise and individuals. Even with respect to hydroelectric projects, their powers have been very limited. Waterfront and shoreland in urban areas remain a complex of parcels, mostly private, often obsolete in function, and of marginal economic value.

Many of the cities that planners today seek to shape and revitalize owe their form to a proximity to water. In the historic urbanization pattern of the United States' described by Glaab (1963), most older American cities, including New York, Boston, Philadelphia and Cincinnati, to name a few, were founded and grew up as ports. In the eighteenth and early nineteenth centures, rivers provided the best means for movement to and from the hinterlands. Water access was an important factor in city growth, diminishing only as transportation technology improved and shifted the earlier advantages of port' cities to landlocked sites. Early in the nineteenth century federal funds were given to harbor and canal development to stimulate interstate commerce. Once installed, these facilities encouraged private investment in industrial wholesaling activities which, with the introduction of the steamboat,

opened the great rivers to the inland cities and promoted growth that heretofore had been reserved for coastal settlements.

Shifts in transportation caused changes in land use. As these shifts occurred many former uses were rendered obsolete by changes in accessability and land values. From 1840 on, railroads were connected to ports and lined the older harbors, canals, and rivers. Although rail transport meant that industrial activities could be dispersed, many remained in waterfront areas. Water was sometimes part of their manufacturing process, and access to water transportation was a useful bargaining point in negotiating freight rates. Still, the economic supremacy of the coastal port cities was weakened as the rail network spread west. Cities with older waterfronts, which at first were transshipping points for basic commodities, gradually became places where such commodities, particularly those high in bulk, could be incorporated into the manufacturing process. Water-using manufacturing activities included oil refining, steel manufacturing, and chemical processing. Waterways provided transport, water for steam generation, and outlets for waste disposal. As a result, water pollution greatly increased.

The railroad rate structure had some impact on waterfront industrial location. There was a tendency for industries with high-value commodities to shift entirely to railroad transportation (which was usually faster) and to relocate away from the water. The "bulk commodity" industries that remained often used large amounts of space inefficiently (Solzman, 1966). Increasing city tax rates also tended to push mobile industries out to suburban, nonwaterfront locations.

In many cases railroads were given eminent domain, or grants of land and cash, by state legislatures. Their location today along many urban shorelines, based on earlier special advantages, seems unwarranted, but so many regulatory agencies are involved that obsolete rail lines tend to stay in place, even when abandoned.

Before the wide use of streetcars and the automotive era, housing was built on or near industrial waterfronts. Often, these districts became "blighted" neighborhoods when economically disadvantaged, and minority populations succeeded the original inhabitants after alternative cheap housing was made accessible to white working-class people by better transportation. Transfer of ownership, coupled with rental of some of the old residences as "income" property, has until recently kept these neighborhoods relatively weak politically, so that shoreline park development has tended to be neglected.

Railroads, which often preceded housing, were supplemented by shoreline freeways which often removed ("cleared") some residential developments for their rights of way, and severed inland residential areas from the waterfront. Such freeways—and there are many—have accelerated the shift from manufacturing to distribution activities in old waterfront areas, and this in turn has worsened the conflicts of "mixed use." Commodity transfer by truck and rail are particularly inimical to pedestrian- and child-related neighborhood uses.

Another pattern of residential land use along waterfronts is the result of the wealthy residents rather than the poor ones. Luxury residential developments spread in many cities to nearby high ground or along lakes, bays, rivers, and ocean fronts where such areas were flood-free and not industrial. This housing often remained as estates for the elite, and as cities grew the owners usually forbade public access, except on a fortuitous occasion when a public benefactor donated his estate as a park.

ADJUSTING LAND USES AND DESIGNING LIVABLE CITIES: A CRITICAL REVIEW OF LOCAL PLANNING TOOLS

Summary

The history of contemporary planning is closely linked with that of landscape architecture. Parks and greenways were early seen both as buffers and as relief to urban development. During the twentieth century the scope of planning has broadened to include consideration of the circulation system of the city (streets, freeways, rails, transits, even trails and paths), public facilities, (schools, libraries, police and fire stations), and the layout of working and living areas of the city. The attitudes of urban dwellers and their choices in these issues have become increasingly important to planners; but the capacity of planners to measure these attitudes, or to get a widespread response to planning work, is limited to what is expressed through conventional political channels. A vital aspect of all planning should be consideration of the physical resources of an area, including water (see McHarg and Clarke, in this volume). As mentioned previously, however, the logical geographic units for consideration of resources are often not local, but regional. The idea of a regional agency for planning problems, which flowered in the 1930s, is exemplified by the Tennessee Valley Authority, but the programs of such agencies have since proven difficult to integrate with others.

As the scope of regional planning and government continues to evolve, the form of the urban general plan has become more or less standard, with certain associated regulations, such as zoning and subdivision, becoming well accepted. Tax incentives, capital budgeting, urban renewal, and "Model Cities" programs have also recently become means for implementing general plans. Aspects of the Model Cities approach, particularly its coordination of diverse programs and attention to public opinion, have become important models for planners. Revenue sharing procedures for larger geographic units may be one of the legacies of this program.

The following section reviews the use of these various tools, and provides the primary basis for recommendations made in the final section.

Park Acquisition: A Direct Approach to Plan Implementation

At the turn of the century, community "elites" concerned with planning generally advocated public recreation and other "progressive" causes. The public recreation movement, led by such pioneers as Frederick Law Olmstead, was in some ways a precursor to planning. Today, more than seventy years later, the advocates of recreation and conservation (although not as well represented on municipal planning commissions as such self-interested parties as real estate professionals, engineers, and aspiring politicians) have again stimulated awareness of urban recreational needs.

Landscape architecture applied to a city scape at the turn of the twentieth century was often called "civic art." It prompted a concern with boulevards, parks, statuary, fountains, arches, and adornments. In a few cities, like Chicago and Seattle, the public recreation and "civic art" movements influenced development of waterfront parks. In crowded cities like Chicago and New York, parks were seen as green relief from tenements and "industrial blight." At the time this movement was in vogue, much of the shoreland affected was of only marginal industrial character. Thus, the waterfront element of the plan for Chicago and its support for funding by the people of that city is one of the successes of early planning.

Parks, of course, were no real solution to most urban problems, notably slums, and how much symptomatic relief they provided is debatable. Many of the parks were valuable mainly to the middle and upper classes. Residential developments contiguous to new parks recognized the value of the amenity and were priced for upper income groups.

Local General Plans — Advisory Documents

A widely used planning tool is the general plan which shows in broad terms planners' recommendations for future urban land uses.

Parks, including those in waterfront areas, are shown as part of the land use scheme. If the waterfront is already a "working" area, it is likely to remain so in the general plan. If the plan is recent, or if it was prepared sixty years ago in the era of civic art, there may be emphasis on recreational access—an esplanade in 1910, a marina in 1970.

The general plan, among its other uses, should be (but often is not) the basis of local capital improvement expenditures. Capital improvements usually have their base in the property tax, but they are increasingly supported by shared federal and state revenues. The tempting opportunity to be awarded federal money skews local priorities, and the general plan may not be implemented in the sequence intended. Starting with the Economic Opportunity Act of 1964, the Economic Development Act of 1965, and Demonstration Cities legislation in 1966-1967, federal assistance has helped to shift priorities toward the poor. Yet the support for capital improvements, including new street access to waterfronts, parking or sitting facilities, and landscaping, has traditionally come from home-owning, middle- and upper-income voters. Decision making on expenditures is in the hands of local city councils, to whom the planner is only advisory. It is worth noting that most waterfront development proposals of the 1950s and 1960s were for parks, yacht harbors (marinas), and commercial recreation development geared to middle- and upper-class populations.

However, the scope (and the audience) for general plans seems to be changing. The idea of a policy rather than a general plan has gained favor; the city is now thought to be too complex for a two-dimensional map. A policy can go beyond stating where certain activities will be located; it can better handle questions of timing and peoples' needs, which may not be spatially distributed.

When, in 1967, California legislation added to general plans an element that would provide housing for all economic segments of the community, planners soon found that policies for housing did not fit neatly on a map. In 1970, also in California, two new mandatory elements of general plans were added for open space and conservation. Linked to the requirement for open space is one for the adoption of open space zoning. However, penalties for not implementing such plans have not yet been devised. For housing, the Department of Housing and Urban Development made priorities for certain grant programs, such as water and sewers, conditional on local and regional adoption of housing elements. But because HUD programs are such a small part of all federal assistance to cities, this strategy is not effective.

Zoning and Subdivision Ordinances

Regulatory powers (at a local, county, or state level) are the strongest tools that planners have. These are the traditional tools of zoning and subdivision ordinances. Unfortunately, they only limit what may be developed, rather than bring about the desired developments. However, zoning around the margins of lakes and bays not used for industry has been a fairly effective conservation tool, even when adopted late in the sequence of population growth (see Yanggen, in this volume). A regulatory procedure which may be preferable to regular zoning is to review the uses of waterfront land case by case by administrations or planning commissions. Such a procedure has been successful for the San Francisco Bay Conservation and Development Commission.

Subdivision ordinances, because they pertain to new housing, are not likely to be invoked for urban waterfronts. However, a requirement for public access in all new shoreline subdivisions was ordered into law by the California State Legislature in 1970.

A regulatory tool which combines aspects of both zoning and subdivision—called "planned unit development" or "planned area districting"—can be utilized in urban water-

fronts. Within such a district, there can be a mixture of activities, types of housing, and commercial uses. Usually there is a tradeoff of density incentives for open space and commercial uses. Usually there is a tradeoff of density incentives for open space and other desired features between developers and regulators. Since this device is most often used for undeveloped land, it can be adapted to an urban waterfront where cooperating landowners can be brought together. However, the difficulty of arranging such a consortium short of redevelopment has limited the use of this flexible regulatory device.

Tax Incentives

Another means by which planners can influence waterfront development and conservation is through recommendations on tax policy. Often, however, the power of taxation that may be influential in a local waterfront area resides in the state or federal government; hence, reforms must take this into account. For a local government, the hope of an increased tax base (through increases in assessed value) will often lead to favoring industrial or commercial land uses over recreational uses or conservation. From a practical standpoint, the best solution may often be to combine uses, some of which produce tax revenues and some of which do not; the opportunity for a lower tax rate through deferment or limitation in proposed development may lead a landowner to favor land conservation in his decisions.

Several kinds of incentives can be used to induce landowners to retain or provide undeveloped shoreline land for public use: (1) tax exemption for dedication of portions of land or water for public use or for conservation; (2) preferential assessment for marshy areas retained as such. (California's Williamson Act, providing for preferential assessment of agricultural land placed by contract in an agricultural preserve, was amended in 1969 to include marsh areas as well.); (3) tax deferral for land remaining in "open" land use until development occurs. This device tends to reduce the market value of the land when it is removed from open use because of the large tax bill which will then be due; the low price, however, may encourage its purchase for development.

Capital Budgeting

A "capital improvement program" is a formal method for programming large-scale physical improvement projects, such as streets, public buildings, schools, and parks over a period of several years. It integrates funding for the projects, and provides a review of timing, location, and financing. Financing is usually both local and federal, through local taxes and bonds and federal grants and loans. Opportunities for coordination of certain projects, such as a combined library, school and playground, public building and park, or a port with recreational facilities, often are more apparent after review in such a program. Ideally, planners should be included in the capital budgeting process, and should have an opportunity to advocate capital projects that will implement adopted plans, including those for waterfront areas. Allocation of money and assigning of priorities for particular projects should follow a political consensus on the needs of the community. If the needs of the community are well expressed in widely read planning documents, then planning professionals will be influential. If there is no plan and no consensus, the capital budgeting will be a less rational exercise.

Urban Renewal

Beginning in 1949, clearance of blighted areas could be accomplished through the use of eminent domain by a local redevelopment agency and with federal financial assistance. Parks and open spaces in redevelopment areas could be credited to cities as part of the local share of project costs. (The federal government bore two-thirds of the cost; the local government one-third.) Unfortunately, the residents of these areas usually were not the beneficiaries of renewal. Often they were displaced and given some relocation help, but then left to face a scarcity of housing because their former housing had been removed without being replaced. After many reforms in the program, more relocation benefits and guarantees for replacement housing are now built into it.

Although redevelopment is usually accomplished not by planners but by administrative specialists together with special interest groups in central business districts, many planners advocate the use of this technique for urban rebuilding.

Apart from the many other problems of redevelopment, open spaces and parks in project areas have sometimes been criticized for lacking warmth and proper human scale, notwithstanding the provision of new views of water for dwellers in redevelopment highrises. Few renewal areas have been directly on waterfronts. Where they have been proposed for waterfronts (Sacramento, Seattle) a newly fashionable concern for historic sites appears to be more important (to the redevelopers) than the human populations of the waterfront.

However imperfect, renewal remains a potent tool for the rationalization of fragmented ownership by amassing developable parcels.

Model Cities: A Paradigm for Coordination

The Model Cities program is a tool by which planners, with the help of Model Cities planning grants, can pull together a number of state and federal assistance programs, thus supplementing or creating new services and providing physical improvement not previously available to a particular area of a city.

The focus is on a particular geographic unit—usually a low income community within a larger city. The stress of Model Cities planning is on more than the physical improvements that an urban renewal or local area plan would provide; it emphasizes a wide range of social and economic needs. However, since the Department of Housing and Urban Development is the parent federal agency for this program, some stress is laid on physical improvements for which HUD grants are available, such as open space acquisition. Model Cities funds from HUD can also be used by local programs to "match" local shares of assistance programs from other federal agencies. Another innovative aspect of the program is to require involvement of local citizens, particularly in the determination of priorities for treatment of locally defined problems.

Planners usually find a general shortage of recreational facilities in low income areas. Residents of these areas may have priorities for their neighborhoods other than more recreational space. But to administrators and politicians, open space will often be an attractive part of the package for the first or second "action" year of a Model Cities program, because physical changes are visible and gratifying and bring tangible credit to elected officials.

The Model Cities program can "sign off" or review HUD grants to other agencies within the Model City's boundaries. This seemingly innocuous power actually gives Model Cities programs a substantial lever by which to control a portion of the program of other agencies or to stop what they consider to be an undesirable program. But at present this power does not extend to federal water development programs except those administered by HUD.

Of the 150 or more Model Cities only a few have waterfronts, although many are near water. Examples of projects relating to waterfronts which have been proposed in Model Cities are: control of flooding (by the Corps of Engineers) to promote community development; organization of local economic development corporations capable of undertaking commercial recreation development; applications for designation as a national seashore; applications for open space acquisition on shorelines; application for Economic Development Administration (Department of Commerce) funds for port development; relocation of a former racially impacted school to a waterfront marsh area next to a Model Neighborhood so that this school could become a center for outdoor education for an entire school district.

Model Cities has become a pattern for a form of revenue sharing in which local citizens, with the help of planners, determine priorities for programs with a careful eye to the existing categorical grants available. As the revenue-sharing concept emerges, practice in pulling together ("coordinating") diverse federal programs, and in some cases setting up new locally based programs, will be valuable to the urban areas that were involved in Model Cities projects.

REGIONAL APPROACHES TO SHORELINE PLANNING

Shoreline Planning as a Function of Regional Government

Regional government is widely proclaimed as a solution to the problems that arise from competition among multiple local, state, and federal agencies. But in some respects a regional government simply increases the number of interest groups with which the implementation of a regional plan must contend. The more comprehensive and ambitious the regional plan, the greater the number of special interests and agencies involved, and hence the greater the difficulty in accomplishing anything.

The fact that the Bureau of the Budget designates voluntary regional councils of governments or regional planning agencies as "clearinghouses" for the review of various

TABLE 1

Waterfront Programs of Federal Agencies

Agriculture Department
    Financial assistance to small towns and rural groups for water projects
    Watershed development and flood protection projects

Commerce Department
    Development of ports
    Economic development districts
    Grants/loans for public works and development facilities
    Public works and economic development
    State marine schools

Defense Department
    Beach erosion control
    Drainage improvement
    Flood control
    Flood, hurricane, and abnormal tide protection
    Hydroelectric power development
    Limited water resources development projects
    Navigation in rivers and harbors
    Recreation facilities at federal water resources projects
    Water supply

Health, Education, and Welfare
    Solid waste programs

Housing and Urban Development
    Advance acquisition of land
    Historic preservation grants
    Model Neighborhoods in demonstration cities
    Neighborhood facilities
    Open space land
    Public facility loans
    Urban beautification
    Urban mass transportation
    Urban planning assistance
    Urban renewal projects
    Water and sewer facilities

Interior Department
    Outdoor recreation assistance
    Real property for public parks
    Water resources investigations and small reclamation project loans (Bureau of Reclamation)

Transportation Department
    Airport development
    Coast Guard services
    Highway beautification
    Highway planning and construction

Federal Power Commission

General Services Administration
    Disposal of surplus federal real property

---

federal assistance programs (for a listing of various federal programs concerning waterfronts, see Table 1) is a step toward coordination. Such coordination ideally should have as a frame of reference an adequate regional plan with appropriate streambelt, shoreline, and floodplain elements, and allocations of recreational lands according to need. Unfortunately, not all federal programs concerning water come under the review of clearinghouses and sometimes the clearinghouses themselves seem to serve only as a means to speed the flow of federal assistance to their members, who continue in other respects to guard the prerogatives of home rule.

Although it may be hard to influence water-related land use directly with a regional plan (most traditional land use controls continue to be administered locally), concern for water quality has been a strong force in pulling together embryonic forms of urban metropolitan governments, as in Seattle's "Metro" (see Edmondson in this volume), and to a lesser degree the government of Toronto, Canada (Canada having many of the same problems as the United States), and Dade County, Florida. Water quality and air pollution within water and air sheds are widely acknowledged as problems of regional scope. The pressure for their solution will continue to favor development of regional forms of government.

Regional Special Purpose Agencies and Water Planning

An alternative approach, which uses the region as an economic base, consists of the formation of a region-wide special purpose agency related to water. Recreation, per se, has generally not been the focus of such special purpose agencies. Two examples of such agencies are the Tennessee Valley Authority, formed in the 1930s, and the San Francisco Bay Conservation and Development Commission, formed in the late 1960s.

TVA in particular is often regarded as a commendable model for comprehensive planning on a regional basis, but early in its history the agency compromised much of its ability to attain public policy goals in order to come to terms with entrenched and politically shrewd local interests. Selznick (1966, Chapter 6) describes the controversy in the TVA project over creation of a protective strip of public waterfront land to permit the realization of opportunities for public use. The issue of whether such a broad land acquisition policy would carry out the purpose of the Act establishing TVA was not resolved in the beginning 1940s because minimal shoreline was acquired. Further, in the four decades since its founding, the mission of TVA has come increasingly to be defined in terms of the technologically exacting and economically visible task of generating electric power, and its ability to serve as a vehicle for comprehensive planning has been diminished greatly as a result.

The TVA was a federal effort; the San Francisco Bay Conservation and Development Commission was first organized as a study commission by the California State Legislature. Its task was to formulate a plan for the shoreline land uses of San Francisco Bay, which is surrounded by a number of municipalities and counties. It was later given interim regulatory powers over fill projects in the Bay. With subsequent adoption of strong public support for the Bay Plan (which gives much consideration both to public access to economically important water-related land uses), the regulatory powers were made permanent by another act of the legislature. This special purpose regional agency was able to regulate activities that the regional voluntary associations of governments in the Bay Area could not have regulated. Through the composition of the BCDC board, a cross section of local, state, and federal agencies act on regulatory issues but not on funding of federal grant programs. A separate, voluntary "Association of Bay Area Governments" attempts to mediate in this area. The strength of the special purpose agency, its efficiency in accomplishing limited tasks, is also its weakness. It controls only one aspect of water and land use (land fill) and only indirectly does it influence the expenditure of money in capital budgets, except as permits for land fill would be required.

POLICY RECOMMENDATIONS

1. Federal water development and conservation programs, including those of the Federal Power Commission, Bureau of Reclamation, and Corps of Engineers should be consolidated and coordinated.

2. Provision of public access should be made a condition of federal assistance programs in shoreline areas, particularly for the departments of Defense, Commerce, and Housing and Urban Development.

3. Environmental impact statements, required at federal, some state (e.g., California), and local levels under the National Environmental Policy Act of 1969 (42 U.S.C. 4321) and other laws, should also consider the potential for public access in each project.

4. Shoreline and coastal regulatory elements should be required in general, regional, and state plans under state planning enabling laws when geographically relevant. Such elements should review the potential for public access, and be correlated with corresponding elements for land use and transportation.

5. When public access is provided by a private owner, both local and federal tax relief should be available. For example, California's Williamson Act provides for tax relief when certain privately owned agricultural or recreational lands are reserved under contract for open space use.

6. Modern transportation economics and technology has shifted the necessity for continuing right-of-way (eminent domain) privileges for railroads. Railroad rights-of-way that traverse city or county boundaries, and often shoreline areas, should come under increased local jurisdiction. If they are now owned in fee, rights-of-way should be converted to franchises or leases with the relevant cities within a certain time period. Public access, visual barriers, and grade crossings could then be better negotiated with railroad companies to the public's benefit. Many old lines are obsolete and could be condemned at no revenue cost to railroads.

7. New federal assistance should be made available to states, counties, and cities for purchase of less-than-fee easements to shorelines for public access.

8. If port authorities are part of the state government, statutes controlling their operation should be amended to require public access in new projects, particularly when bonding powers are used.

9. If access to distant water recreation facilities limits their use by poverty populations, then transportation subsidies, special busing, and other programs could be considered as an alternative to new close-by shoreline access. Aid for transportation to water recreation facilities within one or two hours travel time from metropolitan areas might be included in budgeting for these projects, and might be cheaper than providing water recreation in urban areas.

10. Model Cities programs should be given "sign off" powers for all water development programs across federal agency lines to assure their input and participation in these programs. This would require further amendment of the Demonstration Cities Act of 1968.

11. More federal and state incentives for regional government should be developed.

References

Borchert, John R., 1967. American metropolitan evolution. *Geog. Rev.*, July 1967.

Burby, Raymond J., and Weiss, Shirley F., 1970. Public policy and shoreline landowner behavior. *Rept. 38, Univ. North Carolina, Water Resources Research Institute,* Raleigh, July 1970.

Cicchetti, Charles J., 1971. Some economic issues in planning urban recreation facilities. *Land Economics, v. 47, no. 1.*

Glaab, Charles N., 1963. *The American city: a documentary history.* Homeward, Ill., Dorsey Press.

Selznick, Philip, 1966. *TVA and the grass roots.* New York, Harper and Row.

Solzman, David M., 1966. Waterway industrial sites. A Chicago case study. *Univ. Illinois Dept. Geog. Res. Paper 107.*

CHAPTER 19

A significant part of Wisconsin's economy depends upon tourists who are attracted to the state's thousands of miles of streams, lakes, and shorelands. The Shoreland Protection Law of 1966 is an imaginative effort to protect natural values through joint state and local regulatory zoning.

This chapter describes the conditions leading up to the enactment of the law, the unique provisions of the legislation, the contents of the suggested shoreland protection ordinance, and the factors considered in developing the ordinace. To ensure smooth implementation of the law, the general public and officials of the local governments were indoctrinated in its provisions and the manner in which they could best be carried out, although legal constraints were placed on the local governments to guarantee their compliance.

Also discussed are the legal framework for a state-local regulatory program, other shoreland protection approaches, and the strengths and weaknesses of the Wisconsin program.

WISCONSIN'S SHORELAND PROTECTION PROGRAM: A STATE-LOCAL REGULATORY APPROACH TO NATURAL RESOURCE PRESERVATION

Douglas A. Yanggen

INTRODUCTION

Control of land use in accord with environmentally sound principles can be an important tool for protecting our endangered natural resources. Major deficiencies in the present system of land use regulations in the United States are in its decentralized structure and its insufficient focus on natural resource protection. These inadequacies stem in large part from the absence of any clearly defined federal and state policies. Two federal and legislative proposals to bring about greatly increased state action in land use planning and controls were on the agenda of the 92nd Congress (S632, "Land and Water Resources Planning Act of 1971" and S992, "National Land Use policy Act of 1971"). The administration proposal (S992) provided financial assistance to states to develop a land use program which, among other things, required regulation of "areas of critical environmental concern." Shorelands and flood plains of rivers, lakes, and streams of state importance, and coastal zones and estuaries were listed among these areas of critical environmental concern. The more general language of the Jackson bill (S632) would also have encompassed these areas. Alternative techniques set out in S 992 for strengthening the state regulatory role were state establishment of standards and criteria for local regulation, direct state regulation, and state administrative review and approval of local regulations (Sec. 104). S632 used more general language to describe the state-local regulatory relationship by providing that the state agency must have" the power to prohibit, under state police powers, the use of lands which is inconsistent with the provisions of the plan" (Sec. 305) but permitted the state to delegate authority to local units to plan for and enforce land use pursuant to the state plan as long as the state retained ultimate responsibility for approval and coordination of local efforts (Sec. 305). Neither bill became law although a modified version of S632 entitled "The Land Use Policy and Planning Assistance Act of 1972" passed the Senate but died in the House. The extensive Congressional deliberation on land use policy which took place in the 92nd Congress has laid the groundwork for what will be one of the most significant environmental issues facing the 93rd Congress.

However, the Congress did pass a less ambitious land use measure—the Coastal Zone Management Act of 1972. It is concerned with "the coastal waters . . . and the adjacent shorelines . . . strongly influenced by each other and in proximity to the shorelines" (Sec. 304) and provides for coordination with "any Federally supported national land use program which may be hereafter enacted" [Sec. 307(2)]. It seeks to encourage the coastal states to undertake development and administration of coastal zone management programs through grants-in-aid. The Act requires eligible states to have the ultimate authority to control development within the coastal zone [Sec. 306(c), (d) and (e)].

Some states have already asserted regulatory control over certain land uses which significantly affect the environment. Wisconsin's Shoreland Protection Law, which was enacted in 1966, is an attempt to protect the natural resource values of shorelands through a joint state and county regulatory effort. It illustrates an approach under which the state establishes minimum standards for local land use controls and retains the authority to adopt regulations if the local government fails to act. This paper describes the conditions which led to the enactment of the law, the unique provisions of the legislation, the contents of the suggested shoreland protection ordinance designed to meet its statutory objective, and the factors considered in developing the ordinance. The legal framework for a state-local regulatory program, other shoreland protection approaches, the strengths and weaknesses of the Wisconsin program, and its implications for federal water resource policy are also discussed.

THE IMPORTANCE OF SHORELAND AREAS

Wisconsin is blessed with an abundance of recreational waters including more than 8,800 inland ponds and lakes, numerous recreational rivers and trout streams, and about 725 miles of Lake Michigan and Lake Superior shoreline in the state. These waters are important to the state for environmental, economic, and legal reasons.

The outstanding natural features giving form and variety to the landscape in the state fall into linear patterns. Termed "environmental corridors" these relatively narrow bands lie near lakes and major river and stream valleys in most of Wisconsin (Lewis, 1967). The importance of these environmental corridors was revealed by a statewide inventory of 220 natural and manmade resource values. Natural values inventoried included such features as wildlife types, unique geologic formations, waterfalls, and springs. Among the manmade attractions identified were archaeological sites, museums, historic buildings, swimming facilities, and reservoirs. When these values were plotted on maps, 90 percent of them lay within environmental corridors, giving graphic evidence of the environmental, historical, and recreational importance of these areas.

Outdoor recreation is a big business and represents one of the most important sources of income in Wisconsin, particularly in many of the economically depressed northern counties where most of the recreational waters of the state are found. Water is the focal point for many of the recreational activities and the dream of many city dwellers is to own waterfront property. Subdividing shorelands for cottages and homes adds to the local property tax base. Most recreational lot owners are not permanent residents but their needs for goods and services help the local economy during the tourist season. As seasonal residents they place little demand upon the public coffers for school costs and public welfare, two of the largest items of expense of local government.

There are legal as well as environmental and economic reasons for concern with shorelands in Wisconsin. The Wisconsin Supreme Court has asserted that the navigable waters are held in trust by the state for the public. The state has a duty to protect these public rights, which include fishing, boating, swimming, sailing, skating, and enjoyment of scenic beauty (Muench vs. Public Service Commission, 1952). Improper shoreland

development can destroy scenic beauty and can cause pollution which interferes with the recreational use of the water.

Although the development of lakeshores for recreational use began in the 1920s in northern Wisconsin, it accelerated after World War II. The scattered buildings which first appeared began to be replaced by ribbons of development—a trend sharpened with the increasing demand for water-based recreation. Improved highways, increasing leisure time, earlier retirement, a rising standard of living, and changing consumer preferences continue to make these areas increasingly attractive to the expanding metropolitan populations of Wisconsin and other states. Recreational development burgeons as the willing buyer meets the willing seller.

SHORELAND PROBLEMS

Development causes many problems. The amenities of a natural shoreland are replaced by ribbons of development. Dwellings may be squeezed onto undersized lots. With the removal of shoreland vegetation, native plant communities are destroyed and wildlife habitat disappears. Scenic values are diminished and the rich beauty of a natural shoreline may be changed to a sterile succession of piers and buildings when viewed from the water.

Improper shoreland development can also contribute to water pollution. Usually each dwelling has its own well and is equipped with a septic tank system for disposal of domestic wastes. Too often these systems are incorrectly constructed or installed in unsuitable soil. As a result, sewage may pollute nearby wells and surface waters. Purchasers of lots often give little thought to potential pollution problems until after buildings have been constructed and waste disposal systems fail.

Erosion is another shoreland problem. Road building, grading, and filling during development exposes raw earth and causes erosion. Silt muddies the water and impairs aquatic life. In some places, municipal and industrial wastes and agricultural runoff are the major polluters, but many lakes are free from these sources of pollution.

THE ENABLING STATUTE

In 1966 the Wisconsin legislature enacted Chapter 614 to establish "a comprehensive action program directed at all present and potential sources of water pollution" (Ch. 614, Wis. Laws 1089-1113). This act reorganized and strengthened state pollution abatement and water resource management powers, with major responsibility given to the Department of Natural Resources (referred to as "Department of Resource Development" in Chapter 614). Provisions authorizing and requiring counties to adopt shoreland regulations designed to protect the amenities of shorelands and control water pollution are an important part of this law. The broad policy objectives of shoreland protection are set out in the enabling statute, which contains several unique provisions.

1. The 1969 statute recognizes the interrelationship of land and water resources and the state's responsibility to protect its navigable waters (Wis. Stats. Sec. 144.26):

> To aid in the fulfillment of the state's role as trustee of its navigable waters and to promote public health, safety, convenience, and general welfare, it is declared to be in the public interest to make studies, establish policies, make plans and authorized municipal shoreland zoning regulations for the efficient use, conservation, development and protection of this state's water resources.

The typical regulatory approach to water quality is to initiate a program in which the state controls industries and municipalities that directly discharge wastes into lakes and streams. Indirect pollution from land runoff is usually not regulated. (Kusler, 1970, has an excellent discussion of a number of the physical and legal aspects of the shoreland protection law and their relationship to water quality.)

The most common form of control of land-use depends upon local governmental efforts, based upon zoning, sanitary codes, and subdivision regulations. Rural government units having jurisdiction over the lands adjacent to most of the nation's water bodies have not adopted such land-use controls. The local regulations which do exist usually fail to take into account unique characteristics of the shoreland area concerning ecological values and effects on water quality.

2. The statute sets forth special zoning objectives to be met both in maintenance of water quality and in preservation of shoreland values (Wis. Stats. Sec. 144.26):

> The purposes of the regulations shall be to further the maintenance of safe and healthful conditions; prevent and control water pollution; protect spawning grounds, fish and aquatic life; control building sites, placement of structure(s) and land uses and (p)reserve shore cover and natural beauty.

A statutory section directing a state agency to prepare recommended standards and criteria for local navigable water protection regulations gives further insight into the purposes of the law (Wis. Stats. Sec. 144.26):

> . . . shall give particular attention to safe and healthful conditions for the enjoyment of aquatic recreation . . . requirements necessary to assure proper operation of septic tank disposal fields near navigable waters; building setbacks from the water; preservation of shore growth and cover; conservancy uses for low lying lands; shoreland layout for residential and commercial development.

The statute does not list regulations other than zoning that are required to carry out these objectives. It does, however, indicate the need for an expanded concept of what is ordinarily included within the term "zoning."

358

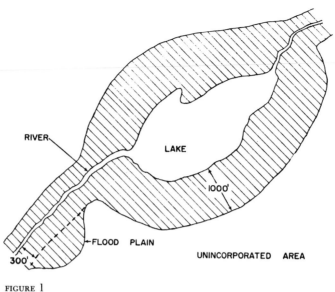

FIGURE 1
Diagrammatic representation of county shoreland jurisdiction that
is 1,000 feet from a lake, pond or flowage; 300 feet from a river or
stream or to the landward side of the flood plain, whichever distance
is greater.

The model ordinance approach discussed later in this article responds in two ways. First, it includes special provisions such as tree cutting, grading and filling, and lagooning and dredging controls that are not typically found in local zoning ordinances. Second, it interprets the use of the word "zoning" in the statute to include provisions more commonly found in sanitary codes and subdivision regulations.

3. The statute creates special shoreland corridors for county zoning of unincorporated areas adjacent to navigable waters (Wis. Stats. Sec. 59.971):

> counties may . . . zone all lands . . . in their unincorporated areas from the normal high-water elevation of navigable waters . . . 1,000 feet from a lake, pond or flowage; 300 feet from a river or stream or to the landward side of the flood plain, whichever distance is greater. [See Figure 1.]

The broad definition of navigability in Wisconsin makes the statute applicable to practically all streams and lakes in the state.

The special shoreland corridors constitute a management unit within which land use controls protect both the water and land resources. Conventional land use controls typically apply to the entire area of the enacting unit of government, whereas the shoreland regulations apply to a limited geographic area.

The 1,000-foot distance from lakes was chosen on the basis that it was the minimum distance necessary to control development that would substantially affect lakes and their shorelands. Lakes are more sensitive to sediment and pollution because they lack the degree of water exchange found in rivers and streams. In addition, lakes typically are subject to greater development pressures, which sometimes result in several tiers of lots along their shores. It was felt that 300 feet on either side of the less ecologically delicate rivers and streams was sufficient distance to provide the necessary environmental protection. The inclusion of the flood plain was based upon two considerations: these low-lying areas are periodically inundated by floodwaters and are thus ecologically part of the adjoining watercourse; and another statutory portion of Chapter 614 requires cities, villages, and counties to adopt flood plain zoning to reduce flood losses, and coordination of regulatory measures was deemed desirable (Wis. Stats. Sec. 87.30).

4. The statute authorizes state-level zoning by the Department of Natural Resources at an unprecedented scale if the counties fail to adopt adequate ordinances meeting minimum state standards (Wis. Stats. Sec. 59.971):

> If any county does not adopt an ordinance by January 1, 1968, or if the department, after notice and hearing, determines that a county has adopted an ordinance which fails to meet reasonable minimum standards in accomplishing the shoreland protection objectives . . . the department shall adopt such an ordinance.

Regulation of land use traditionally has been primarily a local function. The zoning-enabling legislation of most states permits but does not require local governmental units to adopt zoning. The local adoption of subdivision regulations and sanitary codes is also an optional matter under most state law. Most statutes do not authorize a state agency to establish minimum standards for evaluating the adequacy of local regulations.

There was precedent in Wisconsin for state control of land-use in the form of review of subdivision plans and specifications for private domestic sewage systems. However, loopholes in the law and insufficient funds and staff to carry out these functions permitted widespread evasion. The shoreland protection law made important changes by establishing concurrent county responsibility. State regulation by the department was required if the county failed to adopt controls that met minimum state standards. The cost of state adoption could be charged to the county and collected in the same manner as are state-levied taxes.

THE SUGGESTED REGULATORY APPROACH

Constraints and Informational Input

The enabling legislation created special shoreland protection corridors, specified general objectives for protection of water quality and shoreline amenity values, and required the state to adopt land use controls to achieve these objectives if counties failed to adopt adequate regulations by January 1, 1968. To implement the broad mandate of this law a number of difficulties had to be overcome: (1) there were only eighteen months from the time the law was enacted in August 1966 to the January 1, 1968, deadline for county compliance; (2) the regulations had to be capable of being applied on a statewide basis involving many miles of lake and stream shores; (3) few counties had modern zoning, subdivision control, and sanitary regulations, or experience in adopting and administering them; (4) there was a lack of detailed resource data on specific shoreland characteristics such as soil types, slope, vegetative cover, land use development patterns, direction of ground water flow, and water quality parameters, which may vary widely for individual water bodies; (5) limited scientific data made it difficult to generalize about the potential pollutional effects of various uses; (6) constitutional limitations on the use of the regulatory powers, such as those that prohibit the taking of private property without payment of compensation had to be considered; (7) it was necessary to strike a balance between the concern with shoreland problems and the desire for economic revenue from shoreland development in order to maintain political support for the regulatory program; (8) the regulations had to be designed to be feasibly administered and enforced.

The Department of Natural Resources, which was charged with supervising county compliance, was assisted by the University of

Wisconsin, and state and federal agencies in the preparation of a shoreland protection manual and model shoreland protection ordinance (Wisconsin Department of Natural Resources, 1967). The purpose of these publications was to provide those counties lacking professional planning assistance with information to help meet the January 1, 1968, deadline.

In designing a regulatory approach to the law and its purposes, relevant court decisions pertaining to land use controls from Wisconsin and other jurisdictions, available resource data, and the technical, financial, and administrative capabilities of the counties were considered. Experts representing many fields, including hydrology, geology, forestry, economics, sanitary engineering, civil engineering, soil science, limnology, land use planning and law were involved. They provided information and reviewed draft materials from their respective perspectives. Early draft materials were taken out for discussion with the residents of several counties, and using the resource data available, attempts were made to determine the administrative feasibility of various approaches. Finally, after several drafts and numerous discussions, agreement was reached in the summer of 1967 on a shoreland protection manual and ordinance.

The Shoreland Protection Ordinance

The recommended shoreland protection ordinance is essentially a natural resource oriented development code (Yanggen and Kusler, 1968). The basic land use controls available to local government, that is, zoning, subdivision regulation, and sanitary codes, are combined in an integrated package. Special provisions not usually found in these regulatory devices are added to meet the special objectives of the shoreland protection law. Many of the regulatory standards are keyed to the physical characteristics of the site. This information is generated at the time of an application for development permission. Certain special uses with potential problems require a case-by-case evaluation by an administrative agency according to standards set forth in the ordinance. The resulting ordinance consists of broad regulations applicable to all shorelands, together with a basic three-district zoning use classification.

Regulation Applicable to All Shoreland Areas. Certain controls apply to all shoreland areas regardless of the zoning district in which they are located. These regulations include minimum standards for water supply and waste disposal, tree-cutting controls, setbacks for structures from highways and navigable waters, minimum lot sizes and widths, filling and grading limits, lagooning and dredging controls, and subdivision regulations. These provisions constitute the central core of the recommended regulations. It was concluded that the manner in which common shoreland uses are developed usually presents a more pressing threat to the quality of shoreland areas than does the encroachment of incompatible uses. Typical lakeshore development consists of cottages, residences, and resorts, with occasional taverns, groceries, or other commercial buildings on some lakes. Few recreational areas are threatened by severe nuisance uses like factories or junkyards. The main problems in these areas are overcrowding, deterioration of water quality, and destruction of shore cover and natural beauty, stemming from: (1) inadequate lot sizes, side yards, and setbacks from the roads and water; (2) improperly functioning sewage disposal facilities; (3) development practices which lead to extensive erosion; and (4) indiscriminate tree cutting and filling of wetlands. These problems result not so much from the particular use placed on the lot, but from the size of the lot, its suitability for on-site waste disposal, and the manner and placing of development. The basic development code is geared to meet these problems.

The water supply and waste disposal provisions are designed to promote "maintenance of safe and healthful conditions" and "prevention and control of water pollution." These provisions relate to the construction and location of wells and private sewage disposal facilities and the dumping of liquid wastes or rubbish into navigable waters. The on-site septic tank and soil absorption system is the most commonly used method of private sewage treatment in recreational areas. A septic tank disposal system is a sinple sewage treatment facility. In a correctly operating system, bacteriological action in the tank destroys some of the organic matter and disease-causing organisms. The liquid effluent discharged from the septic tank is generally directed to an absorption field, where effluent is filtered by the soil and oxidized. This removes most remaining organic material and bacteria but not certain nutrients. The soil of the absorption field is an integral part of the system and a source of frequent failure. When a system fails, the bacteria-laden effluent backs up into the house or runs out onto the land surface, causing health hazards. This is particularly serious when the effluent reaches a water supply or open water.

Failing septic tank systems and even those operating efficiently may also contribute to a more subtle type of pollution. As septic tank effluent seeps through the soil, certain nutrients are not filtered out. Depending on the direction of the ground water flow, these nutrients may enter a lake or river where nutrients adequate for aquatic plant growth are naturally supplied. With additional nutrients from the effluent, weeds and algae may overproduce and cause nuisances. This problem is particularly serious on lakes, which do not have the assimilative capacity of streams. Since domestic waste disposal is a serious problem in shoreland areas, a sanitary permit for private sewage disposal facilities is required prior to the construction of any structure intended for human occupancy. A permit will not be issued for areas which cannot properly absorb septic tank effluent (that is, steep slopes, high bedrock or ground water, and impermeable soils) unless these

limitations can be overcome. Sites are to be checked for limiting conditions by on-site inspection, including soil borings and percolation tests, and the use of detailed soil surveys where available. Assuming that a site exists with suitable physical properties for soil absorption of liquid wastes, there are additional provisions in the "sanitary code" portion of the ordinance. Detailed standards pertaining to the construction, location, and maintenance of septic tanks systems are included. Private wells are also regulated.

Tree-cutting regulations apply to a strip paralleling the shoreline and extending 35 feet inland from the water (see Figure 2). No more than 30 percent of the length of this 35-foot-deep strip may be cleared to the depth of the strip. The cutting of the 30 percent must not create clearcut openings greater than 30 feet in width. In the remaining 70 percent, cutting must leave sufficient cover to control erosion and to screen cars and structures (except boathouses) visible from the water unless a special cutting plan is permitted by the board of adjustment.

Tree-cutting regulations are designed primarily to protect the scenic beauty of timbered shorelines while still allowing a view of water from the lot. There are important secondary benefits. Retaining shoreland vegetation makes land less vulnerable to erosion. Substantial shoreland cover can also reduce the amount of nutrients and other pollutants reaching the water. The shoreland vegetation uses nutrients contained in effluent and fertilizers as food. The vegetation can block other pollutants and debris from entering the water. Shade from trees along streams helps maintain the cool water temperature necessary for trout and other desirable forms of aquatic life.

In addition to setbacks from highways (typical of conventional zoning) all structures except piers, wharves, and boathouses must be set back from the water. Setbacks help preserve shore cover, natural beauty, and wildlife along the land-water fringe. A 75-foot setback from the water is required

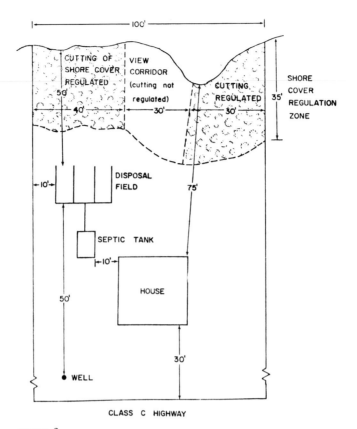

FIGURE 2
Typical shorefront lot (minimum size 20,000 sq. ft.) without public sewer.

of all regulated structures. Increased setbacks are recommended for bodies of water that possess outstanding fish and aquatic life, shore cover, natural beauty, or other ecological attributes.

A minimum lot size of 20,000 square feet and minimum width of 100 feet are required for all new shoreland lots not served by public sewers. This is the minimum size considered necessary to achieve other dimensional requirements such as setbacks from the water and roads, separating distances between private sewage disposal facilities and wells or navigable waters, side yards and parking areas, and the shore-cover protection strip along the water.

Filling and grading provisions are aimed at reducing erosion from raw soil and control-

ling filling of wetlands. Land that has surface drainage toward the water and is within 300 feet of a navigable waterway can be filled or graded only by special permit if the exposed area and the slope exceed a minimum figure. The permit must be obtained from the board of adjustment, which can attach a variety of conditions to minimize erosion.

Lagooning and dredging provisions are designed to protect wetlands, prevent slumping of the sides of excavated areas, and protect fish from oxygen-depleted conditions which may prevail in improperly constructed lagoons. A special permit contingent upon overcoming these problems is required for dredging or constructing any waterway, lagoon, or pond within 300 feet of a navigable water.

Subdivision controls regulating the division of land into lots for sale or building are an important part of the shoreland protection ordinance. Percolation tests, soil borings, detailed soil surveys, and other physical data are used to determine that a specified percentage of each lot within the subdivision is free from physical limitations such as impermeable soils, high ground water, near-surface bedrock, excessive slopes, and flooding. Lot size is geared to the degree to which an area is free from a combination of these limiting conditions. The 20,000-square-foot lot area and 100-foot width is the minimum size permitted. Lots with less favorable physical site factors must have a correspondingly larger size. The presence of limiting factors beyond a certain point prohibits subdivision.

"Planning unit development" provisions allow a developer greater flexibility to arrange lots in clusters rather than in long strips along the shore. The minimum lot size for each dwelling can be reduced if an equivalent portion of the subdivision is restricted to permanent open space. Clustering lots on suitable terrain reduces land improvement costs and makes common sewerage and water systems economically feasible. Wetlands, steep slopes, and other difficult-to-develop areas can be perserved as scenic assets. One subdivision in northern Wisconsin is laid out with all residential development in offshore clusters. The entire lake is buffered by undeveloped land extending back 200 feet from the shoreline. This shoreline strip is owned in common by purchasers of residential lots. The residential clusters, in turn, are linked with each other and certain recreational facilities by the shoreland buffer and other commonly owned greenways. The profit the developer foregoes by not subdividing the high value shoreline property is more than compensated for by the increased value of the more numerous offshore lots. Planned unit development provisions can permit thoughtful design which preserves environmental resources while enhancing property values.

The Use Districts. The model approach suggests three zoning-use districts to supplement the general regulations which apply throughout the shoreland area. The three districts are: (1) a recreational-residential district for most lake shorelands and the shorelands of certain recreational rivers and streams; (2) a conservancy district for all shoreland wetlands; and (3) a general purpose district for the remainder of the shoreland areas. This simple zoning scheme was designed for counties without enough information to permit a more elaborate use classification. When data permits, a more detailed districting scheme is recommended.

Within each district there are permitted uses and special exception uses. A special exception use is one which poses potential health, safety, erosion, water quality, or other problems to the shoreland environment and existing development. An application for a special exception permit must be filed with the county board of adjustment prior to the establishment of such a use. The board is authorized to investigate the effects of the proposed use and, after public hearing, decide whether to refuse, grant, or conditionally grant the special exception permit. If needed, technical assistance is available to the board from field representatives of the Soil Conservation Service, Division of Health, Department of Natural Resources, and other agencies. Standards for the board's investigation and conditions that may be attached to the special exceptions are set out in the ordinance. If it approves a special exception, the board may impose a variety of conditions to minimize the detrimental effects of the proposed use.

The model approach suggests that all substantial wetlands in regulated shoreland areas be placed in "conservancy districts." Wetlands are defined as areas where ground water is at or near the surface of the ground much of the year. These areas are wetlands which are either delineated on U.S. Geological Survey maps or detailed soil survey maps. Some wetlands along water provide fish spawning grounds, whereas others may be prime wildlife habitat. Wetlands are seldom suitable for building because of septic tank failure, unstable soil conditions, and seasonal flooding. For these reasons the conservancy district regulations limit building development.

Permitted uses of land in conservancy districts include harvesting of wild crops, forestry, wildlife preserves, hunting, fishing, the display of certain signs, and other uses that do not include resident structures and that have relatively minimal effects on the natural environment. Special exception uses include dams, flowages, removal of topsoil or peat, general farming, cranberry bogs, and other uses may substantially affect the environment. Filling and drainage are also special exceptions and may be used to overcome the natural development limitations of some of the areas. If the board of adjustment grants a special use permit for filling or drainage, and if the wetland area is made suitable for building development in conformance with the conditions imposed, the county board can then amend the district boundaries to place the area within one of the two other districts.

The shorelands of most named lakes and flowages and stretches of rivers and streams with recreational potential are suggested for "recreational-residential districts." Existing development along those waters is predominantly residential and resort, and such areas are best suited for these uses. Residential, recreational, and conservancy uses are permitted, and a limited number of commercial uses serving recreational needs are allowed as special exceptions. The permitted and special exception uses are, within limits, compatible with one another and are consistent with the recreational use of the water and its shorelands. Permitted uses include seasonal and year-round single family dwellings, accessory uses, the display of certain signs, and any use permitted in the conservancy district. Special exceptions are largely for recreational-commercial uses such as

hotels, resorts, motels, restaurants, taverns, recreational camps, campgrounds, gift and specialty shops, marinas, boat liveries, mobile home parks, and travel trailer parks. To minimize land use conflicts, additional requirements for special exceptions include larger minimum lot areas, greater separating distances, special screening, and increased setbacks.

The "general purpose" districts include the remaining shorelands of lakes, ponds, flowages, rivers, and streams that are not included in the conservancy districts or recreational-residential districts. General purpose areas are potentially suited to a wide range of uses, including commercial, agricultural, residential, recreational, and industrial. Many shorelands, particularly of the rivers and streams that meander across a county, cannot be separated into more detailed use districts without countywide comprehensive planning. Such planning is not and will not be available to many counties in the near future. Therefore, permitted uses include commercial, agricultural, residential, and recreational. Potential conflicts between different forms of land use are minimized by requiring adequate separation distances. Special exceptions include industrial uses, junkyards, dumps, and sanitary fills.

Although the general purpose district is a minimal zoning district relying upon separating distances to reduce the conflict of potentially incompatible uses, the general provisions of the ordinance apply to this district as they do to the recreational-residential and conservancy districts. Minimum lot sizes, setbacks, tree-cutting regulations, and other general provisions will assure that a substantial number of the special shoreland zoning objectives are met, despite a lack of detailed use districts.

The Shoreland Protection Manual

A manual was prepared to explain the basic rationale of the ordinance, and the mechanisms for preparing and administering it on a county level. The first part of the manual describes common water-related problems, and local and state roles in cooperating to achieve shoreland protection. The second part sets forth a logical sequence of steps directed toward implementing the ordinance. It contains a general overview of the organizational procedure, sources of technical help, available base maps, types of regulatory tools, methods of informing the public, and suggestions for administering the ordinance. The final portion describes in detail the structure and purpose of the ordinance and procedures for adopting and administering the zoning, subdivision, and sanitary regulations for shoreland protection.

EDUCATIONAL COMPONENT OF THE SHORELAND PROTECTION PROGRAM

Passage of the general enabling statute and development of a suggested regulatory approach in the ordinance and manual were important steps in initiating the program. A two-faceted educational effort was also developed to inform the general public, and to supply technical assistance to local officials and resource technicians responsible for adopting and administering the regulations on the county level.

The first step was a broad effort to educate both the general public and special clientele groups about the provisions of the Water Resource Management Law (Chapter 614) of which the shoreland protection program was a part. A series of eleven newspaper articles was printed by many daily and weekly newspapers throughout the state. Reprints of these articles were used as handouts at educational meetings held by University Extension personnel at the state and county level. To reach those directly responsible for implementing the law, a two-hour program was carried over the Educational Telephone Network (ETN) to county board members,

county extension personnel, and other local resource technicians in each county. ETN is a private telephone network operated by University Extension and used to transmit educational programs throughout the state. Each ETN station (located at courthouses, campuses, and hospitals in over 100 Wisconsin communities) has a telephone handset and a loudspeaker which enables a person at any station to hear transmissions on the network and to participate in discussion with persons at all other network points. Subsequently, four additional ETN programs were used to disseminate information and answer questions.

The shoreland protection ordinance and manual were distributed and discussed at a series of all-day meetings for local officials and technicians held throughout the state. Prior to passage of the law, the University Extension had prepared a sound-color film, *What's Happening to Our Lakeshores?* that pointed out the consequences of unplanned shoreland development, and offered suggestions for preserving environmental quality in these areas. This film was shown at the beginning of each meeting and then discussion of the manual and ordinance was led by some of the people who participated in their preparation. Similar meetings were held in most counties by county extension personnel who coordinated local efforts.

Another manual that discussed the administrative functions of the zoning administrator, board of adjustment, and county planning and zoning committee was also prepared. This publication, which includes sample forms useful in the administration of the regulations, was distributed and discussed at a series of regional meetings. Other specific educational programs designed to provide inservice training for local administrators were developed. The close working relationship continues between University Extension, the Division of Health, Department of Natural Resources, Soil Conservation Service, and other agencies that assisted in initial implementation of the shoreland program.

An example of a specific program is teaching the proper installation of septic tank systems, which is an integral part of shoreland regulations. A film, *Installing a Septic Tank-Soil Absorption System* was prepared by the University of Wisconsin. This film shows how to make percolation tests, details construction procedures, outlines state standards for septic tanks and soil absorption systems, and shows correct installation of several systems from initial excavation to final inspection. An ETN program explaining proper installation of soil absorption systems was developed, and included the showing of this film, distribution of recently revised state administrative regulations applying to septic tanks, a discussion and question period by a panel of experts from various agencies over the ETN, and further discussion led by a resource technician at each listening location. Three such ETN programs reached over 2,000 local officials, plumbers, surveyors, engineers, and architects from all counties. A series of nine one-day field training sessions was held the following summer to help technicians identify soil conditions important in proper installation of septic tank systems.

The Flood Plain-Shoreland Management Section of the Department of Natural Resources continues to assist counties by working with them on an individual basis and by publishing a periodic newsletter. The department has also distributed a pamphlet explaining the highlights of the regulatory provisions to prospective lot purchasers.

Public and Private Interests

Public regulation of the use of private land to protect water quality and shoreland amenity requires a thoughtful balancing of public and private interests. On the one hand, the shoreland owner has private property interests in his land. He has the right to keep others off, the power to dispose of his holdings, and the privilege of using his land in a wide variety of ways—on the other hand, the privilege of use of private property is subject to regulation under the "police power" of the state. The police power, an inherent attribute of state sovereignty, permits public restrictions upon the privilege of use of private property without compensating the owner for any loss of value.

The power of government to regulate the use of land to achieve protection of natural resources at little direct cost to the taxpayer is an appealing prospect. However, the economic dimension is not the only consideration. It is also important to weigh the social costs of severely restrictive regulations, including political conflict, erosion of controls through the administrative process, possible injustice to landowners, and loss of individual freedom. These are elements in the considerations of legislatures and courts in the dynamic remolding and reshaping of the institution of private property to achieve social goals.

The Legislative Role

The control of land use is primarily a state responsibility under the Tenth Amendment to the United States Constitution. State legislatures are empowered to enact laws regulating the use of private property under their respective constitutions. Although there could be direct state regulation of land use, states commonly delegate much of this power to local governmental units by enacting "enabling" legislation. These statutes permit, but usually do not require, local legislative bodies to enact local regulations. State and local legislatures commonly establish administrative agencies to administer and implement regulatory programs.

Local governmental bodies usually have no inherent powers except those delegated by the enabling statutes. An attempt to exercise power without express authorization and careful compliance with the procedures of the statutes is generally considered *ultra vires* and invalid. Regulation of shoreland areas could thus potentially be authorized at either the state or local level, or both. In Wisconsin, counties were authorized to adopt regulations meeting minimum state standards but failure to exercise this power required state regulation.

The statute authorizing shoreland regulation in Wisconsin attempted to do the following things:

1. Specify additional special objectives to be achieved in the shoreland area through the exercise of land use controls (zoning, subdivision, and sanitary regulations) which counties had previously been authorized to enact.
2. Require a state agency to establish minimum standards for the county shoreland regulations and adopt regulations if counties failed to adopt local controls by a statutory deadline.

The statute, the department's administrative regulations establishing the minimum state standards for determining county compliance (Wis. Adm. Code, Chapter NR115, (1970), and the shoreland protection ordinance as a suggested regulatory approach are all affected by the judicial function.

The Role of the Courts

The courts play a role in the legislative process in several ways: (1) by interpreting the meaning of ambiguous statutory language; (2) by "legislating" in the sense of court-made law that has evolved through settling legal disputes not covered by statutes; (3) by enforcing regulations through the imposition of sanctions; and (4) by determining the constitutionality of legislation.

In determining the constitutionality of land use controls, the courts arbitrate conflicts between the public power to implement social goals through regulations and the individual's decision-making power implemented through the institution of private property.

Through the regulatory power an individual property owner can be constitutionally deprived of some of his privileges to use his land without compensation in order to promote the general welfare. However, because the owner is not compensated courts, carefully scrutinize regulations which severely restrict the use of private property.

The judicially determined limits of the regulatory power are imprecise and vary from state to state. The United States Supreme Court set broad guidelines for determining the constitutionality of land use controls in the 1920s. Since that time they have left the determination of constitutionality up to the state supreme courts. Various state courts have adopted different views as to the validity of similar restrictions. In addition, there are numerous regulatory precedents that have not been judicially determined. It then becomes necessary to reason by analogy from a case that has been decided. Courts typically restrict their review of the validity of regulations to the reasonableness of specific restrictions as applied to a particular parcel of land, so it is difficult to generalize from one instance to another.

Constitutional Constraints

A detailed discussion of the complexity of the constitutional issues in regulatory attempts to preserve the natural environment is beyond the scope of this article. However, the general overview of selected constitutional issues that follows should give some insight into the legal analysis that was a part of the considerations involved in drafting the suggested ordinance.

Although there is no single test of the constitutionality of police power regulations, courts consider: (1) whether the regulation is adopted for a valid public objective (public need); (2) whether the regulation is reasonably related to a valid objective (responsiveness of the regulation to the public need); and (3) whether a "taking" has occurred (regulated land is deprived of all reasonable use). It is easier to state these elements as isolated items than it is to apply them as separate considerations in a given fact situation and court decisions do not always analyze them as separate factors.

Validity of Objectives. Courts generally give considerable weight to legislative discretion in identifying regulatory objectives as a valid public need. The objective of protecting the public health or safety is considered a particularly important public need. Protection of aesthetic values is viewed less favorably and some state courts have held that regulations cannot be adopted solely for aesthetic purposes. In many instances, however, a given regulatory provision serves multiple objectives. In addition, cases which invalidate regulations for lack of valid police power objectives often involve restrictions that prohibit all reasonable use of land.

Reasonable Relationship Between Regulatory Methods and Regulatory Objectives. Besides being enacted for a valid public objective, the regulatory methods must have a reasonable tendency to accomplish these objectives. There is a presumption of constitutionality in favor of the legislative determination that the restrictions are a suitable (although not necessarily the only or best) means to solve the problem.

This presumption is especially important in light of two major problems that were encountered in preparing the suggested regulatory approach: (1) imperfect scientific knowledge of the complex ecological interrelationships found in shoreland and water quality protection; and (2) lack of detailed resource inventories of important shoreland and water characteristics such as soil type, slopes, vegetative cover, direction of ground water flow, and water quality parameters.

Regulations Must Not "Take" Private Property. Regulations that severely restrict private land raise the question of possible violation of provisions in the United States Constitution and in the state constitutions which prohibit taking of private property without payment of compensation (Ryckman, 1966). (The Fourteenth Amendment of the United States Constitution requires that no state shall "deprive a person of . . . property without due process of law." Several considerations are important in determining if a taking has occurred: (1) the relative public benefit conferred by the regulations compared to the individual hardship caused by diminished property values; (2) do the prohibited uses threaten the public health or safety or have nuisance-like characteristics which would substantially interfere with others' lands; and (3) whether the restrictions deny all reasonable use of the land.

Regulations which attempt to restrict land to open space uses to preserve natural amenities are especially subject to being considered a taking. In these instances a court may recognize the existence of a valid public objective but declare the deprivation of use to be so severe that compensation through the use of the eminent domain is required.

Although it is impossible to predict the reaction of a particular state court, the following examples illustrate likely general response to open space zoning under differing situations. (1) A stream shore lot has an attractive cover of trees but no severe physical limitations, such as unsuitability for waste disposal, flooding, and the like, which justifies the prohibition of constructing buildings. Open space zoning that prohibits all structural use would probably be considered an invalid taking. (2) Another stream shore lot is located in an area subject to flooding, making structural use unsuitable under those conditions. The only feasible means of overcoming this physical limitation is by filling, but this would obstruct flood flows and inundate other lands. Since the proposed use has nuisance-like effects and threatens public health and safety its prohibition may be upheld. (3) A third stream shore lot is located in an area of wetland characterized by poor drainage but not subject to flooding. These physical limitations can be overcome by a combination of draining and filling but the regulations prohibit taking this corrective action. Since the land has little private value (although there may be public value as wildlife habitat) in its present state and the regulations prohibit proper corrective action to overcome limitations on building, the regulations may be considered an invalid taking. This latter situation is one in which major evolution of present judicial doctrines will be necessary if regulations are to play an increasing role in preserving certain natural resource values.

A recent Wisconsin Supreme Court case (Just vs. Marinette County, 1972) upholding the constitutionality of shoreland zoning is a big step in that direction. The case involved filling a wetland designated as a conservancy district under the county shoreland zoning ordinance. Under the terms of the ordinance, a conditional-use permit was required but was not obtained. The basic question before the Wisconsin Supreme Court on appeal was whether the conservancy district provisions and the wetlands filling restrictions were unconstitutional because they amounted to a taking of private land without compensation. The court responded to the "taking" question in the following language:

> This case causes us to reexamine the concepts of public benefit in contrast to public harm and the scope of an owner's right to use of his property. In the instant case we have a restriction on the use of a citizens' property, not to secure a benefit for the public, but to prevent a harm from the change in the natural character of the citizens' property. We start with the premise that lakes and rivers in their natural state are unpolluted and the pollution which now exists is man made. The state of Wisconsin under the trust doctrine has a duty to eradicate the present pollution and to prevent further pollution in its navigable waters. This is not, in a legal sense, a gain or a securing of a benefit by the maintaining of the natural *status quo* of the environment. What makes this case different from most condemnation or police power zoning cases is the interrelationship of the wetlands, the swamps and the natural environment of shorelands to the purity of the water and to such natural resources as navigation, fishing, and scenic beauty. Swamps and wetlands were once considered wasteland, undesirable, and not picturesque. But as the people became more sophisticated, an appreciation was acquired that swamps and wetlands serve a vital role in nature, are part of the balance of nature and are essential to the purity of the water in our lakes and streams. Swamps and wetlands are a necessary part of the ecological creation and now, even to the uninitiated, possess their own beauty in nature. . . . An owner of land has no absolute and unlimited right to change the essential natural character of his land so as to use it for a purpose for which it was unsuited in its natural state and which injures the rights of others. The exercise of the police power in zoning must be reasonable and we think it is not an unreasonable exercise of that power to prevent harm to public rights by limiting the use of private property to its natural uses.

Drafting Techniques to Overcome Constitutional and Informational Constraints. To take into account constitutional constraints and informational limitations a number of techniques were used in drafting the ordinance: (1) The objectives of the regulations are set forth in considerable detail in an introductory statement of purpose spelling out the relationship between various objectives and the means used in the ordinance to accomplish them. Further elaboration of the rationale of various regulatory sections is contained in portions of the ordinance, and wherever possible, their relationship to public health and water pollution control is indicated. (2) Many of the regulatory standards are keyed to the physical characteristics of the site. This information is generated at the time of an application for development permission. For example, proposals for all uses involving on-site sewage disposal must be accompanied by detailed information about soil permeability, slopes, depth to bedrock, and height of ground water. This information is based on percolation and on-site inspection and soil boring tests conducted by a licensed technician. (3) Uses which are potential sources of pollution or could have other adverse effects are evaluated on a case-by-case basis. The applicant for a special exception permit must supply detailed information about the proposed use to the county board of adjustment. The board investigates the likely effects of the proposed use and decides whether to refuse, grant, or conditionally grant the special exception permit. Standards for the board's investigation and conditions which may be attached to the permit to minimize detrimental effects are set out in the ordinance. If needed, technical assistance is available from field representatives of the Department of Natural Resources, Division of Health, Soil Conservation Service, and other agencies. This combination of detailed standards and availability of technical assistance lessens the likelihood of arbitrary decision-making and the attendant danger that a court will find an invalid delegation of a legislative function to an administrative agency.

OTHER SHORELAND PROTECTION APPROACHES

The Minnesota Shoreland Protection Program

The Minnesota shoreland protection program authorized by Minnesota Statutes (Section 105.485), enacted into law in 1969, is similar to the Wisconsin program in many respects. Special shoreland corridors for county regulation of unincorporated areas adjacent to public waters are the same. A state agency is directed to establish minimum standards for county shoreland regulations and prepare a model shoreland protection ordinance. Failure of a county to adopt regulations meeting minimum state standards by July 1, 1972, requires that the state agency adopt shoreland regulations, the cost of which can be charged to the county and collected as a special tax levy.

The Minnesota program differs from Wisconsin's in two important respects: (1) there was more detailed inventory data gathered prior to preparation of the state standards and model ordinance; and (2) in some ways the state standards and model ordinance provisions are more stringent.

A Minnesota Lakeshore Development Study (carried out by the University of Minnesota in 1970) surveyed approximately 2,000 lakes containing almost two-thirds of the state's water acreage. The system for lake classification used three basic criteria: (1) the dominant types of lakeshore soils and vegetation; (2) the size-shape relationship of lakes; and (3) water ecology based upon dominant fish type. The basic geographic unit of data collection was a 40-acre parcel.

The inventory of shoreland soils classified into six basic soil groups was compiled from previously mapped soil surveys. For unmapped areas air photo interpretation supplemented in some cases by on-site investigation was used. Other physical characteristics of shoreland areas inventoried by air photo interpretation were onshore slope, offshore slope, aquatic vegetation, tree size, tree type, and tree density. Lake characteristics surveyed were sized in acres, shore length in miles, depths to the nearest 10 feet, and dominant fish type. Totals of resorts and seasonal and permanent homes were collected from assessors records and highway maps.

A computerized data bank permits retrieval of this information. The computer can locate and produce a map of each lake and show within the nearest quarter mile the physical properties about which information is desired (for example, wet soil, gentle to flat offshore land slopes, weedy bottom, and lowland brush vegetation onshore). The availability of data on the number and location of lakes, type of shoreline, and extent and location of private development facilitates management and regulation.

The 1970 Minnesota shoreland standards and ordinance provisions are similar to the Wisconsin standards in most respects, but there are differences. Based in part upon the lake inventory study, Minnesota lakes are classified into four groups determined by the suitability of each lake for future development and the desirable level of development. The classification system consists of Natural Environment Lakes and Streams, Recreational Development Lakes, General Development Lakes and Streams, and Critical Lakes.

Natural Environment Lakes and Streams are the highest quality waters, where regulations are designed to maintain a low density of development with high quality standards. Recreation Development Lakes are intended to provide for a mixture of recreational uses. General Development Lakes and Streams, to which the least stringent regulations apply, are designed for areas presently developed at a high density. Critical Lakes are those that are badly deteriorated and will require further study to determine appropriate standards. Until the studies are completed the most stringent standards, those for Natural Environment Lakes, apply. The standards for the Natural Environment (and Critical) classifications require an 80,000-square-foot minimum lot size, a 200-foot frontage, a waterline setback of 200 feet for buildings and 150 feet for sewage disposal systems. The standards for the Recreational and General Development classifications, respectively, are 40,000- and 20,000-square-foot minimum lot size, 150- and 100-foot frontage, water setbacks of 100 feet and 75 feet for buildings, and sewage systems setbacks of 75 and 50 feet.

The Brandywine Plan

The Brandywine Plan, developed for a rural watershed 30 miles west of Philadelphia, is an example of a shoreland protection program placing major reliance on the purchase of conservation easements as the main imple-menting tool. Under the easement approach a landowner retains title to his property but sells certain privileges of use of his land as specified in the easement. The amount of compensation the landowner receives for giving up these use privileges is measured by an appraisal of the difference of the fair market value of the property with and without the easement.

The plan was designed with a holding capacity for a population growth from 4,500 to 38,000 over a 50-year period. Increased population was to be accommodated by cluster developments unrestricted by easements. Important objectives were: to protect water resources and amenities by preventing or limiting construction in flood plains, stream buffers, steep slopes, and forests; and to control sewerage, drainage, and grading of development to protect the natural environment.

The Institute for Environmental Studies of the University of Pennsylvania undertook the study. Consultants in hydrology, limnology, sanitary engineering, landscape architecture, law, real estate appraisal, and resource planning were involved. The estimated cost of producing the plan was about half a million dollars. A detailed technical report provided supporting data and studies underlying the final recommendations was published by the University of Pennsylvania in 1968.

The final plan and program made the following basic recommendations:

1. Land in the flood plain or within 300 feet of streams or swales (constituting 26 percent of the watershed) could have no further development, except for the extension of existing uses and in hardship situations.
2. Wooded land and land with slopes of 15 percent or greater, which was more than 300 feet from the stream (constituting 20 percent of the watershed) would be restricted to a maximum gross density of one dwelling unit per four

acres. Construction of structures could not increase the area of impervious ground cover beyond 2,000 square feet or 5 percent of the lot, whichever area was greater. Solid waste disposal, filling, grading, and tree cutting would also be covered by the easements.

3. These restrictions would be placed on the land through purchase of permanent conservation easements at fair market value. The total value of easements was estimated to be $3 million, or 48 percent of the estimated cost of outright purchase of the entire fee simple. Funding from other sources was anticipated so that local governmental units would not bear any of the acquisition cost. No easements would be purchased unless owners of 80 percent of the land within a subwatershed voluntarily agreed to the plan. (This was a modification of an early recommendation that the county's eminent domain power be used where necessary.)

4. All municipalities would agree to plan and construct water supply and sewage disposal systems and adopt erosion control regulations to maintain water standards specified in the plan.

Despite intensive educational programs, the fact that property owners were to be compensated for any reduction in property values, and that local governmental units would not bear the cost of acquiring easements, the plan was rejected by the residents and local governmental units (Keene and Strong, 1970).

The Comprehensive Plan for the
Fox River Watershed

The comprehensive plan for the Fox River watershed illustrates how the protection of water quality and amenity values of shoreland can be accomplished as part of a comprehensive planning process. The watershed plan for the 924 square miles of the Wisconsin portion of the Fox River was undertaken as an integrated part of a broader regional planning effort for seven counties in the rapidly urbanizing southeastern area of the state. It is a comprehensive, multipurpose approach to water-related problems focusing on the watershed as a planning unit. This two-volume plan prepared by the Southeastern Wisconsin Regional Planning Commission in 1970 identifies and attempts to quantify the developmental and environmental problems of the watershed. Extensive inventory and analysis permitted forecasts of future levels of economic activity and population growth and concomitant land use and natural resource demands. Coordinated proposals for land use, flood control, pollution abatement, and water supply within the watershed serve to refine and detail the regional plan. (The following discussion focuses on selected highlights of portions of the watershed plan.)

Based upon previous study of population factors and the economic base, the amount of land devoted to urban uses within the watershed is expected to double within the next twenty years. If present trends continue, new urban development will not be properly related to surface water resources, wetlands, woodlands, soil capabilities, or utility systems. The land use plan element proposes a spatial distribution for new growth which emphasizes cohesive urban development on suitable soils, efficient utility services, preservation of prime agricultural lands, and protection of the natural resource base.

Areas which contain concentrations of scenic, recreational, and historic values were identified and mapped. Natural resource elements inventoried include lakes and streams, flood plains, wetlands, woodlands, wildlife habitat, topography of high relief, significant geological formations, and wet or poorly drained soil. These elements of the natural resource base are essential to ecological balance (Kabat, 1969) and natural beauty. "Primary environmental corridors" which contain three or more of these elements are found in linear patterns occupying approximately 21 percent of the total watershed area. Most of the primary environmental corridors lie in the area surrounding major lakes and major river and stream valleys. Additional values, including existing and potential open space and outdoor recreation sites, historic sites and buildings, and significant scenic areas are closely related to these primary environmental corridors, making them the highest concentrations of prime resource values.

The natural resource protection plan element recommends public acquisition of all the remaining undeveloped primary environmental corridors expected to be in urban use by 1990, together with all the primary corridor along the main stem of the Fox River. Public ownership of these areas would protect them from urban development and serve the need for resource conservation, protection of flood plain areas, parks, parkway and related open space needs, and multipurpose reservoir sites. In other rural areas of the watershed, shoreland, flood plain, and conservancy zoning would be relied upon to protect primary environmental corridors from urban encroachment.

Recommendations for pollution abatement of streams involve advance waste treatment (including nutrient removal) at all major waste discharge locations within the watershed. A single large treatment plant for the entire upper watershed is suggested. The following measures to abate lake pollution problems are suggested: (1) Provision of sanitary sewage facilities on selected lakes to eliminate sanitary hazards and nutrient input where there is serious malfunctioning of septic tank systems. (2) Soil and water conservation practices to reduce nutrients and sediment from agricultural runoff. (3) Algae control and weed harvesting to alleviate aquatic nuisance conditions. Specific measures for improving lake water quality, including cost estimates, are proposed for 22 of the most important lakes in the basin.

STRENGTHS AND WEAKNESSES OF WISCONSIN'S SHORELAND PROTECTION PROGRAM

Strengths

The Wisconsin Shoreland Protection Program has been successful in a number of respects: (1) In the years since passage of the law the state land-use control picture has changed substantially. Previously there were only a few scattered instances of effective rural regulations. Today all of the Wisconsin counties have fully complied with state standards for zoning and sanitary and subdivision regulations for shoreland areas, and all have appointed a county administrator. (2) Involvement with the shoreland protection ordinance has encouraged counties to enact basic land-use controls for all of the unincorporated areas within their jurisdictions. Although the state could only require adoption of land-use controls within the shoreland area, a majority of counties have adopted countywide sanitary and subdivision regulations. Counties within regional planning commissions, as well as some other counties, are preparing comprehensive and detailed zoning ordinances. There is less widespread geographic coverage for zoning because the present enabling statute permits unincorporated towns to remain outside the county zoning ordinance. Nevertheless, progress is being made and legislation to eliminate the town "veto power" has been introduced. (3) The regulations are being satisfactorily administered. Since counties are the general purpose unit of local government with the broadest geographic coverage, their demonstrated capabilities to adopt and administer land-use controls is encouraging. (4) Although there were some instances of friction in the implementation of the shoreland program, it has generally been well accepted by the public and local government. On the basis of experience gained, prospects appear relatively promising for further environmentally oriented regulatory programs with joint participation by counties and the state.

Weaknesses

The inadequacies of the shoreland program stem in large part from basic limitations of special purpose regulations and lack of prior physical planning. In addition, a relatively uncomplicated approach was necessary to facilitate administration of the program.

1. The geographic coverage of the protective shoreland corridors is too limited to take into account the influence of land uses within the drainage basin that may adversely affect water quality. Sediments and nutrients contributed by agricultural runoff are not adequately regulated within the protective corridor owing in part to lack of readily feasible alternatives. Even if technically feasible, the area of regulatory jurisdiction would have to be substantially expanded for effective control. Similarly, urban storm water drainage is uncontrolled because incorporated municipalities are not subject to the law. Again, broader geographic coverage would be desirable, assuming there are feasible measures for dealing with the problem.

2. The protection of aesthetic values could be strengthened by controls over the exterior color of structures and more stringent regulation of the removal of vegetative cover. A more logical (although administratively unwieldy) boundary for regulations attempting to deal with aesthetic values would be the line-of-sight distance from the water rather than the present arbitrary figure.

3. To achieve certain shoreland objectives regulations may need to be supplemented by governmental tools that compensate the private owner. For example, if large areas of land are to be preserved in a completely natural state, purchase of conservation easements may be the answer. If public access and use for recreational purposes is desired, fee-simple purchase appears to be the best long-term solution.

4. Regulations can be substantially strengthened both logically and legally by their underlying factual basis. Sound planning and scientific data can document the need for regulations, establish that the regulatory provisions are appropriate methods for dealing with the problem, and establish the extent to which private land use is impairing the public interest.

5. Basic resource inventory data such as that collected by the Minnesota Lake Development Study can provide a basis for classifying lakes rather than attempting to apply a single set of regulatory standards on a statewide basis. This information should be supplemented by water quality data, particularly for streams and lakes that receive stream inflow, so that shoreland management can be fitted into the state's total water quality program.

6. Each lake has unique physical characteristics. Ideally, regulations should be part of a tailormade management program based upon a detailed plan for each water body.

7. Detailed lake planning and management is best undertaken within the framework of comprehensive watershed planning. This permits taking into account the many factors that impinge upon the resource base within the watershed. The Southeastern Regional Planning Commission approach of preparing natural resource oriented watershed plans within the context of a regional planning program results in a more comprehensive perspective.

IMPLICATIONS FOR FEDERAL WATER RESOURCE POLICY

Protection of the nation's water resources will require planning and regulation of land activities which affect water quality. In addition, land areas adjacent to water have important ecological and scenic values worthy of protection in their own right. Federal legislative proposals designed to bring about greatly increased state land-use planning and regulation on a broad front recognize the pivotal role of the states. Local units with restricted geographic boundaries, limited technical expertise and dependence on property tax revenue from land development cannot be expected to have the necessary perspective. The existing institutional structure for determining land-use which is too heavily weighted in terms of local interests is clearly in need of reform. Yet there are many land-use decisions that are predominantly local in character and do not substantially impinge upon the national or state interest. In addition, states may differ in their problems, ways of perceiving them and their institutional mechanisms for problem solving.

The Wisconsin approach to shoreland protection illustrates one technique which can be used. It has included both state and local government in an active program to protect natural resources by controlling land use in environmentally sensitive areas. The discussion of its strengths and weaknesses in the previous section has many implications for federal policy. There are other considerations as well. A true national policy will require more than a composite of state land-use plans and controls. National objectives must be more clearly formulated as a framework for state action. Comprehensive planning at a state or regional level will ultimately be required. This means substantial commitment from the federal government in money and technical assistance. It will take time for the states to develop comprehensive planning programs. In the meantime, priorities must be established and necessary action taken. The initial focus could be on selected classes of critical environmental concerns which are of statewide significance.

It will be no easy task to determine the appropriate level of responsibility and most satisfactory methods for planning and controlling land use in varying situations. However, the difficult challenge presented in determining specific institutional arrangements can and must be met.

References

Installing a septic tank—soil absorption system. Bureau of Audio and Visual Instruction, University of Wisconsin, Madison, Wisconsin.

Just vs. Marinette County, Nos. 106 and 107, (S. Ct. Wis. Oct. 31st, 1972)

Kabat, C. 1969. The role of ecology in comprehensive watershed planning in southeastern Wisconsin. Proceedings; Water Resources Planning Conference. Rhode Island Water Resources Center.

Keene, J. C. and A. L. Strong. 1970. The Brandywine Plan. *Journal of the American Institute of Planners, vol. 36, no. 1.*

Kusler, Jon A. 1970. Water quality protection for inland lakes in Wisconsin: a comprehensive approach to water pollution. *Wis. L. Rev. 35.*

Lewis, Phillip H., Jr. 1967. The environmental corridor. Proceedings—Scenic Easements in Action, University of Wisconsin Extension, Law Department, University of Wisconsin, Madison, Wisconsin, pp. 23-34.

Muench vs. Public Service Commission. 1952. 261 Wis. 492, 53 N.W. 2d 514.

Ryckman, W., Jr. 1966. Eminent domain—conservation—evidence necessary to determine if a regulation restricting the use of property is invalid as a taking without compensation. Natural Resources Journal, 6:8–12.

Yanggen, D. A. and Jon A. Kusler. 1968. Natural Resource Protection through Shoreland Regulation: Wisconsin. *Land Economics, vol. 44, no. 1.*

CHAPTER 20

Contemporary welfare economics, although in some disarray, has a vital place in technical planning for water development and environmental quality. However, "It seems that there is no simple rule to be found in economic theory which will make difficult choices for us."

Money cannot be used as the ultimate expression of all planning variables. For example, willingness to pay for nondevelopment of water cannot be assessed with present or even prospective techniques—certain problems must be solved in other avenues of the decision-making process. In a critique of cost-benefit analysis, as it is presently used, the authors point out that agencies generally approach the correct value for benefits but are very low on nonmarket costs. The resultant overbuilding leads to several serious problems. Cost-benefit analysis is used primarily to obtain consent for water development projects rather than as an integral concept in project formulation.

The authors also discuss compensation tests, the monetization of nonmonetary costs and benefits, secondary benefits, effluent charges, and the use of economics in the political process and multi-objective planning.

THE ECONOMICS OF WATER DEVELOPMENT AND ENVIRONMENTAL QUALITY

David J. Allee and Duane Chapman

INTRODUCTION

Economics, as an approach to evaluation, has made a contribution to the decision-making process that to the present has balanced water development and environmental quality by providing an important component for formal evaluation, a basis for some of the values employed, and a focus for value judgments that must be applied in the political process. We will try to explain some of the reasoning that economists bring to the prob-

lem of balancing environmental and developmental values, but we will not pretend that this reasoning is always well used. Finally, we will try to show some of the differences that exist between economists because in any discipline everyone does not agree on where the truth lies.

We will also try to include the role of economic analysis into the political context as well as show some of its conceptual linkages to other approaches to evaluation. Because benefit-cost analysis is the traditional application of the economist's approach to water development, we will start there. Largely developed and applied by engineer-planners, benefit-cost analysis rests on the reasonableless of marginal analysis and the notions of welfare economics—both powerful but limited concepts. Marginal analysis as applied to water development projects may not tell the whole story, and policy makers must know when the parts of a project do not equal the whole. Welfare economics is in some disarray and the problems debated by economists raise important issues for the serious student of a balanced approach to water policy. A discussion of compensation tests, welfare functions, social costs, and equity, as distinct from efficiency, suggests that no simple rules are to be found in economic theory which will make difficult choices for society.

Economics can be used to generate ideas whose application society may or may not find useful. Is the ultimate test of these ideas agreement by society to use them, or is it internal logic or other criteria provided within the discipline from which they come? Society has used a multiplicity of criteria in its decision-making processes and we will review what has come to be called multiple-objective evaluation. We feel that the implementation of just such a concept is at the heart of achieving a balance of environmental and developmental values, a balance that is responsive to both the values of society and the imperatives of survival.

TRADITIONAL BENEFIT-COST ANALYSIS

A student once wrote the term as "BENEFIT-CO$T ANALY$I$." In the late 1950s and early 1960s, leading figures in the field viewed money as the numéraire for all problems in benefit-cost analysis. Environmental problems were generally ignored or dismissed by reference to opportunity cost techniques where the decision-maker would be asked to consider the net dollar effect of some environmental "constraint" upon the dollar maximizing solution.

For example, Otto Eckstein (1958) stated, "a change in social welfare is equal to the change in national income." Eckstein defined net social welfare as equal to net benefits or the difference between benefits and costs of the project at hand. Costs were what the labor, capital, and natural resources would have earned in some other use. Benefits were what output would be worth if exchange for money were possible. Both benefits and costs would be calculated by taking the sum of the quantities times their prices over the life of the project, discounting future values through the use of the appropriate interest rate, and adjusting for interest during construction.

It is interesting to contrast Eckstein's national income criterion with Stephen Marglin's (1962) "willingness to pay" criterion that Marglin defines as "representing how much the beneficiaries of a system output would purchase at successive prices if the output were sold in a market." This is "equal graphically to the area under aggregate demand curve" and is more than a single price times the quantity demanded at that price.

For example, in Figure 1, A represents consumer expenditures and is equivalent to a quantity times its price. But A plus B represents willingness to pay. (These definitions often appear under different labels; B is often termed "consumers' surplus" and A plus B is occasionally termed "consumers' value." We will not pursue these niceties here.)

Both approaches reflect an adherence to consumer sovereignty as an ethical judgment. The person affected is presumed to reflect the value of either benefits or costs by making his own comparisons of alternative ways to use income. Someone else's judgment of what is good for him is ruled out and consumers are democratically viewed as one man, one vote, if you ignore income differences.

Although it may be the best we have, prices are not the perfect way to compare

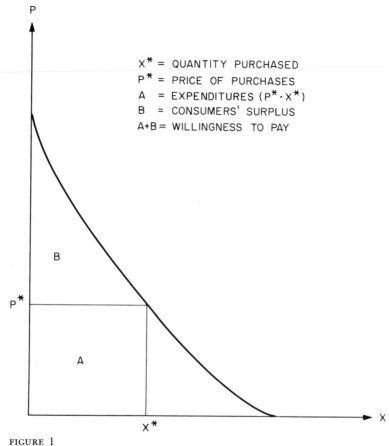

X* = QUANTITY PURCHASED
P* = PRICE OF PURCHASES
A = EXPENDITURES (P*·X*)
B = CONSUMERS' SURPLUS
A+B = WILLINGNESS TO PAY

FIGURE 1
Willingness to pay.

values. Note that most output from water projects is not sold in markets that even approximate competitive conditions. Where prices exist, as for power and municipal water, they are apt to be highly regulated. As we shall note later, these prices often do not function by themselves as fully effective ways to ration output between users, nor do they usually reflect all social costs. And for much output, such as flood control, recreation, and irrigation, prices must be synthesized by one ingenious device or another. Suppose a price is devised and multiplied times the quantity to be produced by a particular project design (area A in Figure 1). The resulting value may be less than the sum of the costs of that design. But if the consumers have no alternative, it is logical

that they would be "willing to pay" more than A (up to the area B in Figure 1). This simply follows from the definition of the relationship between quantity demanded and price.

But if you jump from the project level to the total society level, as some are inclined to do, the "willingness to pay" for the developmental values of water is infinite. Without water we would all die. The point is that such a fact is almost always irrelevant to the total effect. Note that by the same kind of reasoning it is argued that there is an infinite willingness to pay for environmental values. However useful either national income or willingness to pay approaches to benefit and cost values may be at the project level, this discussion should raise the question of whether these approaches should be supplemented for decisions at the national policy level.

Numerous controversies center around these criteria, although the most important is probably the assumption of constant marginal utility of money between all individuals and for a single individual for all amounts of money. In other words, both the national income and willingness to pay criteria assume that an additional dollar gives equal satisfaction to a wealthy man or a poor man, and every individual gets the same satisfaction from each dollar if his income increases from $5,000 a year to $60,000 a year. Seckler (1966) and Chapman (1970) have argued that this assumption may bias public investment toward higher income groups.

Evaluations that stress monetary estimates of either version of the efficiency criterion may implicitly assume that the project at hand will distribute good and bad effects in such a way as to make no significant change overall when clearly it is just such a change that must motivate the supporters (and opponents) of a project. But if you do not assume that a dollar of income has equal value to different people how are the adjustments to be made? Where are the weights to come from? Taking from one group to give to another is often at the heart of the matter, and the few ways to evaluate this "market" are restricted to judging exchanges between rich and poor—for example, tax rates. But that is one way in which affected groups differ. Analysis can identify something about the effects of public action on different groups. However, traditional efficiency analysis gives only a limited amount of such information; indeed, it may obscure more than it reveals as these value judgments are part of the political process.

If we can use willingness to pay as a basis for estimating the benefits for canalizing a stream, why not use it for the values lost as a result of losing the free-flowing stream? The canal may move goods more cheaply than does a railroad, thus limiting the willingness to pay of freight movers. The users of the free-flowing stream and their willingness to pay indeed can be estimated. But what about those who would not use the stream in either form yet have a real willingness to pay to have the stream stay in its natural state? It is unlikely to stay natural unless some action is taken to keep it so, although the point here is how do we decide to take action to obtain or secure values that are different from the sum of individual actions when taken independently of the whole society. Calling these *public* goods or values obscures the fact that they may only be appreciated by a subset of society. Nonetheless, "preservation" should be placed "within the framework of these basic economic principles."

But these values do not fit within the framework described here. We shall return to this problem in our discussion of social cost.

COMPENSATION TESTS

The theory of compensation tests was developed as a response to the need to judge alternative private and public economic policies. The theory places those persons affected by policy into two groups: those who gain and those who lose. The most basic assumption is that a new situation is socially preferable to an existing situation if the gainers offer the losers sufficient income or commodities so that all members of the society are at least as well off as before and some persons are definitely better off.

The original authors of the concept were Nicholas Kaldor (1939), J. R. Hicks (1939), and Tibor Scitovsky (1941). Scitovsky offers a detailed definition which deals with what is sometimes called the index number problem as follows:

> We must first see whether it is possible in the new situation so to redistribute income as to make everybody better off than he was in the initial situation; secondly, we must see whether starting from the initial situation it

is not possible by a mere redistribution of income to reach a position superior to the new situation, again from everybody's point of view. If the first is possible and the second impossible, we shall say that the new situation is better than the old was. If the first is impossible but the second possible, we shall say that the new situation is worse; whereas if both are possible or both are impossible, we shall refrain from making a welfare proposition.

In other words, if both before and after the event we can see how bribes might be used to remove objections, it must be a worthwhile change. It would seem on first inspection that this concept might provide some very valuable tools to judge environmental quality policies as compensation is widely used in the political process. A common problem in water resource development, however, is balancing environmental damages against the gains in water use, and because the damages and gains are distributed to different groups, the groups may not assign the same values to the same goods.

Welfare economists have struggled with the logic of these tests to determine if they are sound. Gorman (1955) and, in a more modern context, Mishan (1967) have shown that compensation tests are inherently unreliable in a particular sense for all contexts. The compensation test is not transitive and is made even less valid owing to problems caused by shifting preferences. Because of the human trait to shift preferences with changes in availability, the use of present preferences is risky and the prediction of future preferences is even riskier. But even with constant preferences it is not difficult to construct reasonably hypothetical examples that show alternative A is superior to B after the development of bribes, B to C, C to D, yet have D preferred to A proving that in compensation tests transitivity is not present.

But all of this presumes that the analyst will decide if indeed A could be made more agreeable than B, B than C, and so on. In fact, planners make many of the choices

because the political system does not process the information for all of the available examples. The planners must therefore display the range of information needed to obtain approval. After negotiation with the interest groups represented in the planning process the planner often displays only one choice for a "go, no go" decision. Within the available means of implementing water-based projects the planner then offers the bribes needed to obtain agreement. Beyond that, at several points in the political process, there are opportunities to make exchanges to gain government support (Ingram, 1970) from quite unrelated agencies. In other words, bribes are offered to the gainers from the resources available to the gainers perhaps to compensate some of the losers—at least those who hold veto power in the decision-making process.

In the use of compensation tests economists have argued if compensation actually had to be paid for one situation to be better than another. An evaluation report stating that the value of the gains far exceeds that of the losses if compensation is not paid implies certain assumptions about compensation. Not only has the report presumably settled (more likely ignored) the before and after index number problem and the transitivity problem, it has probably assumed that unmet compensation to the losers will somehow be worked out through the political system. Environmentalists will lose a little on this project, but they will make up for it someplace else—either where the environment is enhanced on a net basis or through some unrelated redistribution or welfare. For this to be true, information, access, and bargaining power must be distributed between groups proportional to the way in which they may be affected by government.

Alternatively, this would create odd relationships between reversibility and demand. For example, when some mileage of a wild river is lost it is clear that the wild river mileage cannot be replaced elsewhere. What then can and will be substituted in the lives of those who do value wild rivers now or would value them in the future? Until we can answer that question the environmentalist who replies "nothing" has one end of the stage to himself along with a growing share of the audience.

The most important lesson to be learned from the debates over compensation tests as a way to approach the problem of taking from some to give to others is the widespread lack of empirical, quantitative applications in actual analysis. There seems to be no way out of the problem but to apply subjective value judgments whose acceptance or rejection is based on consent. But whose role is it to do that? Are there specially designated decision-makers for including value judgments in planning? We suggest that the total decision-making process must be considered for major changes in balance.

WELFARE FUNCTION: THE IMPOSSIBILITY OF EASY CHOICES

In the preceding two sections, we have seen that the traditional formulations of benefit-cost analyses and compensation tests are of little value in examining environmental externalities of water resource development. In this section we shall note the question

raised by Kenneth Arrow in 1950: "Is [there] *any* method available for ranking social preferences?" and shall translate Arrow's formal analysis into the context of water and environment. The hypothetical example will also display the problem of transitivity.

Suppose there are two groups concerned with a reservoir site—conservationists and irrigationist-tourist store owners. The conservationists rank the scenic and recreation value of three alternatives as follows: (1) no dam, (2) a recreation dam, (3) an irrigation dam. (See Table 1.) Since the conservationists receive little monetary profit from any of the alternatives, their overall evaluation follows their scenic evaluation as shown in column 3 of Table 1.

The irrigationists and tourist store owners prefer reservoir recreation to stream recreation for themselves, and they rank scenic and recreational value differently from the conservationists (see column 4). As column 5 suggests, their financial stake is significant. Their overall evaluation follows their profit, as shown in column 6.

How might a society of conservationists and irrigationists-tourist store owners rank the three alternatives? First, because both groups prefer the recreation dam to the irrigation dam, the society should also. Second, the two groups' preferences are reversed: one preferring no dam and the

TABLE 1.
Conservationists and Irrigationists-Tourist Store Owners

Alternatives	Group 1 Conservationists			Group 2 Irrigationists-Tourist store owners		
	Ranking of scenic and recreational value	Annual Profits from irrigation and tourism	Overall preference ranking	Ranking of scenic and recreational value	Annual Profits from irrigation and tourism	Overall preference ranking
A. No dam	1	$4	1	2	$400	3
B. Dam with releases stabilized for recreation	2	$100	2	1	$20,000	1
C. Dam with releases for maximum irrigation use	3	$50	3	3	$15,000	2

other a recreation dam. If this society is not to be dictatorial and does not impose social preferences on dissenting groups, it must express impartial indifference between no reservoir and a recreation reservoir.

Transitivity would now require that society prefer no dam to an irrigation dam because society takes no sides in the choice between no dam and a recreation dam, and if society prefers a recreation dam to an irrigation dam, then it must prefer no dam to the irrigation dam. The overall evaluations in columns 3 and 6 indicate that the conservationists prefer no dam to the irrigation dam, while the irrigationists-tourist store owners prefer the irrigation dam to no dam. Therefore, impartial indifference requires society to be indifferent to the choice between no dam and the irrigation dam.

The last paragraph contains two contradictions. We cannot simultaneously have society prefer no dam to an irrigation dam and also be indifferent to the choice between the two. The thrust of Arrow's analysis is that we cannot have both transitivity and impartial indifference to group conflicts in a criteria for social choice.

The argument is, of course, applicable to water resources and environmental quality. It seems, therefore, that there is no simple rule in economic theory that will ease our having to make difficult choices.

SOCIAL COST AND SOCIAL VALUES

Throughout this discussion, we have made frequent reference to environmental costs which leads us to an examination of the concepts of social cost and social value. As early as 1952, Ciriacy-Wantrup considered extra-market costs to be a problem in resource use, and discussed market cost and extra market cost as components of social cost. This and other factors led him to note "a possible difference between private and social optima . . . ."

Our discussion is moderately similar to an earlier analysis of the social cost and social value of electricity by Chapman and O'Neill (1970) and may be expanded as follows:

Social Cost. The cost of an economic activity relevant to societal preferences: the sum of market cost, external diseconomy, subsidy, and nonmonetary cost.

Economic Activity. The process of producing or consuming a commodity or a leisure time activity.

Market Cost. The monetary cost of production of a commodity incurred by the producing enterprise.

External Diseconomy. A nonpurposeful by-product of one economic activity that raises the monetary cost of another economic activity.

Subsidy. A payment, tax deferment, or commodity offered by some public body to producers, thus increasing their profit per unit of output, or to consumers, thus lowering the monetary cost of the economic activity.

Nonmonetary Cost. A negative nonmarket effect upon consumers resulting from a non-purposeful by-product of an economic activity. It is potentially measurable as the payment (in higher prices or taxes) consumers would be willing to make to eliminate the by-product.

Monetary Cost. Components of social cost that are included in a national income concept of social cost: market cost, external diseconomy, and subsidy.

Nonmarket Cost. Components of social cost that are not included in the market cost or market price of an economic activity: external diseconomy, subsidy, and nonmonetary cost.

TABLE 2.
Social Cost and Social Value

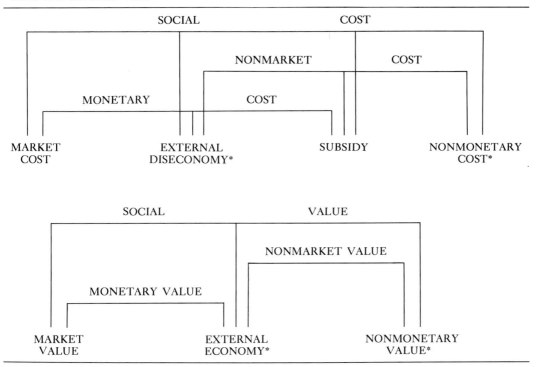

*Substantial environmental significance.

Social Value. The value of an economic activity relevant to societal preferences: the sum of market value, external economy, and nonmonetary value.

Market Value. The price which would have led purchasers to demand the quality consumed. Recall that the price demand function is the inverse of the quantity demand function:

$$P(X) = X^{-1}(P).$$

External Economy. A generally nonpurposeful by-product of one economic activity that lowers the monetary cost of another economic activity.

Nonmonetary Value. A positive nonmarket effect upon consumers resulting from a generally nonpurposeful by-product of another economic activity. It is potentially measureable as the payment (in prices or taxes) consumers would be willing to pay to ensure the continuation of the by-product.

Table 2 may help clarify these relationships. While social cost and social value are partly symmetrical, they are not wholly so. Subsidy is a component of social cost but there is no comparable component of social value. External diseconomy and nonmonetary cost are always nonpurposeful, but external economy and nonmonetary value may occasionally be purposeful.

With reference to the traditional benefit-cost analysis discussed above, the Eckstein-Marglin approach is often associated with an emphasis on monetary cost and monetary values and with a de-emphasis of nonmonetary costs and nonmonetary value.

Past experience with monetizing the nonmonetary in water resource development has

TABLE 3
Social Cost, Social Value, and Water Resource Development by Reservoir Impoundment and Long Distance Transport by Canal or Pipe

I. *Social Cost*	II. *Social Value*
A. Market cost of reservoir bed clearing, dam construction, auxiliary facilities (turbines, picnic tables, etc.), maintenance, and borrowed capital.	A. Market value to agriculture, industry, residences, commerce, and government.
B. External diseconomies. Net loss of wages and profits from destroyed agricultural land, destroyed stream fishery services, destroyed stream recreation services, especially to canoeing and kayaking.	B. External Economies. Net gain in wages and profits from employment of otherwise idle human and capital resources, flood control, navigation improvement, reservoir recreation services, water quality improvement, and electricity production.
C. Nonmonetary cost. Population relocation, species extinction, loss of unique vegetation or landform, interference with or loss of certain recreational experience, such as canoeing, fishing, mountaineering, etc., and loss of scenic attractiveness.	C. Nonmonetary value. Aesthetic value of water quality improvement, security from death through flooding, and satisfaction from reservoir recreation.
D. Subsidies. Low interest charges, federal participation, and agricultural price supports.	

been mixed. Reservoir recreation (an important nonmonetary value) has achieved some degree of accommodation with benefit-cost analysis. Monetary values are imputed to various forms of recreation days, and reservoir recreation is now usually a purposeful by-product of water resource development.

Nonmonetary cost, on the other hand, remains beyond the monetizing ability of agency benefit-cost analysis. Preservation and ecological values have been the political shoals of many a recent water resource proposal, but we shall return later to this problem.

The same physical phenomenon may affect social cost or social value through more than one component (see Table 3). The elimination of stream recreation is a nonmonetary cost to the former recreationists and may cause an external diseconomy in the form of a reduction in wages and profits from stream recreation consumer service to unemployed labor and capital. (Gross National Product is the sum of earned income and ownership income from each economic activity. The external economy and diseco-

nomy concept used here are derived from the national income measures of benefits and costs.)

Secondary Market Benefits and Costs

Direct and indirect monetary effects can be evaluated with increasing ease. Water planners have long debated over the monetary benefits (less loudly over the costs) that "stem from" and are "induced by" a project. If the provision of water and power was a chosen strategy to develop the West, why shouldn't the agencies take as a benefit to set against costs at least the income created in selling to irrigators and processing their crops? Obviously there is a problem of cause and effect. Development is not the result of only one action. Just as we are driven to arbitrarily allocate joint costs in multiple purpose projects, so it is arbitrary to allocate the benefits of economic development to any one of the components needed to produce a project. One of the most appealing rules to emerge from this problem is an insistence on symmetry and system integrity in what is being evaluated. Like costs and like benefits must be compared, and the same system limits for both costs and benefits must be sought. If secondary effects of primary benefits in the project region are to be considered, then secondary effects outside the region—which are apt to be negative in character—should also be considered.

The usual argument against the use of secondary benefits is that federal funds invested in water projects transfer secondary effects from other areas where those funds might otherwise be used. Thus, nationally these effects, however real, cannot be used to offset direct costs. The symmetry rule is violated. As long as the role of evaluation is to add up costs and benefits "to whom so ever they may accrue" (1936 Flood Control Act) with the net value to be used as a criterion, ignoring indirect or multiplier effects is not unreasonable. But if the role of evaluation is to provide an information base to assist the decision-making process in making value judgments about who is to gain or lose, and how much, then perhaps such a display of effects is crucial. It should be noted that the direct benefits from water projects are inherently local while other effects are not.

Obviously, proponents of one set of values will seek to have the displays rigged in their favor. If navigation project reports have not always identified the primary losses to other navigation facilities as a result of a proposed facility, why should they identify both these and the multiplier effects of such losses now? Such indirect effects have long been major motive forces behind water development projects. When the local Chamber of Commerce suggests a dam, it is these effects that motivate it. "Boomer" psychology being what it is, it seems quite likely that such effects are greatly exaggerated in the minds of many and almost any attempt to estimate them may tend to deflate their bubble a bit. Such estimates would go far toward influenc-

ing greater consideration of complex interactions in water resources planning. In terms of economic development, these system-wide input-output effects are analogous to the interactive systems that characterize environmental systems.

SOME EFFECTS OF SUBSIDIES

The economic meaning of the water resource development subsidies has environmental significance which we will discuss with the help of Figures 2 and 3. Figure 2 shows a typical regional supply-demand equilibrium. P_{am} is the market demand function. We have drawn it to reflect the long-run relationship between price and quantity demanded for municipal water of about 0.4, as Hirshleifer and Milliman (1967) and others suggest. C_{am} represents a more hypothetical average market cost function, and C_{as} represents the average subsidy. Water utilities generally follow average cost pricing and avoid rationing; surplus capacity is not uncommon, reflecting lumpiness for new units of capacity, and hydrologic variation in supply as well as demand peaks. Rewards and punishment for water supply managers are not symmetrical between over and under supply. The incentives for new capacity are on the side of avoiding shortages, but that means unused capacity for much of the time. Consumers will purchase supply only at price P_{as}^* to encourage fuller utilization and less apparent unused capacity; shortages are then also made more likely.

As Tables 2 and 3 indicate, the primary significance of environmental effects is in the external and nonmonetary effects. In general, agencies attempt to include all significant external economies as well as estimated monetary worth of nonmonetary values. Agency definitions of benefit probably approach social value. But such is not the case with costs: significant external diseconomies and nonmonetary costs are usually excluded

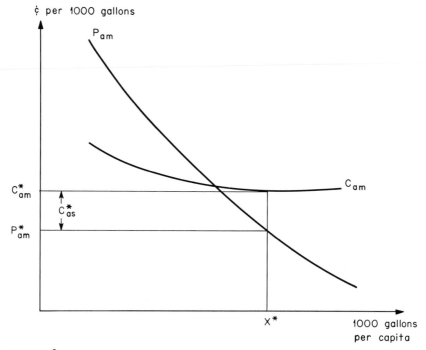

FIGURE 2
Typical supply/demand equilibrium.

from agency calculations. Hence, net benefit maximization in the context of traditional benefit-cost analysis is equivalent to maximizing social value less market cost. In Figure 3, X_{ap} represents the agency preferred supply. It is defined by the intersection of the declining marginal social value function V_{ms} and the rising marginal market cost function C_{mm}.

Table 3 demonstrates substantial external diseconomies, nonmonetary cost, and subsidy. Therefore, marginal social cost C_{ms} is substantially greater than marginal market cost C_{mm}. Maximum net social value is defined by the intersection of marginal social value V_{ms} and marginal social cost C_{ms}. This socially optimal supply would be X_{so}. In response to the discrepancy between social optimum X_{so} and agency preference X_{ap}, conservationists organize to oppose through political means specific construction proposals. The capacity actually built is some compromise X_{ab}^*.

Referring to the preceding discussion of supply-demand equilibrium, actual supply X_{ab}^* can be sold at market price P_{am}^*. Given average market cost C_{am}^*, the water supply industry utilizes subsidy C_{as}^*.

This analysis explains some paradoxes and raises other questions. Expected consequences that flow from this analysis are (1) agency dissatisfaction with actual water supply, (2) conservationist dissatisfaction with actual supply, (3) satisfaction with adequate supplies at given prices from the view of most users, and (4) substantial public subsidy.

Agency managers, more sensitive to the effects of shortage, will still hanker for their preferred supply X_{ap} and beyond. Conservationists will still recognize the gap between marginal social cost C_{ms} and marginal market cost C_{mm}. Once reconciled to the need for water supply to affect that particular set of environmental values, they will still argue for X_{so}. If not reconciled to this need, they

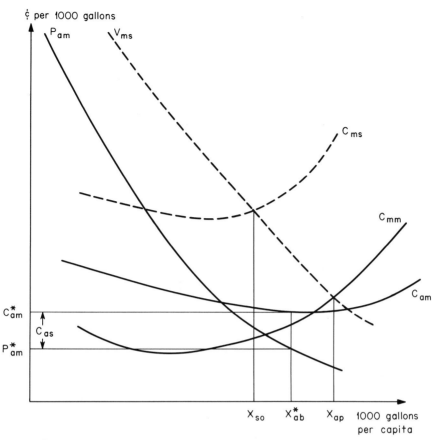

FIGURE 3
Social optima and actual water supply.

cannot be expected to take comfort in the fact that X_{so} is a social optimum and will still agitate for something less. They are not society after all, or are they? Without the subsidy either price would be allowed to rise to C_{am}, or rationing or shortages or both would have to be tolerated more frequently.

EFFLUENT CHARGES

Note that, conceptually, effluent charges act much like the removal of subsidies and raise the price to equal C_{ms}, the marginal social cost. As proposed by most economists they would be used to charge the polluter for the external costs he creates. If it is cheaper for

him to treat, he will. If it is not, then it is better for society (from the Eckstein-Marglin efficiency and constant marginal utility of money, nonequity, everything is reversible point of view) to go ahead and bear the externality caused by the polluter. Even though existing mechanisms to control polluters may be less than effective, it is not clear that everyone would accept the substitution of this system of judgments for them.

But recognize that this system appeals to economists for some features that should not be ignored. First, effluent charges would use the price mechanism as an impersonal rationing device. Prices perform this function for other activities supplemented by other devices such as zoning and property rights; why not make use of it here? This assumes, of course, that there will be some environments where some discharge of wastes will be permitted, which seems likely. Second, the cost in foregone opportunities due to preventing pollution will be minimized. Those who best know the processes that produce the external effect will be provided with incentive to prevent them. Surely, they will find the cheapest mix of process and timing changes and treatment.

Effluent charges will have a useful future. Obviously, charges have long been used where treatment is provided but increasingly the character of the waste is being taken into account in setting the charge. Charges as a control or penalty that do not reflect a service rendered are quite uncommon. Accurate and accepted reflections of the value of the external effects would seem to be as unlikely here as in the monetization of environmental values in traditional benefit-cost analysis. But the logical and operational requirements for accuracy and acceptance may be less demanding. If it is agreed that total waste discharges should be reduced to a given level greater than zero, using a cost of treatment rule to decide how much each should discharge has much to be said for it in terms of equity as well as efficiency. Everyone meeting a rule that calls for the same proportion removed puts quite different cost burdens on different waste producers. Raising a charge to the point where the desired reduction is achieved means that only those who have the greatest interest in avoiding the waste will remain. The test, of course, is whether the application of this rule will produce agreement and at what price for whom.

The problem is to find administratively feasible ways to implement such finely tuned controls. With hundreds of pollutants to be detected, with little in the way of a monitoring system, and with major organizational hurdles and few resources to overcome these problems, pollution agencies will not give up their "works in place" strategy. It is much easier to check on the existence of each treatment plant than to identify the source of each particular pollutant. By spending less on the enforcement system we may spend much more to solve the pollution problem. As long as environmentalists stand alone in support of enforcement and are joined by the construction interests and city administrations only in support of hardware pollution control grants, such an imbalance can be seen as likely to persist.

WHAT KIND OF AN ANSWER IS MULTIPLE OBJECTIVE EVALUATION?

We have not been kind to evaluations which limit themselves to market values. No one believes they are perfect, although many believe they would prefer the outcomes that would result if they were applied more stringently. There is no doubt that the benefit-cost analysis of a project and such related features as the interest rate, choices for projections, and techniques for deriving proxies for market-like values are all effective points at which to attack project justification. But we do have some doubts about the effectiveness of stricter enforcement of the national income or willingness-to-pay criterion leading unambiguously to enhanced environmental quality.

There seems to be no obvious reason why low monetized net returns should be associated very closely with high environmental costs. It does seem likely that wherever the planners are working with a wide benefit-to-cost ratio they can be freer with the inclusion of costs to "mitigate and enhance" environmental features. The opposite of that is that if political support is strong for a project close to the B/C margin and market benefits to costs are being strictly held, there is less room within the project limits to include such compensation. If the planners and the decision process are sensitive to dollar values, then the more environmental values that can be monetized, the stronger the bargaining power will be in the planning period of those who value them. And a correlation between high environmental costs and low net market returns as currently estimated should increasingly shut out the highly damaging projects. But this may be giving the benefit-cost analysis a larger role to play than is warranted.

What is the role of technical screening devices such as benefit-cost analysis? Ingram (1970) argues that they are part of our mechanisms to build consent. Agencies cannot get agreement to undertake every proposed project so they need accepted ways to say "no" to those who would benefit from and promote many of the possibilities. There are also well accepted engineering and financial screens and we have gone far toward identifying a few inviolate environments through the designation of parks and wilderness areas. Once the screens are past, strength of support and lack of conflict may have more to do with real priorities than does technical performance. Obviously, few screens are perfect and it is this very consent process that breaks them down. If a project has strong support and little conflict, is it likely to have problems with the screens, and vice versa? Is there a strong correlation between high support and high market net returns on the one hand and low conflict and low environmental damage on the other? These seem to be reasonable possibilities, but is it enough to view the use of evaluation techniques as simply technical screens? Should we ask for more in a nation that values open democratic processes?

This is not to suggest that water projects have been planned in a manner unsuitable to the values and decision-making structure of the times and places involved. Rather it is to recognize that values and decision-making arrangements are changing, and we must ask what adjustments in planning and evaluation procedures might be considered. The developmental values of water projects are largely local in character and the problem for federal program development is building a pattern of consent across the regions of the nation. This has meant primary Congressional interest with White House interest particularly when the White House is seeking Congressional support on more national issues. The benefit-cost ratio as a technical screen suits this arrangement, and the Office of Management and Budget—the White House's main coordinating agency—was and still is the major proponent of the strict national income point of view.

As a technical screen it also suits the view of a hierarchical decision-making process in which a small number of people at the top of the formal and informal power structure locally and nationally provide the value judgment input—the goals and objectives—for planning. Then the planner is only a technician, applying technical feasibility tests, telling the decision-makers how to do what they have already decided should be done.

But these views of the decision-making situation may not be correct, if they ever were. Environmental quality issues are becoming of more interest on a national level. Does this mean that any time there is a strong environmental conflict in a water development project that it will attain national significance? This would mean reducing Congressional dominance and bringing in White House interest on a different basis, and there is some evidence that this has happened in recent years.

There is some doubt, however, that a monolithic power structure image and the view of the planner as simply a technician is very realistic. Rather, the planner's role may be that of at least a broker between interest groups, and perhaps that of a mobilizer of support if any action is to take place in a highly fragmented and apathetic political situation. This suggests that the "screening device as a way to say no" view of evaluation is at least incomplete. At the very least we should recognize that agencies are themselves groups composed of professionals with articulated value systems and that technical performance standards, including benefits to cost ratio, and many other measures, play a real role in winning their enthusiasm and support for a project. Should this be made more explicit?

If economic evaluation is to play a part in a different kind of planning process the implementation of what has come to be called multiple objective planning and evaluation may be the first step toward achieving it. The basic proposal is to evenhandedly evaluate each project from points of view other than that of national income and to formulate project alternatives that are responsive to other objectives, such as environmental quality. Regional development and social well-being are some other objectives proposed. The elucidation of regional effects would respond to the major motivations for project development that is touted as a way to reduce poverty. Certainly it is unreasonable for us to spend taxes doing so when we can get more poverty reduction for the same amount some other way. But the opportunities for obfuscation are not small now, indeed it is hard to believe that the agencies could effectively use more scope for misuse. Under existing criteria they have well over a 10-year backlog of authorized projects. How many of these have sufficient support and low enough conflict to be built?

More to the point, maybe the opportunities, as seen by Kalter (1971), are for internal change with greater access and information flow that might follow from multiple objective planning and the reduction in decision costs. The present planning process starts with the collection of engineering information and the screening out of a set of feasible engineering solutions. Then economic tests are applied. The last data to be collected and applied are environmental. Considering the staff and expertise available to the planners, this procedure is not unreasonable. There is more engineering knowledge than economic, more economic than environmental. But if environmental values were made more useful to the planner, both in terms of supporting some solutions and rejecting others earlier, fuller and earlier

development of such information should follow. Perhaps fewer never-to-be-funded projects would make it past the authorization stage. Also, it is argued that if environmental problems are seen earlier in the process there will be both the agency realization of and the potential support for innovative means to solve some of the water problems presented to the agencies.

BASIN PLANNING

The above discussion has concerned the agencies, old and new interest groups, the Congress, and the White House. But nothing has been said about basin planning and operating agencies, although since the creation of the Tennessee Valley Authority these have been a part of the debates over water policy. What is their role? Basin planning has done much to increase the inventory of proposed agency projects. This larger inventory has broadened the scope for bargaining between conflicting affected groups. In recent plans there has been a greatly increased attempt to be environmentally responsive at least within the limits available once it was assumed that some level of overall development would take place.

But by and large, there has been little or no shifting of the real intergroup accommodation function to basin entities. As long as the limits of what can be affected are water investments and related regulatory activities, is there scope for effective consent-building? If state and federal executives and legislators are very much the focus for effective decision-making, how does this limit the basin groups and the developers of other schemes for independent evaluation? It raises the suspicion that whatever other planning is done there will be a close relationship between the arena where the final bargain is struck and the agency that will carry it out. To be effective, any other arrangement must have greater consent-building capability. There is at least the suspicion that such consent-building may require considerable planning and construction capacity under one agency roof.

Perhaps of greater concern is that the planning role may be a technical exercise rather than part of the decision-making process, such that the large backlog of authorized but unfunded projects suggests that the steps up to that point are that much less relevant than previously thought. But how much difference is there in what is planned and what is actually constructed? With rapidly changing values and technology it would not be surprising to find that final designs after funding vary drastically from what was approved in the planning years up to the actual funding. But the final design stage is by definition in the hands of the construction agency. Little study has been given to the control and bargaining processes at work there, nor will we do more than raise the issue here. The point is that evaluation is a process that should never be absent from the "gleam in the eye stage to the ribbon-cutting stage."

Perhaps it is suitable to omit a summary of the preceding discussion and conclude with E. J. Mishan's summary of welfare economics:

> Although welfare economics is in a quandary right now, it does not follow that we do nothing until we have found a way out of the current impasse. . . . In certain situations, the welfare economist may reveal the nature, and even guess at the magnitude, of conspicuous external economies or diseconomies, making it apparent that . . . current production determined by commercial considerations is too small or too large . . . I should, therefore, be pleasantly surprised to know if anything in this volume (*Welfare Economics*) has led to some occasional head-scratching on some fundamental questions about the value of economic growth, or perhaps, in more cynical moods, about what it is after all that the world economy is maximizing right now— other than gross productive power, or human population on this planet.

References

Arrow, Kenneth J. 1950. "A Difficulty in the Concept of Social Welfare," in *Readings in Welfare Economics*. Edited by K. J. Arrow and T. Scitovsky, pp. 147–168, Irwin, Homewood, Illinois, 1969, reprinted from *J. of Polit. Econ.*, 58, 328-46.

Chapman, Duane. 1970. *Income Bias, Benefit Cost Analysis, and Consumers' Surplus: Logical Problems in the Evaluation of Public Benefit*. U.S.A.E.C. Report ORNL-4477. Oak Ridge National Laboratory, Oak Ridge, Tenn.

Chapman, Duane, and Robert V. O'Neill. 1970. *Ecology and Resource Economics: An Integration and Application of Theory to Environmental Dilemmas*, U.S.A.E.C. Report ORNL-4641 Oak Ridge National Laboratory, Oak Ridge, Tenn.

Ciriacy-Wantrup, S. V. 1952. *Resource Conservation: Economics and Policies*. University of California Press, Berkeley.

Eckstein, Otto. 1958. *Water Resource Development, The Economics of Project Evaluation*. Harvard University Press, Cambridge, Mass.

Gorman, W. M. 1955. "The Intransitivity of Certain Criteria Used in Welfare Economics," *Oxford Economic Papers, N.S.7,* 25-35.

Hicks, J. R. 1939. "Foundations of Welfare Economics," *Econ. J.,* 49, 696-712.

Hirshleifer, Jack, and J. W. Milliman. 1967. "Urban Water Supply: A Second Look," *American Economic Review,* 57(2):169-78.

Ingram, Helen M. 1970. *Patterns of Politics in Water Resource Development: A Case Study of New Mexico's Role in the Colorado River Basin Bill*. Publications of the Division of Government Research, No. 79. The University of New Mexico.

Kaldor, N. 1939. "Welfare Propositions in Economics," *Econ. J.,* 49:549-552.

Kalter, Robert J. 1971. *Multiple Objective Planning: Reflections on the Current Scene.* Cornell Agricultural Economics Staff Paper No. 28, Cornell University, Ithaca, New York.

Knetsch, Jack L., *et al.* 1969. *Federal Natural Resources Development: Basic Issues in Benefit and Cost Measurement*, Natural Resources Policy Center, The George Washington University, Washington, D. C.

Marglin, Stephen A. 1962. "Objectives of Water-Resource Development: A General Statement," Ch. 2 in *Design of Water-Resource Systems*, Arthur Maas *et al.*, Harvard University Press, Cambridge, Mass.

Mishan, E. J. 1967. *Welfare Economics: Five Introductory Essays*, Random House, New York.

Scitovsky, Tibor. 1941. "A Note on Welfare Propositions in Economics," *The Review of Econ. Studies*, 9:77–88, reprinted in *Readings in Welfare Economics*, op. cit., pp. 390–401.

Seckler, David W. 1966. "On the Uses and Abuses of Economic Science in Evaluating Outdoor Recreation," *Land Econ.*, 42: 485–494.

U.S. Water Resources Council. 1968. *The Nation's Water Resources*, Washington, D.C.

CHAPTER 21

One of the most important components of the decision-making process in a complex field like water resources development is the use of technical expertise. As Dr. Eipper's previous articles on this subject were very perceptive, we invited him to prepare a contribution for this report on how best to use technical experts for incorporating considerations of environmental quality into the planning and evaluation of water development. Unfortunately, Dr. Eipper's superiors in the Bureau of Sport Fisheries and Wildlife showed considerable reluctance to allow his views to be articulated, and delays in the processes of gaining approval to publish his contribution resulted in our being unable to include it. We feel strongly that his opinions are of real value to this report, and if the present system represents a general federal policy, it is a serious detriment to the quality of the entire decision-making process.

There is no doubt that federal bureaucracies must be able to depend upon the loyalty of their members to be assured that present policies be carried out in an orderly and efficient manner. However, it is widely recognized that no policy is perfect, and that many are in need of considerable change. If federal employees, who often are those best acquainted with intimate details of the effects of policies and who are often most cognizant of field problems, are unable to participate in such reasonable, deliberate discussions of policy questions as those covered in this book, the improvement of federal policy will be seriously handicapped.

We urge the National Water Commission to recommend that no review procedure for the statements of federal employees be used as a device to inhibit free discussion of needed policy improvements. Orderly, constructive dissent should not be considered as disloyalty on the part of federal employees any more than dissent by other citizens is disloyal.

In order to present some of Dr. Eipper's views, we have assembled a collage of his previously published work bearing on our theme.

THE ROLE OF THE TECHNICAL EXPERT IN DECISION-MAKING

Alfred W. Eipper

INTRODUCTION

Natural resource management problems have reached a level of complexity and interrelationship where no one category can be realistically considered in a vacuum. Faced with the challenge of developing meaningful policies and genuinely useful plans, the resource manager's first—and perhaps greatest—problem is to identify those processes in the human ecosystem that make it no longer possible to isolate the management of any one natural resource from that of others—the processes that accelerate conflicts in the size, complexity, and occurrence of resource use.

POPULATION, TECHNOLOGY, AND WATER USE

The interacting effects of unchecked population growth and industrial and agricultural expansion cause most of our environmental problems. Although man has taken some half-million years to reach his present population, he will double this within the next forty years; the projected increase of 100 million in the U.S. population over the next thirty years (U.S. Department of the Interior, 1965) can be represented as the addition of a new city of 270,000 inhabitants each month between now and A.D. 2000; four of our states already have population densities substantially higher than India's.

Demands on natural resources are increasing much faster than the population. In the case of water, per capita use in the United States, exclusive of use for transportation and recreation, appears to be doubling every 40 years (U.S. Water Resources Council, 1968). This means that in the 65 years it will take our population to double, *total* water use will increase sixfold. Hence, the Department of the Interior's statement in 1965 that under existing use patterns, the total amount of water needed just to sustain the present U.S. population for the remainder of their lives is greater than all the water that has been used by all people who have occupied the earth to date.

We tend to think of water supplies as fixed. In fact, increasing amounts of water are being rendered unusable through various forms of pollution. Although some uses do not make water unfit for certain purposes, our total usable water supplies are being reduced by pollution while demands for water accelerate sharply in response to the combined effects of population increase and technological development.

SOME BASIC PRECEPTS GOVERNING WATER RESOURCE DECISIONS

Because we are being forced to make increasingly critical decisions about ecosystems for which reliable predictive data are often lacking, we must collectively develop a frame-work of genuinely useful principles to guide our dealings with natural environments.

1. There is an upper limit to the carrying capacity of man's environment.

2. Survival of even a steady-state population depends upon maintenance of its natural environment.

3. Changes in an ecosystem caused by man are generally disruptive, and the occurrence and character of such disruptions are frequently unpredictable.

4. Costs of correcting damage to an ecosystem usually far exceed the costs of preventing it.

In addition, there are certain basic shortcomings of humans—including technical experts and decision-makers—which are particularly important to recognize in this decision-making context:

1. A tendency to oversimplify.

2. Difficulty in recognizing, acknowledging, and acting on future possibilities which lie outside the realm of past experience (for example, limited carrying capacity of man's environment, and new pollution problems).

3. Overconfidence in man's abilities to correct environmental problems with technology.

4. Failure to appreciate necessity of ecological diversity.

5. Tendency to rely on adapting old solutions for solving new problems.

6. Tunnel vision: failure to appreciate necessity of compromise and wide public representation in solutions of natural resource conflicts, and failure to consider a sufficiently wide range of possible alternatives.

7. Reluctance to participate in discussion and debate of policies and programs affecting the environment—such as fear of exposure, fear of ridicule, fear of reprisal.

8. Inadequacy of man's understanding of ecological complexes to predict many environmental effects of resource management schemes, or to recognize occurrence of these effects until their later stages.

ALLOCATION FROM A COMPOSITE OF VIEWPOINTS

One conclusion from the preceding remarks is that any resource manager should unreservedly support and help promote measures to reduce the rate of increase in the human population. To do less implies a failure to comprehend the single largest, most fundamental problem in every subdivision of natural resource management.

Second, the exponential proliferation in kinds and intensities of pressures on natural resources indicates the need for more skillful allocation. On what basis do we allocate the use of a lake or stream for fishing, water supply, boating, industry, swimming, electricity, residence, scenic beauty, flood control, water skiing, sewage treatment, camping, shoreline development, hunting, and so on? Any such complex allocation decision requires the use of a *variety* of "yardsticks" or criteria for estimating values and deciding on priorities.

In the past, dollar values have been widely used by natural resource planners and biologists as a sole basis for weighing (or justifying) all elements in an allocation complex. Today, we recognize many limitations of using the monetary yardstick alone for water resources planning.

Unrealistic results from attempts to force all elements of a water resource complex into a dollar framework have led critical resource economists to describe benefit-cost analysis as "an accumulation of absurdities" or "expedient self-deception," and others—with tongue in cheek—to define an economist as "a man who assumes everything except responsibility." The basic difficulty is that conflicting demands often cannot be compared in one common unit of value.

This does not mean that we should discontinue the use of economic analysis on resource allocation problems, any more than we would throw away a screwdriver because it makes a poor drill. To devise the best possible solutions for today's complex allocation problems, we must employ all available tools that are useful in some capacity. Economic analysis is one of these. Natural resource economists have been among the first to recognize certain limitations of economic analysis generally, and the "classical" form of benefit-cost analysis in particular, for single-handedly solving multiple-use problems.

Today's basic approach to natural resource problems must be a diversified yet coordinated one: jointly to employ a variety of criteria and methods in estimating environmental impacts and charting environmental management.

In short, the policy-making and planning so much needed in natural resource management require a team of imaginative experts representing various disciplines.

THE SCIENTIST'S ROLE

Global ecologists point out that our planet is, in fact, a space vehicle with a mushrooming human population and a balanced, continuously recycling life-support system. Because key elements of this system are increasingly threatened by man's pollution activities, we must develop an effective early-warning process. Scientists must be willing to involve themselves in this process by detecting and publicizing foreseeable threats to the environment. It is encouraging to note the growing recognition of this necessity by scientists such as R. S. Morison (1969) and O. M. Solandt (1969). This is not to suggest any lessened importance of long-term research on the causes and effects of pollution. Our focus here is simply on another dimension of pollution: those impending problems which require preventive action now.

What are some of the functions required of the scientist in this early-warning approach to a potential pollution situation? First, this approach involves ferreting out and analyzing all pertinent data that are available *now.* Frank Di Luzio (1967), former Assistant Secretary of the Interior for Water Pollution Control, stated the concept well,

> all of us would like to know all the facts about the problems we are dealing with. Since we never will know all the facts, we've got to do the best we can with the facts at hand. To a considerable extent we must forego the satisfaction of dealing with incontrovertible scientific data and be guided simply by prima facie evidence.

Next, the scientist must be willing to publicize his tentative conclusions from the data, his assessment of alternative management measures, and the likely effects that these conclusions suggest to him. It is not enough to "let the facts speak for themselves." The scientist, as a trained and experienced specialist, has an obligation to give society his professional interpretation of those facts. It is also essential to the validity of the decision-making process that he identify this as *his*—not *the*—interpretation. When scientists disagree in their interpretations, they should discuss and analyze the sources of disagreement, for the ultimate benefit of society.

I suspect a majority of scientists are disquieted by at least some aspects of the role outlined above. It stipulates the unpleasant necessity of going out on a shaky limb of tentative conclusions. It often involves a kind of limelight the scientist would rather avoid, and it may involve him, at least peripherally, in unaccustomed controversy. Nevertheless, the scientist must face the fact that he is now living in a different ecosystem with critical new problems, on a new time scale that requires new approaches. Only the dedicated scientific recluse can totally ignore these new responsibilities. The early-warning approach requires that scientists call the shots as they see them and remember that debate is central to scientific progress. They should recognize that straddling a fence too long can produce sterility, and that when one has reached the point of making all his communications noncontroversial there is no further need for him to communicate.

The role of the scientist, as such, should not extend beyond presentation and defense of his estimate of pollution hazards and an assessment of alternatives. He has an obligation to make available information from his profession that will help the voter make a more enlightened decision, but he must scrupulously avoid telling him how to vote. Because decisions on environmental management are so complex, they must represent the best possible reconciliation of many different interests; hence, they must be public decisions. The scientist can contribute much to the *basis* for a public decision, but in *making* that decision, he has only one vote. He is no more entitled—and no more qualified—than any other citizen to elect which of various alternative courses should be followed.

On the other hand, he is no *less* entitled or qualified to choose. The scientist should not, from fear that his professional identity will give him unfair advantage, shrink from exercising the political rights of a private citizen to express his personal views on a controversial issue. Although quite properly concerned about his credibility as a scientist, he should not disregard his credibility as a human being and voter with genuine convictions.

MAXIMIZING THE TECHNICAL EXPERT'S CONTRIBUTION

Suggestions for decision-making bodies:

1. Keep the expert's conclusions in perspective.

2. Don't silence your scientists directly (orders, threats, etc.) or indirectly (misuse of "neutrality," "impartiality," etc.).

3. Involve as many technical experts representing as many different views as possible in a decision, *not* just the ones you want to hear from.

4. Start early enough to allow extra weeks for secondary discussions, and for conclusions reviewed by all participants.

5. Create and maintain an atmosphere promoting maximum lively exchange of useful information and constructive opinion among the experts: (*a*) make sure the context and framework of assumptions are realistic, but not confining; (*b*) stimulate and be especially receptive to totally new ideas; (*c*) get the experts to discuss their differences, to define them and, where possible, work through to resolutions of differences; (*d*) avoid the formalized, adversary constraints of differences; (*e*) also avoid a meeting that produces a benign compendium of "motherhood" statements; (*f*) listen intelligently to everything all your experts have to say—if you disagree, be sure your reasons are valid, and that you get their response to your disagreement.

6. Act responsibly on your experts' advice: (*a*) avoid taking only the advice you wanted anyway; (*b*) where a compromise between opposing views is required, be sure it's an intelligent (as opposed to expedient) compromise.

References

Note: This paper is a composite of sections from two articles previously published by Dr. Eipper, and from an outline of a proposed chapter for this report.

De Luzio, Frank. 1967. Quoted in: *A new era for America's waters.* Fed. Water Pollut. Contr. Admin. Publ.

Eipper, Alfred W. 1968. A multiple approach to water management planning. Introduction to *Aspects of Planning, Evaluation, and Decision-Making in Sport Fishery Management.* 4th N.Y. Fishery Biologists' Seminar, Ithaca, New York. Department of Conservation Extension Series No. 1, Cornell University, Ithaca.

Eipper, Alfred W. 1970. *Pollution problems, resource policy, and the scientist.* Science 169: 11–15 (3 July 1970).

Morison, R. S. 1969. *Science 165:* 150.

Solandt, O. M. 1969. *Science 165:* 445.

U.S. Department of Interior. 1965. *Quest for quality.* U.S.D.I. Conservation Yearbook. Washington, D.C.

U.S. Water-Resources Council. 1968. *The Nation's Water Resources.* Washington, D.C.

CHAPTER 22

There is a role for water resource decision-making at all levels, though each has unique problems. Most decisions in the United States will probably continue to be made at the federal or regional level because of the widespread ecological, social, and economic impacts of most projects, and as a result of the greater resources available in terms of money and manpower. In the light of rapid technological and social changes, decisions should, whenever possible, allow for flexibility–that is, leave options open should priorities change in the future.

The major problem in decision-making is the lack of public confidence in the present system, which must be remedied by allowing all interested and affected parties to participate, as well as by improving the caliber of the oligarchy chosen as "the decision-makers." To insure protection of the public interest and to improve the quality of decisions, full, open, and honest procedures are required with adequate communication between all parties. As a last resort, citizens should have the right to sue on environmental grounds, and the establishment of an ombudsman may be necessary to reinforce this right.

DECISION-MAKING AT LOCAL, STATE, FEDERAL, AND INTERNATIONAL LEVELS

Charles R. Ross

INTRODUCTION

Water, its exploitation and its development, has determined the course and direction of our nation's growth throughout history. Occasionally, during the past two hundred years or more, attempts have been made to subject this development to the overriding interests of the public at large.

The Federal Power Act, for example, sought to provide general guidelines under which parties seeking to exploit our water resources were required to act. These standards were generally conceived not for restricting development, but for guiding institutions in promoting further development while recognizing that future generations might wish to reassess the manner of use of this resource. It soon became apparent that the impact of decisions about water could determine the long-run future of the nation, not simply the future of the paper industry, nor the future of a national park, nor the future of conservation or recreation, but the future of man himself.

In recent years, therefore, beginning with initial attempts by such special interest groups as the conservationists, the decision-making process has undergone a dramatic change. No longer could the nation be casual about the methods used to reach water development decisions. All interested parties (removed as they might be from the direct consequences of a decision), including those expressing a concern for future generations, demanded not only the right to be heard, but also that the decision-making process itself be the one best adapted to arrive at a result which would balance fairly the competing interests of all groups. The developers and the environmentalists alike need a forum where they can present their positions, confident that the final decision will be one which has been arrived at as a result of an adequate presentation by all sides, including staff and decision-makers who are expert and independent. Such decisions will have the credibility necessary to command the respect of all, which is vital to the preservation of all our private and governmental institutions.

Over the past ten years or more, I have had a unique opportunity to participate in many decisions at different levels in which the development of water resources has come directly into conflict with the environmentalists. Needless to say, there are a number of these decisions which could be substantially improved or revised. In the hope that there is a lesson to be learned from my experiences on decision-making bodies in Vermont, the Federal Power Commission, and the International Joint Commission, I offer the following comments.

ACQUISITION OF KNOWLEDGE AND EXPERTISE

Administrative agencies such as the FPC were formed because of technological advancement and rapid growth early in this century. Congress was at a virtual standstill because of the time, effort, and knowledge required to license every hydroelectric facility proposed for our navigable streams. Ten years of controversy gave rise to the famous conservation message of President Theodore Roosevelt in his veto of the Rainy River project and to the principle that our water resources were to be held in trust for the people of the United States and not to be exploited by a few special interests (Shad, 1962).

On the passage of the Federal Power Act of 1920,[1] Congress delegated overall responsibility to three already overworked Cabinet members, the Secretaries of War, Interior, and Agriculture, in a committee similar to the present Water Resources Council. Ten years later Congress decided that it needed full-time decision-makers who could be expected to keep themselves informed in the special areas involved, and an independent Federal Power Commission was created.

Fundamental to the administrative process is the procedure by which an administrative body and its staff acquire the necessary knowledge and expertise. During the early 1930s a number of alert, dedicated, and intelligent public servants came to work for the FPC, and the stable staff of knowledgeable experts that evolved has been of great value to the Commissioners ever since. However, above everything else a staff must be independent of the industry which it seeks to supervise. Too often a staff becomes over-imbued with the concept that its principal function is to serve industry and to be as accommodating as possible. This may be the result of too much exposure to industry, or simply of a human desire to impress industry's representatives with its importance in the scheme of things.

To hire a competent staff it is imperative to have adequate funds. Often the much-praised independence of the staff of the so-called independent regulatory agency is, in fact, illusory. The Bureau of the Budget (now the Office of Management and the Budget) repeatedly cut our funds to the bone when its members thought we were being too ambitious; or persons like the late Albert Thomas, Chairman of the House Subcommittee on Appropriations for Independent Agencies was able by virtue of his position, to make us almost subservient to his wishes. Inevitably the FPC had to plead with the Senate Commerce Committee to restore the funds cut by the House.

A staff also needs the support of its agency's members. Recently the Water Resources Council's staff asked for a budget increase and the Council itself cut the request by almost three-fourths before forwarding it on to OMB.

On the international level, lack of money for a staff has effectively prevented the United States section of the International Joint Commission from making an equal contribution. It is ironic that the powerful and wealthy United States should continually be forced to ask its Canadian colleagues to do most of the staff work. Clearly, an adequate American staff could contribute to a more intelligent review of international water pollution problems.

When state regulation works, it is often because the state can afford to hire skilled personnel. This is true in the regulation of industry in New York State. Former FPC chairman Joseph C. Swidler learned the lesson well, and when he assumed his present position as head of the New York Public Service Commission, he hired away many of the most competent members of the FPC staff. In Vermont, as in a few other states, the contesting sides are more nearly equal

financially since the Public Service Board has the right to backcharge to the utilities costs incurred in representing the public in rate cases. This gives the state a great deal more leverage in dealing with companies under its jurisdiction.

Frequently resource agencies simply react to crises; seldom do they seek to anticipate problems. The most effective method of handling controversial matters is to acquire a competent staff and investigate and study the problem well in advance of any deadline and well before emotions take over. However, the staff needs the authorization and backing of the decision-makers, which may be lacking, particularly if the decision-maker is a single individual. It is a distinct advantage to have the responsibility of deciding whether or not to institute investigation vested in more than one person. In any case, a credible answer is almost impossible to achieve when one side or the other, whether the power industry or the conservation movement, seeks to use procedural blackmail to whipsaw an agency and its staff.

The typical decision-maker devotes far too little time to acquiring a real expertise of his own, or relies too much on the expertise he brings to the job without keeping up to date. It might be thought that the staff could read and summarize all the latest law review articles, and keep abreast of the latest technical information on phosphate control or eutrophication, for example. Usually, however, not even the staff has time to sit down and digest all this information. I have often seen cases of particular problems settled on the basis of some article or news report that accidentally came to our attention. This was particularly true of matters which were interdisciplinary in nature. At the FPC, outside personal interests or background often influenced the course of action.

In an effort to compensate for the limitations of time as well as the narrowness of the interests of a particular commissioner, several members of the FPC sought to have personal assistants responsible to them only and not beholden to the chairman, as is the staff. This move was resisted by Chairman Swidler partly because it would enable commissioners to dissent more frequently. Led by Commissioner Lawrence O'Connor, however, we were able to secure the right to hire a second staff member, an action that turned out to be well worth the expense. The surest way to improve the quality of their work is for the members of the staff to know that the decision-maker, whether through his own personal efforts or through advice from his personal staff, may show them up in their own field. An independent source of advice also enables a commissioner better to keep up with technology, and at the same time keep his fellow members on their toes. In general, it improves the quality of the discussion if not of the decision.

This experience is not exactly comparable to the problems of an executive agency, where there is one man at the top accountable in fact and in theory to the chief executive. However, I cannot subscribe to the suggestion of reducing the number of decision-makers to one man in most administrative agencies, particularly in these times when the interrelationship of many disciplines is vital to the final decision.

So long as many administrative agencies consist of several policy makers, every effort should be made to keep open the line of communication between the regular staff and the other members of the agency. Frequently a chief administrative officer is able to reward or penalize members of the staff for certain actions, while other members of the commission are left in the dark.

The most neglected aspect (and the most important) of decision-making is feedback on the impact of a particular decision upon the general public. Until the conservation movement began to flourish and citizen groups started demanding a right to participate in policy formation, the average specialized body seldom got a consumer reaction. Industry groups who follow FPC actions closely understand the subtleties of each decision, and most decisions are made in light of the dire consequences predicted for the industry. The general press usually could not care less. The trade press, on the other hand, not only cares but makes sure that subscriptions go only to persons or organizations which might benefit their cause. For example, after leaving the Commission I had considerable difficulty in subscribing to the *Electrical World*, which is indispensable to anyone following the industry, and which covers Commission activities quite well.

Fortunately the intimacy which has characterized the relationship of the regulator and the regulated is dissolving under the glare of citizen scrutiny. Beneficial as this is, we must be careful that these citizen groups remain independent and not become a part of the system, and we must encourage greater reverse flow from the man on the street. In the January 1971 issue of *Technology Review*, Chandler Stevens says:

That the need for grievance investigation, public discourse on problems, and formal articulation of issues and answers is urgent is demonstrated by the overload on the present system. Other forces besides the media, working to expose inadequacies in bureaucracies and in "the System" in general, are so deluged with inquiries, complaints, and suggestions that most go unanswered. This is true even of the thousands of letters received by the number one ombudsman in the United States today, Ralph Nader—a self-appointed individual who has no more than the power of the law and the public opinion at his disposal. Mr. Nader's effectiveness suggests that the Communications Revolution may well be tipping the balance of power in favor of such individuals and against large corporations.

The current interest in the role of state and local government reflects the concern that government is getting too far from the people. Even the city alderman or the minor state official becomes so engrossed in daily tasks that he hasn't time to bother with individuals. Even if he has time, he is apt to avoid confrontation with an aroused citizenry when his position varies from theirs. In any case, seldom does government get enough citizen input. Again in the words of Stevens (1971):

> The private citizen suffers not only from limitations of perspective—as the specialist policy adviser does—and of knowledge—as the generalist elected representative does—but also from limitations of time and incentive if he is not paid or otherwise significantly rewarded for pondering societal problems. It is only because modern communications make it feasible for all citizens to have easy access to inexpensive receivers and transmitters of information that any citizens who in fact have a stake in, some experience on, or a deep concern about particular societal problems can they make real contributions to the solution of such problems.

Some years ago, while I was in Washington, I was invited by the citizens of Burlington, Vermont, and the local press to comment on a proposed 50,000 megawatt coal-burning generating station on the shores of Lake Champlain in the heart of the city. I weighed very carefully the pros and cons of responding, and finally spoke at length against the project. The bond issue, which needed a two-thirds majority, was a revenue one, and thus the typical reluctance of taxpayers to approve a tax increase was not at issue. It was defeated, much to the chagrin of its supporters, and according to local newspaper ads an outsider, a "Man From Washington," was responsible. Today the decision makes sense because it prevented increased air pollution and thermal pollution, and there are now alternative sources of power, but it illustrates how difficult it is for a local community to take on the power structure without the assistance of a mediator. In this case, the Electric Light Department had hired a large consulting and engineering firm (who would profit from construction) to present their side. Moreover, as in many local issues, many persons were politely blackmailed into publicly supporting the project.

A most unpleasant task in a small community is to displease a neighbor, a friend, or a fellow businessman, and there are subtle pressures brought by the Establishment against those who are willing to stand up and dissent. Unfortunately, facts and the expertise and ability to present them properly (or the means to hire someone to do so) are the key ingredients in resource decisions, and frequently such skill is unavailable when problems are left to a local community for solution.

INPUTS TO THE DECISION

Today's decisions are now profiting by the increased participation of citizen groups, although some people claim that this participation has effectively prevented timely decisions. One of the landmarks in the history of citizen participation is the Scenic Hudson case[2] in which I was involved. My concern in this case arose from an ill-advised attempt by some of the Commissioners (on recommendation of the staff) to short-circuit intervention by persons in the Hudson Valley who wanted to protest the construction of a pumped storage plant at Storm King and wanted the FPC to hold a hearing in the area. The usual contemptuous remark about "little ol' ladies in tennis shoes" holding up progress raised my hackles since it appeared to me that a decision—quite presumptuously—had already been made to grant the license. However, the Second Circuit Court of Appeals not only recognized the rights of conservation groups to intervene, but also reminded the FPC in very forceful language that the purpose of the Commission was not simply to umpire, but to act affirmatively to develop a fair record of the case.[3] Ever since this decision, government agencies have had their feet held to the fire, and legitimately so. Not only does the decision-maker profit from a more aggressive staff position, but he also benefits from well-reasoned arguments by intervener groups.

The staff now faces a lively competition of ideas. Even though it may owe its existence to the decision-makers, it knows that an independent third party is providing a legal yardstick with which to measure the depth of its public interest. Before the advent of public interest law firms and citizen groups, there was a pressing need for Congress to create a Consumer's Protector. This possibility still exists (see McCloskey, in this volume), for some of our public interest law firms are failing to live up to their potential. I fear that the sense of battle and a win at any costs, rather than a broad and constructive record, are becoming the goal in many cases.

Our legal structure has always been based upon the adversary process. The forceful advocacy of narrow positions by differing clients before wise and learned judges is supposed to provide us with proper social and economic judgments. In a typical tort or criminal case the judge can usually rely upon the opposing attorney to keep the other side honest, while the judge himself, with the benefit of many similar cases and his own legal experience to draw upon, can make sure that an adequate and fair record is secured. In the newly developing resource field, however, counsel is often unfamiliar with nascent technology, and one side may not know whether or not the other is being honest. The judge, unless he has taken pains to acquire a working knowledge of the new field, may not have the expertise to aid the parties in developing a fair record.

In a resource case, decision-makers must concern themselves with the consequences of the decision upon the general public, as well as upon the parties to the case. They cannot afford the luxury of a decision which fails to anticipate social and technical impact. For this reason, we must encourage interveners, public interest law firms, unbiased advisory panels of experts, and early public investigation of technological resource problems.

Many state and federal agencies have begun appointing advisory committees or task forces to assist them in handling complicated technical problems. This action should be applauded, provided such committees truly represent consumers as well as a cross section of the experts. Frequently the experts are picked because (1) they are not controversial, (2) they represent important economic interests, (3) they can be expected (from previous cases) to come to certain conclusions, (4) they belong to the right political party, (5) they are employed by someone who can afford to let them appear, or (6) they have a prestigious name but obviously will not have time to bother the people who want to influence the decision. Seldom, if ever, will such a committee have average citizen-consumers as members because their lack of expertise and personal stake in such decisions cause them to be the most critical judges of all.

These remarks are made in light of my experience with the FPC in setting up the Electrical Advisory Committee, the Natural Gas Advisory Council, and a number of special task forces. In the case of the electric industry, we deliberately ignored the wishes of Edison Electric Institute (this industry's trade organization) and picked a chairman who was not a part of the "in" group. With the Natural Gas Council we went along with industry and appointed the heads of large trade groups. In neither case did we concern ourselves with the preliminary conversations as to the industry position. The Commission refused to appoint to one task force a particular well-known, vigorous, and articulate proponent of the conservation movement.

One method of insuring an adequate record would be to hire qualified experts as consultants or expert witnesses. It is a worthwhile objective, but hard to accomplish. First of all, many experts are reluctant to expose themselves to the petty, drawn-out cross-examination which characterizes many administrative proceedings, especially in those cases for which the public pays the bill. Second, many experts are employees of nonprofit institutions such as universities or foundations, and economic pressure may be brought on their employers by the other side. Third, the expert may be retained by one party to prevent him from testifying for the other side. Fourth, witnesses are reluctant to testify if there is a chance that it may kill opportunities for future jobs or appointments. However, there are professional witnesses who enjoy the fame and glory of seeing their names in print.

We are beginning to encourage more and more participation by intervener groups, indicating a recognition by both judges and administrative agencies of the far-reaching impact of modern technological problems. It is an important development and must be allowed to flourish, but under carefully controlled conditions. Unfortunately, interveners, like some professional witnesses, may find that they enjoy the limelight so much that the purpose of the intervention is lost to sight. Conservation groups adopt the same tactics as their opponents. For example, utilities would apply for a license at the last minute in order that they might argue that time was of the essence, thus cutting off development of an adequate case record. Now conservation groups use procedural blackmail by deliberately seeking to delay a hearing, thus vesting economic penalties not only upon the applicant but also upon innocent bystanders.

Despite these tactics, we must seek ways to help interveners make an intelligent presentation. It would be helpful to establish a procedure by which counsel for these groups could have access to the memoranda prepared by the staff of the agencies involved, thus shortening the hearing process and diminishing the competitiveness which develops during trial. The tendency to think of a trial as a competetion may often be the cause of lengthy proceedings, with counsel losing sight of the real objectives and their employers too often refusing to intercede, either

because they don't know enough about it or because they won't accept the responsibility for shutting up their lawyers.

Trade and academic journals often attempt to influence the decision-makers. It is a recognized practice for attorneys to publish articles in law journals in hopes of influencing the outcome of a trial, and trade journals frequently publish flattering articles about a decision-maker from whom they hope to obtain a favorable decision or, conversely, try to "soften him up" by attacking him. Planted newspaper stories designed to influence reluctant colleagues are considered fair tactics by some: many reporters are willing to oblige, since they know that cooperation may gain them an inside track on future stories.

There is little question that actual payoffs are few if we speak in terms of money. However, if by payoff we mean a favorable image, enhanced prestige, laudatory publicity, or whatever, then they are common. Good press notices can lead to many opportunities for advancement, and they are sought as much by decision-makers as by industrial executives or movie stars. Further, it behooves the decision-maker to know what is said in leading newspapers (for example, the *Washington Post* and the *Star*, the *New York Times*, the *Wall Street Journal*) to be able to anticipate future positions and events. Often an exposé in these papers forces the staff to react to a problem, and staff members who are being ignored may go to the press with juicy details, in an attempt to keep their bosses honest. It is a devious and dangerous way to insure a full and fair record, but it is done whether we like it or not.

THE HEARING

The hearing itself is a matter of great importance to all parties, and is probably the most vital protection the public has. Without hearings, the public may never be informed and self-interested parties are much freer to advocate limited and biased positions. It is far easier to arrive at a foregone conclusion if one does not have to fear that the facts will be presented publicly by persons qualified to interpret them: for example, the AEC and the FPC are prone to avoid a public confrontation if at all possible (see the so-called Yadkin case).[4]

The place of hearing is also a matter of importance. At one time the FPC would refuse to go into the field for hearings. In the Scenic Hudson case[2] the Commission originally refused to have a hearing in Cornwall or in any nearby community because it might cause trouble, and this action was the first indication I had that some members of the staff, as well as some members of the Commission, might already have made up their minds. Fortunately, many agencies are learning the lesson and showing less reluctance to hold hearings in the home territory of a particular dispute.

Another procedural aspect of the hearing process is prior notice. All too often every effort is made to minimize public participation rather than to maximize it, by complying literally (and that is all) with notice requirements. At the federal level notice of a public hearing is generally required in the *Federal Register*; but this is hardly what is needed if one is seeking a fair representation by all segments of society. It may make for a more orderly hearing, but it does not make for a better one.

In the early 1960s, a party interested in resource and conservation decisions usually had difficulty locating the results of important cases. Hearings were virtually unreported, and one had to rely upon word of mouth to know what was going on. Since one of the purposes of a hearing is to encourage the development of a well-informed public, every effort should be made to publicize the results. Normally this is not a problem on the local level. On the state level, however, it depends on the size of the state and the degree of concentration of ownership of the communications media On the federal level, hearings and the resultant decisions used to be reported well in Washington and by the trade press, but there was little effort to get news back to the locality affected, if the hearing involved a technical subject. In Canada, the actions taken by the International Joint Commission are usually well reported. The Great Lakes are important to Canadians environmentally, industrially, politically, and aesthetically; moreover, Canadians are constantly concerned about being swallowed up by the patronizing neighbor to the south. On the other hand, the United States often seems to ignore its neighbors, so little is written about mutual problems except along the border. The trials and tribulations of the IJC since 1918 in calling the nation's attention to the deteriorating state of Lake Erie is a good example. More recently, the residents of Windsor, Canada, complained bitterly about the failure of Detroit papers to report the results of a hearing involving the pollution of Canada from sources across the border in Michigan.

THE DECISION

Everyone who has participated as a decision-maker is aware of the highly personal nature of the process. Background, personality, and biases all enter in (Craik, 1970). The very mechanics of decision-making—the time and place of the significant discussion—are often determinative. Even the question of specifying someone to be publicly responsible for decisions makes a great difference. One takes more care and has more pride in a decision when his name is on it, and so I become concerned when I see a decision made for which no one is willing to assume the responsibility.

I should mention briefly the role of dissents. On the FPC, in spite of the pressures stemming from normal group loyalty, I dissented quite frequently. Perhaps I should have been able to convince my colleagues of my position, but I was unable to. However, even the threat of a dissent has a very modifying effect upon the majority. On the other hand, the IJC has functioned for over sixty years virtually without dissents. This harmony is a result of the sense of pride and tradition that its members have, the excellent staff work done by the advisory technical boards, and the recognition of the need to find a satisfactory decision because there is no body to appeal to in case of dissent. War is hardly a worthy or honorable alternative.

There are conflicting views on the desirability of restricting decision-making panels to engineers and scientists rather than include concerned laymen such as lawyers. Although a scientist should not be prohibited from serving, such a background should not be required. Scientists may have preconceived ideas about the outcome; in other cases, their concept of the social impact of various alternatives will be so limited that any decision they make will be attacked by the general public. (This is one of the major criticisms of the AEC.)

The greatest deficiency of all in decision-makers (whether scientists or not) is the failure to anticipate. As Harvey Wheeler has said, the more profound a scientific innovation, the more universal are its potential applications—and the more difficult it becomes to foresee its effects. In the resource field, a decision-maker must now worry about population shifts, advantages and disadvantages of scale production, and the second, third, and fourth level consequences of the possible alternatives (Hertz, 1970). With the lessons of DDT, mercury, cadmium, thermal pollution, *ad infinitum* before us, we must do a better job of predicting.

However, we must not resist innovative proposals simply because unforeseen consequences may occur. Concern for future generations means concern for developing improved methods. It also means avoiding, as far as possible, irreversible decisions, and preserving flexibility. Every resource decision has to be analyzed to determine whether or not it provides the opportunity for changing course in the future. Such an analysis may dictate a different decision, or it may allow society to have a development with a degree of insurance built in. Congress, when it passed the Federal Power Act of 1920, assured such flexibility for hydroelectric development by limiting licenses to fifty-year terms. The debates prior to the adoption of the Act led Congressional leaders to realize that they ought not to try to predict resource development for a longer period. With the ever-increasing compression of time brought by technological developments, I would urge that the FPC limit renewals or new licenses to a term much shorter than fifty years.

A good example of the type of water resource problem which faced the FPC during the 1960s was the so-called Rumford Falls case,[5] in which we stated:

Rapid changes in the technology of power production and in the relative urgency of the need for water for various uses make it impossible to foretell with assurance, when a license is issued, what will be the best use of the water resource throughout the next fifty years, the usual term of a license. In these circumstances, some continuing control to promote comprehensive development is necessary. Our objective in Article 31 is to provide such control with respect to policy for future use of project properties for water supply which may enhance optimum utilization of the water-way while carefully safeguarding the licensee's interest in his development.

In this case we also noted the possibility that future joint use of a water project, such as the use of a reservoir for cooling a fossil fuel plant, might require certain payments in addition to damages or expenses incurred by the licensee. It was our hope that such payments might be used for general development of the river basin.

"To compromise or not to compromise, that is the question." There is hardly a decision-maker alive who has not been faced with this perplexing problem. It can be the easy way out because one is able to bury the essential issues in a mass of settlement detail, but often it simply postpones the inevitable tough decision. In general, settlements should not be encouraged. Frequently, the parties who agree to the settlement are not the only ones who have to live with the consequences. The *quid pro quo* usually cannot be ascertained. Of course, many decisions are the result of a series of compromises. In this case, however, the decision-maker must set out the final compromise for everyone to evaluate, and if it is not in the public interest, appeal must be possible.

Often decision-makers are criticized for failing to achieve certain social or economic objectives, but seldom is it recognized that decision-makers operate under a number of constraints, the most obvious being legal. The FPC once attempted to secure jurisdiction over pumped storage plants. At the time, we were warned that precendent, if not the Federal Power Act itself, would prohibit a favorable decision. We went ahead, nevertheless, and the Supreme Court upheld us. Some groups today wish we had gone even farther and asserted jurisdiction over all thermal generating plants using navigational streams which produce power for interstate commerce. Possibly, in order to win the Taum Sauk case,[7] which gave the FPC jurisdiction over this relatively new method of hydrogeneration, the FPC may have foreclosed itself from securing an even more important victory.

Almost without exception, attempts to develop fully the jurisdiction of a regulatory position are criticized as moves not only to circumvent the legislature, but even to destroy the foundation of our legal system by failing to respect precedent. For example, in the case of the pollution reference for Lake Erie and Lake Ontario, the governments and the IJC were charged with making a study in depth to determine whether or not there was cross-boundary transmission of pollutants to the detriment of the receiving country. We had to analyze the lake currents very carefully in order to report that the

necessary jurisdictional finding could be made. Unfortunately, the Boundary Waters Treaty of 1909[7] was quite restrictive—in those days people were not thinking in ecological terms. If the Treaty were amended today, it probably would include an international ecological bill of rights, and jurisdictional limitations would not be so restrictive.

Frequently, as with the Treaty of 1909, there is pressure to modify jurisdictional restraints in the resource field. Contemporary assumptions which reinforce legal constraints are always in a state of flux. Growing technology and a diminishing natural resource base put continual pressure on decision-makers to institute change. The FPC went through a long, important period of developing hydro facilities with the primary aim of generating power. As use of the reservoirs increased, it became apparent that the Commission would have to reshape its philosophy as to what was "best adapted to a comprehensive plan for improving or developing a waterway . . ."[8] It was no longer possible to take for granted the unrestricted development and use of hydroelectric facilities and associated transmission lines. The FPC began to recognize the public's rightful claim that such resources have to be used in a responsible manner, with recreational needs and aesthetics taken into consideration.

More than ever, the FPC, the IJC, the AEC, the Department of the Interior, and now the Environmental Protection Agency, as well as a host of other agencies, are facing the long-term consequences of their decisions. In many cases, priorities are being debated for the very first time. Through rulemaking, and through constructive comment such as that provided by Section 102 of the Environmental Policy Act (P. L. 91–190), through Congressional committees, through executive task force as well as separate decisions, the resource questions and issues are being publicly debated. We need more, not less, discussion of priorities. Congress, the courts, and the Executive Branch must be challenged to do their part; it should not be the exclusive problem of any one body. To the extent that each branch of government keeps the other branch alert and on its toes, today's public and our descendants will prosper. Each branch must be free, however, to pursue its own course constructively.

DECISION-MAKING AT LOCAL, STATE, AND INTERNATIONAL LEVELS

As the various branches should be encouraged to seek answers to resource problems, so should each level of government. At present, the initiative seems to be in the hands of the federal decision-maker. The key decisions will probably continue to be made at this level even though many people would prefer otherwise.

During the 1970 session of the Vermont Legislature, a bill was passed which provided for local environmental districts.[9] Anyone seeking to construct a development is now required to seek approval from the appropriate district.[10] There is an appeal to a State Environmental Board, which has the right to retry the matter almost *in novo*.[11] During the debate on the role of local interests, it was argued that it was imperative to have local boards to reflect such interests. The proponents of the boards said that the role of the state must be minimized to let environmental problems be handled by local people who know them best. Ironically, the proponents of this philosophy, who after passage of the bill assumed seats of power, were forced to reverse the decision of a local board that wished to establish restrictive discharge conditions before granting a permit for factory construction. The State Board felt that it would set a bad precedent for the state as a whole. Needless to say, this stand caused a great deal of controversy since the local board in this case wanted to improve the quality of the receiving waters. This particular stream originates in Massachusetts

and flows through Vermont and thence into New York. The state's decision intimated that since Massachusetts would not clean it up, there was no reason why Vermont should do so. Officials were also concerned about the economic future of Vermont if local districts could independently prescribe restrictive discharge standards in an effort to upgrade their streams. However, these are the same officials who are seeking the right to overrule AEC radiation discharge standards, and complaining about the state of New York and the International Paper Company.

Although it is imperative for decision-makers to secure local input in resource matters, it is impossible to ignore ecological principles to gain political advantage. The jurisdiction of the decision-making body must correspond to the environmental impact of the proposed action (National Academy of Sciences, 1969). In addition, the local, state, national, and even international economic impact of the decisions must be considered. The environment need not be sacrificed on the altar of economic progress, but if the consequences of a proposed action have wide-scale economic repercussions, it may be necessary, in order for society to enjoy the benefits of a long-term ecological solution for the nation, the region, or the state to provide financial relief to those adversely affected. While it is true that our nation has long minimized the importance (especially in environmental matters) of weighing intangible costs and benefits to society, the pendulum should not swing too far the other way. During the 1960s we were slow to realize that our exploding power consumption was encouraged by artifically low prices that did not assign proper costs for using our land, water, and air. That situation is being corrected, but let us not, in our eagerness to correct a wrong, make a similar mistake in the other direction. Environmentalists cannot blithely call for an absolute lid on energy consumption or population size or economic growth without considering all of the consequences of such decisions. The developing nations, or the have-nots (whether they be black, yellow, red, or white) are entitled to economic and social consideration if we are drastically to change our direction. Furthermore, the implications go far beyond the willingness of an individual to make personal sacrifices in his own life style. The elite, the affluent few, must help finance the transitional period for the unfortunate ones who may be the real victims in our effort to correct past sins of omission and commission. It is easy to lose patience with those who fail to foresee the environmental consequences of our actions, or who want time to implement the changes. But it is far more important to encourage a dialogue between all segments of society so that a meaningful set of priorities may be developed. Victory in itself cannot be made more important than achieving a rational future.

These considerations require that decisions lie with the governmental body with the greatest authority, one with jurisdiction over the entire area of environmental impact. A decision so made will cover most of the interests affected, and it will be enforceable as well. Also, the further the decision-maker is from the local scene, the less likely it is that the decision will be improperly influenced by local power structures (Kneese, 1970). Frequently, the caliber of the decision-maker will be higher, since the larger the responsibility, the greater the chance that the best talent has been employed. However, if a greater number of important decisions were made at the local level, interest in local government would increase and the chance of attracting better talent would be improved.

Local, state, or regional resource decisions have an important role and often do provide a valuable precedent for decisions at a higher level. Foundations and the federal government have often provided seed money to test a concept on the state or local level. It is valuable to have a small manageable area where problems and solutions are easily ascer-

tained and new approaches more quickly instituted. Progressive legislation has often been tried first in the local or state arena (see Yanggen, in this volume); the disadvantage of failing on a national level is obvious. The local press and other communications media will normally give much broader coverage to solutions for resource problems which have an immediate impact on the quality of their readers' lives.

At present, there are movements toward such a compromise solution as regional decision-making: water basin commissions, the New England Regional Commission, and the Regional Medical Program, are good examples. There is considerable debate about this solution, and many persons would rather promote the role of the state or local decision-maker. I believe that as far as resource questions are concerned, the danger that federal or regional decisions may be insulated from public participation can be mitigated by proper institutional structuring. The danger that state or local decision-making will be influenced by self-seeking interests and insufficient expertise, as well as the costs of duplication and the probably narrowness of the decision, are much more difficult to overcome.

CONCLUSIONS AND RECOMMENDATIONS

I have no magic solution to the problems of resource decision-making. Basically, we must improve the quality and social responsibility of the decision at each level, since there is a role for each.

Most of the frustration, cynicism, and disillusionment prevalent today with all of our institutions stems from the lack of public involvement. The sense of helplessness of the average citizen can lead only to a further erosion of confidence in our system. It serves no purpose to say that the public can participate if they want to badly enough. On the contrary, the Establishment must go to the public, and if the problem is technical or complicated, then both financial and manpower resources have to be made available to persons or institutions in which the public has some confidence. Unless such confidence is promoted, whatever the cost, it will be almost impossible to secure cooperative reactions to solutions which require a sacrifice by present generations to assure a livable world for future generations. It is hard enough to ask people to make sacrifices when the reasons are clearly and definitely established. It is much harder to ask it when there is debate as to their necessity—for example, when the remedy is not quantifiable, as in a reduction in phosphate use which may lead to a reversal in the rate of eutrophication of Lake Erie, thus benefiting future generations.

How shall we promote confidence in our decision-making? First, we must take great pains to provide the decision-maker with an expert staff. Second, the decision-maker himself must be intelligent, well motivated, and altruistically dedicated to serving his fellow human beings. Third, we must provide an adequate forum for discussion, via hearings which are held far enough in advance of the decision so that the participants will have an opportunity to make a meaningful contribution. Fourth, the greatest possible public participation must be encouraged, even if it means discomfort to the decision-maker and his staff. Fifth, steps should be taken to institutionalize consumer advice (while recognizing the dangers and problems inherent therein). Advisory panels of local citizens must be formed particularly when federal and state agencies are to make the decisions. Sixth, local, state, regional, and federal agencies must be encouraged to hire outside experts as consultants. In this rapidly moving technological age, we must be careful that we do not ignore the views of those outside the decision-making system just because they may possibly be controversial (National Academy of Sciences, 1969); often these viewpoints will prevail in the future. Seventh, it is imperative that every effort be made to publicize the decision-making process and the results. This cannot be left to chance. If private media fail to do the job or it is too costly, then it may be necessary to subsidize a continuing program to disseminate resource management information. Furthermore, we must take every step possible to encourage greater feedback from the public to the decision-maker and the staff so that the impact of the decision is known to those responsible for it: advisory bodies can be helpful, but they are not enough. Lastly, decision-makers should be trained and instructed in the art. Emphasis should be directed toward encouraging imagination, innovation, flexibility, and the establishment of more explicit priorities. The decision-maker must concern himself with second, third, and fourth level effects and must be capable of anticipating potential problems and suggesting solutions before a crisis is reached.

Unfortunately, even the adoption of every one of these proposals will not solve some basic problems. Local special-interest groups will still seek to influence decisions. Legislatures will fail to provide funds for an adequate staff and skillful decision-makers. Expert witnesses will be cornered. Some staffs will feel that their primary responsibility is to industry. Some lawyers will become so engrossed in the battle that it becomes the most important factor, or there will be no knowledgeable attorneys available to offset industry's battery of hired mouthpieces. A few decision-makers will accept payoffs; others may seek different methods of feathering their financial nests or promoting their egos. Knowledgeable interveners will fail to come forward for fear of controversy, and the whole process will be so technical that only an elite few will understand what is going on.

Therefore, it is necessary to develop a number of alternative procedures to counteract these pressures. The first solution to come to mind is the legal remedy (National Academy of Sciences, 1969). Although it is not the only one and may also be abused, the mere threat of a citizen's law suit can be very beneficial, as demonstrated by Professor Joseph Sax of the University of Michigan Law School (Sax, 1971). The state of Michigan has already passed legislation incorporating the idea, and further state and, perhaps, federal legislation can be expected, and we can only hope that the advantages of this adversary process will not be exploited in a way which would constitute environmental blackmail.

The same admonition applies to public-interest law firms; to date, their record has been excellent. The dedication, vigor, and intelligence which the members of these firms have brought to the adversary process have been an outstanding credit to the legal profession. These firms are handicapped by insufficient funds, but this might be overcome with financial aid channeled through grants to regional agencies such as the New England Regional Commission, a federal-state-regional agency which has firmly resisted political influence.

The problem in selecting an organization to award such funds is in choosing one which is free of politics and willing to engage in embarrassing law suits. The wisdom of promoting these firms is seen in their successful record today, as well as in the fact that the Office of General Counsel is often dominated by the decision-maker. Furthermore, in some agencies (such as the FPC) the staff is prohibited from appealing a decision which overrules its position. One way to minimize political influence and advance the public cause would be to establish an assisting resource advisory panel.

However, these public-interest law firms and other intervening groups must be required to disclose the identity of all financial sponsors. Our resource history is replete with instances of intervening groups operating under false pretenses. The coal industry has not been averse to setting up front groups nor has the power industry backed away from sponsoring conservation groups that object

to public hydroelectric projects. Even today, some strong-willed and well-heeled conservationists or scientists are willing to finance so-called public-interest law suits merely for the purpose of delaying and confusing the issue. Disclosure of their interest might influence the weight given to their position.

A further remedy which has received a great deal of attention has been the establishment of an ombudsman (see McCloskey, in this volume). Since there are problems in allowing an outsider access to governmental memoranda, and since most laymen do not know their way around the agencies, an experienced ombudsman with the legal right to inquire into complaints and the authority to enforce remedial action would serve to re-establish the confidence of the average citizen in our government. The success of this remedy would depend primarily on the person selected and the legislative backing given him.

An ombudsman is hardly the "cure-all," however. Serious consideration should be given to establishing a traveling group of professional decision-makers, chosen not necessarily because of their expertise in a specific field, but because of their experience in handling complex problems. This corps of decision-makers should not operate out of Washington, but live close to the people and their problems. Nor should they be chosen by the agency involved. The experience of the AEC in picking their own examiners is a good reason not to follow their practice: in recent cases the AEC has been criticized for choosing examiners who have had prior association with the Commission and, in some cases, their credibility has suffered because of possible bias.

Obviously, the selection of these individuals should be nonpartisan. The individuals should possess an abundance of creative imagination coupled with strong political acuity. Such individuals should be able to make extremely accurate projections and to take into account the interests of the public at large, even those who may not know they will be affected (see Fox, in this volume). A procedure which regulates the development of conflicting interests and values certainly demands participants who can make rational judgments as to the proper course of action, and who will insist that alternative courses be assessed. A system notoriously loath to change can be moved only if we oversee its course and hold it accountable for the consequences.

Above all, the administrative process upon which I have concentrated must learn from its sister institutions, the legislative chamber and the courtroom, that the dissidents, the disadvantaged, and the idealists in our society must be given their forum. If this is done, decisions to implement change will engender confidence and trust in the general public. Increasingly, the public is being asked to accept on faith the soundness of far-reaching decisions involving complex technological, scientific, and social factors. No one is going to agree to make the necessary sacrifices without confidence and trust.

References

Craik, Kenneth H. 1970. "The environmental dispositions of environmental decision-makers." *Annals of the American Academy of Political and Social Science.* 389(May), 87.

Hertz, Davis B. 1970. "The technological imperative—social implications of professional technology." *Annals of the American Academy of Political and Social Science,* 389(May), 95.

Kneese, Allen V. 1970. *Protecting Our Environment and Natural Resources in the 1970's.* Reprint No. 88. Washington, D.C.; Resources for the Future, Inc.

National Academy of Sciences. 1969. *Technology: Processes of Assessment and Choice.* Report to the Committee on Science and Astronautics, U.S. Congress, House of Representatives, p. 32.

Sax, Joseph L. 1971. *Defending the Environment.* New York: Alfred A. Knopf.

Shad, Theodore. 1962. "Perspective on national water resources planning." *Proceedings of the American Society of Civil Engineers.* 88:HY4.

Stevens, Chandler. 1971. "Citizen feedback: the need and the response." *Technology Review,* January, p. 43.

CASES

1. Federal Power Act, 41 Stat. 1063, 16 U.S.C. 791–833.
2. Consolidated Edison Company of New York, Inc., Project No. 2338, FPC Opinion No. 452, March 9, 1965.
3. United States Court of Appeals, Second Circuit, Scenic Hudson Preservation Conference, Town of Cortlandt, Town of Putnam Valley and Town of Yorktown v. Federal Power Commission, Respondent, and Consolidated Edison Company of New York, Inc., Intervenor, Docket No. 29853, No. 106—September Term, 1965, 354 F. 2d 608, Cert. denied, 384 U.S. 941 (1966).
4. Yadkin, Inc., Project No. 2197, Order Further Amending License (Major), October 3, 1963.
5. Rumford Falls Power Company, Project No. 233, FPC Opinion No. 465-A, September 9, 1966.
6. Union Electric Company, FPC Opinion No. 356, Docket No. E6927, April 19, 1962.
7. Treaty Between the United States and Great Britain Relating to Boundary Waters, and Questions Arising Between the United States and Canada, Signed at Washington January 11, 1909; ratification advised by Senate March 3, 1909; ratified by Great Britain March 31, 1910; ratified by President April 1, 1910; ratifications exchanged at Washington May 5, 1910. 36 Stat. 2448.
8. Federal Power Act, Section 10(a), 16 U.S.C. 803 (a).
9. 10 VSA, Section 6026.
10. *Ibid.,* Sec. 6081.
11. *Ibid.,* Sec. 6089.

CHAPTER 23

The possibility of transfers of enormous quantities of water across the continent, disregarding natural drainage patterns, raises concern that our political and legal systems are inadequate to control such transfers successfully.

Many interacting groups concerned with interbasin transfers have varying political power and influence, although all do not necessarily take part in the decision process. As a rule the transfer costs are too high to be paid for by the users; thus, some means must be found by transfer promoters to impose the cost on other segments of the population who may or may not benefit. A variety of techniques is employed in this process, and is described by the author. The fact that many, or even most, of the individuals or groups affected by the decision have no representation is of concern. Development agencies, originally formed to represent these interested parties, can no longer generate valid alternatives with real attention to environmental problems, as they are caught in the middle of the political maneuvering. The decision-making process should provide a better forum for consensus, and new institutional arrangements in the public interest should generate and communicate effective environmental alternatives, and be representative of all interests.

SOME POLITICAL ASPECTS OF THE RELATIONSHIP BETWEEN LARGE-SCALE INTERBASIN WATER TRANSFERS AND ENVIRONMENTAL QUALITY

Irving K. Fox

INTRODUCTION

Inter-basin transfers of water supplies are not new, as indicated by the number already in operation. San Francisco, Los Angeles, Denver, and New York City all secure water from outside the basin in which each is located. California is transferring water statewide on a substantial scale, and in Colorado and New Mexico water is being diverted from the western to the eastern side of the Continental Divide. Such facts lead us to wonder why the current proposals for interbasin transfers are attracting so much attention. This is doubtless related in part to the large scale and extensiveness of the developments being proposed, in addition to a number of troublesome problems these interbasin transfers pose.

The size of the investments in water transfers raises one issue. In recent years all levels of government have found it difficult to meet their growing financial obligations. Much public debate has focused on the idea of changing priorities to meet these growing needs in a more satisfactory fashion. Large-scale interbasin diversions would entail one type of readjustment in priorities because they could not be undertaken without making enormous increases in capital investments for water resources.

Another issue relates to the institutional structure for planning, deciding upon investments, and managing water resource projects. For several decades we have considered the river basin as the appropriate geographic unit for planning and management. Since river basin areas generally do not coincide with states—the basic political jurisdictions of our federal system—we have struggled to establish federal-interstate arrangements which would reconcile state geographic areas and responsibilities with the river basin management unit. The TVA, the Delaware River Basin Commission, and the structure provided by the Federal Water Resources Planning Act of 1965 are the results of these efforts. The idea that enormous quantities of water might be transferred from Canada to the United States, from the Columbia to the Southwest, from the Mississippi to the High Plains, and among the basins of the East Coast raises doubts about the applicability of the basin as the geographic area for management. This in turn raises a serious question about the adequacy of existing legal, administrative, and jurisdictional arrangements for water management.

The effects of interbasin transfers upon the physical and biological environment are of grave concern to many people. Large-scale transfers will most certainly entail major engineering works which will alter the landscape, and in some instances even threaten to disrupt the natural condition of wilderness areas. By shifting the locations where water reaches the sea, the aquatic environment of bays, estuaries, and sea coasts could be modified in ways difficult to envisage (see Hedgpeth, "Estuaries" in this volume). We can only hope that groups which plan such programs will develop good information about these consequences and weigh them carefully.

The large-scale transfers now being contemplated thus suggest a range of institutional issues—apart from engineering problems—which heretofore have been considered on a relatively restricted ad hoc basis. These issues merit careful investigation and study as a part of the total picture to be considered. This paper does not presume to examine them in any comprehensive way; instead, its general purpose is to propose a framework for studying the institutional arrangements[1] for making decisions about large-scale interbasin transfers. Since the effects of such programs upon environmental quality constitute a major issue, this analysis gives special emphasis to this problem.

Thus, the specific objectives of this paper are:

1. To provide a framework for analyzing and evaluating the institutional aspects of large-scale interbasin transfers with special emphasis on the effects of such transfers upon environmental quality.

---

[1] "Institution" is used as a generic term to refer to a culturally established entity or rule which influences individual or group behavior. Thus it includes organizations, laws, regulations, subsidies, and taxes. "Institutional arrangement" refers to an interacting pattern of institutions.

2. To apply this framework in a general way to the kinds of transfers now being suggested, and to identify the institutional deficiencies revealed by such an analysis.

There exists a reasonably good basis for studying the institutional implications of large-scale transfers in advance. Many of the political, legal, and administrative aspects of transfers differ little from other large water management projects. As already noted, we have had substantial experience with interbasin transfers. On the other hand, our ability to predict the performance of alternative institutional arrangements remains rather primitive. Therefore, an effort of this kind must be based in part upon rather weakly established assumptions about the behavior of organizations, groups, and individuals as they interact within a specified institutional context. This limitation, together with the fact that the review of past experience is based largely upon general observation rather than empirical study, means that the conclusions reached cannot be considered definitive.

THE POLITICAL PROCESS OF DECIDING UPON INTERBASIN TRANSFERS

This analysis is based upon the theory that in the American political system, groups—formal or latent—largely determine the course of political events (Truman, 1951). Through bargaining, certain accepted courses of action and the decisions made reflect the interests of the different groups affected and their relative political strengths (Holden, 1966). In accordance with this concept, legislators and executives, although often participants in the bargaining process and often taking the lead in conceptualizing policy and programs, have the primary function of legitimizing the political agreement.

Groups may be classified in many different ways, but for the purposes of this paper a useful classification must relate to the prospect of an interbasin transfer. The American political system, relying as it does upon the principle of geographic representation in the Congress and the independent roles of states in a federal system, has many regional as well as national groups. If a transfer is proposed, it is reasonable to assume that some type of bargain must be worked out among these regional and national groups to permit action. With this in mind, and in view of the nature of existing water development institutions, a useful classification of groups follows.

1. Groups within the region of water origin: those who perceive that they would benefit from a potential transfer bargain; those who perceive that they would lose from a potential transfer bargain; and those who have only a peripheral interest, or no interest, in the decision.

2. Groups within the region receiving the water supply: those who perceive that they would benefit from the transfer; those who perceive that they would suffer some disadvantages from the transfer; and those who feel that they will be affected in only a peripheral way.

3. The developers (these may be regional or national organizations): public development agencies such as the Corps of Engineers and the Bureau of Reclamation; consulting engineers who might become involved in the transfer program; and construction contractors who might help build the transfer facilities.

4. Certain national groups of people: citizens and general taxpayers who may share the cost of the facilities; and national interest groups such as the environmental interests, public power advocates, and private power advocates.

In view of the importance of regional interests in water transfers, it would appear essential that the bargain to achieve a transfer must involve some type of compensation to the region of origin.

If the transfer were from Canada to the United States, compensation might be provided partly or even largely through a financial payment. If the transfer is intranational, groups favoring the transfer might agree to support a project politically—another water project or a defense facility—in the region of origin in return for agreement to the transfer. If such a bargain is proposed, some within the region of origin will benefit and, depending upon the nature of the compensation, some may be adversely affected by it. Within the receiving region the configuration of interests favoring and opposing the transfer will depend in part upon how the financial costs are to be assigned, in part upon how the structures will affect various parties, and in part upon the incidence of benefits from the project itself.

One must also expect certain groups located outside the regions involved, or extending beyond them, to have a direct interest in the transfer and to participate in the bargaining process. The national water agencies, consulting engineers, and contractors, all of whom may be involved in some way in the development program, will have a voice in the bargain. If the project is to be financed in part by the federal government, the general taxpayers (operating through the Presidency) will have an interest. If the transfer threatens an historic site or a scenic area of national significance, those groups seeking to preserve these values will become involved. All transfers will have some important environmental effects, so that the groups organized to promote the preservation and enhancement of the environment will undoubtedly take an active interest in any transfer proposals. If certain national policies are affected—for example, marketing of power—national groups concerned with these policies will become active.

As in the Central Arizona Project (which had many of the political characteristics of an interbasin transfer), negotiation and bargaining of an extremely complex nature among these several interests will become

necessary to achieve agreement on a given transfer program. Success depends upon the relative strength of the various groups, the extent of the interest of each one, and the strategies that are pursued. Whether the transfer involves an interstate compact or a Congressional act, the bargaining process will have essentially the same characteristics, although some structures may give greater strength to some groups than to others.

STRATEGIES FOR ACHIEVING INTERBASIN TRANSFERS

To consider in a relatively concrete way the strategies that might be adopted for achieving interbasin transfers, certain assumptions will be made about the nature of the demand for the water provided in this manner. First, it is assumed that the major diversions contemplated will be designed primarily to serve one or all of the following objectives: (1) to preserve an agricultural economy or expand agricultural production; (2) to deal with water quality problems; and (3) to improve navigation.

Certainly the proposed transfers to the High Plains of Texas and the Southwest serve no other purpose than to preserve or expand agriculture even if, in the first instance, some of the water is purchased by industries and municipalities. In the absence of large-scale interbasin transfers one would expect a gradual transfer of water from agricultural to municipal and industrial uses in these areas so that new water, in reality, could serve to preserve and expand agriculture. Proposed large-scale transfers among river basins in the East would hardly be called for in the absence of water quality problems, and in the Great Lakes water quality and navigation are the major demands to be met. This is not to say, however, that modest interbasin transfers would not be desirable for other purposes.

It is assumed further that transfer costs will be high—probably much higher than the immediate beneficiaries can afford to pay. It seems quite unlikely that agricultural water users could pay the full cost of transferred water. In the East the transfer costs may be more than could be paid by those who are responsible for the decline of water quality (although this is not entirely clear), and it is doubtful that navigation interests could afford to pay for high-cost water. The important point here is that both in the West and in the East it will be essential to involve interests other than the direct beneficiaries in paying for the costs of the water transfers. In both areas, it would appear that a major share of the costs must be borne by the national government, and that some portion of the cost will be shifted to municipal water users.

Leadership to achieve a transfer generally will come from those who perceive an opportunity to benefit substantially from the bargain, usually the benefiting groups within the receiving region in alliance with the developers. They must adopt one of the following general strategies (or some combination of the second and the third): (1) achieve sufficient net benefits so that the direct beneficiaries can afford to pay the costs imposed on all parties adversely affected; (2) impose a portion of the costs upon those who are politically disadvantaged; and (3) convince those who receive limited or no benefits that they receive certain hidden benefits from the transfer and therefore should share the costs.

Our assumption with regard to the high cost of the transfers suggests that it is unlikely that the direct beneficiaries will be able to repay all costs. Furthermore, the political bargaining process offers an opportunity to impose part of the costs upon others, as demonstrated by the large federal investments in flood control, navigation, and irrigation. Therefore, one should expect a strategy that is a partial combination of the second and third specified above. The promoters of interbasin transfers thus face the task of satisfying groups in the basin of origin whose political support or acquiescence is needed to gain approval of the transfer, while at the same time working out an acceptable distribution of the costs and benefits. In view of the groups that are affected in one way or another, a successful strategy would probably entail the following components:

1. *Finding some way of compensating politically important groups in the region of origin to secure their support for the transfer, or at least acquiescence in it.* This may mean no more than convincing these groups that the transfer will not affect them adversely and that the broader public interest will be served. It may entail a trade whereby the region of origin receives support for a project it wishes. If the project is an international one, direct compensation of the country of origin may be necessary, or alternatively (or in addition) the receiving country may make some concession on a quite unrelated matter.

2. *Finding a way of distributing a portion of the direct costs to groups that will not benefit directly from the water transfer.* In the transfer of water from the Colorado River to Southern California, the property taxpayers of Los Angeles paid a substantial share of the cost (Hirschleifer and others, 1960). The outlook now is that substantial portions of the costs will be borne by users of municipal and industrial water supplies and by the national government. This distribution of direct costs among other than the direct beneficiaries must be handled in such a way as to forestall opposition from these groups. Here the usual strategies are to indicate that the municipalities that are the recipients of the water are the direct beneficiaries, when in fact the purpose of the transfer may be to avoid upgrading polluted streams or to preserve agriculture; and to indicate that the transfer is in accord with long-standing repayment policy inasmuch as the agricultural water users will repay all capital costs—even though this may take 100 years or more.

3. *Achieving a united front among those who will benefit.* In the West this means the agricultural interests, the business interests that will enjoy secondary benefits, and the

developers. In the East, the navigation interests and the municipalities and industries that will avoid costs of pollution abatement will be included.

4. *Designing the transfer, including the associated policies, to avoid arousing the opposition of a politically effective national interest group or to achieve a bargain that neutralizes possible opposition.* In view of the amount of structural work involved, and the effect of such transfers upon aquatic environments, it will be difficult to avoid arousing the groups concerned with environmental quality. If they are aroused, other latent groups may join them, and opposition to the transfer may reach serious proportions. If the costs imposed on the federal taxpayer are large, the President and his staff (such as the Office of Management and the Budget) and certain members of Congress may oppose the program. This may make it necessary for influential supporters of the project to strike some kind of special bargain with the President. For example, the President might be promised needed support for a foreign aid authorization if the transfer is permitted.

If water is transferred from Canada to the United States, it will be necessary to consider the full range of relations between the two countries as well as the interests of the regions directly affected within each country. The history of negotiations between the United States and Mexico and the United States and Canada on water matters amply demonstrates that quite unrelated issues between the negotiating countries influence the character of the agreement. A water transfer from Canada to the United States may hinge not only upon payment to Canada of a substantial amount as compensation for loss of water, but also upon the general status of relations between the two countries.

This description of the strategy which transfer promoters may pursue is a delineation of the pattern that has been followed on numerous large-scale water projects. Furthermore, this kind of pattern is typical of American political institutions, and there is nothing sinister or evil about it. It does suggest, how-

ever, that a decision will not be based primarily upon the results of a technical economic analysis that indicates the course of action which will maximize net national benefits. Benefit-cost analyses should provide vital information to be used by the negotiators, but such analyses will be only one element in the complex framework of decision-making.

AN ANALYTICAL FRAMEWORK FOR APPRAISING INSTITUTIONAL ARRANGEMENTS

The institutional arrangements for planning and deciding upon large-scale interbasin transfers are of paramount importance, as they determine who participates in the bargaining process, the strength and relationships of participants, what information about opportunities is generated, and how this information is evaluated. Study of these factors leads to the question of how to determine what constitutes a desirable institutional pattern. There is no objective answer to this question. In this paper it is assumed that a set of institutional arrangements should express the values inherent in a democratic society, and that the institutional pattern should therefore meet a set of normative criteria based upon democratic thought. To achieve this objective the pattern must take into account not only the physical character of the problem, but also the organization, group, and individual behavior within the pattern.

Criteria for Evaluating Institutional Arrangements

A study of democracy suggests that a given institutional arrangement for planning and choosing programs is functioning well if it meets the following criteria:

1. Information is generated about the physical, biological, and value consequences of alternative courses of action,

and the information is communicated with fidelity to the groups affected.

2. Those affected are represented or have genuine opportunities for representation in the decision-making process.

3. Decision-making proceeds with reasonable efficiency and dispatch.

4. Decisions are made in such a way that sharp cleavages in society are not engendered.

Little need be said about the basis for selecting these criteria. In our society, it is assumed that decisions should be made on the basis of good information. There is also an underlying premise that each individual affected by a proposal should be able to participate directly or be represented by someone else in the process of making the decision. At the same time it is important in a democracy to avoid polarization. Instead, the objective must be to facilitate understanding and unified values, and this is extremely important at a time when powerful forces are attempting to alter conventional values and life styles in this country.

Relevant Principles of
Organization, Group,
and Individual Behavior

Whenever a law is enacted or an organization established, there are underlying assumptions about how individuals, organizations, and groups will respond. Whereas the study of human behavior is not advanced enough to enable us to predict it unequivocally, a basis does exist for making estimates concerning the likely effects of alternative institutional patterns. The literature on this subject suggests that the following assumptions are reasonable conclusions about behavior which could be applicable to arrangements for planning and deciding upon large-scale water transfers.

1. The perception of relevant opportunities and the receipt and interpretation of information varies greatly among individuals as a result of differing experiences and other factors in the psychological environment (White, 1966, and in this volume). It follows that the alternative courses of action perceived as relevant in a water transfer situation will be determined by the experience and value preferences of the planning organization. In short, if the Bureau of Reclamation does the planning with regard to water transfer, the perceived alternatives will be determined by the background of reclamation planners and the environment in which they work.

2. Not all individuals can take an active part in matters that affect them. The costs of acquiring the information required for active participation and the costs of negotiation would be much higher than the prospective benefits. Thus, the general taxpayer who would pay a small share of the cost of a water transfer could not afford to assume an active role in the decision. These individuals usually will support the views of others who do take an active part and become their representatives, so that finally the decisions are made by an oligarchy.

3. Some individuals lack sufficient interest in a decision to organize and select representatives (Olson, 1965). These are the "latent" groups and are not generally represented in the decision. Where subsidies are involved and costs are diffused over a large group (as in most water projects), those who pay the subsidy tend to be poorly represented in the decision-making process.

4. To survive, a public agency must be supported by groups in society. When there is a wide range of objectives and value preferences among members of society on a given matter, it is extremely difficult for an agency to serve the divergent interests. Thus, a public agency can serve all groups in society only when objectives and value preferences are reasonably well unified. In water transfers an important issue is whether a single planning agency, such as the Bureau of Reclamation, can serve the wide range of interests affected by such diversions.

5. Legitimatizing organizations—such as the Congress—are reluctant to choose between widely divergent courses of action and are motivated to find a compromise or consensus which avoids polarization of group positions. This is so powerful that the decision-making process (it would appear) should provide a forum to foster consensus among the divergent interests. In the absence of such arrangements, decisions are often held in abeyance, and if decisions are reached, better feelings on the part of groups adversely affected may result.

In summary, if the institutional arrangements for making decisions about large-scale interbasin transfers are to serve the public interest, they must meet the criteria specified with regard to information generation, the communication of information, representation, efficiency, and consensus. To do so the institutional design must take into account the basic characteristics of organization, group, and individual behavior outlined above.

APPLICATION OF ANALYTICAL FRAMEWORK TO CURRENT INSTITUTIONAL ARRANGEMENTS

The fundamental policy issues of interbasin transfers do not differ significantly from those of other large-scale water resources projects. Existing national water development agencies certainly have the technical competence to plan and implement large-scale transfers, and as they are not limited geographically in their coverage, their capability to undertake such programs is not restricted. Large states—such as California and Texas—could, no doubt, marshall technical agencies to undertake large-scale programs of this nature through agreements with adjoining states. Some laws inhibit transfers, and complex economic issues and problems of

technical analysis and design can be troublesome, but if negotiations among the affected groups provide a basis for agreement, these factors will not necessarily be insurmountable.

In view of the behavioral characteristics of organizations, groups, and individuals described in the previous section, a more basic question is whether current institutional arrangements can be expected to meet the specified criteria. More explicitly, can one expect existing planning organizations to generate information about courses of action considered important by those concerned with the preservation and enhancement of the environment? Will such information be communicated with fidelity to those affected, and will the environmental interests be adequately represented in the decision-making process?

To answer these questions, one must identify the important characteristics of the current institutional structure. These characteristics are best reflected in studies being led by the Corps of Engineers for the East Coast and by the Bureau of Reclamation for the western United States. Both of these studies involve regional water programs covering several river basins and *could* result in recommendations for largescale interbasin diversions, with evaluations being made in accordance with procedures of the Water Resources Council (WRC), and these provide for consideration of the alternative which will do the most for preserving and enhancing the environment. Each study makes specific provision for participation by state governments and federal agencies, and each study provides for periodic consultation with private interests including those concerned with environmental preservation. Each would also be subject eventually to "coordination" by the WRC, the Council on Environmental Quality (CEQ), and the Office of Management and Budget. Whether we may expect this pattern to meet the criteria specified depends upon the conclusions one reaches from three questions:

1. Can environmental interests organize themselves to represent faithfully the views of those concerned with environmental preservation, and participate effectively in the planning and deciding of such matters as large-scale water transfers?
2. Can existing planning organizations—the Corps of Engineers and the Bureau of Reclamation—adequately represent the environmental interests when it is time to provide alternatives for consideration?
3. Are existing arrangements—provisions for consultation with interest groups in the field, the WRC, and the CEQ—adequate for achieving consensus and for fostering unification of views?

Definitive answers to these empirical questions cannot be provided, but experience suggests what the answers are likely to be.

Organization and Participation of Environmental Interests

In considering the answer to the first question, it must be remembered that the environmental interests are not by any means a single, unified, and well-organized interest group, but include a broad range of views and feelings. Some elements—such as the wilderness devotees—are reasonably well organized, but no one group can presume to speak for the full range of environmental interests. These organized groups tend to represent the views of an upper-class, well-educated minority, and not the general citizenry (see McEvoy, in this volume). Thus, any formal participation in the decision-making process will not tend to reflect the full spectrum of interests in environmental matters. It is certainly better to have these groups participate rather than not have environmental interests represented at all, but we cannot consider such partial representation to be adequate.

It still remains to be seen whether all of the public agencies—such as the two major planning organizations, the fish and game agencies, the park and recreation agencies, the CEQ, and the Environmental Protection Agency (EPA)—reflect the broader environmental interests. My estimate is that their activities only slightly extend the representation of the organized private groups. The role of the two major water planning agencies will be examined in the response to the second question. The fish and game and recreation interests have been responsive to a quite limited clientele—the fishing and hunting interests and those particularly concerned with outdoor recreation opportunities. The role of the EPA remains unclear. Although this agency will be deeply concerned with pollution issues, it is not clear that it will take an active part in broader environmental problems, and this, together with an examination of the probable role of the CEQ, is explored further below.

The Generation of Alternatives

The introduction of alternative courses of action which reflect the perceptions and interests of environmentalists is a critical question. Although the environmental interests have demonstrated that they can defeat certain proposals—such as dams in the Grand Canyon (see Nash, this volume) or a jetport in the Everglades—a major handicap has been their lack of resources to develop detailed, alternative programs. If the range of choices is to be fully explored and the interests in the environment accurately expressed, it is essential that such alternatives be precisely defined and evaluated. To provide alternatives when a water transfer is being proposed, a staff of engineers, economists, biologists, and other specialists is required. Will the Corps of Engineers and the Bureau of Reclamation —operating in accordance with recently adopted WRC requirements that they take account of environmental values—examine the alternatives perceived as relevant by the environmental interests? If these two agencies do not develop alternatives, will they be developed directly by the environmental interests or by environmentally oriented agencies such as the CEQ, the EPA, the fish and game agencies, or the recreation agencies?

It seems doubtful that the environmental interests will be well enough organized and financed to produce technically sound alternative courses of action in water transfer problems. It is simply too difficult to raise sufficient funds to employ the required technical staff. The fish and game and recreation agencies have not been staffed and financed to engage in this kind of activity. Certainly the CEQ is not equipped to undertake such large-scale planning studies, and it does not seem that the new Environmental Protection Agency was established to develop plans that are alternatives to those of the Corps of Engineers and the Bureau of Reclamation. The issue is, then, whether the Corps or the Bureau, operating in the new climate of concern about the environment and in accordance with the new standards of the Water Resources Council, can produce alternatives which faithfully reflect the objectives of the environmental interests.

It is not possible to say with assurance what the answer is, as past experience is not entirely relevant because the climate in which these agencies function has changed and the leadership of these agencies is earnestly seeking to be responsive to the concern about the environment (see McCloskey, in this volume). As long as groups with interests in large-scale water transfers continue to have such widely divergent objectives and value preferences, it is doubtful that any single agency can objectively conceive and analyze a range of alternatives that reflects the perceptions of the different groups.

First, the two federal planning-construction agencies are dependent upon certain well-organized, developmental interests for survival. If, in planning, they depart from the objectives of these interests, they run a serious risk of losing the support on which they have been dependent. The planning agencies are powerfully motivated to pursue the kind of strategy outlined earlier in this paper. This strategy will include at least a partial accommodation with environmental groups, which means proposing plans that will not arouse the opposition of most of the environmental interests. The emphasis would be upon achieving enough agreement that the program could proceed, rather than upon illuminating the range of possibilities considered relevant by committed environmentalists. To the extent that a range of alternatives are presented by the planning agencies, past experience suggests that those alternatives not consistent with the objectives of the developmental interests will be more in the nature of straw men to be knocked down than alternatives presented for serious debate. Inherent pressures upon the planning agencies simply would be too great to pursue any other strategy.

The second consideration is that the kind of staff and the traditions of the two major federal water planning agencies make it difficult for them to perceive courses of action and strategies other than those which lead to development. These agencies have a long tradition of pursuing developmental programs, and are staffed and led largely by engineers whose interests are primarily in construction. whose interests are primarily in construction. It will be difficult indeed for them to conceive alternative courses of action acceptable to the more committed environmental groups.

In short, one should not expect the planning agencies to propose alternatives which reflect a broad range of interests. Instead, it is only reasonable for them to search for a coalition to minimize the opposition of the environmental interests and also to support a plan reasonably consistent with the goals of the developmental groups that traditionally have given political support to these agencies. This plan may lead to an early decision and action, but what is more likely—in the current climate of concern about the environment—is that it will lead instead to endless debate and stalemate.

ADEQUACY OF CONSENSUS ACHIEVING ARRANGEMENTS

Under the present framework, consensus will be sought and achieved in the process of conceptualizing and planning the program. However, we should not forget that this process may leave the more committed environmental groups embittered. If, as expected, acceptable alternatives are never even presented at a hearing, the risk is created that this sector of society will be increasingly disenchanted with decision-making about environmental affairs. The process would not be consistent with the normative criteria posited earlier in this paper, although this seems to underlie much of the disenchantment of young people with current social institutions (McEvoy, in this volume).

CONCLUSIONS

What kinds of changes in our planning and decision-making arrangements does this analysis suggest? Is it possible to design arrangements which will meet the criteria proposed? Apparently, desirable changes should be based upon the following considerations:

1. Since the environmental interests are broadly diffused through society, and since they constitute a recognized set of important interests, they should be organized and represented by a major federal agency. It would appear that the only way that the "latent" sectors of these interest groups can become satisfactorily represented is in such a manner.

2. A technically equipped planning organization within an environmental agency should undertake the development of plans which are in accord with the perceptions of the environmental interests. A qualified staff of engineers, economists, biologists, and soil scientists, are needed to formulate such plans

because only by placing this kind of expertise in an agency which looks to environmental interests for political support can we expect plans to be formulated which reflect the perceptions of these interests.

These considerations lead us to conclude that the federal government should have a separate environmental resources planning agency which would take the lead in developing regional environmental resource plans in consultation with other federal and state environmental agencies. Such an agency might include the fish, wildlife, park, and recreation agencies, but not the developmental agencies such as the Bureau of Reclamation, the Corps of Engineers, or the minerals development agencies. Neither should it be given regulatory responsibilities and sit as judge. Instead it should be an advocate of the views of the environmental interests.

Such an agency would develop regional land and water programs consistent with the perceptions of the environmental interests, which would then enter into bargaining with other interest groups such as those supporting the plans emerging from studies of the Corps of Engineers and the Bureau of Reclamation. The environmental interests would have strong representation in such bargaining by having a well-staffed planning agency, and then the representation and alternatives criteria postulated in this memorandum presumably would be met.

It seems likely that this approach would also foster more expeditious decision-making. The alternatives would be known, and the environmental interests would have well-qualified representatives to participate in the bargaining process. In this situation consensus might be realized more quickly than it was over the Central Arizona Project, for example.

Most likely, consensus would be achieved at field level. Furthermore, since the full range of interests would be involved in the bargaining process, important groups would not be bitter and feel excluded. At the Washington level the environmental resources planning agency would certainly need to have representation on the Water Resources Council or whatever consensus-achieving institution is established to take its place.

For these changes to occur, society must first accept the view that special institutional arrangements are necessary to assure presentation of the range of choices in large public decisions and to assure representation of politically disadvantaged groups. Because of limitations in their interests and capacities, we cannot expect existing agencies at the federal, state, or local level to perform this function. Special institutions designed to provide representation of the politically disadvantaged in our political system would appear necessary if we are to achieve substantial improvements in public decision-making processes related to water development. Large-scale interbasin transfers have not yet given rise to this problem, but the scale contemplated emphasizes the need to find a solution.

References

Hirschleifer, Jack, James C. DeHaven, and Jerome W. Milliman. 1960. *Water Supply —Economics, Technology and Policy.* University of Chicago Press.

Holden, Matthew, Jr. 1966. *Pollution Control as a Bargaining Process: An Essay on Regulatory Decision-Making.* Cornell Water Resources Center, Publication No. 9, Ithaca, N.Y.

Olson, Mancur. 1965. *The Logic of Collective Action: Public Goods and the Theory of Groups.* Cambridge, Mass.: Harvard University Press.

Truman, David. 1951. *The Governmental Process: Political Interest and Public Opinion.* New York: Alfred Knopf.

White, Gilbert F. 1966. "Formation and role of public attitudes." Chapter 5 *in* H. Jarrett, ed. *Environmental Quality in a Growing Economy.* Baltimore: The Johns Hopkins Press.

CHAPTER 24

The context of water development in the United States has changed from that of an expanding nation which used such projects in the West to encourage settlement of empty lands and to provide employment. In the face of rising demands for a healthy natural environment and abundant, varied recreation land it is time to consider new values. However, federal development agencies and public utilities are pushing ahead with plans for new hydro, irrigation, and flood control projects and navigation facilities, while nonconstruction alternatives receive inadequate attention. The rationale for development usually is to keep pace with economic and population growth; such plans, however, may be self-fulfilling prophesies.

Specific examples of present construction-oriented trends in water resource management are discussed. This paper also describes the differences in ecological and spiritual values between a free-flowing stream and an impoundment.

To balance environmental quality in water resource management, the initial planning process should have three independent components: engineering aspects, economic evaluation, and judgment of aesthetic values to be gained or lost. Adequate environmental impact reports would be prepared for evaluation by the Council on Environmental Quality. After full consideration of possible impacts of and alternatives to the proposal, Congress would receive each proposal for consideration individually or in related sets to avoid present omnibus bill abuses.

ALTERNATIVES IN WATER PROJECT PLANNING: ECOLOGICAL AND ENVIRONMENTAL CONSIDERATIONS

Michael McCloskey

INTRODUCTION

As a reflection of the environmental movement, the context for planning water projects is changing drastically, particularly in the West and in rural areas. It is an appropriate time to take a comprehensive look at the status of water development and to make some suggestions for future planning. In doing so there is an admitted risk of oversimplification, but we hope the value of a general view will make the risk worthwhile.

AN HISTORICAL REVIEW

Projects to develop water resources have a special place in this nation's political history.

From the earliest times, internal improvements, especially in the form of public water projects, have been controversial. Questions of constitutional authority and the respective roles of public and private agencies have dominated the controversy, yet on the frontier and in the less developed portions of the country these projects have generally been popular. They have offered a ready stimulus to economic development. At the very least, construction has provided employment, and usually more enduring benefits ensued: navigation, flood control, irrigation, and hydroelectricity. While the already developed regions of the country might question the economic efficiency of dollars invested in these projects instead of in other areas, this investment could always be justified as a matter of political equity. As each region of the country passed through successive economic stages, it got subsidies of various sorts: the South got cotton, the Midwest corn, the East tariffs and armament purchases, and the West received water project subsidies.

The setting for this rough and ready method of keeping the political peace was that of a developing nation. Internal improvements in water were used to advance settlement, to secure claims to new territories, and to promote agriculture in all regions. The aim was to promote widespread settlement in what was an empty land, and to promote the growth of an emerging economy. Later, in the depression of the 1930s, these goals were reinterpreted to place emphasis on putting unemployed people to work. In place of the goal of regional development, income redistribution through public works became dominant as a new matter of political equity. Moreover, in this period and earlier, prevention of private monopoly and exploitation as part of the political program of the Progressive Party period were continuing goals in public development of water resources. Conversely, these projects were resisted by those who held either a different view of regional equities or who believed that the role of government should be more limited.

At any rate, by now most of the politically desirable projects have been built. The political controversies of the first half of this century over public participation in water development are fast becoming part of ancient history. This is so not only because most of the easy or profitable projects have been built, but also because the whole context has changed—in economic, historical, and political terms. What was once an empty land is now full, and all regions have been sufficiently settled; in fact, rural depopulation is now the trend (see Hollis and Teclaff, this volume). With social overhead investments in rural areas being abandoned with depopulation, what sense does it make to continue to invest in local service water projects? An economy of scarcity has now given way to an economy in which our prodigious productive capacity is causing more problems than it solves. A large degree of public control over resources, including water, has now been achieved, and remaining fears of monopoly control have been lost in an abundant economy. Because of a tendency toward chronic inflation, there is strong competition for investment dollars.

This radical change in circumstances has now produced an overriding concern for intangibles—all those amenities of the environment which are enjoyed as common goods outside the market economy (see McEvoy and Nash, this volume). Because they are pressed too hard by the force of an overly dynamic economic system, these resources are now in short supply. On the extent to which natural amenities now survive, however, rests the quality of our lives. Planning for environmental preservation, and the population stability that will allow it, is now the overriding goal that conservationists feel public policy should pursue.

In an earlier period public policy gave the benefit of the doubt to the case *for* constructing water projects. Conditions then may have warranted this presumption in favor of rearranging natural conditions, but conditions have now changed entirely. Much of nature has been rearranged, conditions now reflect a shortage of natural amenities, and the benefit of the doubt should be shifted in favor of retaining remaining vestiges of nature—unaltered watercourses in particular—unless engineers can sustain a heavy burden of proof in showing an incontestable need for their projects. And where watercourses have already been altered, we should maximize the opportunities for more complex flora and fauna to exist. Pool levels should be kept as constant as possible, steps should be taken to prevent nitrogen build-ups, to provide cool water releases in the summer, and to landscape the settings with native flora.

Changes need to be made in the procedures of political and economic evaluation to effect this shift in the burden of proof. Before discussing them, however, it may be pertinent to examine further the continuing concern over water project construction.

THE PROSPECTS AHEAD

In the first place, all should understand that environmental conservationists have not been a major party to past controversies. They have not objected to more than 90 percent of the projects that have been proposed and constructed. They have not been "obstructionists" to "economic progress." They have not objected to governmental intervention on ideological grounds; in fact, they advocate such intervention in many environmental fields, as in water and air pollution abatement and the provision of parks, open space, and ecological reserves. They do not object to the use of welfare economics; they merely think the "merit wants" and the beneficiaries have changed with the changing nature of our society. The needs of "economic man" have been replaced by the psychic needs of harassed members of a mass industrial society (see Swan, this volume).

It may be suggested that their concerns over further water project development are moot in that the era of dam and canal building is over. Certainly the great period of construction does seem to be behind us, but powerful agencies have vested interests in continuing these activities. Diminishing returns may be setting in in terms of total public values stemming from further projects, but the sponsoring agencies have developed great expertise in attributing economic and political benefits to these projects. Special clienteles in our economy are organized to promote projects of these agencies. Their expertise, the power of their clienteles, and the inertia of political habit combine to give substance to their ambitions.

What then are the ambitions of these agencies? The Federal Power Commission lists 154 hydroelectric projects which it feels could be economically constructed by 1980 (U.S. Federal Power Commission, 1964). Conservationists will probably object to construction of between 15 and 20 percent of these. In any event, the FPC says that only 30 percent of the hydropotential of this country has been developed in some 1,500 plants. The U.S. Water Resources Council (1968) predicts an increase of about one-and-one-half times in hydro capacity by the year 2000, which is at a somewhat slower rate than the Federal Power Commission hopes. Hydro agencies look to the use of hydro projects to supply peaking power at low load factors, to pumped storage plants, and to low-head turbines to keep a place for hydro in the future total energy supply picture. Nevertheless, by the year 2000, according to these estimates, hydro will be supplying less than 5 percent of our electricity.

Presently, some 42 million acres are under irrigation, 95 percent of them in the West. Eight million of these acres are irrigated by water from the Bureau of Reclamation's 113 projects. The U.S. Water Resources Council (1968) projects a 40 percent increase in land to be brought under irrigation by the year 2000. Presumably much of this increase would be facilitated by new storage and diversion works. It should be pointed out, alternatively, that new water could be provided through increasing efficiency of existing works. Presently, 50 percent of irrigation water is wasted by farmers, but could be easily reduced to 30 percent with sufficient incentives, according to the Water Resources Council.

The Corps of Engineers alone by 1980 wishes to double the storage capacity of America's reservoirs (Krutilla, 1966). It suggests that this water could be useful for what is euphemistically called "water quality control," which means, among other things, diluting sewage and other effluents. Needless to say, other ways of maintaining water quality exist. If the pollution control methods used in Germany's Ruhr Valley were adopted here, for instance, all of America's industrial output in 1980 could be supported by the low flows of the Columbia River alone (Krutilla, 1966). Nevertheless, a three-fold increase in industrial water supply is foreseen by the Water Resources Council; the same increase is seen for municipal water supply facilities (U.S. Water Resources Council, 1968).

The Corps of Engineers also wants to expand its inland waterways for navigation. A 20 percent increase is forecast by the year 2000; 5,000 new miles of waterway, dredged to at least 9 feet, are projected on top of the 22,500 miles already available. Although the increase is modest in relation to other projects, the investments projected by then are astronomical: $21 billion of public monies by the year 2000 (U.S. Water Resources Council, 1968).

By 1980 the Corps of Engineers also hopes to have more than doubled the 1960 capacity of the country's flood control works, moving from 219 to 738 reservoirs, from 9,047 miles of levees and floodwalls to 16,408 miles, and from 7,430 miles of so-called channel improvements to 10,613 (U.S. Army Corps of Engineers, 1960). Presumably these figures are destined to go up, because continued

encroachments on flood plains present new economic values "needing" protection. It should be noted, of course, that flood plain zoning, flood proofing, early warning systems, and insurance often can handle the problems just as well.

Obviously the projections are predicated upon continued population growth and economic expansion. However, an increasing number of observers feel that planning to facilitate growth operates as a self-fulfilling prophecy. If growth is not a good in itself and is in fact undesirable, failure to facilitate it may work as a deterrent. In this light, negative planning—that is, planning to prevent growth—may be the best policy. In any event, many of these projected goals are merely self-serving efforts to promote a continued role for an agency. Any "real" needs can be served, in most cases, through a variety of alternative means. Capital available for dam projects should be able to filter into these alternative approaches.

In the face of these projections, however, one can readily wonder whether any wild and natural streams will survive if these agencies' ambitions are not checked. To some extent, the Wild and Scenic Rivers System Act of 1968 will help. Of the 725 rivers of appreciable size in the United States, some 35 may be protected by the Act, though only eight are completely protected initially. Probably conservationists will work to have about 100 of these rivers ultimately preserved in the system; 71 were inventoried by the Bureau of Outdoor Recreation in its 1964 study. Another 13, not in study, were inserted in the Act before it passed, and some others figured prominently in debate. Moreover, additional protection may come under state action under the terms of the Act.

CURRENT ABUSES

Despite the fact that only fragments of these streams will be protected under the Wild and Scenic Rivers Act—those reaches of 20 miles or more—there will probably be intense competition for sites between developers and those who wish to keep some streams completely wild, which, then, will be exacerbated by the realization that many projects are not being proposed to serve consumer needs directly. In other words, if these projects were not built, no discernible damage would be experienced by local consumers. This pattern is illustrated by the following increasingly common practices among federal agencies:

1. A project is devised to provide a role for competing agencies, as in the Eel River basin of northern California, to keep peace between the Corps of Engineers and the Bureau of Reclamation so that each can have an equal role.

2. A project is justified primarily to serve recreational "needs" despite the fact that no bona fide recreational group expresses any need or wants the dam. The Gilbert Dam in northern Arkansas is an example where important recreational values would be lost. Flat reservoir water, which is not in short supply there, would replace fast-running water, which is lacking.

3. In arid regions a common practice is to build a reclamation project to sell water at far below its actual delivery cost. This underpricing, as with the Central Arizona Project, maintains an artificial agricultural demand for water that would not exist in the absence of the heavy subsidy.

4. In the Grand Canyon where certain dams were defeated, we see an even more questionable extension of these subsidies. Hydro dams were proposed to be built in the canyon to generate profits from electrical sales so that the profits could be stockpiled to finance later diversions of water from the Northwest. Construction of these dams thus was designed to produce a subsidy two steps removed from the actual beneficiaries.

Nonfederal agencies are guilty of proposals just as egregious in their remoteness of purpose:

1. As potential sites for hydro projects decrease, utilities have begun to file claims on sites with the Federal Power Commission to protect their territorial control, and unless a fear of counter-filing arises, they may never develop these sites. Chelan Public Utility District, for instance, has filed a claim to Washington's Wenatchee River for this reason despite a large surplus of power to sell outside its service area, and San Francisco wants to expand its Hetch Hetchy Project, ostensibly for the same reason.

2. This is also related to the practice of expanding hydro projects as a money-making enterprise of a public agency, and has nothing to do with serving the agency's own customers. The additional capacity is designed solely to generate surplus revenues to enrich the utility, with the implied promise that rates or taxes may ultimately be reduced as a customer benefit.

3. Somewhat related is the fixation which some utilities have on squeezing the last drop of hydro out of their production territory, regardless of environmental damage and despite most new large increments of power in their supply systems being nuclear. Seattle City Light is trying to do this with its plan for raising Ross Dam and developing Thunder Creek in a recreational area at the edge of the new North Cascades National Park.

4. Another dubious practice related to protective filing is the struggle to get the last major hydro sites developed before nuclear power renders them economically uncompetitive, as in the battle to get any kind of license in Hells Canyon. Many believe that in another few years sites in Hells Canyon will not be able to produce power as cheaply as nuclear plants can. The financial and emotional commitments of that 15 year struggle keep public and private utilities alike fixed in their determination to salvage something from the long-term effort.

5. Finally, we see utilities whose projects have expiring 50-year licenses struggling to get renewals despite the projects' obsolescence. Instead of realizing that it is time to start cleaning up and clearing our streams of needless obstructions, they work to find ways

to renovate the projects for extremely marginal benefits. For instance, San Francisco wants to flood out the old Lake Eleanor Dam that it got in Yosemite National Park as part of the Hetch Hetchy project and construct a new, larger dam. It admits, however, that the power revenues would be insignificant.

If fewer areas had been dammed, these practices, unnecessary as they are, would still not be too unpalatable. But dams already dot our landscape, and wild rivers are increasingly scarce. If there is to be a proper mix of development and preservation—of quantity and quality in our use of water resources—the line must be drawn to protect many of the natural watercourses that remain.

When a natural watercourse is converted into a reservoir, quality is exchanged for quantity. In ecological terms, complexity and stability are exchanged for simplicity and instability. In esthetic terms, subtlety is exchanged for uniformity. And in recreational terms, sport forms which require an understanding of the environment are exchanged for those that look away from it as much as to it. Machinery and athletics become the focus, as these exchanges increasingly deprive us of resources in short supply, and give us features that are already abundant, so that balance is also lost in the process.

The losses these exchanges entail can be seen by comparing the characteristics of a natural watercourse to a reservoir. A natural watercourse is the product of slow evolution. Riparian vegetation lines the banks, arranged by species according to proximity to the water. The processes of evolution have created a great many specialized habitats for flora and fauna, ranging from bottom species to water-loving trees on the banks which control the amount of light reaching the water. The habitats within the stream vary immensely too, as the stream changes from fast to slow water, from rapids to pools, from gravels to rocky bottoms to sands and muds, from wide channels to narrow ones, from straight courses to bends and eddies. Each habitat has its own limitations on the life it can support, and these habitats produce a visual subtlety too.

For the human visitor, this variety and complexity are full of spontaneity and surprise. The patterns of design open and close and shift and deepen in an intriciate tapestry. This variety often stands as a sort of counterpoint to the greater uniformity of the vegetative patterns on the slopes above. The riparian vegetation is distinctive, more limited, and is the thread of life which organizes the geological story of the eroding landforms in the watershed. And the setting of the watercourse makes sense geologically, whether meandering on a flood plain, entrenched in one, or cutting a new canyon.

The recreationist who comes to the watercourse often sees it as the culminating center of the landscape. Stream bottoms and ridgetops are the two central features of most recreational landscapes. Fly fisherman, canoeist, kayaker, hiker, photographer, or naturalist—the recreationist who comes there wants to lose himself in the uniqueness that these special environments afford. Whether in a placid stream or whitewater canyon, he has a sense of enclosure, of privacy, of primal encounter with a moving force that suggests significance of life itself. Whatever his recreational form, it is one which tends to rely on an appreciation of the rare qualities of that environment. And he tends to become a subordinate and integral part of it: one who is usually governed by a code of conduct having ethical implications, one who reveres, respects, and wants to understand his environment.

In contrast, a body of impounded water is deficient in almost all of these respects. Riparian vegetation is usually absent because there has not been time for it to grow, or because the water level fluctuates too much. The area is open, lacking shelter and cover for both men and animals. A varied flora and fauna does not exist as there are only a few simple habitats. The geological processes which produce alluvial benches, bends, and riffles have not been at work. Spawning gravels are, for the most part, absent. Downstream watercourses are deprived of flushing flows, silts, and nutrients, and without flushing bedloads build up. Within the impoundment, there are poor opportunities for bottom flora and fauna because conditions have not evolved properly and pool levels fluctuate irregularly. There is little variation, too, within the water body, with marshes possible only in a few shallows in the heads of coves if the water level remains constant enough. Mostly there is just one large body of still water, as in a bathtub, with rings around the edges marking fluctuations. Flat water replaces flowing water, and fewer types of living things can find niches to support them, though a few species of fish may find the habitat just right and thrive in number. Most often these are the so-called "trash fish."

Visually, the scene is usually dull. The setting is rarely appropriate geologically for a lake-like body. There are no alluvial benches, so the water abruptly meets the side slope or aimlessly floods out flats, with no riparian shrubs or trees, and rarely any beaches. From a distance, the pool may look interesting, but up close it almost never is. At best the meeting of land and water is dull, and at worst ugly. All too often, drawdowns reveal terraced waterlines or mudflats. In some instances, they reveal seas of stumps, snags, and trash. At the inlet, growing sandbars catch the siltload that is dropped when the gradient ends, and the carrying capacity of the water dwindles with diminishing velocity.

With the disappearance of varied flora, fauna, and visual interest, the interested recreational clientele that used to come no longer does. And a new one will only come if certain features are present. A large open surface will attract power boats if they are sufficiently protected from wind, and if water levels stay constant long enough to make moorage and navigation reliable. Boating of this type is not possible if docks are suddenly deposited on mudflats, and if shoals keep shifting with the water level. Bathers may come if beaches can be created, and if water temperatures and quality are adequate. Trolling fishermen may come for a warm-water fishery if one exists, but usually these are erratic. Water skiers may come too, if they can avoid conflict with fishing boats, and if water conditions are right. In many cases, conditions are not right—for any of these. But when they are, the people come primarily to use their machines, to congregate, and to take easy, coarse fish. They do not come because they hold the environment in esteem, or because they wish to understand it. An environment that might invite them to do so has been taken from them.

NEW PROCEDURES

At this point in our history to give the benefit of the doubt to nature, a number of institutional reforms need to be made in our planning process for water projects. These are primarily applicable to federal projects, but could be adapted, in part, for use by the Federal Power Commission and state licensing and planning authorities.

Present practice is unduly weighted in favor of construction because all basic data is organized and evaluated by the sponsoring agency in partnership with forces in Congress which have an interest in seeing a project go forward. To reverse the weighting, separate institutions should be established to handle the three basic aspects of project evaluation: engineering, economics, and intangibles. Engineering evaluation could be handled by the construction agency, but economics and intangibles should be evaluated by agencies which are completely separate and could be variously lodged either in the Water Resources Council or within the executive office of the President, or they could be independent. Thus, to be recommended to Congress, a project should have to (1) be recommended by engineers who felt it represented the best engineering solution to accomplish goals assigned as part of a larger plan, (2) pass muster at the hands of a board of economists who would apply rigorous economic tests, and (3) approved by a board of people chosen for their experience in judging intangibles such as ecological, natural, recreational, and social values. They would look both at intangible benefits and at costs. For instance, they would try to evaluate the scenic importance of an area like the Red River Gorge in Kentucky where limestone arches and Daniel Boone's cabin would have been flooded by an originally proposed Corps project. A project would have to clear these three hurdles to reach the Office of Management and Budget and the executive office of the President, and public hearings should be held before the reports are forwarded.

This approach would be distinctly different than that most recently recommended by the U.S. Water Resources Council (1970). It suggests that a project be evaluated in the light of four different objectives: national economic development, environmental quality, social well-being, and regional development. The benefits and costs in terms of each objective presumably would be derived in some fashion and then be added together. If total benefits exceeded costs, then authorization would be recommended. The problems with this seemingly enlightened approach are manifold, but three stand out. First, in any of these calculations, there is always a greater impetus to quantify benefits than costs, and with an expanded calculation this tendency is magnified. Second, the formulation invites repeated double counting for elements that can be quantified in dollar terms. The full significance of these economic elements should be counted only once, in the national income account. Third, the elements in these four accounts are simply not additive. Some are purely subjective and, although others may be expressed in quantifiable terms, they will not always be in firm numbers or in dollars. Any effort to add these elements is purely illusory. Instead, one should be able to legitimately demand that a project make sense both in economic terms—without double

counting—and in terms of subjective values, whether environmental or others.

Following the procedure recommended here, once a project has cleared each planning hurdle, it should then be scrutinized further by the Council on Environmental Quality to test its conformity with overall environmental goals and the National Environmental Policy Act, and to verify the adequacy of the threefold evaluation at lower levels. It is particularly important that fully adequate reports be prepared in compliance with Section 102(2) (c) of that Act. These reports need to set forth a detailed account of the project's environmental impact, including those that are adverse, a description of irreversible commitments, a discussion of long- and short-term effects, and a list of alternative approaches. These reports should be prepared early in the planning process to help guide an agency in choosing the method it will follow, and must not be merely "boilerplate" reports prepared to survive all legal challenges. Also, the record that is forwarded must show that all other affected and interested agencies have been consulted.

The discussion of alternative methods of achieving the same goals is a key provision in this reform, and it will help remedy the problem that John Carver, former Undersecretary of the Department of the Interior and Federal Power Commissioner, articulated in 1966 as follows:

> Present procedures do not provide an adequate comparison of such alternatives. . . . Classically, legislation whether it be for a project or a government policy has been presented by the executive branch as an act of advocacy, the best possible case for a particular course of action or a single project. The process of identifying alternatives—indeed of discovering whether any exist—is left to the arena of countervailing powers in the political process.

Congress thus should be given a recommendation with alternatives, and then proceed to study and authorize each project separately, or at least in related sets, as in the practice of the House and Senate Interior Committees with respect to projects of the Bureau of Reclamation. However, projects of the Corps of Engineers each year are grouped together in one huge omnibus bill that the Public Works Committees consider. This omnibus package is carefully constructed by the Corps to garner the greatest possible support, so if possible, each committee member is given a project in his district that will gain his support for the entire package. As a result, the package often receives less than adequate scrutiny.

To remedy this it has been suggested that the package be broken into smaller segments to encourage exposure and thorough investigation of each project, to prevent "pork-barrell" politics and logrolling commitments from playing a role in the approval of the large package. In fact, Senator Frank Church has introduced a resolution aimed at changing current procedures (see Senate Concurrent Resolution 3, 91st Congress, 1st Session, 1969).

In addition, Congress should greatly expand its own review staff. An analysis branch, either in the Library of Congress or as an adjunct of the committees, should exist to carefully examine the mountain of paperwork that the agencies send up. The presumption that a project's merit is suggested by the size of the backup report can only be challenged if such a staff exists, and presently there is only a skeleton staff to check obvious weaknesses.

A final defensive tool should also be provided to give nature the benefit of the doubt. A public defender for the "rights of nature" should be established in the executive office of the President, perhaps as an adjunct of the President's Council on Environmental Quality (see also Ross, in this volume), and would be available to hear pleas of citizens who felt an agency had drastically underestimated the values of a wild river. If convinced, he could help plead their case to the Office of Management and Budget and the Congress. His expertise, and that of his staff, would be counterposed to that of the agency and its clientele, in and out of Congress. As Fox has suggested (this volume) this office should be adequately staffed in a variety of disciplines, particularly in the natural sciences, and then as a matter of fairness, the one-sided advocacy proceeding, where all the powers of government are ranged on just one side, would be ended.

Now one may reasonably ask how realistic these proposals are. Admittedly they are far-reaching, but there are stirrings in these directions. Greater economic rigor is reflected in the increased interest rates put into effect by the Water Resources Council on December 23, 1968. By raising the rate from 3¼ percent to 4⅞ percent, all projects which formerly had cost-benefit ratios of less than 1.4 to 1.0 have now been ruled out of consideration, and the interest rate has since been raised to 5½ percent. Former Federal Power Commissioner Charles Ross has suggested having an independent review board to advise the Federal Power Commission, and bills to provide this have been introduced. The Water Resources Council is struggling with efforts to modernize planning procedures. The National Water Commission has 5 years to try to cut through the fog of self-serving and self-fulfilling projections of need. The National Environmental Policy Act (P.L. 91–190) has now been enacted and the Council on Environmental Quality is demanding "102 reports," a requirement which the courts have upheld. Increased surveillance by the Office of Management and Budget and a public environmental defender are logical outgrowths of the work of the Council. Articulation of alternatives is already beginning to emerge in the work of the Corps of Engineers. In its planning for the upper Missouri River, various alternative sets of dams, including no-dam alternatives for certain reaches of the river, were presented, and an even more refined approach to planning for alternatives, in consultation with the public, is being employed by the

Corps in its Susquehanna River Basin Survey (U.S. Army Corps of Engineers, 1970).

Basic to the success of the scheme of screening that has been suggested is the creation of strong and truly independent boards of analysis—both for economics and intangibles.

Economists agree that, in the main, current benefit-cost calculations are not sufficiently rigorous and are misused to provide a seal of "political approval." At best, the calculations can do little more than weed out obviously inferior projects, and cannot really prove that a project should be built. Arthur Smithies discussed their limitations in these words (Prest and Turvey, 1965):

> First, judgment plays such an important role in the estimation of benefit-cost ratios that little significance can be attached to the precise numerical results obtained . . . . Second, competition is likely to drive the agencies towards increasingly optimistic estimates; and far from resolving the organizational difficulties, computation of benefit-cost ratios may in fact make them worse.

The most prominent of the specific criticisms customarily leveled by economists has been that the interest rate, used to calculate repayment of the federal investment from revenues, is below the cost of the money that the federal government must borrow. This has been partially answered by the recent series of rate increases. (Attempts, however, are underway to dilute the effect of these increases by inflating benefit estimates, as by imputing various secondary benefits and placing dollar figures on claimed wildlife enhancement.) Despite the increases, some maintain that an even higher rate should be used, between 7 and 10 percent, to reflect the efficiency of the same money in the general market if it were not taken out of it in the form of taxes. Currently OMB wants a 10% rate schedule to go into effect soon if it is not blocked by Congress. One study showed that 64 percent of the Corps' projects would not have been economically feasible at a 6 percent rate of interest (Krutilla, 1966). Another criticism is that there is no allowance

for risk in the interest rate, as there are many uncertainties in a project's lifespan.

There is resistance also to extending lifespan estimates from 50 years because of the uncertainties in projecting prices and benefits, and because it is recognized that projections of more than a few years into the future are mainly an exercise in guesswork. On a variety of grounds, too, economists feel that current methods of calculation encourage construction of excessively large projects, which stems from a bias in methodology toward low operating expenses but high capital costs, from interest rates below market rates, and from underpriced benefits, such as irrigation water.

Most economists are united in censuring the Bureau of Reclamation for including secondary benefits in its calculations because a form of double counting results inasmuch as the context of the investment decision is the national economy. Now this problem is being compounded by the Water Resources Council's proposal that secondary benefits be used in calculating the benefits for all federal water projects. The use of Senate Document 97 (U.S. Congress, 1962) by the Bureau of Reclamation to calculate benefits by savings in comparison to "most likely" alternatives, rather than "least cost" alternatives, is also censured, as is the use of higher interest rates and taxes in calculating the costs of private alternatives. Other even more esoteric criticisms are made in a voluminous literature which has blossomed since the early 1950s (for example, Prest and Turvey, 1965; Hammond, 1960; Krutilla, 1966; Carlin, 1967). Without attempting to assess the validity of each criticism, it would only seem reasonable to suggest compliance with those procedures on which economists, outside of the agencies, are in general agreement. After all, economic tools should be used properly.

In 1967 the Corps of Engineers rephrased its formula for evaluating projects to provide that it would "recommend developments only when convinced that the sum of the prospective economic and esthetic gains would exceed the sum of the economic costs and esthetic losses (U.S. Army Corps of Engineers, 1968)." While this formulation expresses an admirable goal, to be realizable it requires superhuman powers of objectivity, unique blends of skills, and unavailable technology. While we can be grateful that the Corps now has established environmental planning branches, it is unlikely that these branches can be more than a leavening influence at best; at worst they may be little more than window-dressing.

Esthetic gains and losses must be evaluated by experts in esthetics—by landscape architects, naturalists, artists, and conservationists—those whose reputations are made by their esthetic judgments, not by their prowess in constructing dams. Independence of judgment here is the touchstone of authenticity. Methods of analysis and comparison in the field of esthetics must be genuine to the esthetic professions, not techniques devised by engineers and economists to fit their formulations. Some progress in systematic consideration of esthetic values can probably be made (see McEvoy and Henwood, this volume), but the results will not be in a form that can be added in with economic gains and losses. Some instructive lower limits of values might be obtained through refined economic techniques, as with shadow prices, but these techniques will not produce additive values, nor full values. In particular, shadow prices should not be used to calculate recreational benefits if recreational losses are not also computed in the same manner. Some interesting comparisons of opportunity costs for recreational losses might be inferred by examining past decisions to forego economic development, as with gorges in national parks and monuments and with wild rivers. Where decisions to save such areas for esthetic reasons have the blessing of a national consensus, one could assume that the esthetic resources are valued by at least as much as the amount of the economic benefits expected from the development that was disallowed.

The hopes that conservationists share for reform of the planning process for water

development may be dismissed as wishful thinking. What then are the prospects for the dam builders? By their own admission, they are worried. The Bureau of Reclamation feels that at least $500 million per year should be appropriated to make adequate progress in constructing projects already authorized. Instead, it has been getting less than $200 million. In the words of Congressman Wayne Aspinall, Chairman of the House Interior Committee: "I cannot recall a time when the future for water resource development—insofar as federal dollars are concerned—was ever bleaker . . . The urban areas don't even know about the meaning and value of such projects . . ." He was quoted further as saying: "The tight budgeting situation, opposition from conservation groups, and the heavy urban complexion of the country combine to make for lean pickings for water resources projects." (Interview in *Grand Junction* (Colorado) *Sentinel,* July 16, 1968). Congressman Harold Johnson, who chairs the Subcommittee on Irrigation and Reclamation, says, "The Western bloc of Congressmen is not enough to influence appropriations to get these projects started." (Report of address to California Water Resources Association, *Sacramento Bee,* December 4, 1968). While at one time urban Congressmen were willing to support large reclamation outlays as a matter of regional equity and income redistribution, they are increasingly inclined to believe that the equities have changed and that there are more pressing needs in cities for federal monies. The recalcitrant attitude of rural Congressmen toward projects for parks, wilderness, wild rivers, and the open space that urban Congressmen want, makes urban Congressmen less and less disposed to continue voting large sums for rural reclamation projects.

The Corps of Engineers is also failing to achieve announced goals in constructing its projects. One observer in Congress (Hart, 1968) recently lamented that: "In more than one-third of the time period between 1954 and 1980, only about one-fourth of the additional storage projected by the select committee [the Senate's Select Committee on National Water Resources, which reported in 1961] has been added, and with the objections that are continually being raised to construction of new reservoirs, it is likely that the rate has slowed down even more in the last several years. . . Instead of the expansion needed in our water programs, it appears to me that there has actually been a relative slowdown."

It appears, too, that the tide in the intellectual community has turned against large water projects. Whereas once opposition was limited mainly to fiscal conservatives, now much of the intellectual community and the liberal, urban press is also inveighing against the crudities of "pork barrel" and "boondoggles." Even the Senate Interior Committee, which is completely dominated by westerners, is exhibiting a somewhat critical attitude toward the rationale for new reclamation projects. Its chairman is increasingly skeptical of plans for new reclamation projects in the Southwest that will create growing pressures for water diversions from the Northwest. He was responsible for a provision in the Lower Colorado Project Act that bars any studies on water importation into the Colorado River system for 10 years. In changes in the committee's alignment in 1969, the Colorado basin states lost two seats while both of Alaska's new senators were placed on the committee. While all northwestern states have representation on the committee—and two of these states have two senators—no southwestern state has two Senators on it, and California now has no representation. Clearly, powerful political defenses are being built against water diversions from the Northwest.

It is time that promoters of water projects take a hard look at their political future, as their political base is eroding as their historical rationale weakens. Probably, future success will depend upon the extent to which they can make peace with conservation groups and urban interests. The rigidity of established outlooks may make peace-making difficult, but their greatest hazard may be in not even trying.

ACKNOWLEDGMENTS

Portions of this chapter have appeared in the Sierra Club *Bulletin*, 55(7):8–11 (July 1970), and in *Environmental Quality: The Forensic Quarterly*, 44:433–446 (August 1970).

References

Carlin, Alan. 1967. "The Grand Canyon controversy: lessons for federal cost-benefit practices." *Land Economics* 43(October).

Carver, John. 1966. "Grand Canyon dams: Interior to ask, 'Are they necessary?'" *Science* 154:134.

Hammond, R. J. 1960. *Benefit-Cost Analysis and Water Pollution Control*. Food Research Inst., Stanford University.

Hart, Philip. 1968. "Remarks: Implementation of the work of the Senate Select Committee on National Water Resources." *Congressional Record* (September 6, 1968), S. 10447.

Krutilla, John V. 1966. "Is public intervention in water resources development conducive to economic efficiency?" *Natural Resources Journal* 6:70.

Prest, A. R. and R. Turvey. 1965. Cost-benefit analysis. *The Economic Journal* (December).

U.S. Army. Corps of Engineers. 1960. *Floods and flood control*. Submitted to Senate Select Committee on National Water Resources as Report 15.

U.S. Army. Corps of Engineers. 1968. *Consideration of aesthetic values in water resources development*. Regulation No. 1165-2-2, Feb. 15, 1968.

U.S. Army. Corps of Engineers. 1970. *The Susquehanna communication-participation study.* Institute for Water Resources, Report 70-6.

U.S. Congress. Senate. 1962. *Policies, standards, and procedures in the formulation, evaluation, and review of plans for use and development of water and related land resources.* Senate Document 97 (U.S. Water Resources Council).

U.S. Federal Power Commission. 1964. *National Power Survey.*

U.S. Water Resources Council. 1968. *The Nation's Water Resources.*

U.S. Water Resources Council. 1970. *Report to the W.R.C. by the Special Task Force.*

CHAPTER 25

Intense controversy arose when the Pacific Gas and Electric Company decided to construct a nuclear-fueled power plant on Bodega Head, a small peninsula north of San Francisco, California. With scenery unique to the California coast and rich marine life, Bodega Head had been considered as a site for a national or state park, and for the University of California's marine laboratory. Park and laboratory proponents came into conflict with the proponents of the power plant. Wary landowners on Bodega Head and local citizens then joined those favoring a park–laboratory to determine the effects of construction and any radioactive and thermal plant effluents on the environment and the local fishing industry. Also at issue was Bodega's location on the geologically active San Andreas fault.

Hedgpeth traces the complex course of events from 1956 through 1964, when the combined forces of citizen outcry and fears of disaster-compounded by the destructive Alaska earthquake—caused the power company to abandon plans to construct the plant at Bodega Head. Among other things, this study illustrates the frustration of ordinary citizens who attempt to take part in decisions by government agencies and large public utilities.

BODEGA: A CASE HISTORY
OF INTENSE CONTROVERSY

Joel W. Hedgpeth

INTRODUCTION

Bodega Head is a small peninsula north of San Francisco Bay projecting southward like the thumb of a left hand laid palm down on the map of California, with the greatest width being about a mile. Its northern end is low, obscured by sand dunes, whereas the southern end rises to heights of 200 to 250 feet above the sea like a Cornish moor ending abruptly in cliffs a hundred feet high. Near the northern end, facing westward, there is a small symmetrical indentation, unimaginatively named Horseshoe Cove, where the bluffs are low and the land around the cove almost level. No trees and very few bushes grow on the headlands except for the inevitable cluster of Monterey Cypress around an old farmstead.

In a 1955 National Park Service survey of potential park sites along the Pacific coast the area was not considered to have outstand-

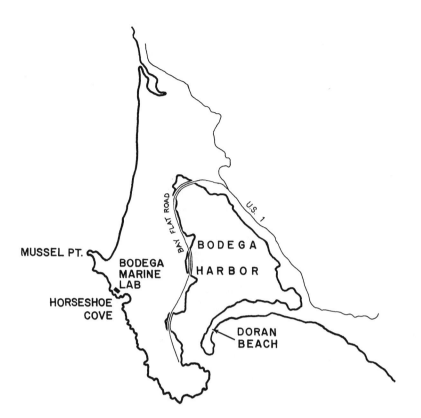

MUSSEL PT.

BODEGA
MARINE
LAB

HORSESHOE
COVE

BAY FLAT ROAD

BODEGA
HARBOR

U.S. 1

DORAN
BEACH

FIGURE 1
Map of Bodega Head.

ing scenic quality, although it was rich in history and archaeology and was also one of the areas of biological significance on the Pacific Coast, and therefore justified preservation from that standpoint alone. The report did not mention that the headland is geologically a sort of island, composed of a coarse, friable Monterey diorite separated from the serpentines, jaspers, and shales of the mainland by the San Andreas fault. The fault line is easily apparent because of the difference in soil types and consequent vegetation on the headland. At the time of the Park Service study, Bodega Head (Figure 1) was included in the Sonoma Master Plan and the Five Year Master Plan of the State Division of Beaches and Parks. It would be the logical and natural termination of a park system extending southward from the mouth of the Russian River.

Today, of course, every inch of seashore is valuable and we no longer hear the argument advanced by subdividing interests that this is a windswept, unpleasant, and useless coast and could not justify public funds for purchase as park land. In the afternoon of the same hearing, so to speak, the promoters would then argue against diversion of such potentially valuable residential property into public hands. But now, with thousands of people seeking access to the sea every weekend, and condominiums springing up like toadstools, no one denies the prime value of ocean shore property for parkland as well.

For years biologists had gone to Bodega Head for observation and collecting, where there are many productive tide pools on the rocks near Horseshoe Cove, and clams and worms abound in the mud and sand flats in the shelter of Bodega Head. The opening to the harbor is maintained by two small jetties, containing a rich development of crevice and cranny—dwelling creatures among the rocks, and since there are no permanent streams flowing into Bodega Harbor, the fauna is essentially marine. Along the eastern shore of the harbor are the docks and sheds of a small fishing industry, and at the northern end of Bodega Head is Salmon Creek, a small permanent stream with an estuarine reach, closed off in summer by a sand bar. To the south of Bodega, beyond a 6-mile gap, lies Tomales Point and Tomales Bay. Thus the area has many kinds of marine habitats, and in 1956 and 1957 the University of California rented rustic facilities at the edge of the town of Bodega Bay for its summer course in marine invertebrates. After the experience of 1956, discussions were opened with the State Division of Parks for possible joint use of the Bodega Head area as a marine biology field station and park.

But it seemed that for many years Bodega Head had impressed another group of people as a prime place for a different use. A narrow, basically granitic peninsula projecting into a cold sea was an obvious site for the foundations of a massive power generating plant and for the tunnels needed to convey the cooling water from one side of it to the other. Furthermore, it was undeveloped, and only a few cattle grazed upon it. In all, Bodega Head was an ideal location for industrialization, once the economics could be justified. Atomic power seemed to be the answer, and in 1956 the plans of the Pacific Gas and Electric Company began to take shape. In that year officials of Sonoma County were approached individually by representatives of the Pacific Gas and Electric Company and were encouraged to remain inactive with respect to the proposed master plan for including Bodega Head in the state park system, for without county approval the State could not proceed. It would be far more advantageous to the county to have a large installation that would generate tax revenue,

rather than remove the property from the tax rolls for park purposes. Whatever the exact words may have been, the substance of the argument remained the same until the end and was reiterated by editorials in the county's principal newspaper, the Santa Rosa *Press Democrat*, with the monotonous sterility of a well-wound metronome.

In the following year, not long after the University of California began to make serious inquiries about Bodega Head as a marine laboratory site, there was friendly communication to rather high levels of the univeristy administration from the hierarchy of the PG&E, to the effect that Bodega Head had already been spoken for by a higher power.

During these preliminary skirmishes, the land of Bodega Head was in private hands; the southern half of it was owned by the Stroh family, and all the rest—including the dune fields—was owned by Rose Gaffney. Such ownership meant as little to the Pacific Gas and Electric Company as it did to the California Division of Beaches and Parks, for both possessed the power of eminent domain. The strength of the power company was perhaps the greater, for as a licensed monopoly it could claim to act in the name of public convenience and necessity, and by approaching local officials on the grounds of bettering public treasuries it gained powerful sanction to exercise its power of eminent domain.

CONFIRMATION AND CONTROVERSY

On February 21, 1956, the Sonoma County Board of Supervisors adopted a master plan for the improvement and development of Bodega Harbor. This plan provided for better roads, improvement of a small air strip at the southeast corner of the bay on filled land, a small marina, concessions, and the like. Probably not long after the adoption of this master plan, the PG&E made its approaches to members of the Board, and confided to them its interest in Bodega Head as the site for an atomic power plant.

In any event, the harbor plan seemed to drop from sight after adoption, until it was recalled in a series of articles in the Santa Rosa *Press Democrat* from January 5 to January 12, 1958. In this series, entitled "The Bodega Dream," there were such separate headings as "Sonoma Seaport Undeveloped and· Ignored;" "Harbor business ventures founder in the rough seas of county apathy;" and "Bay harbor master plan allowed to gather dust." Why was nothing happening? asked the articles. Nobody seemed to know. However, it is probable that the author of the series knew that the PG&E power plant was in the offing, and the series may have been in part an effort to smoke this matter out into public.

It was not until May 23, however, that the first definite news appeared, a brief confirmation of rumors by President Norman Sutherland of the PG&E's interest in the Bodega Head site. Later, on July 20, the company's intentions were confirmed by the state. According to a paragraph in the Santa Rosa *Press Democrat*, "Long rumored plans by the Pacific Gas and Electric Company and the State Division of Beaches and Parks to buy up separately most of the private holdings on Bodega Head have been confirmed by the State agency."

The article also stated, "University of California interest in establishing a marine science branch on part of Bodega Head was not mentioned yesterday. University officials once said they felt an arrangement could be made for that branch on state park land there, although some doubt has been reported recently that the university installation would be placed near a steam power plant."

The following week PG&E confirmed its intentions to purchase property on Bodega Head, and suggested that the Board of Supervisors hold up development of the air strip until the company decided what the county might do if it interfered with power lines from the Bodega plant.

President Clark Kerr of the University of California was questioned on the university's plans at Bodega shortly after he took office. I remember that the university became aware of the company's plans sometime late in 1957, a recollection confirmed in the Emerson Report of November 29, 1960 (a letter from Ralph Emerson, Chairman of the laboratory committee, to Chancellor Seaborg), which stated, "Most unfortunately, however, progress on this plan virtually ceased in the fall of 1957 when it was learned that the Pacific Gas and Electric Company was planning a power installation on Bodega Head." I understand that Emerson suggested this matter be carried to the highest state levels for resolution, but he was overruled.

A number of us along the waterfront had some idea that PG&E had designs on Bodega Head late in 1957 or early in 1958. I was informed of these plans by colleagues at the University of California in a manner that indicated their unhappiness with the apparent unquestioning acquiescence of the administration. In fact, they were advised to keep the matter "confidential," but this was not possible. Perhaps there were some information leaks from the Sonoma County offices. Without some official statement, however, the situation was like that of waiting in a hospital for news about a patient; only the company would not even admit there was a patient. When PG&E finally admitted that it indeed had plans for Bodega Head, it was possible to raise open questions. At first, the company spokesmen were vague about the exact location they had in mind, although there were rumors that planning was much farther ahead. There was, however, no clear statement about the possible location of the plant until mid-October of the following year when the *Press Democrat* headlined on October 16, 1959, "PG&E tells location of Bodega Bay Plant."

Immediately after the announcement of interest in the Bodega area, I wrote to the President of the Pacific Gas and Electric Company in my capacity as Director of the Pacific Marine Station, located about 6 miles downwind of Bodega Head:

May 26, 1958

Dear Mr. Sutherland:

The possibility of a large scale power plant, whether atomic or steam generation, in this vicinity is of vital concern to the program of this laboratory or any other laboratory that might be established near Bodega Head. We are considering a program of long term study of changes in the composition of common certain seashore organisms, for a minimum period of perhaps 25 years, and preferably at least 50 years. If a large power plant were to be built within 10 or 15 years at the mouth of Estero Americano (one of the rumored sites), we should know this immediately in order to plan our program, utilizing other sites, or instituting a research program of a year or two for a study of the shore currents along Bodega Bay to estimate the possible course of warm water from your outlets. This information would also be necessary if your cooling outlets were on the inner side of Bodega Head.

. . . Our principal asset here is the rich and varied shore fauna of the rocky, sandy and muddy regions of Bodega Bay and Tomales Bay regions. There are indications that changes in mean water temperatures near the shore of only one or two degrees centigrade have marked influences on the presence or absence, and reproductive survival, of certain marine organisms. I would consider the establishment of a large power plant . . . if done without proper study of its local effects, a major calamity for this or any other marine laboratory in this region. It would also be a sad impairment of biological and scenic values to use Horseshoe Cove for such an installation (as some rumors have it). I also wonder if the AEC would consent to the installation of large scale reactors on top of an active fault, as any such installation on Bodega Head would be. Indeed, this whole region seems a bit too close to the San Andreas fault for comfort, and I wonder if you have adequately considered this

aspect. If you have considered this and plan to construct a plant which would be unaffected by possible shifts of twenty feet or so (as happened at Pt. Reyes Station [nearby] in 1906) along the fault, it is still in order to consider a survey of nearshore currents to determine the possible course of warm water from the various possible sites that the company has in mind.

Sutherland's reply to this letter indicated a complete lack of understanding of long-term studies of the natural environment and how such an industrial development as a power plant would impair the value of such studies and, even more significantly, it indicated that the Pacific Gas and Electric Company had not considered geological factors in its initial decision:

June 11, 1958

Dear Mr. Hedgpeth:

I can only give you general answers in reply to your letter of May 26, 1958, since our search for a steam plant site in the [area] is in its preliminary stages and may not be settled for some time to come. Circumstances might develop, however, that would permit a decision on a plant location within a year's time. Actual operations of the proposed steam electric plant, wherever located in the North Bay area, will probably not occur before five to ten years from now.

We have been studying the possibilities of Bodega Head, as well as other locations along the coast. We have not considered a plant location at the mouth of the Estero Americano, unless you consider the Head to be within the area of the mouth. We have retained a geologist to report on the effect of the San Andreas fault in this area as a plant site for either atomic or conventional steam plant development. His investigations have not been completed, and are awaiting the results of field surveys and calculations now under way.

If a site on Bodega Head is found to be feasible, studies made up to the present time indicate that cooling water will be taken through the plant and discharged into the ocean on the westerly side of the island. It appears to be almost certain that the discharge would not be on the inner side.

We expect to have more definite information on which to proceed with our studies as soon as our geologist has completed his investigations. In any event, there should be ample time for you to institute the research program you suggest before we would be ready to proceed with any development in the area, if it proves to be feasible at all.

According to a short news item in the Santa Rosa *Press Democrat* for June 11, 1958, "A thorough geological study of the Bodega Bay area—possible future site of a 200,000-kilowatt steam-electric plant—is now under way." However, I was advised later in a meeting with company engineers in San Francisco on November 22, 1958, that their geological report was based on general information, that they had no precise information about the structure of Bodega Head other than that it was split up into blocks and that the rock was "soft" granite that would require reinforcement for construction. Apparently no original field work was to be done by the Pacific Gas and Electric Company until after it had dug its famous "glory hole" in Bodega Head in 1963 and until after geologists inspected the excavation late in that year. However, for several years the geological aspects of the site received remarkably little notice in the public press.

The exchange with Sutherland was the beginning of a 5-inch stack of correspondence about the Bodega affair from 1958 through 1963. On August 11, 1958, the first of my many letters to the editor appeared in the *Press Democrat*; I suggested that if the plant were built at Bodega PG&E would be supporting more than half the assessed valuation of the county, a situation which could reduce the county to vassalage. The original series of articles on Bodega Bay in the *Press Democrat* in January 1958 caused me to begin a scrapbook of newspaper clippings that ultimately filled four large books and became one of the principal sources of material for the campaign in defense of Bodega Head.

However, there was comparatively little overt opposition or even opinion concerning PG&E and its approach to Bodega Head during 1958. The official attitude was substantially that indicated by an account of a meeting of the Sonoma County Harbor Commission on August 14, 1958. At this meeting the acting chairman, Robert M. Harkness, brought up the need for information concerning the plan; other commisioners, however, contended that many of the questions with which Harkness was concerned were not the business of the commission, but of other agencies, and tabled Harkness' move for investigation. Harkness' concern may have been primarily economic; he visited me after reading my letter of August 11 in the *Press Democrat*. In part his remarks at the Harbor Commission meeting were inspired by conversations with me, but he was also concerned about the Commission's lack of authority and the manner in which county government decisions had been made behind the scenes without respect to the responsibilities of the Harbor Commission.

When it made its overtures before the Sonoma County Supervisors about the air strip at Bodega, the Pacific Gas and Electric Company owned no property on Bodega Head, as it was negotiating with the formidable Rose Gaffney—who was not interested in anything less than $1,000 for each of her 407.5 acres. PG&E finally abandoned this approach to file suit in eminent domain for her entire holdings on August 22, 1958. I went to the Court House and read the terse and uninformative document, which seemed to have been written in the tone of a sovereign ruler. I also found that I could file my own opinion for $3. Just a few days previously our library had received the September issue of *Nature*, with the account of the fallout of radioactive iodine over the Lake District of England from the Windscale "incident" of the previous year.

On October 30, I filed an *amicus curiae* statement, which opened with: "Bodega Head is a unique feature of the California

CUMBERLAND

CALIFORNIA

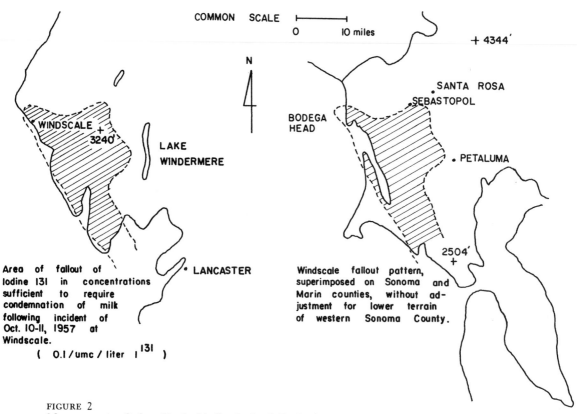

COMMON SCALE

0   10 miles

N

WINDSCALE +
3240'

LAKE
WINDERMERE

BODEGA
HEAD

+ 4344'

• SANTA ROSA
• SEBASTOPOL

• PETALUMA

2504'
+

• LANCASTER

Area of fallout of
Iodine 131 in concentrations
sufficient to require
condemnation of milk
following incident of
Oct. 10-11, 1957 at
Windscale.

(0.1/umc/liter I^{131})

Windscale fallout pattern,
superimposed on Sonoma and
Marin counties, without adjustment for lower terrain
of western Sonoma County.

FIGURE 2
Map comparing Bodega Head with Cumberland, England.

coast, displaying to best advantage one of the greatest geological features of the North American continent, the San Andreas fault, whose activity caused the disaster to San Francisco in 1906, and being an extraordinarily favorable site for the study of marine shore life." The statement pleaded for proper studies, and included a diagram (Figure 2) of the extent of the Windscale fallout over Sonoma and Marin counties (mostly dairy farms). Subsequent events confirmed my opinion and the substance of my statement:

We are no longer in an age when a power company should have the right to decide the location and type of power installation without adequate public notice and control. It should be required to state plainly what type

of power plant it intends to build, well in advance of actual construction, in order to establish, equally well in advance, an adequate monitoring system to determine the present and future levels of radioactivity.

I sent copies of this document to the county supervisors of both Marin and Sonoma counties, and to the Sierra Club, but nothing much happened. There was no acknowledgment from the Sierra Club, and the document and its covering letter are missing from the files. In fact, I observed no reaction from the Sierra Club for two years. The original petition was later modified when the Pacific Gas and Electric Company joined forces with the University of California and the state parks people to divide Mrs. Gaffney's property, and the document was, I suppose, technically moot.

My function as a witness in the case was to attest to the scenic and biological values of Mrs. Gaffney's property. Careless comments that beyond this spot was where the power plant outfall was planned, or that a chain link fence would be built along the proposed property line were objected to strenuously by the attorneys for the PG&E. However, a friend of mine on the jury later told me that the jury thought the attorneys—and the judge—made themselves a bit foolish by objecting to such remarks as unjustified conclusions of the witness. As he said, everybody knew PG & E would build a big fence around their property, they always do.

Reaction from the Pacific Gas and Electric Company was immediate; President Robert E. Burns of the University of the Pacific was approached by his lodge brothers, who happened to be company officials, and told in a most friendly way that it was possible I did not know what I was talking about, and that continued expression of this sort could embarrass the university. In this matter I owe a great deal to the position taken by the late Dr. Burns, who told company officials he could only ask me to inform myself, that he could not control my thoughts. As the controversy wore on an effort was made to cast doubts concerning my competence and, I daresay, emotional balance, among county and state officials.

In response to this encouragement to inform myself, I attended a meeting with various company engineers and their chief land department man, Stanley Barton, on November 22, 1958. It was not a very informative meeting; I was told that their consulting geologist's report had no new information as they had made no test borings. I was congratulated on exercising my citizen's duty of calling attention to the Windscale affair, but assured that a boiling water reactor does not leak radioactivity, and was given the impression that they knew very little about near-shore oceanography or the uptake of radionuclides by marine organisms. Sometime later the company did retain Dr. Ernest O. Salo of Humboldt State College to study these matters, but his studies were incomplete and did not cover enough time to demonstrate adequately the circulation pattern off Bodega Head.

A photograph taken in March of 1953 showing the circulation of water off Bodega Head (Figure 3) would have been of great assistance in preparing an adequate study of the region, but it did not come to light until 1963. For that matter, it might have induced Professor Robert Wiegel to qualify his opinion of the mixing process off Bodega Head, which was to have a key influence within the university. His opinion seems to have been derived from general considerations rather than such primary data or actual field reconnaissance.

Although my statement received conspicuous notice in the local newspapers, little else happened in 1958 except for a few letters and murmurs at county meetings, most of which were concerned with the changes to the harbor from such a large construction project and the possible effects of the accompanying high power lines on fishing and navigation in Bodega Bay. Scattered letters to the editor appeared, and by the end of 1959 there was a steady flow. Mrs. Gaffney was an especially voluminous contributor, asserting her rights under the treaty of Guadalupe Hidalgo to accreted lands, and her disdain of the Pacific Gas and Electric Company and various members of the Sonoma County Board of Supervisors. She got some extra space with equally long and similar letters under the name of Virginia Devereaux (her daughter), until someone told the editor of the paper and he ordered rationing of her space.

On October 16, 1959, according to a front page story in the Santa Rosa *Press Democrat*, PG&E had decided just about where it would put its plant on Bodega Head, and some questions were answered "for the first time since the power plant came under discussion in 1957 [sic]." The plant, according

FIGURE 3
Circulation of water off Bodega Head.

to this story, was to be placed "on the southerly part of the headlands." The Horseshoe Cove site could not be used "because of branches of the San Andreas fault." At the time, however, PG&E did not have title to its proposed site, and the deed for the Stroh ranch was not filed until November 19. But according to a headline in the *Press Democrat* for December 20, 1959: "Type of Bodega Bay Plan Still Undecided by PG&E"

PROGRESS OF THE MARINE LABORATORY

After deciding that it could not locate its plant on Horseshoe Cove, the site desired by the University of California for its marine laboratory, the PG&E suggested that this part of the property was again available to the university for laboratory purposes. On December 13, 1959, I was visited at Pacific

Marine Station by two colleagues from the University of California, Daniel Mazia and Roger Stanier, who indicated this development and inquired about knowledge of the possible effects of the power plant. The biologists interested in a marine laboratory for the Berkeley campus were beginning to convince themselves that even if Bodega were now to be considered a second class site because of the possible proximity of power plant, it was the best of all second class sites since it had originally been the only first class site. This conviction is in essence the tenor of the famous Emerson Report, actually a memorandum to Chancellor Seaborg dated November 29, 1960. However, before that opinion was completely firm, help was requested from the oceanographers at Scripps Institution of Oceanography. On May 12, Douglas Inman, a specialist in coastal circulation, and Jeffrey Frautschy, a marine engineer, visited Bodega Head with me, and we watched the surface indications of nearshore containment of water along the face of Bodega Head. A report by Frautschy and Inman suggesting that "Horseshoe Cove will from time to time be bathed for periods of some hours in unmixed effluent at near discharge temperatures" was written in the form of a letter to Roger Stanier on June 14, 1960, and suggested that the proposed schedule of diversion of water into the cooling system would materially alter the ebb flow and possibly accelerate sedimentation within the harbor.

The Frautschy-Inman report caused consternation, or at least was considered a "severe blow." Nevertheless, as far as the Emerson Report indicated, without further expert opinion (but after some more soul searching) the committee recommended to Chancellor Seaborg that the Horseshoe Cove area of Bodega Head be acquired for the laboratory site.

None of this, of course, answered my objection that the site would not be useful for natural studies of long-term environmental variables, or for certain types of basic studies

of the biology of seashore animals; but it became the informal position of the acting director of the laboratory, Cadet Hand, that the site would of course be an ideal one for the study of the effects of a large power reactor on the seashore. It was partly on these grounds that the National Science Foundation awarded more than a million dollars for construction of the Bodega Marine Laboratory in 1964. The university's position unfortunately became one of the greatest obstacles to conservationists who opposed the power plant, because it served to weaken their case.

Formal announcement of the university's decision to return to Bodega Head was not made until September 1961, and the Emerson Report of November 29, 1960, was finally published in the *Daily Californian* (Berkeley) on December 14, 1962. Unwillingly, the marine laboratory committee had effectively aligned itself with the Pacific Gas and Electric Company, as they reluctantly realized. The company's public relations people made the most of this turnabout, not only to advance their own cause but also as evidence of the possible incompetence of critics of the university decision. As one company press release in January 1963 put it: "As for the concern expressed about the possible effects of the atomic plant on marine biology in the Bodega area, the University of California's selection of a site adjacent to the atomic plant for its Bodega Marine Laboratory is of great significance."

Matters proceeded slowly. The Sierra Club at last appeared on the scene, when Mrs. Taylor Sloan of the Redwood Chapter came before the Sonoma County Board of Supervisors on September 9, 1960, requesting a public hearing of the Bodega project; the reaction to this request was that such a hearing was not necessary. Later in the year, the Sierra Club called on me for information. At the public utilities hearings in 1962 they again appeared.

The power plant itself was not the only negative aspect of the situation from the marine laboratory viewpoint; there was also the matter of access. This access was to be achieved by a road along the tidelands shore of Bodega Harbor. It was heavily supported by county interests, and the protests by Cadet Hand that it would obliterate some of the biological assets of the region evidently outraged a number of county officials. Behind the scenes, amicable arrangements seem to have been made, and Professor Hand found that the rug—or in this case the mud flat—had been pulled from beneath him, and his further protests about the tidelands road had a zombie-like quality.

Planning went ahead, and a formal request for funds to construct the Bodega Marine Laboratory was submitted to the National Science Foundation in 1962, despite the uproar that reached its climax in that year. In this proposal some mention was made of the possible effect of the proposed PG&E installation, but an attempt was made to place the matter on a rather folksy basis by referring to "our southerly neighbor." Requests for such large sums of money as $1.5 million must be investigated by a committee that visits the institution and the site. I was invited to be a member of this committee, and declined.

I entered my reasons for refusing in my diary for January 25, 1963: '. . . have decided to ask NSF not to involve me. I do not think I should be on record as saying anything for or against this. This will not be easy as dearly as I love to meddle in other people's business." I was upset by the cocksure attitude of some of my colleagues, and still felt keenly that the university's position had impeached environmental witness against the project.

Members of the committee—whom I joined on the following day in Oregon on another site visit—indicated that they were justifying their decision to approve funding on the basis that the laboratory would provide a good opportunity to study the effects of the power plant, and that in such a great university the laboratory would undoubtedly be put to use by many scientists. While in Washington in the spring of 1963 visiting NSF, I was informed that the only justification the Foundation would possibly make for funding would be the opportunity the site provided to study the effects of the reactor. There was also word that the Atomic Energy Commission was worried about the faults on Bodega Head.

The laboratory was finally built. It had become, through the years, a much more pretentious project than the informal scientific seashore resort originally envisioned in the 1940s, and indeed by the original laboratory committee of the mid-1950s. Perhaps as part of the growing controversy over Bodega Head the laboratory grew in importance to its $1.5 million magnitude. Also, the nervousness about the proximity of the San Andreas fault was contracted by the university architects, and a structure was designed and built to withstand severe stress. From a distance it has the unfortunate appearance of a fortification—lying squat on the land, with narrow, embrasure-like windows and a solid flat roof. The Assyrian massiveness of the buildings conveys an impression of isolation, although the interior courtyard lightens this effect at close quarters. The heating bills for this type of structure are such that one wonders if PG&E has not in the end won after all.

There were Faustian overtones to the University of California's increasingly ambiguous position. Having once decided that the power plant might not be incompatible with a marine laboratory, our modern Fausts realized that further criticism of the project within the university would reflect upon their own scientific acumen; indeed, it might possibly raise the question of their competence to select a laboratory site at all. We have recently become less altruistic, and applied or relevant research is more respectable than it used to be, but at the time the decision that they could "live with the PG&E" was an immoral surrender to expediency in the opinion of many bystanders. In this context it is still not entirely clear whether Mephistopheles was retained by the Pacific Gas and Electric Company, the University of California, or the Atomic Energy Commission.

THE CONTROVERSY REACHES A CLIMAX

The Battle of Bodega Head reached its peak during 1962. It began with meetings in Bodega to plan strategy for the Corps of Engineers hearing on February 15 concerning the mud flats access road, and did not quite end with a meeting in Santa Rosa on November 10, during which Governor Brown's advisor on atomic energy matters advised our citizens group that we really had no business meddling in such matters—decisions were for the experts, not the people. Between these events came the climactic action before the California Public Utilities Commission in San Francisco. Most significant of all was the rallying of public opposition to the plant, the appearance of organizations to fight the designs of the power company, and the escalation of the controversy beyond the shores of Pacific Marine Station and the tidelands of Bodega Harbor. During the first years we had not made much of an impression, but by the end of the year we knew that we were getting close to some nerves.

The first event was a local affair, the hearing by the Corps of Engineers concerning the application of Sonoma County to build a road along the tidelands to Bodega Head. Actually, the road was to be built by the Pacific Gas and Electric Company, partly from material to be excavated from the reactor site on Bodega Head. This hearing was scornfully regarded by the editor of the Santa Rosa *Press Democrat*, who suggested that since it could concern only the effect of the road upon navigation, it would be something of a waste of time, and the late Congressman Clem Miller was never thanked for having persuaded the Engineers to hold the hearing.

According to the extended account of the hearing published in the *Press Democrat* for February 16, fifty speakers offered opinions about the road. Testimony was offered about the destruction of biological values. A great deal of the testimony was political, and as the presiding officer stated at the conclusion of the hearing (which lasted from 2 P.M. to 10 P.M.), those matters not bearing directly on navigation would not be considered. Mention was made in the account of the statement by one resident that "dumping rock in the bay would push mud up elsewhere." According to my own notes he was not the only Bodega Bay native to suggest that the weight of the road would cause movement of mud into the harbor and consequently shoal the bottom. However, since these people were not recognized engineers their testimony was apparently disregarded, and the road was approved in March 1962. Not quite two years later, in December 1964, the Corps of Engineers in a letter to the County of Sonoma called attention to the impairment of navigation by mud waves caused by the weight of the road on the tidelands, and requested the county to remove the mud waves.

The Corps hearing sapped the energies of the Bodega natives, and the hearing of the California Public Utilities Commission in San Francisco on March 7-9 was almost unnoticed by those most directly concerned. This meeting was held to determine whether the application for a power plant on Bodega Head was indeed in the public interest. Most of the witnesses were PG&E company representatives and while some protests were made, notably by the environmental columnist Harold Gilliam, approval of the application by the Commission seemed certain. Approval was indeed inevitable under the regulations, but not before a dramatic event. If there was a single turning point in the affair, it was the letter by Karl Kortum, Director of the San Francisco Maritime Museum, published in the San Francisco *Chronicle* on March 14. Without this letter the battle might well have ended on the somewhat whimpering note of the first PUC hearing. Kortum's letter, inspired by Harold Gilliam's article "Atom vs Nature at Bodega" (San Francisco *Chronicle*, February 11, 1962) and his lifelong knowledge of Bodega and its people, was in large part a hypothetical dialogue between the engineers of a "public utility," scheming to "grab Bodega Head." His concluding plea that people concerned write to the Public Utilities Commission was extraordinarily successful; more than 2,500 letters of protest were received by the Commission, and it reopened the hearings. Before the hearings were reopened on May 21, however, the condemnation proceedings against Mrs. Gaffney took place in Santa Rosa and an organization to Preserve Bodega Head and Harbor was founded in the Tides Restaurant at Bodega Bay on May 2, 1962.

The reopened hearings took place on May 21-22 and, after a recess, from June 6-8. More than 150 people appeared, including the natives from Bodega, and the testimony ran to 1,500 pages. The hearing was a public forum for all sorts of opinions and warnings, with very few concerning atomic energy. Toward the end of the hearing, after offering testimony on potential effects of the cooling effluent, I had the opportunity to denounce my colleagues as idiots (as I was so thinking) but instead stated the university would be unwise to build a laboratory on Bodega unless it could control plant operations. My remarks were somewhat misconstrued, although I was correctly quoted as stating, "if something untoward happens, at least it will be a base of operation." This was actually part of the rationale for the university's acceptance of Bodega. At the time there were still doors ajar, and I did not want to close them.

It was only on the last of the seven days of hearings that the issue of earthquake faults began to be mentioned. The hearings were not only significant in bringing the issues of wise use, site selection, and behind-the-scenes maneuvering to public attention, but also in

recruiting the Sierra Club to the cause. David Pesonen, the conservation editor for the Sierra Club, called attention to the vacuum of responsibility in state government for the public welfare in the matter of power plant site selection. Soon after, he made a study of the affair that was published serially in the Sebastopol *Times* and was brought together in brochure form and widely circulated, as "A Visit to the Atomic Park."

On November 9 the Public Utilities Commission issued a Certificate of Convenience and Necessity to the Pacific Gas and Electric Company, subject to certain conditions, including a research program to reassure the Commission that there would be no serious effects on the flora and fauna of the region. On the night this decision was announced in the papers a meeting was held in the Odd Fellows' Hall in Santa Rosa. It was intended to be an informational meeting for concerned citizens to present information about the possible effects of a nuclear reactor at Bodega Bay, and was sponsored primarily by the Northern California Association to Preserve Bodega Bay and Harbor, the Unitarian Fellowship, and the Bodega Bay Chamber of Commerce. It promised to be something of an anticlimax; one newspaper account termed the coincidence "almost ironic." It was a rather dull meeting for the first two hours or so.

Then came one of those rare catalyzing moments. The Governor's Coordinator of Atomic Energy Development and Radiation Protection, in response to some routine questions, proceeded to discuss things as they really were. In a dry, humorless manner he informed the audience that only the opinion of qualified experts would carry any weight in the forthcoming Atomic Energy Commission hearings on the Bodega Head project. He would do his part to see that the hearing would be held in Santa Rosa, but it would of course do them little good: "The general public will not be permitted to testify because they will not be able to demonstrate the expert competence that will be required."

In the informal cross examination that followed, it became obvious that as far as the state coordinator of atomic energy was concerned the only criterion for judgment was whether or not the installation would be safe; all other considerations, especially the first one of location, were for other jurisdictions.

It was all well and bluntly said and for the first time the full implication of the procedures that had developed around the application of atomic energy in a democratic but uninformed, nonexpert society became obvious. Some of us were shocked, as were many who heard the tapes of the meeting broadcast from a Berkeley radio several times after the meeting. Money began to flow into the coffers of the Association to Preserve Bodega Head and the organization functioned on a full-time basis. It was undoubtedly the last thing that the state coordinator expected from his earnest effort to tell us how the world really was. The reaction of my friend Evan Evans, no stranger to the atomic labyrinth, was pithy and revealing:

> The Bodega Head issue assumes a much deeper political significance. As Pesonen [the Sierra Club representative] clearly brought out, no public body or private individual can effectively oppose the A.E.C.'s decisions . . . in matters of conservation there is as yet no watchdog at all.

The polarization of opinion by the unwitting coordinator was not, however, the last event of 1962. In late November came the first of what developed into a continuous barrage of petitions to the Public Utilities Commission to reconsider or revoke its permit to the Pacific Gas and Electric Company.

The crescendo of the year 1962 never quite decreased during the following two years; the basic battle lines had been drawn and the issues of earthquake danger, radiation leakage, and denial of public hearings were fought out as a war of attrition by petitions and publicity releases. Every petition to reopen the hearings was turned down, and every attempt to gain a public hearing in

Sonoma County was denied. But some sort of publicity or straight news item appeared in the papers almost every day. Letters to the editor became a steady flood. A spontaneous counter-organization sprouted from the grassroots of Sonoma County, where letters to the editor were written in behalf of the project and assailing the motives and intelligence of the opposition. Mrs. Gaffney lost her land—at $1,000 per acre—but never gave up her criticism of the PG&E and its ways, although she was wooed with tasteless Season's Greetings and potted plants.

The Pacific Gas and Electric Company kept on its ponderous course, apparently a rhinoceros shrugging off pebbles tossed by pygmies. It built the road along the mud flats and began to dig an enormous hole in Bodega Head. This hole was not "construction," but "site preparation"; construction could not begin until the Atomic Energy Commission had held its hearings and issued its permit, the last hurdle in the process of expert approval. It announced that the plant would be three times as large as originally suggested. The servile Supervisors of Sonoma County, finding it impossible to avoid a property owner's suit to invalidate the use permit for PG&E on grounds that no public hearing had been held, adopted a "precise" zoning plan for Bodega Bay. According to this plan the headland was rezoned for agriculture from its "interim" status. Under agricultural zoning, farmers may build their home generating plants for barnyard power without a permit from the county. Since no size limit was set on this construction, PG&E no longer needed a use permit from the county and the court proceedings became moot.

Shortly after this low comedy, the former jazz trumpeter Lu Watters released some balloons from Bodega Head to the blast of his battered horn. The balloons carried a tag which said that this balloon could have been a radioactive molecule. A couple of them were found in the fountain of the elegant Civic Center Building in San Rafael, about

40 miles downwind. It was a diversion which greatly discomforted the public relations people of PG&E. At about the same time there was indication of concern by the Department of the Interior, and professional geologists were reported beginning an investigation. Lu Watters later held a benefit concert at Earthquake McGoon's in San Francisco which brought a heartening sum to the Association to Preserve Bodega Head and Harbor.

In September 1963 PG&E dedicated its prototype reactor at Humboldt Bay with glowing predictions of the new dawn and a statement by Senator Pastore: "You have built a temple to the advancement of mankind." The glowing press releases of 1963 now read somewhat oddly in view of the troubles of 1966 at the Humboldt reactor, which suggest that the company had bought an engineering lemon; not only was there excessive leakage from the fuel elements, but they had applied to the AEC for permission to increase their allowable discharge of radioactive gases from the stack.

The digging of the hole at Bodega went on and in October the excavation revealed some old cracks. The company's geologists said that they did not amount to much, but both the opposition and impartial geologists did not agree. Shortly after this discovery the research vessel *Baird* from Scripps Institution of Oceanography appeared off the coast of Bodega, making seismic refraction studies of the San Andreas fault complex, and preliminary results of this study became public in January 1964. A very complex faulting structure was indicated by the instruments, including a possible vertical displacement of about 90 feet not far offshore in the underlying rock structure.

Undoubtedly these preliminary results reached sensitive desks in Washington in advance of the usual slow procedure of progress reports and formal analyses, and it may have been that minds were made up about the risks of the project some weeks before March 27, 1964, when the Alaska earthquake on Good Friday reminded everyone of the potential destruction from a moderate earthquake. After this, there were indications of sharp questions from the AEC, especially concerning the possibility of a tsunami associated with a major earthquake, and what it might do to a nuclear reactor.

There followed a sort of diapause. Hearings were postponed, and although letters and publicity releases continued, they seemed to be at a lower key. By October it was obvious that something was going on—"What's delaying AEC hearing on Bay A-Plant?" asked the heading of an article in the Santa Rosa *Press Democrat* for October 11. On October 28 it was announced that in the opinion of the AEC's Division of Nuclear Licensing, "Bodega Head is not a suitable location for the proposed nuclear plant at the present state of our knowledge." On October 29, Governor Edmund G. Brown of California urged that the project be abandoned. Finally, on October 30, the Pacific Gas and Electric Company announced that because of the reasonable doubt raised by the AEC committee they were withdrawing their application in the interest of public safety.

Subsequently, PG&E leased its property with the famous "Hole in the Head" to Sonoma County for $1 per year as a park, and in May of 1972 it was purchased by the State of California as part of the park system. Now, at the time of this writing, PG&E is preparing to seek a permit to construct a massive reactor installation about 50 miles north of Bodega, at Point Arena where the San Andreas fault at last bends westward out to sea.

EPILOGUE

Almost before the dust had settled on Bodega Head the significance of the controversy was being assessed. According to Harold Gilliam, the most important lesson was the demonstration that there was no agency in

California "to protect the people's interest in maintaining open space." The power company said that parks were not their business, the Public Utilities Commission said that selection of a site was not its business, and the Park's people said thay could not move without county approval. But the long fight and its publicity did convince the Pacific Gas and Electric Company that it would be best in the future to avoid such a confrontation if possible, and it endeavored to reach a meeting of minds with the Sierra Club in subsequent site selections. The desirability of long-range planning for use of the seashore was obvious, and the discussion stimulated by Bodega is still going on although definite statewide plans are yet to be adopted.

There were—and still are—indications that within industry and the Atomic Energy Commission the implications have been misunderstood. It was considered a case of ill-justified public reaction to something not well understood, poor preparation on the part of the company, or even a matter of questionable motivation by the opponents. A member of the AEC declared in a speech in Vermont in 1968 that those opposing the Bodega Head project were financed by the fossil fuel interests. The idea that some people may fight a battle for altruistic motives is simply not comprehended in some circles.

Yet much of the opposition generated against the Bodega project was inspired by the political skullduggery and contempt for peoples' opinions on the one hand, and on the other a conviction that this use was not the wisest and best use of the landscape. Bodega's attraction to many people was immediate and overwhelming. As soon as marine geologists from the Scripps Institution of Oceanography saw Bodega Head, they were dedicated to its defense. I have no doubt that this dedication may have influenced the ready manner in which their preliminary results became available to the anonymous people within the decision-making process.

To those who may think that the Good Friday earthquake of 1964 in Alaska caused an adverse decision, it can be suggested that there were indications of uncertainty before the event. Certainly, some people were worried about radiation and its effects, and would oppose a nuclear reactor anywhere, and it must be said that subsequent events have justified some of their concern.

The effective decision that arose out of concern for the safety of the power plant was made by the people who were supposed to be the experts, but who had originally claimed all would be well. Public concern and publicity helped them arrive at the opinion that a nuclear reactor on a major fault structure was not a good idea. At the critical moment, almost to the point of no return, our experts, the specialists on whom we are supposed to depend, did not have the courage of their knowledge, and in the end had to respond to public opinion just as the politicians did.

I still think, as I did immediately after the surrender of the Pacific Gas and Electric Company, that the most significant moral to the tale is concerned with the manner in which these things are done in our society. As I wrote in a letter to the editor of the Santa Rosa *Press Democrat*, November 9, 1964):

> Undoubtedly there was a preliminary conditioning of our county government by the great corporation, which has cultivated and no doubt honestly believes the image that it can do no wrong, that whatever it does is for the best interests of the people. With this is the corollary notion that the company could not possibly make an error in judgment—a statement made to me many times by advocates of the project. But corporations are made of people, and all people make mistakes. I think that a better system of regulating and examining projects of this type at the outset would have prevented the mistake that has been made . . . . In a real sense the P.G.&E. has been as much a victim of the present system as the people . . . The frightening power of condemnation which the P.G.&E. has must somehow be limited.

Another moral concerns the people of our local governments—both elected bodies and . . . voluntary organizations . . . There are other values than tax revenues in our society, and one of the most disturbing aspects of this affair has been the willingness of many people to be concerned with tax revenue at the expense of the county's unique scenic and recreational and scientific assets. The reappraisal may be agonizing to some but it must be made, for these intangible values . . . are the values which attract people to Sonoma County.

The Battle of Bodega has turned out to be a landmark in the endless struggle of citizens against the Establishment and against Progress, if you will. When it first began, few people were aware of the manner in which we were witlessly destroying our environment, and fewer people believed that anything could be done. Not only did they believe that one could not lick City Hall, but also that a corporation like PG&E could not possibly make a stupid mistake. Both ideas have proved false, and the public relations people of large corporations are a little less careless about calling their opposition bird watchers and lily pickers. Their hearts may not always be with their words, but they too talk of the environment and how they are concerned about the preservation of our amenities. However, there seems to have been little change in such local political entities as the Sonoma County Board of Supervisors, and until there is, the preservation issue symbolized by Bodega Head is still not resolved. Perhaps this is the vital issue in our democratic decision-making process: the real decisions are controlled at a local level while the repercussions of the decisions are far-reaching.

References

Several articles have been published about Bodega, and the affair was given some notice in Sheldon Novick's *The Careless Atom* (Houghton Mifflin, 1969), but there is as yet no definitive history. It has been used in a novel, *Galleon Bay*, by Neill C. Wilson (William Morrow, 1968), but this is strictly a light fiction effort for summer hammock readers; all the author seemed to know about the situation, despite his residence in Sebastopol, was dimly remembered from the newspapers. However, the testimony of Dr. Deems of the "University Marine Laboratory" does, in a somewhat oversimplified manner, echo popular understanding of this unfortunate position: "I have absolutely no fears," Dr. Deems responded from the audience. "All the heated water you plan to pour out into the ocean, perhaps two hundred thousand gallons a minute, won't seem like a spurt from an eye-dropper. The combers will dissipate it. The ocean is too big and restless to be bothered by such a trifle. I promise everyone that our laboratory will keep close tabs on all threats—real or imaginary—to our shoreline's ecology."

The more important articles are:

Hedgpeth, Joel W. 1965. "Bodega Head—a partisan view." *Bull. Atomic Scientists*, pp. 2–7.

Hedgpeth, Joel W. 1966. "The battle of Bodega Head." *Ibid.*, pp. 42–47.

Marine, Gene. 1963. "Outrage on Bodega Head." *The Nation* (June 22), pp. 524–527.

Pesonen, David E. 1962. *A visit to the Atomic Park.* 38 pp., Copyright by David E. Pesonen. (Reprinted from the *Sebastopol Times*, September 27, October 4, 11 and 18) Photographs by Karl Kortum.

Pesonen, David E. 1967. "Science and public power: Bodega Head." *Medical Opinion and Review.* pp. 20–27.

CHAPTER 26

Major conflict was precipitated when hydroelectric development was proposed for Switzerland's only national park. It involved not only the ecological and aesthetic effects of such construction on a delicate alpine life zone, but concern for the sovereignty of local government, the water rights of local residents, legal rights of the land owners from which the park is leased, and the issue of preservation in a technological society. The latter concern became a focus of national controversy between proponents and opponents of the project before a compromise was finally reached.

This history illustrates how costly conflict between preservation and development can be, as well as how conflicts can be satisfactorily resolved provided that all interested factions are a party to the compromise.

WATER DEVELOPMENT: A EUROPEAN EXPERIENCE

Lucas Werenfels and Pierre Meylan

INTRODUCTION

In this chapter a general evaluation of Swiss environmental problems created by water development projects—largely hydropower projects—is made. One of the last major power development schemes in Switzerland, the Spoel Project in the Alps, stirred controversy before and during its implementation because of encroachment on the National Park. The environmental values discussed are mainly aesthetic, but to some extent they are biotic. The controversy surrounding the proposed project must also be seen against the background of decreasing demand for hydro-power projects owing to increasing competition from thermal power.

The sociological and the environmental aspects differ from most hydro-power developments in the USA, but because of the similar political structures of Switzerland and the United States, the democratic processes at work in such developments are pertinent to this discussion of water development.

EXISTING SWISS LAWS REGARDING WATER DEVELOPMENT

Water Rights

As a consequence of the Swiss federal political system, laws concerning the use of water are not uniform. Under the federal constitution, the use of water is subject to the jurisdiction of the Swiss confederation, and Congress must issue decrees safeguarding public interest and ensuring rational utilization of water for hydropower. As a rule, however, a state, or even a district or a commune (the political equivalent of a township) is entitled to develop water directly or to grant concessions, so that detailed legislation concerning the granting of concessions for water utilization remains the privilege of the states. In case there are water disputes between states, the federal government has the right to intervene.

Minimum Flows

Minimum flows are necessary to keep fine particles in suspension and prevent river beds from silting up. Coarse particles can be evacuated by increased releases, which may cause erosion of spawning beds.

In general, the greatest controversies have occurred over minimum flows. As development of the water resources of a river nearly always implies modifications of the water levels—at least in certain sections of the river—concessionaires are required to ensure minimum discharges during the whole year, or at least part of it; however, in 1961 the federal government was requested to study the possibility of stiffening federal regulations aimed at establishing standards for minimum discharges because of the dependence of other environmental variables on a good supply of water. In its answer the government pointed out that the problem of minimum discharges was complex and not only related to the safe yield of diverted rivers, but also to the economics of hydraulics as a whole, such as irrigation, water pollution, fishing, and supply of drinking water. No satisfactory solution has yet been proposed.

Water Quality

A federal anti-pollution law was passed in 1955 and began to be enforced in 1957. It applies to surface and ground water, either natural or artificial, public or private, and includes springs. It calls for all necessary measures to be taken to protect the health of man and animals, and to make sure that ground and spring water remain potable. According to this law, used water may be spilled into rivers only when treatment plants exist. If there are none, specific minimum discharges for dilution to safe levels are mandatory.

Scenic Beauty

Another important aspect related to water development is the protection of scenic beauty—a most important prerequisite in providing for tourism and outdoor recreation. A law on this subject was passed in 1966, after the Spoel controversy was decided.

ENVIRONMENTAL PROBLEMS CREATED BY SWISS WATER DEVELOPMENT IN GENERAL

The main problems brought about by water diversion for hydropower development such as the Spoel project are the following: (1) variation in discharge flows of streams; (2) lowering of the water table and decreasing flow of springs; (3) negative influence on vegetation, particularly river bank vegetation; (4) increase in water pollution through less dilution; (5) damage to fish populations; (6) spoiling the beauty of the landscape; and (7) sedimentation of river beds. These factors should be taken into account when fixing the minimum discharge in the original water course. These negative aspects vary greatly according to each water development scheme, and a required minimum discharge is not the only means useful to counteract them.

Influence of Minimum Discharges on Energy production

The decrease in energy output caused by minimum discharge requirements is negligible, as it is only a few percent. The loss in revenue can, of course, be much larger in countries with topographic and climatic conditions different from those in Switzerland.

Effects of Hydroschemes with High Head

These projects generally affect large areas with many rivers in the mountainous parts of Switzerland. It is rare that the water levels in such rivers have an influence on the ground water table. However, diversions may directly or indirectly affect some springs used for the supply of drinking or mineral water and the supply in the river itself.

Socioeconomic Effects

Once the Alps were densely populated and the discrepancy in living standards between dwellers in the mountains and plains was relatively small. The onset of the industrial revolution drastically steepened the economic gradient, causing a heavy population shift from the mountains toward the plains, although this negative trend has been somewhat alleviated by the increase in tourism.

THE SPOEL PROJECT

The Spoel project, intimately associated with Swiss National Park, is located in southeastern Switzerland in the State of Grison (see Figure 1). The Swiss National Park covers an area of approximately 160 km^2, and is the only federal nature preserve in the country.

The physical features of the project are typical of hydropower developments in the Swiss Alps: valleys are steep, and as the watersheds of any particular valley are small, they justify construction of small reservoirs only. Very favorable dam sites, however, often permit construction of large dams and storage facilities, and it is therefore economical to tap neighboring watersheds by diverting water via diversion tunnels into the watershed concerned. An example of this is the Grande Dixence project in the State of Valais, which taps and diverts the waters of about six major watersheds. The ecological problems thus created are extensive, and although some water is left in the rivers, it is sometimes inadequate to prevent dropping of the water table and cleansing of the river beds. Among the most serious problems are the aesthetic ones, as wild watercourses become unimpressive trickles having no resemblance to their once mighty rushing and gushing white rivers.

Legal Background

In Switzerland, each hydroproject is complicated by the question of water rights, which differ in every state. In the State of Grison, the Civil Code established in 1862 requires a concession from the commune in whose territorial boundaries the watershed is located. The watercourses themselves are public domain.

In 1906, a special water rights law was adopted by public vote in Grison, bestowing the property rights of public watercourses on the communes. However, each concession granted by a commune to an entrepreneur

458

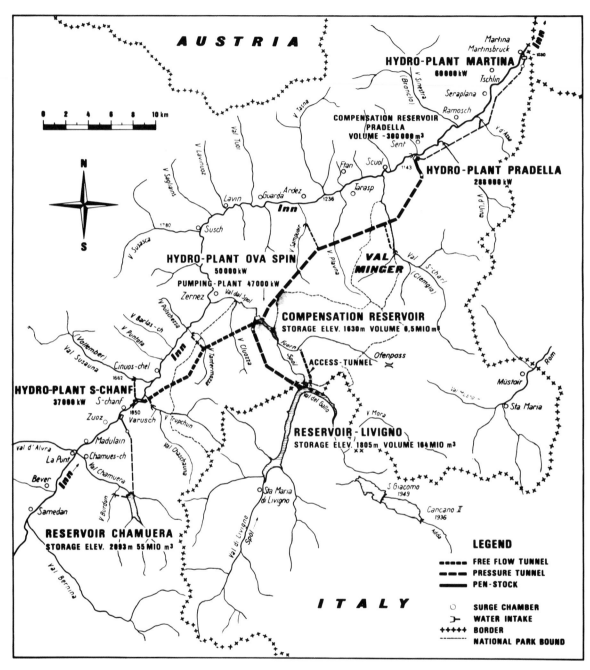

FIGURE 1
Map of Swiss National Park and the Spoel Hydroelectric Project.

may be revoked by the state, should it violate public interest.

In 1916, a federal water rights law was passed, limiting the royalty on water to be charged by the communes.

In 1947, a decree by the federal government concerning the "Protection of Nature and Landscape" bestowed on the state the responsibility for granting concessions, which could be denied if the environment was not sufficiently protected. This decree has prevented financially poor communes from selling their water rights with no regard to environmental consequences.

CREATION OF THE SWISS NATIONAL PARK

In 1913 the Swiss federal government, acting legally as a private party, entered into negotiations for land for a national park with the Commune of Zernez, the largest of the three communes whose territory now covers the park. The result was a treaty, which was ratified in 1914, in which the federal government merely was granted an easement, not the right to acquire title. Although hunting, fishing, and picking of wildflowers were to be banned on park grounds, cutting timber and pasturing the meadows were still permitted. The Annual rent paid by the federal government was $4,000, until it was later increased to $7,000.

Enlargement of the Park

The Commune of Scuol, being more conservative than Zernez, limited its arrangement to leasing the Val Minger to the federal government, with the provision that the lease could be broken in 30 years.

In the first few years of the park, flora and fauna developed beautifully, but one wildlife species that once was abundant in the area was still lacking by 1920. An attempt made to re-establish the ibex was without success:

its ecological requirements were not met by the conditions within park limits at that time, although an ideal feeding and breeding ground for the ibex existed adjacent to the park boundaries, in the Commune of Zernez. In 1920, the commune entered into a further agreement with the federal government, leasing the desired lands on the condition that "the commune's right to hydropower development within park limits must be respected." This treaty was signed by the President of the National Park Commission, the executive agency entrusted by the federal government with the administration of the park. Not long after a few of the animals were brought to the area, a marvelous ibex colony developed, and the park addition could truly be considered a success.

THE CONTROVERSY OVER THE DEVELOPMENT

From the beginning the Commune of Zernez was fully aware of the consequences of its provision for hydropower rights in the new treaty. In fact, in 1919 a project had already been designed to build a dam at the site where the Spoel River leaves the park boundaries (Praspol). The resulting reservoir (160,000,000 m^3 in size) would have extended to the other boundary of the park, where the Spoel enters it (Punt dal Gall). Little demand for power and more suitable projects elsewhere caused this to be shelved until after World War II.

In 1947, a new project was proposed which turned out to be the forerunner of the one finally adopted (Figure 1). The main features would be a large dam at Punt dal Gall, which is also the boundary with Italy, a reservoir on Italian territory, and a regulating reservoir at Ova Spin which is on the Spoel where it leaves the park. The Fuorn River, which is a tributary to the Spoel, was to be captured upstream and diverted to the Punt dal Gall reservoir through a tunnel. The reservoir at Ova Spin would have encroached on the park.

The Position of the Conservationist Groups

The Swiss Society for the Protection of Nature, and the Park Commission strongly opposed the project on the grounds that it was a "flagrant violation of the Federal Decree of 1914 which stated that the National Park was to be protected from any influence not being in the interest of the Park." The main fear was that wildlife and wildflower populations would be decimated by the hordes of construction workers expected to be hired for the project.

However, the Swiss Society for the Protection of the Landscape, after careful study, reached the conclusion that the project would not hurt the park if the Fuorn River was not diverted. By taking this stand it was accused of treason by the Society for the Protection of Nature, whose argument was that if you give the devil your little finger he takes your whole hand, and that consequently one should not let any unrelated development touch the park.

The Society for the Protection of Nature suggested that the water royalty lost to the communes by nondevelopment would have to be compensated by the federal government. The affected communes, primarily Scuol and Zernez, violently opposed this idea. They stressed that their rights for water development must not be violated and that they did not want to live on subsidies. Scuol threatened not to renew the lease on the Val Minger addition, thus virtually eliminating the large deer colony which had developed as a result of the fertile feeding grounds.

A Famous Biologist's Viewpoint

Frey-Wyssling, world-renowned plant physiologist, in his inauguration speech as chancellor of the Federal Institute of Technology brought the issue of conservation in a technological society before the people. He emphasized the fact that the communes of the National Park would earn fifty times as much water royalties than from rent money provided by the federal government for the park, thus underlining the disparity between the power of the promoters and of the conservationists.

Frey-Wyssling advocated a compromise, because he realized that water development could no longer be stopped owing to the pre-existing legal and moral rights of the communes. Furthermore, he reminded his audience that development would have meant the end of the Val Minger deer colony, because the Commune of Scuol would then have broken its lease of park land. He described a possible alternative to the present system: that all power and industrial development taking up land should contribute 1 percent of its investment cost toward a fund for acquiring land (not only for leasing) destined to become national parks. He made the comparison between Switzerland and California: the latter spent about a hundred times as much per person for acquiring land than the former. Unfortunately, his proposal has not been taken up.

Finally, the speaker pointed out that two kinds of reserves must be created: (1) reserves in which human influence is completely eliminated; and (2) reserves preserving archaic ecosystems that have developed under the prolonged influence of man, which would be eliminated should the sustaining influence of man be withheld. An example of the second type is the preservation of bogs by annual removal of the reed growth. This reed removal was accomplished throughout centuries by farmers who used the reeds for litter straw. Without removal of the new reed growth, surface elevation gradually rises, thus drying up the bog and eliminating, among other things, the breeding grounds for waterfowl. The beautiful subalpine meadows of Switzerland are another example.

ITALY'S INTERVENTION AND THE COMPROMISE SOLUTION

Italy entered the discussion about the Spoel Project in due course and declared that unless a solution was reached, it would divert the

Spoel itself by pumping it back to Italy whence it comes. The Swiss federal government, under this pressure from Italy, appointed a committee to work out a compromise. It consisted of six members: the mayors of the three communes concerned, the president of the National Park Commission, the president of the Swiss Society for Research in Nature (one of the oldest and most prestigious scientific organizations), as well as a member of the Council of the Swiss Society for the Protection of Nature, the largest of the conservation organizations.

The committee worked out the following compromise: (1) part of the Spoel water would be stored and pumped back to Italy; (2) in return, all electricity produced would belong to Switzerland; (3) no construction would be carried out on park grounds, the diversion tunnel carrying the water from Punt dal Gall to Ova Spin being constructed from the two ends only, all lateral access galleries being prohibited, and excavation materials being deposited outside park limits; (4) the Fuorn River would not be diverted into the Punt dal Gall reservoir; (5) certain minimum releases would be guaranteed, allowing for year-round flow in the Spoel for scenic, biotic, and health reasons; and (6) the Val Minger would be permanently included in the National Park.

THE THREE NATIONAL ELECTIONS ON THE ISSUE

In Switzerland, as in some of the United States, the right of the people to take action on issues of national concern is granted through two possible alternatives, namely the initiative and the referendum. Either can be solicited by a petition consisting of 50,000 signatures, asking for a popular vote on any new issue—an initiative—or a reconsideration of a proposition already passed by Congress—a referendum.

The Swiss Society for the Protection of Nature was the promoter of all three national votes, collecting the necessary signatures. The

first issue was the so-called Spoel Initiative 1 which was intended to incorporate into law an act requiring ratification by Congress of all power developments involving international rivers. This initiative was designed to kill two projects which conservationists opposed, the Rheinau and the Spoel projects, and in 1956 it was defeated by a large margin.

The second vote was a referendum brought about by the relentless *Bund fur Naturschutz* who raised sufficient signatures to contest ratification of the international treaty with Italy concerning the waters of the Spoel. At the same time, before waiting for the result of the referendum, it began another initiative, in case the referendum did not bring about the desired result. The initiative proposed that the land of the communes that was within the national park be expropriated, and that the federal government acquire title to the land.

In 1958 both the referendum and the initiative failed by a large majority, and it became evident that the Swiss people did not consider the possible impact of the Spoel Project on the national park large enough to warrant interfering with the commune's right of self-determination.

ENVIRONMENTAL AND FINANCIAL RECORD OF THE PROJECT

During construction, many precautions were taken to protect the park. All excavated materials were deposited outside park limits, and the only access to the diversion tunnel was at the two ends. The dam construction site at Punt dal Gall was reached by an underground access road from the existing highway.

Protective endeavors occasionally failed because of carelessness, as when a rocket was used to shoot a cable across the Ova Spin gorge, setting off a forest fire the scars of which are still visible ten years later. Not all agreements were rigidly respected; for example, in the first stages of construction a large gravel wash installation spilled large amounts of suspended material down the Spoel, and it was only after vigorous protest by the park management that a polyphosphate coagulation process was incorporated.

During construction an incident occurred—the kind of incident that is amusing to some and cause others to adopt an I-told-you-so attitude. The planned entrance of the diversion tunnel coincided with an ant hill, and the president of the Scientific National Park Commission asked that the projected entrance be shifted to protect the biological values of the area since a long record of observation on the ant hill was in process. In the end, the tunnel alignment was not changed and the ant hill was destroyed.

A general increase in construction costs caused an overrun in the budgeted investment costs for the project. Furthermore, a large segment of the diversion tunnel had to be abandoned because of heavy water intrusion, forcing the construction of a costly by-pass in its place. The protective measures for the park also proved to be costlier than projected.

Then in 1964 the EKW (Engadin Power Company) ran out of money. Initially no one was interested in refinancing EKW because of the anticipated kilowatt price (20 mills/kwh)—at that time more than double that of thermal plants. It was not until another large power company, the State of Grison, and the concessionist communes contributed funds that construction could be resumed. Therefore the minimum economic returns of the project once more became important and renewed pressures to capture hitherto untouched tributaries were applied. As a result, the waters of the Vallember, which is outside park limits, were included in the project, so that all of the unused waters still equal 32 percent of the mean annual flow out of the project area (26 percent unappropriated waters, 6 percent minimum discharges). In the final analysis, this accounts for the project's economic marginality.

The local population stopped declining—it has even registered a small increase. About a hundred new permanent jobs were created. The annual income from royalties is approximately $400,000 and permits the three communes of Scuol, S'chanf, and Zernez to improve their infrastructure. New schools and water treatment plants have already been built. And now, because of the project, more people who otherwise would be condemned to live in a city have been able to settle in a beautiful and healthy environment.

Biotic Effects

As only two years have elapsed since completion of the project, it is too early to make a final statement about the resulting environmental changes. Microclimatic changes can be picked up in no less than twenty years because if there are changes, they would be comparatively small.

So far, the altered hydrological regime has had no effect on the fish population, and the much feared decimation of deer and chamois populations by poaching laborers did not take place. Among the negative effects, sudden massive releases due to operational procedures at the Punt dal Gall reservoir have eroded banks and destroyed spawning grounds. It is, however, believed that during normal operation of the reservoir such releases will no longer be necessary.

Aesthetic Effects

No negative effects from the Ova Spin dam and reservoir have been observed, mainly because the canyon is so narrow and deeply incised that it prevents the structures from being seen from most places. The functional design of the arch dam at Punt dal Gall must be considered to be beautiful, by all but the most extreme preservationist standards.

In the realm of aesthetics the most serious impairment caused by the project is the loss in natural runoff. The sight and sound of powerful torrents is something we intimately associate with our first experience in the Alps. Anyone ever having slept in a mountain resort or camped nearby knows the wonderful feeling of comfort the steady sound of rushing water offers at night. In this respect, the Spoel Project has done much less damage to aesthetics than larger and less restricted ones like the Grande Dixence. In the former a minimum of streams were captured; in the latter almost every trickle—sometimes even those underlying glaciers—was diverted.

SOME COMPARISONS BETWEEN U.S. AND SWISS PROCESSES OF WATER DEVELOPMENT

The Promoters

It is interesting to compare the type of water resource development promotion practiced in Switzerland and the United States. Water development in the Swiss Alps so far has been mostly for the single purpose of electric power production, whereas in the United States it is usually multipurpose (such as hydropower, flood control, or irrigation). Single-purpose development is, of course, much more suitable for private enterprise, because multipurpose development often requires the administrative and financial support of government institutions.

Switzerland's Semi-Private Power Companies

Power companies are semi-private utilities in Switzerland; states, communes, and private persons are the shareholders. In general, these companies issue bonds to finance their projects. Development of new hydropower facilities has been achieved mostly through private local initiative. The project is designed by private consulting engineers, who also draw up bid specifications so that afterwards when the contractors are selected on the basis of low bid and qualifications, the consultant also supervises construction.

As the opportunity to develop further hydroschemes diminished through the years in Switzerland, the private consultants had to diversify and went into highway and tunnel design, thermal and atomic power, and sewage treatment plants. Finally, they offered their experience in hydropower and dam design and construction work to the developing nations. Unlike the United States, Switzerland has no self-perpetuating construction institution which must be maintained. In addition the Speol Project is proof that the Swiss public has many possibilities of controlling the power companies.

Development in the United States

In the United States, hydropower development was initially private enterprise. This type of development is relatively easy to regulate by the restraining organizations. Some years ago, however, (see Teclaff, in this volume) hydropower development became multipurpose, especially in the West, with the Bureau of Reclamation having been largely responsible.

The legislative mandates which established the Bureau of Reclamation spelled out what this organization was to engage in—simply to develop the arid lands of the West. The Bureau is now facing the problem of having constantly to search for new irrigation projects. Because it is publicly funded it can work up much technical background information in support of its projects, and it can also gain support from most states because it is "offering something for nothing." This would be called bribery in private industry, but in the public sphere it is considered in the "interest of the people."

The Bureau of Reclamation is not staffed by avid anticonservationists, but it is often a party to questionable multipurpose schemes, because it is prevented from activities other than irrigation. This is a very unfortunate circumstance, for the preservation of the environment, as attention to maintaining environmental quality is the government's responsibility. This becomes a difficult task for a government having a branch which by its very nature is not primarily interested in conservation.

THE CONSERVATION MOVEMENTS IN THE UNITED STATES AND SWITZERLAND

The conservation movement in these two countries appears to have developed according to need. In the United States abundant natural resources were available for unlimited exploitation in the beginning stages of settlement, and it was only recently that the American public has begun to realize that its natural resources are being depleted and pollution is everywhere. Finally environmental deterioration has become so apparent that many concerned citizens have begun to be personally affected, and this also explains the cry for environmental protection and the tremendous momentum the conservation movement has gained.

In Switzerland, however, resources were already scarce at the beginning of the Industrial Revolution, and water development has always been more restricted than in the United States, and aesthetics have been far more important. One reason for the latter is that water development was always carried out in populous areas of Switzerland where *tradition* often controlled government and business and so development was seldom aesthetically unacceptable. For this reason, a countrywide conservation movement did not develop rapidly.

Switzerland may not have suffered as much aesthetically from water development as has the United States, but this is not true biologically. Lacking a powerful fisherman's lobby, the pollution of streams and lakes in Switzerland has not been controlled for years. The cry for conservation came too late: all rivers and lakes in Switzerland, except those in the mountains far from urban centers and industry, are so polluted that swimming in many of them is prohibited by health officers. Although some lakes, such as Lake Zurich, no longer receive untreated effluent and are showing signs of improvement, it is not safe to say that Switzerland has overcome the majority of its environmental problems.

The Sierra Club is certainly the most powerful instrument in the United States for the preservation of nature. Its counterpart in Switzerland is the Swiss Society for the Protection of Nature. In their goals and methods of struggle the two organizations are similar in that they set their goals rather high to gain at least something for their cause—both prefer defeat to conformity.

CONCLUSIONS

It is doubtful that financial backers would be found if the Spoel Project were proposed today. It was submarginal during construction, and it certainly would be uneconomical to build it today. Nevertheless it permitted local government to develop its economy, perhaps at a cost to the country as a whole. Opponents of the project point out that it would have been cheaper to hand out the subsidies directly instead of via Spoel. They forget, however, one important technical factor: the main purpose of hydropower plants is to produce peaking energy. This they can do more economically than other power sources for some time to come, and in Switzerland hydropower is a natural resource which can be exported.

If the economy of the project had left no room for criticism, what lesson can be learned from the Spoel? It took the combined action of all interest groups finally to lead to a project that truly is a compromise. All the parties involved have left their marks, be it by action or reaction, and this seems to us the important point. Whereas conservationists apparently lost their battle to stop the project by losing all three popular votes, the National Park has greatly benefited from their interventions by keeping the negative effects of the project to a minimum.

CHAPTER 27

At a public hearing in Sacramento, California in 1969 the U.S. Army Corps of Engineers presented a plan for a flood control project on a system of streams just outside the city. The land traversed by the streams is owned in part by subdivision developers who want increased flood protection for their lands, although the area, which is regularly flooded, is a rich habitat for wildlife and waterfowl and provides scenic open space close to a crowded metropolis. Conservationists expressed strong dismay at the prospect of channelization and levee systems, which they felt would destroy these natural values.

The Corps (for which Miss Petersen is a planner) felt that conservationists' concerns that nondevelopment alternatives were not being considered were justified and proceeded to generate several alternatives to the project. The Corps took the initiative to include all interested and affected parties. Citizens, civic organizations, and local, state, and federal agencies subsequently took part in discussions.

As a result, one alternative plan for the area in question was selected with full decision-making participation by all interest groups. It is a balanced plan recognizing flood protection and environmental and recreational needs, and is accepted by the public as a reasonable compromise and a desirable future for the area.

CASE DESCRIPTION: MORRISON CREEK STREAM GROUP BASIN, CALIFORNIA

Margaret S. Petersen

CHRONOLOGY OF STUDY

In 1963 Congress authorized the U.S. Army Corps of Engineers to investigate flood control and related problems in Morrison Creek Stream Group Basin through a study initiated by the Sacramento District in 1964. After several years of preliminary work conducted in coordination with local, state and other federal agencies, the Corps developed a tentative plan for flood protection and recreation in the basin that was presented for public consideration in May 1969. The plan was strongly criticized by conservation and wildlife interests because private agricultural land inhabited by wildlife could feasibly be converted to urban use. In an effort to develop a plan acceptable to the public, private interests, as well as public agencies, were included in the Corps' planning process in 1969. Additional alternatives were developed, and major features of the plan were reformulated. A report recommending Congressional authorization of the modified plan was submitted by the Sacramento district in June 1970, but was returned from Washington in September 1970 for further coordination with the State of California. Major events in the study flow are listed in Appendix I.

DESCRIPTION OF STUDY AREA

The study area is in the Central Valley of California, about 90 miles east of San Francisco. The basin, shown in Figure 1, covers 192 square miles. The northwest corner of the basin is densely developed and includes the southern part of the City of Sacramento. The urban area is rapidly spreading south, farther into the basin. Most of the basin is not high-grade agricultural land; soils are of moderate to low fertility, with severe limitations for agricultural use. The basin has a two-season climate, with arid summers and moderate rainfall in cool winter months.

The upper basin, east of the Western Pacific Railroad, is drained by a network of small streams. Flood problems in this area are quite different from problems in the Beach-Stone lakes area in the lower basin. Natural streams in the upper basin have little slope; channel capacities are inadequate; and the area is subject to extensive shallow flooding. These creeks are intermittent, with no natural flow in the summer, and there are few native trees and shrubs along the stream banks. In developed urban areas the City and County of Sacramento have enlarged the channels, but many of these reaches do not have adequate capacities for runoff from major storms.

The Beach-Stone lakes area receives runoff from the entire watershed and serves as a natural temporary ponding basin. The area is flooded to some extent each winter and, therefore, has remained in agricultural use and as vacant land. Channel and lake bottoms are below sea level, and water surface elevations are influenced by tidal action through the San Francisco Bay-Delta system. The lakes, thus, have a dependable source of fresh water throughout the year, and abundant vegetation along the banks of the lakes and connecting channels provides a range of habitat which supports a diverse population of birds, fish, and small mammals. The area is the outstanding environmental resource in the basin and is an important part of the Pacific flyway, providing a seasonal home for large numbers of migratory waterfowl of many species.

WATER RESOURCES AND RELATED PROBLEMS

Initial studies were made in 1965 and 1966, at a time when the primary emphasis in planning was on economic efficiency. Much of the basin is forecast to be developed for urban use in the future, and a high degree of flood protection is economically justified. The Sacramento County General Plan shows part of the basin west of proposed Interstate Highway No. 5 in the Beach-Stone lakes area as permanent agricultural-recreational reserve. Detailed studies, however, indicated that this land would be developed for urban use in the near future because of its accessibility to the downtown Sacramento area and because large blocks of land are owned by developers. Sacramento County had indicated that urban development would be permitted when the flood hazard was removed. Before 1969 it appeared that, unless the 7,800 acre Beach-Stone lakes area were purchased for parkland or some other public

FIGURE 1
Recommended Plan of Improvement for the Morrison Creek Stream Group.

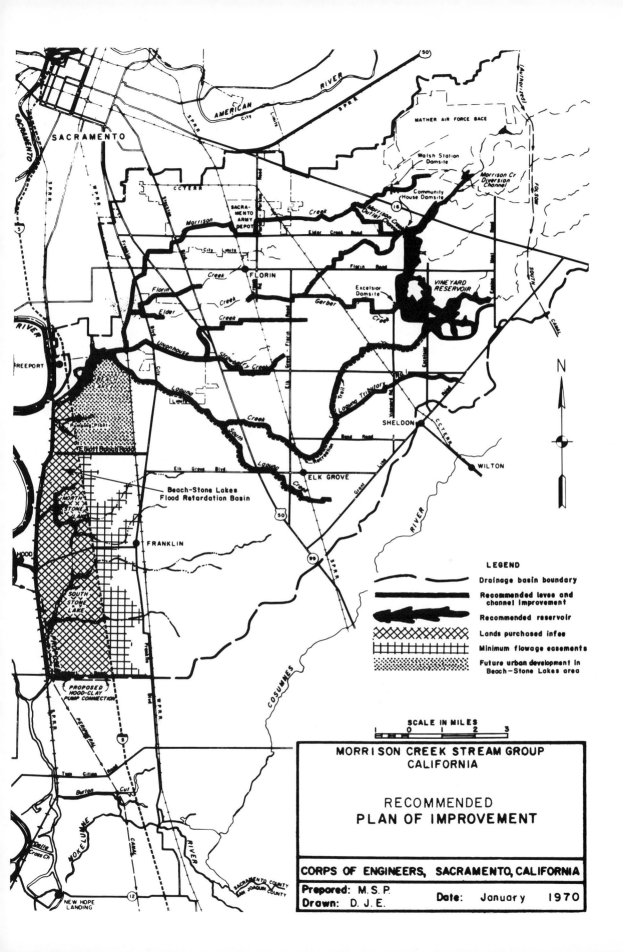

LEGEND

Drainage basin boundary

Recommended levee and
channel improvement

Recommended reservoir

Lands purchased infee

Minimum flowage easements

Future urban development in
Beach–Stone Lakes area

SCALE IN MILES

1   0   1   2   3

MORRISON CREEK STREAM GROUP
CALIFORNIA

RECOMMENDED
PLAN OF IMPROVEMENT

CORPS OF ENGINEERS, SACRAMENTO, CALIFORNIA

Prepared: M.S.P.
Drawn: D.J.E.   Date: January 1970

use, it eventually would be privately sold for urban use.

In consideration of these factors early Corps studies, requiring North and South Stone lakes to remain natural lakes, were done to provide flood protection for the Beach-Stone lakes area. The tentative plan under consideration in 1969 is shown as alternative 1 on Figure 1. With projected future urban development and increased channel capacities in the upper basin, peak inflow to the Beach-Stone lakes area would be significantly increased over inflows under present conditions. To check the flood hazard in the Beach-Stone lakes area after construction of the project, the plan included a wide leveed floodway across the area.

Conservation and recreation aspects of the 1969 tentative plan had been coordinated with responsible agencies, and the plan was designed to mitigate fish and wildlife losses on project lands and to provide some scenic value as well. In the Beach-Stone lakes area, the plan provided for public access for nature-oriented recreation in the 1,000-foot wide floodway, a significant improvement over existing recreational opportunities in the area. Special effort was made to insure that the reservoir and channel work would have a minimum adverse impact on the ecology of the basin and would be aesthetically pleasing.

It was recognized that the same flood control project that would reduce flood damages in Morrison Creek basin would also increase the potential value of lands so frequently flooded now that they are unsuitable for development. In an area rapidly changing from agricultural to urban use that is made up of flat terrain drained by a network of small channels—such as Morrison Creek Basin—the cost of flood-proofing existing development would be greater than the cost of flood control works. The obvious but more costly alternative to proceeding with a flood control project in such an area in the early stage of development is to delay providing flood protection until development is such that a project is justified by flood damage reduction benefits alone.

The tentative plan was presented for consideration by local people at a public meeting in May 1969 and met strong criticism from non-governmental conservation and wildlife interests whose primary objection was that future conversion of private agricultural lands in the Beach-Stone lakes area to urban and suburban uses would represent an irretrievable loss of valuable wildlife habitat and open space. Conservationists stated that the direct impact on lands to be acquired for the project would not be nearly as adverse as the effect on the private lands adjacent to the floodway where natural beauty and the habitat for major concentrations of wildlife, particularly waterfowl, would be lost. This potential change from agricultural to urban use under project conditions apparently was not fully realized by conservation organizations until shortly before the May 1969 public meeting when features of the plan were made public. At the same time there was no indication of how conservation interests proposed to prevent such development in the future if these lands in private ownership were privately sold.

Conservation interests were also critical of land enhancement benefits of the project and of Corps of Engineers' procedures in making only limited information available for public review before presentation of the plan at the public meeting.

In the climate of changing priorities in water resources planning in 1969, the Corps felt that criticisms by conservationists with regard to loss of wildlife habitat and open space in the Beach-Stone lakes area were valid. Subsequent to the public meeting five alternatives for the lower basin were developed and were discussed informally with conservation and wildlife interests and affected local landowners.

Landowners in the Beach-Stone lakes area favor the 1969 tentative plan and unani-

limited public meetings, with a free exchange of information, and formation of a Citizens' Environmental Advisory Committee to represent the interests of a range of public organizations and the academic community in discussions with the Sacramento District. Major events of public involvement are included in the study flow presented in Appendix I. Not listed in the appendix are innumerable telephone contacts and office visits by individual property owners throughout the basin and by conservationists, routine coordination with other agencies, and correspondence in reply to questions raised by congressional representatives at the behest of conservationists.

These techniques were used in recognition of the crucial need for expeditious development of citizen-planner communication within existing authorities. The techniques proved successful in a number of ways. Of primary importance to the Morrison Creek study was development of additional alternatives, which recognized the importance of intangible aesthetic benefits related to preservation of the open verdant environment and ecological values of the Beach-Stone lakes area, and modification of the proposed plan of improvement.

Probably of greater importance to the overall planning effort of the Sacramento District, however, was establishment of the Citizens Environmental Advisory Committee by public-interest groups to work closely with Corps planners on all studies. In the past, the Corps has relied on local and state agencies to express the needs and desires of the general public. With Morrison Creek, public concern for environmental values had not been reflected in the policies and procedures of these agencies, and direct communication with citizens was essential to determine their values and preferences.

The limited public meeting technique was less successful with local landowners than with conservationists; however, the open discussions and information furnished those attending the meetings gave landowners a more complete picture of the complexity of plan formulation than had been possible up to that time.

Through the avenues of communication established with conservationists, Corps planners have become more aware of latent environmentally sensitive areas and now have ready recourse to citizens who can speak for public groups on such matters. Coincident with the establishment of cooperation and free exchange of information, has been the realization by local conservationists in the Sacramento area that they are most effective in commenting on facets of water resource development within their areas of expertise and the recognition by them that continuing water resource development is needed and can be achieved with due consideration for preservation of the environment.

RECENT CHANGES IN
PLANNING PROCESS

The study program utilized for the Morrison Creek investigation in 1964-69 has been substantially modified by the Sacramento District in the past two years in an effort to obtain maximum involvement of pertinent sectors of the public in the planning process so that their needs and desires—with regard to problems and alternative solutions—can be recognized and understood and given full consideration in development of the most balanced plan for water resources development. For studies recently initiated, public sectors are involved early in the study at the time of the initial public meeting, and continue to be involved throughout the study period by informal contacts, coordination with representatives of the Citizens Environmental Advisory Committee, limited public meetings, and formal public meetings. With early and continuing public involvement, it is expected that potential conflicts will surface early enough so that they can be most effectively resolved.

Appendix I

STUDY FLOW MORRISON CREEK INVESTIGATION

Date	Item
1952	Local interests first expressed concern over flood problems.
19 Jun 1963	Study authorized.
10 Jun 1965	Initial public hearing.
20 Jul 1967	Preliminary draft of U.S. Fish and Wildlife Service report received. Report recommended major modifications of project in Snodgrass Slough.
26 Jul 1967	Tentative plan discussed with South Pacific Division (SPD), Office of the Chief of Engineers (OCE), and Board of Engineers for Rivers and Harbors (BERH), particularly with regard to land enhancement.
Oct 1967	Plan modified in Snodgrass Slough area to meet suggestions of Fish and Wildlife.
26 Apr 1968	Draft report #1 submitted to SPD for concurrence in cost sharing.
16 Aug 1968	Draft report #2 submitted to SPD.
10 Dec 1968	Conference with SPD and OCE on cost sharing.
1 Apr 1969	Draft report #3 issued for field level review to State and Federal agencies.
2 May 1969	Public hearing on proposed plan of improvement—major objections by wildlife interests.
28 May 1969	Meeting with State agencies to discuss prospective State comments on April 1969 draft, primarily with regard to fish and wildlife losses in Beach-Stone lakes area with urbanization under project conditions.
1 Aug 1969	Meeting with Sacramento County to discuss preliminary alternative plans in Beach-Stone lakes area. County in favor of Plan 4 (later adopted).
28 Aug 1969	Meeting with Sacramento County and conservationists to discuss problems and preliminary alternative plans.
4 Sep 1969	Meeting with representatives of Sierra Club and Sacramento Audubon Society to discuss Morrison Creek and Corps review and hearing procedures.
11 Sep 1969	Meeting with Sacramento County and California Reclamation Board to discuss alternatives.
25 Sep 1969	Meeting with SPD to discuss alternatives.
26 Sep 1969	Office Study on alternatives released to conservationists and local interests.
22 Oct 1969	Conference with conservationists to discuss alternatives. Conservationists in favor of Plan 4.
30 Oct 1969	Meeting with landowners in Beach-Stone lakes area to discuss alternatives. Landowners preferred Plan 1 (original plan).
6 Nov 1969	Meeting with California Department of Water Resources (DWR), U.S. Bureau of Reclamation (USBR), and Sacramento County to discuss impact of alternatives on a coordinated joint plan with Peripheral Canal.
19 Nov 1969	Meeting with landowners in Beach-Stone Lakes area to discuss alternatives. Landowners still favored Plan 1.

Date	Item
16 Jan 1970	Revised draft #4 issued for completion of field level review by State and Federal agencies.
31 May 1970	Meeting with California Resources Agency and Sacramento County regarding State comments. Sacramento County asked if it would be feasible to submit report to higher authority without State comments. Sacramento District indicated this might be done. State personnel appeared doubtful that State comments would be submitted at an early date.
7 Apr 1970	Meeting with Reclamation Board and Sacramento County to brief Board on County's views on revised plan. Sacramento District stated higher authority had indicated they would consider a statement of intent to provide assurances of local cooperation from California Reclamation Board as adequate for processing of report prior to Washington level review of Chief of Engineers' report.
10 Apr 1970	California Reclamation Board passed resolution stating intent to provide assurances of local cooperation and endorsing Morrison Creek project.
15 Apr 1970	Submitted environmental impact statement to SPD.
30 Apr 1970	Meeting with DWR staff to discuss State questions on January draft of report.
8 Jun 1970	Final report formally submitted to SPD.
12 Jun 1970	Division Engineers' public notice issued.
15 Jun 1970	Meeting with DWR to discuss State concern over coordination with Peripheral Canal.
16 Jul 1970	County Board to Supervisors overruled Planning Commission to rezone 5,200 acre North Stone Lake area from agricultural with 20 acre minimum lot size to agricultural with 2 acre minimum lot size.
22 Sep 1970	Landowner announced plan for a new town (Stonelake) of 50,000 on 5,200 acre North Stone Lake area.
29 Sep 1970	June 1970 report returned by BERH for further coordination by Sacramento District with State.
26 Oct 1970	County Planning Commission hearing on Stonelake development continued to 28 December 1970.
13 Nov 1970	Meeting with DWR staff to discuss major concerns of State.
22 Dec 1970	Landowner withdrew application for change in county master plan to accommodate Stonelake developmant.
8 Jan 1971	Meeting with DWR staff to discuss major concerns of the State.

Appendix II

STUDY PARTICIPANTS FURNISHING WRITTEN COMMENTS

Item	Date
Federal Agencies	

Item	Date
Department of Agriculture	
Forest Service	10 Apr 1969
Soil Conservation Service	18 Feb 1970
Soil Conservation Service	22 May 1969
Department of the Air Force, Mather Air Force Base	13 May 1969
Department of Health, Education and Welfare	
Public Health Service	17 Feb 1970
Department of Housing and Urban Development	
Program Coordination and Services Office	18 Apr 1969
Department of the Interior	
Bureau of Land Management	11 Feb 1970
Bureau of Outdoor Recreation	9 Mar 1970
Bureau of Outdoor Recreation	29 May 1969
Bureau of Reclamation	11 Feb 1970
Bureau of Reclamation	27 May 1969
Federal Water Pollution Control Admin.	11 Feb 1970
Federal Water Pollution Control Admin.	29 Apr 1969
Fish and Wildlife Service	9 Mar 1970
Fish and Wildlife Service	2 May 1969
Fish and Wildlife Service	28 May 1965
Fish and Wildlife Service	29 Apr 1968
National Park Service	26 Jan 1970
National Park Service	9 May 1969
Department of Transportation	
Bureau of Public Roads	9 Feb 1970
Bureau of Public Roads	25 Apr 1969
Federal Power Commission	15 May 1969

State Agencies	
Resources Agency of California	28 Jul 1970
State Regional Water Quality Control Board, Central Valley Region	14 Feb 1967
The Reclamation Board	13 Apr 1970

Local Agencies	
Sacramento Regional Area Planning Commission	28 May 1970
County of Sacramento, Department of Public Works	11 Feb 1970
County of Sacramento, Department of Public Works	18 Jun 1970
City of Sacramento, Office of the City Engineer	8 Apr 1970

Item	Date
Interested Groups and Individuals	
Mother Lode Chapter, Sierra Club	2 May 1969
Sacramento Audubon Society	28 Apr 1969
California Wildlife Federation, Inc.	2 May 1969
Mother Lode Chapter, Sierra Club, and Sacramento Audubon Society	8 Dec 1969
McKeon Construction Company (landowner)	19 Nov 1969
Downey, Brand, Seymour and Rohwer (representing landowner)	30 Dec 1969
Downey, Brand, Seymour and Rohwer (representing landowner)	28 Apr 1969
D. J. Pisano (conservationist)	10 May 1969
Gene Knapp (conservationist)	18 May 1969
Rita A. Dowell (conservationist)	May 1969
David Trice (landowner)	21 Jan 1970

CHAPTER 28

CRITIQUE OF WATER RESOURCES COUNCIL'S PROPOSED PRINCIPLES AND STANDARDS FOR PLANNING WATER AND RELATED LAND RESOURCES

John G. Coy, Robert A. Johnston, and Peter J. Richerson

INTRODUCTION

The 1971 proposal of the Water Resources Council is the most recent water and related land resources planning methodology designed to guide federal water development.

Historically, this proposal is the latest in a succession of attempts to rationalize such development practices beginning in earnest with the 1936 Flood Control Act which established the principle that the benefits of projects must exceed the costs. The 1936 Act set forth the objectives of National Economy, Regional Development, and Social Security. This methodology was elaborated in 1952 by Bureau of the Budget Circular A-47 which required all water development agencies to use their guidelines and standards. In 1962, new executive guidelines, printed as Senate Document 87-97 (known as Senate Document 97), were adopted. This document added a fourth planning objective, "preservation" of the environment. In addition, the "well-being of people" objective was restated and strengthened. Senate Document 97 dropped the existing requirement that monetary benefits exceed monetary costs, but left the Bureau of the Budget free to add this constraint. The bureau has informally required a positive monetary benefit-cost ratio since 1962.

The Council itself is a result of the 1965 Water Resources Planning Act (PL 89-80). Its full members included the secretaries of Interior, Agriculture, Army, HEW, Transportation and the Chairman of the Federal Power Commission. The secretaries of Commerce and HUD are associate members as are the Attorney General and the Director of the Office of Management and Budget. The administrator of the EPA was later added as an associate member and the chairmen of the Council on Environmental Quality and the various river basin commissions were added as observers. Unlike the National Water Commission, which is to prepare a high level "blue ribbon" study, the WRC is an interagency group whose proposals, upon signature by the President, become the actual executive policy governing water resources decisions.

The work of the WRC is carried on by an independent staff and representatives of the members and associate members. Two early versions of the 1971 proposal were developed by a special task force which presented their recommendations in June 1969 (WRC 1969) and August 1970 (WRC 1970 a,b,c,d). The council then made further alterations of the proposal which were presented for final public comment in the Federal Register in December, 1971 (WRC 1971). As of this writing the proposal awaits final revision and adoption by executive order.

The major thrust of the 1971 Proposal is to broaden the formal base of water resources planning and evaluation beyond narrow consideration of economic costs and benefits which have dominated past planning methodology to include much more detailed considerations of environment, regional development and social effects, which have received much less attention. This broadening of planning methods is, in part, a response to specific legislative actions such as the National Environmental Policy Act and the Appalachian Regional Development Act (WRC 1971; 24150-24151), and is also a response to the heightened awareness by the public and many interest groups.

In the three years since their original formulation, the proposals have been vigorously debated by interested parties and have undergone many changes in response to these challenges (Corrigan and Clark 1971). Major issues have included the role of economic methods in the total planning and evaluation process, the proper interest rate to apply to economic evaluations, and questions of environmental impact analysis.

Environmentalists and economists, especially economists of the powerful Office of Management and Budget, have opposed certain features of the proposals because—as we see it—they do not wish to broaden the evaluation objectives and give development agencies more latitude to justify dubious projects. Development interests, on the other hand, have viewed portions of the proposals, especially the increased discount rate, as placing unreasonable constraints on water resources development. The WRC has recommended raising the discount rate first from 3.250% to 4.625% then to 5.125% and finally to 7% to satisfy economists' arguments that the discount rate should reflect the rate of return to private investment (about 10%).

All of these debates have taken place in a political climate in which environmental concerns and general public questioning of the value of additional water development has been growing. (See McCloskey and McEvoy, this volume).

In this paper we attempt to point out the most important strengths and weaknesses of the 1971 WRC proposal and to suggest reforms that would enable more effective planning and evaluation and better representation of the needs and desires of the nation.

IMPROVEMENTS EMBODIED IN THE PROPOSAL

The most significant reform in the 1971 proposal is the 7% discount rate which will diminish the overall subsidy long given to water development. This rate increase probably reflects society's changing resource values as well as the objections of OMB economists to low discount rates for water development. If major federal water resources development subsidies were once useful and popular expenditures of federal tax money, they clearly are no longer, because of the questionable environmental and economic effects of such projects. Clearly, a minimum condition for future construction should be a strict demonstration of the economic utility of projects.

Another major planning improvement in the 1971 proposal is the requirement that agencies generate and compare alternative plans for realizing development objectives. There is no doubt that the careful formulation and consideration of alternatives will help ensure better plans. The proposal would require alternative plans to be developed for different assumptions concerning the future (population growth and the like) and for each of several component needs associated with the several "multiobjectives" described below.

The major deficiency evident in the proposal's discussion on alternatives is the lack of a requirement for alternatives which optimize or emphasize each of the several objectives *solely* through nonstructural means without the construction of dams, channels, and the like. In this way, engineering agencies

could be encouraged to "think small" and explore new approaches. In general, nonstructural projects would employ more people per budgeted dollar, since such projects would be more labor intensive. Construction projects such as dams do not employ large numbers of local workers with most of the budget being for engineering and materials, whereas small scale projects, such as watershed rehabilitation, should be encouraged because they employ large numbers of local people, and would spread spending benefits across more geographical areas and employment types and provide long term economic stability when staggered in time. One major problem with large structural projects is that the economic boost is short-lived and often disruptive to long-term stability in declining or low-income regions. These and other benefits should be considered in identifying and evaluating non-structural alternatives. The preoccupation of water development agencies with long-term, highly structural solutions to water problems has been strongly criticized by White (1969).

The major methodological improvement developed in the final WRC proposal is the multiobjective concept. The multiobjective planning procedure attempts to identify the several kinds of motivations for water development projects and judge projects with a balanced consideration of all of these objectives. The objectives originally proposed by the WRC (1969) included national income, environmental quality, regional income and social well-being. In the final proposal (WRC 1971), the social well-being objective has been downgraded to a subsidiary account of an ambiguous advisory nature and regional income objective analyses will be prepared only in special cases.

The WRC proposal requires that important social and environmental issues which have been only informally included in the past be taken into consideration in the planning process. There is some hope then, that the WRC multiobjective procedure is a substantial reform which will considerably broaden the information available to decision makers and the public for judging the desirability of particular water projects.

Several other improvements in planning methodology are contained in the 1971 proposal. The following items are illustrative of these:

1. The proposal requires the specification of opportunities irreversibly lost in all multiobjective accounts.

2. A broader identification of potential adverse effects is to be included in the evaluations of the multiobjectives.

3. Quantitative non-monetary and qualitative costs and benefits for all objectives are to be fully evaluted to provide more complete information than has been provided in the past about important but technically difficult areas, as are alternatives which include "both structural and nonstructural measures to achieve desired objectives." (WRC 1971: 24147).

4. The requirement of alternatives which "optimize" national income and "emphasize" environmental quality is likewise a significant broadening of alternatives examination (WRC 1971: 24148).

5. Accounting for costs and benefits for the project region, the adjacent region, and the rest of the nation is a sound step in the direction of identifying the spatial distribution of beneficial and adverse effects.

6. Disaggregating costs and benefits by components of the national income objective is a positive move toward identifying the incidence of both beneficial and adverse effects on various economic groups. This accounting should be carried out in sufficient detail to identify the individual persons, firms, agencies, and interest groups (including taxpayers) benefitting from, or paying for, the water project.

OBJECTIONS TO
THE PROPOSAL

The primary political uneasiness created by the WRC proposal is a result of trying to broaden the ostensible objectives of water resources development while at the same time the net marginal economic, environmental, and social benefits of projects appear to be decreasing. The most efficient dams and canals were built years ago in this country. The relative benefit of new projects is constant or declining, while the relative environmental costs are increasing rapidly as the remaining wildlands and fisheries diminish with each new project (McCloskey, this volume). Whereas it is commendable to increase the scope for evaluation of water projects, the WRC should realize that water projects are declining in economic usefulness and are creating greater environmental disruption each year. These projects can only be properly evaluated by comparing them with *non-water* projects and programs.

As Bromley *et al.* (1971) point out, the objectives as defined by the WRC are too broad to be operational ends. The real objectives of water development, they suggest, are largely specific local problems for which federal aid is sought by certain interest groups. The higher order multiobjectives identified by the WRC and the modifications of these suggested by Bromley *et al.* (1971) and ourselves in following sections are more accurately identified as impact accounts than as immediate objectives.

The purpose of multiobjective accounts should be to broaden the information available to various interest groups whose participation in water development decision-making has been hampered in the past because such information has been lacking. The most important of these interest groups are presently the environmentalists whose political power can no longer be ignored. Potentially as important are such groups as recreationists for whom water developments have diverse impacts and the poor with whom water development interests compete for federal budget dollars. No doubt the general citizen as a taxpayer and the groups organized to represent him in the decision-making process such as public interest law firms, Ralph Nader's Raiders, and John Gardiner's Common Cause could also benefit from such information.

To the extent that federal agencies and their associated interest groups attempt to use the WRC proposal objectives as operational objectives and prepare long lists of benefits contributed to these objectives by water development without reference to the very broad range of other public and private alternative expenditures which might better realize the objectives, the proposal will hinder rather than advance the course of wise resource development.

WEAKNESSES OF
THE PROPOSAL

The most important underlying weakness of the WRC proposal is its assumption of the continued desirability of economic growth. The statement that gains in national output "are generally regarded as favorable" is perhaps correct but is not the whole truth (WRC 1971: 24152). There is an emerging national debate on the facile assumption that a growing economy is inherently beneficial.

Economists such as Barkley and Seckler (1972) have pointed out that the rise in GNP as a measure of increase in the net social benefit of economic activity is very poor. Many kinds of external costs are not netted out of GNP as in the case of pollution. Increased production which pollutes the air adds to GNP, but the pollution costs to society are not subtracted from GNP. This is, of course, the weakness of a gross product indicator. The mere transfer of non-market to market goods will increase the GNP without increasing social benefits as when a previously free recreation site has a fee placed on its use to discourage crowding. The costs of administering an increasingly complex economic and social enterprise are added to the GNP, although they do not represent effective increases in goods or services. Boulding (1970) has also pointed out that the GNP is a flow concept, whereas many of the satisfactions provided by goods are at

least partly a function of static wealth. For example, living in a house provides the basic satisfaction, not building it, but the consumption of materials and labor is what goes into GNP. Thus planned obsolescense increases GNP but does not necessarily increase net social benefit.

Even to the degree to which a growing economy is providing more net goods and services to consumers it is by no means clear that it, in like measure, is increasing social welfare. The marginal increases in the consumption of goods and services for the satisfaction of most needs must decrease as overall consumption increases. In fact, using the orthodox marginal utility arguments of economics, we might expect per capita economic growth to come to a halt of its own accord as consumers place less and less value on goods and services vis-a-vis non-consumptive values such as leisure amenities, even if increased consumption was without rising costs. The aggregate consumption of all goods and services might be expected to behave like any particular good or service; consumers should be willing to pay less and less for more per capita GNP as GNP rises until supply balances demand.

This expectation of declining growth is, however, based upon a misunderstanding of one of the chief values of consumption. As Thorsten Veblen (1899) pointed out, people consume goods and services not only to satisfy basic needs but also to display status. The most important motive force behind a growing economy in a wealthy country is competition for status. The problem with status needs is that they are relative, not absolute. Thus economic growth can become a status race much like an arms race in which everyone strives to have more goods for display but in which the relative distribution of wealth remains the same. Total consumption goes up but on the average no one is relatively better off than anyone else, so net satisfaction owing to status display is static.

Of course, some components of economic growth do lead to increases in satisfaction.

People are no doubt better off to some degree, status considerations aside, because of modern consumer goods like automobiles and stereophonic, high fidelity equipment. The thrust of this argument is not that economic growth is wholly undesirable in wealthy consumer goods societies, but only to suggest that the common measures of economic growth, (GNP per capita, disposable income per capita) vastly overstate the true growth of social welfare

One of the commonest arguments for economic growth is that it is a method of satisfying the poor without tackling the knotty problem of income redistribution. To the extent that wealth and consumption satisfy status rather than basic needs, this argument is fallacious. The relativity of status needs precludes any satisfactions by merely increasing consumption without changing relative levels of income and wealth. Indeed, conservative critics of social welfare measures often point out that the poor of the United States are quite well off compared to the poor of underdeveloped nations; this argument is not satisfactory to our poor people *because* they compare themselves not to the poor of Asia or Latin America, but to the middle class and upper classes of our own nation. Again, this argument cannot be taken to the extreme of disparaging the basic needs of our many poor which are very real. It is true, however, that the deprivation of status which the poor suffer cannot be corrected merely by economic growth. Any real attack on poverty in an industrial state must make income redistribution, rather than economic growth, its primary component.

The growth economy debate has begun in earnest not so much because of the above-mentioned fundamental criticisms of the concept and its measure, but because many conservationists see a direct tradeoff between economic growth and environmental quality. Their model argues that economies, like populations of organisms, cannot grow indefinitely, esecially at exponential rates, in a limited environment. They further believe that our present scale of environmental degradation is evidence that economic growth has already begun to encounter such limits.

Whereas this debate addresses complex issues which cannot be settled by appeals to simple models of growth based upon biological analogies, the conservationist point is a serious one, deserving of very exhaustive analysis. For example, it is clear that a fairly simple growth limitation model does apply to increases in human population, the extraction of non-renewable resources, and energy consumption. To the extent that these increases are linked to economic growth, the conservationists have a very strong point. If economic growth can be redirected from primary resource mobilization and population growth toward service sectors, economic growth can take place in much less conflict with environmental quality. Technological improvement, such as pollution control, which can reduce tradeoffs between resource utilization and environmental quality is also a means by which economic growth could continue. These issues are treated in some detail by Barkley and Seckler (1972).

The proposal ought to reflect the increasing importance of this issue. Within a decade, fundamental changes in federal policy will be necessary to reflect economic growth problems. Federal agencies have the responsibility to participate constructively in such debates rather than ignore them.

The major institutional weakness of the 1971 proposal is the lack of an adequate mechanism for the independent and intensive review of agencies' plans. As Fox (this volume) and McCloskey (this volume) point out, the natural self interest of development agencies tends to lead to the preparation of self-serving plans.

Major reforms are necessary within agencies in order to produce multiobjective plans. For example, the teams preparing environmental impact statements and plan components related to the proposed Environmental Quality objective must have a much broader range of expertise than impact statements to date have shown and must have substantial independence from the engineering and economic planning offices. The review procedures (WRC 1971: 24189-24191) currently in use are diffuse and inadequate. Review procedures must be developed in which all phases of the plan are examined for adequacy and accuracy by independent review staffs. Maximum separation of planning, review, and construction responsibilities must be achieved. Agency staff and line authority for environmental and economic evaluation should have considerable independence from engineering staff and line authority. Present Army Corps' practice in regional offices of housing the environmental impact staff in engineering sections, for example, almost makes the writing of critical, high quality, objective impact statements impossible (Henwood and Coop, this volume).

For the short term, the WRC might, in cooperation with the OMB and the Council on Environmental Quality, set up a single office of plan review with specific responsibility to carefully examine all phases of plans and hold appropriate hearings before approval is granted. Staff expertise and support must be sufficient to ensure a high level of quality control, including spot field checks of all components of analysis. The independence and staff resources of reviewing units must be increased in order to ensure fair, accurate, and complete review of plans and evaluations produced by public works agencies.

A SUGGESTED SET OF MULTI-OBJECTIVES

The major *methodological* weakness of the proposal is the muddled nature of the multi-objectives. They are unclear and overlap conceptually, which invites double counting (of benefits) and makes the identification of tradeoffs among objectives difficult. The value of the accounts prepared for the four

objectives is diminished greatly because as they stand the proposed multiobjectives are poorly conceived. If the usefulness of the multiobjectives lies in their display of the effects of a particular proposed project will have upon the quality of life in the regions in question and the nation as a whole, they should be exhaustive of all aspects of the quality of life potentially affected by each project. The various objectives should also be as mutually exclusive as is conceptually feasible, so that tradeoffs occasioned by projects between different components of the quality of life can be identified as clearly as is possible.

The WRC objectives are: national economic development, environmental quality, regional development, and social factors. We would maintain the first objective but modify the measures for it. The second objective should be redefined as "natural environmental quality" and would exclude economic considerations. We would eliminate the third objective, regional development, for reasons which follow, and replace it with an objective for democratic decision making. It is felt that this procedural objective is an end as well as a means and deserves explicit recognition as an objective. The fourth object, social factors should be elaborated to include the value of equality. The specific reasons for redefining the objectives to be mutually exclusive and more comprehensive are more fully explained in the following discussions of each recommended objective.

NATIONAL ECONOMIC DEVELOPMENT

This objective remains the same in our revised set. The standards for measuring effects on the national economy need to be revised, however. The proposed use of Census "C" projections and OBERS population forecasts reflects an attitude of development (WRC 1971: 24165). The Water Resources

Council should use Census "D" or even "E" projections in the future. The Series D projections are based on fertility levels which are more in line with predictions of future child-bearing behavior (2.45 births per woman during her lifetime). The Series C assumption of 2.775 is definitely too high when current attitudes, recent trends, and long-term social changes are projected. Estimated annual births per 1000 females have been dropping steadily since 1957, from 123.0 (1957), to 97.6 (1965), to 86.6 (1969). Some very recent 1971 demographic data indicate that we may have to turn to the Series E projections for the nation (constant population), in a few years. Series E forecasts are probably appropriate now for use in many regions of the nation.

The discount rate should be 10%. The proposal states that "The full cost of federal long-term borrowing, for generally prevailing economic considerations, is at least 7 percent and can be as high as 10 percent. . . . Thus the 7 percent rate established above, approaches both the opportunity cost and the total cost of federal borrowing." (WRC 1971: 24167). We should not be merely "approaching" the total costs of borrowing in project evaluation. This would not reflect a balance of economic and environmental considerations as called for in the NEP Act of 1969. Plan selection will reflect "the priorities and preferences expressed by the public" (WRC 1971: 24148), and will "accommodate changing national needs and priorities" (WRC 1971: 24150). The public and the courts are seeking a balanced approach. This balance requires a 10% discount rate.

The "net benefit generated by Government is maximized only when the marginal rate of return on Federal investments is equal to the marginal rate of return on investments by other institutions in this Nation" (WRC 1971: 24166). The proposal explicitly calls for the use of the private sector average interest rate in evaluating projects.

The rationale for subsidizing water resource projects at a 7% discount rate is inconsistent with the overall national policy of efficient government spending. The subsidy rationale is based strongly on arguments for regional development and assumes that water resource developments are a collective good of high social value in the long run. These arguments are being challenged, as shown above. The main reason to stress economic efficiency so strongly in this objective is to maintain exclusiveness. Arguments for subsidies for water projects should have careful justification in the social amenity and equality objective. As we argue below, there is serious doubt that most water development projects actually provide the non-economic benefits necessary to justify economic subsidies.

Qualitative long-term costs such as siltation of dams and salinization of soil and groundwater, should be included in this category.

ENVIRONMENTAL QUALITY

This objective should be defined as "natural environmental quality" and benefit measured in terms of restoration and maintenance of natural ecosystem characteristics. Attention should be paid to such characteristics of natural ecosystems as biotic diversity, long-term productivity, and stability. Biotic diversity is an expression of the number of kinds of organisms present. Long-term productivity is the capacity of the ecosystem to return benefits indefinitely. Stability is the ability of an ecosystem to withstand impact without being radically changed through time. Biotic diversity is closely related to ecosystem stability. A more extended discussion of these issues can be found in Richerson and McEvoy in this volume. By defining this objective as ecosystem-centered instead of man-centered, the conceptual and economic confusion of including recreation benefits under this objective is ended.

An ecosystem-centered means of evaluating environmental quality reflects the intent of recent legislation and the 102 Statement concept. In this fashion, by making this objective biosphere-oriented (man-included, instead of man-centered), we can have a clear set of standards of beneficial effects which is truly environmentally oriented and is conceptually separate from the other objectives and measures.

The environmental quality objective in the proposal is seriously weakened by the inclusion of several elements related to man's immediate use of the environment rather than to inherent characteristics of the environment itself. Recreation, for example, uses the environment as a resource but recreational benefits may result in environmental costs, just as any other use does. The inclusion of increases in recreational access as a beneficial effect on environmental quality should be eliminated.

In order to be useful a category, environmental quality must have an independent definition and valuation. As redefined it places stress on those inherent qualities of natural environments man values *per se*, rather than for derivative benefits like recreational and economic uses. This revised objective measures natural ecosystem health, not direct usefulness to man. Certain subsystems will have high value because they are critical links in larger systems, maintaining overall viability.

In the mid-1970s, the intrinsic characteristics of natural environments will be increasingly valued for two reasons. First of all, natural environments have many poorly understood functional attributes which are necessary for the continued prosperous existence of human life apart from direct use benefits. The whole biosphere functions in an integrated manner to produce a tolerable climate, for example. Many direct use benefits are dependent upon the proper functioning of this integrated biosphere. We understand enough of these processes to know that the antientropic (matter, energy and information accumulating) nature of biological processes, which produce the observed diversity and stability of the earth's biota, must be respected if long-term viability and productivity are to be maintained. Because of our ignorance of the details of these functions, we must place high value on them, even though we often cannot translate natural environmental quality into direct use values. Man has become the most powerful single biogeochemical agent on earth and he must exercise this power with considerable respect for natural environments, lest catastrophes ensue to constrain his long-term economic and social well-being. The example of the potentially disastrous effects of the widespread contamination of the biosphere by DDT and related compounds is a lesson which must be taken very seriously.

Secondly, many Americans today have a religious or quasi-religious regard for natural environments. Values associated with this regard form a part of preservationist conservation attitudes which are at the root of the political mass movement which in turn has resulted in such partial reforms as NEPA and CEQ. Only if a fair consideration of these values is made in the planning process can water development agencies expect to be spared the political and legal opposition of environmentalists.

This redefinition of the environmental quality objective makes possible an evaluation of natural environmental quality in clear terms which can be balanced against other objectives with a minimum of confusion. Planners must realize that most environmental effects of developments will be counted as costs in a revised environmental quality objective. The only exceptions would be actions such as certain forms of pollution control and the rehabilitation of man-damaged ecosystems. The man-included nature of the revised objective does, however, potentially allow man to make positive contributions. To the extent that human activities increase such qualities as the diversity, stability or permanent natural productivity of the biosphere they could be counted as benefits to this objective.

No discount rate should be used at all in the calculation of costs and benefits under this objective. Discounting has a clear meaning and usefulness only when applied to dollar values. The discount rate is used to express the present value of future dollars and is thus roughly equal to the return on invested capital (the amount received by someone willing to forego present rewards for future value). Money as a measure of value has its utility in its interchangeability. The exchange value of many otherwise unrelated things can be expressed in common (dollar) terms. Discount rates are thus used to extend this common unit of value from the present into the future.

Environmental quality cannot be evaluated adequately in money terms and there is no other common unit of measure of environmental quality comparable to money. If environmental effects do have unambiguous monetary values, they should be included in the national economic development objective.

The fundamental problem with the use of ordinary economic evaluation techniques in dealing with environmental quality is that people do not treat environmental quality as having exchange value to be expressed in monetary terms. Absolute values are often placed upon it (Richerson and McEvoy, this volume). For example, most people probably believe that it is wrong to destroy scenic places like the Grand Canyon, no matter what the money value that might result from such destruction might be. In general most people would probably hold that present generations should not irreversibly degrade the planet as a place for future generations to live, regardless of how much benefit they would receive. Values of this kind cannot be expressed in monetary terms and cannot be subjected to economic analysis.

REGIONAL DEVELOPMENT

The idea that water projects are valuable in stimulating regional growth (WRC 1971: 24162) is subject to doubt. Cox, *et al.* (1971) studied water projects in the northeastern United States (61 counties) in which large water projects were built between 1948 and 1958.

They measured economic impact of the projects by studying indicators such as difference in total employment and difference in median value of owner occupied dwellings.

Their data showed no relationship between size of project and the rate of economic growth. This finding implies that the size of projects should be held to a minimum needed to fulfill other goals in order to reduce costs. Rural areas showed no significant correlation between the building of a project (of any size) and economic growth. Cox's study covered three of the specific criteria proposed by the WRC as indicators of economic benefit to a region: regional income, regional employment and changes in population distribution.

Since this study indicates that water projects were ineffective in the stimulation of regional growth, alternative methods should be studied for achieving the desired results. We would suggest that methods other than water resources development are more efficient and more effective in the stimulation of the economies of the depressed rural areas of this country.

Not only is it doubtful that water projects are particularly effective in stimulating economic growth rates on a regional basis, it is also doubtful that the growth that does occur serves to aid the lower income groups in the U.S.

Tolley (1959) estimated that the billion dollars of federal reclamation development in the Southwest displaced one out of every twenty low income farm workers in the Southeast. And as Gaffney (1969) pointed out, since many of the resource development benefits become directly capitalized in land values, such projects constitute a subsidy to the extremely rich.

Howe (1968) in studying "Water Resources and Regional Economic Growth in the U.S." for the period 1950-1960 concluded that "water did not constitute a bottleneck to rapid economic growth in the water deficit areas of this country, nor did its presence in large quantities in other regions guarantee the rapid growth of these regions."

He also found that areas with large inland waters (Tennessee excepted) showed relatively poor economic growth rates in spite of the very large past and present public investments in waterway improvements in these areas. Howe concludes that water availability itself is only a minor variable in economic development and that its availability did not outweight the other economic attributes in a region which were responsible for industry locational decisions. He quite clearly indicates that water projects are likely to be poor tools for accelerating regional economic growth if markets, factor availability and other amenities are lacking.

Although the council's proposal seems to take cognizance of the need for factors complementary to water availability, the council also appears to be suggesting that investments be made along with water project investments to stimulate growth in a region (WRC 1971: 24162). If such investments are necessary for a water project to be effective, then the costs of such investments should be weighed in as cost of the water project (since the benefits of such complementary investments would be included in the water project benefits).

Both Tiebout (1962) and Howe (1968) state that the most important consideration when studying regional growth is the advantage of industry in that region (indicated by rate of growth of that industry in the region) relative to the industry average for the nation, or its relevant competitors, since this gives an indication of the competitive advantage of the region in question. If industry in the depressed region does gain an advantage due to water resources development, any loss of income to any other depressed region which results would have to be subtracted from the benefits to the advantaged region to prevent a false picture of the net regional prosperity generated.

DEMOCRATIC DECISION-MAKING

At the root of this revised third objective is the need for open public determination of the value judgements made in water development planning. The restriction of the planning process to inputs of technical experts (predominately) has clearly failed to adequately reflect the value judgements of the public. The achievement of the democratic ideals of this nation is dependent upon major reforms in this area.

The Water Resources Council should require local and state hearings on all projects before beginning a study, before tentative selection of an alternative, and before final selection. Public participation was seen as a major national land management problem by the Public Land Law Review Commission. Their report, *One Third of the Nation's Land*, Recommendation No. 109 was for increased public participation in all resource decisions. (1970, pp. 253–6).

The Institute for Water Resources (of the Corps of Engineers) Report 70-7, "Public Participation in Water Resources Planning," (1970) recommended broader participation in water resources decisions and specifically recommended local community participation in goal setting through community workshops, local public hearings on proposals, public inquiry proceedings, and opinion sampling.

Planning meetings should be held by citizen boards with tapes of the proceedings sent to the water resources planning team. This technique allows the public to transmit its ideas about the proposed project before any alternatives have been formulated. These meetings are for public input, not for the planners to defend their plans. The meetings should be run by non-project persons, preferably persons known to be unbiased by local or regional residents.

After plan alternatives have been formulated and general accounts drawn up, then actual hearings should be held with two-way communication between the citizenry and the planning team. This double round of meetings and hearings enables the public to enter into the planning process in its early stages, before alternatives are designed, and allows the planning team to be better prepared for arguments during the hearings. Adequate notice of hearings and meetings must be given. Hearings and meetings should be held at the two largest cities within 300 miles of the proposed project, as well as at local cities.

All bills in Congress should be separately considered for both authorization and appropriation to ensure a stronger democratic system. The Omnibus Rivers and Harbors Act, which annually groups water projects (good and bad) into one bill, has gone a long way toward undermining public faith in water resources planning.

Independent review of the cost/benefit analyses of proposed projects and of all other phases of planning should be institutionalized. Proposals would then be reviewed by commissions of industry representatives, scientists, and conservationists for example, or by an office created by the WRC, OMB, and CEQ. Access to the courts by citizens should be encouraged also to provide a fair hearing of all the issues. During the 1970s when our national values are so rapidly changing, these increases in public participation will be essential, if informed public interest is to be developed, identified and protected.

SOCIAL FACTORS

This objective should be redefined to be "social amenity and equality." Components of this redefined objective would be:

Community Health. This component includes continuous personal physical health factors such as clean air and psychological health factors such as quiet residential areas.

Recreational Social Amenity. Broadly defined, recreational social amenity includes not only visual conditions which satisfy people, but also environmental factors which promote physical and psychological recuperation through activities which relieve urban anxieties and refresh the spirit. Solitude and natural diverse surroundings are chief environmental attributes promoting recreational amenity, for both physical and psychological healing. Recreation is the activity generally associated with this recuperation. These two components include the benefits which result from decreases in personal and social stress concommitant with the decentralization of urban settlement. In other words, this objective also includes the benefits resulting from increasing the satisfaction of persons who can find a place to live in smaller urban centers in which it is possible to have greater identity and are more pleasant communities, rather than in major metropoli.

Social Equality. Project effects on intra-regional distribution of job opportunities and incomes and on recreational opportunities should be examined carefully. Condemnation of land and dwellings or businesses owned or used by various population groups should also be predicted for possible changes of relative status of various socioeconomic groups. The benefits of this objective must be carefully defined and calculated, since water resources development has only a modest role to play in increasing amenity in small cities and towns, because in decentralizing overall urbanization patterns, it often decreases recreational social amenity and social equality.

MEASURES OF RECREATIONAL BENEFITS

Since recreation is a conceptually unclear category of project effects and one which is sure to receive greater attention by development agencies in searching for benefits to estimate, we will examine this set of effects in some detail. Our essential argument here is that the currently used measures of recreational benefit are inadequate. Economic benefits used as measures of recreational social benefits are seriously misleading.

The majority of our population lives in metropolitan areas, and the majority of the excess demand for constant price recreational facilities is found within a 0 to 2 hour travel zone from these metropolitan areas (Outdoor Recreation Review Commission, 1962; California Department of Parks and Recreation, 1966). The Water Resources Council's proposal should favor recreational facilities in these areas.

The present system biases in favor of hunting and fishing recreation, when, in fact, the above mentioned studies indicate that the greatest need for recreation facilities is for camping, horseback riding, and nature walks. The federal government should provide water related recreation near to urban areas to reduce automobile pollution and travel costs even if added land costs exceed the dollar difference in transportation costs in the short run. Public recreational user fees should be subsidized to fulfill demands for recreation by the urban poor who do not have automobiles and have fewer recreational choices than persons with higher mobility.

The market fails properly to evaluate the benefits of recreation. One cause is the abundance of public facilities making it difficult or impossible to find existing market prices which accurately indicate recreation value. Where private facilities do exist, the difficulty in comparing prices for facilities is exacerbated by the problem of comparing recreation facilities with widely differing qualities and accessabilities.

Most economists agree that the Trice-Wood method (travel cost method) is at best an extremely gross approximation of the benefits received by recreationists. The other methods used in Senate Document 97 to compute theoretical values for both general and specialized recreation-days are based on crude averages which stem from highly con-

troversial indicators of willingness to pay (Clawson & Knetsch, 1966, and Lerner, 1962). All of these methods are biased in favor of artificial "improvements" that are fine near metropolitan areas but of dubious aesthetic value (sanitation facilities excepted) when constructed in heretofore unspoiled areas found some distance from major population centers. Wilderness recreation experiences lose much of their inherent scenic qualities when development of sites occurs. Basic to the recreation experience is relief—relief from urban "improvements."

In areas which are presently unspoiled by human embellishments and are of high scenic quality and uniqueness, the project proposals should attempt to encourage only those facilities which allow uses compatible with the goals of environmental preservation and enhancement. This strategy looks toward the future when relatively primitive recreation areas will be under greater demand pressure because they are of limited quantity. The national forests in California have already begun a wilderness permit system to limit use of fragile wilderness areas. The future development of an area that is used as a wildland recreation site would transfer wilderness demand to other wilderness-type areas. This social cost should be taken into account in the generation of alternatives and in decisions. Recreation areas near urban centers should, however, be developed intensively (Scott, this volume). Thus, we see that improvements cannot be considered a recreational benefit without considering the type of recreational experience to be provided for and the character of the environment involved, whether it be rural or urban.

Since benefit-cost analysis is at best a contrivance when applied to the field of recreation, it should be discarded as a planning device for recreational aspects of water projects. Instead, relative supplies of and demand for recreation facilities should be the relevant criteria for consideration when evaluating a water project under the social amenity and equality objective. Monetary evaluations under the national economic development objective should be utilized only in efficiency studies of the alternatives proposed to supply various amounts of recreation with the priority of recreation type and location to be determined by non-monetary methods in the earlier stages of planning.

Surplus (excess, unfulfilled) demand for various types of recreation in a metropolitan region should be the primary standard for determining recreational need in that region. The highest percentage unfulfilled demand category gets the highest need rating. Since pricing of public recreation is economically arbitrary, demand can be measured using the same price for recreation in different land value locations. These ratings can be ranked ordinally. Recreation categories will be designated according to use type and distance from the cities under consideration. Recreation is far more important to the citizens of the United States as a social process than as an economic development process and should be so valued. The important benefit of recreation is the psychological and physical relief afterwards allowing a refreshed return to family life and work.

Recreational benefits should be measured in satisfied person-days, preferably to reflect percent excess person-day demand to be satisfied by a project for each activity type and region. Actual person-days are measured by counts at existing facilities and are estimated by projection for proposed projects. Person-day demand for facilities by type and location can be estimated from sample surveys of large populations, such as metropolitan areas, or can be inferred from surveys at existing facilities and from national recreation studies. Person-day supply can be determined from analysis of existing facilities and estimated for proposed recreation areas. Often, person-day use at existing sites will exceed their calculated capacity. In other words, certain facilities are currently overused. This valuation scheme would favor near-urban recreation and thereby lessen the rise in resource consumption, smog, and automobile deaths which occur under the proposed WRC system since it favors rural

recreation and the use of the travel costs and expenses method of shadow pricing. Unfulfilled person-day demand will be highest in and near urban areas and mass transit could often be used for these recreation areas, thereby lessening economic and environmental costs.

As an example, let us say that the 3 to 4 hour time-distance ring of Los Angeles has a picnic area deficit of 5000 person-days per year. Total picnic area person-days in this ring are 50,000 person-days per year. The 4 to 5 hour ring of Fresno has a hiking trail deficit of 500 person-days per year and this time-distance ring has 2,000 hiker-days per year. Most current planning systems would give development priority to the picnic function in the Los Angeles 3 to 4 hour ring, since that deficit is largest, absolutely. We believe that the absolutely smaller, but *relatively* larger, hiking deficit for Fresno's 4 to 5 hour ring should get higher priority for development. The relativistic basis is because users can enjoy most types of facilities even when they are crowded. Therefore, the uses with relatively high crowding should be expanded first.

In any valuation of recreation, all adverse costs attributable to each alternative such as pollution, recreator transportation, siltation, and government maintenance costs, should be subtracted from some arbitrary base benefit figure or from the highest benefit figure in any alternative under consideration. This treatment of recreation as a social amenity need not conflict with evaluation of the economic effects of recreation which can be partially evaluated by revising pricing techniques. Such economic techniques must be considered as subordinate to social amenity measures of the sort suggested above.

BALANCED CONSIDERATION OF OBJECTIVES

The relative importance of the objectives in terms of the amount of information to be collected and considered is not specified in the WRC proposal. Is the environmental quality objective advisory, or is it to be considered in "balanced" fashion with the National Economic Development objective? What general weight does the social factors objective get in the information system? How will regional development be included in the accounts without double-counting benefits with the national economic development objective? We believe that the WRC objectives for national economic development, environmental quality, and social factors should be given equal consideration in the information accounts for all alternatives. Furthermore, minimum constraints on the achievement of each objective should be incorporated into the formulation of alternative plans.

This equal weighing of information regarding the three WRC objectives (excluding regional development) holds for our recommended ones: national economic development, natural environmental quality, democratic decision-making, and social amenity and equality. The strongest set of tradeoffs will occur in most cases, however, between the national economic development objective and natural environmental quality objective. Then at least for the next decade these objectives will receive the most scrutiny. Improvements must be made in the generation of alternative plans and in the decision-making itself in order to ensure adequate examination of the economic/environmental tradeoff.

The National Environmental Policy Act of 1969 (PL 91-190) calls for "a balance between population and resource use which will permit high standards of living and a wide sharing of life's amenities . . ." (Sec. 101, (b) (5)).

A recent memorandum dated July 30, 1971 from the Office of Counsel for the Council on Environmental Quality concerning the *Calvert Cliffs* opinion (2 ERC 1779, July 23, 1971), states as follows: "The opinion makes a number of points which are relevant to agency procedures to implement Sec. 102 (2) (C):

"A balancing of economic and environmental costs and benefits is a required part of the 102 process. The *Calvert Cliffs* opinion states (p. 1788):

'. . . In each individual case, the particular economic and technical benefits of planned action must be assessed and then weighed against the environmental costs; alternatives must be considered which would affect the balance of values. . . The magnitude of possible benefits and possible costs may lie anywhere on a broad spectrum. Much will depend on the particular magnitudes involved in particular cases. In some cases, the benefits will be great enough to justify a certain quantum of environmental costs; in other cases, they will not be so great and the proposed action may have to be abandoned or significantly altered so as to bring the benefits and costs into proper balance. . .'

This decision requires that alternatives be developed which balance economic and environmental values to differing degrees along a "broad spectrum." An *equal* balance between environmental and economic values certainly lies along this spectrum. Since this "equal balance" alternative should result from a subjectively "equal" weighting of the national economic development and natural environmental quality objectives (A and B), we feel that explicitly including this middle-of-the-spectrum alternative would aid decision-making. This project alternative, roughly "halfway" between the alternative which optimizes national economic development (A) and the alternative which strongly emphasizes natural environmental quality (B), would indicate the tradeoffs more clearly to the decision makers by identifying the nature of the alternative which roughly balances economic values and environmental values. An "equally balanced" alternative should, therefore, be considered in the water resources evaluation process. This requirement, combined with the prescription to include one alternative which optimizes national economic growth (A) and one which *strongly* emphasizes natural environmental quality (B), creates an overall demand for a spread of alternatives, one of which emphasizes A, one which balances A and B, and one which strongly emphasizes objective B.

The value tradeoff between objectives A and B must be examined in more detail than other tradeoffs among objectives, since the appropriate economic/environmental tradeoff is going to be the most difficult to determine politically in the near future. This tradeoff requires the most detailed analysis, in order to effectively reconcile competing values.

Objectives A and B, as well as the others, are subject to minimum constraints, of course. One existing political constraint is that the economic benefits exceed the economic costs substantially, usually by a ratio of 1.4:1.0 or more, using a given discount rate. Environmental quality constraints are also feasible and appropriate. Air and water quality standards are examples of these.

BALANCED WEIGHTING OF OBJECTIVES A AND B IN DECISIONS

Recent changes in federal air and water quality legislation affirm nondegradation as an environmental quality objective. The Environmental Quality Improvement Act of 1970 (PL 91-224) emphasizes government responsibilities for environmental improvement. It would seem appropriate, in light of the clear trend in national policy toward a balancing of economic and environmental values in decisions, for the WRC to state in unambiguous terms in its proposal that objective B will be given "roughly equal weight" to objective A in project decisions. This balanced decision *value-weighting* would, we believe, properly reflect public opinion in the 1970's.

We realize that there are no exchange ratios available from which an "equal balancing" of economic and environmental values could be formally calculated. We feel, however, that this lack of common dimensionality does not excuse planners,

economists and decision-makers from the responsibility they have to seek ways of minimizing environmental degradation by mitigation and rehabilitation and by shelving projects which provide for economic growth by degrading our natural environment.

We believe that the WRC multi-objective process, with the objectives redefined as we have done can lead to considerably better water resource decisions than are presently being made. By requiring new kinds of information to be made available, by making tradeoffs between various kinds of values as explicit as possible, and by encouraging a thorough exposure to public judgement, decisions can be both technically superior and more responsive to national values.

The changes suggested will make planning and evaluation more expensive and more contentious, but we are confident that these costs will be more than compensated for by increased public satisfaction and confidence in federal decision-making processes.

References

Barkley, P. W. and D. W. Seckler. 1972. *Economic Growth and Environmental Decay.* Harcourt Brace Jovanovich, Inc., New York.

Boulding, K. E. 1970. Fun and Games with the Gross National Product—The role of misleading indicators in social policy. *In*: H. W. Helfrich Jr., *The Environmental Crisis.* Yale University Press, New Haven.

Bromley, D. W., *et al.* 1971. *Procedures for Evaluation of Water and Related Land Resource Projects: An Analysis of the Water Resources Council's Task Force Report.* Center for Resource Policy Studies and Programs. University of Wisconsin.

California Department of Parks and Recreation. 1966. *Planning Monograph Series, 1966-1968.*

Clawson, M. & J. L. Knetsch, 1966. *Economics of Outdoor Recreation, Resources for the Future, Inc.* Baltimore: Johns Hopkins Press, 1966.

Corrigan, R. and I. B. Clark. 1971 Resources Report: Budget Office, agencies struggle over standards for new water projects. *C.P.R. National Journal* (June 2).

Council on Environmental Quality. 1971. Memorandum to Agency Liaison on National Environmental Policy Act (NEPA) Matters from Timothy Atkeson, General Counsel, Regarding "Calvert Cliffs" case. July 30.

Cox, T. P., C. W. Grover, and B. Siskin. 1971. Effect of water resource investment on economic growth. Water Resources Research. 7: 32–38.

Gaffney, M. M. 1969. Benefits of farm programs. *Am. Jour. of Econ. & Soc.* 26: 236–30, 417–24, JL-0, 1967.

Howe, C. 1968. *Water Resources & Regional Economic Growth in the U.S. 1950-1960.* Johns Hopkins Press.

Lerner, L. T. "Quantative Indices of Recreational Values", *Water Resources and Economic Development of the West: Economics in Outdoor Recreational Policy*, Report #11, Conference Proceedings of the committee on the Economics of Water Resources Development, Western Agricultural Economics Research Council jointly with the Western Farm Economics Association (University of Nevada, Reno, 1962).

Outdoor Recreation Resources Review Commission, 1962. Report to the President. Also, various Study Reports.

Public Land Law Review Commission, 1970. *One third of the Nation's Land.* June.

Tiebout, 1962. The Community Economic Case Study: New York Committee for Econ. Development.

Tolley (1959). Symposium on the Economics of Watershed Planning, Knoxville 1959. Sponsored by the Southeast Land Tenure Research Committee, the Farm Foundation and the T.V.A., Ames, Iowa State University Press 1961.

U.S. Army Corps of Engineers. 1970. Public Participation in Water Resources Planning. *Institute for Water Resources Report* 70-7.

Veblen, Thorstein. 1899. *The Theory of the Leisure Class: A Economic Study of Institutions.* The Macmillan Co., New York.

White, G. F. 1969. *Strategies of American Water Management.* Univ. of Michigan Press.

Water Resources Council. 1969. Procedures for Evaluation of Water and Related Land Resource Projects.

Water Resources Council. 1970a. Principles for Planning Water and Land Resources. A Report to the Water Resources Council by the Special Task Force.

Water Resources Council. 1970b. Findings and Recommendations. Report to the Water Resources Council by the Special Task Force.

Water Resources Council. 1970c. Standards for Planning Water and Land Resources. A Report to the Water Resources Council by the Special Task Force.

Water Resources Council. 1970d. A Summary Analysis of Nineteen Tests of Proposed Evaluation Procedures on Selected Water and Land Resource Projects. Report to the Water Resources Council by the Special Task Force.

Water Resources Council. 1971. Proposed Principles and Standards for Planning Water and Related Land Resources. Notice of Public Hearing and Review. Federal Register 36: 245.

INDEX

INDEX